New and Revised 10th Edition, Second Printing
Custom collection of resources
Expert Interviews, L. A. Hangouts
Go to **www.actingiseverything.com** for latest updates

Yes, You Can Live Your Life As An Actor!

Acting Is Everything you do, you are,
you have been or hope to be in your life.

Welcome to *Acting Is Everything*. In this Tenth edition, I will guide you toward fulfilling your dreams, giving you important information about developing the actor inside you. I share ideas, facts and many special secrets for establishing your career.

If your dream is to live your life as a professional actor, your first tool is your basic acting craft. Good training helps you discover the power, control and confidence to act. Once you have confidence and know how to interpret a script and develop a character, then the business side of acting begins. It takes desire, guts, preparation, discipline, talent and luck to have an acting career.

This advice has helped bring a great deal of success to countless readers and many of my students over the years.

I hope it will do the same for you.

Judy Kerr,
Studio City, California

"*If you really want to know how to make it in Los Angeles, this book is a must.*" Bill Macy, Actor

"*An actor's roadmap to the ins and outs of what truly is a business.*" Dee Wallace Stone, Actress, Acting Coach

"*The best reference book of its type on the market.*" Steven Nash, Personal Manager

"*Excellent. Helpful and direct.*" Bud Cort, Actor

"*Rich with the wisdom of a dedicated professional.*" Eve Brandstein, Casting Director/Producer/Director

"*Practical information and sound advice. I use it myself.*" Joel Asher, Acting Coach/Director

"*A great handbook for every actor, beginner or pro!*" Beverly Long, Casting Director

"*A must-read for actors who are serious about a career.*" Eric Morris, Acting Coach/Author/Director

"*For any actor who wants to know the who's, what's and where's of L.A.*" Deborah Kurtz, Casting Director

"*More real help per page than stacks of other books on the subject!*" Al Burton, Producer

"*Don't make the mistake so many actors make. Read this book.*" Dan Gauthier, Actor

"*Very informative—a must for all actors.*" Lou Ferrigno, Actor *(The Incredible Hulk)*

"*It took me fourteen years to discover the Hollywood secrets that Judy Kerr gives you.*" Dianne Kay, Actress *(Eight Is Enough)*

ACTING IS EVERYTHING

An Actor's Guidebook for a Successful Career in Los Angeles

by Judy Kerr

Tenth Edition, Completely Revised

Spring, 2003

September Publishing

Studio City, California, USA

www.ActingIsEverything.com

Distributed By:
SCB Distributors
15608 South New Century Drive
Gardena, California, 90248, USA
800/729-6423
www.scbdistributors.com

ACTING IS EVERYTHING
An Actor's Guidebook for
Successful Career in Los Angeles
by Judy Kerr

Published by: **September Publishing**
                  Studio City, California, USA
                  www.actingiseverything.com

Distributed by: **SCB DISTRIBUTORS**
                  15608 S. New Century Dr., Gardena, CA 90248, USA
                  800/729-6423
                  www.scbdistributors.com

Copyright © 1981, 1989, 1992, 1994, 1997, 2000, 2003
1st Edition 1981
2nd Edition, 1983, updated
3rd Edition 1988, updated
4th Edition 1989, completely revised
5th Edition 1990, updated
6th Edition 1992, completely revised and expanded
7th Edition 1994, completely revised and expanded
8th Edition 1997, revised, updated and expanded
9th Edition 2000, completely revised and expanded, first printing
9th Edition 2000, Fall, second printing, updated
10th Edition 2003, completely revised and expanded
10th Edition 2004, second printing, updated
Publisher's Cataloging in Publication Data
Kerr, Judy
Acting Is Everything: An Actor's Guidebook for a Successful Career in Los Angeles by Judy Kerr.
—10th edition, completely revised.
Bibliography: k.
Includes index
1. Acting—Guidebooks, handbooks, manuals, etc.
2. Career—Guidebooks, handbooks, manuals, etc.
Library of Congress Catalog Card Number: 99-60713
ISBN: 0-9629496-5-5

Buckets of gratitude to my husband Ron Gorow—without his love and support you would not be reading this; my daughters, Christina, Cynthia and Catherine for their encouragement and enthusiasm; friends Robin Gee for her time, inspiration and start-up skills; Steven Nash for his valuable opinions, and Samantha Harper for her magic; assistants Blythe Baten, Tricia Gilfone and Carol Hernandez—couldn't have done it without you; proofreaders Ron and Bonnie Howard; my teacher, Joan Darling, for her continued guidance and all my students over the years for whom this was written.

Thanks to the following for their many contributions:
Bonnie Gillespie
Bonnie Howard
Steven Nash
Caryn West

Cover Design: Thomas Cobb

Table of Contents

SECTION ONE

Developing Your Talent

SECTION TWO

Pictures and Resumes

SECTION FOUR

Professional Tools

ABOUT THE AUTHOR

Photography by Michael Maron

Accomplished acting coach, actress, director Judy Kerr brings over 25 years of experience to this edition of *Acting Is Everything.*

Judy is recognized in Hollywood for her unique gift of nurturing talent and helping actors succeed. She used that gift brilliantly as the dialogue coach on the hit series *Seinfeld,* working with all of the cast members, as well as guest stars. Coaching one-on-one with some of the top names in the business, Judy works to enhance the artistry and technical skill necessary for an actor to deliver their best performance.

Judy's credits include dialogue coach on *The Michael Richards Show, Bob Patterson, It's like, you know..., The Single Guy,* and *Alright Already.*

Her television show in Los Angeles, *Judy Kerr's Acting Workshop,* is in its 18th season. She is the bestselling author of nine previous editions of *Acting Is Everything,* contributing to the success of thousands of readers.

With this Tenth Edition, Judy opens the doors of Hollywood to a new generation of acting hopefuls and professionals with a straightforward road map for building their careers. Judy Kerr takes special pleasure helping young talents grow as she continues to coach privately and on sets, teach workshops and conduct seminars worldwide.

Email: Judy@JudyKerr.com

HOW TO USE THIS BOOK

• **You are holding a workbook.** It is meant to be studied, highlighted, marked in and pages turned down. Using this book as a guide, many actors and potential actors have traveled from all over the country to fulfill their dreams by seeking their fame and fortunes in Los Angeles. I love to see their well-used copies of *Acting Is Everything*.

• **This book is big—think of each section as almost a separate book.** This is not necessarily a book to be read cover to cover. Study and take the appropriate actions for what is most important to you. I've tried to give you some information on most aspects of the acting/entertainment business. Discover your own favorite people and services.

• **To get the full benefit** from this book you must have a computer and computer skills, a printer, an email address and be *online savvy.*

• *Acting Is Everything* is protected under copyright law but you have my permission to make copies of pages you need to keep with you and to share with your friends. I think they'll need and want a book of their own.

• **I can't resolve the he/she pronoun issue** so I have broken the rules; I use *they* and *their* as singular pronouns meaning *he* or *she.*

• **I love beginnings and helping you make your dreams come true.** Now is the time to turn your dreams into goals and to aim your heart toward them.

• **William Shakespeare** said, "Our doubts are traitors, and make us lose the good we oft might win by fearing to attempt."

• **Anthony Hopkins,** when asked if he had doubts, replied, "Yes, but you can't let them get in your way. Just do it, be bold. Mighty forces will come to your aid."

• **Let the fears and doubts be there** and still go for your dreams. You deserve it.

ABOUT THE RESOURCES
LISTED IN *ACTING IS EVERYTHING*

All of the resources for actors included in *Acting Is Everything* have been personally researched by me. I have used most of the services myself or have had excellent reports from my students and friends who have used them.

In this Tenth Edition, many new resources have been added. Others have been reviewed and updated and some deleted. In Los Angeles, phone area codes change fairly often; we do our best to have the latest ones for you. When you reach a wrong number, try using one of the newer area codes. New information and updated resources will be downloadable from the web site, as well as many links to other informative sites. (www.JudyKerr.com)

If you have a problem with any of the businesses listed. please let me know by email: judy@JudyKerr.com.

I provide resources to help you begin your own list of special people and services. Always research all your contacts carefully; prices and integrity have been known to change. This book will point you in the right direction and help you get the maximum value for every dollar spent.

This book is about doing all you can to build your artistic acting career and living your life as an actor...

so the journey begins...

I BELIEVE . . .

- That we can fulfill our dreams.

- We must accept responsibility for our actions and choices.

- We choose our paths daily and are offered many opportunities.

- It takes extreme focus and clear intentions to fulfill our dreams.

- We need tenacity not to give up and to see adversities
  as opportunities.

- It takes extreme curiousity.

- We must use time and organizational skills to our advantage and
  respect them for the power they give us.

- When we operate from poverty thinking, we will always be lacking.

- Without a developed spiritual life and fundamental values/beliefs,
  we will not experience real joy and are likely to feel empty.

- Having fun is the most important goal in life.

I have written this book for you.
With love,

Judy Kerr

SECTION ONE

DEVELOPING YOUR TALENT

PREPARING FOR SUCCESS
AND
LIVING YOUR DREAM

• **Making a living as an actor** is a worthy goal and a grand dream. I believe it is attainable for many. However, most actors never achieve this dream. From what I have observed, actors who make a good living, or even become wealthy, always seem surprised and grateful.

• **My goal, my dream is to help you become a working actor**; an actor who is enjoying the process of being an actor, one who understands that the process is the journey. During this process you reset your goals over and over, even though the dream may remain the same. Living life as an actor can mean earning a living doing something else. You may have years of working as an actor and also years of acting without having a paying acting job.

• **By following the advice in this book** from the experts I quote and from my experiences, you can create opportunities to make money as an actor.

• **If you have chosen this career** because you want to be rich and famous and you think this book will have the answers, choose another book. You can sacrifice your whole life chasing after those dreams without achieving them. There are many other professions, even in show business, that if done well, can bring wealth. Fame can come in many ways—get on a reality show.

• **Spike Lee**, when interviewed on *Inside The Actors' Studio,* spoke of how difficult an actor's life is when dealing with the many rejections actors face. "It's a very, very tough business, but if this is what you want to do, if it's what you love, then you're not going to let that stop you from doing what you want to do."

• **Whatever your acting career dreams and goals are**, creating a successful business to support and propel your career is necessary and exciting. Simply speaking, an acting career consists of three components: the acting (which is the art), the business and your dream. As you begin to develop your career, you are in fact, setting up a small business in which you are both the President and CEO. When setting up your business, you'll be making many decisions and purchasing quality goods and services for, hopefully, the best price. This book will guide you as you make those decisions. The best career choices are made when you follow your instincts and use your own good judgment, based on who you are and what your values are.

• **To be an actor you must act.** Study, always study, and find places to express your art; act for audiences and for the camera. If you have the business but not the art, you are likely to feel something is missing in your life. Discover the ways to satisfy the artist within your soul.

• **Lucille Ball, in speaking of why she succeeded:** "I acted anywhere and everywhere they would let me."

• **Develop the art and the business** so you will have a well-rounded, enduring acting career. Labors of love (usually jobs without financial reward) often lead to life-changing career paths.

• **Lili Taylor** (*imdb.com*) when asked by *Backstage West* what she would say to actors trying to break into the business, said: "Have faith and trust. And know that there are no rules. Knock down rules."

• **Robert Ellenstein, artistic director of the Los Angeles Repertory Company:**

> • **We must rearrange the priorities.** Namely, put the god of our art first and our career second. It means we must pursue our craft every day. We must learn a new speech every day. We must keep our voice and body in shape every day. We must live our lives alert for how we can use it for our craft. We must dedicate ourselves to what we feel is the highest, not the best paying. We must work at it despite self doubts, disdainful smiles, approval or disapproval from others, showbiz expediency—dedicating ourselves to the perfection of our craft, with faith that this will give us life.

> • **Such purposeful, active dedication is so rare** that we will stand out of the crowd of toadies to the system almost immediately and become a choice morsel that the buyers would like to have—thus satisfying our material needs.

• **Joan Darling, Emmy-award winning director, acting coach and actress:**

Q: What does it take to be a success in this business?

> • **There are two things** you have to make a delineation between. One is to succeed in the business, which takes one set of skills, and the other is to succeed for yourself as an artist, which is another kettle of fish altogether.

> • **To succeed in the business,** you have to come to where the business is happening, which is either New York or Los Angeles. Get yourself into an acting class; that is how you meet people and begin to network. You need a resume, good pictures and an audition scene, three minutes long, that shows you off. Show the scene to anyone who will let you. Go to all the open calls and start to get used to auditioning; work breeds work.

> • **If you can't get in the door** anywhere, then get together a little showcase, rent a theater and invite as many people as you can. Start networking, which is why class is very helpful—any kind of class that gets you in touch with other actors, because that's where you begin to get the information about how to do it. Learn everything you don't know; study body movement, voice and speech. The more skills you have, the more chances you have to succeed.

> • **Make a list** of anyone you or your parents know who is connected with the business. Contact them all and see if there is anyone they can introduce you to, so you can start making your own connections in the business. Keep performing someplace and get people in to see you. And the rest of it is: pray a lot.

• **Jay Bernstein, manager, writer, publicist, producer, director** and EMMY winner, taught a course called *Stardom, the Management of, the Public Relations for, and the Survival and Maintenance In*. He has managed careers for many stars, including Farrah Fawcett, Drew Barrymore, Suzanne Somers, William Shatner, Donald Sutherland, Stacy Keach, Mary Hart and Linda Evans.

Q: What does it take to be a star?

• **To be a star,** everything has to be 100% with your talent, your representation and your presentation. For example, if you're talented and you present yourself well but you don't have an agent, it's going to be pretty hard to get a job—so your representation is failing. If you're very talented and the representation is the best you can get but you dress like a rock star, they're probably not going to hire you to play a nun—so that's your presentation.

• **If your presentation** and your representation are wonderful, maybe you need some work on your talent. If talent is a problem, maybe there won't be stardom. There's nothing you can do with just representation and presentation. I think that talent is 35% of making it. The other 65% is having the right team with you.

• **The team** is the right agent who gets you the jobs, the right personal manager who gives you direction, the right business manager who makes sure your money grows as your career grows, the right entertainment attorney because there's an awful lot of small print in Hollywood, and the right public relations person that will help you maximize what you've done.

Q: What if actors are shy about asking for help?

• If you don't ask, the answer is already no. The worst thing that will happen if you ask is, the answer will still be no.

• **Scott Sedita of the Scott Sedita Acting Studios.** KTLA-TV calls him: "One of the hottest coaches in town." I asked what he thought it takes to make it in Hollywood. Is it luck?

• **During my 20 years in the business** as a talent agent, casting director and acting coach, I've seen many actors become very successful. They all had the same three things in common: talent, perseverance and confidence. I believe you can't take one component out of the equation. If you have confidence, perseverance but no talent for acting, you'll never make it; and I don't care who your Daddy is.

You can't just have talent and confidence without perseverance, because no one is going to knock on your door and hand you a three-picture deal. And equally as important is self-confidence; you have to always believe in yourself. If you let the business regulate your self-esteem, you'll be in big trouble.

• **In class, I talk a lot about the "I want"** (objective) of a character and the obstacles he/she endures in order to get what they want. The same is true for actors. You have to want it. Passionately. If you can enjoy the process and stay on the path, no matter what obstacles come your way, you will make it.

• **Many people believe that luck** should be part of this equation. I believe luck is when opportunity meets preparation. If you study hard, put yourself out there and believe in yourself, you'll be prepared when the opportunity arrives.

• **Antwone Fisher's first screenplay,** based on his life, was made into a movie. The first-time director was Denzel Washington, who also had a starring role in the movie. Another success story is how Derek Luke landed the starring role playing Antwone Fisher.

• **Antwone Fisher was an abused child and homeless teen.** He began his career in show business in 1992 as a security guard on the Sony Pictures lot. His boss became interested in his life story. Several producers were interested too but wouldn't hire Antwone to write the script. He had been taking a screenwriting course. Producer Todd Black said he would hire him and helped him write 41 drafts of the screenplay. The picture was shot in 2002, ten years after Antwone's arrival in Los Angeles.

• **Derek Luke in 1997 had started working as a clerk** in the gift shop on the Sony Pictures lot. Antwone was now writing the screenplay and would often stop by the gift shop to visit. They became friends and many times talked about their life stories. When they were doing the first open-call auditions Derek couldn't get an appointment, so he crashed it. He says he was "horrible." But the production of the film was stalled for two years allowing him time to prep himself and again go after the role he felt he "had" to play. When the time came for the next round of auditions he was ready, he got callbacks and finally to read with Denzel. Then he waited to hear.

• **Denzel Washington** two months later came into the gift shop to tell Derek he had the part. Denzel said, "Derek was jumping, screaming, crying, laughing." After shooting *Antwone Fisher* and before it was released; Derek landed two more films—an independent film, *Pieces of April,* and an action movie, *Biker Boyz.*

• **Derek encourages actors to continue to pursue their dreams.** "There have been so many dreamers like me. Everyone out here [in Hollywood] has a mission."

• **During the above process** these individuals had to make a living; they had hardships. Derek says, "There was a time when we [he and his wife] were homeless, living out of her car, because all I had was a BMX bicycle." He kept working on his craft so he would be a better artist when the opportunities came along. This is the process, the journey.

• **Steven Nash, personal manager, producer** and president of the Talent Managers Association says, "Actors and creative people who aim to make it in Hollywood have to trust that being true to the journey is the real measure of a successful life."

• **Personally, I haven't known any overnight successes.** It can take years to get a big break but along the way you work on projects that encourage you. You have fun acting. Many times you have to create the break by writing a part for yourself or finding a project and producing it on your own.

• **You will have your dreams, you will set your goals.** This is what starts your adventure. You will accomplish goals but the mystery, the unexpected, the surprises are what the adventurous path is all about. You never know what the final destination might be.

• **Salma Hayek** was Oscar-nominated for *Frida.* This was a project that took her many years to bring into being. Her next project was as a first time director of *The Maldonado Miracle* staring Peter Fonda, Ruben Blades and Mare Winningham. When Showtime asked her to direct, she said, "You're crazy, I don't know how to do that." Then she found a script she liked and said, "Yes, I'll direct." Salma, when talking about dreams, says, "You do something, you give it your best, and then when it's done you let it go and then you dream a new dream."

• **Choices are where the real talent lies.** If you choose to love the process, life can be so much easier. You can learn and grow through pleasure as well as pain; both are simply choices. Try to choose pleasure whenever you can; it's more fun. You will be able to observe people all around you who choose to take the painful road. Acting, though it takes work, is fun and easy; getting the job is tough, but possible. Lots of actors get roles each and every day.

• **Acting is an art and a craft.** Some people make a living at acting while others act and make their living doing other things. Both ways are valid and artistic. Being an actor takes dedication, desire and ambition beyond reason. Most actors are gamblers—there is something about gambling with your life and your security that is attractive to you. An actor must be a survivor, must persevere.

• **James Gandolfini** (*Sopranos*) when receiving his Best Actor Statuette at the SAG Awards said, "To all the actors who are working hard and struggling, things can change very quickly. Hang in there. Enjoy what's happening to you now 'cause things get pretty weird later on if it works."

• **Show business is the most exciting business** in the world and no one can keep you out of it. No matter how big your dreams are, how long it takes or what paths there are to follow, you are willing to do it. Why? For the THRILL of putting yourself on the line, jumping off the cliff, wonderful close-ups and actors you respect telling you they enjoy your acting work. A career break can be a phone call away; don't let anyone convince you differently. Make your choices and commit. You can have everything you *intend* to have.

• **Abraham Lincoln** said, "Always bear in mind that your own resolution to succeed is more important than any other one thing."

WHAT IS ACTING?

• **Acting is living your life**, then using those experiences to enable the audience to experience their own lives and emotions.

• **Acting** *in the moment* is always the goal. The *moment* is that instant in time when the actor's imagination and talent create a flash of truth. The audience recognizes and identifies with this truth and is transported and moved.

• **Robert De Niro** said, "Sometimes I get moments I know are right on the head, almost an epiphany, knowing you're exactly there; you're in the moment, in character. Most of the other times it's just a struggle to get through it and hope that it's right."

• **Emmy Award-winning Director Joan Darling** says, "Acting, when it is done at its best, is behaving as if you were alive in a set of given circumstances that are different from your own given circumstances."

• **Richard Dreyfuss** said, "An actor's job is not to feel things, it is to make the audience feel them."

• **Meryl Streep, when asked about spontaneity.** "It's the only thing worth looking at, what nobody expected to happen. In a play, when somebody drops something, forgets a line, suddenly it all becomes electric, alive, it all feels real. The spontaneous is what you dream of, wish for and hope appears."

• **Actors cannot always depend** on this *spontaneous moment* happening by accident or luck. By learning the craft of acting, you can *deliver the goods* on demand, whether you feel like it or not. In acting classes, you can learn the craft of using your own life experiences as your acting tools.

• **Acting is a physical, athletic event.** As you are always in a changing, growing process, you need to develop an awareness of what is going on in your life at all times; be aware of every emotional and physical fiber in your body.

• **Your face, body, voice and spirit** are your billboards—what sells you. They are what the casting directors who interview you notice first. You cannot have the right *look* for every role, nor can you figure out what each director, producer or writer has in mind for each role. However, you can make the best of every casting meeting by figuring out who you are and giving of your whole self at each and every meeting.

• **To discover the *inner you*** takes time spent thinking, reading and soul searching. Finding the physical you takes honesty when looking at yourself in the mirror and on camera. Presence, vocal quality, hair, makeup, clothes, weight, height, and your spiritual development are all important aspects of the presentation of your unique self. Only you can decide who you are and then make the commitment to perfect and fine-tune your acting instrument—you.

• **The best part** about all this self-discovery is that it makes you an actor every minute of the day. Even though it may have been a long time since a job or interview, you are still working, studying, preparing all the time. Actors usually don't work as much as they would like, so it is very important to enjoy the process, the privilege of living an actor's life. If you become discouraged and unhappy, the great destroyer—negativity—sets in.

• **Tom Hanks, on acting as a profession.** "It requires a knowledge of why you're doing it in the first place. If it's power, well, you'll never be able to hold on to that. It it's money, eventually they are not going to pay your price; it's going to drift away. If it's influence, that's going to shift as well. If your sense of purpose for doing it is because there is no life like it and it's more fun than you can imagine and you'd be doing it anyway, then you might be a little ahead of the game. I think that's why I do it."

• **Michelle Danner of the Larry Moss Studio** is an acting coach as well as a stage and film director. She says: "Acting is to be interested in going deeper into what it's like to be human."

• **Susan Batson, head of the New York based Black Nexxus Acting Studio**, who has coached many Oscar nominated actors, said in a *Hollywood Reporter* interview: "A great actor can—with great artistic ease—create a walking, talking human being. To make a walking, talking human being, you have to be connected to the need of this character. A great actor can determine the need of the character and is then able to experience internally the need of that character. The actor is then capable of crafting the expression of that need."

• **Dee Wallace Stone**, wonderful, talented actress and acting coach, says: "Acting is being joyful, trusting, committed and willing to share every ounce of your soul with millions of people."

• **Nicholas Cage** said about shooting *The Rock* with Sean Connery, "It's like playing cops and robbers in the backyard." This is the ideal for every actor to reach in each role. The dialogue and movement will be absolutely believable for the audience.

• **Leonardo DiCaprio**, says: "I don't really understand the process. The main thing is just getting into the reality of what the character is, finding all the suitable things to go along with it. I often look at a situation from the outside, like I was a camera."

• **John Malkovich**, says: "Acting is a job; if it's not fun, why do it?"

• **Kimberly Jentzen**, acting coach, film director and director of Living The Art Institute, says: "Acting is an art form of compassion. It is an act of courage. Great acting will move the audience from thinking to feeling, from judging to identifying—giving us subtle but sacred permission to feel when we are too proud to release our own fears, laughter and tears, creating a pathway to experience our connection to each other. When this occurs, a performance is truly memorable."

• **Sally Field** says, "Being an actor is both wonderful and horrible. . . You never know what's next. After my children, acting's the love of my life, my best friend, my lover, my companion."

• **Harrison Ford**—when speaking of why acting is fun—said, "There is a certain foolish pleasure in having these experiences."

• **Richard Gere** said, "This is what we do in acting—we embarrass ourselves all the time. You have to be able to make a fool of yourself regularly to do this; otherwise it is not going to be any good."

• **Warner Loughlin**, acting coach, director and actress says, "Rather than the putting on of masks, acting is the willingness to rip them off and allow the passion of the inner life to be exposed. It is the great unveiling. Choosing to be an actor is brave and courageous. When you choose to be an actor, you have chosen to be a giver of life."

• **Anthony Hopkins**, says, "My goal, principally, is to always get into the technical relaxation that Stanislavski talks endlessly about in his books and just listen."

• **Leigh Kilton-Smith**, acting teacher, coach and director says, "For me acting is listening. Actors are storytellers who work very hard to make it look as though they haven't worked at all. They trust their homework is present and listen. If an actor is listening, they are telling the truth."

• **Cherie Franklin**, actress, coach and on-set dialogue coach says, "Acting is creating 'life' from the written word. A successful actor must master the ability to create and sustain this 'life' while respecting the script, director's vision and always taking into consideration the specific medium, i.e. feature film, sit-com, episodic, stage, or commercials, wherein this 'life' must live."

• **Steve McQueen** said, "Acting was hard; playing a role was like reaching inside you and pulling out broken glass." He "treated every script like an enemy."

• **Willliam H. Macy** told *Back Stage West,* "I think an actor's task is to read the script, figure out the action—the objective—and do that and let everything else go hang. We can never forget acting is a big fat trick that we play on the audience. You're standing in a set. It's not real, but it's real enough, and the audience is willing enough to suspend disbelief that there you are in the setting and you're wearing somebody else's clothes that have been designed. So it's the actor's job to figure out what his character wants and to do something that's similar to that so that it looks like you're making it up as you go along. The emotions will follow; they will be there as you need them."

ACTING TECHNIQUE

• **This is the most important section of this book.** A solid acting craft or technique is what makes a career possible.

• **You will probably remember your first acting class session.** Mine was at El Camino College in Redondo Beach. I took a basic acting class in my thirties as a fluke, I thought. In my first class, the teacher presented a scene from *Applause* with two experienced actors. One of them, Bob White, remains a close friend. When I saw those actors on stage my life changed. I knew I had to learn to act so I could *try* to move an audience like I was moved. That moment in time led me on this adventure.

• **In basic acting class, you learn specific acting tools**—how to develop characters and how to interpret a script. You can decide where to study by going to watch different classes or interviewing teachers to discover who might teach the best techniques for you. There are many acting coaches to choose from. I would encourage you to pick a coach who is supportive, not abrasive or negative. There is no reason to be humiliated in order to learn.

• **If you can afford it**, study basic craft, improvisation, voice and scene study at the same time. Four classes a week and all the homework in between for a year or two would give you a solid foundation. If you could also work in the theater and do student films, you would gain actual experience too. I know this isn't possible if you have to make a living at the same time. If you are not one of those actors who are lucky enough to be funded for a year or two, take on as much as your time and money will allow. Think of it as financing an advanced degree in professional acting. Taking professional classes and landing professional acting roles is what makes you a professional actor.

• **Scene study classes** are often taken after you've honed your basic craft. The actors prepare scenes and present them to the teacher for critique. It takes personal motivation and homework.

• **Jason Alexander** (*Seinfeld*) in a *Back Stage West* interview, gives an understandable explanation of what acting technique is. If you are willing to study what he is saying and to do all that he says, you will become an actor who can deliver.

• **Technique for me is:** How do I do enough crafting so that I can rehearse intelligently, and how do I then make choices that will sustain me for a run? That's all it is. It's nothing that a studied actor has not heard before; it's just very clear-cut. You have to answer four questions: Who am I speaking to? What do I want from them? How am I going to get it? and What is standing in the way of what I want?

• **But it's not just answering the questions**—you have to answer them so incredibly specifically that it can take weeks to come up with answers for these things. You not only have to make choices that are smart but fit the material. And ideally you're making choices that once you get them, they make your instrument do things so that you don't have to manufacture a performance—they're so strong that when you plug in the right thought, or the right word, or whatever it is, your instrument starts to respond. And that's hard.

• **That's the difference between a craftsman and a non-craftsman.** Actors have to take the responsibility that any artist makes in saying, "I choose that color, that stroke, right there. Right or wrong, there it is." Actors have to say, "I'm not winging it, I'm not waiting to see what happens; I'm making this choice right here with my intelligence and with my instrument."

• **It's especially good when you're preparing sides for auditions.** No one's gonna tell you different; no one's gonna direct you out of it. So you have to be able to craft this material so that it shows you in a great light, shows your range, shows your ability, and shows your everything. How do I walk into that room and be undeniably more masterful than anyone that's walked in before me? It can't just be cockiness, it just can't be, "I know I'm good." It has nothing to do with me being good or not. It's that I'm doing things that the average schmo on the street is not doing. They don't know how. I craft, and they hope. That's the difference.

• **Caryn West, acting coach, actress, director** and teacher of a well-respected Audition Technique class speaks of acting technique.

> • **Good acting is good acting**, in any medium. The foundations of good acting are all found organically in thorough training. The beginning actor learns the skills to pursue objectives, moment-to-moment tactics and actions, factoring in internal and external obstacles to those actions. They learn to inhabit an acute sensory world with physical and vocal skills, to be sensitive to text and subtext, to be a keen listener, to glean information from given circumstances and back-story. They learn to create character detail and nuance, to open the channel of one's being to psychological truth, organic impulses and spontaneity. Actors further learn to foster and fan a comic idea in farce or commedia and to serve the story.

• **Director Martha Coolidge** said, "Acting is an art form and is probably one of the toughest. You need to learn as much about it as any musician knows about their instrument. Ironically, it's a career chosen by people who need to be loved, people who will probably receive 98% rejection in their lives. Without a craft to back you up, you're riding for a fall."

• **Brad Pitt** worked as an extra in 1989 on *Cutting Class*. He says, "I am the living testament that you can learn anything, because I was so bad."

• **Jason Alexander** was doing a scene on *Seinfeld* about why he had to postpone his wedding. It wasn't getting the laughs. The writers changed a line to include the name of the hall the reception was to be held in. On the next take Jason got a huge laugh. I asked him how he did that so fast. He said he immediately identified the reception hall with a place he knew that was specific, eventful, truthful and full of history. The audience couldn't help but identify with his wedding dilemma, believe it, and laugh at his uncomfortableness.

• **Lisa Kudrow** of *Friends* says about her character, Phoebe: "She's operating out of a huge amount of denial; so many horrible things have happened to her that she would not be able to even breathe another breath if she took it all in. She's in search of whatever feels good. I think Phoebe thinks she's a very talented, struggling artist, but she's just not." When you know the truth of the character you are playing, it will make your acting choices specific and identifiable for the audience.

• **Dustin Hoffman said**, "If an actor can find the personal rhythm to a character, he's home free."

• **Director Martin Scorsese says about Harvey Keitel**, with whom he has worked five times, "He pays scrupulous attention to the smallest detail of a role. I've seen him get deeper and deeper into himself. Harvey travels into very forbidding regions of his soul for his work, and he's able to have that experience and put it on the screen in an absolutely genuine way I find very touching."

• **Laurence Fishburne**, Oscar nominee, says about acting, "I want to startle people in a subtle kind of way—the way people are startled when they catch sight of themselves in a mirror. That's the goal of my work: communicating with people on a much deeper level than whatever is obviously going on. It's not so much about finding the truth as *revealing* it. Getting to the truth requires a tremendous amount of patience because things are only revealed to you when you're ready to deal with them."

• **Sally Field** said, "Anyone who isn't terrified of acting is a liar. I'm always terrified when I know I have to be emotional."

• **Dinah Manoff** says: "My process is to use whatever works. I studied method and it is wonderful. And sometimes I have an onion in my purse in case I have to cry."

• **Dustin Hoffman's colleague, Jessica Lange** said, "Dustin has obsessive curiosity." Meryl Streep said, "His mantra is specificity, specificity, specificity."

• **Danny Glover** said, "Listening is the key [to acting.] Listening and relaxing, because if you're not relaxed you can't listen."

• **Joan Allen** said, "If you lose your focus, regain it by really listening."

• **Billy Wilder**, legendary director, said about an actor's preparation, "You can tell how good an actor is by looking at his script. If he's no good, the script will be neat as a pin. Charles Laughton's script was so filthy it looked like a herring had been wrapped in it."

• **Anthony Hopkins** told Ed Bradley on *60 Minutes* that Katharine Hepburn gave him his most valuable piece of advice on his first movie, *The Lion In Winter*. She said, "Don't do anything; don't act. Just be what you are. Acting is reacting; just listen."

• **Albert Einstein said**, "Imagination is more important than knowledge. Knowledge is limited."

• **Dee Wallace Stone**, actress and acting coach, answered when I asked her how actors act: "Well, five-year-olds do it 50 times a day. They just get up, have fun, jump in and believe. It ain't the cure for cancer, its just play time. Most of us lose our joy and go into fear. Everything shuts down when we ask 'My God, am I good enough?' When you are in fear you can't go to where your instinct takes you because you are always afraid you are going to go the wrong way. Be in the moment!"

• **Jeffrey Marcus, acting coach** and very sensitive, caring human being asks his actors in class to work with an open heart. I asked Jeffery to explain what that meant.

> • **Open hearted means that the fear and defenses are down** so the love and passion can come to the surface. It's when you're more concerned with what you have to give than what you can receive. It's when you're willing to be seen without artifice, raw and vulnerable. When you are in the moment, trusting the moment and trusting that your talent and being are sacred and non-rejectable. Basically, the fear of rejection or judgment or criticism is overruled by the responsibility of bringing more love into being. It's the first mandate of true creativity.

• **Mala Powers, actress, author and acting teacher** in her Discovery-Guide to the audio CD and cassette titled, *Michael Chekhov: On Theatre and the Art of Acting,* says:

> • **The actor should train himself** to notice the *atmospheres* which exist around him in life—a library, cluttered antique shop, a street fair or the waiting room at an audition. Ask yourself what happens to your psychology and feelings when you are open to these atmospheres.

Q: How do you create what you notice?

> • These *atmospheres* are simple to create on the stage or for film through the use of your imagination. Imagine the space, the very air around you to be filled with whatever atmosphere you wish—impending doom, the color blue, a cathedral, a graveyard at midnight, ecstatic

joy, a street accident, springtime, champagne bubbles; the choices are endless. Once created, these atmospheres then begin to influence the actors, often guiding their character's reactions and behavior. Emotional nuances are added to the performance. In addition, the audience senses the invisible, but very present atmosphere created by the actors, and an additional bond is formed between them.

Q: What is a good exercise to start with?

- **Most great performances appear to be effortless.** It is important for the actor to practice the *feeling of ease*. Practice walking with the feeling of ease. Lift your arms with the feeling of ease. Pick up an object, even a chair or a table while consciously employing the feeling of ease. Once you have exercised this many times, you will begin to notice when you tighten-up or are pushing. You can then immediately call up the feeling of ease to come to your rescue.

- **Joan Darling, my teacher,** has been nominated for an Emmy, three times as a director and once as an actor. She won for directing. She was the original director of *Mary Hartman, Mary Hartman*—one of the first women to direct film and television in the 1970s. She is a legendary acting teacher in Los Angeles, New York and Sundance.

Q: Can acting be taught?

- **It is possible to teach someone** the techniques of how to wake up different portions of their own personality in order to create a set of given circumstances inside the actor that are similar to what the character is experiencing. That is a craft that can be taught to anybody; everybody knows how to be alive. It is easier for some people to immediately understand and process this craft almost innately without thinking about it and to be able to do it right away.

- **People tend to think that actors** who can do it right away, because it is easy for them, are talented and other people who can't do it right away aren't talented. I've taught long enough to see that if people work hard enough they will learn everything they need to learn to really be wonderful. I think the measure of whether a person can do it or not is totally dictated by how much they want it.

Q: What are some specific acting tools you teach?

- **Acting is a sport** and you have to learn the tools and techniques in your body. Everything that you know and understand is stored in your body through information you got from your five senses. There is an acting technique called "sense memory" which teaches you how to evoke that memory. When you let yourself remember the different sensory stimulus surrounding a particular event, it wakes up the memory of that event and makes it present for you to use in an acting scene. While people know how to do this by just thinking about an event that is similar to the event in the play, "sense memory" is a real craft technique that wakes up the information of the event for you in a much deeper and much more reliable way.

- **Another acting technique** is called "personalizing." If the other actor on stage is your sister in the play and it is a sister your character hates, then you might "personalize" that other actor as someone you hate, meaning you would deal with them as if they were that person you hate.

- **"Relaxation"** is one of the single most important acting techniques. You really need "relaxation" because when you have impulses come into and go out of your body, any physical tension you have will prevent that flow. Just so you don't make a mistake: "Relaxing exercise" in acting is not like Yoga or meditating. You are not trying to calm yourself down; you're simply trying to get your body to let go, relax and be curious about what emotionally is going on with you and to not meddle with it. Don't think you are supposed to become calm when you are "relaxing."

Q: What does "being in the moment" mean?

- **Briefly, "being in the moment"** means that not only does the actor deal with all the stuff they have awakened, with whatever acting technique they use that makes them similar to the play, or allows them to function as if they were in the play, but the actor is also relating to themself at that moment in time on stage. The actor that allows himself or herself to be totally conscious of their experience at a given moment on stage, along with the work they created as an actor, is much more compelling to watch.

Q: What should new actors focus on?

- **I think new actors should read a lot of plays**, get acquainted with what their appetite is, what parts they love, the little child in them that really wants to be the princess or the athlete in the story.

- **If you are really serious about acting** you need to gather information. Try all kinds of acting techniques. I strongly recommend that new actors be insistent that their teachers are not punitive (punishing) and that their teachers have real information for them. If teachers ask you to do something, they have to be able to tell you how to do it. If they can't tell you how, then they are not teaching you.

- **Look around and see the actors you admire.** Make it a quest to find out how they do whatever you can't do and teach yourself how to do it.

Q: Is acting magic?

- **Yes and no.** I believe there is something magical in acting; in the communication between a person standing on a stage and the people sitting in the audience. An actor can stand on stage in a 1500 seat auditorium and have a wave of jealousy go through her and somebody from the back of the audience will say, "Oh, she's jealous," without the actor saying anything or making a face to show it. That is kind of magical.

- **In terms of learning to act,** there are very pragmatic things you can learn to do. If you do them like a recipe, you will be able to act a scene and act it well. So in that regard, I don't think it's magical at all. The magical question relates back to: do some people have talent and others not? I don't believe that's the case: I believe anybody can learn anything about acting that they need to know to be a good actor.

- **Michelle Danner of the Larry Moss Studio** is an actress, coach, stage and film director. She teaches a weekend *Acting Technique Breakdown Workshop* where she thoroughly discusses using back-story and trigger techniques.

Q: Why is it good to have a back-story for your character?

- **A complex, personal and imaginative back story** on stage and on film will ground in a foundation that gives you authenticity and a freedom to play because you know who you are.

- **To have a diary that you know inside out,** ask a zillion questions and let each one bring out an emotional response. That is how you'll find the physical life, the behavior and the emotional river of your character. Having a back-story is what enables you to listen with the thoughts and point of view that your character would have. This is what makes your performance riveting to watch. Everyone is different; you find your own way to write your back-story whether it's using your personal life, your imagination or a combination of both.

Q: What are triggers and how do you find them?

- **Triggers are tools** that you use to create the emotional river of the character.

- **They're sensory realities** such as visuals, smells, sounds, tastes, textures from your life and from your imagination that produce emotionality in you.

- **Every time you read an article**, watch a movie, the news, a homeless person on the street and you're moved, that's your golden box of triggers and no one has the key to that box but you.

- **You have to live your life, be open, be affected**, stay responsive and dare to feel all the time. It takes courage to do that.

• **Alan Ball** (*American Beauty, Six Feet Under*) **tells this story** of Annette Bening during the shooting of *American Beauty*: "During one rehearsal, director Sam Mendes asked the actors where they were before the scene begins. Annette didn't lose a beat: 'I was at the dry cleaner's, and I'm *very* upset because they lost my cream-colored blouse and they shouldn't be allowed to get away with that because it's the second blouse they've lost, and I'm going to write a letter! This can't happen anymore!' Our jaws dropped. It was as though she was channeling." As actors we all need to be this thorough in knowing where we are and who we are at every moment of the character's full life.

• **Kim Darby**, veteran actress, three-time Emmy and two-time Golden Globe nominee.

Q: In your view point, what is most important in acting?

- **You must learn a technique** that doesn't involve playing the words, the emotions or the feelings. Actors are afraid the audience won't feel or understand that conflict is going on. You have to play the action in the scene and deal with the resistance you are getting from the other character. When you put the action and obstacle on the other person then the drama and conflict come out of trying to change that person. Acting is not self-absorbed; it is the interaction that is important.

- **This technique shouldn't be academic and complicated.** What do I want and what is keeping me from getting it? There is always preparation. How do I feel at the top of the scene, what am I thinking about, what is my rhythm? You do your preparation and when the scene starts you drop the preparation and play the action again. If you play the results it will not be truthful and the audience will not be involved.

• **Larry Moss is the acting teacher Helen Hunt thanked** when she accepted her Golden Globe, SAG, and Academy Award for *As Good as It Gets*. When Karen Kondazian asked him in a *Back Stage West* interview about acting techniques, he replied:

- **The three things that actors need the most** are relaxation, imagination and the ability to analyze a script.

- **I work enormously with intentions.** And to find those, you need to know who the character is. You've got to understand their background. I'm a great believer in building a character's biography, because once you've done that, you walk into the play or screenplay with a full life. Things like the character's education, religion, relationship to parents, past events that were troubling or exciting, politics, dreams, etc. And what you create should be a combination of your own experiences and your imagination. If you just use yourself and not your imagination or you just use your imagination and not yourself, you're going to come off half-baked. I think it's absurd for any teacher to say that an acting student could just walk in and be themselves in any play. It's almost sophomoric and it's very, very destructive to the actor.

- **Film acting is all about containment,** but you have to have something to contain. The problem that some people have is they have nothing to contain and that's when you see bad acting. All good film and television acting has an enormous volcano in it that's being held back.

- **Janice Lynde, prominent Emmy-nominated,** Obie Award-winning actress and acting coach for actors as well as faculty members at the American Film Institute, teaches directors how to work with actors.

Q: How do you create a character that is very different from yourself?

- **Do research; it grounds you in authenticity.** Choose personalizations, where you may have behaved in a similar way as the character, imitation and sense memories to support the imitation. I find animal exercises enormously valuable. Imitate someone you know who is like the character. Dress like them—I always insist on the right shoes. How do they move? What mannerisms are keys to their psychology? Then personalize the other characters and each "event."

- **Example: When I played Marilyn Monroe,** I watched films and newsreels and read everything I could about her life. I began to imitate her physicality. Then I found a sense memory of a feather tickling my lips, which not only made me look "as if" I were her, but gave me an inner glow. My secret "acting work" tickled me which resulted in giving me an incandescent sparkle. I also did an animal exercise of Kitty, the brown skunk who lived next door. She would taunt my dog, brushing her tail in his face and moving in a slow luxurious, sensual way. Then from scene to scene, I personalized the other characters as people with whom I was very sensual, or vulnerable. My "event" was to get them to love me, including the audience.

- **Example: A heroin addict.** I found a drug rehab center, watched someone in withdrawal and talked to people who had been addicted.

I chose a sense memory of an itch I couldn't scratch and a migraine headache for when the character was in need of a "fix." For right after a "fix," I chose a smell from a place remembering thunderous applause and a specific smell after orgasm. For the "high" state, I also did an animal exercise of a gorilla after a nap.

- **Once you have the craft to support your ideas,** your artistry guides you in your choices. It's fun. To me, character work takes me to the edges and depth of my own spiritual being. As a result I "own" more of myself, I am more whole. The process of becoming whole is the most fulfilling aspect of acting.

• **Warner Loughlin,** acting coach, director, and actress, teaches classes and coaches privately. Many professionals, award winners and celebrities are in her master class.

Q: Is there a formula for acting?

- **I believe there is no set formula for acting,** but if some essential elements could be described, I would characterize them as: a) the actor's complete suspension of disbelief, wholly immersed in the moment; plus b) total, specific and extremely detailed knowledge of the character through specific analytical and emotional investigation; plus c) a hefty dose of willingness to focus only on the task in front of you; minus d) the fear of negative comment.

- **One universal formula would be difficult to pinpoint.** Because we have all lived our lives with individual experiences and perceptions of the world, each of us possess a unique inner voice. When we choose to immerse ourselves in the life of a character, our uniqueness of being simmers within that character, allowing that character to be unique as well. The actor therefore constantly births unique gifts into the world. The actor celebrates life.

• **John Kirby, acting coach, director,** teaches classes as well as privately coaches many top industry actors, including international and Broadway personalities.

Q: What are the mistakes you see in actors' work?

- **One of the biggest problems** actors have in their work and especially what they do on auditions is to *suggest* the work! They suggest the character and the events of the script, but never reveal a life—a true living person. They go on automatic and stay in the *event* of the audition. The actor is so caught up on being good or not being bad that they forget these thoughts are of no concern to their character and have nothing to do with what their character wants or is happening in their character's life. The greatest lesson an actor can learn is to own the room and make the place safe to live in!

• **Anita Jesse, acting coach, author** of *Let The Part Play You: A Practical Approach To The Actor's Creative Process* and *The Playing Is The Thing: Learning to Act Through Games and Exercises.*

Q: What would you say is the best method for improving an actor's concentration?

- **It takes time and patience to master concentration.** However, you can learn to choose a mental target, place it at the center of your awareness, and hold it there regardless of distractions. Script exploration, remembering lines, audition pressures, staying in character—all these become manageable only if you master concentration.

- **Sometimes you consciously order your mind** to focus on a particular mental target, then struggle to screen out distractions. Other times it's almost as if the mental target chooses you and everything else seems to automatically fade from awareness. For example, you effortlessly become enthralled by an appealing movie or book, a person you find attractive or your favorite music. It's almost as if you have *unconsciously* hit the switch that focuses attention on a particular object or train of thought.

Q: Would you explain how to do one of the concentration exercises from your book, *Let The Part Play You?*

- **A favorite seems to be,** "Doing My Job." While driving, make that activity the center of your awareness. When your mind wanders, refocus. When you find yourself thinking about what you will do when you get to your destination or replaying past events, gently redirect your attention to *this* moment—to what is happening right now. Pay attention to the cars around you, the feel of your car, everything happening on the road and exactly how it relates to you. Use variations of this exercise anytime during the day—while reading, eating, talking to a friend, or washing dishes.

• **Eric Morris, actor, acting coach** and author, travels the world giving seminars on acting.

Q: What is your approach to teaching technique?

- **I do something that Lee Strasberg** was terrified about, which he would have called "therapy." Psychotherapy it isn't. It's a behavioral-modification therapy. The circle of the work is the instrument, which is the actor—his mind, body, voice, and his emotions. Truth can only come from a place of truth, and unless you accomplish your "being" state, your place of truth, you cannot act from an organic place. So largely the instrumental emphasis of my work is to eliminate obstacles and liberate the actor to be free, to be who he or she is.

- **I ask actors to do the hardest things** for them to do first. To people who are very proper and socially obligated, I give exercises that break down that propriety, antisocial exercises. My work is profoundly life-changing because an actor is liberated to be a free person, to enjoy life on an impressive and expressive level.

- **I teach actors to be professional experiencers.** Your responsibility as an actor is to fulfill the author's intentions, obligations and responsibilities. You have to be able to really experience, from your own frame of reference and inner, organic fabric of emotions, what the character is experiencing. You become, not an actor who acts, but an experiencer who really experiences. You have to be able to discover the next moment of behavior in the next moment, at exactly the same moment the audience does. That's true acting, true experiencing.

• **Joel Asher, well-respected acting coach** and director of film and television, produces training videos for actors.

Q: What acting techniques do you teach?

- **I use many techniques.** Just as a carpenter wouldn't go to a job carrying only one tool, an actor can't do that either. If an actor uses the same technique to audition for a soap opera as a situation comedy, it's not going to work. So I give actors different scenes with different styles, different challenges, so they can constantly be expanding their techniques. I teach weekly technique, professional and master scene study classes. We do exercises and improvisations that grow out of the scene work. These are improvisations that are done to isolate a specific skill and work on that issue.

• **In Don Richardson's book**, *Acting Without Agony: An Alternative to the Method*, he has an extensive list of emotions that may help you when making your acting choices. Here are a few he lists: admiration, amazement, anger, awe, boredom, curiosity, desire, desperation, disbelief, disgust, embarrassment, envy, expectation, fascination, fear, grief, hatred, hope, anger, horror, hysteria, indignation, jealousy, loneliness, lust, panic, pity, pride, relief, remorse, respect, serenity, shame, suspicion and terror. It is absolutely essential to figure out what your character is thinking and feeling. As an exercise, pick any sentence and try using a different emotion each time you say the sentence. This will help you to realize it is the acting that is most important, not the words.

• **On the set of** *Seinfeld* one day, Jerry, Julia and Jason were playing around, thinking of all the ways you can say *all right* or *okay* and which one should be used in specific circumstances. During the laughter, Jerry said, "Hey, Judy, that would be a great exercise for your actors." It is a great exercise. Try it with your friends.

ACTING TRAINING: COACHES AND TEACHERS

The mediocre teacher tells. The good teacher explains. The superior teacher demonstrates. The great teacher inspires. William A. Ward

Great teachers have always been measured by the number of their students who have surpassed them. Don Robinson

• **It takes many teachers** in life to develop an actor. Following are teachers, tools, suggestions and recommendations that have helped me and others to develop lives and careers. There are countless paths, and part of an actor's job is to keep exploring new ones.

• **You should always be studying.** Your training will be a constant expenditure so don't skimp in this area. Your technique and acting knowledge will make you more employable.

• **Choosing an acting coach** is an important choice, but it is not a life or death one. Choose one, take a month's classes, give it your all and then evaluate what you have learned. If you've improved and others in class have grown and improved, then stick with it.

• **Jeffrey Marcus, an inspired acting coach, answers, "Why train?"**

  • **An athlete, musician or doctor** would never ask such a question. If acting were such an easy career, why wouldn't everyone want to do it?

  • **Acting is a discipline that demands such skill**, and yet, can be done without any. Of course, we can all act passionately and emotionally all by ourselves. But when the stakes are high and tension and self- consciousness creep in, we need techniques to fall back on in order to soar.

• **William H. Macy** in *Back Stage West,* when asked about what kind of teachers actors should seek out said, "I believe that an actor is held in better stead if he doesn't rely on his talent. What you rely on is technique. Talent is given by God and there's no negotiating. Technique is something anybody can learn, and for a technique to be a valid technique, it's got to be scientific. It's got to be repeatable. It's got to be testable. That's what they should look for in a teacher."

• **Eve Brandstein, Casting Director, Producer, Career Coach,** says about choosing an acting coach, "I think you have to see a teacher work. You could have heard that this is the greatest teacher in the whole world and they've taught some of the biggest names in the business, but if there's no chemistry, forget it. Some actors are better off in a negative situation and others in a positive one. One teacher says, 'Why do you bring that piece of s— into class? You're a terrible actor; who ever said you could act?' And this inspires the actor to greatness. Another teacher says, 'That was beautiful work, but what about this?' And that works for that actor. You have to find out if the teacher and you are magical together."

• **Joan Darling, legendary acting teacher and director:**

Q: Should working actors still go to class?

   • **If you find yourself starting to be disappointed** after you finish a job instead of feeling that you grew and things are wonderful and you can't wait to act again—then you should get into a class where the working on one's art is respected and you have fun. If you don't exercise your acting muscles at top capacity, you'll lose them.

Q: What if an actor can't afford to study?

   • **Find a teacher that you can apprentice yourself to.** Or get other actors with the same desire and meet in your living room once a week. Ask a friend who knows about acting to conduct this workshop for you.

• **Larry Moss, respected acting coach,** in a *Back Stage West* interview when asked about acting teachers said:

   • **I believe that the aim of a teacher** should be to help the individual students find the tools to realize their greatest potential. When you try to teach from a singular point-of-view or method, you're going to hurt the student.

• **About the expense of acting classes.**

  • **I have actors who hold down two jobs** in order to take class. I think that your education as an actor is something that you pay for because you care about it. It's like therapy. I had a therapist who once said to me, "If you don't think enough of yourself to pay for therapy, how do you think you're going to get well?" I don't think the classes would be as productive for the students if they weren't making some sacrifices. I don't think that life is about getting it easy. I don't think being an artist is easy. I think you get to earn things in life.

• **Cherie Franklin, actress, acting coach and well known dialogue coach on feature films and television:**

Q: **What should an actor gain by working with a coach?**

  • **The value of working** with an acting coach on an ongoing basis is this: they can offer a safe environment that can allow you to reveal your fears and bring your work to a place where you can face your truths. This work state will invite you to trust in yourself, creating confidence and steering you clear of self-sabotage throughout your journey as an actor.

Q: **Who is your ideal student?**

  • **One who is committed to excellence,** to daily homework, to investigating his emotional levels, to understanding his blocks, and understanding what he does and doesn't do well. Someone who wants to be the best actor they can be, who is willing to do all that it takes to get what they want. Homework might include journal work to discover emotional blocks, practicing cold reading, vocalizing, the reading of a play, seeing a TV show or a new director's work and so on. Bottom line, an actor should remember that perfect is an end state. Therefore, as actors, we have the privilege of becoming a better craftsman with each new day, whether working on set or at home. We can continue learning and advancing as the business changes.

Q: **How does an actor stay prepared to work between auditions and jobs? Are you an actor when you are not acting?**

  • **Daily homework and classes** keep an actor prepared. If you are not acting daily on-set, in class or in your bedroom, you are not an actor.

• **Leigh Kilton-Smith, director, teacher** and well respected on-set coach comments on choosing an acting coach, and what she looks for in a student.

- **Find the acting coach that speaks your language** and addresses the issues you are currently dealing with. No actor should have to compromise, ever. As in all decisions regarding their craft, actors should feel empowered.

- **I look for a student to be committed**: committed to the work beyond their fears and insecurities. Committed to a life of *process*. Actors who are willing to recognize that they are not half-empty vessels waiting to be filled, but are actually artists who seek out teachers, not gurus, as a form of collaboration.

- **Anita Jesse, acting coach and author:**

Q: How can actors make the most of class?

- **Be professional.** Be on time. Be prepared. Be "present." Fully commit all your energies to learning. I'm amazed at how many actors throw away their time and money. If you aren't ready to commit to the training, save your money and wait until you are.

- **Learn to listen.** Learn to take what you can from every comment given you and don't waste time arguing with the teacher. If you disagree with the majority of what a particular coach has to say, you are in the wrong workshop.

- **No one can teach you to be an artist.** Whether or not you become an artist must be left to you and your creative spirit. You hope to find a workshop where you can learn your craft.

- **Dee Wallace Stone, actress and acting coach:**

Q: What is important for the actor to learn in class?

- **It is important to know** that everyone is looking for you to bring your own essence, your own idea and your own self to the material. I think we spend half of our careers trying to figure out what *they* want. *They* want you to come in and bring to the piece *yourself*, totally committed and in the moment.

- **Eric Morris, actor, acting coach and author, says:**

- **My ideal student** is a person who commits himself to acting on a level of artistry. Somebody who is so committed to the work that it becomes a way of living. Unless you must act, because it's a calling, something you need to do, forget it! It'll break your heart.

• **Joel Asher, well-respected acting coach, describes his ideal actor:**

> • **Someone who is so hungry to grow** constantly that they will be eating, sleeping, and breathing acting 24 hours a day. When an actor is walking down the street, it's a sense memory exercise. You can constantly be training yourself as an actor by being alive in the space that you inhabit. Preparation is the key to spontaneity.

• **John Kirby, popular acting coach,** makes observations regarding actors studying:

> • **It feels like there is a breed of young actors** who want a "quick fix approach" to learning their craft. They run to any cold reading class or gimmick to keep themselves from doing the real kind of work that's going to raise their abilities to greatness. This can be very detrimental to anyone who does not already have a strong foundation in training. Their work becomes automatic, cranked out and extremely technical. They may feel they have given a great audition, what they have produced is slick, and may appear perfect because they did not drop a line or held their sides [script] correctly, but they have revealed nothing in the room that could blow anyone away with their performance. Their audition will lack dimension and effective moments. I love the actors who are in acting for the long run, who invest themselves in the work and take all the time necessary to be truly great.

• **Terrance Hines, acting coach and personal manager,** Hines and Hunt Entertainment, explains why he thinks training is so important:

> • **Whether you are one of the Three Tenors,** a member of the Bolshoi Ballet, an Iron Man in baseball, an Olympic swimmer or a waiter at Denny's, you have a coach and a trainer who warms you up, guides you and prepares you for the physical and emotional struggle that lies ahead that day. For an actor, it is important to be in a class so that your instrument stays flexible and focused. Unlike a violinist who plays an instrument, you the actor are the instrument you play. It is as wrong to mistreat your body with alcohol and smoke as it is to deny this same instrument the opportunity to be nurtured by exposure to good writing, risk taking and the emotional communion that happens with other artists in a safe landscape. Class offers you the opportunity to share your losses and gains with others who will understand. Compliments or criticism from a fellow artist you trust are the highest form of support and sharing.

• **Scott Sedita** (featured in a KTLA-TV story titled "Where Young Hollywood Goes and Studies") talks of the kind of training that best helps an actor.

> • **I believe in the development of the well-rounded actor.** Every actor needs to start with a good foundation class to learn the techniques of acting. When you have your foundation take a Scene Study class to work on character development and script analysis. An On Camera class is a must for those actors seeking a career in TV and Film. A Cold Reading class is essential for audition preparation. At my studio we also offer Comedy Improvisation. I find this class really helps actors get out of their heads and be spontaneous in auditions. We also offer Voice and Speech, because an actor should be able to say anything boldly and with confidence. Your voice should be heard and your words should be understood.

• **The following list of teachers are experts** and have good reputations. These few are just a small representation of what is available in Los Angeles. Extensive lists of teachers are in the *Working Actor's Guide*, *The Selective Hollywood Acting Coaches and Teachers Directory* and in special issues of *Back Stage West.* Follow your intuition on choosing a teacher and also when it is time to move on. Some actors change teachers every few months. Find the way that is best for you to study and grow.

• **If you are reading this outside of Los Angeles,** use these guidelines to pick your teachers in preparation for your move to a bigger market. Good and bad acting coaches teach all over the country. See the teachers in the *Cities Outside of Los Angeles* Section.

• **After each acting class, make notes in an acting notebook** on what exercises you did and what the reports were from your teacher and the other actors; put your feelings down too. The exercises you learned in class will be helpful in choosing acting work for your scripts; they are your acting tools. When you are looking for a piece of acting work to help you interpret a script, you can look in your notebook to see if one of the exercises will help you.

• **Keep a copy of all monologues and scenes you do.** They will come in handy when someone asks you to bring in a scene at the last minute.

Resources

FOUNDATION, BASIC TECHNIQUE AND SCENE STUDY TEACHERS

Judy Kerr's Acting Workshop, 818/505-9373. www.JudyKerr.com. $500 for a 10-week class. I only teach one 10-week group class a year, in the spring. Basic, auditioning and camera techniques. The camera is used in every class so you can see how your acting tools are working. You keep and review your tape each week. Many students appear on my cable television show, gaining three-camera experience. For the group class, I only take actors who are working on professional careers, have their headshots, resume and some experience. A very strong commitment is expected. Call to discuss the classes, schedule a time to audit and to get on my mailing list. I'm always available to work with actors privately and on-set. I coach all levels of actors privately and do career counseling. I love beginners.

Joan Darling's Acting Class, 323/964-3410. $350 for four weekends, from 8-5. She is a master teacher, director, actress. She usually teaches scene study classes four times a year in Los Angeles. Don't miss out on the opportunity to have at least one session with her. Very supportive and insightful. Her scene study classes are great even for beginners because she incorporates her very valuable basic exercises. She is also wonderful for working professionals who have been beat up on their jobs; she will help you heal. Lots of homework in this fast paced class. Auditing permitted.

Caryn West Scene Study, 323/876-0394. Los Angeles website: http://groups.yahoo.com/group/CarynWest-ActorsLA. The website for New York actors is: http://groups.yahoo.com/group/CarynWest-ActorsNY. You can subscribe to her very informative, instructional yahoo groups, and receive more information about her classes. $660 for 12 weeks. Four to six scenes an evening. She co-teaches the Scene Study Workshop with director Jessica Kubzansky. Script analysis; actions; character work; comedy dynamics; physicality; pursuing truth; genre/style work; risk taking and acquiring a new skill. A terrific opportunity to hear two different insights. Not designed for the beginner but for those who know the Stanislavsky basics and are looking for growth. Caryn also teaches a very well known and respected six to 12-week Audition Technique Workshop. "There is emphasis on script analysis, breath, presence and spontaneity." There is also a beginning acting class taught at her studio. Privates are $80. She regularly teaches at Michael Howard's studio in New York.

Actors Studio, West Coast, 323/654-7125. West Hollywood. Anyone over 18 can audition and it takes three votes to get in. Sydney Pollack, Martin Landau and Mark Rydell are the executive directors in Los Angeles. Arthur Penn is New York president. The combined membership in both venues is $950.

The Acting Corps, 323/464-2228. www.theactingcorps.com. 6425 Hollywood Blvd, 4th Floor, Hollywood, 90028. I first noticed this group at Back Stage West's Actorfest and I am very impressed with their website. I like the idea of going to school all day. They do a four-week Boot Camp including voice work for $550. They have many other general classes and the prices are reasonable. The staff all has very impressive credentials. This may be a good place to get your feet wet when you are new in town, if you can afford it and you have the stamina to take full advantage of the program.

Catlin Adams Acting Lab, 323/851-8811. $235 a month for one class per week, $385 for two classes per week. Strasberg trained director. All levels, improv, cold reading, sensory work, scene study. Endorsed by Melanie Mayron, Lee Grant, Ellen Burstyn, Dinah Manoff, Joe Bologna and Lily Tomlin. After interview, $25 fee for a working audit.

Janet Alhanti Studio, 323/465-2348. She and her associate, Iris Klein, teach two 20-week session professional technique classes a year, one in January and one in July. Students must be recommended by agents, managers, casting directors or actors who have studied with them. Janet also teaches a poetry monologue class and a master class. She is one of the most respected teachers in the business.

Joel Asher Studio, 818/785-1551. www.Joel-Asher-Studio.com. $225 a month, one class a week plus unlimited private work at no charge. Takes beginners. Four ongoing, different level, scene study classes. He incorporates as many techniques as possible with an emphasis on film and television work. His 6-week on-camera cold reading class is $195. He also offers Jeff Doucette's "Acting on Instinct" improvisation class, $150 a month. Private coaching $100 an hour, but free with Scene Study Class. His informative, instructive video tapes are *Getting the Part*, *All About Cold Readings*; *Casting Directors "Tell It Like It Is;"* and *Agents "Tell It Like It Is."* The newest is: *Directors on Acting!* He has a great little theater in the valley which he designed and built. Uses video in classes.

Tony Barr's Film Actors Workshop, 310/442-9488. www.filmactorsworkshop.com. $175 per month and first time registration fee of $55 includes copy of *Acting for the Camera*. Classes are held once a week. Taught by Eric Kline. Held in a three-camera video studio. Students cold read, rehearse and tape scenes from feature films. Emphasis is on the listening technique Barr developed in his book, *Acting for the Camera*. On-going beginning and advanced classes. Actors must interview for the class and no auditing is permitted.

Ron Burrus, 323/953-2823. 4646 Hollywood Blvd. Beginning acting technique is in two formats: the day program is six weeks, four times a week, 3 hours a day, $800. The evening program is three months, twice a week, 6 hours a week, $233 a month. Cold Reading class: $150/month, Character Scenes and Monologues $150/month. The advance class is $275 a month, with script interpretations and character development, culminating in a showcase production after two months. Emphasizes imagination as an actor's primary tool and stresses the ability to live in the present. The only technique teacher personally trained by Stella Adler. "It is up to the actor to convey what language cannot. The technique I teach pushes the actor beyond words." Admittance by interview.

Sharon Chatten, pager: 213/486-4229. In Venice. Relaxation, sensory work. Larry Moss trained. My student Dave Roth raves about her classes and the Cold Reading Sundays.

Ivana Chubbuck, 323/935-2100. Author of *Script Analysis*. $250/month for Ivana's class. There are several other instructors who teach at the studio. Scene study, beginning, advanced and master classes. Several of my students have studied with her organization and they gave glowing reports.

Lisa Dalton's Chekhov Connection, 818/220-3074. www.chekhov.net. $175 for four classes. You can take one trial class for $40. Lisa strongly suggests first reading *On the Technique of Acting* by Michael Chekhov. If the book feels "right," call her. You'll then schedule your first of five private or semi-private foundation lessons. The Foundation Course covers the "Chart for Inspired Acting" found in the preface of *On the Technique of Acting*. She teaches several on-going group classes as well as coaching privately. Her website has further information on Chekhov and links to other sites.

Kim Darby, 818/985-0666. $200 a month. Scene study and cold reading. Actors work in every class on camera. All levels and beginners are very welcome. She is a veteran actress, three-time Emmy and two-time Golden Globe nominee. To keep a "safe atmosphere," she limits the class size and requires auditions for admittance. "My class is based on a listening process, always honoring the author by learning the words but not letting the words tell you how you feel; you learn to listen to full implication."

Wayne Dvorak, 323/462-5328. www.actingcoachdvorak.com. $125 a month. On-going classes for all levels, incorporating techniques from Meisner to marketing. Interview, audition and free audit are required for admittance. Class sizes are limited. The highly selective professional networking class showcases in front of top casting directors and agents on a regular basis. This class offers the next step, once you have done serious training.

Fairfax Adult High School, 323/653-4085, in the Greenway Court Theatre. If you can't afford the other classes listed, you can keep your acting tools sharp and learn new ones by taking this class. Classes are extremely reasonable, beginners welcome and are taught by the very respected actor/director/coach Gary Carter. He also teaches a "Digital Kitchen Video Co-op Class for Filmmakers." To reach him personally for information, 323/697-5499.

Howard Fine Studio, 323/951-1221. www.howardfine.com. $650 for a 12-week basic technique class taught by Howard. 12-week introductory scene study class for $220 a month with another teacher and ongoing intermediate and advanced classes for $220 a month. Other teachers and classes are available. An audit, referral and audition are required.

Cherie Franklin, 818/762-4658. $200 to $250 a month, all levels. Cherie is a very inspirational coach. She teaches classes for feature films, comedy, situation comedy, dramady and episodic television. In addition, she teaches privately and on-set, emphasizing confidence, pacing, behavior, developing a character and how to remove fear. Her on-camera awareness classes include audition technique and especially how to identify the emotional arc of the character and how to nail those emotions throughout the filming process of shooting out of sequence. She travels giving seminars and teaching workshops worldwide.

Laura Gardner, 323/957-4764. Caryn West Studio: 323/876-0394. Email: laura17mae@aol.com. $540 for 12 weeks, Level One. A Film and TV Preparation Toolbox for anyone lacking basic technique or anyone who wants to reevaluate their foundation. This class gives the beginning actor the techniques to bring themselves to any role and opens the way to strong auditions and work choices. Each class will focus on different tools that include physical relaxation, ability to play, take risks, gain creativity, and build self-esteem. Much of the work is based on Uta Hagen's book, *The Challenge For The Actor,* which is required reading. Laura is currently on the faculty of the Howard Fine Acting Studio and has taught in NYC at HB Studios, Stella Adler Institute, and the American Academy of Dramatic Arts. Laura also coaches privately.

Brad Heller, "The Acting Without Agony School," 323/503-8262. www.abwag.com. Classes held Tuesdays and Thursdays, $195 a month for once a week, and $295 a month for twice a week. Brad was a longtime protege of the late director Don Richardson, who wrote *Acting Without Agony: An Alternative to the Method.* I don't know Brad but I was a big fan of Don and I'm glad to see his work carried on. Brad is also a professor at UCLA.

Lorrie Hull, Ph.D. and **Dianne Hull Acting Workshops,** 310/828-0632. www.actorsstudio.com/hull/class. Her workshops offer intensive training in a broad spectrum of acting tools. Techniques of relaxation, concentration, sense memory, affective memory, emotional recall, improvisation, cold reading, preparing and learning the role, motivating and justifying behavior. Auditing allowed for a fee. Author of *Strasberg's Method: As Taught by Lorrie Hull: A Practical Guide for Actors, Teachers and Directors* and video: *The Method.*

Laura James, 818/754-4705. Ongoing acting workshop, "A safe place for the novice to learn, develop and practice your craft, and the experienced actor to be challenged and grow in your craft." Exercises, improvs, scenes, monologues, cold reading and audition techniques are taught. Small classes with individual nurturing attention. First class is free. Private coaching available.

Jill Jaress, coach and career consultant, 310/828-7814 or 888/576-4695. www.actorsconsultations.com. $240 a month. Scene study, small group. Actors work every week, which is essential to every actor's development. When the class is completed, each actor will have a monologue and two scenes on tape that can be used as an audition tape. She also teaches a three-month intensive class covering the information you need to break into the business and the acting skills you need to book the job.

Maria Elesia Jenson, 310-823-9973. www.visualizethis.com. $500 for the 12-week Acting From Depth Workshop. Payment plans available plus she offers two work-study positions. This workshop explores the connections between imagination and acting. Maria approaches acting practically, giving actors, writers and directors a range of perspectives rather than any one technique. Through use of your imagination you will learn to make stronger choices, to create unforgettable characters and to focus on the meaning of the story hidden in the subtext. Everyone works on scenes and monologues, sometimes on-camera, and there are writing exercises, along with improvs. Participants can produce their own digital video shorts as an extra-curricular activity. There is a screening of the shorts at the closing party. She also works on audition techniques with occasional video review. With this class actors will gain a variety of tools to face the challenges of the profession. Maria teaches in a lovely space in Venice.

Kimberly Jentzen, 818/509-1311. www.kimberlyjentzen.net. On-going classes as well as the Cold Reading Weekend Intensive, the Comedy Intensive, the Essence Weekend Intensive and Far Day. Award-winning director and acting coach, creator of audio tapes *Fearless Acting* and *Coming From Love*. "My goal is to create a safe place for actors to take risks, explore and develop skills, stretch their emotional range and learn how to make choices that allow their own individuality, depth and power to emerge." Training covers: scene study, monologues, cold reading, improv, concentration, imagination, audition technique and film acting. Admission by interview/audition. Beginning master classes. Auditing available.

Anita Jesse Studio, 323/876-2870, www.anitajessestudio.com. The author of *Let The Part Play You: A Practical Approach To The Actor's Creative Process* and *The Playing Is The Thing: Learning to Act Through Games and Exercises*. Through her classes and books, Anita Jesse has been providing a practical approach to the actor's creative process since 1978. Anita says: "We offer a technique that prepares you to get work in film and television, yet celebrates and nurtures your creative spirit. It's a delicate balance, and we welcome a limited number of fearless and determined actors who are willing to embrace the challenge." Classes are taught by Anita Jesse and James Ingersoll. Six ongoing classes, actors work every week. Placement in classes is by audition only. Twice a year, the studio hosts a film festival to showcase original short films produced by the members. Anita tells her students to produce a three minute or less short film, on their own without her help. There were 16 at the recent festival where the acting was wonderful in each one. The production values were mixed but on an acting reel it is always most important for the acting to be good.

Leigh Kilton-Smith Scene Study Class, 323/650-4204. $225 a month. I first met Leigh on the set of *Its like, you know...* She was Jennifer Grey's acting coach, working with Jennifer to help her attain the performance she wanted. I respect Leigh's view on acting very much. She is mainly an on-set coach but teaches one Monday morning scene class for nine months of the year. She accepts experienced and inexperienced actors working side by side as is often the case on sets. Current client list includes recognized celebrities. Auditing is permitted.

John Kirby, 323/939-5284. $450 for a 12-week commitment, classes ongoing. Intensive scene study classes for the professional, as well as newcomer. Classes are extremely disciplined and require a strong commitment. No gimmicks, exercises or class member critique. Homework and rehearsals required. Uta Hagan fundamentals. Auditing, $10. John does take out of town on-set coaching jobs.

Ken Lerner Studio, 818/753-7744. www.kenlerner.com. 12215 Ventura Blvd., Suite 111, Studio City. $200 to $250 a month. Ken uses methods culled from his own acting experiences as well as his own teachers: Stella Adler, Peggy Feury and Roy London, who handpicked Ken as his first student teacher. All classes are ongoing, beginners to advanced. Free audits by appointment. Scene study and cold reading. He gives you his insights into script interpretation so that you learn to make the "hottest" choices that will deepen your acting. See his website for many celebrity endorsements.

M.K. Lewis Workshops, 310/826-8118. www.mklewisworkshops.com. $200 a month. Author of *Your Film Acting Career*. Teaches an ongoing "Acting for the Camera" class. Also a 10-week film technique for professional and mid-level performers.

Warner Loughlin, 310/276-0555. www.warnerloughlin.com. $210 monthly. She was trained by Michael Kahn (head of Juilliard), Sonia Moore and Strasberg. Intensive on-going scene study with an emphasis on growth in skills. Focus also includes basics of camera technique, cold reading and performance fear. Her technique melds several schools of thought with her own unique concepts developed through her experience as an actress, teacher and director. Classes are small with a concentration on a safe environment to create. Strong commitment to the craft required. Fast paced and intensive. Committed beginners; intermediate; advanced and master classes. Many professionals, award winners and celebrities in the master class. Admittance by audition. Auditing is required.

Janice Lynde, 323/650-0515. $200 a month on an ongoing basis. She teaches Joan Darling's technique. Working with all levels of actors, she teaches exercises and scene study in a loving, safe environment. Class limited to 15 actors so everyone works every week. She also teaches an audition formula involving three simple acting choices that helps actors book the jobs. Janice is a working, two-time Emmy nominated actress, winner of an Obie award and director. She is also on the faculty at the American Film Institute teaching "Directing the Actor" for directors, screenwriters and producers. Also private coaching.

Mala Powers 818/980-5400 Email: chekhovpower@earthlink.net Mala holds two 8-week scene study classes each year; she gives an occasional weekend Intensive Workshop and coaches privately. Mala Powers (www.imdb.com) is an actress, Hollywood Walk of Fame honoree and has been directing and teaching the Michael Chekhov Technique of acting for the past fifteen years. She studied intensively with Chekhov and is the Executrix of the Chekhov estate. She conducts workshops in her home base of Los Angeles and throughout the United States at various Conferences and Universities. Mala teaches all aspects of Chekhov's techniques including the development of Stage Presence, Imagination, and the creation of interesting and believable Characterizations through the use of Imaginary Center, Imaginary Body, and Psychological Gesture.

Jeffrey Marcus, 323/965-9392. www.jeffreymarcus.com. $150 for four classes. Jeffrey teaches ongoing basic and advanced technique classes. When I sat in on his workshop I was very impressed with the actors' work and Jeffrey's teaching style. To quote from his website: "My belief is that each actor has talent, wisdom, courage and boldness locked inside him or her. I aim to train the artist to unlock their potential using methods I've gleaned from Stanislavsky to Tantric Yoga." My favorite quote is, "Wanting to learn to act by taking Cold Reading classes is like wanting to learn to paint by using a 'paint by number' kit." Classes are small so actors can work each week. Free auditing.

Allan Miller, 818/907-6262. $150 a month. Author of *A Passion for Acting* and instructional video *Auditioning*. Ongoing classes in techniques to refresh the creative imagination. A very passionate, experienced teacher and accomplished director. Class limited to 15 people.

Eric Morris Actors Workshop, 323/466-9250. $250 for four classes. He offers three ongoing weekly classes focusing on group exercises, instrumental work, craft work, scenes and monologues. Auditing permitted. He has developed his own system and has written some excellent books about how acting works: *No Acting Please, Being & Doing, Irreverent Acting, Acting From The Ultimate Consciousness, Acting & Imaging.*

Larry Moss, 310/399-3666. wwww.Edgemar.com. 2437 Main Street, Santa Monica, 90405. $225 a month for his Professional Class. Very famous acting coach from New York, he taught at Juilliard Studio and Circle in the Square. Helen Hunt and Hilary Swank thanked him when they accepted their Academy Awards! Many well-known professionals study scene work with him. Jason Alexander of *Seinfeld* says that classes with Larry Moss are what made his acting career. Highly recommended! No auditing; acceptance is by interview.

Michelle Danner of The Larry Moss Studio, 310/399-3666. wwww.Edgemar.com. 2437 Main Street, Santa Monica, 90405. $225 a month for an advanced class or an intermediate/advanced class. Her on-camera cold reading class is $215 a month. Michelle teaches a weekend $195 *Technique Breakdown Workshop* that should be taken by all actors who love acting. For beginners it brings you to an understanding of what it is to act. For seasoned actors, even those (me) who have been teaching for 25 years, she reminds you what all actors are capable of. Her seminar is required if you are going to study with this organization. **John Cirigliano** is also a very respected teacher at The Larry Moss Studio.

Brian Reise Acting Studios, 323/874-5593. 7954 Fountain Ave., West Hollywood, 90046. $190 a month. Brian's classes specialize in Acting and Cold Reading for beginners through professional levels. The focus is on the reality of the acting business, teaching actors how to develop their acting skills so they can audition more effectively, book jobs, get agents and guide them in their careers. Ongoing classes are held in the afternoons and evenings. No auditing due to lack of space but the studio offers free bi-monthly orientations for information about the classes. James Lew, a successful working actor, who is interviewed in the *Action Actor section* has been studying with Brian for five years. He is a big fan of the classes, says he enjoys being able to work in every class.

Stuart K. Robinson, of Robinson Creative, 310/558-4961. $140 for four sessions, on Monday and Tuesday evenings and Saturday afternoons. Stuart is the kind of teacher who inspires his actors to greatness. As a commercial teacher, he is a genius, His theatrical classes are very special too. Many of my students have taken his class and loved it. He gets to the heart of figuring out why the producers/directors need this character in the script and what is the character's function. He teaches a motivating, positive acting philosophy, very focused on actors landing the jobs. His classes always have waiting lists—good luck.

Sal Romeo, 323/665-6360. $175 a month. A workout for working and intermediate actors. Based in Stanislavski, classes focus on relaxation, self exploration, voice and speech, camera technique, cold reading, improvisation and building the character. Free workshops on weekends for his students in Improv, Grotowski, Feldenkreis bodywork, voice and speech. Sal has 25 years of experience in stage, television and film directing, as well as professional teaching. I really like the way Sal thinks and talks about acting. One of his "team teachers" is Michael Nehring, who also teaches at Chapman University. This is definitely a class to check out!

Scott Sedita Acting Studios, 323/465-6152. www.scottseditaacting.com. 526 N. Larchmont Blvd., Los Angeles, 90004. Scott says, "Our goal is to help the actor discover their own unique talent, realize their greatest potential and provide them with knowledge to successfully 'market' themselves in today's competitive industry." Six staff teachers. Professional Classes: On Camera Television and Film Acting Classes; Cold Reading and Audition Techniques; Scene Study; Master Scene Study; Voice and Speech Classes; Acting Foundation/Technique Courses; Comedy Improv and Commercial Workshop. Industry showcases presented regularly. Public performances presented once a year. Admittance is through the monthly Free Audit Seminar or a one on one interview with Scott Sedita. Speak to Jorge for an appointment.

Scott Tiler of the Scott Sedita Acting Studios, 323/465-6152. www.scottseditaacting.com. 526 N. Larchmont Blvd., Los Angeles, 90004. $500 for 10 weeks of Nuts and Bolts. Focuses on developing the actor's foundation, technique and the ability to prepare. Incorporates elements of relaxation, repetition, improvisation, imagination and sense memory. Actors work several times each session. Recommended for the new actor and those who need to re-invigorate their technique. Scott also teaches a scene study class focusing on character analysis, emotional depth and living the part. Learn to utilize intentions, objectives and beats. Assigned scripts from plays and films, scene partners are required to have 5 hours of outside rehearsal per week. This class is $300 for six weeks.

Tom Todoroff, 310/281-8688. www.tomtodoroff.com. His actors use primarily classical text (anything written pre-1900 or translated from another language) in class, unless they have an audition. He believes that if you learn to use language properly with great writing, you can easily work your way through any contemporary script. After training at Julliard, he specialized in voice placement and dialects for many years. Tom says, "It's my belief that whenever the voice is blocked it is always emotional; witness that babies have big voices. Teaching is deeply gratifying as it transforms people's lives; suddenly their work is free because their life is." Attendance is mandatory. He is now producing films (seven in the last four years). Six of his class students were in his last two films. Some of Tom's famous clients are: Liam Neeson, Lolita Davidovich, Jimmy Buffett, Tony Goldwyn, Robert Wagner, Roma Downey and Bob Hoskins.

UCLA Extension, 310/825-9064, www.uclaextension.org/entertainmentstudies. Many weekend intensives and weekly evening classes; a typical 12-week course is $465. Classes taught by working professionals. It is good to get on their mailing list just to see the wide array of classes.

Dee Wallace Stone's Acting Studio, 818/876-0386, ext. 3. www.dwsactingstudio.com. $210 a month. Put the joy back in acting. Dee is a very special person, actress and teacher. She is interested in the spiritual side of the actor and in helping each actor achieve their best. "A positive approach to fearless acting." Her technique is loosely based on Meisner and Charles Conrad, but she has developed her own way of acting that works under all the pressures you will encounter on the set. The actors are encouraged to treat the class as an on-set working environment. Her required and suggested reading list will be of great value. The class is held in a theater in a church basement. Auditing is required.

Doug Warhit, 310/479-5647. $200 for the first month (which includes one private session) $170 a month thereafter. Author of *Warhit's Guidebook for the Actor*. Casting Director Junie Lowry-Johnson of *NYPD Blue* says, "I wish I could see actors trained by him at every casting session." My student, David Roth, found the showcasing to be very valuable. Scene study and cold reading classes, beginning through advanced.

www.studioactreel.com. Bruce Ducat has a good site with many links to other actor-friendly sites.

SECOND PRINTING ADDITIONS:
Ron Burrus's website: www.ronburrus.com. He also teaches in New York.

Joanne Linville Studio, 310/248-4825. Michael Richards credits Joanne for his work on *Seinfeld*. She was accidentally left out of the 10th Edition.

Bernard Hiller, 818/781-8000. www.bernardhiller.com. "Change your thinking, change your career. Acting is a living challenge. Overcome personal blocks and recognize self-defeating behaviors. Learn to overcome emotional blocks. Find joy in the process, take charge and get started." Bernie teaches many types of classes including beginning, commercials, dialects, career guidance and his Acting Masterclass. Also private coaching $75 an hour.

WORKSHOPS OUT OF THE LOS ANGELES AREA:

KD Studio Actors Conservatory of the Southwest, 214/638-0484. www.kdstudio.com. Dallas, Texas. They have a four-semester program where you can earn an AA degree. Includes every phase of actors' development, including opportunities for gaining actual working experience. They have evening and weekend classes for actors not involved in the Conservatory program. My daughter, Cynthia Kerr, loved this conservatory and was able to pay her way through it with the acting jobs and commercials she landed while studying there. Their website provides actors a great deal of information including many Texas organizations.

Acting Studio in South Florida, 954/929-4553, www.actingstudio.org. 2450 Hollywood Blvd., #308, Hollywood, FL 33020. They have a full conservatory program as well as classes for adults and children and summer programs. I taught a weekend seminar at the Acting Studio and was very impressed with the high level of actors trained there. They also produce plays and showcases.

Ft. Lauderdale and Miami, Florida, www.acttrue.com. Acting coach Marc Durso has a wonderful site for all actors. Concepts and exercises that are useful for everyone, no matter where you are located.

In San Francisco:
Joie Seldon at Full Circle Productions, 415/982-2024.
Richard Seyd 323/665-9782.
Robert Weinapple 510/559-1029.

For more, see Section 10, Cities Outside of Los Angeles.

Audition Techniques and Teachers

• **Cold reading is an old fashioned term**. It means you pick up a script and actually read the words off the page for the very first time. It doesn't take an actor to do that; almost anyone who is not dyslexic can do it. At cold reading workshops you will be doing lukewarm readings; you will get the script and have twenty minutes to work on it before you present it to the casting director, agent, manager or director that is the guest that evening. In order to do an audition in twenty minutes, you will have to make many acting choices plus memorize as much as you can. It doesn't really give the full report of how good you are as an actor. Many actors have been fired from the set because they were good at auditioning but couldn't deliver on the set.

• **You can become an excellent auditioner** but it most likely will be because you have the sides at least overnight as SAG guarantees in our contract. Where cold reading or quick audition skills will come in handy is at auditions for student films when the script isn't available ahead of time. The students haven't learned yet that they are unable to cast the best actor from that type of audition. They will learn. You will learn too that if you can't see the script ahead of time you'll go in early, pick up the sides, take them out to your car, and work on them for twenty minutes.

• **On actual auditions, you should never be asked** to cold read because we get our sides the day before. Casting directors' jobs depend on them calling in good actors to read. The exception might be if you come in to audition for one role and they think you would be better in another role. Again, take the script away from their office and prepare it using your quick skills then go back to the office and tell them you are ready.

• **I would suggest studying your basic acting technique first**, then take an audition technique class to enhance your acting skills. You will be able to get the most for your money because you will understand the acting skills your audition teacher is talking about. There are special skills for auditioning. Recently, I took Caryn West's Audition Workshop and learned so much. I've been auditioning for years but it was great to stretch myself; it was exciting.

• **Caryn West taught me about "butt breathing."** The name alone tickles me and keeps me thinking about it. Conscious breathing is essential in all acting in fact in many life situations it is helpful. We use our breath to find our center, to allow the tension to drop from our bodies through the floor. When we hold our breath, it short circuits our acting instincts; we lose power.

• **Caryn gives her explaination:**

  • **Having been an athlete most of my life** and at one time a world class Alpine skier (National Alpine ski team for 4 years), I learned a lot from my years of competition about "peak performance" skills under pressure. My ongoing investigation of that phenomenon has really helped both myself and other actors prepare for auditions and with their acting in general. It has a lot to do with centering and breath.

  • **Auditioning as a process has similarities to acting** in rehearsal, onstage or in actual shooting, but with a big, confusing twist: The actor is necessarily put into a "proving mode," yet the conundrum is the only way he/she will get the job is to "not need the job." The actor can often feel threatened by the authority figures in the room. The "fight or flight syndrome" of the situation can physically and psychologically overwhelm the actor. And the trouble starts when the actor walks in holding their breath. Or starts holding his/her breath the minute they begin their lines. Even the well-trained and talented actor can "choke" and audition badly coming from this place. Basically, the actor in not breathing or in taking very shallow breaths has to sprint to get to the end of the material.

  • **I teach actors to use a bigger "uber breath,"** not unlike the large, diaphragmatic ways opera singers train to sustain a legato phrase or produce the big high note. I rather comically refer to good audition breathing as "butt breathing." Because if you consciously breathe very low and deep and pull in a large of volume of air, you will indeed feel it, ever so slightly, in your anal sphincter. So your "butt" essentially clues you in to whether you are really breathing deeply.

- **In fact, when you do breathe deeper in auditions,** it seems easier to center oneself, stay in your body and commit to physical choices, to listen more acutely, to assimilate emotional stimuli, to think a sub-textual thought that we could read on your face, to access your courage and spontaneity. In other words, deep "butt breathing" is the essential lubricant to a well-oiled acting engine. Without it, we choke, we sputter, we get all "gummed up" and awkward, we run out of gas in the room or spin out of control.

- **Deep breathing is the simple key** to correcting many problems that appear to be more complicated.

- **Cherie Franklin**, noted audition and on-set coach, answers: Are there different styles to auditioning for films, soaps, episodics and sitcoms?

  - **For feature films,** the actor must remember the screen is 30 feet high, and tailor his/her movements and expressions accordingly. The old adage "Less is More" is never more true than in acting for the feature film.

  - **Soap Opera** is a very personality-driven medium, and the audition must show a character with a full personality. Knowing your lines for the soap audition is essential.

  - **Episodics** play heavily on the 2 shot/3 shot and single reaction shots. Audition with these shots in mind, not the master. Episodics feature one to three story lines, and knowing to what story line your character belongs is necessary to deliver an audition appropriate to the show as a whole. Some story lines are resolved each week, others are on-going, and still others are set-ups for resolution down the line. Know your spot.

  - **Sit-Com** has a specific timing and rhythm and pace, and your audition must include all of these. Recognize what attitudes, emotions and/or behaviors are necessary to support the 22 minute show.

  - **For all mediums, the story is like a puzzle.** It is essential for the actor to recognize exactly where his/her character fits into this puzzle and to provide an audition that delivers the "missing piece" his/her character has to provide. Providing too much or too little will lose the job.

- **Caryn West answers,** Do you audition differently for different types of projects?

  - Yes! and no. Some elements are essential in all forms, but styles and genre dictate a lot of your choices. One cannot approach a noir film or an edgy cop drama as you would a broad commedia based sitcom or even a silly Rob Schneider or David Spade farcical comedy. You certainly approach Moliere or neoclassicism differently than Odets or Arthur Miller, so too must an actor adapt and learn the world of a film or TV genre. How a show is shot and the size of frame also dictate much about choices. Many stage-trained actors when auditioning for camera, don't realize they are 'muscling' a part and showing and telling too much about a character when the simplicity of the communication can speak for itself. Trusting subtext and inferences best left to the audience to decipher for themselves are essential camera skills. They are some of the hardest lessons to learn, as I had to suffer through them myself, but once mastered makes the actor even more versatile.

AUDITION TEACHERS & WORKSHOPS

Judy Kerr, 818/505-9373. www.JudyKerr.com. $80-$100 an hour. Private coaching for film and television. We study the audition material and decide how to portray your character. We work on camera until you can deliver the performance that could land the job. You keep the tape.

Caryn West's Audition Workshop, 323/876-0394. Los Angeles Web Site: http://groups.yahoo.com/group/CarynWest-ActorsLA. For New York actors: http://groups.yahoo.com/group/CarynWest-ActorsNY. $600 for 12 weeks. Not designed for the beginner but for those who have their basic technique and are actively auditioning. "There is emphasis on script analysis, breath, presence and spontaneity." Privates are $80. She regularly teaches at Michael Howard's studio in New York. Sign up online to receive her informative, instructive newsletters.

Michelle Danner of the Larry Moss Studio, 310/399-3666. wwww.Edgemar.com. 2437 Main Street, Santa Monica, 90405. $215 for four weeks. Emphasis is placed on developing strong intentions, fully realized relationships and specific clear environments. Overall, this workshop focuses on making creative and powerful choices, while bringing your unique personality and your professional best into every audition. Call for class times.

Brian Drillinger of the Larry Moss Studio, 310/399-3666. wwww.Edgemar.com. 2437 Main Street, Santa Monica, 90405. $215 a month. This ongoing class is especially recommended by Jode Leigh Edwards. Learn to clarify the audition process as well as strengthen your ability to prepare and execute a great audition by learning how to make physical and emotional choices. Learn the Do's and Don'ts of an audition and how to break down a scene. Experience the freedom and energy of making bold choices.

Joel Asher, 818/785-1551. Teaches a 6-week cold reading class for $195, all on camera. Joel has a lovely theater he has built.

Lori Cobe-Ross, CSA, 562/938-9088. Film and television casting director. Lori has a small class once a week in Brentwood, 8-10 people in the class. You work with the sides, put it on camera, she critiques it and you tape it again.

Cherie Franklin, 818/762-4658. $85-$200 an hour private coaching for auditioning. Cherie is a very inspirational teacher and on-set coach. She teaches seminars, classes and privately, emphasizing confidence, pacing, behavior, developing a character and how to remove fear.

Margie Haber Studio, 310/854-0870, www.margiehaber.com. Very well respected audition technique teacher. Author of the book: *How To Get The Part Without Falling Apart*. Several teachers teach her technique at the studio.

Sandy Holt, 310/271-8217. $400 for 8 weeks. She is a *Second City* alumni. She will point out what is working or not working in the characters you create. She teaches how to take care of yourself at auditions, how to switch gears in a second, "how to be interesting and specific, get to the heart of the character, and audition with power." Hones in on what is special about you so you can totally rely on yourself. She says, "80% of the actors who work with me are landing the jobs. They're prepared, open to taking risks and committed to going full out with their characters. They make an impression; they stand out."

Kimberly Jentzen, 818/509-1311. www.kimberlyjentzen.net. Award-winning director and acting coach. On-going classes as well as *the cold reading weekend intensive, the comedy intensive, the essence weekend intensive* and *fear day*. Admission by interview/ audition. Beginning-master classes. Auditing available.

Kip King, 818/784-0544. One of the original Groundlings. Private coaching $75. Helps you bring yourself to each character you play. Especially helpful with comedy. *See Commercials and Improv sections.*

Karen Kondazian, at The Lee Strasberg Institute, 323-650-7777. www.strasberg.com. 7936 Santa Monica Blvd., Los Angeles, 90046. To register contact Victoria Krane by above phone or admissionsLA@Strasberg.com. $450 for a 12-week class. Advanced actors only. Beginners must study at least six months at Strasberg's before joining the class. Karen works with the actors on cold readings and monologues. She also brings in many industry guests, such as casting directors, agents, managers, theater directors, commercial teachers, career advisors, and has them lecture and teach a class. Karen is a lifetime member of The Actor's Studio and studied with Lee Strasberg. She's a winner of the LA Drama Critics Circle Award, journalist for Backstage West, and author of *The Actor's Encyclopedia of Casting Directors*. Karen's website is: www.KarenKondazian.com.

M.K. Lewis, 310/826-8118. $200 per month. Author of *Your Film Acting Career*. Teaches a 12-week cold reading and interview technique workshop on camera. Auditing permitted.

Joey Paul, CSA, 818/784-6500. On the staff at TVI. She is a casting director, and teaches basic technique, cold reading, improv, scene study, all geared toward getting the job or the audition process. On camera. Also great insights on "the biz."

Scott Sedita Acting Studios, 323/465-6152. www.scottseditaacting.com. 526 N. Larchmont Blvd., Los Angeles, 90004. $300, for a six-week Audition Intensive taught by Scott Sedita tailored for the professional actor who is represented and is currently auditioning. All aspects: working the sides, preparing the character, coaching for the role, the callback, the screen test, group auditions, entrance and exits. Scott's motto for this class, "Be prepared but expect the unexpected."

Melissa Skoff, CSA, 818/760-2058 or VM: 310/262-8651 for her assistant, Larry Woods. $150 a month. Respected casting director. Industry guests. $40 for a paid audit.

Clair Sinnett, head of Clair Sinnett Casting, 310/606-0813. E-mail: sinnett@earthlink.net. $250 for a Weekend Intensive; includes marketing, cover letters, interview techniques, cold reading, script analysis, screen tests, etc. All sessions videotaped, followed by in-depth critique. Author of *Actors Working: Marketing For Success*. Private sessions $100 an hour.

COMEDY AND STAND-UP

ACTING COACHES

• **Judy Carter—standup comic, author, and master teacher** has appeared on over one hundred TV shows. She is the author of *Standup Comedy: The Book* (Dell Books, 1989) which has sold over 150,000 copies. Her latest book—*The Comedy Bible* (Simon & Schuster; September 2001)— the definitive guide to making a career out of making people laugh, was featured on *Oprah* and *Good Morning America*. Ten years ago she formed Comedy Workshop Productions, which runs comedy classes nationwide. Carter also produces the annual California Comedy Conference in Palm Springs, California, which is attended by top Hollywood VIPs including executives from HBO, Warner Bros, William Morris Agency and others. Her web site, www.comedyworkshops.com, has valuable information for standup comics and actors, including listings of agents, job and casting opportunities, and video clips.

Q: Tell me about the book.

> • *The Comedy Bible* **is the ultimate guide** for anyone wanting to know how to turn their sense of humor into a comedy making career whether they want to do standup, write, or do a one-person show.

Q: Do you have specific things to say about actors doing stand-up?

- **If you look at TV sitcoms, they are all using stand-up comics** because they know audiences don't lie. There's a certain confidence that stand-ups have to bring to a producer. They can make an audience laugh right there and then. Or an agent can bring an actor to a producer and say, "Yes, this person knows how to make an audience laugh. I saw it myself."

- **As a stand-up, it is much easier to showcase** your talents because when you have an act, you don't have to wait to be cast in a play. You can go to a showcase yourself. It's obvious why casting directors prefer to go to a club. At a showcase at the Improv, they'll get to see 20 people in two hours, eat nachos and drink. It's true. They talk, schmooze, mingle and maybe have sex with someone they've met when they are done. That rarely happens in waiver theater.

- **You can have a video of yourself** doing stand-up and get work that way. I can't tell you how many students I have with development deals because they sent a video tape to someone who showed it to someone else.

- **Create an act.** Decide what the sitcom would look like that you are in. For example, if you look at *Roseanne's* show and then you look at her first HBO special, you can see that everything was there. All the characters that she talked about and acted out in her stand-up act became real actors in the sitcom that she became the center of. Who are the people that are in your arena of life? What is your life like? Who is your family? If you look at Mary Tyler Moore, her family was the people she worked with. Her problems were due to being a single woman.

- **Back to *Roseanne*,** it was her immediate family, trying to eke out a living and deal with men in this sexist world. If you put yourself in the center, who are the people that you have issues with? You start acting them out in your life and you start showcasing that. It's a great way to empower your career and hold the reins on your creative destiny. You're not waking up each day saying, "How can I get somebody to see me to give me a job?" You wake up each day creating material that will lead someplace.

Q: How do they learn to create material if it doesn't come naturally?

- **We have an audio tape workshop** that has four tapes. The first tape is "Creating your material," which asks a lot of self-help things like "It bugs me when my mother..." It bugs you with what isn't right with your immediate relationship. On tape two, we cover those "ranting and ravings," which all come from what bugs you about people that you are in relationships with. We talk specifically about how to arrange that material in stand-up material format. It's a very specific formula and structure that has to have a set-up to interest the audience and relieve itself in a laugh within 30 to 40 seconds because of the nature of television. You've got to keep people from channel surfing. Tape two goes into those techniques.

- **Tape three is "How not to bomb."** Once you've put your act together and you're going to go out and perform it, you need specific techniques to let go of fear. Tape four is how to go and market your act and start making money, which is a very separate issue.

- **CD ROM, Five Steps to Writing A Joke, comes with a little workbook.**

Q: What about the fear?

- **Actors that I speak to are dealing with fear.** "Oh, there's no one else on stage." What they find is the audience is their friend, and they become the other character in a scene. They learn that it's not about giving a monologue, but having dialogue with the audience. You just don't know how the audience is going to react. The same way in a play. You really don't know how the other actor is going to read a line, but you just have to be alive and respond.

Q: Do you have to be funny yourself?

- **Most people who make good stand-up** comics are people who aren't the center of attention but are the people who are watching. They are the ones outside of their family, the ones who have a crazy family and who aren't very involved, but watch and comment later on what happened. It's the observers of life, but not necessarily the ones that are very funny, who are the stand-ups.

- **Steve Kaplan, "The Stanislavski of Comedy,"** teaches a Comedy Intensive Weekend Seminar. He has taught comedy at Yale, NYU and UCLA. He created the HBO Workspace and ran HBO's New Writers Project. His class is for actors, writers, directors, producers and studio executives.

Q: What is the key element of comedy?

- **Comedy is about an ordinary person struggling** against insurmountable odds, without many of the required tools with which to win, yet never giving up hope. Great comics share their own imperfections with us without ever giving up. The art of comedy is telling the truth about people and it's also about hope.

Q: What can a comedian do to develop their act?

- **The best thing is to watch great comedians,** such as Charlie Chaplin, Buster Keaton, Jack Benny and Bob Hope. Notice the music of comedy—the rhythm. It's a form of jazz with timing, rhythmic and musical elements.

Q: What makes a joke work?

- **There are two elements:** the jokes themselves and the character they are written for. The jokes are the expressions of a character who most commonly has a unique, or sometimes warped, point of view. For instance, Jerry Seinfield has a routine about socks. The topic is ordinary; you put socks in the washer, you put them in the dryer, but you always seem to lose some along the way. Where do they go? What's happened to them?" The joke is in his strange analogy: he says they are prisoners and the lost ones "escaped." If you see a stray one lying in the gutter, it's one that didn't make it. He takes it to the logical/ illogical extreme.

- **Stand-up comedy is a theatre piece with a very small cast** so it's still about creating character: Emo Phillips and Howie Mandel are idiots; Jerry Seinfeld and Paul Reiser are observers. Find the voice for that character or persona and let that character speak about the world in a specific way.

Q: What about the *Seinfeld* characters? What made them funny?

- **They were all funny in different ways.** They were the four most horrible people in New York, but what was funny is they admitted to the worst sides of themselves. They did it in a way that put us at ease and we can say "It's okay I'm this neurotic; it's okay that I'm this cranky." George was the biggest, most neurotic loser in the world. Kramer was the biggest idiot. Elaine was the crankiest woman; her lover said, "Let's do it again," and she said, "You're not sponge-worthy." This is a woman we hope we don't meet on a date. And yet, there are parts of these people in each of us.

- **The genius of comedy is that it loves humanity without forgiving it.** The audience says, "It is okay for George to be a neurotic loser," and then they say, "Look at him; he's a neurotic loser." And the gift that those actors brought to those characters is that they did it with such inventiveness, truth and specificity.

Q: How do you play a comedic character?

- **Comedy depends on things being the way they are in real life,** which is untidy and inconsistent. The comedic character is usually one that the main characters can react to. You should let your character be as imperfect and honest as you can. Actors will often argue and say "this character is not stupid," but the comedy in the scene depends on the character not being perfect, so play that imperfection. Just being weird won't get a laugh because people can't relate to that.

- **There is a difference between funny and comic.** If you laugh at something, it's funny, no question, but that doesn't necessarily make it comedy. If you're not laughing at it, it's not funny to you. In a play, what's comic is to see a character be in a pickle and not really know what to do. When an actor who isn't getting a laugh panics and says "Oh, no, I'm not getting a laugh" and makes it bigger, it becomes less real and less funny. If you think you're doing something funny and the audience isn't laughing, they could be enjoying it but just aren't laughing out loud. However, if they never laugh, you might have a problem.

Q: How do I choose a comedic monologue?

- **Many people choose things that are silly** or as far from them as possible, thinking that comedy is about exaggeration. I would look for a monologue that speaks to you—that reflects some of your experience. You can speak your own truth through the character. What makes it comic is the fact that you share the confusion, befuddlement, lack of certainty or neurosis of the character. Comedy gives you the permission to make mistakes in front of people.

Q: Where should you look for comedic monologues?

- **Look at plays that speak to you**; if you're a young girl from Brooklyn, you don't want to do Tennessee Williams. It's not about showing how you can stretch; it's more difficult than that. It is about showing and really speaking about what's going on with you. If you're a young girl, find a young girl who's confused about the same things you are. If you're a guy who's not good with girls, find something from a Woody Allen movie. A lot of people find great monologues in comic novels. Comedy tells the truth about people, so you have to get material from a great writer who has written a great character who is a complete human being.

Q: How do you find comedy in a drama?

• **By focusing on the character, rather than the dialogue.** That is also how you find comedy in a sitcom. What is funny is what is human about this character. We would like to be as romantic as Kenneth Branaugh in Hamlet; most people are more like Ray Romano—just ordinary guys who are confused by the things that happen around them; trying their best to get through the day.

• **Performing stand-up comedy** is a good way to be noticed in Los Angeles. Take a chance; hit all the open mikes at the many comedy clubs listed in *Backstage West* and *L.A. Weekly.* Many comedians have been signed to development deals or cast as regulars on sitcoms because of characters they portray in their acts.

• **Buy the DVD of *Comedian,* the movie about Jerry Seinfeld** getting his act together. Some video stores carry tapes of stand-ups doing their acts. Watch the comedy channel. Read books the comics have written. *SeinLanguage* by Jerry Seinfeld is one of the best. Figure out why you laugh on each page. His sense of language and vocabulary is extraordinary; he can turn a phrase better and funnier than most. Jerry just walking around is funny; his thought process is funny. One thing I like most about him is his loyalty to all of his stand-up friends. He looked for roles on the show where he could hire them, and then always appreciated their work.

• **Rita Rudner** analyzed the science of comedy by playing all of Woody Allen's albums from his stand-up comedy years, listened to Jack Benny albums and every comedy album she could get at the library. She tried to figure out what was funny. She would try a joke out on her friends and if they laughed, she would use it. "It's hard, yet you do feel a tremendous power."

• **Tom Dreesen** occasionally teaches comedy seminars. He tells of sleeping in his car in an alley in the Valley and hitch-hiking to the Comedy Store and begging for the chance to get on stage. He used to perform at The Show Biz. Some of the other comics there were Michael Keaton, David Letterman, Jay Leno, Robin Williams, and Debra Winger was the waitress. "Whatever the mind can see and believe it will also achieve. I used to go to that car every night and see myself on *The Tonight Show* and Johnny Carson laughing and telling me I was funny. Now I have a picture on my wall of that happening."

• **Eve Brandstein, who has managed several comics,** says, "You can develop characters or material in an improv, acting, writing or stand-up workshop. Work your material among your colleagues. Then go to one of the small clubs on their audition night, get up and try it. If it's for you, you'll know it; you'll get bitten by it. Bingo!"

• **Bernie Young of the Bernie Young Agency** has managed many comics over the years. Currently, his only client is Rosie O'Donnell. He is her manager and was the executive producer of her talk show when it was on the air.

Q: Do most comedians have a manager?

> • Yes. **Certainly the person that is the self-motivator** and a very good organizer really can serve as his own manager. But most entertainers are so focused on their work that they don't have time to spend on those little things that make a difference in moving their careers forward. It's pretty important that comedians have that other voice, that manager who can give them career guidance and help move their careers in the right direction.

Q: Do you help comedians with their material?

> • **If they are working on new material, I'll give them my input.** They respect my opinion and that I'll be objective in looking at that material. We always discuss what they intend to do, should and shouldn't do, but the final decision is theirs.

Q: What advice would you give for someone wanting to get started in stand-up comedy?

> • **You need to have your own point of view, your own style.** Comedy is personal. My advice would be to understand who you are and develop your ideas around that. That's going to be the thing that sets you apart from everybody else. For so long, the industry didn't look at stand-up comedians as actors. The industry now realizes that these people are acting every night. They write their own material, perform it, and promote their own shows. It's perfect training for sitcoms and feature films.

Q: Then what do you do?

> • **You have to get on stage, in front of an audience.** Wherever you are in this country, there's a comedy club somewhere close by. Work the material and the audience will judge whether or not it's good. In stand-up today, you can be "discovered" in any city in America. If you really want to get into TV and film, you need to be in Los Angeles or New York.

Resources

Also look at the Improvisation Teachers Section.

Judy Carter, Comedy Workshop Productions, 310/915-0555. www.comedyworkshops.com. She guarantees a performance at a comedy club and a video of your act. *The Comedy Bible* includes a test to find out if you're funny. She offers free class auditing as well as regular emails about up-to-date casting info. Call or email for her brochure info@comedyworkshops.com or 800-4COMICS (800-426-6427). Private consultation also available.

Sandy Holt, 310/271-8217. She is a *Second City* alumni, has a looping group and teaches improvisation, character work and on-camera sketch comedy. I asked Sandy for advice for struggling actors. She laughed, "Marry a rich person so they'll pay for your classes. Be willing to do whatever it takes. I don't care what age you are or what you've been through; follow your dream." Private coaching to work on material, timing and on-camera persona. $80 an hour.

Kimberly Jentzen, 818/509-1311. www.kimberlyjentzen.net On-going classes as well as *THE COLD READING WEEKEND INTENSIVE, THE COMEDY INTENSIVE, THE ESSENCE WEEKEND INTENSIVE* and *FEAR DAY.* Award-winning director and acting/comedy coach. Admission by interview/audition. Auditing available.

Steve Kaplan's Comedy Intensive, 818/728-6951. www.comedyintensive.com. $425 for 10 weeks. Workshop for professional actors, writers and directors designed to "move beyond intuition and guesswork" and give artists "the tools to understand why things are funny, how to adjust things that don't work, and how to make sure that your audition or performance succeeds." He created the HBO Workspace, founded New York's famed Manhattan Punchline, developed writers such as David Ives, Howard Korder, Peter Tolan, David Crane and Ted Tally, and directed and coached actors such as Mercedes Ruehl, Illeana Douglas, and Oliver Platt. He has taught comedy at Yale, NYU and UCLA and has been called the Stanislavski of Comedy.

Harvey Lembeck Comedy Workshop, 310/271-2831. www.harveylembeckworkshop.com. $200 a month. Three levels but aimed for the trained working actor who wants to specialize in comedy. Teaches how to play comedy legitimately in a scene. Using improv as a method to teach comedy, work on stage 3 to 4 times a night. Robin Williams said, "I looked around the class and said I'm home, they can't hurt me now, forget therapy." Former students include John Ritter, Jenna Elfman, Bryan Cranston, Kim Cattrall.

Mark Lonow, Improv co-owner 323/936-9550. Mark is an actor/writer/director. He teaches four 10-week classes for $400, one on acting and one on standup comedy point of view—which culminates with a performance at the Improv. Claudia Lonow is available for private coaching.

Paul Ryan's Comedy Studio at CBS Studio Center, 323/936-9524. www.paulryanproductions.com. CBS Studio Center, 4024 Radford Avenue, Studio City, 91604. All levels. Classes start at $195 a month. Master comedy acting classes, sitcom character development, comedy improvising, comedy timing, sitcom auditioning techniques, cold readings, comedy scene work.

Scott Sedita Acting Studios, 323/465-6152. www.scottseditaacting.com. Scott teaches a Comedy Intensive one-day Sitcom Boot Camp. Includes: Eight Characters of Situation Comedy; How to breakdown a comedy script; How to identify and deliver a joke; How to find your "Comedic Note." Many other classes taught at the Studio as well as a six-week sitcom class.

Janice Kent's Sit-Com Audition Technique Intensive, 818/906-2201. www.janicekent.com. Hone your audition technique by: Finding your signature; Facing your fears; Learning script analysis; Finding the HOT choices. 2003 Students have appeared in *Raymond, Will & Grace, Friends, Grounded for Life, Frasier, Reba, According to Jim, Miss Match, What I Like About You*, partial list. Also works privately; great for those important sitcom auditions.

Comedy Dojo, Chris Barnes, 310/393-6686. www.comedydojo.com. Chris has put together an acting technique you can take from the classroom to the stage, to the audition and onto the set. Actress Aimee Garcia recommended this class to me when we worked together on *All About The Andersons*. She found his comedy character definitions very helpful.

Cynthia Szigeti, 818/980-7890. Former head of the Groundlings' training program, and of Acme Comedy Theatre's improv workshops. Students have included Lisa Kudrow, Conan O'Brien, Alex Borstein and Julia Sweeney. She coaches actors and stand-ups privately. $50-$75 an hour.

BOOKS

Order:
Samuel French Bookstore, 323/876-0570 or 818/762-0535 or the website: www.samuelfrench.com.

Stand-Up Comedy: The Book by Judy Carter

How To Be a Stand-Up Comic by Larry Charles and Richard Belzer

SeinLanguage by Jerry Seinfeld

Successful Stand-Up Comedy: Advice from a Comedy Writer by Gene Perret

VIDEO STORES

Video West, 818/760-0096. 11376 Ventura Blvd., Studio City, 91604.

Video West, 310/659-5762. 805 Larrabee Street, West Hollywood, 90069.

These video stores are the best! Bargain days Tuesday, Wednesday and Thursday, $1.29 a tape. Have them give you a tour of the store; they've got classics, independents, foreign, art house, comedies, stand-up comics. Just about anything you need to research. Fantastic!

Private Acting Coaches

• **Many actors routinely use an acting coach** when they are auditioning for an important role. The time to get your coaching is before your first reading. If they call you back, they liked what you did. Sometimes, though, the casting director or director will ask you to take the script and bring a character back with a whole different attitude. Your coach can help you discover a new way to approach the character.

• **Actors when working on projects** will often hire their coach to prepare them for the role before shooting starts. They will work on the entire script so when they are shooting out of sequence the actor will know and remember the work they had planned for each scene. Often on a film or a single-camera television show, you may shoot the first and last scene the same day. You may be shooting the nude love scenes your first day on the project, even the first day of meeting your partner. For several seasons of *Seinfeld,* Michael Richards worked with his coach, Joanne Linville, for each show.

• **Working with an acting coach** privately will help you progress faster, as every moment will be concentrated on you. However, there is no audience to work off of, as there is in an acting class.

• **Your first consideration** will probably be the cost. The average price is $50 to $100 per hour and at least twice that much if you are being coached on the set or for a role you're being paid for.

• **A beginning actor** who is very shy may want to have private sessions before joining a class.

• **You may need coaching** if you are a new actor and have been given a job as a result of your fame in another field, such as sports or modeling. When I was Joan Darling's assistant, she coached, among many others, Joe Namath, for his first film after his football career. Some of the personalities I've worked with are Catherine Oxenberg when she was on *Dynasty;* Miss America, Debbie Maffett, when she landed her first television job hosting *P.M. Magazine* and Thea Vidale, a successful stand-up comic who had her own ABC television show, *Thea.*

• **A good time to seek a coach** is when you are getting lots of callbacks but not landing the jobs. The coach may be able to give you that extra edge of confidence to put you over the top.

• **I usually video tape when coaching.** I believe actors learn faster if they are able to see their work and observe their own strong and weak points. They also take the tape home and continue to learn from their work and my notes.

• **Many of the coaches** listed below are also written about in greater detail in the *Acting Coaches* section.

Private Coaches

Judy Kerr, 818/505-9373. www.JudyKerr.com. $80-$100 an hour. All levels, acting techniques and audition work. I coach actors for auditions. I also coach actors who want to study acting privately. A beginner who wants an understanding of what it is to act before taking classes; or an experienced actor who wants an hour devoted to them to further develop their technique. I give the actor a script ahead of time; they work on it and bring it in having done the best preparation they know how. I coach on video so they keep a tape of their acting along with my critique and instructions of how to make and deliver stronger acting choices. The actors then review their tape at home and learn more. I also teach a private one time, one-and-a-half to two hour career coaching/ guidance meeting for $120-$150. This is based on the principles in the book but geared for you individually—what works for your particular needs.

Caryn West, 323/876-0394. $80 an hour. Los Angeles website: http://groups.yahoo.com/ group/CarynWest-ActorsLA. For New York actors: http://groups.yahoo.com/group/ CarynWest-ActorsNY. $80 an hour. She is sometimes available in New York.She is great at preparing you for your auditions. Caryn has coached me many times.

Rae Allen, 310/396-6734. Tony Award winning actress and director. $125 per session on camera.

Joel Asher, 818/785-1551. www.Joel-Asher-Studio.com. $100 an hour, but free when you are taking his scene study class.

Sandra Caruso, 310/476-5113. www.tft.ucla.edu. Private coaching and audition preparation, $45 an hour. Professor of Acting at UCLA School of Theater, Film and Television. Author of three books, *The Actor's Book of Improvisation: Dramatic Situations for the Teacher and the Actor* by Sandra Caruso and Paul Clemens, *The Actor's Book of Improvisation: Dramatic Situations from Shakespeare to Spielberg,* Book 1, Ages 12-16 and Book II, Ages 7-11.

Brian Drillinger, 310/828-9107. $75 an hour. Some actors Brian has worked with privately are Traylor Howard, Jennifer Grant and Stacey Dash. He helps the actor strengthen their ability to prepare and execute a great audition by learning how to make physical and emotional choices. Learn how to break down a scene and experience the freedom and energy of making bold choices. His group classes are taught through The Larry Moss Studio.

Wayne Dvorak, 323/462-5328. www.actingcoachdvorak.com. Private coaching is $60/session.

Cherie Franklin, 818/762-4658. $85-$200 an hour. Cherie is an inspirational teacher; I've worked with her often. She's also an on-set coach.

Nina Foch Studio, 310/553-5805. $200 an hour for consulting and coaching for actors and directors. She is an Oscar and Emmy nominee, a working actor since 1942, a professor at USC and a director of documentaries and MOWs.

Jill Jaress, coach and career consultant, 310/828-7814 or 888/576-4695. www.actorsconsultations.com. $120 an hour. Private coaching for audition preparation as well as designing cover letters, submitting to agents and casting directors, and other business techniques.

Sandy Holt, 310/271-8217. $80 an hour. Audition preparation. Geat with sitcom material.

Leigh Kilton-Smith, 323/650-4204. $150 an hour for consulting and coaching. Also an on-set coach.

Janice Kent, 818/906-2201. A very experienced actress, director and coach. She specializes in sitcom, but coaches everything. She emphasizes taking the risks to make bold choices.

John Kirby, 323/939-5284. $65 an hour, unless paid by a studio or agency. Works privately on auditions, bookings and on-set coach. Also does career consulting.

Warner Loughlin, 310/276-0555. www.warnerloughlin.com $125 an hour, unless paid by studio. On-set film and television coaching for actors and directors. She works with many celebrities and adores beginners.

Janice Lynde, 323/650-0515. $75-$150 an hour. Teaches a wonderful, fast, simple audition technique, as well as coaching for a specific role you have been cast in.

Jeffrey Marcus, 323/965-9392. www.jeffreymarcus.com. $75 an hour. "My coaching is practical, workable and designed to give specificity and clarity to finding the behavior in the dry dust of the words; and to find the 'fun' in what can otherwise be a fearful experience of auditioning. We find the arc and logic of behavior." Jeffrey is hired by studios to coach actors for film and television roles.

Allan Miller, 818/907-6262. $125 an hour.

Mike Muscat, 818/904-9494. $50 an hour, he coaches on camera and offers a money back guarantee. He is especially good at helping stage actors adjust to film acting. He works as an on-set film coach.

Mala Powers, 818/980-5400. Email: chekhovpowers@earthlink.net. $75 an hour. Mala is a Hollywood Walk of Fame honoree, author and director specializes in the Michael Chekhov Technique of Acting. Audition preparation and coaching for specific stage and film roles. She studied intensively with Chekhov and is the Executrix of the Chekhov estate. She teaches all aspects of Chekhov's techniques including the development of Stage Presence, Imagination, and the creation of interesting and believable Characterizations through the use of Imaginary Center, Imaginary Body, and Psychological Gesture.

Stuart K. Robinson, 310/558-4961. $100 first time and then $80 an hour after that. Great with commercials, auditions, script writing and directing for demo reels and business strategy.

Scott Sedita of the Scott Sedita Acting Studios, 323/465-6152. www.scottseditaacting.com. $75 for an hour and $40 for a half hour. Now a coach, he's been a casting director and an agent. KTLA-TV says, "One of the hottest coaches in town."

Clair Sinnett, 310/606-0813. E-mail: sinnett@earthlink.net. $100 an hour for career counsulting and audition preparation. All levels. "If you don't get cast, no one gets to see how talented you are." Clair teaches creative audition choices and conversational dialogue. "Once you're cast, who gets to be creative? The director!"

Cynthia Szigeti, 818/980-7890. $50-$75 an hour. Former head of the Groundlings' training program, and of Acme Comedy Theatre's improv workshops. Students have included Lisa Kudrow, Conan O'Brien, Alex Borstein and Julia Sweeney. Coaches actors and standups.

IMPROVISATION

• **I believe every actor** should have some improvisational training. Many casting directors look for the ability to improvise on your resume. I have been hired for several acting jobs solely because I knew how to improvise. In television it is almost essential because you have very little rehearsal time; nor is there time for the director to tell you how to play a scene.

• **Improv is also good** for breaking down barriers you might have in revealing yourself, so it is helpful to study it at the beginning of your acting career—you get off to the right start.

• **Jeff Doucette**, founding member of the ongoing "Improv at the Improv" and veteran of Chicago's Second City.

Q: How does improvisation help actors?

> • There is a common misconception that improvisation is about being funny. When actors are working on their feet, they often make the more comic choice, but that is not by any means the only valid one. Wonderful improvisations often center on more dramatic situations and emotions. Improvisation is a technique of acting. Acting is playing. As actors, we play parts in plays, screenplays, or teleplays. Spontaneity is the natural by-product of play. Improvisation opens the door to spontaneity by focusing on playing and solving problems in the moment. Through the process of improvisation, actors learn their own acting technique naturally by learning how to push their own buttons. They learn scene structure and character development. They unlock their creativity and open their imagination.

• **Learning the lines and breaking down a scene** can only give an actor a game plan. Once the camera is rolling, once the lights come up on the stage, the actor must trust his choices and find the truth in the moment. He must play the part. Improvisation teaches an actor to trust his instincts. An actor trained in improvisation learns to love being out on a limb. He's not afraid because he knows that if the branch gives way, there will either be a net to catch him or he will discover that he can fly.

• **Improvisation also helps the actor in everyday life** and in almost any audition situation. By learning to play with people and trust his instincts, an actor can overcome fear and learn to project his personality in a positive and constructive way.

Q: How should an actor pick an improv teacher?

• **First of all, the actor has to decide what he wants.** There is comedic-performance oriented improv and there is improv aimed more at the acting process. Both are good, but many actors are intimidated by the comedic improv classes. They feel that they have to be clever, quick and funny, or are intimidated by the competitiveness of the class.

• **Obviously you should talk to the teacher.** But ask specific questions and listen carefully for the answers. The more you know what you want out of a class the more specific you can be with your questions. You're not going to "get" the whole course in an interview, but how you relate to the teacher will give you a feeling of how it might be in the class.

• **Take advantage of an audit.** You can get a feel for the teacher, the class and the other students. If auditing isn't permitted, try to talk to as many students as possible. Most will say they love it, but try to pin them down and find out why they love it. See if you can get them to be specific. This will give you a better idea of what it is they look for in a class. It may or may not be what you are looking for.

• **Sandy Holt improv/cold reading teacher**, acting coach, actress, comedy writer and co-owner of a voice casting company, began her career performing with *Second City*.

Q: Why is improvisation important for the actor?

• **Improvisation is the springboard to your imagination.** I get actors to unlock the part of their brain where the creativity is, to break through the cliches. Improv is like jazz—you pick up on the riff that's happening and go with the dance and bring your magic to it.

I get actors to find their own magic. Sandra Bernhard told me when doing *King Of Comedy*, she used all the skills she learned in class. She got the part because she brought her own excitement to the work, her own stamp.

• **Improvisation is also valuable for writers and stand-ups.** If a writer is having trouble with a script, we improvise to see what isn't working. Is it the action? Too wordy? Are the characters authentic? I had writers from *Cheers* come to my class. They were having trouble pitching ideas. By getting them into improvising and playing different roles, they really increased their pitching skills. Stand-up comedians find out what's funny about them and what makes them special.

Q: How would you describe your ideal student?

• **Someone who wants to play,** is willing to take direction, wants to participate, loves to get up and is willing to work through resistance. Actors should use their improv class as a safe place to make mistakes, work through blocks, get their courage up, take risks, go through their discomfort, and move through fear, so they can tap into the most wonderful, craziest part of themselves. When I interview actors wishing to join my classes I ask what they need to work on. Some people say, "I'm going up for auditions but I don't nail the job." So we work on how to nail the job. I work with actors on camera because this is a film business. I work on appearance and image. When you walk into a room, what do they see?

Resources

Jeff Doucette, 818/769-3767. $120 per month—3 hour class. Founding member of the ongoing "Improv at the Improv" and veteran of Chicago's *Second City*. He is the winner of the Drama Critics Circle Award for best lead performance, appeared in hundreds of TV shows, over 30 films, 70 stage productions. Acting on instinct, scene structure, character development, sense memory, all levels. "Through various acting/improv exercises actors learn to trust and develop their own workable acting technique."

Gary Austin, 800/DOG-TOES. Gary is the original founder of The Groundlings. He is a famous coach and teaches around the country. His prices are very reasonable and you should take at least one session with him. Many stay for years.

Comedy Dojo, Chris Barnes, 310/393-6686. www.comedydojo.com. Actress Aimee Garcia recommended this class to me when we worked together on *All About The Andersons*. She found his comedy character definitions very helpful.

Andy Goldberg, 310/479-1498. 12—16 week classes. Author of *Improv Comedy* as well as member of the *Off the Wall* improv group since 1975. Ongoing class applying improv techniques to character development.

The Groundlings, 323/934-4747. 7307 Melrose Ave., in Hollywood, 90046. www.groundlings.com. $395 for 12-week class. A performing group producing many working actors specializing in comedy. Go see a performance and get an idea of what is possible in improvisation. Students audition for the basic level, then are invited to the intermediate class. Auditions are not required for the pre-beginning-level class.

Sandy Holt, 310/271-8217. See the *Audition Technique Section*. She combines improv with audition technique.

Kip King, 818/784-0544. $350 for 10 weeks, returning students $300 for 11 weeks. One of the original Groundlings. Helps you bring yourself to each character you play. Especially helpful with comedy. Uses improv with commercials and comedy.

Improv Underground, 310/451-1800. Based on *Second City* school of comedy. Classes and live performance. Games, scene work, character development and long-form improv. $300 for eight weeks.

Harvey Lembeck Comedy Workshop, 310/271-2831. www.harveylembeckworkshop.com. $200 a month. Three levels but aimed for the trained working actor who wants to specialize in comedy. Teaches how to play comedy legitimately in a scene. Using improv as a method to teach comedy, work on stage 3 to 4 times a night. Former students include John Ritter, Jenna Elfman, Bryan Cranston, Kim Cattrall.

Mark Lonow, 323/936-9550. Mark is an actor/writer/director and co-owner of The Improv. He teaches four 10-week classes for $400, one on acting and one on standup comedy point of view—which culminates with a performance at the Improv.

Second City Training Center, 323/658-8190. 8156 Melrose Avenue, Los Angeles, 90046. www.secondcity.com. Lots of different classes at varying prices. See website for information. "No comedic or presentation acting form in America has been unaffected by Second City."

VOICE AND
VOICE TEACHERS

To an actor a word is not just a sound, it is the evocation of images. Your job is to instill your inner visions in others. . . and convey it in words. Constaintin Stanislavki

The voice is the audio reflection of your soul. Expanding the voice opens the artist and the soul. Bob Corff

• **Acting is a vocal art**; our voices are used to interpret and depict scripts. Most actors need voice training in order to have complete control of their speaking voice. In many plays, actors need to use their voice for a considerable length of time. In film and TV, a big yelling scene may come after 12 or 16 hours of work; your voice should last through all of that. Another skill that must be in the actor's tool kit is the ability to speak with a general American accent; without it you will be very limited in the roles you will be considered for. You can add other accents and dialects for even more versatility. Of course, speaking other languages helps too.

• **Sal Romeo, a popular acting coach says:**

  • **As an actor it is necessary to free one's natural voice** so the truth of feeling comes through. Much of what is done in film and television today is shot in close up and really all you've got is your voice to bring the nuance and emotional truth to the work. Vocal relaxation and use of language enhances and brings truth to one's performance. Many of us have been raised with tension in our voices; we put on a nice personality that hides our feelings in order to please. Often that voice is pitched from two or three notes to even an octave higher than our real, natural, true voice. When you learn to relax the tension in the voice, the emotional truth rings out in a richer, more resonating sound.

- **Tom Todoroff, film producer, acting, dialogue and dialect coach, says:**

  - **Basically, all you have to act with is your breath.** If you're not connected to your breath, it's possible to speak but you are saying words that don't come from where you feel things. I can understand you, but I'm not receiving your words where I feel things. The breath sends off vibrations that the other actor and the audience feels.

- **Gary Catona, voice builder, says:**

  - **The voice is a character,** as identifiable as your physical appearance. Your voice should be an expression of who you are, as an actor and as a person. When a person acts and a singer sings, they are indulging in an athletic activity. It is athletic because you are using muscles. In a sense, an actor is somebody who is a vocal athlete and you have to look at his or her voice in that light. Vocal exercises are important; exercise is necessary to improve your voice.

- **Bob and Claire Corff, well known voice teachers, say:**

  - **Enriching and improving your voice alters the way you feel** about yourself and the way people respond to you. Voice is the purest representation of you, revealing levels of confidence and attitude. The voice is one of the first and most powerful characteristics people respond to. A strong and self assured voice commands attention and respect.

  - **Developing an effective voice is as important** to a person and an artist as developing a toned and healthy body. Practicing the proper exercises from one to three weeks can make a striking improvement in any actor's voice. This can have as dramatic an effect on their performance and confidence as having plastic surgery.

- **Godeane Eagle, speech pathologist and voice teacher, says:**

  - **Actors are their own instruments,** and in order to play that instrument, it has to be in tune. Some of the problems are: not using the voice to the fullest, lack of confidence, vowel shapings or vowel projection, and the sound of the voice. If, at the end of a performance or rehearsal, the performer is feeling strain or pain in the throat area, he or she is doing something incorrectly. Voices can be stressed to the point where they simply stop.

• **Ben D'Aubery, dialect and accent coach, explains the difference between dialects and accents.**

  • **Dialect is regionalism**—as far as emphasis on the words and pronunciations as used in language. You have an accent when you use your own language regionalisms on someone else's language. For instance: a German learning to speak English would be speaking with an accent. But if a Californian goes to the South and speaks as a Californian, it would be considered a dialect. If English is your native language and you go to another country where English is spoken, you would be speaking a dialect, because your "English" would be a regional difference on that country's "English"—Irish, Scottish, Australian, etc.

  • **Accent** means when you take on a foreign language, you're speaking with an accent—Spanish, Italian, Russian, etc.

• **When listing dialects and accents** on your resume, make sure you list them correctly.

• **Godeane Eagle,** when working with accents, believes ear training is the first step.

  • **It's necessary to take the actor to the piano** and check how he or she recognizes pitches; it must be known if they can match a pitch, or even hear a pitch. Ear training makes people aware of fine-tuning differences in sound, such as between 'pen' and 'pin.'

• **You can train your ear for the proper language or dialect** you wish to use. A good source is Dove Books on tape. The books are read by well known actors and authors. If someone says they want you to play an Elizabeth Ashley or Tom Hanks type, you can get a tape of that actor reading a book or parts of a book and pick up some of what their essence is.

• **Shopping for the right voice teacher** is important because working with your voice is extremely intimate and personal.

• **Godeane Eagle believes:**

  • **It's necessary** that the voice teacher be someone with whom you feel comfortable, someone who cares about you and is interested in your voice. The speaking voice is very sensitive, delicate, and will respond negatively to negative teaching. Actors can learn both privately and in small classes, though beginners frequently need one-on-one because they need total attention.

- **Tom Todoroff recommends:**

  - **Meet with three different coaches** and take a class with each—see who you connect with.

- **He also spoke of the discipline required for voice work:**

  - **Your voice is a series of muscles** like other muscles in your body and it responds to exercise. When you go to the gym or take a dance class, your body becomes more elastic, more coordinated; your voice is the same way. If you don't work on it, it doesn't take care of you. An actor needs to work 20 minutes each and every day on their voice. To be an actor and not work on your voice is akin to being a dancer and saying, "I don't go to dance class" or a pianist who says, "I don't believe in scales or practicing." So much of what I teach beginners in the first classes has to do with the benefits of discipline. Discipline allows you incredible freedom.

- **For information on work in voiceovers,** read *Voiceover Work* in Section 3.

Resources

• VOICE TEACHERS

Bob Corff, 323/851-9042, www.corffvoice.com. $75 a half hour. If you mention this book he will give a special rate of $65 a half hour. For actors and singers, works on giving your voice color, strength and stamina. Working on breathing, diction, accents and accent reduction, sibilant "s" and other speech problems, proper placement, lowering your voice and widening your range. Small group classes and private sessions. Author of the tape, *The Bob Corff Voice Method.* Some of his famous clients include Antonio Banderas, Glenn Close, Heather Locklear, Jenna Elfman, Faye Dunaway, Sally Field and Salma Hayek.

Claire Corff, 323/969-0565, www.corffvoice.com. $45 and up. She teaches the Bob Corff method. Singing, speaking and accent reduction. She's fun and easy to be with. Many of my students as well as my husband, Ron Gorow, and I have improved greatly while working with her.

Sam Chwat, In New York, 212/242-8435. (Pronounced schwah.) www.nyspeech.com. People Magazine says: "Speech pathologist to the stars, accent-uates his celebrity clients." Adam Sandler in *The Waterboy;* Julia Roberts in *Mystic Pizza;* Leonardo DiCaprio in *The Basketball Diaries;* Robert De Niro in *Cape Fear.* He's recorded three audio books about accent elimination. They can be ordered through New York Speech Improvement Services, 1/800/SPEAKWELL.

Ben D'Aubery, 818/783-1951. $45 to $60 an hour. Private and group lessons, specializing in accent reduction and acquisition. I worked with him at the West Coast Ensemble Theatre to develop a North Carolina accent; he was excellent. He can deliver a crash course to get you ready for an audition in a short amount of time. Standard English, Cockney, Scottish, Irish, Aussie, French, German, Russian, Italian, Spanish, Yiddish, American Southern, New England, New York and Caribbean. On *Seinfeld*, he helped the Jamaican jogger (whom Elaine fouled up) create his accent.

Bill Dearth, 818/761-1051. www.Sqlman.com/SpeechMech. $60 per session, $295 for six lessons. Specializes in learning and losing accents and developing speaking voices. "Your voice is as important as your picture!" Highly recommended by commercial teacher Carolyn Barry.

Brian Drillinger, 310/828-9107. $50 an hour for private coaching. $35 a week for the group class. Recommended by acting coaches Larry Moss and Michelle Danner and actress Jode Edwards. Brian begins by working privately. You learn to connect with your full breath and work through a series of exercises that become a vocal warm-up you can use the rest of your career. Once you've learned the warm-up, you join the advanced class and work on acting material from a vocal perspective. In class you will work to create a clear channel of breath, emotion, and voice. Brian believes, "You must have an emotionally connected, fully expressive voice; it is the primary connector between you and the audience."

Godeane Grace Eagle, 310/450-5735. $50 to $75 an hour. Godeane holds an M.A. combination in music, theatre, and clinical speech. She teaches singers and actors who want to sing. She teaches stage voice, projection, and is very mindful regarding voice and throat protection. She works with students of all ages, including young children and is trained in speech defect correction and accent reduction. She was my special teacher and helped me find my real voice. I am eternally grateful.

Libby Jordan, 310/428-2992. $75 an hour. American dialect coach, she works almost exclusively with Australian, English, and New Zealand actors who require a natural-sounding American accent. She also works with American actors who need to perfect a new dialect, whether British or American. Her technique focuses on how the breath, tongue, lips, placement of the jaw and intonation all determine how our dialects sound. Libby says this method quickly teaches you how to physically change your speech patterns effortlessly so you can slip into any American dialect easily.

Patrick Munoz, 323/512-3841. $85 an hour. Teaches privately and in group classes at the Scott Sedita Acting Studios, 323/465-6152. Four week session, $200. Learn to breath properly and lose any regionalism and accent reduction. He incorporates several techniques including Skinner and Linklater plus his own unique approach. Also works as an on set dialect coach. Very highly recommended by Talent Manager, Steven Nash. Private clients include Penelope Cruz.

Elizabeth Sabine, 818/761-6747. www.elizabethsabine.com. Call for rates. Voice strengthening specialist. She teaches at the Lee Strasberg Theater Institute and UCLA Extension. Some she's worked with: Kathy Griffin, Chuck Norris, Elisabeth Shue and

Priscilla Presley. She trains her students to replicate the physical and emotional manifestations of extreme emotions by taking short breaths and holding their abdominal muscles tight, the same as they would if they were yelling at someone in anger, or like a hungry infant when it cries for a bottle.

Tom Todoroff, 310/281-8688. www.tomtodoroff.com. See Acting Coach section.

• VOICE AND DIALECT TAPES AND WEBSITES

The **Bob Corff Voice Method**, www.corffvoice.com. *Bob Corff Speaker's Voice Method; Bob & Claire Corff's Achieving the Standard American Accent* and *Voice Method for Singers*. Sold on the website or at Samuel French Booksellers, Take One! and Skylight Books. "With the confidence that comes from having a strong, powerful voice there are no limits to what you can achieve in your career." Casting director Reuben Cannon says, "Your success as an actor or singer will be greatly determined by your vocal skills. Study with a master—Bob Corff."

Sam Chwat's SPEAKUP! Programs, 1/800-SPEAKWELL, M-F 9-6 EST. Three different tapes: *American regional accent elimination; Spanish regional accent elimination; Asian Middle Eastern, Hindi-Indian-Pakistani, Chinese, Japanese, Vietnamese, & Pacific.* Call for more information.

Jerry Blunt audio tapes of accents and dialects available at theatrical bookstores. These tapes are very conversational and easy to learn from.

David Alan Stern, 800/753-1016. www.dialectaccentspecialists.com He teaches from a very academic point of view on these tapes, but many actors use them. His books and audio tapes are available at theatrical bookstores or by mail order. Call for catalogue; they will probably have a tape for any dialect or accent you need.

www.iwasthere.org.uk/page_18.htm. Click into Links then into International Dialects of English Archive. You will find two different printed texts and then downloadable voices reading the text in many different dialects. MP3 files. You can study these and train your ear for the dialect.

www.uncc.edu/english/clc/index1.html. Oral histories from different parts of the country.

www.dialectresource.com/. They give a very brief sample of some dialects but have tapes of many different dialects to purchase.

polyglot.lss.wisc.edu/dare/dare.html. On this site, Dictionary of American Regional English, click on Audio Sample and you will hear several different people with accents reading a short passage.

http://web.uvic.ca/ling/resources/ipa/handbook.htm. Downloadable audio files of language illustrations. Many languages.

www.ling.upenn.edu/phono_atlas/home.html. Samples of New York speech. Download and listen.

• SINGING TEACHERS

Morgan Ames, well known composer, singer and producer, recommends the following two voice coaches to the professional and studio session singers she produces and arranges for. They work strictly with the singing voice.

Liz Lewis, 818/623-6668. www.thesingersworkshop.com

RosemaryButler, 310/572-6338. www.rosemarybutler.com. Works also with teens. Call for rates.

• BOOKS AND MATERIALS

The Total Singer by Lisa Popeil, 800-BEL-VOCE
The Secrets of Singing by Jeffrey Allen, 800/644-4707, ext. 22.
Tom Todoroff's recommended reading list: **Voice and the Actor** and **The Actor and the Text** by Cicely Berry; **Freeing the Natural Voice** by Kristen Linklater; and **Speak With Distinction** by Edith Skinner.
The Brand Library, 818/548-2051. 1601 W. Mountain Street, Glendale, 91201, at the top of Grandview Ave. Hours: T & Th 1-9, W & F 1-6, Sa 1-5; W 1-5. They have a vast supply of records, tapes, CDs, print music and art books available for loan-out.
Theatrical bookstores sell books and tapes to help you with standard American speech as well as dialects.
Travel Stores, for tapes of instruction on how to speak other languages. Usually the instructor on the tape has the accent of the language they are teaching.
Working Actors' Guide lists voice teachers for speech and singing.

• **Tongue Twisters** can sometimes be a very good warm-up for your voice on the way to auditions or before getting ready to act in class, on the stage or set. Memorize your favorite ones to be able to use them anytime. Godeane Eagle gave me these two favorites of mine: "Blueberry pie with peach ice cream" and "Strawberry shortcake with whipped cream." Really move your mouth, pucker and smile. Tom Todoroff's favorite is: "Eleven benevolent elephants." Try some of the following twisters. Use a tape recorder to make sure your pronunciation is correct.

TONGUE TWISTERS

- The lips, the teeth, the tip of the tongue.
- Which witch, what watt?
- A big black bug bit a big black bear.
- Loving Lucy likes light literature.
- Some shun sunshine, do you shun sunshine?
- Bad blood (ten times very quickly.)
- Flesh of freshly dried flying fish.
- I slit a sheet, a sheet I slit. Upon a slitted sheet I sit.
- Lemon liniment, lemon liniment, lemon liniment.

STAGE PRESENCE,
BODY AWARENESS,
BODY MOVEMENT

• **The moment you step on stage** or in front of a camera, you must become larger than life. This ability comes from the control you have over your body. We are born with the capacity to use our bodies perfectly but somewhere along the way, many of us learn bad body habits. I don't think there is an acting institution or acting teacher who does not recommend some type of body movement class. We act through our bodies; acting is an athletic event.

• **In the beginning of my career**, an acting coach told me I would never be able to work as an actress because I was "sunk into myself," I had no presence. I had spent a great deal of my life trying not be seen—very detrimental for an actor. Your presence, your appearance, really does make the difference in getting jobs. It is the way you present your *package* when you walk in the door that will make a lasting impression.

• **He was the right kind of acting teacher** because he not only told me the problem but gave me the solution: The *Alexander Technique*. It took me about four lessons before I began to get an understanding of how to hold my body properly. Once you learn the technique, it is yours. I studied constantly for two years because I was in bad shape, but then it became mine.

• **Good stage presence becomes a habit**, just like bad posture was. This technique has helped me in everything I do, whether it's yoga, ballet or weight lifting. It is a specific, unique body technique that will increase the amount of space you take up in a room and what you *radiate* in person, on the stage, or in front of a camera.

• **After about ten years I had to go back for more lessons;** I was "sinking" again. This time I went with the Sike Technique that incorporates Alexander Technique and other traditions. It took me about a year to really discover good stage presence again. There are also many other health and pain relieving benefits with the Sike Technique.

• THE ALEXANDER TECHNIQUE

• **F. M. Alexander was an Australian actor.** When he lost his voice while performing, he went to specialists and was told there was no solution. He decided to look for the cure himself. He spent many months in front of a three-way mirror to try and detect the exact reason for the hoarseness in his voice. He discovered the hoarseness came as a result of vocal misuse and an overall pattern of body misuse. He could clearly see it in his mirror but he couldn't feel it. It became clear he could not correct his voice without changing his mental concepts and the way he used his whole body. He noticed the muscles at the back of his neck pulled his head down and caused a chain reaction of pressure down his spine. This created tension throughout his entire body.

• **Alexander then developed a technique** to help himself and over the years trained many actors and taught others to teach his technique. The changes he noticed in himself and his students included: a release of excess tension in the body, a lengthening of the spine, greater freedom and flexibility in movement, more efficient breathing, elimination of vocal problems and improved posture and appearance. His most famous directive and one his teachers give over and over again is: "Let my neck be free to let my head go forward and up, to let my back lengthen and widen." When you learn to move in this fashion you will acquire better posture, grace of movement, better balance and coordination in your body for all of your activities.

• **The *Alexander Technique* is taught** at many institutions, including The Juilliard School in New York, ACT in San Francisco, SMU in Dallas, UCLA and USC in Los Angeles. Juilliard graduate Kevin Kline says, "The many obvious benefits that the technique afforded us as actors included minimized tension, centeredness, vocal relaxation and responsiveness, mind/body connection and about an inch and a half of additional height." Andre Rotkiewicz, movement teacher at KD Studio Acting Conservatory in Dallas, says, "It makes you, the actor, aware of your mannerisms so you can control and change your actions. You will become more neutral and able to take on more characters. The connection with the mind and body will let you become more universal." Alexander said, "Every man, woman and child holds the possibility of physical perfection; it rests with each one of us to attain it by personal understanding and effort."

- **Lyn Charlsen, certified *Alexander* instructor says:**

  - **Performers need to be conscious of what they're doing** with their bodies, because that is their means of expression. It really becomes the tool for the expression of their art—whether that's somebody holding a violin, an actor on stage, or a singer. The way that we are using our body translates into the sound of the guitar, the sound of the voice, or the expression of the face.

  - The *Alexander Technique* can increase an actor's physical coordination and allow him to express himself fully. The elements of choice and consciousness enliven performance skills and make it possible for people to do what they intend. What's so wonderful for actors to know is that their instrument is so finely tuned that they can really be spontaneous.

- **THE SIKE TECHNIQUE**

- **Dr. Mallory Fromm and Therese Baxter of the SIKE Institute** explain this unique body work, which is a healing art and a means of correcting poor body behavior, harmful to the quality of presence, movement and voice.

  - **The *SIKE Technique* combines two healing and alignment techniques.** The first one is *Physio-Synthesis*, created by an osteopathic physician to restore structural balance in order to improve the body's contour, grace in movement, circulation and breath control. The second technique comes from Japan and is based on the precise use of Ki (or Chi) Energy to send energy directly into the nervous system to command muscles and ligaments to move and shift bones and organs.

  - **This technique relaxes the upper body,** head and neck by strengthening the actor's body from the ground up. Inner core muscles extend the spine which lifts and supports the head up and off the top of the neck, producing a "floating" sensation. The body is grounded and light at the same time. Application of Ki Energy to the head and solar plexus produces mental clarity and heightened concentration. Thus a unity of mind and body is achieved. In this way stage presence is enhanced through the natural projection of character, substantiality, and intensity.

  - **The *SIKE Technique* for actors** is a series of weekly or bi-weekly treatment and instruction that, as the actor gains confidence, tapers off to seasonal treatments to maintain an integrated body structure. The ultimate goal is to make the actor independent of the practitioner.

• MOMENTUM

• **Ebba-Marie Gendron, acting teacher** and practicing, registered dance/movement therapist has developed *Momentum*. She works with actors and other artists who wish to strengthen their art and deepen their self-knowledge through movement. She explains *Momentum*:

> • **It is in connecting to the body through movement** that we connect to the deepest part of who we are—the place in us from which our creativity as artists springs. Movement allows for open, honest and spontaneous connection to both ourselves and others.

> • **Our feelings, past experiences and imagination** are directly held in the body. Opening the body to this material sets the stage for deeper internal awareness and subsequently, greater spontaneous flow of impulses through action. This ability directly translates to character development, scene study and performance.

Resources

North American Society of Teachers of the Alexander Technique, 800/473-0620. www.alexandertech.com. Check website for classes and prices. There is a wide selection of classes offered. This is the only organization of authorized or certified teachers of the technique in the United States. You can call this number, leave your name and address, and they will send you a list of all certified teachers. Teachers can only be a member of this society if they have gone through a three year, rigorous, approved training course. The booklet also includes societies in other countries.

Dr. Mallory Fromm and Therese Baxter of the SIKE Institute, 818/992-0713, www.sikehealth.com. $65 per treatment. Workshops are announced on the website. Mallory is the author of "The Book of Ki: The Healing Principles of Life Energy" and "Qi Energy for Healing and Health." Therese is a graduate of England's Royal Academy of Dramatic Arts and has experience with Feldenkrais Technique, Alexander Technique and is a certified practitioner of *Physio-Synthesis.*

Momentum, Ebba-Marie Gendron, 323/935-7666. Classes are held at the Sal Romeo Acting Conservatory. Open to all actors. This ongoing movement workshop focuses on the freedom of expression achieved through relaxation, kinesthetic (bodily) awareness and the use of voice. The classes are led by Ebba-Marie Gendron, MA, DTR. She pulls from her extensive and varied movement training to uniquely synthesize the work of Jerzy Grotowski together with dance/movement therapy, yoga, creative movement and voice to create a powerful creative exploration for the actor. Private sessions are available for $50 an hour.

Lyn Charlsen, Alexander Technique, 818/786-3944, Van Nuys. $60 for a private class. She is my special teacher and has worked with many actors.

Debby Jay, Alexander Technique, 818/769-9171. She teaches an introductory course on the Alexander Technique at the Howard Fine Acting Studio. Open to all actors. Privates available in Studio City. Sessions are $70 and a sliding scale is available. Call to get on her mailing list to receive her very informative newsletter.

Larry White, Alexander Technique, 310/394-3177. $50 an hour, in Santa Monica. Specializes in scoliosis.

UCLA, USC, Howard Fine Acting Studio and many other colleges offer group classes.

South Florida: Roberto Mainetti, 305/438-9379. $50 hr. 1918 Southwest 17th Terrace, Miami, FL 33137. Highly recommended by one of the actors from The Acting Studio.

SCRIPTS FOR WORKSHOP SCENES AND MONOLOGUES

• **Choosing the work you want to do in class** takes effort but it is very rewarding; you get to act the roles that attract you, roles you may not otherwise have the opportunity to portray.

• **Take chances! Stretch! Can't hurt!** It also really helps you to read scripts. Even if you read 15 scripts to find one scene, you will have learned something.

• **Videotapes are a great source for scenes**, as are books. When you pick a scene from a book, chances are no one has seen it before, which is a big plus.

Resources

SCRIPTS ON-LINE
www.whysanity.net. There are hundreds of monologues that have been transcribed from movies. My lovely student Carol Hernandez told me about this site and the ones below. This one solves the, "where to find a short monologue" question.

www.script-o-rama.com. Drews Script-O-Rama.

www.dailyscript.com. Daily Script features a new script every day, or search the huge database. Free.

www.screentalk.org. Screen Talk.

www.movie-page.com. Movie Page.

www.vl-theatre.com. The Virtual Library for Theatre and Drama.

www.screenwriting.about.com. Free Scripts.

www.zzippeddskripptzz.com. Many film scripts. A one-time $15 sign-up fee. You have to remember your password to get back in after signing up.

www.chezjim.com/writing/monologues.html. Free adult and teen original monologues. Actor Jim Chevallier has written many monologues he invites others to use. He also sells a book *The Monologue Bin*.

Academy of Motion Picture Arts & Sciences Library, 310/247-3035 for general information; 310/247-3020 for general reference. 333 S. La Cienega, at Olympic, West Hollywood. M,Tu,Th,F 10-5:30; closed Wednesday and weekends. You must present a valid ID such as a passport or driver's license. No personal belongings are permitted, but they provide storage lockers. For film scripts: read the scene into a tape recorder or hand-copy and take home to type—there is no photocopying unless the script has been published. Laptop computers are permitted, but no carrying cases. Great place to go.

The American Film Institute, Louis B. Mayer Library, 323/856-7654. www.afionline.org. 2021 N. Western Ave., north of Franklin, Hollywood. M-F 9:30-5:15; W till 7:15; Sa 10-4:30. Library is closed during the summer and odd hours during Christmas and Spring breaks. No copying of unpublished scripts, but you can copy published ones. Books, periodicals, clipping files, festival files, motion picture collections, seminar transcripts, oral history transcripts, special collections.

Movie World, 818/846-0459. 212 N. San Fernando, Burbank, 91502. Every day 11-6. Books, posters, magazines, photos, autographs, memorabilia and scripts.

Script City, 818/764-4081. www.scriptcity.com. Outside of California 800/676-2522. Ask them for a catalogue; it's all mail order. They have thousands of movie and TV scripts, directories, guides, books, audio/video seminars, etc.

Samuel French Theatrical Bookstores, www.samuelfrench.com. 323/876-0570. 7623 Sunset Blvd., Hollywood. M-F 10-6; Sat. 10-5; Closed Sunday. Valley store: 818/762-0535, 11963 Ventura Blvd., just East of Laurel Canyon, Studio City. M-F 10-9; Sat. 10-6; Sun 12-5. For plays, get their free catalogue. They also sell many published film and television scripts.

Take One Film & Theater Books, 310/445-4050. www.take1filmbooks.com. 11516 Santa Monica Blvd., West Los Angeles. A great bookstore and knowledgeable staff. They have several free events every month; seminars and book signings.

Larry Edmund's Theatrical Book Shop, 323/463-3273. 6644 Hollywood Blvd., Hollywood, 90028. M-Sa 10-6.

Dramatists Play Service, 212/683-8960. 440 Park Ave. South, New York, NY 10016. Call, ask for a catalogue; they will mail it.

• SCENE AND MONOLOGUE BOOKS

• It's a good idea to buy two copies of a scene book; then you and a partner can read all the scenes together—good practice.

99 Film Scenes For Actors edited by Angela Nicholas. The interview with acting coach Mark Monroe on how to pick scenes for class is worth the price of the book. I love this book. Definitely buy two.

The Ultimate Scene and Monologue Sourcebook: An Actor's Guide to Over 1000 Monologues and Scenes from More Than 300 Contemporary Plays by Ed Hooks. This reference book should be on every actor's and acting teacher's bookshelf. No monologues, but where to find them.

The Monologue Index: A guide to 1,778 Monologues from 1,074 Plays edited by Karen Morris.

The Perfect Monologue by Ginger Howard Friedman. Forward by Michael Shurtleff.

Contemporary Movie Monologues: A Source Book for Actors edited by Marisa Smith and Jocelyn Beard. Over 95 monologues from contemporary films.

50 Great Scenes for Student Actors edited by Lewy Olfson.

Film Scenes for Actors edited by Josha Karton.

Scenes and Monologues from the Best New Plays edited by Roger Ellis. A sampling of the more recent works of playwrights.

The Actor's Book of Movie Monologues edited by Marisa Smith & Amy Schewel.

Uptown Character Monologues for Actors: Powerful Original Audition Pieces by Glenn Alterman and many other monologue books. www.glennalterman.com.

• **Many screenplays are in book form**—usually several scripts by the same writer or director.

How to Rehearse and Prepare for Scenes, Monologues, Audition Material and Acting Jobs

• **Your job as an actor is to make dialogue sound like the truth.** Sometimes that's easy, other times not. It is always doable. You decide what is the truth of the script; you choose how to tell that truth. When you don't really figure out the script your performance won't look truthful—it will look general, non-specific, vanilla, like you are just saying the words with a fake attitude.

• **Eli Wallach, (imdb.com), talking of creating the reality in acting,** said: "If I ask you to sing *Happy Days Are Here Again,* the same words but I change the circumstances—If I say to you, 'Sing it like you've just been given a raise or won the Academy Award,' you'll sing one way; if I say to you, Your wife of 30 years just died—now sing *Happy Days Are Here Again.* You sing it without me prompting you as how to sing it. . . and that's one of the secrets of good acting."

• **You making the choices for your interpretation** of the script is your "acting work." How you choose your acting work will come from what you have learned in basic technique acting classes, from what has worked for you in the past and from your instinct. As always, making these choices is what allows you to give a very specific, unique performance, whether for a finished project or an audition. I am instructing you from what I have studied, used in my own acting and taught my students. I ask you to use acting tools that come from your own life experience, your own reality. Other acting techniques are just as valuable; use what works for you.

• **Never start to memorize lines until you have chosen your acting work.** If you memorize the words before choosing the work, it will tie you up so you won't be able to really investigate all that is waiting to be discovered. This is true whether you have twenty minutes to work on a script or three weeks.

• **Read the whole script** (if available), then read your scenes again out loud to hear the words, all the roles, not just your lines. Read the copy or sides over many times. Don't use any acting at first, listen to what your instincts tell you about the script.

• **When you are auditioning for a television series** that you haven't seen or don't know the tone of, you can view an episode or several at Jan's Video Editing, 323/462-5511. Jan's has all of the shows. The charge is $20 an hour. No charge if you are a client of Jan's.

• **Look up any word you are not familiar with** at www.m-w.com, Merriam-Webster's Collegiate Dictionary. Enter your word, write down the meaning and then click on the little speaker icon and a voice will pronounce the word clearly for you. If it is a new word you need to learn to pronounce it, record it several times on a tape recorder. Listen to the word and speak it many times so it will sound like your everyday language. When your character is a doctor, lawyer, politician or in the military, they will have a specific vocabulary that rolls off their tongue.

• **Decide what the given circumstances of the script are.** This means: what, when and where are the circumstances of the script? Look for every clue possible. It is important what the other characters say about your character. *Given circumstances* are all the things the story (script) tells you about the events taking place and the characters taking part. Such as: What happened right before and after this scene? What was I doing? What was I saying? How old am I and the other characters? What is my relationship to the other people in the scene and to the people mentioned in it? How do I feel physically? Emotionally? What do I want? What is standing in the way of my getting what I want? What is the emotional event going on in the scene? What is the place like? Is it home? Is it a place that is uncomfortable and why? Are the ceilings high or low? Is it hot or cold? Ask and answer every possible question you can think of.

• **When all the given circumstances** aren't in the script or scene, use your imagination to create them. Your choices should be *hot* ones: passionate, filled with feeling. You either *love or hate* yourself, the situation and the other characters. Be specific: this character is afraid of the dark, has hot flashes, is sexually aggressive, shows affection by teasing, feels betrayed by his sister, hopes the sweat stains under his arms aren't showing, has to go to the bathroom but doesn't want to leave the room, etc. The more specific you are the more you will be able to pack into your interpretation of the script.

• **If the role you are auditioning for is a day player part** with just a few lines, then you may have to make up all of your given circumstances. For instance: This is an accountant who loves his job, a bank teller who has a hangover, a garbage collector who is an opera buff, a doctor who is very proud of his education, a socialite who has a drinking problem, a musician who is afraid of becoming deaf, a ballerina who is obsessed with her feet. For most day player roles you will be the only one who knows these things about the character.

• **Nina Foch, famous actress, director** and private acting coach who charges $200 an hour says, "I never tell people what to do. But I ask them every possible question and I get them to ask themselves every possible question. When they leave me, it's unlikely they'll be asked any questions they're not prepared to answer. They're prepared." Be as thoroughly prepared as if you were paying $200 an hour. It may help you to write the given circumstances on your script as you discover them.

• **You must figure out what the author means** in each and every line so you know how to personalize it, or relate it to your own life.

• **To *personalize* the scene** is to make the lines mean something to you personally so it looks like you are speaking the dialogue truthfully. Use the lines of the scene as a *code* for what you would say, did say or wished you had said in your own life. If the scene situation is like a situation that you have experienced in your life, it's fairly easy and there won't be much acting work involved. If it is different from your own life, then choose a similar or parallel situation.

• **When you are personalizing,** you will be talking to the other character in the scene "as if" they were your: sister, father, lover, person you hated, someone you betrayed, who betrayed you, and so on. It doesn't matter if the scene says you are talking to your sister and you (because of the circumstances) decide to talk to a male principle you had in grade school. If need be you can personalize one part of the script as one person and then switch talking to another person more appropriate for another section.

• **Harvey Keitel, speaking of** *acting as if*:

> • **Improvisation was always a very good tool for me to use.** It helped to bring me closer to the role; to find the role in me. To learn about the life of a pimp *(Taxi Driver)*, I found myself a pimp and we improvised. I played the girl and he the pimp, and he showed me how a pimp would treat one of his girls and then we would reverse the roles. So first I had to research what a pimp is; then I can play it *as if* I'm a pimp. The notion of improvisation, the notion of *as if* is very simple: to do it as if I'm your brother, as if I'm your father, as if I'm your husband—sort of a jumping-off spot, the *as if*.

• **For auditions, now is the time to start rehearsing the lines,** thinking of the pieces of acting work you've chosen. Try several different ways and personalizations; if the director gives you some direction during the audition, you will not be fixed on just one way of acting the role. Now you can highlight your lines, saying them as you are highlighting. Underline your cues. Sometimes it is not a line, it is a phone ringing or a kiss or a doorbell. You want to memorize those cues so you have a reaction planned, even though they don't actually happen in the audition room.

• **The lines are not the most important thing;** they can get people off the street to simply read the lines letter-perfect. They are looking for an actor who can create a *relationship* with the person they are reading with. Most of the time you are not reading with an actor so you will usually have to create the whole relationship yourself. You can do this by being very specific about the choices you make. You may be reading with an actor who is good or not so good. Play "in the moment," listening and reacting to your fellow actor but also keeping your work specific.

• **I believe you must memorize the script** for an audition and only look down at the script once or twice during the interview. (Always hold the script—even if it's memorized.) I know for some actors this skill isn't easy to acquire, but to compete, you must give a full performance of the material. Anything less and someone else gets the job.

• **Memorize in a flat monotone**; say the lines over and over but don't use your acting work. By using a flat monotone to memorize, the words will just be instruments to get across the script's meaning and you will never get stuck doing just a line-reading audition.

• **The next step will be to choose some sensory work.** This means using one or more of your five senses to make the circumstances or your personalizations more vivid for the audience. When you are auditioning you may not have time to get to this step. Or a great piece of sense memory, maybe the smell of your first lover, will come to mind as you step into the auditioning room. These types of inspirations are a gift from the universe; use them.

• **When you have rehearsal time, choose sensory work** to make the given circumstances and your personalizations very specific and unique to your own life. The way to choose sensory work is: if the character is insecure, macho or afraid, think of a *real* time in your own life when you felt insecure, macho or afraid. Then *make an effort* to wake up the memory of that time through one or more of your five senses: the *smell* of the room; the *touch* (what your fingers remember) of an object from that place or a piece of clothing you were wearing; the *sound* of music that was playing or a horn honking; the *taste* of food you had eaten; the *pain* in your heart or foot; the butterflies in your stomach; how the moon *looked*; from that specific event in *your life* when you felt insecure, macho or afraid.

• **Rehearse the scene** a few times, trying some of the pieces of sensory work you've chosen; see how each piece can change the way the scene plays. Try several different pieces. Then when you're ready to perform the scene, monologue or audition material, you'll have an idea of what works best. You must still remain free enough to act *in the moment* when everything is working beautifully and you are living the scene; or free enough to choose a new piece of sensory work at the last moment because you had a wonderful flash (driving in your car) of what the scene is really about. Trust your instincts.

• **If this is a scene for an acting class** or a rehearsed scene for an agent's office or a showcase, now is the time to get with your partner to rehearse. Discuss and agree on the given circumstances that are the same for your two characters. Remember, the events that you are personalizing from your own life will be very different from your partner's and you should never discuss them; you can defuse your personal choices by talking about them. Your choices are your tools, your treasures, your actor's secrets; they can't possibly help anyone else and the only way you can lose them is to discuss them.

• **Next, if you must, cut the scene.** A showcase scene should be four minutes or less and a class scene five or six minutes (acting minutes not reading minutes) with a beginning, middle and end. Do not add lines or words unless you must to set up or end a scene.

• **Rehearse in a professional way;** be considerate of your partner. Never be late. Arrive with your homework done. Scene partners may find it very useful to improvise scenes that could have happened outside of the script. Such as: when they first met; last Christmas; two years later; when they were caught in a snowstorm, etc.

• **Sally Field says:**

> • **Rehearsal is a most exciting time for me,** delving into what you can create, and when the director calls 'Action,' you take flight, leave your body, and are no longer on this planet.

• **Never give or ask another actor for acting notes. It is most unprofessional, and will not be appreciated by anyone.** Community theater actors are famous for this. You may discuss the scene or script endlessly but you must make your own choices. Tell your partner, "I'm going to try something different this rehearsal." Never ask anyone for a line reading and decline when someone wants to give you one—these are choices *you* must make. That is what being an actor is all about. If you need some help thinking of choices to make, call your coach or an actor friend and ask for help. I still have to do that, even though I'm hired as a coach to help actors make their choices. Sometimes you need that outside perspective.

• **Find an activity to be doing during the scene or monologue.** *Never pretend* to do something. One time when I was directing a very important show, an actress during rehearsals always pretended to be embroidering. I had assumed that during performances she would really be doing it. On opening night she was still pretending and I sat in the audience, dying. There is so much pretending in acting; anything you can really do—do it. Pick an activity that is logical for the character. Fix food, cut up an apple or cheese, find an article you really want to read in the paper or magazine, repair your radio, polish your nails, clean your gun, wax the furniture, shave, put makeup on, etc. Again, try several different things; never settle on the first one. Always investigate.

• **Next, memorize the lines.** The work above will give you a good idea of what the scene is about and what you are talking about; it will make the memorization much easier. *The lines are not the important part of the scene; the relationships are what is most important.* Yes, you learn the lines word-perfect; that is the only way to be professional. The lines are more like the costume; they are just tools to help get the story across, but not the whole story. The actors who bore us are the ones who are just saying or reading the lines.

• When you have been *hired* for an acting job, *always* show up on the set or sound stage with your lines memorized. That is your job as a professional actor. The exception is a stage play where you have the opportunity to rehearse and grow in the character before you learn lines. This luxury is what makes working in a play so much fun. You are allowed to discover your character.

• **Memorize word-perfect: it is a valuable habit.** (*See the next section for more details on memorizing.*)

MEMORIZING

• **Many actors who come to me for private coaching** show up without their lines memorized. They usually say, "I've heard it's best not to have the words memorized so it looks like you can do more with the script when the lines are memorized." Either the actors have been taught by a teacher who doesn't know what auditioning in Los Angeles is all about, or what they really heard was, "Always hold your script in your hand during the first audition." You hold it in your hand because, in case of nerves, the lines fly out of your head or you hit an unexpected emotional moment and lose the lines. It is always acceptable to look at your script to pick up a line. You stay in character and in the moment, look at your script, see what the line is and go back to playing the part.

Bonnie Gillespie, casting columnist for *Back Stage West,* author of the best-selling book, *Casting Qs: A Collection of Casting Director Interviews*, consultant on the business of acting, and owner of Cricket Feet Management, has given me a few quotes of how certain casting directors feel about actors showing up for auditions without their scripts memorized.

"Material is available way ahead of the audition. I put the script in the lobby, I put the sides up on the fax services. There's no excuse. We know how many people want this job, so it's awful when someone who has booked an audition isn't prepared for the opportunity. Get all the sides for all the characters. If you're up for a lead role, you can bet you'll learn about your character from reading all the sides."
Michael Donovan, CSA, CCDA

"**Be prepared, obviously. Have the lines as memorized as you can.** Some actors need the security blanket of holding onto those sides, and that's fine, but have a good handle on the material." **Julie Selzer, CSA**

"**I want to see you invested in your career.** I want a performance, I don't want to see you doing a cold read." **Bob Morones, CSA**

"**I personally want you off book.** This is so my director can work with you. Ninety percent of the time, we don't prescreen. I want you at performance level because when you read for me, the director is there." **Donald Paul Pemrick, CSA**

"**I can smell a cold reading in an instant**, generally at the end of the actor's first or second line. I'm more than happy to give you the time to work on it." **Lisa Miller Katz, CSA**

"**To come in, especially for a producer session**, and not be prepared? It's inexcusable. You wouldn't do that in any other profession. You wouldn't do that with a board meeting. This is the career you've chosen. Take it seriously." **Michael Greer, CSA**

"**You can tell who's winging it.** Get the sides as soon as you can, and really make a choice, even if it's wrong. Just let me see that you've made a choice. We can always redirect you." **Lori Cobe-Ross**

"**Don't come in here saying you just got the material.** Remember that producers don't ask the scattered actor back. Without exception, I find it's the well-prepared actor who gets the part." **Julie Ashton**

• **If it is hard for you to memorize—never, never mention it.** No one wants to hear it. Actors who memorize easily may not understand and think you are a fool. You'll hate them because it seems they'll have an advantage. Other actors who have trouble learning lines will resent you for bringing it up. They also won't trust you to learn yours because they know what the fear is like. So for your own sake, keep it to yourself how hard or easy it is for you to memorize. It is the *ultimate* actor's secret. Discussing it does nothing but damage. Assume that other actors memorize and you can too; it just takes practice, time and effort. Being a good actor has nothing to do with how easy or difficult it is to learn lines.

• **Some actors go through torment memorizing**. So what! We really do not care. You go through this trial alone or with a loved one at home who will hold book for you. Memorizing is just a mundane part of your acting craft that must be conquered silently, without complaint.

• **William H. Macy** says, "It should look as if you're making up the words and you've never said them before and it's happening in real time right before your eyes, even though it's not. It's scripted."

• **An industry insider** said he wished actors would conduct themselves like Richard Gere—who arrives on the set at the beginning of a project with "two suitcases and the script memorized."

• **Memorize lines in a flat monotone.** Do not memorize in an acting way or you'll be stuck with that rehearsed line reading. You won't be free to add sensory work and personalizations to change the meaning of the piece. The writer's words are a code for what *you* are feeling and experiencing from your own life. The actor gives the piece meaning by using specific, personal acting choices. When a director asks you for a different reading of a line, be able to change your acting choice immediately. Make several choices before settling on one so you'll be prepared. Keep trying different acting work with the same words to see what unique things, what new insight, you can bring to the script.

• **Highlight your lines in yellow** and draw a dark line underneath so they stand out. Memorize the writer's lines word-perfect. This is professional. No one is holding book in acting class but on the set, the script supervisor is watching each word.

• **Set aside blocks of 15 to 20 minutes** of solid, concentrated memorization time. Hold a piece of paper over everything but the first line. Say the line, then look to see if it's right. When it is, add the second line and do both together until they're memorized, then add the third line, etc. Memorize your cue line also; if you don't know the cues you won't know when it's your turn to speak. Another good way (to augment the above) is to tape-record the piece in a *flat monotone* voice. You can record all the parts; just change your voice for each one. You can act the other roles if you want but, again, yours is spoken in flat monotone. Now play the tape over and over—in your car or while you're doing the dishes. When you have the lines down, record a tape leaving a blank space for your lines, then say your lines with the tape; you'll learn the cues this way.

• **When I was the dialogue coach on** *Seinfeld*, Jerry used to love to be tested. He felt the key was learning all the cues. So if I could give him a cue from any place in the script and he knew the line—he won. He would also take Ginkgo Biloba (said to be a memory enhancing herb) in the afternoon on show day and then right before we started shooting the show.

• **Still another technique**—write or type out all the lines except yours. Just type the character's name where your lines go. Have a bunch copied, then write in your lines like filling in the blanks. Then check to see how accurate you are. Writing the lines in long hand helps get them in your memory.

• **Speed drills are good—on your own or with your scene partner.** This is Joan Darling's "bla bla" exercise. Say the lines as fast as you can, NO ACTING. If you can't think of the line, say "bla bla bla" till you do or it's the other actor's line, then jump back in with yours. The secret is: the words tumble out of your mouth with no meaning— then you are free for acting.

• **Get the words into your body.** Set up a rehearsal space similar to where you'll be acting. Move around the space as you are doing the lines.

• **To practice, memorize something every day** until you perfect the memorization craft. Soap opera actors have to memorize a new script every night.

• **Look for books on memorizing** and learn other people's techniques. All is fair in the pursuit of learning lines—more tools for your tool kit.

• **I also believe it helps** to put your script under your pillow when sleeping.

• **Not knowing your lines can stop you from being an actor— toughen up!**

Resources

www.m-w.com is the Merriam-Webster OnLine Dictionary. Look up all words you don't know the meaning of. Click on the speaker icon and hear the word spoken correctly.

www.learningannex.com. They offer many courses of industry related topics including memorizing.

Vicki Mizel, "Brainspouts," 213/963-1275. www.vickimizel.com. Private is $75 an hour with discounts if you sign up for a series. $99 for the memory tapes. She offers a three week, 12 to 16 hour beginning acting intensive class called "Off Book . . . in Minutes." $300, plus advance workshops. Vicki says, "Through stimulating and strengthening your mind, you will turn the main ideas into tangible pictures allowing you to memorize, retain, and recall monologue and script copy easily. You will be able to get off book in minutes for auditions or once you've landed the part. Besides just learning to get off book, the memory system truly deepens all aspects of the work: character development, understanding the scenes, playing the different levels, improving auditions because of increased clarity in making strong choices with confidence." She continues, "Using the combination of the three-week class and the audio tape program, you can integrate all the techniques necessary to use these methods of memorization forever."

Here is a letter I received from an actor about Vicki's technique.

> I just took a day-long seminar on the memorization technique that is listed in your book through The Learning Annex. I had my doubts but the method clicked for me. Later in the day when we ran through the first section of a monologue, it was easy to remember the text using the method.
>
> Of course, it takes practice but I think it is a valid way to memorize as fast as the business requires. Just thought it might be useful feedback for the next memory-impaired actor you come across.
>
> Christine Sang

ACTING BOOKS
AND
TAPES

All of the following theatrical books may be purchased or mail ordered through the following theatrical bookstores and www.amazon.com.

Samuel French Theatrical Bookstores, 323/876-0570. www.samuelfrench.com. 7623 Sunset Blvd., Hollywood. M-F 10-6; Sat. 10-5; Closed Sunday. Valley store: 818/762-0535, 11963 Ventura Blvd., just East of Laurel Canyon, Studio City. M-F 10-9; Sat. 10-6; Sun 12-5. For plays, get their free catalogue. They also sell many published film and television scripts.

Take One Film & Theater Books, 310/445-4050. www.take1filmbooks.com. 11516 Santa Monica Blvd., West Los Angeles. A great bookstore and knowledgeable staff. They have several free events every month; seminars and book signings.

Larry Edmund's Theatrical Book Shop, 323/463-3273. 6644 Hollywood Blvd., Hollywood, 90028. M-Sa 10-6.

www.backstage.com. $9.95 a month. Four years of archived articles.

• ACTING BOOKS AND TAPES

Acting For The Camera by Tony Barr. Excellent.

Acting In Film by Michael Caine. Excellent—I quote him all the time in my classes.

Acting Is Believing by Charles McGaw.

Acting: The First Six Lessons by Richard Boleslavski

Acting Truths and Fictions: Straight Talk about the Many Myths, Myth-Conceptions and Mistakes that Affect Actors' Development and Professional Careers Today! by Lawrence Parke. This is several books in one, a wealth of practical knowledge. Treat yourself.

Action! Acting For Film & Camera by Robert Benedetti.

Act Right: A Manual for the On-Camera Actor by Erin Gray & Mara Purl.

An Actor Prepares by Constantin Stanislavski

Audition by Michael Shurtleff. Memorize this book. He is a fabulous teacher!

Call Back: The Complete Guide to Preparing and Performing the Audition that will Get You the Part! by Ginger Howard Friedman.

Chekhov, Michael—books and tapes:
On the Technique of Acting by Michael Chekhov. Preface by Mala Powers.
To the Actor by Michael Chekhov. Edited by Mala Powers. Includes a biography of Michael Chekhov by Mala Powers.
Michael Chekhov: On Theatre and the Art of Acting (audio) Edited with **A Guide to Discovery** by Mala Powers

The Craft of Acting: Auditioning. A video tape by Allan Miller. The next best thing to reading is watching. Very practical tape.

Hitting Your Mark: What Every Actor Really Needs to Know on a Hollywood Set by Steve Carlson.

How To Audition by Gordon Hunt. Helen Hunt's father.

How To Get the Part Without Falling Apart by Margie Haber.

If You Don't Dance They Beat You by Jose Quintero.

If You Want To Write by Brenda Ueland.

The Inner Game of Tennis by W. Timothy Gallwey. using your thinking self and your intuitive self in balance.

Killer Monologues by J.P. Pierce.

Let The Part Play You by Anita Jesse. She is a teacher, famous for her audition techniques. Her exercises will make you a better actor and give you an understanding of what the acting process actually is.

Method or Madness? by Robert Lewis. Explores what the method is and is not as a workable theory of stage techniques.

My Life in Art by Constantin Stanislavski.

The Mystic in the Theater by Eva Le Gallienne. A biography of Eleonora Duse.

No Acting Please by Eric Morris. This is the best explanation of relaxation and preparation for an actor that I've seen. Author of **The Craft Of Acting** and **The Meg Approaches.**

On Acting by Sanford Meisner.

A Passion for Acting: Exploring the Creative Process by Allan Miller. Innovating acting exercises to help the actor develop his or her craft. I love this book!

The Playing Is The Thing: Learning to Act Through Games and Exercises by Anita Jesse. "These games and exercises thrust actors into situations where they are inclined to interact naturally, and without self-consciousness."

A Practical Handbook for the Actor by Melissa Bruder, Lee Michael Cohn, Madeleine Olnek, Nathaniel Pollack, Robert Previto, Scott Zigler. Introduction by David Mamet. He says, "This is the best book on acting written in the last twenty years."

Screen Acting: How to Succeed in Motion Pictures and Television by Brian Adams. A broad range, practical guide to film and television acting.

Sense of Direction by Bill Ball. San Francisco's ACT longtime artistic director's book for actors and directors.

Stanislavski's Legacy by Constantin Stanislavski.

Strasberg At The Actors Studio: Tape Recorded Sessions Edited by Robert Hethmon

Strasberg's Method, As Taught by Lorrie Hull: A Practical Guide for Actors, Teachers and Directors by S. Lorraine Hull. Comprehensive and detailed guide to Strasberg's work. She also has a two hour video tape examining the acting techniques. Included are relaxation techniques, four basic sensory and concentration exercises and scene critiques. To order: 310/828-0632 or 805/682-0638.

The Technique Of Acting by Stella Adler.

Towards A Poor Theater by Jerzy Grotowski.

Your Film and Acting Career: How to Break Into the Movies and TV and Survive in Hollywood by M. K. Lewis and Rosemary R. Lewis. M. K. Lewis is a prominent Los Angeles acting teacher whose career spans 25 years in theater, TV and films. Rosemary Lewis has worked in the print media as well as TV and films.

• BOOKS LISTING TEACHERS

The Selective Hollywood Acting Coaches and Teachers Directory by Acting World Books. Detailed information. Do not purchase these types of seminar books produced by Keith Wolf. They have a picture of a wolf on the cover. The information is not current.

Working Actors Guide, published every year.

Back Stage West ads. Request their latest back issue featuring the workshops and teachers in Los Angeles. They also feature some Northern California teachers. There are issues with all the college training programs and summer training opportunities.

• GUIDE BOOKS, HOW-TO BOOKS AND TAPES

Acting as a Business by Brian O'Neil.

Acting Out: Your Personal Coach to a Money Making Career in Televisiom Commercials by Stuart Stone.

Acting Strategies for the Cyber Age by Ed Hooks.

The Actor's Encyclopedia of Casting Directors by Karen Kondazian.

The Actor's Guide to Getting The Job, an audio tape, By Carolyne Barry and Kevin E. West. $24.95. www.carolynebarry.com.

The Actors Guide to the Internet by Rob Kozlowski

Actor's Interview Log: *Where Am I Going? Where Have I Been?* This is a great way to keep track of all your interviews, location, what you wore, tax information, etc.

The Actor's Picture/Resume Book by Jill Charles with photographer Tom Bloom. Very good advice and illustrations.

An Actor Succeeds by Terrance Hines and Suzanne Vaughan. This is a most valuable book; they have a real working knowledge of the business.

The Agencies: What the Actor Needs To Know by Acting World Books. If you don't have this guide, you aren't really looking for an agent. This is the authentic, well-researched agent guide. There are other publications that look like this one—don't be fooled. Don't get the one with a wolf on it.

Agents "Tell It Like It Is!" a video tape by Joel Asher. See actual agents in their offices. Great tape.

The Audition Book by Ed Hooks. The Rolls Royce of audition information. I think any actor who has not read this book is not doing everything possible to get work.

The Backstage Guide To Casting Directors by Hettie Lynne Hurtes. 56 top casting directors interviewed here offer convincing evidence that the more you know about their jobs, the closer you'll come to your dreams.

Back To One: How To Make Good Money As A Hollywood Extra by Cullen Chambers. This is the book you must have if you want to work as an extra. He gives all the answers, the agencies, tells you what to do on the set.

The Book: An Actors Guide to Chicago.

Book on Acting: Improvisation Technique for the Professional Actor in Film, Theater & Television, by Stephen Book. Endorsed by many celebrities.

The Camera Smart Actor by Richard Brestoff. You must have this book. It clearly explains what it takes to act in front of a camera. This book is like a good friend; take it on the set with you.

Casting Directors "Tell It Like It Is." video tape. Famous acting coach Joel Asher has produced this informative tape all about casting directors. $19.95. Get $5.00 off by calling 800/652-7437 and mentioning this book.

Casting Qs: A Collection of Casting Director Interviews by Bonnie Gillespie. She's the current writer for Back Stage West and this is right up to date.

Curbside L.A.: An Offbeat Guide to the City of Angels from the pages of the L.A. Times by Cecilia Rasmussen

Directors on Acting, video tape by acting coach, director Joel Asher. Six well known film and television directors talk about actors working on the set. Joel really does a wonderful job with this video tape series. 800/652-7437.

Discover Yourself in Hollywood by Lilyan Chauvin. The ins and outs of coming to Hollywood. Mail order only 323/877-4988.

Dreams Into Action: Getting What You Want by Milton Katselas.

From Agent to Actor by Edgar Small. A well informed perspective from both sides. Tells how careers are established and nourished.

Getting The Part, video tape by acting coach Joel Asher. Actual casting meetings and interviews. Very informative. The tape is very well produced and filled with information. $29.95. Get $5.00 off by calling 800/652-7437 and mentioning this book.

The Glam Scam: Successfully Avoiding the Casting Couch and Other Talent and Modeling Scams by Erik Joseph. Glam scams occur everywhere—beware.

Hollywood Agents & Managers Directory by Hollywood Creative Directory. Over 1000 talent, literary agencies and managers in L.A., N.Y. and across the nation.

Hollywood, Here I Come!: An Insider's Guide to a Successful Acting and Modeling Career in Los Angeles by Cynthia Hunter.

Hollywood Scams and Survival Tactics by Lilyan Chauvin. She tells of all the scams!

How To Be A Working Actor: The Insider's Guide to Finding Jobs in Theater, Film and Television by New York casting director Mary Lynn Henry.

How To Get Publicity by William Parkhurst.

How To Sell Yourself As An Actor by K Callan. How to merchandise your craft after you've learned it. K was Superman's mom on *Lois & Clark. (Blythe Baten loves this book and also regularly consults K's The Los Angeles Agent Book.)*

How To Work a Room by Susan RoAne. For those actors who may struggle with the schmoozing part of the job. Practical information on how to overcome roadblocks to this important element of being a professional actor in Los Angeles.

The Job Book: 100 Acting Jobs For Actors edited by Glenn Alterman.

L.A. from A to Z: The Actor's Guide to Surviving and Succeeding in Los Angeles by Thomas Mills. www.heinemanndrama.com.

The Los Angeles Agent Book: Get the Agent You Need for the Career You Want by K Callen.

Making It in New York City by Glenn Alterman.

Meditations for Actors: for the actor within us all by Carra Robertson.

The Practical Dreamer's Handbook: Finding the Time, Money and Energy to Live the Life You Want to Live by Paul & Sarah Edwards.

Ross Reports: TV Commercial Casting guide, Comedy Casting Guide and Personal Managers Directory are among the great ones. Subscriptions only, 800/817-3273. Special Directories, 212/536-5170. Check out all these reports.

Seminar Books by Acting World Books. I love these and recommend all of them: **The Selective Hollywood Acting Coaches and Teachers Directory, The Agencies, Publicizing Yourself, Personal Managers**, etc.

Survival Jobs: 118 Ways To Make Money While Pursuing Your Dreams by Deborah Jacobson.

True and False: Heresy and the Common Sense for the Actor by David Mamet.

Voice and the Actor by Cicely Berry. Speaking is an expression of inner life and of emotion.

Walking in This World: The Practical Art of Creativity by Julia Cameron.

The Working Actor's Guide edited by Karin Mani. If you live in L.A. or are planning to move here, you must have it! Lists all the services available.

Working in Hollywood by Alexandra Brouwer & Thomas Lee Wright. It describes the jobs of everybody you see in the credits. Great!

The Writer's Journey: Mythic Structure for Writers by Christopher Vogler.

Your Handwriting Can Change Your Life by Vimala Rodgers.

FAKE CIGARETTES, SMOKING, FAKE TEARS, SWEATING AND FUNNY TEETH

CIGARETTES

• **Many people say** that you have to be or have been a smoker to be believable smoking in a role. I don't know this to be true. When I think of Daniel Day-Lewis in *My Left Foot* portraying the feisty Irish artist Christy Brown born with cerebral palsy, I believe a great actor can do anything. Smoking while you are acting without using nicotine is definitely possible and believable. I was a smoker and it took many tries and years to rid myself of the longing. If you don't smoke, I encourage you to not start; if you do, quit.

• **Health issues aside, the craving can hurt you as an actor.** You will be on a set where no one in the cast smokes and you can't get out to have a cigarette; the distraction can hurt your performance. On an audition your preoccupation with when you will be able to have your next smoke will take needed energy away from your focus. You may have to leave acting class to have a smoke just at the moment when the teacher has something to say that will help to transform your acting.

• **When you must smoke in a play or film**, use herbal cigarettes; they are nonaddictive. Even if you are a smoker, it is wise to use the herbals for take after take. They burn faster, look real. The only drawback when working on stage is they may smell like marijuana. Many health food stores sell the herbals as well as smoke shops. When working on a set, let the prop people know well ahead of time that you will need herbal cigarettes. As a safety measure, have some of your own.

• **On a set, matching the length of the cigarette** for each take is an issue. The prop people will take care of the proper length for the master and close-ups which can start at different spots in the scene. Ask props to use the gizmo that lights the cigarette, so they can get it going at the right length and hand you the lit herbal cigarette. You must keep track of the drags you take, your attitude, the placement of your hands, when you use the ashtray.

• **William B. David was a reformed smoker** and had to smoke during his seven seasons on *The X-Files* as the "smoking man." He used the above methods in order to remain a non-smoker. He says, "For any given scene one might smoke 30 to 40 cigarettes."

• **Magic-trick cigarettes are an alternative for stage.** They are expensive and bought in magic shops. You blow in them and they emit a powder that resembles smoke. They really are believable and the audience doesn't suffer from the second-hand smoke.

TEARS

• **You learn in acting class** how to reach the emotions where tears are likely to come from. When they don't come and the director wants them or the audition script calls for them, you will have to create the tears however you can.

• **Some actors tell me they learn to look out of their eyes** in a certain way that the tears just flow. Actress Janice Allen, when looking at a person, adjusts her eyes as if to see a picture in a mass of dots to bring tears. If you are not familiar with that type of picture, do some research and find one and practice.

• **On a sitcom, you can get away** with giant sobs and putting your hand over your eyes and make it look like you are wiping away the tears. There is a famous *Seinfeld* show where Jerry's girlfriend never stops crying. The actress was worried about not really crying. I asked what she did in the audition she said, "I just faked it." I said, "well, continue doing it; you got the job." She was hilarious.

• **Ammonia Inhalants, by North Health Care**, at most drugstores, can help. They are for reviving people when they have fainted. One sniff makes your eyes water.

• **Also try liquid Binaca** loaded up on your finger or knuckle. Rub your eye with it to start tears.

• **A fresh cut onion** in a plastic bag in your pocket can help. Get the juice all over your hand and rub it in your eye.

UNDERARM SWEATING

• **Prescription Drysal applied once a month** will change your life. Shots of Botox have been talked about to help with sweating by paralyzing the glands, but my Botox guy, Rand Rusher, says it is dangerous and not advisable.

• **I know several women**—I haven't heard from the men—who use a product from Sav-on Drugstores called Certain Dry. They apply it two to three times a week at night. With any product like this you do have to be aware of the risks with certain deodorants and antiperspirants that have been reported by health experts. A natural deodorant is always best, but you will change your life if you are not sweating during your important meetings and when you are acting.

FUNNY TEETH

• **Dr. Bukks for personalized funny, fake teeth**. Many styles, including hillbilly, homeless, missing teeth and buck. Most are $35. 800-925-BUKK. www.drbukk.com. Call for a brochure. Chris Cooper did it best in the movie *Adaptation*. What a hoot!

SECTION TWO

PICTURES AND RESUMES

HOW TO TAKE
GREAT PICTURES

• **Your 8x10 pictures put you into the acting business**; they are your most important career marketing tools. An 8x10 picture is usually your first introduction to the people who will be calling you in for interviews and auditions, and casting you in their productions. You must have pictures, they must look like you, and you must like them so you never have to apologize when handing them out.

• **Color pictures are now necessary in order to compete** in Los Angeles. Black and white pictures are becoming old fashioned. Color reproductions usually cost just a little more than the black and white.

• **Agents, casting directors, producers and directors** will pick up the telephone to arrange to meet you because of something they see in your eyes, attitude, look or style. An actor always brings an 8x10 picture to every interview; the people you meet need it in order to remember you.

• **As your collection of pictures grows**, you will be able to show the interviewer a portfolio of different looks: body and stunt shots, glamour looks, character shots on a set or in a play, riding a motorcycle, with or without a mustache, lighter, darker, shorter or longer hair, etc.

• **Mark Malis, former head of Universal Casting.** "I tell actors they must look like their pictures on a daily basis. Otherwise they are wasting the casting director's time. They should attempt to find a photographer who can capture their personality. If they can accomplish those two things, they will get what they need."

• **Your first step is shopping for a photographer.** It is good business to interview at least three. Look at the people in their books who look like you. If you have blue eyes, see if their blue-eyed actors look like they have light eyes. How do they handle your gender, ethnicity and age bracket? If you are 18, don't look at the 30 year olds. If you are 40, don't look at the 20 year olds. If you are a woman, don't look at the men's shots.

• **The most important feature in the photograph are the eyes.** They must be saying something. We must be able to see inside you, see your thoughts. Models eyes for the most part fade into the picture. Actors' eyes must draw the viewer in, move them in some way and make them curious about you. The viewer needs to think they can read your thoughts.

• **The photographer's personality and environment are very important.** You must feel comfortable in order to take the risks of letting the camera see inside you. Certain personalities click with our own and others make us uncomfortable. Your instincts will tell you what feels right. Don't ignore your gut feeling and go with someone because all your friends got great shots or the photographer is very famous.

• **Respected photographer Tom Lascher** advises:

  • **The goal of the head shot is to suspend the disbelief** of the casting director, so that he or she sees beyond the photograph and feels the presence of the person/actor it represents.

  • **The three issues to consider when choosing a photographer are:** first, look at the pictures and imagine whether you would fit in this photographer's style. The second factor is whether you and the photographer want to go in the same direction. If you're thinking femme fatale and he's thinking ingenue or you're thinking villian and he's thinking leading man, you may spend the whole session tugging in different directions. Third and most important is whether or not you can have enough of a relationship with the photographer to be able to use the photographer not just as a technician but as a scene partner.

• **Consider your photo shoot** an important acting assignment. You will be investing a great deal of money, time and energy. Preparation is the key. Research various looks, characters and attitudes you can play, tear pictures out of magazine ads, watch TV shows, commercials and rent movies.

Make a list of looks and attitudes you would like the photographer to capture. Gather the appropriate clothes for these aspects of yourself from your wardrobe, thrift stores and new purchases. Don't borrow clothes; what you use for your photos will soon be your audition wardrobe. Have the clothing items altered, cleaned, ironed and ready.

• **Have your hair styled, colored, permed and treated** at least a week before the shoot. The exception is men doing long and short hair looks in the same photo session; they will shave and get their hair cut in the middle of the session. If you are planning on doing your own makeup, have a makeup designer show you how to do it and purchase the right products. *See Make Up Artists, Section Two.* Do this a couple of weeks ahead of your shoot and practice, practice, practice. This also applies to having a facial; do it at least one week before the shoot. *See Age Defying Techniques, Section Six.*

• **To look as good as you can on the day of your shoot**, get at least two weeks of daily vigorous exercise and the three or four nights before, plenty of rest. You don't want a tan on your face for B&W pictures, so wear sun block. Avoid foods that darken your blood: meat, carrots, beets, sugar. They darken the circles under your eyes. Be alcohol and drug free for at least a week before the shoot. Train for the session as a highly competitive athlete would.

• **The price for a photo shoot** is usually $100 to $600 plus makeup for women and also men who need it, though some photographers do their own. The price seems to be based on reputation and what the market will bear. My students and I have obtained good pictures from photographers in all price ranges. If the picture helps you get interviews, it has done its job. In your teens and 20s, you may need new pictures every year; after that, every two to five years. Pictures are one of your biggest expenses and greatest payoffs. This is the place to use a good percentage of your available promotion dollars.

• **The most important thing about your picture** is that you are looking straight into the lens, eyes open. Pretend or personalize the camera as someone you are eager to talk to, for a specific reason. Let your guard down, no defenses; be at your most vulnerable. Let the camera see inside you and let it see you project the attitudes you and your agent, acting coach or the photographer think are appropriate for you to portray—the characters you will be cast to play. The focus should be *very sharp*.

• **Photographer and working actor Frank Bruynbroek** talks about the photo session:

> • **I approach the head shot session** as if it were a publicity shoot. By nature a head shot says, "please hire me," it puts the actor in a begging mode. A publicity shoot means you are on top of the world. You have your series or your big movie coming out, it changes your attitude and influences the way you look at yourself. You don't have anything to prove, you are enough.

> • **Pick your favorite actor** and try to imagine how their photo shoot goes. They control the session with their "star quality," with their personality. Do the same. Play the game, don't be afraid to be private in public, have fun. Be your own photographer, know what you want, know how you want to market yourself. Know in your heart before you shoot with a photographer, you will have the greatest shots ever.

• **Glamour photographer Michael Maron says:**

> • **Actors are used to having a character** to hide behind so they freeze up in front of the camera when they have to be themselves. The key is to let everything go, just be present, be who you are. Use your acting abilities, your technique. Think of a role you enjoyed playing, the time somebody did something wonderful for you or a funny situation that happened. Be in that moment so you won't be self-conscious.

• **Casting director Clair Sinnett says:**

> • **Don't just do smiling and non-smiling looks.** What you need in a picture is attitude, feeling, thought behind the eyes. Actors should have two monologues prepared when they go to a photographer. One, a dramatic piece that really touches them, makes them angry, hurt or even makes them cry. And second, a comedic monologue that makes them laugh. When actors don't have monologues, as a short cut they can think of the worst day they've ever had, for theatrical pictures; the best day, for commercial pictures.

> • **Do your own hair and makeup** the way you do them on a day-to-day basis. You want to look like your picture when you walk into the casting director's office.

• **Caryn West, respected Los Angeles and New York acting coach,** advised one of her shy students this way:

  • **For shyness issues, shoot your pictures with** Barbara Benvil. She is an actress, coach, wonderfully empathetic and works very slowly. Tell her the "types" you plan to play: smiley commercial dad, haughty aristocrat, executive businessman, casually dramatic.

  • **Make up a 4x6 index card** with some expressions of attitude or one sentence thoughts to say to the camera; use these when you are feeling self conscious or feel you've dried up.

  Sentences such as:

  • I love your eyes too.
  • I have a wicked sense of humor.
  • I butt breathe and love this. (*See the Audition Technique Section for Caryn's explanation of "butt breathing"*)
  • Life is short and precious and I take myself all too seriously in these situations, so I'm giggling now.
  • Do you come here often?
  • My wife loves me so there.

  • **In general, Caryn advises:** Get a teeth whitening/cleaning. Bring a small boom box and your favorite CD. Get a full body massage, finishing one or two hours before the shoot. It really relaxes your face and eases overall tension.

• **Well-known photographer Mary Ann Halpin says:**

  • **Actors arrive at my studio under pressure** from their agents, managers, mothers and the world to get the perfect photograph. They are carrying so much weight on their shoulders that it is hard for them to just be themselves. I see portraiture as an emotional dance. When an actor lets go and goes with the dance, it can be magical. I'm convinced that when someone reacts positively to a photograph it's because of the actor's energy rather than just the aesthetic beauty of the photograph.

  • **The casting directors all want "slice of life" photos.** What is the actor feeling, not what do they look like. The most interesting shot wins. I shot an actress from New York sitting on the floor barefoot in jeans; we created a look. She called to tell me she got cast because they loved her feet. The producers, after seeing the picture, restyled the character on the soap to reflect the way she looked in the photograph.

• **Here is Mary Ann's list of clothes** to wear for different styles of pictures. She says, "Bring everything."

Wardrobe List

Men

• **Sporty Look:** Tennis shirts, Izod shirts, T-shirts with white collars, sweat shirts and jackets, ski jackets, zip-up cotton jackets are great.
• **Rugged Outdoor Look:** Plaid shirts, woolen Pendelton shirts, blue denim shirts and jackets, down jackets or vest, sheepskin, leather or big old funky jackets, safari shirts and jackets are good too. Also, big bulky sweaters like ski and fisherman knits.
• **Street Look:** Tight black T-shirts or shirts. Black, navy, or gray sweat shirts. Again, denim or rough looking jackets, undershirts.
• **Clean-Cut Look:** Cotton dress shirts in lighter colors and patterns, V-neck sweaters, crew-neck sweaters, sports jackets in lighter colors, casual ties, light leather or suede jackets. Also a couple of pairs of good fitting jeans or pants with a belt to finish off the look.
• **Businessman/Executive Look:** Three piece suit, pin stripe, tuxedo and tuxedo shirt for a dressier look. Dress shirts, vests, and a variety of ties. Also, bring some tie clips/pins and cuff-links to finish off the look.

Women

• **Casual/Earthy:** Men's shirts: cotton type dress, denim, Pendleton, plaids. Patterned blouses if they're not too busy. Sweaters: textured, lacy, angora, V-necks, crew necks, boat necks, and turtle necks. Vintage clothes are unusual and interesting. Bring a pair of jeans or leggings and an assortment of belts.
• **Business/Spokeswoman:** Business suits and jackets: tweeds patterned or plain: dark or light colors are great. Blouses: silk, lacy, or tailored; interesting colors. Vest with a tie or suspenders are fun. Bring interesting tailored pants or skirts.
• **Upscale/Sexy/Dramatic:** Silk shirts, men's shirts, tuxedo shirts, lacy things. Black sweaters and dresses, off the shoulder or low necklines. Romantic dresses: vintage, flowered or lacy. Lacy camisoles and romantic lingerie. It is preferable to work with texture, pattern, style and design. Avoid plain fabrics in medium reds, blues and greens that rely purely on color for their effect.

• **The first picture you need** is a commercial and/or a theatrical B&W or color head shot (currently, that means from the waist up) that looks just like you will look when you walk in the office. Your next picture may be a 3/4 shot (down to at least your knees), usually with a little more projection of your personality by the clothes you are wearing and your attitude. There are really no hard, fast rules; you and your photographer can be creative in designing the shots you wish to have. I'm giving you the following descriptions and photo examples as guidelines to opening your own imagination. Styles in photos change. Sometimes the most interesting shot is one where rules have been broken.

• **Study the photographers' web sites** in the following listings. They put up their best pictures in the latest Los Angeles styles. You can learn a lot by finding the actors who look like you and asking your photographer to shoot that kind of shot. When preparing to have Marina Rice Bader shoot me for this book I chose a couple of character shots from her site, printed them out and took them along with other print and trade ad pictures I liked. This gave her an idea of how I see myself cast.

• **A theatrical head or 3/4 shot** is used for film and television auditions and for seeking a theatrical agent. This shot, in general, should not have a full smile; often quite an intense look is required, such as the soap opera bitch or the gang leader, if that's how you will be cast. All pictures need attitude. Look in the camera lens, let the camera see inside of you, and then imagine you are talking to someone you know who would make you say things like:

"I want you."	"You make me angry because..."
"Come here."	"I'm so embarrassed."
"Get out of here!"	"I'm ready."
"I hate you."	"I love you."
"You devastated me."	"You feel so good."
"I'll pay you back."	"You're so sexy."
"I'm bad."	"You're so cute."
"Please forgive me."	"Come on, let's play."
"You are so bad."	"Let's party!"
"I'll never forgive you."	"Where's the party?"

• **Your commercial B&W head or 3/4 shot** will be used in seeking a commercial agent and on commercial auditions. This picture should be honest and upbeat, usually a smile that looks happy, perky, in love with life, with lots of energy in your eyes. When looking in the lens, say things like,

"Hey!"	"This is the best!"
"Oh!"	"Yummy!"
"What a great day!"	"What a bargain!"
"What a surprise!"	"I got the job!" etc.

• **Do whatever it takes to get your energy up.** Talk to the camera as if it is your puppy, pet bird, best friend or mom; find what works for you and then do the acting.

For much more about commercial pictures, go to Commercials in Section Three, where there are commercial photo examples and more information.

• **After you have your basic shots,** you will want to add pictures of characters you can play. Some I always have are businesswoman, waitress, tough madam-hooker, country grandma, prison warden, quirky commercial, and soap-opera glamour looks.

• **Makeup artist Rita Montanez** designed the following clothing list for photographers she works with.

Clothing List

Bring a lot of clothing so we figure out what works best!
• Solid colors work best (no prints, patterns or stripes), we've been using more white, texture works well.
• Long sleeves are best for headshots, short sleeves can work for 3/4 shots, never wear short sleeves if you are uncomfortable with your arms.
• Mock turtlenecks, nothing bulky.
• White, black and gray t-shirts work well under denim shirts, sport jackets, etc.
• Dark blue and black jeans as well as regular blue jeans.
• For women, jewelry is simple, studs and small earrings. No watches or rings.
Commercial
• Think The Gap, Banana Republic, J.Crew, etc. Casual and comfortable. I also like layered looks.
Theatrical
• Dark colors are inherently more dramatic. We love black.
• For women: bodysuits, simple shirts with clean lines. Cleavage is not always appropriate. if a suit has been suggested, again, simple clean lines. Large shoulder pads are out.
• For men: blazers with collared shirts or t-shirts. Suits for an upscale look. Ties are good for a detective, a cop and a business look.

• **If you have a great body,** male or female, and like to show it off, you will need a body-shot picture. Consider tennis, bike riding, dance, work-out clothes or one of your own personal skills that require body-fitting clothes. If you do stunts, you need pictures of you doing martial arts, jumping from a building, firing a gun, whatever your specialty is. If you want to be considered for sexy roles where nudity or partial nudity is required, take pictures in a tiny bathing suit or an outfit that plays up your body. Do not mail these shots. Give them out personally when it is appropriate to the role.

• **The above descriptions** of pictures are for the Los Angeles market. If you are in another city, research the trends in your area. If you are moving to Los Angeles, plan on having your professional pictures taken here. If your pictures are from New York, chances are they will work. If they are from San Diego, San Francisco, Seattle or your home town, they most likely will not be useable.

• **For commercial interviews in some parts of the country** (not Los Angeles), your agent may want a composite. These can be three or four shots on one side or a commercial head shot on one side and several commercial-type situation shots on the back: horseback riding, grocery shopping, selling fast-food, cheerleading, holding a baby, playing baseball, doing laundry, typing, etc. When my martial artist daughter, Cynthia Kerr, lived in Dallas, she used a one-sided composite made up of two pictures—one wearing a tank top and karate pants, doing a perfect side kick, the other a glamour head shot. Composites always have your name, your agent's name and oftentimes your measurements. *See commercial shots, in Section Three.*

• **When you have your first pictures** taken and your funds are limited, contact art schools and colleges and investigate how to become a model for the photography students in exchange for photos. *See the Art Center under the Photographer listings in this section.*

• **Or ask a talented friend with a good 35mm camera** to shoot a B&W trial roll in an outdoor setting with nice light. You can rent an appropriate lens from a camera supply store. A good lens is a 105mm F-2.5 Nikon portrait lens. In Hollywood, try Samy's Camera at 431 S. Fairfax Ave., Los Angeles. 800/321-4726 or 877/297-1223. www.samys.com. *See Hank Tovar's directions for amateur photographers, in Section Nine, Child Actors.*

• **Have the roll developed and printed** as 3x5 or 4x6 prints or an 81/2 x11 or 11x14 proof sheet at a photo lab. A proof sheet can have up to 36 exposures on it. *See Photo Labs, Section Two.* When you have a proof sheet you must purchase a photographer's loop for a few dollars at a camera store. It is the only way to look at your proof sheets. You must use these professional tools. Look at the proofs with the loop to check lighting and focus. Pick a few shots and have them made into 3x5s or 4x6s to see the real quality. When the shots are 3x5 or 4x6 proof prints from the beginning, it is much easier to pick out the good ones. All this can be done cheaply and may result in a fine head shot to get you started.

• **When you have the money** to invest in professional pictures, choose the right photographer for you. Ask your friends, look at ads in the trades, and check out the ones I've listed here. Although I've worked with most of the following photographers, I have never found one that everyone has been satisfied with. This could be a reflection on the actor as well as the photographer. Make sure the photographer you choose guarantees their work. This means if you and your agent did not get the shots you need, they will reshoot for the price of the film and makeup artist only.

• **Try not to be discouraged** if it takes more than one photo session to get an 8x10 you love. It is unusual to have a truly successful first shoot. Use these picture-taking events as a time to learn something about acting in front of the camera. Your personal preparation and ease with the photographer will make all the difference in the success of the shoot. It can be very tough not to have your pictures come out as you dreamed they would. I have been through some agony myself and with my daughter, Cynthia, and many of my students. It can be a situation where you spend a great deal of money and have a product that you hate or that your agent says won't work for you. Try to diagnose what didn't work. This isn't to look for blame, but to educate yourself. Blame will not solve anything and can lead to self-pity, which can kill your spirit. Pick yourself up, save more money and go for it again.

• **Hugh Grant** says, "I'm terrible at having my picture taken. I'm always furious and unpleasant."

• **The next step is choosing the right shots** from your proof sheets, 3x5s or 4x6s to be blown up to 8x10 masters. Ask your photographer to pick their favorite choices. They will mark these with a grease pencil, which easily wipes off with a Kleenex. Equipped with your grease pencil and loop, ask three or four people their opinions of which pictures look most like you. It's best to ask someone in the business: your acting coach, a working actor, an agent or casting director. Keep track of each person's picks and then make your choices.

• **I suggest you choose last** so you can see how others perceive you. If you have selected a lot of shots, see if your photographer can save you money by having 3x5s blown up and then make your final choices for 8x10 masters from those. Blow up your selections into 8x10 borderless (four-way bleed) matte finish masters or use interesting, artistic borders your photographer, agent or photo lab may suggest. The rejects can be gifts to your family members.

• **Now you are ready to reproduce your master picture.** Again, take the masters to three or four people and ask their opinions. Some pictures will be eliminated right away because of flaws that were not perceptible when looking at the proof sheet or 3x5s. Many flaws can be corrected by retouching; a good picture is worth the expense. If there are some pictures you hate, you have my permission to destroy them no matter how much they cost. You don't want a picture you hate to be anywhere in this world; you never know when it will turn up to embarrass you. Next, look at the masters chosen most by your people and see if you agree. Then have them retouched, if necessary, and reproduced. *See Photo Retouching, page 140.*

• **The following pictures are presented here** to demonstrate different types of 8x10s used for theatrical interviews and auditions. I thought it might be informative to show you pictures taken of me; actresses Carly Althoff teens/early 20s, Loryn Phillips, mid 20s, Janice Allen, late 20s and Caryn West late 30s and 40s; actors Jordan Osher teens/early 20s, DJ Johnson late 20s/30s and Keith Johnson in his 30s, by different photographers. Each photographer chose the photo to be used, the makeup artist, and decided if retouching should be done. Notice how each shot tells a different story. Imagine how many stories your pictures will tell.

CHECKLIST FOR A SUCCESSFUL PHOTO SHOOT

Before the shoot:

• Choose your photographer.

• Book the makeup artist.

• Style, curl and color hair.

• Get in shape.

• Gather clothes and makeup.

• Drink water and rest.

After the shoot:

• Purchase photo loop and grease pencil—black, red or green.

• Pick up proof sheets or prints.

• Make picture choices, blow up 3x5s or 4x6s.

• Blow up 8x10s.

• Retouching.

• Reproduction.

• You are now in show business.

On the next few pages are samples of theatrical headshots. The same actors appear in commercial shots starting on page 169. Child actor photos, see Section Nine.

My special thanks to the photographers,

makeup artists and retouchers for their

time, energy, creativity and

the donation of their services.

3/4 Shot

Actor
Judy
   Kerr

Photographer
Frank
   Bruynbroek

Makeup
Rita
   Montanez

Head Shot

Photographer
Frank
   Bruynbroek

Makeup
Rita
   Montanez

Retouching
Nichan
touched up
crinkled neck.

Country/blue collar
Head Shot

Photographer
Marina
Rice Bader

Makeup
Marina

Clothes
Flannel shirt

The Judge/Principal
"You're in trouble"
Shot

Photographer
Marina
Rice Bader

Makeup
Marina

Personality Shot

Actor
**Jordan
    Osher**

Photographer
**Pam
    Springsteen**

This shot captures
Jordan's sense of
humor. His first
photo shoot.

Mood Shot

Photographer
**Pam
    Springsteen**

The darker side of
his personality.

See Jordan's story
in the *Actor Living
His Dream* section.

The Student Shot

Actor
**Jordan
Osher**

Photographer
**Bob
Bayles**

Bob was able to
catch the glasses
with no reflection.

Wrong Side
of the Law
Shot

Photographer
**Jillian
Griffiths**
of
**J.Thomasin
Photography**

I asked for a
Sopranos shot.

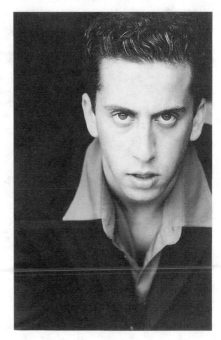

Natural All-American
Shot

Actor
**Carly
Althoff**

Photographer
**Kevin
McIntyre**

Carly did her
own makeup.

Photographer
**Gayle
Garnett**

Makeup & Hair
**Sara
Chameides**

Soap Opera
Shot

Actor
Carly
Althoff

Photographer
Lesley
Bohm

Makeup & Hair
Shawn
Flint
Blair

Photographer
Mara

Makeup & Hair
Mara

Retouching
Mara

Taken a year earlier.

Actor
Loryn
    Phillips

Photographer
Robert
    Raphael

Makeup & Hair
Robert
    Raphael

Photographer
Robert
    Raphael

Makeup & Hair
Robert
    Raphael

Retouching
Nichan
filled in sweater
fabric.

Actor
**DJ
Johnson**

Photographer
**Michael
Sanville**

Retouching
**Mary
Morano**

3/4 Shot

Photographer
**Sean
Kenney**

Actor
Janice
   Allen

Photographer
Mark
   Husmann
      Digital

Makeup & Hair
Dara
   Dupuy

3/4 Shot

Photographer
Diana
   Lannes
      Digital

Makeup & Hair
Naja

Digital Retouching
Randall
   Michelson

3/4 Shot

Photographer
**Mary Ann
Halpin**

Makeup & Hair
**Mary Ann
Halpin**

Retouching
**Charisse of
Retouching
Company**
Whites of eyes and
defined eyelashes.

Photographer
**David
LaPorte**

Makeup
**Laura
Connelly**

Head Shot

Actor
**Keith
    Johnson**

Photographer
**Rod
    Goodman**

This was his first
photo shoot.

3/4 Shot

Photographer
**Rod
    Goodman**

See Keith's story
in the *Actor Living
His Dream* section.

Mood Shot

Photographer
**Rich
Hogan**

3/4 Shot

Photographer
**Carrie
Cavalier**

Makeup & Hair
**Kari
Nicole**

Actor
**Caryn
West**

Photographer
**Barbara
Benvil**

Makeup, Hair
and Retouching
**Barbara
Benvil**

Photographer
**Barbara
Benvil**

Makeup, Hair
and Retouching
**Barbara
Benvil**

These shots
taken on the
same day.

Photographer
**Barbara
Benvil**

Makeup, Hair
and Retouching
**Barbara
Benvil**

Caryn uses these
4 shots on a
5x7 card with
her resume
on the back
for submissions
and to give
casting directors
when she does
showcases.

Photographers

SECOND PRINTING NOTE: Many of the photographers in the last year have switched to digital, color, 4x6 proofs and photos online and CDs. Check the websites. Actors must have color photos to compete in Los Angeles.

PHOTOGRAPHERS ADDED FOR THIS PRINTING:

L.A. Casting Couch Photography and Websites for Actors, 310/379.1828. www.laccheadshots.com. $350 for 3 rolls, 6 changes color or b&w, 35mm, photos digitized. Plus $61 for 4x6 prints, Photo CD, negaitves and online contact sheet. Retouching $10 a picture. My student Brittani Taylor's agent Micheal Zanuck loves their work. Brittani's shots are fabulous, six very different looks.

Nancy Jo Gilchrist,818/780-0803. www.nancyjophoto.com. Read all about her process on her very complete website. I've shot with Nancy and it was a wonderful, easy time and I enjoyed the shots she designed for me.

Wayne Rutledge, 206/550-1820. www.rutledgephoto.com. $350, shoots on film then scans images in photo shop on to CD disk, 3 looks, 4x6 proofs. Wayne works in Los Angeles and Seattle. Very highly recommended by manager Carlyne Grager.

Dana Patrick Photography, 310/854-1135 or 310/704-7493. Highly recommended by acting coach/actress Caryn West.

www.my8x10.com. Takes you to NowCasting.com's photographers' gallery.

www.actorsite.com. Photographer's gallery.

The Art Center College of Design: Photo Office, 626/396-2250. There are over 100 students enrolled in the photography department. If you want an opportunity to shoot for free with their photographers, call and ask for the model form to fill out and then mail it and your 8x10 to Atten: Model Office/Test File, Art Center College Of Design, 1700 Lida Street, Pasadena, CA 91103. I would re-send each year in September. The model receives two black and white or one color print per wardrobe change. This is also a good way to learn about print modeling.

Bob Bayles, 818/997-8518. www.bobbaylesphotos.com $85 per roll. His studio has a very comfortable atmosphere; also location shooting. Use your own makeup artist. He guarantees a proof sheet in two days and 8x10s in two more days. He does his own developing so he really has control. He has shot many of my students and they all have gotten the shots they needed. Bob really tries to help you be fully comfortable before he shoots. *See theatrical of Jordan Osher on page 113 and commercial look on page 171.*

Barbara Benvil of Benvil Photography, 323/969-4944. $250 1 roll, 1 8x10; $375 2 rolls, 2 8x10s; $500 3 rolls, 3 8x10s. B&W and color. Hair and make-up is included! An appointment is necessary before shooting in order to understand the needs of the individual, whether they are just starting out or a celebrity needing a publicity photo for a layout. Barbara usually signs her photographs. I disagree with this; I don't think there should be any distraction on your photo. Request that she leave her signature off your picture. *See the pictures of Caryn West in four different characters from a two roll shoot on pages 122 and 123.*

Lesley Bohm, 213/625-8401. www.bohmphotography.com. $175, one roll black and white or color, with one 8x10, (two roll minimum if shooting theatrical and commercial looks); $350, two rolls with two 8x10s; $495, three rolls three 8x10s; $645, four rolls four 8x10s. 4x6 work prints, $2; B&W 8x10 master, $19.50; color 8x10 master, $25. Makeup and hairstylist, $150. Lesley has a great natural light studio where she shoots all her clients. Two of my students got truly amazing shots from Lesley and Carly says she had a great, relaxed time shooting. She's shot many of the actors currently starring on soaps. Lesley keeps the negatives or they can be purchased for $50 per roll. *See Carly Althoff's theatrical shot on page 115 and commercial shot on page 173. Makeup by Shawn Flint Blair.*

Frank Bruynbroek, 818/755-7933. www.fbsiteonline.com. $425 for six rolls and proofsheets. 4x6s, $2.50; 8x10s, $15. Money back guarantee. He says, "I approach the head shot session as if it were a publicity shoot." By shooting 6 rolls he wants the actor to feel confident they will get the photos they need. Looking at his photos, he seems to discover the person in the actor. In a letter from one of his fans, "His gift is capturing the spirit and soul, Frank's work is so good because it is real and honest." I discovered Frank through actress Maddisen Krown; great photos, many different looks. In my shoot he was easy to be with and interested in who I was. Natural light set up, relaxed atmosphere, you feel confident he will capture you as you need to be seen. *See the theatrical shots of me on page 110, a commercial shot on page172. Makeup by Rita Montanez.*

Carrie Cavalier of Cavalier Photography, 818/840-9148 and 818/566-8291. www.cavalierphotography.com. Adults, $175.00 for one roll; $250.00 for two rolls and $350.00 for three roles. Free negatives, 8x10's are $16. Studio and outdoor available, although most of her work reflects creative locations using natural light. Make-up and hair starts at $50. Color 3x5 or 4x6 pictures for extra work registration. Color fashion, or artist photos start at $200.00 for one roll. Children's headshots are $150 which includes the negatives and one 8x10. *See Keith Johnson's theatrical shot on page 121 and commercial shot on page 171. Makeup by Kari Nicole. Skylar Cavalier in the Child Actor Section.*

David Edwards, 310/364-0130. *See commercial shot of DJ Johnson on page 170.*

Gayle Garnett, 310/712-3911. www.photographybygayle.com. 155 West Washington Blvd. #944, Los Angeles, 90015. Free parking. Three roll B&W package is $325; two roll B&W package is $265. A color roll may be substituted for an extra $10. Additional B&W rolls are $55, additional color rolls are $65. Proof sheets and negatives are included. Accepts credit cards. Makeup for women is $85-$100 for a two-three roll shoot. Light makeup for men is typically included, but could be $15 - $75 depending on what is needed. Gayle shoots in a beautiful downtown loft studio using natural light. Time is spent discussing how you will market yourself; she wants the agents and casting directors to easily see where you fit in. Gayle allows each actor's uniqueness to shine through by creating a comfortable, unhurried environment. "I love hearing that your headshots are getting you called in." Kids under 12 receive discounted pricing. *See theatrical photo of Carly Althoff on page 114 and commercial photo on page 173 Makeup by Sara Chameides.*

Dorothy Goulah, 818/789-6884. $250 for 2 rolls, includes makeup and help with hair. Extra rolls are $75 each. Uses natural and reflected light for a true to life image. Will help define your look and casting possibilities. The most common comment after shooting is, "That was so easy!" Recommended by casting director Stuart Stone.

Rod Goodman, 818/760-0733. $50 per 36 exposure roll of B&W; 4x6 preview prints $3 each; 8x10s $17 each. Proofs available the next business day. $70 per 36 exposure roll of color; 8x10s $22 each. All prints take 3-5 days. Two looks allowed per roll, both studio and natural light are available. Makeup artist $25, no hair. Rod keeps the negatives. His studio is set in a stress free homey environment. Hours: Tu-F 9-5, Sa 9-1. He is usually booked two to four weeks ahead. This is an inexpensive place to try a new look or for that specialty shot. High-end photographer Mark Husmann likes his work. *See Keith Johnson's theatrical shots on page 120 and commercial shot on page 171.*

Greg Crowder of 6 Reel Pictures. 310/472-1515. www.6reel.com. $250 for five rolls, the actor keeps the rolls and takes the film to the lab of their choice for developing. He likes Isgo's Lab. You can get a proof sheet or what I prefer is to develop all the shots into 4x6s. You then have your own 8x10s made. Greg says, "I shoot all around Santa Monica in a relaxed, natural environment and capture a fun, energetic, spontaneous moment that is unique to the head shot world." My student Marcus Patric was referred to him by his manager. Greg ended up shooting seven rolls and they came up with many different looks. Wonderful location shots.

Mary Ann Halpin of Halpin-Croyle Photography, 323/874-8500. www.maryannhalpin.com. $650 including sales tax for four rolls and negatives, three different looks in a three to four hour session; B&W Polaroid shots before each look. Mary Ann does the makeup and styling and helps with hair. A $200 nonrefundable deposit, contact sheet in two to three days. She says, "If an actor says, 'This is the most fun I've ever had having my pictures taken,' then I feel I've done my job!" The music and snacks are great. She is the author of a coffee table book, "Pregnant Goddesshood: A Celebration of Life." *See photos of Janice Allen, theatrical shot on page 119, commercial shot on page 169 and Cynthia Kerr on page 172. Makeup by Mary Ann and retouching by Charisse of The Retouching Company.*

Terri Hanauer, 310/459-1859. $175 per roll for B&W, $195 per roll for color, includes proofsheet and negatives. A wonderful photographer. Terri helps you let your guard down so you are open and vulnerable for the camera. She is a working actress; keeps up to the minute on what the industry needs are in Los Angeles as well as in Canada. If you will be working in both markets, definitely see her.

Rich Hogan, 323/467-2628. $150 for a basic one roll shoot which includes two looks, the proofsheet, negatives and one 8x10. Also offers a premium three roll session for $375. Makeup and hair artist is available for $100. He's shot Tina Turner, Magic Johnson, Big Boy of Power 106, Jay Thomas, Playboy and Penthouse models of the year. He does a good job, along with his special makeup artist Ali Finnie. He does computer imaging with over 400 different borders available to enhance your 8x10. Rich registers non-union extras for Sunset Casting and Union extras for Idell James. *See theatrical photo of Keith Johnson, on page 121 and commercial shot on page 171. Austin and Jackson Tovar's pictures are in the Child Actor Section.*

Mark Husmann, 213/680-9999. www.greatheadshots.com. $550. Shoots digitally so he shoots until you get the shots you want. You view all the shots as you shoot. Mark says, "We keep the good ones and delete the bad ones. My clients leave with 150 to 200 great shots." Every shot is in color and black and white for better marketing versatility. View everything at home online, making your own test prints of your favorites; you can email them to your agent, manager and acting coach for their input. No master shots are needed; all multiples are made from the original digital file. Makeup and hair artist is $175. He shoots inside a studio, using the natural light that comes in through the windows. Mark only shoots two people a day and he meets people prior to shooting so they will feel comfortable with him on the day of the shoot. "I tell people to try and keep the pictures as simple as possible; the photographs should be about them, not the clothing, the makeup, or the background." *See theatrical photo of Janice Allen on page 118 and commercial photo on page 169. Makeup by Dara Dupuy.*

Sean Kenney, 800/505-7698. For adults $250 for one roll, three changes, two 8x10s including minor retouching; $350 for two rolls, five changes and four 8x10s. Makeup artist is available. Guarantees to have 8x10s back in five to seven working days. Extra 8x10s are $25 each. Rush orders are available. You can buy your negatives for $75 per roll. Works with adults and children. Note the savings here because he does minor retouching. Sean travels to other parts of the country, bringing the Los Angeles style. *See DJ Johnson's theatrical shot on page 117 and commercial shot on page 170 which were taken in Phoenix.*

Diana Lannes Photography, Voice Mail: 213/427-8096, Studio: 323/465-3232. $250.00 - $350.00 depending on the package. Diana has been taking pictures for 12 years in New York and Los Angeles. She works out of the Hollywood Raleigh Studios office that she shares with her husband, photographer Randall Michelson. She shoots with natural or studio light and they do all their own printing and retouching with gorgeous, flawless results. Clients are able to view their photos during the shoot and they can take home the whole photo shoot plus finals on a CD for $25. Film and Digital are both available. Professional Make-up available, $100. *See theatrical photo of Janice Allen on page 118, her commercial shot on page 169 and the Photo Retouching Section on page 140. Makeup by Naja. Also check out Carrara and Chance Onody's pictures in the Child Actor Section.*

David LaPorte, 310/452-4053. www.davidlaporte.com. Two rolls for $275, $85 for makeup. Includes proofs and negative. You order your own 4x6s and 8x10s. Unconditional guarantee means you and your agents have to love the photos or he will reshoot. He helps people to just be themselves; that's why agents and managers love his work. "Bringing out the personality helps market the actor." Very likeable, open and truthful. Shoots just two to three people a day. Several of my students have used David and I loved their photos. They said he was great to work with. *See Janice Allen's theatrical shot on page 119 and her commercial shot on page 169. Makeup by Laura Connelly.*

Tom Lascher, 310/581-1980. $250 session fee plus cost of film at about $15 per roll. Actor picks up the negatives and proof sheets, proceeds with master prints and reproductions. "I'm committed to meeting my clients before we shoot in order for us to get to know each other and to better plan a potential shoot. Some of my favorite clients are actors who truly detest having their pictures taken. When things work right we can use the rehearsal process of shooting to create a really strong final 8x10." Acting coaches Sal Romeo and Michael Nehring give Tom the highest of recommendations.

Mara, 818/781-8933. $300 for three rolls of B&W, including makeup and two 8x10s; $8 for each 8x10, you keep the negatives. She's been a photographer for 25 years. Mara loves working with new people and thinks getting the best pictures is the photographer's responsibility. An agent said, "She is the only photographer who is consistently good with my clients." Mara was a New York model for many years; she is beautiful herself and makes you feel beautiful while she's shooting you. *See photos of Carly Althoff's, theatrical shot, page 115, commercial shot, page 173.*

Kevin McIntyre, 818/761-6081. www.kevinmcphotograph.com. $145 for 1 roll and $250.00 for 2 rolls. Special deal for Judy Kerr's readers: 3 rolls for the price of 2. Negatives included. Travels to a location (i.e. the beach) for an additional minimal charge. Proof sheets in 24 to 36 hours. Kevin shoots headshots, fashion and music bands. "His ability to adapt to any pace and personality is complimented by his easygoing manner; the product intensely and simplistically captures the honest essence of a client." He is a natural light devotee and is recommended by many top agents. *See Carly Althoff's theatrical shot on page 114 and commercial shot on page 173.*

Robert Raphael, 310/486-7881 or 310/855-0047. www.robertraphael.com. The West End Salon, 520 N. La Cienega Blvd., West Hollywood, 90048. $165 for one roll including proof sheet and negatives; $275 for two rolls; $375 for three rolls. Makeup for women: $100; men $35. He shoots with B&W or color film. Robert has been a makeup artist for 20 years, working with many of the top photographers, giving him an insight into what a great head shot is all about. Shooting in his salon, The West End, he uses natural light, studio beauty light or theatrical set light. "The color head shots are an added dimension for commercial head shots. Works very well for actors with honey brown or red hair, hazel eyes or to bring out what you really look like. Many managers, agents and casting people are asking my clients to print in both B&W and color." *See the theatrical photos of Loryn Phillips on page 116 and the commercial photo on page 172.*

Marina Rice Bader, 310/859-4687. www.marinarice.com. $375 for three rolls, several looks; two 8x10s and negatives; additional rolls, $75 each. Sessions are three to four hours; she shoots in B&W and color; in studio or location. Makeup for women $50 to $75; men and children free. For optimum results, she approaches each session as a fun and relaxed publicity shoot as opposed to a head shot session, making every client feel like they are already an established working actor. I loved the acting direction she gave me while shooting; I could easily think the thoughts she asked for and the stories of the characters I was living. Wonderful. Highly recommended by casting director Michael Donovan. *See the theatrical shot of me on page 111, commercial shot on page 172.*

Michael Sanville, 323/654-9141. wwwmichaelsanville.com. $485 per session. Hair and makeup $75 for men, $100 to $125 for women. Located in the Hollywood Hills. Shooting one or two people a day using natural light, he books sessions not per roll shoots. Works in depth with select clientele. Top agents, managers, casting directors and acting coaches swear by him. By appointment only. *See photo of DJ Johnson on page 117.*

Klint Spillsbury, 310/721-7225. www.xlint.com. $350-$600 includes makeup and retouching. Acting coach Caryn West highly recommends.

Pamela Springsteen Photography, 323/874-9188. www.pamelaspringsteen.com. $500 for three rolls, no prints included; you keep the negatives. Each 8x10 is at lab cost. Makeup artist available. She shoots many celebrities and CD covers, works in a studio and starts with Polaroids. Pamela also directs music videos and short films. She's taken pictures of me and many of my students; her work is good, and she is fun to be with. *See photos of Jordan Osher on page 112. These were the first photos Jordan had ever taken. She understood his essence and captured it.*

Jillian Griffiths of J Thomasin Photography, 818/769-6998. www.jthomasinphotography.com. $100 for each roll, proofsheets and negatives included. Jillian says, "I think it's important for my client to be specific with their thoughts for each shot. Thoughts translate— they come through the eyes and give a certain amount of genuineness: a moment has truly been captured. No fake smiles allowed." She continues, "I help my clients decide what sort of essence, vibe, character they would like to capture and then we figure out what thoughts this 'character' might have. For example: instead of trying to *look* like a high-powered attorney, this process helps you *become* that character. People often tell me I make them feel comfortable and put them at ease, and I'm certainly not afraid to jump in and act with them as well." Highly recommended by Stuart K. Robinson. *See Jordan Osher's theatrical shot on page 113 and commercial shots on page 170.*

Other Photographers With Good Reputations

Michael D'Ambrosia	310/444-7391	www.michaeldambrosia.com
Brad Buckman	323/466-2700	www.bradbuckman.com
David Carlson	323/656-3324	$95 1 roll; $175 2 rolls, incl. neg.
John Corbett	323/654-9427	www.johncorbettphotography.com
Kelsey Edwards	323/936-6106	
Elliot Photography	323/876-8821	
Erin Fiedler	818/415-1533	www.erinfiedler.com
Michael Helms	818/353-5855	www.michaelhelms.com
Bader Hower	310/472-8584	
Robert Kazandjian	323/957-9575	www.kazphoto.com
Suzanne Karp	310/450-0117	
Kim Kimbro	323/769-5588	
Michael Lamont	818/506-0285	
Harry Langdon	310/859-4900	www.harrylangdon.com
Don Lewis	323/656-2138	$250, 2 rolls, incl. neg.
Michael Papo	818/760-8160	www.michaelpapo.com
Kevin Merrill	818/508-4533.	www.kevinmerrill.com
Cari Lightfoot Pike	310/288-6620	
Chris Prince	310/890-1920	$150, 1 roll, incl. neg.
Peter Solari	323/934-9930	
Maggie Smith	310/454-1545	A lovely person.
Alisha Tamburri	818/998-8838	www.atamburri.com
Adam Sheridan Taylor	323/878-0693	www.velvetartist.com
Handeland Tesoro	818/623-7200	www.handelandtesoro.com
Alan Weissman	818/766-9797	www.alanwiessman.com

In San Francisco: Lisa Keating 415/777-4918. www.lisakeatingphotography.com. Highly recommended—I love what I have seen.

In San Diego: Sandy Spear, 619/234-9728. $90 per roll, $150 for two rolls.

In **South Florida: Bob Lasky**, 305/891-0550. www.boblasky.com. He is wonderful; two of my acting students arrived here with pictures taken by him and were able to use them in the Los Angeles market. I taught a seminar at the Acting Studio in Hollywood, Florida and all the actors who had pictures taken by him had excellent pictures. For anyone acting in this area, check out his web site. Everything you want to know about South Florida —getting work, coaches, networking and general information—is there.

Other Cities: *See the Cities Outside of Los Angeles section.*

MAKEUP AND
MAKEUP ARTISTS

• **While women always need a full makeup** for their B&W photos, men seldom need full makeup, just a little help.

• **Men will need** translucent powder to remove shine and maybe an eyebrow pencil to fill in their brows. It is most important that a man doesn't look like he is wearing makeup in his photos. Other imperfections can be removed in retouching.

• **Makeup artist Lorraine Altamura tells men:**

> • **For photo shoots**, 95% of Caucasian men can use Revlon's Love Pat in the Suntan tone found at any drugstore for about $6. It is a moisturizing powder and can be put on dry or wet. If you put it on wet, just dust off the excess when it dries. Don't put it on your lips. Joe Blasco's Natural Blue Neutralizer I, found at professional beauty supply stores, is a mild beard cover and great for eliminating dark circles under the eyes.

• **Robert Raphael, makeup artist, talks about eyebrows.**

> • The many looks your brows can have would surprise you. Where your arch is placed can make close set eyes appear further apart and can help a heavy lid to appear lifted without cosmetic surgery. Your brows and lashes may need to be colored. Pale blondes look better with a deeper ash brow and redheads need a touch of brown. Men can really benefit from natural eyebrow grooming. Defined brows and lashes will give your eyes a stronger expression when you are acting.

• **Lorraine Altamura, makeup artist,** talks about lips and hints on how to work with your makeup artist.

  • I use a product called Young Lips to smooth on the lips first. This will keep your lip color from bleeding. Next apply lip pencil and then lipstick.

  • **Come with your eyebrows tweezed or waxed.** Don't tweeze the top of the eyebrows—the natural shape duplicates the top line of the upper eyes. When you strip that line away, it takes away your personality. Do your eyebrow, mustache waxing and facials at least a week before the shoot. Your face goes into shock for three or four days after these procedures. Get your hair styled at least two weeks before the shoot to be sure the style works. If you want your hair to grow another inch, then wait; you want these photos to last for a long time.

Rita Montanez, makeup artist, designer and teacher, tells actresses:

  • **Makeup is incredibly important when it comes to photography;** the right makeup shows that you are professional. If you don't have a makeup artist for your photo session, make sure that you know how to do your own properly. In black & white photos you have to create a lot of contrast because normal makeup will not show up. You use more, concentrating on shading, using grays, browns and blacks. Color photography is different because it's more natural; something you can wear everyday.

  • **Always take your own makeup kit on a shoot** so you're prepared if the makeup artist doesn't show up for some reason. In interviews, your makeup can be the same as for color photography. For commercials, you need to look natural. On soap opera interviews, you want a glamour look. If there's a little bit of chubbiness or excess chin area, learn how to contour in order to complement your face.

• **Anne Archer** (*Fatal Attraction, Clear and Present Danger*) thinks actresses should learn to do their own makeup. She likes to do hers at home so she can leave for the studio a little later. She has two complete sets of makeup; one is set up at home and the other is organized in a portable bag she always carries with her.

• **Most makeup artists in beauty salons or department stores** will give free makeup lessons if you buy from them. Hold a mirror so you can watch what they do; ideally, they will draw a step-by-step chart for you. If you aren't buying products, a lesson is usually $35 to $100. Makeup by a professional artist for a photo shoot is between $25 and $150.

• **Rita created the following chart for my readers and students.** Rita has listed commercial products but she has developed her own line of great products that are reasonable and can be purchased in person, by phone or on her web site.

MAKEUP CHART FOR
BLACK & WHITE PHOTOGRAPHS
by Rita Montanez 818/509-5733. www.makeupbyrita.com.

• Use makeup sponges for best results.

• Foundation (use your favorite foundation) should be applied lightly and evenly over entire face. A little foundation on the lips helps keep lipstick on. Make sure the foundation is blended well and there are no lines under your chin.Custom blended foundations are nice, since they're your exact skin color. This is one of my favorite products I carry.

• I like to put my favorite concealer on after foundation. Apply with a small brush and blend into foundation with sponge – very lightly. My favorite concealers are: Keromask, Laura Mercier, MAC.

• Powder over the foundation sets the makeup. You can use a loose powder which is applied with a large brush or a puff. You can also use a powder compact. There are many brands in the Beauty Supply Stores. Some of the brands I like are MAC, LaFemme and Rita's.

• Eyebrows. Keep them groomed, either by plucking, or having them waxed professionally. Fill them in with either an eyebrow pencil very lightly, or a brush and eye shadow powder in a color close to the hair.

• Eyeshadow. A soft color over the entire lid, and a slightly darker color in the crease, blended well, makes the eyes stand out.

• Brush yellow tone eye shadow over the whole lid.

• Eyeliner. I like using a soft eyeliner pencil and going over it with a matching eyeshadow applied with an angle brush to make it stay on.

• Curl eyelashes. Mascara. A light coat of mascara is prettiest. My favorite is Almay, which is found at any drug store.

• Blush and contouring. A powder blush applied with a Blush Brush to the apple of the cheek is fresh and natural. Contouring is usually done to define cheek bones or to make the face look thinner. Contouring along the jaw-line also enhances one's face.

• Lips. Lipliners stay on the lips the longest. I like to fill the whole lip area in with the liner, and use a little lipstick on top to give a creamier look. Sometimes I use a gloss instead of a lipstick.

• Many of the products above are sold by MakeUp by Rita. Lessons are also available.

- **Rita further advises during your photo shoot.**

  - **Check all of your makeup during the shoot.** Use either powder/ foundation on a puff or loose translucent powder on a puff for touchups. A great deal of attention and focus on your makeup will make a world of difference in your black and white pictures. Hint: a little Preparation H hemorrhoidal creme will take down puffy eyes.

- **Lorraine shares further tips:**

  - **RCMA** (Research Council of Makeup Artists) is the best creme foundation for B&W photos; mostly pigment and less grease for more coverage and less shine. MAC cosmetics have very good colors. If you can't go to a beauty supply store and get RCMA, then MAC is a good choice. Actors and models get a 30% discount. The foundation doesn't have to go down the neck but put a little blush or contour powder in the middle of your neck, and to contour the décolletage line.

  - **We use three tones or shades** on the eyes and several tones on the face: foundation, highlight, contour and blush. Also use three tones on your lips. For instance: a deep rose, almost burgundy on the outer edge, a lighter rose to blend it all in together and a beige on the inside bottom lip to highlight and pucker the lips; it makes them more interesting. When you're touching up, use a creamy lipstick pencil that's just a shade or two darker than your lip color; filling in your lips with pencil color is the trendy thing to do. You can use just a tiny bit of foundation on the hot spot of the bottom lip.

  - **Put your lipsticks in little round pots** that screw together or in little plastic flip top pill boxes with several compartments. Buy the pots at the professional beauty supply and the pill boxes at the drug store. Scoop out the lipstick from the tubes with a plastic spatula or knife and put them in the containers, microwave them for a few seconds and the lipstick will quickly melt to the bottom of the containers. Use a brush to combine your own lipsticks for interesting looks.

  - **Cleanliness is very important**, especially for people who have sensitive skin. I sharpen all my pencils as I put them back. I use disposable mascara wands that go into the tube once and are discarded. Bring your own mascara; if someone has conjunctivitis and the wand goes back in the tube, the mascara is contaminated. Use clean sponges with the creme foundations. I use a spatula or side of the brush to take it out of the pot and put it on my pallet (hand) so the sponge doesn't go back into the pot. The Board of Health says the Hepatitis B Virus can stay alive on a piece of paper for eleven days. AIDS virus stays alive on cuticle snippers through general washing; it has to be killed in a 10 part water, 1 part Clorox solution.

• **Robert Raphael is a talented makeup artist.** I had my first makeup lesson from him almost 20 years ago. I still use the special brushes I bought from him. He talks more about makeup.

- • **Makeup can make your best features pop.** When applying your own makeup, bring your best features forward first. Your so-called flaws will diminish without much effort.

- • **For Men:** Base makeup should always go two shades darker for black and white photo shoots and television and one shade darker for film. With this technique, their faces will never be washed out by the studio lights. A second base three shades darker for contouring the cheeks, chin and eye crease area. Concealer for under eye area should match skin tone. Medium to deep translucent powder to eliminate shine.

- • **For Women:** Schedule your eyebrows to be shaped a week before your photo shoot. If there are any areas of facial hair that appear to cause shadows, waxing can eliminate the hair for up to six weeks. You can also have the photo retouched.

- • **Mascara:** From dark brown to black. Painting only the upper lashes is a more youthful look in photos, as well as omitting the liner from the bottom lid. When it comes to television and film this rule does not apply.

- • **Eye Brows:** Fill your brows in with a powder shadow a shade lighter than your brow color. Match only your brow shade if there are no brow hairs, such as at the end of your brows. If the brows appear too dark when finished, simply apply ivory shadow or translucent powder over them.

- • Keep all shadows, blush and lip color matte. Avoid all frost colors.

• **Rand Rusher, R.N., C.N.O.R.** www.randrusher.com. Botox, Collagen, Cymetra, Perlane and Restylane injection specialist of Solutions Skincare Medical Clinic in Beverly Hills talks about the best way to take care of your skin.

- • **Commit yourself to the basics:**
- • **Water**
- • **Cleanse**
- • **Sunscreen**
- • **Moisturize**
- • **Anti-oxidents**—using vitamin rich moisturizers are the best anti-aging effects. Anti-oxidents help eliminate free radicals caused by environment, smoking, pollution. Topical vitamins work faster, within hours, to replenish the body, while oral vitamins can take weeks to show significant effects. This is why Dr. Leaf and I have developed a skin care line, called Leaf & Rusher, to provide necessary anti-oxidents for daily skin regiments. For more information, please visit www.leafandrusher.com.

Resources

EYEBROW SPECIALISTS

Robert Raphael, 310/486-7881 or 310/855-0047 www.robertraphael.com. The West End Salon, 520 N. La Cienega Blvd., West Hollywood, 90048. Brows are $20 and up. Makeup for photo shoot is $100. Lessons are $75.

Diane Barletta of Salon Oases, 818/876-0633. 22941-C Ventura Blvd., Woodland Hills, 91364. Actress Jode Leigh Edwards says, "When I went to Diane, my eyebrows had been destroyed; they were lopsided and I'd been burnt by the wax. Diane is very gentle, and the shape is always perfect for my face. I would drive to Timbuktu for her. I won't let anyone else touch my eyebrows!" Rates available upon request. Diane does all types of body waxing, facials and massage.

Jacqueline Shepard, 323/939-8969. Located at Bleu, 454 S. La Brea, L.A. $32 for eyebrow tweeze rather than wax; Lash tinting, $20; brow tinting, $10; lip wax, $10; individual false eyelash application, $20. Chris and Cathy Kerr say she's the BEST!

MAKEUP ARTISTS
Photographers will usually have professional makeup artists they recommend.

• *The following makeup artists sell makeup and give lessons at their places of business.*

Cynthia Roman Beauty, 310/276-5558. www.leafskincare.com. Solutions Skincare, 436 N. Bedford Dr., #104, Beverly Hills, 90210. Makeup application and lessons; post-op makeup applications and lessons; facial waxing and brow shaping. Endorsed by many celebrities and affiliated with the top Plastic Surgery Office in Beverly Hills. Cynthia has developed her own line of products. "Though inner beauty is timeless, our outer beauty is timed."

Cinema Secrets, 818/846-0579. 4400 Riverside Drive, Burbank, 91505, in Toluca Lake. M-F 8-6, Sa 10-5. $75 to $150 per lesson for a one or two hour session.

Naimie's Film & Television Beauty Supply, 818/655-9933. 12640 Riverside Dr., Valley Village, CA 91607. M-W 9-6, Th-Fr 9-7, Sat 9-6. $55 for makeup application. This is where most of the studio makeup and hairstylists get their supplies. The regular retail store is on the top level. 10% discount with your SAG card. Second, smaller location, 818/763-7073. 12801 Victory Blvd., North Hollywood, 91606. M-F 8:30-6; Sa 8:30-5:30.

The Color Company, 818/760-7798. www.jillkirshcolor.com. Jill Kirsh manufactures her own color coordinated line, has appeared on QVC and many television shows. Kit consists of eight eyeshadows, four blushes, two lipsticks, lip gloss, lip liner, eye pencil, mascara, three brushes, a color swatch booklet, a scarf and a miniature makeup version for travel, $90. *See the wardrobe section for more about her color charts.*

• *The following professional makeup artists will go on your photo shoots to work with you.*

Alicia Ali. Contact her through Rich Hogan at 323/467-2628. Hair, makeup and photo styling. She works mainly with Rich but is available for outside shoots. She also gives private lessons.

Helena Cepeda, 310/991-0422. $100 for makeup and hair. Helena has an extensive background as a makeup artist and stylist. She works often with celebrities; she was the resident makeup artist for "The Vagina Monologues" and does freelance work on Lifetime's "Biographies" and ABC news. She is experienced in working with hair on camera—will go on sets. She has a great eye and can create both a subtle, natural look or go to the other extreme. She also does weddings and special events.

Sara Chameides, 818/400-7229. $100 and up for makeup and hair. Very experienced in styling (fashion background). Sara has been a makeup artist for over 10 years in all capacities, print in B&W and color, film, video, stage, and personal appearances. Happy to consult/shop for an actor getting their makeup kit together. $75 for makeup design and lessons. *She works with photographer Gayle Garnett; see Carly Althoff's theatrical picture on page 114 and the commercial shot on page 173.*

Alisha Chompupong, Pager 213/719-7790. Hair, makeup and photo styling, $150 for four hours. Makeup for special occasions, such as award shows and weddings. Also works in film, videos, print and television.

Laura Connelly, 310/473-3355. Makeup and hair. $85 and up, depending on time and locations, for a general photo shoot. She likes to stay the whole shoot to keep an eye on the hair and makeup for the photographer. If she has to do a complete hairstyle, there is an extra charge. Makeup for a special occasions and private lessons, $100 and up. *See Janice Allen's theatrical photo taken by David LaPorte on page 119 and the commercial shot on page 169.*

Dara Dupuy, 310/403-9233. $150 for hair and makeup. She says, "I feel it is important to stay for the whole shoot, sustaining perfection. Making subtle changes such as flipping the hair gives you different variations to choose from. I believe it is in your best interest to shoot multiple 'looks' ranging from natural to glamorous during your photo session." Janice said "Dara was very willing to make changes and she stayed right next to Mark during the whole shoot." *See Mark Husmann's photos of Janice Allen; theatrical shot on page 118 and her commercial shot on page 169.*

Shawn Flint Blair, 323/856-6105. www.makeupbyshawn.com. $150 and she stays the whole shoot, approximately two hours. A true artist, she works in all media (video, film, photography, commercials). Trained at Joe Blasco's, she has created her own style through 20 years of experience. Shawn says, "I work with each client, giving them the look they want with makeup and hair. The only thing I do not offer is blow drying hair straight; I use a straight iron for that." She works with photographers doing promotional shots, head shots, catalogues, music, etc. Available for private lessons, $150 about an hour and a half. There is a FREE step-by-step makeup lesson on her website plus many other features including before and after shots. Also private sessions for any occasion including weddings, special events, award shows, etc. She is the only makeup artist that is a professional photo retoucher as well. Samples are on her website. www.artist2design.com. *See Lesley Bohm's photography: Carly Althoff's theatrical shot on page 115, commercial shot on page173.*

Ivy Halford of Ivy's Skincare and Makeup Garden, 310/451-7780. 522 Wilshire Blvd., Suite G., Santa Monica, 90401. Transformational skincare and makeup. Makeup Union Local 706. The art of corrective makeup to treat blemished skin and to cosmetically camouflage irreparable damaged surface tissue and scars. She has her own line of transformational skincare and makeup products. Written diagnostic skincare and makeup analysis and customized at-home maintenance regimen. Eyebrow design, shaping and waxing, $20 comes with micro-dermabrasion and lash and brow tinting, $20. Helps you prepare for auditions, head shots and special occasions.

Eryn Krueger, 818/414-1314. $150 for a 4-hour shoot. $200 for hair and makeup. $75 for an hour makeup and hair session at the photographer's. She'll leave you instructions on how to change for a more glamorous look. Eryn certainly knows the glamorous look; Emmy nomination for helping to create the "looks" on General Hospital. She also works in video, commercials, film, stage and print.

Anne Marso, 310/281-1904. $150 for hair and makeup. In the business for 15 years, she does B&W and color print; also videos, commercials, features, fashion and weddings.

Rela Martine, 323/878-0675, Pager 213/303-5122. $75 and up, makeup and hair, depending on how many rolls and looks. Color and B&W print. Rela has traveled the world doing the fashion runways in Spain, France, Italy, Germany, etc. Member IATSE Local 706, doing film, TV and commercials. Available for private sessions showing you how to apply your makeup easily and makeup tips. "This industry is all about having fun!"

Rita Montanez, 818/509-5733. www.makeupbyrita.com. Hair and makeup: $100 for a general shoot. I've worked with her many times. Besides being available for your photo shoot, she gives seminars and private lessons in how to do your own makeup. Private lesson, $75. She teaches color and B&W photography look, natural and glamour looks. $75 for a special occasion or bride's makeup. You get a 25% discount on her professional line of cosmetics. She will put your makeup kit together for you. Rita works with many photographers. *See Frank Bruynbroek's theatrical shots of me on page 110 and commercial shot on page 172.*

Naja, 310/770-9525. $100, makeup and light hair, from natural beauty makeup to more creative looks. She stays for the whole shoot for touch-ups and bump-ups. She does head shots, commercials, videos and printwork. She believes that it's important to work in a relaxed, friendly and comfortable environment. *She works with photographer Diana Lannes; see Janice Allen's theatrical shot on page 118, the retouching examples on page 140 and her commercial shot on page 169.*

Kari Nicole, 310/592-6914. karidoll3@yahoo.com. $75-$100 for makeup and hair at the photo session. Extensive professional training in all aspects of makeup: fashion, beauty, fantasy, character and special effects. Makeup for film, television, theatre, fashion and weddings. Call or e-mail for scheduling. *See photographer Carrie Cavalier's pictures of Keith Johnson; theatrical shot on page 121 and his commercial shot on page 171.*

Robert Raphael, 310/486-7881 or 310/855-0047. www.robertraphael.com. The West End Salon, 520 N. La Cienega Blvd., West Hollywood, 90048. $100 for a photo shoot. He does great eyebrows $20 and up. Makeup lesson is $75. He carries a great line of makeup, still gives lessons and the salon has all the services, plus he's a very wonderful photographer. *See his theatrical photos of Loryn Phillips on page 116 in the commercial section on page 172.*

Sandy Williams, 818/752-2582. Pager: 818/327-9036. Makeup and hair for photography sessions, $90-$150. "I believe actors should have a real say in how they want to look, especially their hair, because they have to duplicate it. We go from looking very natural to upscale glamour." Special occasion, award show makeup, $300. She also does, film, rock videos, commercials, television. *See Cynthia Kerr's shot on page 172.*

Yolanda Frye Skin Care, 310/275-3981. 632 1/2 Doheny Dr., Los Angeles, 90069. Black and white photography and special event makeup, $50 at the shop, $100 at the photographer's location. See her special facials and notes about her full service skin and nail services, in the Age Defying section.

PROFESSIONAL BEAUTY SUPPLY STORES

For regular or stage makeup and hair supplies, beauty supply stores are your best bet. All of these stores will give a 10% discount to actors. They also provide mail order service.

Cinema Secrets, 818/846-0579. www.cinemasecrets.com. 4400 Riverside Drive, Burbank, 91505, in Toluca Lake. M-F 8-6, Sa 10-5. Owner Maurice Stein has been in the business 30 years. Makeup artists and hair stylists work there part time, so you have professionals helping you.

Naimie's Film & Television Beauty Supply, 818/655-9933. (Naimie's Beauty Center) 12640 Riverside Dr., Valley Village, 91607. M-W 9-6, Th-Fr 9-7, Sa 9-6. This is where most of the studio makeup and hairstylists get their supplies. The regular retail store is on the top level. 10% discount with your SAG card. Second, smaller location, 818/763-7073. 12801 Victory Blvd., North Hollywood, 91606. M-Sa 9:30-6.

Frends Beauty Supply, 323/877-4828 or 818/769-3834. 5270 Laurel Canyon Blvd., North Hollywood, 91607. M-Sa 8-6, Su 10-4. Makeup and hair supplies, all brands.

Alcone Makeup Supply, 212/633-0551. 235 West 19 Street, Manhattan, NY 10011.

SPECIAL MAIL ORDER

Alcone Makeup Supply, 800/466-7446. 5-49 49th Avenue, Long Island City, NY 11101. Call and ask Vinny for their great catalogue. They are the largest store and outlet on the East Coast. There is no sales tax for out-of-state sales, which balances the shipping cost.

BEAUTY SUPPLY STORES WITH THEATRICAL MAKEUP

Bay City Beauty Supply, 310/393-3709. 320 Santa Monica Blvd., Santa Monica, 90401. M-Th 10-7; F&Sa 9-8; Su 10-7. Good prices. Big inventory.

Diamond Beauty Supply, 818/761-1778. 12151 Ventura Blvd., Studio City, 91604. One block west of Laurel Canyon. M-Sa 9:30-5:30; Su 11-4:30. Wonderful store, carries all the good products and they are very knowledgeable and helpful. Full service beauty shop in the back including an African-American specialist, hair extensions, facials, waxing and makeup.

MAC Make Up Store, 310/854-0860, 800/387-6707. 133 North Robertson, Los Angeles, 90048, across from the Newsroom Cafe. M-Sa 10:30-7, Su 12-5. They give a 30% discount to actors for a fee of $35 a year—sign up in store; bring a photo copy of your Union card. Also sold in the Beverly Center at the MAC store and at Hollywood & Highland. Without discount, sold at Nordstrom's and Macy's department stores. The creme foundation is wonderful, especially for your photos; covers everything. The powder colors and lipsticks are excellent; I see many makeup artists on the set using all their products.

M.P. Beauty, 323/934-7500. 6244 Wilshire Blvd., L.A., 90048. Corner of Wilshire and Crescent Heights in a strip mall. M-F 10-7, Sa 10-6. Denise does hair. A small store but packed with products.

Number One Beauty Supply, 310/656-2455. 1426 Montana Ave., #3, Santa Monica. M-Sa 9-7; Su 10-6. They have all of the Hard Candy shades. Jennifer Aniston, Courtney Cox, Holly Hunter, Michelle Pfeiffer, Robert Wagner, Mary Steenburgen and Anne Archer visit this store, just to name a few. Body jewelry, a self-painting kit for tattoos, is big with the celebs.

AN ACTRESSES MAKEUP KIT
by Rita Montanez

Foundation in your shade.
Concealer for dark circles.
Pencil concealer for other things to hide.
Finishing powder and puff.
Blush for healthy glow or
Bronzing powder for a natural tan look.
Eyeliner, soft taupe or gray pencil.
Mascara.
Carmex or lip balm on lips before liner.
Neutral lip pencil as lip liner.
Lipstick close to liner color.
Powder brush to blend all of the face powders.
A sponge and Q-tips for clean up.

Actress
Janice
Allen

Photographer
Diana
Lannes

Hair & Makeup
Naja

Unretouched photo.

Diana took this shot
to use as an example
of digital retouching.

Randall Michelson
demonstrates digital
retouching.

He smoothed out stray
hairs, skin shadows under
the eyes, sharpened and
brightened the eyes and
teeth and fixed the fabric
on the right sleeve.

Randall also removed
the distracting window
overhead.

PHOTO RETOUCHING

• **The photos you use for your headshot** should closely resemble you. As you mature, your wrinkles will get you roles but as a young person, lines and shadows on your photos that look like wrinkles will hurt your chances of being called in for your age appropriate roles. Your retoucher can advise you according to what your specific needs are. The cost can range from $10 to $50 for an uncomplicated job. As always, get an estimate of the cost before proceeding.

• **I like to work personally with a retoucher.** I want them to see me in person and to discuss my specific needs. Many photo labs offer retouching services but usually the clerk marks it and puts it in a stack; then you aren't a real person to the retoucher.

• **Digital retouching** has become very popular especially with photographers who are shooting with digital cameras. *See the example on the previous page.* My only caution is to be careful not to take away too much personality. With computers it is very easy to make a picture look perfect which is not always in your best interest. When the photographer is doing the retouching rather than a lab, it is personal because they shot your pictures and know your personality and what you look like in person.

• **Photographer Mary Ann Halpin** believes that most pictures are enhanced by having the whites of the eyes lightened and the eyelashes defined. She further suggests that if you have a great shot but the eyes are slightly out of focus, they can be sharpened by a retoucher and thus save the picture.

• **Nichan, master artist, retoucher.**

Q: Why get pictures retouched?

• **Once you convert the color reality** to a black and white print, blotches appear on the face which copy light and dark. There are shadows of light under the eyes exposing the depths of the wrinkles. We clean the shadow inside the line or wrinkle. We remove any blemishes or undesirable marks.

• **If the mouth is in-between** opening and closing we restore it to normal.

• **When a picture is out of focus,** we sharpen the eyes by adding more lashes and by adding white to the eye, and on the edge of the pupil.

• **If the hair looks thin** because the light hits it very strongly, we can add more detail. We can remove hair that is out of proportion or in the wrong place.

• **When the background is too distracting** or there's something missing, we can change it—even remove the whole background and put in a new one.

Q: How do you shop for a retoucher?

• **The best way is to see the retoucher's work and get the prices.** Your picture is something you are going to use for a couple of years. Five or 10 dollars over a two year span is not going to affect you that much.

Resources

Nichan Photographic Services, 818/508-8566. 12555 Hatteras St., North Hollywood, 91607. B&W and color retouching on headshots. Minimum is $25 a picture. Some services available while you wait. Complete retouching services; his techniques are etching, bleaching, dyeing and airbrushing. Average is $40, unless there is a great deal of work to be done. He is indeed an artist and has been retouching for many years, the favorite of many photographers and my favorite. *See example: Loryn's picture on page 116. Her lighter bra was showing through the sweater, Nichan retouched it in a few minutes, giving her a beautiful, usable picture. In my theatrical picture on page 110, Nichan retouched my neck. The photographer, Frank Bruynbroek, didn't feel it needed to be retouched but it was just a little too much aging for me. Nichan was very careful to leave the neck looking naturally aged.*

The Retouching Company, 818/842-4790. 3412 1/2 W. Magnolia Blvd., Burbank, 91505. M-F 9-6. B&W and color retouching on headshots. Todd Farcau and Charisse Broderick are very caring people; they do good work at a good price. $30 per hour for retouching; $40 per hour for air brushing. No minimum. Also digital capability. *See Mary Ann Halpin's photos of Janice Allen on page 119 and page 169. Charisse lightened the whites of the eyes and defined the eyelashes.*

Randall Michelson, 323/465-3232. $45 to $75 for the average headshot, including a final print. He does digital retouching designed to maximize the impact of your headshot. Complexion, shadows, flyaway hairs, contrast, background, eyes, clothing problems, fat and thinning hair can all be corrected in a natural way. Randall's retouching work is included with the photography of Diana Lannes. *See the page 140 for a demonstration of his work on Janice Allen's photo. Also Janice's theatrical photo on page 118 and commercial shot on page169.*

Shawn Flint Blair, 323/856-6105. www.artist2design.com. Starts at $25. B&W and color photos; manual and digital retouching. Manual etching technique on B&W prints begins at $25. Digital B&W and color starts at $50. A digital file starts at $35. Shawn is the only makeup artist we know of who also does retouching. Her makeup website is www.makeupbyshawn.com.

Mary Morano, 323/466-4079. 424 N. Larchmont, L.A., 90004. Minimum $25 for headshots. M-F 12-5. Drop by or make appointment. B&W and color retouching on headshots. *See DJs picture on page 117.*

Multi Image, Gail Rudy, 323/466-1266. 1607 El Centro Ave., Suite. 14, Los Angeles, 90028. B&W and color headshot retouching. $25 flat rate for digital and conventional; color quoted; free consultation. Two day turnaround. Color, B&W retouching on headshots and any photos used for reproduction. Old photos restored. In business since 1977.

Cameron Murley, 818/760-6756. 12134 Valley Spring Lane, Studio City, 91604. Flexible hours and turnaround time. Free estimate. Full service retoucher; art background. Works on color, B&W; glossy and fiber based papers. B&W and color retouching on headshots. Digital retouching available. Full satisfaction guaranteed. Can reconstruct bodies and faces. Restores and rebuilds old photographs. Treats each picture as an art project.

RJG Photo Retouching, Rodney Gottlieb, 310/202-0150. Los Angeles. B&W and color retouching on headshots, $60 an hour. $30 to $75 for the average 8x10. Airbrushing. Digital retouching. For changing the background, taking fat off the face, removing flyaway hairs, the range is slightly higher. He will quote the price before he does the work. 24 years experience.

Barbara Turner, 323/464-4015. 1570 1/2 Gower, north of Sunset, in Hollywood. Photographer Frank Bruynbroek recommends her work.

Eliott Photography and Retouching, 323/876-8821. 1151 N. La Brea Ave., West Hollywood, 90038. Recommended by actress/coach Caryn West. "Just had my color and sepia pictures done. Lovely people, a fast and terrific job, about $35 a picture, plus they are next door to Isgo's lab in West Hollywood."

PHOTO LABS AND

PICTURE REPRODUCTION

• **Photo labs develop your film** to proof sheets and 4x6 proof prints and produce your border or borderless matte 8x10 masters, plus many other services. All of these labs do multiple prints and some do lithographs. All labs listed here take mail orders.

• **The original 8x10 master picture** must be of excellent quality. When you mass-produce the picture, quality is always lost; you cannot avoid it. Go to a duplication lab that specializes in photo reproduction. Most pictures will need to be retouched at least a little before you bring them in to be reproduced. *See Photo Retouching Section.* Always make a few photocopies of your master so you will have something to give an interviewer, should the occasion arise before the lab is finished.

• **Take very good** protective care of your master and negative. If they get bent you will have to pay for another one. I keep each of mine with a piece of cardboard in an 8x10 labeled envelope, in a labeled folder in my file drawer. I am able to find my master and negative at a moment's notice.

• **Your 8x10 headshots** either B&W or color should be printed on photographic paper or very fine quality digital lithographs like ones done by Reproductions, Isgos or Imagestarters. The photographic paper choices are glossy, matte or pearl, with or without borders. Your duplication lab will show you what is available. Sometimes fancy borders cost more, especially the "sloppy" or "full frame" borders. These borders have the actual sprockets of the film showing and usually must be on your master when you take it to the reproduction house. Use what your agent wants or what you think will sell you and sell the picture best. Be creative; stand out.

• **Now decide how many prints to run.** When you are trying to get experience and have a great shot why not get 300 or 250 quality lithos, whatever the good price break is. You will want to get your pictures to everybody who is using actors. If you have an agent, they will tell you how many they need. Many agents and managers are using electronic submissions and they may not require the large quantity of pictures they once needed. When the demand is not great your best investment is quality photos.

• **If you are looking for an agent,** you may need two different photos reproduced, perhaps 50 of each. Then use photo copies, not lithos. A new agent may want new pictures or new shots mastered and reproduced. Have enough run off to be able to submit yourself for jobs while shopping for an agent. Any picture is better than no picture.

• **Photographer Frank Bruynbroek believes** that pictures are your foot in the door. "This is all you have to make that first good impression. Why compromise the quality of your headshot with a bad litho? It's better to have 100 great photos than 300 mediocre lithos that might end up in a drawer at home."

• **Your professional pictures must have your name on the front.** The photo reproduction service will do this for you. Don't put your agent's name on your pictures because if you change agents the pictures become obsolete. Your agent's and manager's information is always on your resume, which will be securely attached to the back of your picture. When a picture you are sending out is for a very important project, write your phone number in pencil on the back of your picture in case it gets separated from your resume.

• **Do not put the photographers' or reproduction lab's name on your photos.** If the photographer takes your picture for free then you can advertise their service on your reproductions.

• **When you pick up your pictures,** always carefully inspect the negative and prints before accepting them. I believe it's best to keep the master negatives in your possession. Labs have a way of going out of business or burning down. You will take better care of your negatives than anyone else. Of course, if you are not good at keeping things, let the lab store the negative.

• **Go to the places listed here and others.** Look at the papers and finishes and collect samples. Write the name of the lab and prices on the back of the sample picture and keep this in your picture reproduction file. This knowledge will be valuable because you will have pictures run for different uses. Have the reproduction lab do test shots. Test shots are several samples of what the finished reproduced picture will look like. Proof the shots and pick the exact skin tone and look you want. Your educated instinct will tell you which of the test shots is best. Doing test shots usually doubles the delivery time.

Photographic & Reproduction Terms

• **Border:** 1/4" or more of white around the picture.
• **Sloppy Border or Full Frame:** Shows sprockets of the film around the picture.
• **Bleed:** Picture covers all the paper.
• **Black Line:** Added to border around the picture.
• **Overlay:** White name on dark area or black name on white area of picture.
• **Litho Line:** Your name, or other information.
• **Line Negative:** Name in border of picture.
• **Copy Negative:** Negative made from master print.

Resources

Isgo Lepejian Custom Photo Lab (Isgos), 818/848-9001. www.isgophoto.com. 2411 W. Magnolia Blvd., Burbank, 91506, 1/2 block east of Buena Vista. M-F, 9-6. This place is a favorite one of mine for the service. Orders may be taken at their smaller location, (323) 323/876-8085. 1145 N. La Brea Ave. Hollywood, 90038, half block north of Santa Monica. M-F, 10-6, Sa, 11-4. Processing and 8 1/2 x11 proof sheet, $11, with 4x6 proof prints, $13-$17; in by 1:00 back by 4:30 the same day. All 8x10 masters, 4-way bleed, white or sloppy borders are $22, if from a color negative, $15; back in 3 days. B&W and color digital imaging. Copy negative and name border or bleed is $22. For custom multiples of bleed, bordered prints on pearl or glossy paper, 100 for $75; 150 for $105; 200 for $130. The quality is top of the line; I love them. They can repair or restore any photo. For instance, retouching can't remove tattoos but digital imaging can. They can tone prints, sepia or any custom color. B&W print made from color slide is $25. Many of the photographers listed in the photography section say they are the best.

Argentum Photo Lab, 323/461-2775. www.argentum.com 1050 Cahuenga Blvd., Hollywood, 90038. The do every type of photo lab work plus reproductions. $80 for 100 prints B&W prints and $90 for 100 color prints, plus the set up fee; $22 for B&W and $29 for color. They have a wide selection of layouts, fonts and papers. I've heard very good reports about their work and service. I do love their color photos.

Nardulli, 323/882-8331. www.nardulli.com. 1720 La Brea, Hollywood, 90046. M-F 8-10, Sa 9-4. Processing and proof sheet in 5 hours, $8. 11x14 proof sheet, $25.50. 16x20 proof sheet, $30.50. 8x10 master in three days, $13. All work is custom including bleeds, sloppy borders and border with lines. Wonderful lab, wonderful work. All work is custom. 10% discount for repeat customers. The tests are free and ready in three days, then two days to complete the run. Top of the line reproductions. Download their price list from the website.

Paragon Photo & Digital Imaging, 323/933-5865. www.paragonphoto.com 326 S. La Brea Ave., L.A. 90036. Great lithos and photo reproducing. $69 for 100 8x10 photos; $75 for bleed photos, plus the set up fees. $89 for 300 8x10 lithos; $99 for bleed lithos, no set up fees for lithos. Very helpful. Janice Allen loves all of their services.

Reproductions, see listing below and website for information about the beautiful color photos.

FOR LITHOGRAPHS:

I believe lithos from Reproductions and Isgos are equally good. Imagestarter also has good quality; it is just a matter of what you like. Go by and get samples.

Reproductions, 323/845-9595 or 888/797-7795. www.reproductions.com. 3499 Cahuenga Blvd. West, Los Angeles, 90068. Also in New York. 100 b&w 8x10s, $69; 200 for $82, color $115; 300 for $95, color $130. Their prices include all setup fees. They never add on charges for layouts or adding a black line. They keep your scans for two years; call with your reorder, it will be ready in two days. New orders take four working days. I'm sure that is without proofing. I think it is always worth an extra day to proof. Feature Package: 300 8x10s and 300 business cards for $148, color $209. They were the first in town to do these digital scans. I love them. Color photos: 100, $98; 200, $145. Check the website for information on the color photos.

Isgo Lepejian Photo-Digital Lab, (Isgos) 818/848-9001. www.isgophoto.com. 2411 W. Magnolia Blvd., Burbank, 91506, 1/2 block east of Buena Vista. M-F 9-6. Smaller location, 323/876-8085. 1145 La Brea, Hollywood, 90038. M-F 10-6, Sa 11-4. Great lithos. $74 for 150 8x10s; $60 for 300 business cards; $70 for 300 4x6s or 5x7s. $95 for 300 B&W or full color 8x10s. Normal time, three days. Great photos and great lithos!

Imagestarter, 818/506-7010. www.imagestarter.com. 4849 Laurel Canyon Blvd., North Hollywood, 91607. M-F 10-6. Lithos, 100 B&W 8x10s for $75, color for $95; 300 for $95, color $115. 500 business cards for $85, color $100; 4x6 postcards, 1,000 for $129, color $139. Free name, negative and border. I have seen the examples of their lithos and they look great.

In Orange County: Photomation 800/439-6363 or 714/236-2121. 2551 West La Palma Ave., Anaheim. The work I've seen has been very good quality. Lab and re-production. At last, a great resource for people living in Orange County. However, make the trip to L.A. for the best quality.

RESUMES

• **First and foremost**, your resume is selling you and it should represent you in a professional way. The purpose of your resume is to give the reader a brief description of you and your professional experience. You must have one to go along with your picture when you are seeking interviews and auditions.

Resume Form
• **At the top**, centered, put your name in bold letters
• **On the left side** of center, in a column, put:
  Weight:
  Height:
  Hair: (color)
  Eyes: (color)
• **In the center** of the page under your name, include any union affiliations: SAG, AFTRA, AEA. These union titles do not have to be big. Your work on the resume will make it obvious that you belong to the unions.
• **On the right side**, how to contact you: your agent's name and telephone number; if no agent, your home or cell number with a machine or pickup type message service. This is actually the most important item on your resume. List your email address under the phone number. Do not use a phone number on your resume that is shared with anyone. If your agent doesn't mind, you can also include your contact number.
• **Do not** put your home address or age range on your resume.

• **Now comes the fun part**—your experience and training. Always list the latest project first, then the others in reverse chronological order. Do not use all capitals. Small caps can work. You want to make your resume very easy to read. Times font is the easiest to read; it is what newspapers use. Make sure the font you choose is easy to read.

• **List films first.** First column: film title; center column: billing, starring, supporting or featured; third column: the director. When listing a student film, use the director's name, not the school.

• **Television.** Left column: title of show; center column: billing; star, co-star, guest star, featured; right column: director.

• **Stage or Theater.** Left column: play; center column: character name (lead or supporting in parenthesis); right column: the name of the theater—unless the director is famous, then list both.

• **Training.** First, the teacher you are studying with currently; then any other acting teachers. You can list any speciality class, such as voice or commercials, and the teacher's name. Last, your degree and from what college.

• **Special skills**, including any foreign language, accents, dialects, any sports or training that might make you special—computers, medical lab, sharpshooting, pilot's license, CPR, etc.

• **You must have some type of message arrangement; if there is no answer or the line is busy, they will not call again.**

• **If you have not acted professionally**, in place of Film/Television/Stage, put Acting Workshop Scenes and list scenes and characters you have performed in acting class. Now your task is to develop credits to put on your resume; student films, plays and projects you produce yourself are a way for your resume to grow rapidly. Do not think of seeking an agent until your resume indicates that you are able to land work yourself.

• **It can take two years** (after obtaining your union cards and agent) for your resume to reach a fairly comfortable professional place. It does grow! The process is fun.

• **Sylvester Stallone's pre-Rocky resume credits:** *A Party at Kitty and Stud's,* 1970; *Bananas* (unbilled bit), 1971; *The Lords of Flatbush,* 1974; *The Prisoner of Second Avenue* (bit), 1975; *Capone,* 1975; *Death Race 2000,* 1975; *Farewell My Lovely,* 1975; *Cannonball,* 1976; *No Place To Hide,* 1976; *Rocky* (writer and actor), 1976. No wonder he had nothing in the fridge. The legend goes that he turned down $250,000 for his *Rocky* script and got very little for it in order to act in the movie. The reason he wrote the script was to get a break as an actor in the biz, and he didn't sell out.

• **Harrison Ford's early resume:** *Dead Heat on a Merry-Go-Round,* 1966; *Long Ride Home,* 1967; *Luv,* 1967; *Zabriskie Point,* 1970; *Getting Straight,* 1970; *American Graffiti,* 1973 (memorable but too small to lead to anything other than more character work); *The Conversation,*

1974 (just a few moments but very daring); *Heroes,* 1977; *Star Wars,* 1977—this is the role that led to his many leading man roles.

• **Michael Keaton:** *Night Shift,* 1982; *Mr. Mom,* 1983; *Gung-Ho,* 1986; *Batman,* 1989; and then the big time.

• **Some copy services will typeset** and laser-print your resume. There are many services that advertise in *Back Stage West.* If you are computer savvy, typeset and laser print your own resume. Your resume must be trimmed to 8x10 to fit on the back of your 8x10 picture.

• **Have just a few resumes photocopied** each time (you'll be adding things often) unless you're sending out a large mailing. Copy services charge more to use color paper; if you are using color paper it is cheaper if you provide your own. Make sure the color you choose is easy to read. Everything is placed on your resume in order to be easily read and understood. Ask them to charge you the rate for white copies. *See resources for paper.*

• **Always have your resumes cut to 8x10** so they will fit on the back of your 8x10 picture. Attach the resume to your picture, back to back, facing out. Use double-stick tape, spray glue or staples. **Staple from the picture side and hide the staples in the borders so they won't draw the viewer's eye away from your face.** Place two staples on top and two on the bottom about two inches from the left side so when a three-hole punch is used, the picture and resume will go into the punch easily. *Never submit a resume that is not cut-down to the exact size of the picture.*

• **When submitting your package** for a particular role, put a post-it note on your picture with the name of the role you want to audition for. Also put the name of the role on the outside of the envelope. A cover letter is not necessary, unless there is particular reason why you are right for the role.

• **At all times keep pictures**, resumes, and a roll of double-stick tape or stapler in a zippered briefcase in your car! You may get a job because your pictures and resumes are with you.

• **Alex Stone, a 25 year veteran of film and TV,** talks about picture and resume submission packages.

Q: What are some tips to help actors gain interviews?

• **The casting person** will get a huge stack of submissions, so you have about a second for your photo to grab their eye. The choice of a good photographer is crucial: the money you spend there is never wasted. After that, good reproductions. The resume is important. It should be truthful, factual, neat, clean, and the same size as the picture.

• **Some resumes are almost unreadable** because of exotic computer typefaces or faded Xerox copies. One actor listed a special skill as "requitball." Typos or misspellings are not acceptable. You must have a professional looking resume. Duplicate your resumes on light colored paper. Avoid bright orange, red or green; a casting person may need another copy of your resume and these colors won't fax or photocopy well.

• **A lot of people use the "special skills" as icebreakers.** It's an excellent technique because the more odd skills you have, the more chance you get to talk to the casting person.

• Fine art	• Bartending
• Sign language	• CPR
• Canoeing	• Dog showing
• Baton twirling	• Sculpture
• Nursing	• Trampoline
• Wire welding	• Chainsaw and wood splitting
• Skydiving	• Accents and weird noises

• California State Champion Cheerleader
• Beijing opera dance techniques (If I had this person in the office, I'd say, "Tell me about Beijing.")
• For *Dracula*, they were casting people who could speak a middle-eastern language, not just put on the accent. An actress got a role because she knew enough words to string together and they liked the sound.

Resources

Xpedx Paper & Graphics, 818/409-0077; 1220 Air Way, Glendale, 92101; M-F 7:30-5. 818/785-4237; 6947 Hayvenhurst Ave., Van Nuys, 91406; M-F 7:30-5; Sa. 8-1. They have a great selection of papers. I like to pick out my own and not be restricted to just what the copy service provides.
Kelly Paper, M-F 7:30-5. Sa 9-1. Many locations, local and out of state, some are: 323/957-1176. 844 N. La Brea, Los Angeles, 90038. 818/843-0393. 724 Flower St., Burbank, 91502. 818/764-0850. 12641 Saticoy St., No. Hollywood, 91605. 310/452-7590. 1601 Olympic Blvd., Los Angeles, 90404.
Staples Office Superstores, 800/333-3330 for locations. www.staples.com Many stores in the L.A. area. *Business services: photocopying, printing, faxing, envelopes and paper.*
Office Depot Office Superstores, 800/685-8800 for locations. www.officedepot.com Many stores in the L.A. area. *Business services: photocopying, printing, faxing, envelopes and paper.*

RESUMES

See *Working Actor's Guide* and *Back Stage West* for many other resume design businesses.

Firepit Productions, 818/558-6622. Photo resumes; VHS, CD and DVD promotional covers; flyers and postcards promoting events. Photo resume samples are on the next two pages. They are working in conjunction with Imagestarter who offered these sevices for years and have now discontinued them to focus on picture reproductions. $92 for setup and 100 resumes. *See their listing under the Demo Reel Section on page 291.*

Brenda Marshall, 818/766-8735. In North Hollywood. By appointment only. $25 and she does it while you wait; she is very fast. She also does other writing, such as cover letters. Interestingly, she uses a word processor not a computer. *See the beautiful job she did for Mark Winn on page 156. On the left is the resume that he brought when we met for a career coaching. His phone number wasn't even on it; he just wrote it in. His was nice and simple but didn't give his billing. It is hard to tell when using a character name or description how substantial the role is.*

Pink Copy Center, 818/762-8100. 12080 Ventura Place #2 (Laurel Canyon & Ventura Blvd.) Studio City, 91604. $15 to set up a simple resume; go in with it written out. $25 to scan and make a photo resume with up to four pictures. If you have your resume on your computer, bring in the disk and it will just be $25 for the photo setup. Shawn has owned this copy service for years and is always looking for ways to help actors with their marketing skills. Copying, printing, color copying, digital (Fiery) output, digital B&W copying. Discount for actors.

Smart Girls, 818/907-6511. www.smartgirlsprod.com. 15030 Ventura Blvd., #914, Sherman Oaks, 91403. Acting resumes created in a half hour, $25. They save them on computer for easy updating. Many office services for actors and screenwriters.

BOOKS

Order through Samuel French Bookstore 323/876-0570; amazon.com or other bookstores.
Actor's Resumes, The Definitive Guidebook by Richard Devin.
The Actor's Picture/Resume Book by Jill Charles with photographer Tom Bloom.

JORDAN OSHER

Height: 5'6"
Weight: 138
Hair: Brown
Eyes: Hazel

Contact:
(310) 963-

FILM

THE JIM MOORE STORY	Starring	Jessica Conway

TELEVISION

DAWSON'S CREEK	Featured	Frank Waldeck
THE BOB BRAUN SHOW	Co-Star	Cincinnati

THEATRE

GRANDMA MAGIC	Jonathon	Bloomington's Playwright Prods.

TRAINING

Private Coach	Judy Kerr's Acting Workshop
Basic Acting/Scene Work	Sal Romeo
Commercial Workshop	Stuart K. Robinson
Indiana University–BA	

SPECIAL SKILLS

Baseball, Football, Basketball, Track, Golf,
Tennis, Swimming, Ping Pong, Weightlifting,
Spinning, Snowboarding, Skiing, Mountain Biking,
Knee-Boarding, Club Dancing

Jordan Osher's very first resume when he had been in Los Angeles just a few weeks. *See Jordan's story of coming to Los Angeles and then his six-month diary detailing his acting life in Section Three.*

JORDAN OSHER

Contact:
(310) 963-

FILM

BIG MAN	Lead	Stuart Robinson
IN THE TIME OF MY EXISTENCE	Lead	Mesh Flinders
EX-MEN	Co-Star	Anthony Mead
THE SNITCH	Lead	Mark Baydarian
SHARKS	Lead	USC Film
THE JIM MOORE STORY	Title Role	Dorky Art Connoisseur
KATHY	Lead	LMU Film

TELEVISION

DAYS OF OUR LIVES	Featured	NBC
GIANT (Pilot)	Principal	TNN
DAWSON'S CREEK	Featured	Frank Waldeck
THE BOB BRAUN SHOW (Pilot)	Ed, Sarcastic Date	Cincinnati
JGJ MANAGEMENT	Starring Role	Pilot

THEATRE

HALLELU	Lead	Universal Amplitheatre
GRANDMA MAGIC	Jonathon	Bloomington's Playwright Prods.

TRAINING

Private Coach	Judy Kerr's Acting Workshop
Larry Moss Acting Workshop	Michelle Danner
The Groundlings	Steve Little
Basic Acting/Scene Work	Sal Romeo
Commercial Workshop	Stuart K. Robinson
Indiana University–BA	

SPECIAL SKILLS

Baseball, Football, Basketball, Track, Golf,
Tennis, Swimming, Ping Pong, Weightlifting,
Spinning, Snowboarding, Skiing, Mountain Biking,
Knee-Boarding, Club Dancing, Italian, New York Dialect

Jordan's resume as we went to print, early 2003. This represents a driving ambition, fueling his desire to find work as an actor.

Mark Winn
SAG/AFTRA

Height: 6.0 ft.
Weight: 180lbs.
Hair: Brown
Eyes: Brown

Features

Don Juan De Marco	Moroccan	Jeremy Leven
True Lies	Arab Terrorist	James Cameron
Hook	Pirate	Steven Spielberg

Film & Television

American Made	Featured/ Taliban	Andrew Will
The Bold & The Beautiful	Under/5	John Zak
Will Work For Food	Featured/Moroccan	Josh Butler
Gotcha	Co-starring	Ron Kantor
The Guys	Starring	Virginia Capers
True Detectives	Featured/ Black	Ron Brody
General Hospital	Under/5	Gloria Monty
The Move	Starring	Karen Robinson

Theatre

Fiancee of Voodoo	Hunchback	Gallery Theatre
Driving Miss Daisy	Hoke	Santa Monica Main Stage
The Karaoke Man	Roman	Burbage Theatre
Othello	Roderigo	Magnolia Playhouse
One Flew Over The Cuckoo's Nest	Turkle	West Covina Playhouse
The Black American Dream	Luke	William Grant Stills
They're Dying To Hear Me Sing	Amadeus	Inner City Theatre
Shadow Boxer	Announcer	Inner City Theatre
Subtle, Tragic & Domestic Changes	Prentiss Brown	Theatre of Arts
Satch, A folk Musical Comedy	Claude	Variety Arts
Romeo & Juliet	Old Montague	Globe Playhouse
The Male Box	Michael Jenkins	Wilshire Ebell
Black Mass	Jesus Christ	UC Berkeley

Training

LaFayette Players West	Virginia Capers, Artistic Director
Actors Workshop	Estelle Harman
Marla Gibbs's Crossroads Academy	Edmund Cambodge
Facets Acting Process	Peter DeAnda
Actors Workshop	Tracy Roberts
UC Berkeley	Theatre Department

Proficient Skills
Stand-Up Comedy, Running Long Distance
Dialects: British. Middle Eastern. Arabic, Jewish, East Indian, Russian, Armenian, Korean Japanese, and Ethiopian.
Languages Italian

Familiar Skills
Creative Writing, Swimming (Free-Style) Dancing (Soul & Ballet) Fencing, Spanish and German

Mark Winn came to me for a Career Coaching Session using this resume. He wanted to audition for better roles. He had worked for years and had good experience but the way his resume looked you couldn't tell what his billing had been. Casting directors want to know if you have played leading roles. Notice his phone number wasn't on this resume so he had to hand-write it in, which doesn't look professional. Designed on home computer.

MARK WINN

SAG/AFTRA/AEA

Height:	6'
Weight:	180 lbs.
Hair:	Brown
Eyes:	Brown

Cell: (213) XXX-XXXX

FILM:

		Directors :
THE MOVE	Lead	Karen Robinson
9 1/2	Supporting	Mun Chee
AMERICAN MADE	Supporting	Andrew Will
WILL WORK FOR FOOD	Supporting	Josh Butler
DON JUAN DE MARCO	Featured	Jeremy Leven
TRUE LIES	Featured	James Cameron
HOOK	Featured	Steven Spielberg

TELEVISION:

THE GUYS (pilot)	Starring	Virginia Capers
GOTCHA	Guest Star	Ron Kantor
TRUE DETECTIVES	Co-star	Ron Brody
BOLD & THE BEAUTIFUL	Recurring	John Zak
GENERAL HOSPITAL	Featured	Gloria Monty

THEATRE:

DRIVING MISS DAISY	Lead/Hoke	Santa Monica Main Stage
MALE BOX	Lead/Jenkins	Wilshire Ebell
THEY'RE DYING TO HEAR ME SING	Lead/Amadeus	Inner City Theatre
FIANCEE OF VOODOO	Hunchback	Gallery Theatre
THE KARAOKE MAN	Roman	Burbage Theatre
OTHELLO	Roderigo	Magnolia Playhouse
ONE FLEW OVER THE CUCKOO'S NEST	Turkle	West Covina Playhouse
THE BLACK AMERICAN DREAM	Luke	William Grant Stills
SHADOW BOXER	Announcer	Inner City Theatre
SUBTLE, TRAGIC & DOMESTIC CHANGES	Prentiss Brown	Theatre of Arts
SATCH, A FOLK MUSICAL COMEDY	Claude	Variety Arts Centre
ROMEO & JULIET	Old Montague	Globe Playhouse
BLACK MASS	Jesus Christ	UC Berkeley

TRAINING:
Tom Todoroff (currently).
Marla Gibbs Crossroads Academy, Edmund Cambridge.
Estelle Harman.
Tracy Roberts.
Lafayette Players West, Virginia Capers.
Peter DeAnda, Eugene Williams.
Voice, Steven Memel (currently).
UC Berkeley - B.A. Italian Literature.

SPECIAL SKILLS:
Languages: Conversational Spanish, Italian, German.
Accents: British, Middle Eastern, Jewish, East Indian, Armenian, Ethiopian.
Dance: ballet, soul.
Sports: swimming, running.

This is the newly designed resume which is much easier to read. We put all the films together, featured the directors better, spotlighted his impressive training and helped his language talents stand out in the Special Skills section. After our session, Mark made an appointment with resume specialist **Brenda Marshall,** who he found in *Back Stage West.* He paid $25 and she designed it while he waited.

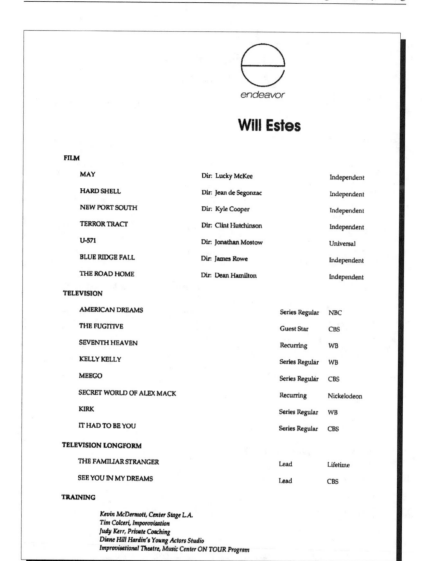

endeavor

Will Estes

FILM

MAY	Dir: Lucky McKee	Independent
HARD SHELL	Dir: Jean de Segonzac	Independent
NEW PORT SOUTH	Dir: Kyle Cooper	Independent
TERROR TRACT	Dir: Clint Hutchinson	Independent
U-571	Dir: Jonathan Mostow	Universal
BLUE RIDGE FALL	Dir: James Rowe	Independent
THE ROAD HOME	Dir: Dean Hamilton	Independent

TELEVISION

AMERICAN DREAMS	Series Regular	NBC
THE FUGITIVE	Guest Star	CBS
SEVENTH HEAVEN	Recurring	WB
KELLY KELLY	Series Regular	WB
MEEGO	Series Regular	CBS
SECRET WORLD OF ALEX MACK	Recurring	Nickelodeon
KIRK	Series Regular	WB
IT HAD TO BE YOU	Series Regular	CBS

TELEVISION LONGFORM

| THE FAMILIAR STRANGER | Lead | Lifetime |
| SEE YOU IN MY DREAMS | Lead | CBS |

TRAINING

Kevin McDermott, Center Stage L.A.
Tim Colceri, Imporovisation
Judy Kerr, Private Coaching
Diane Hill Hardin's Young Actors Studio
Improvisational Theatre, Music Center ON TOUR Program

Will Estes is 23, started working in commercials at age nine and has made the transition from child to adult actor. See his interview in *Child Actors, Section Eight.* His resume looks low key and he has a top level agent. The more status you have in this business the less you have to call attention to your accomplishments. He is currently one of the stars on NBC's hit, *American Dreams.* Resume designed by the agency.

ELI SCHWARTZ

HEIGHT: 5'3"   213/ 555-5555
WEIGHT: 108
HAIR: Brown
EYES: Brown

Films

SNAPSHOTS	Supporting	USC

Theater

THE MIRACLE WORKER	Helen Keller	Fl., Katy Award
WATER ON THE MOON	Leading	F.A.T.E. Theatre
LOVERS & OTHER STRANGERS	Leading	Florida
BYE BYE BIRDIE	Leading	Florida
THE SOUND OF MUSIC	Leading	Maine
YOU'RE A GOOD MAN CHARLIE BROWN	Leading	Maine
THE PRIME OF MISS JEAN BRODIE	Leading	Maine
OLD JED PROUTY OF BUCKSPORT MAINE	Leading	Maine
LETTERS TO KELSO	Leading	Maine
BRIGHTON BEACH MEMOIRS	Supporting	Florida
110° IN THE SHADE	Supporting	Maine
THE MIRACLE WORKER	Supporting	Maine
OLIVER!	Supporting	Maine

Industrial Films

CHILD ABUSE PREVENTION
CPR TRAINING
CAR/BIKE ACCIDENTS

Training

Judy Kerr's Acting Workshop, Class Assistant

Special Skills

Competitive Gymnastics: Bars, Floor, Tumbling
Unicycle Riding, Snow & Water Skiing
Firearms
Drawing, Painting, Singing, Piano
Bartending and Waitressing
Various Southern Dialects, New York accent, British accent

Eli Schwartz, 22 years old, new to Los Angeles and just starting to audition for film work. Meanwhile, she stresses her theater background and her leading roles in major shows out of town. Designed on home computer.

PRINTING AND PHOTOCOPYING

• **A valuable relationship** can be built with your reproduction people. They will be very helpful in the promotion of your career.

• **In the printing department,** you can have postcards printed with your picture and a space for a message. Have five hundred or a thousand printed blank and then when you want to print a message, you can just run off five or a hundred, whatever you need, or handwrite short "thank you for the interview" notes. Let people on your mailing list know what you are doing or wish them a "merry new TV season" or any other idea you come up with. Print your picture and resume on 5x7 cards or on cards the size of business envelopes. Leave an area for the address or label. Since the postage/anthrax scares, it is better to send mail that doesn't have to be opened.

• **Have picture business cards made up.** So important to have these with you when meeting people; later they can see your face and remember who you are.

• **When you do a play or showcase,** send out flyers or cards to let casting directors know you are acting somewhere. Even if they never attend, your name and picture cross their desk. It is good to send something to all the casting directors once or twice a year. The best times, I believe, are mid-July, the beginning of the television shooting season, and the last of January, the start of pilot season.

• **A very clever actress** printed 8 1/2 x11 white mailing envelopes with an inch and a half by three inch imprint of her eyes in the lower right hand corner with "look into my eyes..." underneath.

• **Picture mailing envelopes are available with a clear plastic** side so your picture can be seen before the envelope is opened. Bob The Printer and Pink Copy Center carry these, as well as many other places.

• **You can design your own note cards** with a picture on the front and then open it up to write inside. Christopher Paul Ford sent my favorite.

It was a great picture of him printed vertically, his name and phone number in black in the bottom border. In the left corner, in white, it says, *The journey of ten thousand miles begins with a single phone call.—Confucius Bell.* Clever, fun and inventive.

Resources

Pink Copy Center, 818/762-8100. 12080 Ventura Place #2 (Laurel Canyon & Ventura Blvd.) Studio City, 91604. M-F 8:30-6. Sa. 9:30-3. Copying, printing, color copying, digital (Fiery) output, digital b/w copying. They give a discount to actors. They will copy a message on your picture postcards at a cheaper cost than having them printed. Very helpful. They also do resumes and photo resumes.

Alpha Printing & Graphics, 310/273-9460. 9030 West Sunset Blvd., West Hollywood, 90069. They scanned my resume and put my agent's logo on it, printed 200 copies and trimmed them for $9.65. Seemed like a good bargain, and it only took ten minutes. Validated parking.

Bob The Printer, 818/766-9379. 4850 Vineland Ave., North Hollywood, 91601. M-F 9-6, Sa 10-4. Complete business printing, script copies, color copies, full and self serve copying, faxing, mail boxes. Very helpful, big busy place.

Charlie Chan, 323/650-7699. 8267 Santa Monica Blvd., West Hollywood, 90046. Also 323/850-5407. 7402 Sunset Blvd., L.A. 90046. M-F 8:30-6, Sa 10-4. Self or full-service copying, offset printing, computers and laser printers for customer's use. Friendly, helpful, fast service. Talk to general manager, Alex, for your special printing needs and designs. Postcards, business cards, flyers, velox and halftones, etc. www.charliechan.com.

Copymaster, 323/467-6111. 1553 Cahuenga Blvd., Hollywood, 90028. M-F 8-5. Printing only, no photocopying. Very helpful. Great postcards and business cards.

Copymat, 323/461-1222. 6464 Sunset Blvd., Ste. 100, Hollywood, 90028. At Wilcox. M-F 8-10 Sa & Su 10-7. Color, oversize and laser copies; high-speed duplicating; professional binding; self-service typing and worldwide fax service.

Henry's, 323/464-7228. 6110 Sunset Blvd., Hollywood, at Gower Gulch. M-F 8:30-7, Sa 9-5. Self or full-service copying, offset printing. Friendly, helpful, fast service.

Kinko's, Many locations. Open 24 hours, 7 days a week. I find, in general, their photocopying work is not up to my standards but with their 24 hr. service, in an emergency, they have saved me. Where I find they do have excellent services is in their computer departments. The employees are knowledgeable and helpful and the computers work well.

Legal Source, 213/236-0460. 601 W. 5th St, LA, 90071. 24 hours a day. They specialize in large copy projects, microfilming, exhibit-board design and enlargements.

New Image Copy Printing, 323/876-1102. 7109 Sunset Blvd. at La Brea, Hollywood, 90046. M-F 9-7; Sa 10-5. Self or full service: Color, oversize and laser copies, offset printing, lithos.

SECTION THREE

WORKING AS AN ACTOR

GENERATING ACTING WORK

• **Section Three is about creating acting opportunities** for yourself. You have been training, you've figured out your type, how you see yourself being cast. You have your 8x10 black and white or color photos that look like you and you have your resume. Now you need more experience. Maybe on your resume at this point you only have plays you did in college, high school or in your hometown. Perhaps the only experience on your resume is workshop scenes.

• **Through your training** you know that you can understand a script and you've learned how to breathe life into the dialogue using your unique self. You have delivered good performances in your workshops. Your teachers and the other actors are looking at you with awe and say, "You moved me; you are good." There is a voice inside that says, "Maybe I can get a director to cast me in a project and I can deliver a performance on stage or in film."

• **Many actors want to look for an agent at this point.** Agents are in business to make 10% from the fees you generate. When you are earning money acting, then it is time to put your team together. Now is the time to gain experience and get your career tools in place for this long career ahead of you. *See Section Five about your Career Team.*

162

• **Billy Bob Thornton arrived in Los Angeles struggling and broke.** He took a job as a waiter. First night on the job, as he worked a Beverly Hills banquet, director Billy Wilder, a many time Oscar-winner, walked up to him and said, "So you wanna be an actor? Look, I hate to disillusion you. You don't have the looks for a leading man. Learn to write. Then write your own movie—and write yourself a good part in it." Years later, after Billy Bob had learned to write, he wrote *Sling Blade* and was nominated for best actor and won the Oscar for best writer. He had been kicking around for years but with *Sling Blade,* he became an "overnight success."

• **Amanda Peet,** talking to a group, said, "No matter how many acting classes you take, how many times you stand alone in front of your mirror at home rehearsing, no matter how many Katharine Hepburn movies you watch, the only way to learn your craft is by acting—on stage or in front of the camera. And I'm of the school that work sparks more work, which all actors hunger for."

• **Mars Callahan** at 31 is the co-writer, director and star of the feature film *Poolhall Junkies.* It took him ten years to get it made and then another two years to get its theatrical release. Mars says, "I guess I just never gave up. If anything, that's it: Never, ever give up." He and a poolhall friend wrote the script when he was 19. They did get options over the years because the script was good but it just didn't go. Mars kept working on his acting, landing small roles and started studying directing. He directed a film short, which even got him a small directing job. Finally when the opportunity came he was ready to direct and old enough to play the lead. Originally he wrote it to play the younger brother.

• **Mars advised actors** in an interview in *Back Stage West,* "You've got to be out there doing something all the time. An actor acts. How many monologues do you have memorized? Can you do something from Tennessee Williams? Can you do something from Shakespeare? How many accents can you do? Can you sing and dance? Work at it. Write a one-man show. Do a play. Work begets work."

• **Nia Valdalos** is the actress and screenwriter of *My Big Fat Greek Wedding.* I met Nia on a show I was coaching on; she played a ditsy receptionist. She is so talented; in this little role I saw her create something new for every rehearsal. She had just arrived in town because her script had been optioned. She told me her story and that she was waiting on the go-ahead for shooting the film. I am including part of her interview from O magazine as an inspiration for us all.

- **What I know for sure is** that in your lifetime you will hear the word no much more than you will hear the word yes. People say no when they don't want to think in a different way, and when they don't know what else to say.

- **In my career,** I have been asked to leave theatre school, not gotten past the first round of auditions for an acting job, and then been told I was unattractive and therefore would never make it as an actress. As if looks have anything to do with good acting. They told me that it would be impossible to cast me in a part since there were no roles written for someone who looked like me. So I set out to create that role.

- **I got on stage, and I started telling stories** about the one thing I knew best: my family. When the play sold out, I was approached by companies to turn it into a movie. I asked to play the lead and write the screenplay. They said no.

- **Then Rita Wilson and Tom Hanks** came to my show and what did they say? They said yes. Yes, they were going to make it into a movie. Yes, I would be the writer of the screenplay. And yes, I could play the lead.

- **What have I learned?** That secure people say yes much faster than people who operate out of fear. That some people believe thinking in a different way is an interesting choice. That if you keep saying yes to yourself, one day someone might just say it to you.

- **I am telling you these stories** because I don't want you to play a victim of the industry. I want you to have the kind of courage the actors above have. You will find many actors who whine and say, "I can't get an agent. I don't have any auditons. Someone else has all the luck. I never get any opportunities." I want you to talk about the script or idea you are writing; about the scripts you've downloaded; about the weekly script reading group you've organized; about the volunteer work you are doing; how excited you are over the scene you are rehearsing for class. Yes, create your own acting opportunities when you are between roles.

THE BUSINESS OF COMMERCIALS

• **A commercial career is a tough, competitive,** ever-changing specialty career. In commercials, you must have an agent in order to get auditions. It is rare to find student or non-union opportunities to gain experience. Commercial acting classes are essential. You will also benefit from taking improvisation classes, as well as basic acting craft.

• **Working in commercials** can change your life. One good national commercial can be worth roughly $35,000 a year. If you were to book three or four nationals in the next year, just imagine how much your financial world might change. The security of having money in the bank can give you the confidence to continue pursuing the acting career of your dreams. Some actor's careers consist of just commercials or voiceovers; it is what they love to do.

• **Hugh Leon, successful commercial agent with Coast to Coast Talent Group says:**

> • **If you are not in class, you're not serious about making a living** working in commercials. I don't care how many commercials you book, you still need to study, to get in there and practice. You are always going to learn something new by looking over new copy, getting in front of the camera and staying current. When you take classes from various casting directors, you are no longer just a face on a picture. You learn what is going to get you a call back when you audition for them.

- **Stuart Stone, one of the busiest commercial casting directors,** a great commercial workshop teacher, and author of *Acting Out—Your Personal Coach to a Money Making Career in Television Commercials* says:

  - **When there is no dialogue in the commercial,** it is great to find actors with good improvisation skills. The actors who have "what it takes" can always be counted on and we continually book them. They have developed themselves, are prepared and have taken the appropriate classes and workshops. Understanding the audition process and *how* to audition is what can often make the difference in booking the job.

- **If you want a commercial career, be an expert in commercials.** Watch commercials at different times of the day and night. Where are you going to make your money? Figure out what your type is. Are you the spokesperson, young mom or dad, fast-food counter guy or girl, granny or gramps, blue collar worker, executive, athlete, model type, the comedian? Maybe you fit several types. Knowing your types and the spots you will be cast in will help you sell yourself when you start interviewing with agents.

- **Keep a notebook; study the actors who look like you** and are in the same age category. What is the product, the style of campaign, the type of people, what was their behavior, why did they book the job? Write down the copy (dialogue in commercials) and practice doing the commercial yourself. What type of clothes are they wearing? Clothing terms are usually:

  - **Casual,** meaning what you might wear to clean your house or mow your lawn, dockers and T-shirt. No jeans or denim shirts.
  - **Nice casual,** which is what you would wear out to dinner and a movie with friends—dockers with a nice shirt or sweater.
  - **Upscale casual.** This look is casual and classy.
  - **Upscale.** Dressy and classy.
  - **Business/Spokesperson.** Suit and tie for men, tailored dress or suit for women.
  - **Hip/trendy look** means the latest fashion trend.

- **Your notebook will help you when you get an audition** for Coke, Xerox, IBM, Folgers, Citibank, etc. You will have a sense of what the campaign is and what the client might be looking for when they are auditioning you.

• **Stuart K. Robinson, respected and sought-after commercial coach,** who teaches the skills, techniques and philosophy of how to book the job, says:

> • **The reason most actors are not successful** is that they don't know what the client (the person/people who represent the product which is being advertised) wants. The client will tell you what they want you to do, but they do not tell you what they need. In order to be competitive in the commercial business, the actor must be an expert at three things.
>
> > • **First,** you must be able to diagnose what the client needs without being told.
> > • **Second,** you must be able to create the behavior to answer that need.
> > • **Third,** you must be able to execute that need before the camera.

• **Once you have an idea of the type of characters** you can play and you have taken enough commercial classes to be consistently good, it is time to shop for an agent. You now need a promotional package. This consists of a great head shot, a resume, and a powerful cover letter.

• **Your commercial head shot is the most important tool** in your promotional package; it is your ticket in the door. Your picture will be one in a thousand that passes the desk of a casting director or agent in any given week. You must grab their attention in a millisecond.

Q: What is a good commercial head shot?

• **Commercial agent Hugh Leon says:**

> • **I like personality shots.** I should be able to say 10 things about who that person is, whether this person is a smart-ass, intelligent, crazy, warm and loving or shy—something about that person. A commercial actor can have multiple pictures—a business shot, a casual shot, an athletic shot if you are athletic and a zany/crazy shot if you are a character.

• **Stuart Stone likes pictures that have great energy.** He adds:

> • **Your picture should look like you do** at any given moment of the day. I want to know what I am getting when I call you in. I like natural shots, messy hair is great.

• **Casting director Michael Donovan** has cast over 1,000 commercials,

> • **The picture needs to look like you, as you do** *normally*—not under that specific lighting with that special makeup, etc., and not at your

most glamorous. I should be able to look up at you as you walk in, and not be surprised!

• **In terms of what's most important, your eyes need to connect.** When casting directors are going through hundreds of photos, your picture gets a matter of seconds under their noses. When you look in someone's face, you look at their eyes—same thing applies to headshots.

• **Stuart K. Robinson says:**

  • **Anytime I look at a head shot and I know what the person is thinking,** that is a great photo. A photograph is not meant to capture a look on your face. A photograph has to capture your quality, a specific feeling.

  • **To take a great shot you have to have a thought.** "I am so happy to be here." "It is good to see you!" "It's my birthday!" You have to have a feeling about what is going on, so the photographer can capture that feeling. That thought will be real joy, true pride, warm love, real power, great satisfaction, or whatever it is you are trying to capture.

  • **Thoughts create great photos; posing creates portraits.** Let the picture show your acting ability. Bad pictures do not come from bad photographers. Bad pictures come from bad acting.

  • **To get a great shot you have to prepare for your photo shoot.** Interview photographers. Do not just pick one because someone tells you to go to them. Meet them, make sure you feel comfortable in their company. Look at their work, see what they think a good shot is. Do the eyes talk to you? Are the pictures saying anything? You want a photographer that gives you the motivation, freedom and comfort so you can have specific thoughts. One who knows when to snap the photo.

  • **Before the shoot, decide what categories you want to capture,** what thoughts to have in your head in order to do that. Bring to the shoot your favorite music and photographs from your life that can help you trigger the moods you want to feel. Do not rush your session—take all the time you need. Remember, this picture is going to open up the doors to your career.

Following are good commercial pictures that the individual photographers chose, featuring the same actors you met in the theatrical picture section. *See the individual photographers listings, starting on page 124.*

Janice Allen

Photographer: **Mary Ann Halpin**
Makeup: **Mary Ann Halpin**
Retouching: **Charisse of**
  The Retouching Company

Photographer: **David La Porte**
Makeup: **Laura Connelly**

Photographer: **Mark Husmann**
Makeup: **Dara Dupuy**

Photographer: **Diana Lannes**
Makeup: **Naja**
Retouching: **Randall Michelson**

Jordan Osher

Photographer: **Jillian Griffiths**
of **J Thomasin Photography**

Photographer: **Jillian Griffiths**
of **J Thomasin Photography**

DJ Johnson

Photographer: **Sean Kenney**

Photographer: **David Edwards**

Jordan Osher

Photographer: **Bob Bayles**

Keith Johnson

Photographer: **Carrie Cavalier**
Makeup: **Kari Nicole**

Keith Johnson

Photographer: **Rich Hogan**

Photographer: **Rod Goodman**

Judy Kerr

Photographer: **Marina Rice Bader**
Makeup: **Marina Rice Bader**

Photographer: **Frank Bruynbroek**
Makeup: **Rita Montanez**

Loryn Phillips

Photographer: **Robert Raphael**
Makeup: **Robert Raphael**

Cynthia Kerr

Photographer: **Mary Ann Halpin**
Makeup: **Sandy Williams**

Carly Althoff

Photographer: **Lesley Bohm**
Makeup: **Shawn Flint Blair**

Photographer: **Mara**
Makeup: **Mara**

Photographer: **Gayle Garnett**
Makeup: **Sara Chameides**

Photographer: **Kevin Mc Intyre**

- **Casting director Stuart Stone talks about resumes:**

  - **Put everything you can on your resume** and be proficient in everything you list under special skills. I look under training to see if you have taken commercial workshops. Do you have theatre credits? List plays you have done, no matter how long ago or how small the venue. We want to see on your resume that you are studying and working.

- **The third tool in your package is a powerful cover letter.** *See Cover Letters in the Career Tools section for instructions and examples.*

- **Now your package is together.** How do you get a commercial agent, or at least an appointment to meet with one?

- **There are three ways to get an appointment with an agent.**

1) The standard way. Mail your head shot, resume and cover letter to agencies. This method is not very effective unless your materials are so dynamic that they just have to see you as soon as possible.

- **Beverly Long, casting director and teacher says:**

  - **There are books with the names of agents** and a little blurb about each agent in the city. There are probably 200 commercial agents in Los Angeles. You can't send your picture out to every agent, but with some help you can narrow it down. That is what I try to do in my classes—narrow it down, and give you maybe 10 to 12 choices of agents who will be likely to represent you.

2) The scenic route way. Doing theater or showcases and hoping someone sees your work, that you impress them and they suggest a meeting.

3) Referrals, the most effective way. When an agent is told by someone they respect that they should see you, they will. How do you get referrals? You ask! If you know someone who has an agent or who knows an agent, ask him to introduce you. Make it known that you are looking for an agent.

- **When you get an interview with an agent, you want to go in there** and really sell yourself. What usually happens is, we try to be on our best behavior and answer the agent's questions without letting our personality out. The agent then wonders what is so special about this person? Go into that office knowing exactly where you are going to make your money, act and look your type, dress your type. Be extremely clear about the roles you are going to book and the categories you are going to work in. Talk about commercials you love. Talk about what their part is in the business; you are an expert too.

• **Tell stories about yourself.** Look around the office and learn about them. Try to find a common denominator and establish a relationship. Most agents will take you on because they like you and like being around you. It is not always about your acting ability.

• **Neil Kreppel, long time, respected commercial agent from Commercial Talent Agency.**

Q: How do you build a relationship with an agent? Should you ask them to lunch?

> • **Make an appointment,** come in and just talk so we can get to know each other. As for lunch, at this time in the agency, we are really too busy to go out to lunch. If someone wants to bring in something for us to have lunch together that would be all right.

Q: What is the actor's responsibility?

> • **They should always have pictures here** with their resume stapled on the back. They should immediately confirm with us the information we have given them about an audition. They should always arrive early for their appointment time and of course, they should book some jobs.

Q: How can the actor help the agent?

> • **We expect clients to be very professional.** We want them to have trust in us. It is all right if occasionally you fax or call about a casting that you have heard about and wonder if you have been sent out. Sometimes you have been submitted and sometimes you may not be what the casting director has asked for. We don't like people to be annoying, calling every day about submitting them for projects because they have seen the breakdowns.

• **Commercial agent Hugh Leon** talks about what he expects from the actors he represents.

> • **I expect the actor to give me the right pictures**; I need the marketing tools to get you out there. I don't want to hear, "I don't have the money to get better pictures." Once I have called you with an audition, don't ask me to rearrange the audition time to meet your schedule. Don't miss an audition—this is not a hobby, this is a career; it should be the number one priority. If it is not, get out! Do the best you can, be professional and go into your audition prepared. Don't call me 20 times a day. Keep good records, write down the audition information, who you saw, where you went,

what you wore, so if I call you a week later with a call back you are ready to go. Have a Thomas Guide in your car— I'm not a map. Confirm auditions. Be grateful that I got you an audition. Remember, I work for free until you book a job.

• **Once you have signed with an agent,** it is a good idea to start marketing yourself to casting directors. They are the ones who will call you in to audition.

• **When Cynthia Kerr's agent took her on,** she had post cards printed. Her picture on the left; under the picture her name and under that SAG. The message was on the right with her agent's logo under it. "I'm ready to work! Just signed with Gold/Liedtke Associates for commercial representation. Looking forward to auditioning for you soon!"

• **Stuart Stone, CCDA, casting director, talks about marketing:**

  • **Postcards with your picture on it are a great marketing tool.** I don't have to open an envelope, your picture is right there. Write a note, let me know you just signed with such and such agency, or you will be on a TV show (with date, time and channel) so I can watch, or that you are in a play. You can send postcards or fliers every few weeks. I will become familiar with your face, so when your agent submits your picture to me, I think to myself, "I know her" and I'll call you in. You can also knock on my door and say, "Hey, I just wanted to introduce myself." I don't mind an actor doing that, because most actors do not take the initiative.

• **Casting director Michael Donovan, CSA, CCDA,** when asked about receiving unsolicited pictures and resumes, responded:

  • **No problem with my office.** But I really resent it when an actor does not include a cover note of some sort. It could be very brief, and hand-written. It should *not* be a "form" letter, in which you have written in the casting director's name, or a letter that says "Dear Casting Director." An actor wants to be treated as an individual— so treat the casting person the same way. The same applies to letters sent to agents' offices.

  • **We also accept submissions from actors without agents** or even non-union actors; that is how we meet new people. At one point, I'm sure Dustin Hoffman was non-union. Once in a while we do have a producer who says, "Only call in union actors."

COMMERCIAL AUDITIONS

• **Danny Goldman, CCDA, casting director, director and teacher, describes his job:**

> • **The function of the casting director** is to show the director, the agency and the client a variety of people—the types they ask for and some alternatives. We have seen as many as 200 people for one part. The final decision is made by the client, the agency and the director when the director is a star director. The casting director has no say whatsoever. If the dialogue is really bad, those actors that can come in and solve the problems of the dialogue are the ones who get the job.

• **When your agent calls you with an audition,** they are going to give you some valuable information. They will tell you the date and time of your call, the casting person/company and their location, as well as the product, the wardrobe you should wear and the type of character they are looking for (i.e. young mom, clerk, spokesperson etc.). You must write all this information down and use it to help prepare yourself for your audition.

• **Plan your wardrobe** based on the information your agent gave you and from your own research on the product and type of character they are looking for. Dress for the part. Don't forget your head shot and resume.

• **Use your** <u>Thomas Guide</u> or download a map from your computer with directions to map out your route to the location. Plan to arrive at least 15 minutes before your call time to go over any copy you will need to rehearse.

• **When you arrive at the audition, check the storyboard** (a series of hand drawn pictures showing each scene of the commercial) and see if there is any copy you need to prepare for the audition. Diagnose the script quickly with the techniques you have learned from your commercial training. Don't worry about memorizing the copy.

• **Once you feel prepared to audition, sign in** on the Exhibit E SAG/AFTRA Commercial Audition Report, (sign-in sheet). Print your name, social security number (SAG membership number can be used instead of social security number for security purposes), agent, time of actual call, time you arrived, your initials, whether it is your first call or a call back. The sex, age, and ethnicity questions are optional; the unions use these to track casting trends. Upon leaving, always be sure you sign out.

If the audition runs longer than an hour, you may be entitled to compensation from the production company.

• **Next, fill out the size card if one is available.** This is used for call backs to help size up groups or pairs and also for the wardrobe people when you book the commercial, so be accurate. You do not have to put your address or Social Security number on the card. After you complete the size card, the casting director will probably take a Polaroid of you. These usually look pretty bad—don't get upset over it. The casting people say they only use them as a reference to help match you up with your video audition.

• **When the paper work is done, continue to work** on the audition copy. Rehearse out loud, get comfortable with the words and your actions. Make the material about you. Own it! Keep a positive attitude; do not let other actors in the room distract you. Compete for the job.

• **Carolyne Barry, commercial actress, teacher and casting director says:**

  • **Good commercial acting is good acting, only speeded up**; it is the pauses that are tightened up. When auditioning, you must spend time with the copy as you would a cold reading. You must motivate the copy, know who you are talking to and determine your objective.

• **Casting director Stuart Stone suggests:**

  • **Always know what has happened in this character's life** the moment before you start talking and what is going to happen after the last moment of the scene. Make the piece real to you, then it will be real to us. Give the most feeling you can to the copy and still be honest. This is the ideal in commercial acting.

• **Stuart talks about improvements actors can make.**

  • **It makes things tough when actors arrive at castings** where there is dialogue and they do not take the time to work on their lines. They get caught up in conversations and gossip in the waiting area and forget why they are there. When they come into the studio to audition, they become frustrated or discouraged because they give a bad audition.

• **Casting director Michael Donovan says:**

  • **Be specific in your choices for the commercial copy.** So many actors I see walk into the audition concerned with what the producer or casting director wants. I want the actor to show us what they want to bring to the copy. The most important thing I teach in my classes is to make specific choices.

• **I asked Michael how he felt about actors** hearing about a casting session and arriving and signing in like they belong there.

> • **If an actor happens to come to an audition** with a friend and sees that in the office there is a session going on that he would be right for, I don't mind the actor asking if they can be seen for the spot. There is a big problem though if the actor just signs in, "crashing the session."

• **Stuart Stone also responds to actors dropping by the office.**

> • **I often enjoy actors who stop by to drop off a picture and say hello.** They must realize though, we are usually very busy and do not have time to get into a conversation. When an actor has heard about a part we are currently casting and they want to audition, I request they go through their agent for many reasons. If they do not have representation it is important that they ask before they sign in. To just sign in without asking is *crashing* the audition, it is not professional and very much frowned upon. If the actor is right for the part, I am glad to let them audition, but check first.

• **You are auditioning when you enter the audition room.** Be in character. Your behavior, body language, tone of voice and emotions should reflect the situation in the commercial scenario.

• **There will be a mark on the floor where you should stand.** Most likely it will be a piece of tape in the shape of a T. Stand on your mark with the T between your feet and look into the camera. If a cue card (the copy written in large print placed near the camera) is provided, look it over. Some words may be different from your script. Get familiar with the sentence structure so you know where to look when you need to read the next line.

• **Not all auditions have copy.** Many times you are asked to improvise a scene or tell a funny joke, or the casting director will ask you a question like, "Name three people living or dead that you'd like to have dinner with and why?" Do not panic, just say the first thing that pops in your mind. If the question does stump you, keep a constant connection with the camera. This will allow your personality to show and remember, you can always make something up. The people looking at the tape are looking at your personality and how you will fit it with their product. Many times they watch these tapes with the sound turned off.

• **The casting director or the camera operator will give you directions.** As you listen to them, look into the camera and picture someone you know in the lens and let the camera see inside you.

• **You will be asked to slate your name.** Slating is your introduction and your opportunity to let the clients know, within the first three seconds, you are what they are looking for. After you slate your name, the casting director or camera operator will often ask for profiles. This means they want to see your face from different angles. The director or camera operator will then say "action" and you start the scene. Go for it!

• **The casting director is not always in the room** during the first call audition, but don't think they are not watching. Most casting facilities have video feed from the audition room to the casting director's office down the hall. Listen to all directions given to you and work them into your audition. You must be flexible; they are also looking to see if you are able to take direction.

• **After the audition say to yourself,** "I just took a shot at a $35,000 job today," and then forget about it. You may hear from your agent in a couple of days that you have a call back. Congratulations. A call back means you are a finalist for the job and you get to audition again, this time for the clients, the director, producer and advertising agency. When you go to the call back, dress and look the same way you did for your first audition unless your agent tells you differently. Figure out why they called you back, so you can give them more of the same behavior. The director will most likely be directing your audition. One of the things they will be looking for is how flexible you are, how well you take direction and how easy you will be to work with.

• **After your call back, your agent may call you to say** you are on "avail/first refusal" or they have put you on "hold." "Avail/first refusal" means the casting director wants to know if you are available to work on a certain date. It is not legally binding; the actor can accept other work. When the actor is put on "hold" they are asked to schedule a specific day to work. The actor and employer have made the commit-ment; it is legally binding and payment must be made whether or not the actor works on that day.

• **You booked the job! Your agent or someone from the production company** will call you with the days you will need to be available for the commercial shoot and the time and date of your wardrobe fitting. You will be paid hourly with a one-hour minimum for the fitting. At your fitting appointment you will be given the date, time and location shoot for the commercial.

• **When you arrive on the set, find the second** AD (assistant director), who will have your SAG contract and let you know where you need to be. I suggest asking them for today's call sheet. It will have the names of everybody who is working that day. I also find it helpful when writing my thank you notes because the addresses of the advertising agency and production company are usually on the call sheet. You should file this away. You may need to refer to it years later when you are working with some of the same people again. Make sure you read your contract carefully. If you are unsure about anything, call your agent before signing. Have the production company fax a copy to your agent.

• **Always be professional, polite, prepared and eager to work.** Stay relaxed and comfortable. If you are not working on a shot, stay close by and let the AD know where you are at all times. When they call for you, be ready to work. Have fun; this is what you have been working so hard for.

• **When and how much do we get paid?**

• **An on-camera principle actor gets paid a session fee** for each day of work or for each commercial produced, whichever is greater. Currently the session fee is $500 for an eight-hour workday, excluding mealtime. The ninth and tenth hour are paid at time and a half ($93.75 per hour). The eleventh hour and beyond is known as golden time and is paid at double-time ($125 hour). The session fee must be paid within 12 working days.

• **The session fee allows the advertising agency** the right to use the commercial for 13 weeks. The actor cannot work for a competitive product during the same period of time.

• **Holding fees or fixed payment fees** are paid every 13 weeks to maintain the rights to the commercial and the actor's exclusivity to the product. The amount is equal to the session fee. If you do not get a holding fee after 13 weeks it means you have been released and then you can book another commercial with a competing product.

• **When the commercial is aired, you are due residual payments.** There are several different types of residual payments and they are paid on different scale levels depending on how the commercial is used. Some of the different categories are: network use, cable use, national, regional, local, wild spot, dealer use.

• **It is not uncommon in commercials to receive a "buyout" payment.** This means you will be paid a single fee for the shooting and airing of the commercial. No residuals. These are usually commercials that are sold to foreign markets.

• **Your pay checks usually get mailed to your agent** and they will take out their 10 percent of the session fees, holding fees and residuals. The agent then mails you a check. When you have a good national commercial running, it is fun to go to the mailbox.

COMMERCIAL CLASSES

Stuart K. Robinson of Robinson Creative, 310/558-4961. He teaches a $70 one-night introduction to commercials. Five-week commercial class is $300. Semiprivate classes $35 each, private $80 an hour. I continue to study with him in his semiprivate hour-and-a-half workouts. He is the only teacher who has this type of on-going classes where you can get a chance to work on audition copy on a weekly or by-weekly basis. Stuart is recommended by most agents and casting directors. He usually has a waiting list but it is worth the effort to get into his classes. Also check out his acting classes. He is devoted to helping his actors achieve their career goals.

Stuart Stone, CCDA, casting director, 323/866-1811. www.actingoutinfo.com. $325 for four weeks. His *Acting Out* commercial workshop teaches you how to audition so you get the call back; and then on the call back, how to book the job! Copy reading techniques, cue card skill, overcoming obstacles and working with props. He provides valuable insights and actors seem to book more jobs after taking his class. Stuart is fun and my students have loved his classes. He likes to call in the people he has taught; he doesn't forget you. Because of his busy casting schedule, classes are just a few times a year. There is usually a waiting list. His book, *Acting Out: Your Personal Coach To A Money Making Career in TV Commercials*, is geared to actors everywhere, whether working in your home town area or preparing to move to Los Angeles.

Carolyne Barry's Commercial Acting Workshops, 323/654-2212. www.carolynebarry.com. All workshops are divided into beginner, intermediate and advance levels. Improvisation, Improv for Commercial Auditions, Performance Improv I & II, Intro Commercial, Intermediate Commercial, Advanced Commercial Technique and the unique Agent Showcase Tape Class. Classes range in price from $405 to $425 for eight-week sessions. Recommended by agents. **Carolyne and Kevin E. West of Actor's Network have produced an audio tape:** *The Actor's Guide to Getting The Job*. Great to listen to on your way to auditions.

Terry Berland, CCDA, casting director, 310/571-4141. www.TerryBerlandcasting.com. Author of *Breaking Into Commercials: Complete Guide to Marketing Yourself*. Six-week on-camera, $350. She teaches how to apply your unique personality and develop a confident approach. Learn on camera how to create dimension in this one minute commercial medium. Class includes meeting an agent.

Pamela Campus, CCDA, casting director, 818/897-1588 or310/398-2715. Has cast over 3,000 commercials and taught over 10,000 adults and children. Adults and teens, beginners and advanced. Six-week classes at Westside Studios. Children starting at age three. They are always taught personally by the casting directors. Very highly recommended by agents.

Michael Donovan, CSA, CCDA, casting director, 323/655-9020. www.Michaeldonovancasting.com. 8170 Beverly Blvd. Suite 105, LA, 90048. $200. Michael Donovan has cast over 1,000 commercials and runs this well-respected workshop. Three-week class.

Megan Foley, CCDA, casting director, 818/755-9384. $150. Teaches a commercial intensive, a one day, eight-hour class on camera, that covers all aspects of the commercial audition.

Kip King, www.kipking.actorsite.com. 818/784-0544. On-going, 11 weeks: $350. Commercial copy and improvisation. Successful actor, over 400 movies, TV shows, commercials and voice-overs; one of the original Groundlings. Only class of its kind. On-camera improv for TV and commercials. Guest casting directors, agents, celebrities and voiceover pros. Private coaching, $75 per hour. Chris Katan from *Saturday Night Live* is his son.

Lien/Cowan, CCDA, Michael Lien and Dan Cowan, casting directors, 323/937-0411. www.liencowancasting.com. The office casts hundreds of commercials a year. $125 for a one day, six hour class on either Saturday or Sunday, includes snacks and a pizza lunch. Class is taught by associates Jan Bina and John Smet. 15 actors per class. Two teachers, two studios, lots of on-camera time. They critique pictures and have the actors read actual copy from commercials they've cast. They show the call back tapes of people who got the commercials. *$ In Commercials TV and Movies* is a book they offer online at the website.

Beverly Long, CCDA, casting director, 818/754-6222. I took my first commercial class with Beverly many years ago. She is very knowledgeable, fun and a great teacher. Many of my students have taken her classes with great results.

Blanca Valdez, CCDA, 323/876-5700. Casting director for most of the Spanish speaking commercials. This is a huge market. She teaches a class that can be hard to get into but keep calling. Tell them I sent you. It is worth the wait. If you speak Spanish, you will want to know Blanca Valdez.

BOOKS & TAPES

Order from Samuel French Bookstore, 323/876-0570 www.SamuelFrench.com or Take One Film & Theater Books, 310/445-4050. www.take1filmbooks.com.

Acting Out: Your Personal Coach to a Money Making Career in TV Commercials by Stuart Stone.
The Actor's Guide to Getting The Job, an audio tape, by Carolyne Barry and Kevin E. West. $24.95. www.carolynebarry.com.
The Agencies: What the Actor Needs To Know by Acting World Books.
The Actor's Picture/Resume Book by Jill Charles & Tom Bloom.
An Actor's Workbook: Get The Agent You Need And The Career You Want by K. Callan.
.Acting In Television Commercials by Squire Fridell.
Acting In the Million Dollar Minute by Tom Logan.
Breaking Into Commercials: Complete Guide to Marketing Yourself by Terry Berland.
Commercials, Just My Speed!! by Vernee Watson-Johnson.
Word of Mouth, a Guide to Commercial Voice-Overs, by Susan Blu & Molly Ann Mullin.
Ross Reports Television and Film: Agents, *TV Commercial Casting Guide* By Backstage.
West Coast Performer's Complete Personal Managers Directory by Acting World Books.

FILM AND TELEVISION
AUDITIONS, INTERVIEWS
AND CALL BACKS

• **If auditions scare you,** buy *Back Stage West* each Wednesday afternoon or Thursday morning. To be really on top of it, subscribe on-line at www.backstagewest.com and check daily for new projects. Check at www.breakdownservices.com then to the Actors Access button daily. Send your pictures and resumes to all the projects you are right for, and go on every audition/reading you can. You will be more comfortable doing auditions only after doing a lot of them. Give the interview and reading all of your attention and focus at the time. Then let go of the audition. The casting person or director will either hire you or not. You will get jobs to build your resume.

• **Paul Newman** says, "If you want to survive, you have to show your ass. You can't walk in and play it safe."

• **Luke Perry** (*90210*) had 216 auditions before landing his first job.

• **To some actors,** *interview* and *audition* are two of the most terrifying acting words. To others, they are very exciting words because they are the actions that lead to landing acting roles. Perhaps with more understanding, you will realize how the other people involved (agents, casting directors, directors, producers) do their jobs and what exactly *your* job is as an actor. The fact is, auditions cause stress; it's how we handle the stress that makes the difference in landing the jobs.

• **Get your script or sides ahead of time.** SAG guarantees that you can get them at least the day before your interview. Often, though, in the case of episodic television, the script is still being written. In this situation, make arrangements with the assistant at the casting office to pick up your script as soon as it's available. This may be only an hour or two before the interview. *Showfax.com,* for a fee, will fax your audition sides to you. You can also subscribe online to *Showfax.com, Nowcasting.com, Castnet* and get your sides 24 hours a day. Showfax limits you to downloading six projects a day, they do have the most sides available, the other groups' downloads aren't limited. *See Resources at the end of this section.* This helps when you are working or auditioning across town and you can't get to the casting director's or production office to pick up sides in person. Sometimes your agent has the script and will fax the sides to you. *For instructions on how to prepare your script for auditions go to Section One, page 95: How To Rehearse And Prepare.*

• **When you are auditioning for a television series** that you haven't seen or don't know the tone of, you can view an episode or several at Jan's Video Editing, 323/462-5511. The charge is $20 an hour. When you are a client of Jan's they don't charge for the viewing room. Jan's has all of the shows.

• **Whenever you walk into an office** for an interview, whoever you are meeting is hoping 100% you are wonderful and will:

• **Make them a lot of money,** as in the case of an agent or manager.

• **Make an impression on the producer or director** that a casting director is having you meet. Casting directors' reputations depend on introducing new discoveries (you) to their employers.

• **Fit the concept of the role** the director or producer has. **They are all rooting for you!**

• **This is absolutely true.** I worked many hours in casting sessions as assistant to director Joan Darling. Directors hire excellent casting directors so they will screen out the bad actors and thus save them a lot of time. The casting directors' reputations depend on the caliber of actors they bring in. However bad, untrained and scared, actors do end up coming in for readings. They are usually friends of the producer or director, the director's assistant, someone the network thinks is up and coming, a waiter at Canter's because he has been so nice and has a good look, etc. When you get an opportunity to read, be prepared and take full advantage of it.

• **The one person in the room** who may not be rooting for you could be you. Because: You don't think you're good enough. You don't deserve to get a break. Someone in the waiting room is perfect for the role. You got here by mistake. You are faking it when you act. You are too fat, thin, old, young, short, tall, blonde, dark, ethnic or not ethnic enough. These are all personal issues that need to be faced and worked on. Self-doubt has killed many promising careers.

• **So, if you've met the casting director** and they've called you in to read for the director, you are a good actor or have a great look. That is not in question. If your agent has obtained the reading without you meeting the casting director first, you are a good actor represented by an agent with a good reputation. If you've obtained the interview in one of the other ways, say "thank you very much" and enter the office knowing that you have acting work to do. Let the fear be there—let it be part of the character.

• **Commit to the acting choices** you made when you read the script. Be open and vulnerable, and you will do a good acting job. Listen without any defenses to directions you may be given and deliver them to the best of your ability. This is your job as an actor. You may not get the role (most of the time you won't) but this is not proof of whether or not you did a good job. It may be proof they are not doing a terrific job by not hiring you, or there may have been another actor who was better suited to the role.

• **Mira Sorvino said the first time she auditioned** for the hooker role in Woody Allen's *Mighty Aphrodite,* she didn't get the part. Woody thought she wasn't sensual enough. Then, while she was in London, she found out he was there and still auditioning. She went to King's Road, bought trashy clothes and mules with plastic flowers, fluffed out her hair, dredged up a cartoon voice, went to see Woody and wowed him. She eventually won the supporting actress Oscar for the role.

• **Ned Bellamy**, character actor, played the role of Eddie, Elaine's psychotic employee, on *Seinfeld.* He made the character choice to use a raspy, creepy voice. I asked Jerry if Ned had used that voice at the audition. He said, "Yes, and I was quite surprised when he showed up at rehearsal and that wasn't his real voice." I asked Ned about it.

Moments before the audition, he decided on the voice and asked casting director Marc Hirschfeld if he should use it. Marc said, "Why not?" Ned had a couple of questions to ask about the role and used the same voice to ask them because he didn't want to break the illusion of the character. Besides being a wonderful actor and looking the part, his choice of using that voice may have been what gave him the edge over the other actors auditioning.

• **Katie Holmes** (*Dawson's Creek*) is from Cleveland, Ohio. She had done some school plays and then, in her junior year, she and her mother went to a talent convention. She did a monologue, they liked her, sent her to Los Angeles. She auditioned for the film *Ice Storm* and got it. After shooting it and returning home, she auditioned for pilots by recording her reading on video tape and sending it to her agent. Her mother read the other characters off camera. She said she kidded James Van Der Beek, saying he was good but her mom really knew how to play Dawson.

• **Gail O'Grady** (*American Dreams*) auditioned for the part of the secretary on *NYPD Blue*, wearing a '60s hairdo, false eyelashes, a tight angora sweater, bright stirrup pants and adding a heavy New York accent; she was inspired by characters in the film *Working Girl*. She said, "I know this woman, she's very physical. And I knew nobody else would show up like that." They auditioned over 100 actors for the part. The three-episode role turned into a regular role with Gail receiving an Emmy nomination.

• **David Schwimmer** (*Friends*) wanted the part in the film *The Pallbearer* from the moment he read the script. He was obsessed. A dozen actors were up for the role. One morning the film's director, Matt Reeves, found a tiny coffin on his desk. The message inside: "I'd kill to be in this movie!" It was signed David Schwimmer. Persistence paid off.

• **Debi Mazar** *(imdb.com, GoodFellas, Jungle Fever)*, in an interview, spoke of her audition with Spike Lee for *Malcolm X*. She wore a blond wig, 1940s makeup, platform shoes, and landed the part of Shorty's girlfriend. She said, "I thought Spike would like to see the character the minute I walked in the door. It was a great audition."

• **Poppy Montgomery** audtioned to play Marilyn Monroe for *Blonde*, a CBS miniseries, decided to take a gamble. "I didn't do the breathless Marilyn voice, I came in with a ponytail, a white T-shirt and jeans."

She was playing the younger Norma Jean Baker, the pinup girl. Out of the 100 actresses auditioning, the producers chose her.

• **Casting Director Tom McSweeney** says, "We love actors; they're our livelihood. We love to find new people. There's nothing more fun than giving an actor a break. I don't want to see actors suffer; I want to see them work; I want to see them happy."

• **Tuesday Knight** was working as a receptionist at Orion Television. "Somebody from the show *Fame* saw me. They were looking for a combination Deborah Harry/Madonna–so they had this big cattle call. I saw it on TV, about 3,000 girls. Then the next day they saw me in the office and they hired me. It was like a dream. I was a regular for a while."

• **Director Ron Shelton's original plan** for Woody Harrelson's date in *White Men Can't Jump* was to be a snooty Ivy League girl. Rosie Perez showed up for an interview and blurted out to him, with feeling, "I can't audition today! I'm having a bad hair day!" That grabbed his attention; she got the role.

• **Regina Taylor** auditioned for *I'll Fly Away*. She felt she was very different from the part until she started thinking of her grandmother and her family. "When I finally sat down to audition to a room full of suits in Los Angeles, I told them I wasn't ready to do the scene, that I felt like talking. They said, 'Sure, talk.' I told them about where I came from, about the faces of the people who raised me. When I was done talking, no one said anything. Someone thanked me. I got up and left." A month later she was in Atlanta filming the part of Lily Harper.

• **Anna Maria Horsford** *(Amen)* says when she went to audition for the part of Sherman Hemsley's ditsy daughter, she wore a pink bathrobe, a pair of little-girl teddy bear slippers and carried a supermarket tabloid under her arm. Her reasoning was: if the character doesn't work, then what does she do? She watches soap operas and reads the gossip sheets.

• **Mariska Hargitay** auditioned for the TV series *Tequila & Bonetti*. The executive producer, Donald Bellisario, said, "I vividly remember the day she auditioned and gave a sly twist to a tragic monologue about a dead husband. The other actresses played it straight, but Mariska played it with laughter. She told this horrible story as if it were a joke, and as she continued, tears started to streak past her smile. She got the part."

• **Edward Norton** brought the stutter into the audition for *Primal Fear*. It was not in the script, it was his invention.

- **Kissing and sexual scenes are hard to carry out** when you are in the auditioning room. Bonnie Gillespie, author of *Casting Qs: A Collection of Casting Director Interviews*, told me of an interview situation that casting director **Jane Jenkins, CSA** often shares.

  - **I have vivid memories** of Vincent D'Onfrio's audition for *Mystic Pizza*. The sides called for the character to roll around on the floor with Lily Taylor's character in a heavy make out scene, followed by an abrupt confrontation by her father. Most actors felt the need to grope me, grab me, or roll around on the floor by themselves. Vincent got down on one knee and did the whole scene as if it were his close up. When you have one of those physically demanding, complicated scenes that is impossible to do in an office, do your close-up.

- **Susan Rutan** *(LA Law),* referring to every character she auditioned for said: "You can get away with anything you are comfortable with. If you think you're pushing it, then you are. Never hit a casting director. Never touch them. Commit, commit, commit. I know that whenever I fully commit to a choice, I either get the job or get a chance to do it another way." When talking about her *LA Law* audition, she said:

  - **There was a clue in the script**: "She would chew off her right arm for Arnie." I took that and committed to that part of the personality. I didn't know anything else about her. There were four little scenes. One was where she came in, in the morning, and there was this big smell in the office. I brought an empty spray can with me and I sprayed it around the room and used it. I'm not sure props are always right, but they were right for this moment. As I was leaving, Greg Hoblit said, "You made us laugh." They didn't know she was funny. I made a choice; I risked—but you have to do it. Otherwise when you go in to read and just do what the stage directions say, you're doing what everyone else is doing.

- **It takes guts to go with your instincts** like that; but in these cases, the actors ended up launching their careers with long-running television series. It certainly was worth it. I'm sure there were times these actors didn't get jobs using outrageous choices, but the few successes are worth the many failures.

- **Casting Director Cathy Henderson, CSA**, says:

  - **I think the actor who usually gets the part** will be someone who walks in and does it as if they were walking on the set, somebody said "Action" and they did it. Making it their own and making it real.

• **A great deal of the reason** why one person will continually get a job and someone else won't is very often not how talented someone is, but more that they grasp what the director and producer are doing that day, which is trying to hire several people for specific roles, and not that they're waiting for someone to come in and blow them away. I mean, it's great if that happens, if the part calls for it. But lots of times your part doesn't call for you to come in and blow somebody away. They want somebody natural, somebody who has good chemistry with the rest of the cast and somebody who makes it real.

• **Casting director Clair Sinnett** says actors should ask, "Would you like to see what I've prepared or is there something specific you would like to see?"

• **If you know any directors or casting directors**, you might ask if you can volunteer to be a reader for them. As a reader, you will read all the other roles with feeling to the auditioning actor. You will be a partner to play off of. The time you spend in a casting office will be a real eye-opener to the casting business. It is also valuable to volunteer as an intern in a casting office.

• **Joe Reich, casting director**, when asked how an actor should hold a script during an audition replied, "I only care that the actor does hold the script. It is axiomatic that when you memorize the script you will always forget a line, usually at the most crucial point (and usually at an important audition). So even if you do memorize, please carry the script and spare yourself that agonizing moment."

• **Absolutely, do not look at the script when you are talking or listening.** I cannot say this strongly enough. It could determine whether you get the job. The time to look down is when the other person reading with you has finished their line and you don't know what your next one is. Start your reaction to what has been said to you and then look down and "grab" the words. Look at the other person and take the time to play the lines. Don't just say them. Use all your acting work and choices. Remember, the lines are not important; the acting is.

• **Kathleen Freeman**, the late character actress and teacher, taught me a very valuable exercise for quickly learning to pick up your lines from a page. Read out loud from a newspaper. Hold your thumb near the copy. Look down, pick up words. Look up in a mirror or into the room and try and make real conversation with those stiff words. Newspapers work better than magazines, because they are written in a dryer form. If you do this 10 minutes every day for three months, you will become very good at picking up words off the script.

• **Wallis Nicita, producer** and former vice president of Warner Bros. Casting, says, "In casting, it is a new person every 10 minutes, eight hours a day, five days a week. You get one take to hit your emotional level and then, good-bye, thank you very much."

• **There is nothing to be afraid of except your own ego.** You are a business person, a career person, a professional dealing with other professionals. Take up your full space, ask questions if you don't know something. It is okay not to know.

• **Take care of the people interviewing you.** Interviews are also difficult for some of these people; they are shy too. The reason they ask a question is to find out about your personality and who you are, not necessarily what your credits are.

• **Come to love the question** "What have you been doing?" If you can love that question and come up with an entertaining, positive, happy answer you've got the interview 90% down.

• **Casting director James F. Tarzia speaks of general interviews.**

  • During a general, I'll read the actor's resume and ask them to tell me about themselves. I don't want them to tell me what's on the resume, I can read what's there. I want to know if there is a well-rounded human being here, or are you one-minded and focused on just being an actor? If you're not a well-rounded human being, then there are no dimensions to you. I want people to be three-dimensional.

• **CALL BACKS**

• **When you go back for another reading,** wear the same clothes, hair style and make the same acting choices, unless you have been asked to read for another part. The time to use an acting coach is before the first audition, not for the call back. They have called you back because they liked how you looked and what you did. The exception would be if they told your agent they didn't like your acting and wanted you to play the role in another way. At this point, a coach could be of great help to open your mind to another point of view in choosing your work.

• **Casting director James F. Tarzia says,**

  • Of course, we all know about actors on call backs—they never seem to do it the same way they did it when they first auditioned. There must be this thing about it: "I got a call back, I think I'll rework this totally differently from what I did the last time." But I liked what you did, don't change it, please don't change it, because I'm going in before you and saying to my director, "This is the most brilliant reading

I've seen, I mean he was just absolutely great," and the actor will come in and do something *totally* different, and I'm like, "What are you doing?" My director is looking at me going "Uh huh, okay." It's a surprise and we don't want to be too surprised. So leave it, don't change it.

• **There are acting jobs**, and you will get yours. This is your career path and you must take each one of the steps. There is a natural progression. Yes, some people seem to get luckier breaks. *Yeah!* They will get there faster and help us. Everyone likes to have their friends working with them. It makes for a happier family on the set.

• **After the audition, have an appointment in your book** to go to: facial, dance class, rehearsal, movie, lunch, etc., so the interview becomes just another event in your day. Write down the people you've met, put them on your networking address list, send thank you notes if appropriate. Remember the things that you did right and for the most part, don't talk about your auditions.

• **Try to keep your interview scenes** (sides) from your film and TV auditions and the copy from your commercial auditions. File them in your notebook. When you work on a project, keep the scripts; years down the line, you will love having them. Maybe your career will someday be valuable enough for a library donation. We never know til it's over.

Resources

Breakdown Services, www.breakdownservices.com. Click on the Actor Access link. You can view the daily posting of Breakdowns from casting directors who want you to submit yourself for roles. Many times they are non-paying. Actors can download two pictures and a resume for free on the site and then submit themselves electronically. Their many services are growing and will expand to include many areas of the country. You will be able to audition for roles at a casting office in your hometown and the casting director will be able to watch you and talk with you from their office.

Showfax, 310/385-6920. www.showfax.com. Hours: M-F 8-10, S & S 10-2. Online fee is $68 a year. $45 a year if you are in the Academy Players' Directory. You can download up to six shows a day. To receive sides by fax: $1.75 per page, with a price cap that never exceeds $12. No charge for cover page or any non-dialogue pages, such as maps or character descriptions. It is free to check them out online, the Actor Access Link has many of the nonpaying jobs casting in town. If you have an online membership and request it, they will automatically email you the Actor Access breakdowns as they become available. I love Showfax's services including the Actor's Bulletin Board. They have been around the longest and are related to the Breakdown Services.

The Actors' Network, 818/509-1010. www.actors-network.com. "Where the Serious Actor Does Business." They are a professional, unique, business networking organization, created by actors. Their members receive notices of projects currently casting.

Now Casting, 818/841-7165. www.nowcasting.com. 60 E. Magnolia Blvd., Burbank, 91502. As a member you receive free unlimited sides otherwise they are $25 a year. They post Union actors pictures and resumes on the site for free. Non-union, unrepresented actors are charged $2.50 a month. Members receive casting notices almost on a daily basis and can submit to the projects and roles they are right for online. Now Casting also produces a very informative, monthly Casting Director Guide including the assistant's names. I really like the services and the helpful staff at Now Casting.

www.thecastlist.com. Membership site. They post pictures and have casting notices.

L.A. Actor Site, www.actorsite.com. Membership site but also an abundance of free information and actor chat rooms too. They post casting notices and have links to the Actor Access site. You can sign up to receive the free, very informative newsletter.

L.A. Casting Network, www.lacasting.com. This is the newest online casting service. They started with actors with commercial representation. Agents signed their actors on for free. If an actor wants to change or add a picture it is $25. Set up fee for unrepresented actors is $50, free hosting for six months, then a $10 monthly fee. They've branched into theatrical castings. They plan some free services like sides and mailing labels for all. Check their website for current information.

Mobile Mailbox, 323/969-9853. 1514 N. Formosa Avenue, Los Angeles, 90046. This is an inexpensive messenger service; Biff Yeager is the actor/owner of the company. Actors can submit themselves for projects they hear or read about that are currently casting. To quote the brochure, "We are a unique messenger service developed several years ago as a twice-a-day, fast pickup and delivery service. We pre-sell our own special delivery stamps as low as $.90 each. Anything that fits in a 10 x 13 inch envelope may be sent by affixing the required amount of stamps and depositing the envelope into one of our conveniently located drop boxes around the Los Angeles, Hollywood, Century City, Beverly Hills, North Hollywood and Burbank areas!" You must register with MMB and buy your stamps before you can put your submissions in their drop boxes. Biff has come up with an unique way to get a leading role in a movie. Check it out at: www.ultimatewishgift.com.

GMA Marketing Concepts, 818/708-0242. www.getmoreauditions.com. Doug Eakins heads this marketing service for actors. For a weekly fee, around $12, plus the monthly postage bill, they submit your picture and resume to projects in preparation, pre-production and casting directors. You will receive a monthly notice of where your pictures have been submitted. They use the trade papers and personal sources, not the Breakdown Service, to find the potential work. They say 90% of their people have booked auditions and jobs. I think you can do the same research yourself, but actors with more money and less time like to have someone else do this type of work for them. Students, Terrill Warren, Greta Hill, Jordan Osher and others have found this service valuable.

CONQUERING FEAR

- **John Wayne** said,

  - **Courage** is being scared to death and saddling up anyway.

- **If you haven't** already thought of your own ways to get through some or all of your interview, audition and performing fears, here are some tried and true ones. Use them all and add your own until you can walk through your fears. These are *not* the most important moments in your life; they are just simply moments.

- **Jeremy Irons**, Oscar winner for *Reversal of Fortune,* says about acting,

  - **A lot of it is like hang gliding**—you just hold on and hope it works. When I talk to acting students, I always read them this poem: "Come to the edge, it's too high, come to the edge, you might fall, come to the edge—so they came. And they flew." I want to keep coming to a high edge. That's why I've made the choices I have. Sometimes I will fall, and sometimes, please God, I will fly. But I wouldn't want to get so scared that I come to a low edge I can just step off easily.

- **Meryl Streep** said,

  - **Characters that are in precarious life and death circumstances** are dangerous characters to visit with your body and soul. It's dangerous to go there. We spend our whole lives as real human beings trying to get beyond the fears and the terrors that are there, everywhere, for us. To be an actor is to want to visit those dark places, the scary parts.

- **Patrick Swayze**, when he was still studying, out of work and broke, used to tell himself over and over,

  - **I'm a winner and my life works.**

194

• **Time.** When you know the time and location of your interview, start planning backwards. You want to arrive and park your car one half-hour before your scheduled appointment time. That means checking the address in your Thomas Guide and figuring your exact route and leaving for your destination in plenty of time to find it. As a rule, on your way to the audition, the traffic will be the worst it has ever been in history. Always give yourself a break and allow the most time it could take—not the least.

• **Bill Macy,** (mature character actor) was doing a presentation of a scene from *Maude* at the Television Academy to honor Norman Lear. Three days before the event we were talking and he casually mentioned he had just come back from a trial run to make sure he knew exactly where the Academy was, where he would park and how long it would take him to get there. Now this is from an ex-New York cab driver who starred in his own TV series for seven years and has worked decades in films, television and on stage. Still, this veteran is clocking how long it will take him to get to his destination for this important event. He says, "It makes me feel secure to know where I'm going." He gets secure so he can walk on the edge of the cliff in his acting. He loves taking risks, that's why he's so funny!

• **Keep a coin purse** in your glove compartment so you'll always have quarters and dimes for parking. I also keep a few coins in my appointment book.

• **Keep a magnetic lock box** hidden on the outside of your car with your car key and house key in it—never be locked out of your car or home before an audition or set call. If you haven't already done this, please put this book down and do it right now. You can get the lock box at Rite Aid, Sav-on, Target, Pep Boys, etc. and keys can also be made at most of those stores.

• **In getting ready to leave the house,** whatever preparation it takes to turn you on to yourself, do it. This may involve some of your *actor's secrets* or simply deciding what to wear, ironing it, primping, playing positive tapes or music, reading something inspirational.

• **If you have an early appointment** and you aren't any good in the morning till you've been up for three hours and have had four cups of coffee, it means you are up $3^1/_2$ hours before the appointment. Luckily, when you work in film and TV and your call is for 6 or 7AM, you can just take a shower, wash your hair and go to work. The hair and makeup people take care of the rest and give you a chance to wake up.

• **Okay. You are prepared**, parked in your car one half-hour ahead of time. Now relax. Just sit with any fears, tears, giggles, anger or whatever comes up; you may start to cry or laugh. Experience all of it because beyond those feelings and tensions are the knowledge of who you are and the energy to use all of yourself. Allow plenty of time for this, then take down all of your defenses, be willing to let whatever happens to you happen. Go into the office, sign or report in with the assistant, and check to make sure there aren't changes of dialogue in the sides you are reading today or pick up your copy or sides if you don't already have them.

• **If for some insane reason you weren't able to get your script ahead of time**, find the bathroom so you can say all your lines out loud. Figure out what the scene or copy is about (the situation), who the characters are and to whom they are talking. Find similar experiences and characters in your own life and act as if you were talking to them under these given circumstances. Memorize as much of the material as you can—at least the first couple of lines.

• **Then back to the office**, relax, observe everything going on but don't expend your energy playing with the other actors until you have read and are on your way out.

• **Practice these** *being ahead of time* **muscles** by being at class on time to get ready to act—whatever that takes for you: coffee, socializing, talking to your teacher, etc. Also practice this with any appointments that have to do with your career. This will build your muscles in finding out what it takes for you to be at your most comfortable, relaxed, unique best.

• **On your drive to the interview** or before, start thinking of your stories. Have an answer to "What have you been doing lately?" It is very important to have a wonderful story to tell about each entry on your resume, as the interviewer might use it as a guide for conversation.

• **Stories.** These are _positive_ stories about your life, your career, the weather; it doesn't matter. If anyone mentions the smog, you haven't noticed because of some other positive thing you _have_ noticed. If it's raining—isn't it grand how fresh it smells.

• **Make the stories short,** interesting and geared to show off who you are. You just got back from a great vacation, skiing, surfing, Las Vegas. You're taking a class in anthropology and are going on a dig next week. You can use things that happened a few months back as if they were last week; a story is more exiting if it sounds like it just happened. Funny incidents entertain. The most trivial information can be made humorous. Show biz gossip stories are good: shows you've worked on, stars you've worked with. Just make sure the story revolves around _you_ and not who or what you are talking about.

• **List of questions.** Joan Darling taught me this one. Write out five questions—to find the answers to during the interview—on a piece of paper and put it in your pocket or purse. Find out the answers in the meeting without asking the questions, of course, but by observation. I love sex questions because they entertain me the most. Such as: Who in the room gets the most sex? Who lost their virginity first? Last? Other questions: Who's most ambitious? Who's most in control of the situation? etc. Always include yourself—it is answered between you and the rest of the people in the room. You talk about whatever is appropriate but you are also thinking about finding the answers to the questions you have written down. This device is to keep you involved with the people and uninvolved in your fear.

• **William James** said, "If you want a quality, act as if you already had it." Try the "as if" technique.

• **Love of yourself.** Give yourself the _permission_ to be wonderful. Your uniqueness is the gift, yes gift, you are giving the audience, whomever they may be. Keep putting yourself on the line; don't be afraid to be outrageous, or to be willing to just say the lines. Most of the time you are going up for parts that are exactly like you.

From Nelson Mandela's 1994 Inaugural Speech

Our deepest fear is not that we are inadequate.

Our deepest fear is that we are powerful beyond measure.

It is our light, not our darkness, that most frightens us.

We ask ourselves: Who am I to be brilliant, gorgeous, talented and fabulous?

Actually, who are you not to be?

You are a child of God. Your playing small doesn't serve the world.

There's nothing enlightening about shrinking so that other people won't feel insecure around you.

We were born to make manifest the glory of God that is within us.

It's not just in some of us; it's in everyone.

And as we let our own light shine, we unconsciously give other people permission to do the same.

As we are liberated from our own fear, our presence automatically liberates others.

I've asked my students to make a copy of this speech on a bright colored piece of paper and put it in their wallet. Everytime they take out some money, they see the bright color and think of not being afraid.

DEALING WITH REJECTION

• **Through my spiritual work and inner growth,** I have found positive ways to accept not getting an acting job I've wanted. I don't forget the jobs and I still wish "they" had wanted me, but I have come to accept the fact that they didn't.

• **I hate dealing with rejection** but I can tolerate it, even though it hurts. Sometimes I do stew about it, rationalize that somehow it's for my own good, get angry and/or feel sorry for myself. I've learned, if I'm really in self-pity, to give myself a time limit, whether it's 15 minutes or two days. It usually doesn't last the full time but sometimes it does and then time is up and I let go of it. I really do believe I have a choice in my thoughts.

• **There have been times in my life** when I have allowed the depression to take over for longer periods, but not anymore. Time seems too precious to me now; I've got so many things in my life that fulfill me. I still don't have enough acting jobs. When I do get one, I really celebrate the whole event.

• **Sometimes you can have a job and lose it.** In spirtual work we are taught that events happen for a reason. When we lose one thing, something better will come along. When you have been fired or the pilot you were counting on going to series didn't go, it is hard to see what might be better. This is a time in your life where you really have to do the hard work of keeping yourself in the game.

• **Hilary Swank talks about the day Aaron Spelling fired her** off *Beverly Hills, 90210.* "I was on the eighth season and around the 16th episode, Aaron said, 'Hilary, it's not working.' I went home and cried all day, weeping, 'If I'm not good enough to be on *90210,* then I shouldn't be an actress at all!'" Three weeks later she landed her Oscar-winning role in the independent film *Boys Don't Cry.* Hilary says, "You must trust fate. If I hadn't been fired, I wouldn't have been open to take the role."

• **Bill Macy, a well known mature character actor** was cast as one of the regulars on an ABC show called *Regular Joe* with Daniel Stern. They shot the pilot and word was everyone was hot for the show. At the last minute in May, it didn't make the fall schedule. Then in August it was back on for a mid-season replacement. All Fall the news was, "It was a go." Then they started dropping characters and changing the story line. Then just three weeks before the show was to go into production they told Bill they were replacing him with Judd Hirsch and paying off his contract.

• **Bill has been around a long time** so he was sad but went to play golf and get on with his life. The next week he auditioned for a movie he hadn't been available for before. Callbacks and dealmaking ensued. Finally the deal was signed on the day he had been scheduled to start shooting the series. The movie is *Surviving Christmas* with Ben Affleck, James Gandolfini, Christina Applegate and Catherine O'Hara. This ended up being a great turn of events. Bill believes, "When one door closes, another will open."

• **When we follow** *The Four Agreements* book by Don Miguel Ruiz and not take anything personally we reach a higher level, we learn to trust, we work even harder. Rejection is tough and we get tougher.

• **Dr. Sherie Zander** instructs actors on ways to deal with rejection.

  • **Everyone must face rejection**, but for the actor rejection is a constant companion. It cannot be avoided. No one is immune. It not only affects the beginner, but the seasoned actor as well. Success, fame and fortune don't keep the experience and pain of rejection away. Rejection must be faced and dealt with so that it will not destroy the motivation and self-esteem that are necessary in order to maintain an acting career.

  • **No one likes rejection**. It can be discouraging and hurtful. It may lead to insomnia, depression and despair. Because it is so prevalent and so destructive, it is critical that you, as an actor, discover how to detach from its harmful effect. But, how is that possible? You are told not to take rejection personally, but how do you differentiate who you are from what you do?

  • **When I work with actors who are struggling** with this issue, I begin by taking a look at possible sources of rejection in childhood. Often the healing of early emotional wounds will provide the emotional stability that is required to move through rejection with less pain and stress. You may need to get to a good therapist.

- **I work with attitude and perspective.** Because every success will be preceded by many rejections, it may be helpful to view each rejection as a stepping stone rather than a set back. Remember that every rejection brings you one step closer to success.

- **There are many practical things** you can do to keep rejection from getting you down. Finding a safe way to release feelings of anger, sadness, hurt, fear and guilt is a good place to start. You may need to cry or yell, hit a punching bag or pour out the feelings on paper. This will serve to clear your mind and body and prepare you to carry on in spite of disappointment.

- **You may find a creative outlet** for all of that rejection energy—write a poem, write an article, draw, paint or sculpt. Physical exercise will help. Get the sleep you need and eat regular, healthy meals. Take this opportunity to do things that are fulfilling and refreshing.

- **Turn your focus away from thoughts of failure** and onto improvement. Take time to study and explore your craft. This is the time to continue the mechanics of finding new work—phone calls, mailings, photos, networking. Make a decision to learn what you can from this rejection by doing the following:
  - Make an effort to find out why you were turned down.
  - Notice any positive things that came out of this incident.
  - Make two lists:
    Things I can change.
    Things I can't change.
  - Utilize the practice of meditation and prayer.
  - Decide to go for the next opportunity and try again.

- **I would encourage you to prepare now for that day.** You can do so by making sure you are living a full life. Take time to develop deep and lasting friendships. Nurture and enjoy family relationships. Involve yourself with other actors in study or support groups. These are the persons who will help to lift your spirits when discouragement and despair threaten to bring you down.

- **You have many choices.** Refuse to allow rejection to ruin your day or your future.

LIE ABOUT YOUR AGE?

• **Honesty is always the best policy!** *However,* if you are 30 and look 22 and you are reading for a part that is 22, and *if* you are asked how old you are, give the age the part calls for. You can only do this if you are very comfortable with it. It is hard for a casting director to bring you in to meet the director and producer for a 22-year-old role if they know you are 30. Remember, you will be laughed at if you look 30 and claim to play 20 to 30. You must judge your age according to how those in-the-know in the industry perceive you.

• **On the other hand,** one of the stars I coach has been adding a few years to her real age because she's pursuing roles in an older category, where she has more casting potential.

• **It is usually best, about this issue, to do what your agent wants** you to do. They will be selling you at a certain age. When you are hired, someone in the production office will end up knowing your age because of the ruling that you must show your driver's license, passport, or birth certificate to prove your right to work. SAG has been trying to get this rule overturned.

• **Theatrical agent Terry Lichtman advises:**

  • **I don't recommend lying;** I just recommend side-stepping the question because once you tell someone the age you are, they always think of you as that age.

• **Stuart K. Robinson, noted commercial acting teacher,** acting teacher, successful actor and director highly recommends that you never tell your age. He believes that if you are asked outright, "How old are you?" which is against the law, that you avoid answering. I love watching Stuart teach; he has the perfect body language and verbal language to avoid telling his age. Such as, "I don't tell my age." or "It is a long tradition in my family, we never tell our age." or "You tell me, do you think I look the right age to play this part?" or "Don't you agree, I'm in the age range to play this part?" or "I believe I look the age to play this part. If you disagree, I'm out of here." Stuart is a master at pulling this off with style.

• **I am one to blurt out my age.** You really have to always play it as you see it. We can change our minds on how we see things. If you decide not to tell your age then you will have to keep it a secret from most everyone. Angelina Jolie has been pulling off younger for years. One of my students graduated from UCLA with her younger brother. My student was 25 and Angelina was still selling 22. Every article about her has a slightly different age. I'm not saying she isn't what she says she is, but she may not be.

• **There is no denying the fact: the younger you play** the more opportunities you will have to work. This will not change, so each of us has to make peace with this issue. There is no use in trying to change the business; you can only change yourself, your thinking, your age.

• **In legal terms, according to** SAG, a performer should never be asked their age or ethnicity. The only exception is if the producer needs to know whether or not the performer is a minor or if the actor speaks a certain language.

CASTING DIRECTORS

• **Casting directors are mentioned all through this book** because they are usually the people who bring you in to meet the producers and directors of film and television projects. *(For more about commercial casting directors, see the Commercial Section)*

• **Bonnie Gillespie is the casting columnist for** *Back Stage West*, author of *Casting Qs: A Collection of Casting Director Interviews*, consultant on the business of acting, and owner of Cricket Feet Management. I asked Bonnie to gather some specific quotes to demonstrate to my readers how much the casting directors are on the actor's side. She chose the following from many, many hours of interviews she has conducted.

• **Carol Lefko.** "Actors think that casting directors are not on their side. We are! We have a problem and they are our solution!"

• **Ellyn Long Marshall.** "Our eyes, minds and hearts want you to be what we need. It's not known what is needed. You bring it in and show it to us."

• **Delicia Turner.** "I tell my actor friends, 'Look, if you're good, you're making my job easier.'"

• **Mike Fenton, CSA.** "We don't bite. We don't invite an actor in hoping he'll fail. The sooner we find an actor who scores, the better for us."

• **Laura Gleason, CSA.** "I know how difficult the process is. I respect actors and really enjoy them as people and I want them to do so well."

• **Iris Grossman.** "We want you to be the one who's going to get the part because then the job is done. I want you to come in and get it."

• **Julie Hutchinson, CSA.** "Our fantasy is to make a major discovery and stop looking."

• **Amy Lippens, CSA.** "We want you to be good. We want you to be right for the part. It's about being creative and having fun."

• **Marnie Saitta.** "When an actor comes in and feels nervous, I want to say, 'Hey, you're doing me a favor, coming in here and making good choices. You're inspiring me.'"

• **April Webster, CSA.** "We try to make this a safe place, so that the actor feels that he or she has the right to try something out. I want you to do your best work because that makes my job go smoothly."

• **Every week in *Back Stage West*** Bonnie interviews a casting director in her *Casting Q's* column. Save these articles in an alphabetized file so when you have a meeting with someone you have read about, you will have material to start up a conversation. When you subscribe online to *Back Stage West* you can check into the archives and read her past interviews.

• **There is so much valuable information** that can help you with your career. When you go to showcases, take notes; often the casting director will say something of a personal nature. You can mention it in your thank you letter or when you have an interview two years later. You can, for instance, inquire whether their child won his Little League championship or not.

• **When you see a film or television** show that you especially like the casting of, write the casting director telling them what you liked in particular. Their addresses can always be obtained through Breakdown Services or other membership groups.

• **Joey Paul, CSA, film, television and stage casting director:**

Q: How should the actor approach a general interview, when they are just meeting with the casting director and not auditioning?

> • **For the most part, actors take the wrong psychological approach.** If they walk into a general interview and a casting director has to say to them, "So, tell me about yourself," they're not off to a good start. Part of the reason that a general interview might go very well is that a real dialogue of action and response occurs between two people, just like in a regular scene. If a general interview is one where the casting director is just asking questions and then passively sits there and listens to the

actor talk about their life or their day, etc., it is not very conducive to making a long-lasting impression. Everybody likes to talk about themselves, particularly people in show business, who are oriented toward, and proud of their accomplishments. The goal of a general interview should be to find a common bond, something that both people can jointly discuss. The actor should be asking questions, too.

• **Questions like,** "I am familiar with some of your work; it's amazing what you do. Is casting everything you thought it would be and is it a creative and fun process for you?" or, "I was curious; how did you first get started as a casting director?" I think that if an actor seems interested in the casting director, they'll have a better chance of the casting director being interested in them. People always respond well when somebody says, "You know, I saw such and such film that you cast and I felt... How long have you been casting this project? Are you still looking for such and such? I notice the artwork in your office is of a southwestern taste" Coming from a business point of view, I don't think of that as flattery. That kind of discussion lends itself to being able to remember the actor better, but only if it comes from a real and genuine place.

• **For me, there's nothing worse** than when actors come in, sit in my office and don't say a word. Nothing, not even bad small talk like, "Boy, the traffic was busy getting here today. What was it like for you after the earthquake?" To me a general interview is kind of like a blind date; you have hopes that maybe this time it might work out. You hope there's a possibility that you could make a friend. Maybe this person will like you and remember you. If you were to go on a blind date and all the person did for 20 minutes was talk about himself, you'd walk away saying he couldn't care less about me. All the regular things also apply: be yourself, don't be somebody you're not, be real and honest, have a sharing dialogue. If they ask a question, you ask a question, or start off the conversation with a question.

Q: So you're really talking about personality development?

• **Yes, because ultimately if an actor becomes a major, major star,** one of the reasons may be because they have an incredible personality in addition to their talent. Robin Williams is a perfect example of that. I tell students of mine that they should see a general interview in their mind the same way they would if they were going to appear on David Letterman or Jay Leno. If they aspire to be a celebrity someday, then that aspiration has to be with them today. The reason that kind of success happens is because that's who they are now.

- **Actors who are shy and would rather do the acting work** than be in situations where their personalities must carry them, shouldn't do general interviews. Whoever represents them or is helping them to promote their careers should put the emphasis on trying to get them the audition. Let the actors do their magic in the reading and leave.

Q: When going in for an audition, should the actor immediately start to do the audition or try to get a general conversation going first?

- **I have never been impressed by an actor**, regardless of whether it's a call back or an initial meeting, who wants to try to create a general interview situation prior to their audition. Particularly if they assume that we're going to sit down and talk before they read. I firmly believe that less is more. There are ways actors can develop a certain kind of control over auditions, rather than coming in like victims. One of the ways they can do this is by truly looking at the audition as a journey.

- **With the entrance into my office they have the opportunity** to take me on a little fantasy journey that will be created by what they do. If actors are in control of this journey, they will have a better chance of my going along fully for the ride. When they come in and decide they want to talk, tell stories, do whatever before they read, they've put a heavier burden on themselves. They hope that I am following them, am attentive and they are holding my interest for that entire story, talk or whatever. After we're done with that, they've got to go back to a somewhat neutral place, so they can get into the character that they're reading.

- **Look at that audition as if it were a bunch of line-to-line dots** on a piece of paper. They have to take me along from dot to dot to dot to dot on this journey, which is comprised of their story and all the points of interest. Once they've finished the story there's another dot they've got to carry me to, back to that neutral place so they can be the artist. Then they've got to take me to the next dot when they begin to perform, and all the little dots that are within that performance. They hope for that entire journey, I'm with them. It's a much heavier burden doing all of that, because if they say anything that's the least bit of interest to me, it's going to be much more difficult to get me back on track and hold my attention. Whereas, if they simply come in and just begin to do their magic, the role, it's like the curtain comes up, they do the audition, the curtain comes down and they leave the stage or my office, as it were. They have a greater chance of maintaining my attention and now that they're gone and I was so enraptured with what they did, I have the potential of thinking, "Wow, I want more. That was great." The only way I can get more is by bringing them back.

• **Tony Shepherd was the Vice President of Talent** for Aaron Spelling Productions for 14 years.

Q: What do you see when an actor is entering the casting meeting?

• **If you're in the business of buying talent,** a casting director, producer or director, you can see the talent in the actor in 30 seconds or less; it's that indefinable something. You feel it; you know it. I look for a twinkle in the eye. You can't create that; it comes from within. I think the best actors are people who understand what they are about, understand what is going on in the world around them and how they relate to that world.

Q: How can an actor make the best impression?

• **Boring people make boring actors.** Work on yourself, process your life, examine how you relate to other people, how you communicate. Learn how to work with and motivate yourself and use that person from within. Acting is just a little bit bigger than real life. You are going to use who you are in everything you do. If you aren't focused, centered, honest, a risk-taking person, what kind of an actor can you ever expect to be? What you do in your daily life is directly reflected in what you do as an actor.

• **80 percent of jobs are lost,** not because the actor is right or wrong for the role or they can't act, but because something has gone wrong and they come in less than 100% focused. You don't know why, it's just that the person isn't right. In casting sessions, listen to what we say about actors: "He's cold, he has an edge, he has no warmth, he has no vulnerability, he has no strength." We're not talking about the person's acting ability, we're talking about the person, what they bring of themselves to the role they are playing or reading for. If an actor sits in a room with me and is interesting, exciting and there is a sparkle, a twinkle, an energy and a vitality about them, I can tell you right now they are going to work; it's only a matter of time.

• **Finally, in your auditions** and acting work, find tragedy in the comedy and humor in the drama.

• **Richard DeLancy casts,** among other things, *Unsolved Mysteries*.

Q: What will cause an actor to lose a job or not be called in again?

• **Being late. That's my number one pet peeve.** I believe that an actor's job is the interview. If you can't make the interview, then... A lady was late for her interview with producers. She was so perfect for the role but if she's going to be late for her interview with the producers, I cannot guarantee she is going to be at work on time. In New York, if you are late for your audition, you are no longer going to be considered for that role. That's the discipline I like.

• **Lori Cobe-Ross, is an independent feature film casting director.**

Q: What does a casting director do?

> • **I read the script,** with the director or writer, work up the breakdowns of the characters and specifically what we want or what we need. I submit the descriptions to the Breakdown Service, they send this information over computer or fax to all of the agents. From that, the agents submit actors. That same day, particularly on a feature, I receive hundreds of pictures and resumes. I don't interview all of the actors, but I look at everything.

Q: Do you prefer seeing actors through agents?

> • **Unfortunately, 99 percent of the time, I have to say no to the actors.** If I see a hundred people, only one is going to get the role. So it's a lot easier to talk to the agents, without saying directly to the actor why they weren't right. Also, actors without agents would be at a disadvantage making their own deals because they're not really equipped to do that, whereas, agents are.

Q: Is making the deal the most important part of your job?

> • **For the producer it is;** for the director it's getting the right actor for the part. I work for the producer and the director. To me they are of equal importance, though I would think getting the right actor is more important.

Q: Do you think there's a stigma about doing extra work?

> • **It isn't something you need to put on your resume,** but it's certainly a way to get your SAG card. Lots of films I've worked on, people have been upgraded to a speaking role and get their SAG card, or at least get Taft-Hartleyed, so the next time they work, they can get their card. It's also important to be comfortable around a set. When people only have theater training, I'm very nervous about hiring them for a series, or for a feature. When you work on sets and meet directors or producers that think you're terrific, they may give you a shot at a job; it happens all the time. I think you need to do whatever you can to meet the people that can get you work.

Q: When actors are reading together for a role with kissing and such, should they do it for the audition?

> • **People are afraid to ask questions about physical movement.** Some actors are afraid to look each other in the eyes. You really need to act physical. You should talk about it ahead of time. You could say to the actor, "Is it okay if we kiss?" or "What do you want to do?" Make sure you are both willing to do it. Then ask the auditioners what they would like to see.

• **Lori wrote a letter** to the editor of *Back Stage West*; I thought it important for all actors. She gave me permission to print it here.

> • **Casting is a business.** We casting directors do our part and the actors need to do the same.
>
> 1. **Always bring a picture and resume** with you to every audition. Come on—keep some in your car.
>
> 2. **Get a contact number with a Los Angeles area code.** Some casting directors might not want to make a long distance call. Why risk losing an audition?
>
> 3. **Don't call a casting office** unless you are running late for an audition or it is some emergency. Our job is to find the best actor; we are not career counselors. After talking to agents and managers to schedule, negotiate, and book actors, auditions, preparing and approving sides, and dealing with our producers and director, there is little or no time left in the day.
>
> 4. **Don't make excuses once you are in for an audition.** If you aren't prepared, *don't audition.* Ask for more time. I'd much rather give you time than see you stumble through the material. We don't know who has had the sides for an hour or a week; we assume you've spent time on the material.
>
> 5. **Be kind to the casting assistants.** I don't need to say more.
>
> 6. **It's fine to ask questions in an audition.** If you have unanswered questions about your character, you cannot do a good job.
>
> 7. **One last hint** that I learned from my best friend, casting director Mark Paladini: If you go to an audition and you know the casting director, and it is just the two of you in the room, it is fine to chat, reminisce, schmooze...*but* if there are others in the room just do your audition and answer any questions you're asked. You don't want the producers, director, or others to think that you were brought in as a favor. You want them to think you're there because you are one of the best choices for the role.
>
> **Casting directors want you to do a good job.** We love to call and say, "He/she got the job!"

• Clair Sinnett, independent casting director, says:

> • **Learn the business. See at least one feature film a week,** if that's the area that you want to go into. Watch television. What are some of your favorites? Who does the casting of those shows? That's the "business of the business." Know who the casting directors, directors and producers are in television as well as feature films. Once you know who they are, try to find out a little bit about them so you can send them a personal cover letter that accompanies your picture and resume every time you write them. Remember, your picture and resume is your liaison between their desk and you.

Resources

Casting Society's Website. www.castingsociety.com. Look up the members, many of their resumes are listed. They may be more up-to-date than the www.imdb.com listing. Also check out the "other cool stuff" links on the Casting Society's website.

Casting Directors Directory, by Breakdown Services, 310/276-9166. www.breakdownservices.com. 2140 Cotner Ave., Los Angeles, 90025. $45 a year for a subscription of two directories a year with updates snail mailed every two weeks or emailed weekly. Casting directors move around very fast; this directory is the leader in providing the most current information because CDs use the Breakdown Service every time they're casting a new project. It also gives you a list of all the television shows and who casts them. **Casting director mailing labels** (300) for $16. You can send out notices of a film, television show or play that you would like them to see you in or to just hear that you are working. Again, your name crosses their desks. **Play Flyers,** $80 to deliver one to each casting director. Newer companies are beginning to provide some of the same services Breakdown does. As always, check companies' reputations. You can never have too much correct information.

Now Casting, 818/841-7165. www.nowcasting.com. 60 E. Magnolia Blvd., Burbank, 91502. This is a membership organization run by Union actors. As a member you can download information from their Casting Director Guide; Casting Director Labels, list of current projects and who is casting, casting director interviews, casting notices emailed to you as they receive them: you submit electronically. They also post your pictures, resume and demo reel and qualified members receive a discount at the casting director workshops. Updated agency information and labels.

L.A. Actor Site, www.actorsite.com. Casting director information, workshops, casting notices and online submissions.

Mark Paladini, CSA, taught a UCLA Extension course titled, "Casting for Film and Television." An actor can learn so much by studying and observing what the job of a casting director is. Hopefully he will continue teaching this class—look for it.

Casting Qs: A Collection of Casting Director Interviews, www.castingqs.com. by Bonnie Gillespie, the current casting columnist for *Back Stage West.*

Casting Directors Master Map by Actor's Toolbox. It is a fold out map showing the locations of all the casting directors and whether or not they accept drop-offs or mail-in submissions. Updated monthly.

The Actor's Encyclopedia of Casting Directors, by Karen Kondazian.
The Back Stage Guide To Casting Directors, by Hettie Lynn Hurtes.
Casting Directors' Secrets, by Ginger Howard.

CASTING DIRECTORS TALK ABOUT PILOT SEASON

COMPILED BY BONNIE GILLESPIE, CASTING COLUMNIST FOR *BACK STAGE WEST*

Pilot season is a very big deal in Los Angeles. Over 100 comedy and dramatic pilots may be shot during "pilot season" which runs typically from January into April. All the completed pilots will be viewed by May. That is when the networks decide on their fall schedules. The number of pilots chosen to go into production in July depends on how many returning shows each network has. Typically, 25 pilots will be picked up for the fall schedule. The network will order six to twelve shows to be produced. Many of the shows that premier in the fall will be cancelled before their third episode airs. There are usually several more pilots in limbo for mid-season replacements; they won't go into production until the fall.

For casting directors, agents and many actors, pilot season is the busiest time of year. I asked Bonnie Gillespie to contribute the following chapter because she talks to and interviews the casting directors who are at the core of this frenzy of casting.

Bonnie Gillespie is the casting columnist for Back Stage West and author of the book, *Casting Qs: A Collection of Casting Director Interviews.* www.castingqs.com. She is also a career consultant on the business of acting and owner of Cricket Feet Management.

CASTING Qs PILOT SEASON—TIPS FROM CASTING DIRECTORS

What I've learned, in talking to both casting directors and actors about pilot season, is that the stakes are high, the pressure is on, and the rewards can be unfathomably good. Of course, after six trips to producers, getting told, "We went another way," can be a crushing blow.

My advice on how to keep (relatively) sane during pilot season? Spend as much time as you can in preparation for your auditions; allow plenty of extra time to commute, park, and find your way to the audition location; and be graciously patient. Remember that pilot season affects everyone in this town, and no one should take any of that personally.

In an attempt to uncover the absolute must-haves for actors during pilot season, I contacted several casting directors with track records including TV series and pilot casting. What follows is their advice for the physical tools, the emotional strength, and the perspective on timing essential to weathering auditions through this pilot season and beyond.

CONTRIBUTING CASTING DIRECTORS:

Patrick Baca, CSA, who has cast several pilots and series, as well as many features.

Jeanie Bacharach, currently casting *The Flannerys,* has worked on *Judging Amy, Ally McBeal* and *The Guardian.*

Matthew Barry, CSA, a former actor who mainly casts features.

Deborah Barylski, CSA, currently casting *Life With Bonnie,* plus features and pilots, has worked on *Still Standing, Emeril!, The Lot, Just Shoot Me,* and *Home Improvement.*

Jackie Briskey, CSA, currently casting *Passions,* has worked on *WKRP in Cinncinatti.*

Lori Cobe-Ross, currently casting *PBS's Madison Heights,* has worked on *On Common Ground.*

Donna Ekholdt, CSA, former actor, oversees all casting as Sr. VP, Talent Development and Casting for Big Ticket Television.

Peter Golden, CSA, oversees all casting as Sr. VP, Talent and Casting for CBS Television.

Elisa Goodman, CSA, has cast dozens of MOWs and features.

Cathy Henderson, CSA, currently casting features and pilots, has worked on *That's My Bush!*

Marc Hirschfeld, CSA, oversees all casting as Exec. VP, Talent and Casting for NBC Television.

Lisa Miller Katz, CSA, currently casting *Everybody Loves Raymond, A.U.S.A.,* has worked on *According to Jim, The Ellen Show* and *The King of Queens.*

Mark Paladini, CSA, currently casting features and pilots, has worked on *All Souls, Titans, Babylon 5* and *Beverly Hills, 90210.*

Kevin Scott, CSA, currently casting *The Black Sash* and pilots, has worked on *The West Wing, Citizen Baines, ER* and *Fastlane.*

Mark Teschner, CSA, a former actor who is currently casting *General Hospital* and *Port Charles.*

Katy Wallin, CSA, currently casting features and pilots, has worked on *Santiara* and *Hollywood Off-Ramp.*

April Webster, CSA, currently casting *Alias* and *111 Gramercy Park,* has worked on *The Lone Gunmen, CSI* and *Providence.*

A STRONG HEAD SHOT

"A good picture is your first priority. Good pictures are extraordinarily important. Don't let your lover or your mother pick the one they want on the mantle. Your head shot should say, "I'm a very good actor," to me when I look at your eyes. Let us figure out what to do with your hair. Just look like you can act." **Cathy Henderson**

"There's a certain depth to you that comes across in your pictures. I look at the picture and resume thinking, 'Do I want to get to know this person better?'" **Kevin Scott**

CONFIDENCE

"I'm looking for strong persona, charisma, distinct choices with the character, and star quality. I don't care if it's just one line. I want to see an air of confidence about you." **Marc Hirschfeld**

"[I'm looking for you to have] a comfort level with yourself. You need to feel comfortable in your own skin." **Kevin Scott**

"I like to call it charm, but it's really a sense of humor about yourself or a sense of irony within the role that you need. Remember that it's not a personal issue when you don't get cast. It's not a statement of the quality of your work." **Donna Ekholdt**

"It's often not about talent, but about who's *more right* for the role. Just let it go and trust that you have something unique and when it's your turn, it's your turn." **Mark Teschner**

"[Getting a callback] is an indication of your talent. Be glad. You have to keep your own center and realize that getting a callback is an accomplishment. Every time I work on a pilot, I get thousands of envelopes. Piles and piles and piles! It blows my mind." **Jeanie Bacharach**

"The hardest thing is to stay present. That's a hard process. There's whispering, there's note-taking. Keep your focus. Connect to your reader. Remember who you are, not who they want you to be. Have integrity and fill the room with your energy. Take the space. Know you're a contribution to the project. The right thing will happen. Know that casting directors are nervous at those meetings too. Be clear on your technique and focus on the task. It's not about getting the job." **April Webster**

PREPAREDNESS

"You have to treat an audition like a job. Go in prepared. Be professional. Take that audition seriously. If you're given the opportunity to read the script, read the script." **Katy Wallin**

"Don't feel, in a cold read situation, that complete wardrobe is necessary. It's a cold reading. We don't need sets, wardrobe, or props. Props are a real distraction and they show your lack of experience. Ask whatever questions you have *before* reading. Don't kick yourself after reading by wondering what the answers would've been if you had asked the questions." **Jackie Briskey**

"Get the material ahead of time. Study it. Make a choice. Come in here and do it." **Kevin Scott**

"Try to be as prepared as possible during pilot season. It is about the only time of year that a script should be readily available in the casting director's office, so there's no excuse for not having read and prepared the script as much as possible. Ask questions of your agent or of the assistant in the casting director's office. Know the tone of the show. Is it similar to something already on the air? There's no such thing as too much information. All of this will be helpful during an audition." **Lisa Miller Katz**

"Remember that a sitcom really is just a 22-minute play. When you're preparing for an audition, have two or three ways of doing the role in your back pocket. The producers don't always know what they want, so they may just ask you to try something else. Have something else ready. But know that most of the time in television, they don't want you to deviate from the script." **Deborah Barylski**

"I want to see someone who has an understanding of the text, who is good with the language, who has made strong choices—whether [those choices are] right or wrong. I want to see that you've thought it all out." **Jeanie Bacharach**

"Remember that, in casting a pilot, we are looking for someone that an audience will care about every week. Make your character special, someone we will want to care about and therefore want to see week after week." **Lori Cobe-Ross**

LISTENING

"Do you listen? The most important thing about acting is what's going on in your eyes. Are you listening and reacting or just doing your lines? I know the difference." **Jackie Briskey**

"If I'm reading with you and I pause, mid-line, and you jump in, thinking it's your cue, I know you aren't listening. If the phone rings, you should pick it up after you've *heard* the phone ring or looked to it as if the ring drew your attention there. Those details are important to the reality you should create for us. Be a good observer of people. Borrow from what you observe. It's the little things that could add to a character exactly what it needs." **Peter Golden**

PILOT SEASON TIMING

"We get busy. I will add a casting director to our office for pilot season. The stakes are very high. Actors become overwhelmed and their priorities are skewed out of line. Be fully prepared. Your agent can help by not scheduling 12 appointments in one day. Don't be so attached to the outcome that you are depleted and your energy is gone, and you're not present for your auditions. That just adds tension." **April Webster**

"Within four to six weeks of getting the script, we're shooting the pilot, so sometimes our casting directors hold auditions with just an outline and one scene. The actor will go from reading for the associate to the casting director, to the producer, do a callback, maybe read for the director, get to the studio level, and then final choices go to the network, all just in a few weeks." **Peter Golden**

"Many people have multiple appointments on busy days during pilot season. If you feel the need, ask for more time. Usually that will be an option. If you're an actor who seems like you don't care about giving a cold reading, you'll be quickly dismissed during pilot season; a time when reading 100 actors a day is the norm." **Lisa Miller Katz**

"Limit how many auditions you attend in a day. Preparation for an audition is so important, because things can move very quickly. A preread in the morning can lead to a producer's session, a studio session, and a network session within 24 hours. I don't agree with the mindset that you can *wing it* for the preread and if you get a callback, [then] you'll start preparing. If you connect with the material and confirm your audition, you should show your commitment from the very beginning of the process by preparing for the audition. So many times I've heard actors say, 'I didn't read the script because I had four other auditions today.' That's like going on a first date and saying, 'I would've showered but I had a couple of dates earlier.'" **Mark Paladini**

"Actors need to realize that [although] you may be the single best thing since sliced bread, the director loves you, the casting director wants to marry you, and the producer is about to call his real estate broker for that $11 million house in the hills [that sometimes] the *creative executive* doesn't 'get you' and the casting director has to start all over again. The lousiest actor in your acting class—the one with acne, bad hair, horrid breath, who won't even make his own funeral on time—will get the job because the same *creative executive* thinks that he's 'it.' So, you go home and cry and want to move back to the city from which you came and become an assistant manger at your local Home Depot. But you can't. Because as an actor, you have to keep trying. You have to understand that even if you didn't get the job, the casting director will remember you and push you and insist that smart people hire you because you have talent." **Matthew Barry**

"Pilot season is like [Las] Vegas. It's the one time of year when, all of a sudden, there are more slot machines available for you [as an actor] to play on. Anyone can hit it big. Even the little old lady sitting next to you can land a pilot. If you don't hit the jackpot this time, you know there is always next year. Hopefully, you'll be a more experienced player by then." **Patrick Baca**

"If casting sees a million people and [the pilot] is still not cast, it may work in your favor to go in at the end of their casting process, because at least they've narrowed their choices down and they have probably defined what they really want. The good news is, some things don't happen for a reason—and better, more exciting things come to you unexpectedly: you weren't right for that part, they write you a new part, the writer-producer remembers you on the next project he is doing, someone is having dinner with someone who is having trouble with casting and someone remembers and recommends you, whatever. So always do your best with integrity, commitment, your word. Never take anything personally—and don't forget to bring a cookie to the casting director if you have an appointment at 4 p.m. Chances are, they will need sugar and a good latte to make it through the night!" **Elisa Goodman**

Casting Director / Agent
Cold Reading Workshops
and
Prepared Scene Showcases

• **Showcase workshops give actors an opportunity** and a place to show themselves to people in the industry. Yes, they cost money, but so does everything else you do to promote yourself. Consider showcase costs as marketing expenditures. If you don't have very many credits and don't know many casting people or agents, promotion is the name of the game. I landed my first agent at a "prepared scenes" showcase. I was called in and cast for a situation comedy by a casting director I had met at a cold reading workshop a year-and-a-half before.

• **For a great story of how Casting Director Workshops can help a career,** go to www.itaproductions.com, read the statement, click to enter, click on "Spotlight On Success" then click on Kathyrn Joosten, and read why this successful, working actress continues to attend these workshops.

• **Good things do happen from casting director workshops and show-cases,** but you can't count on anything except getting to act for a few minutes. That, in essence, is what you are paying for. If you are in a play, it is very hard to get a casting director or agent to come see the play. It will cost you to send out your flyers, do follow up calls and offer free seats that you often pay for. It seems like the unknown actor is always paying to be seen. It is one of the facts of our lives. I believe we must make peace with it or ignore the whole thing. It is not valuable to fight it or be angry over the situation.

• **Cold reading casting director** or agent showcases usually cost $25 to $40 each. The casting director brings in sides (part of the script you will read from) for a show they've cast and assigns a part and a partner to you. You then have about twenty minutes to rehearse your scene. I strongly suggest you rehearse on your own first. Decide the given circumstances, what the script tells you about the scene, and what your character needs and wants. Then rehearse with your partner. Most of the actors will pretty well memorize their lines, they will look at the script very few times while performing the scene for the casting director.

• **The term "cold reading" is not an accurate description** of what you are doing. You are giving a warm reading. A cold reading means performing the scene as you are reading it for the first time. Under a true audition situation, you have your script the day before an audition and are expected to give a finished, polished, opening night performance in the office of the person or people you are auditioning for. In the workshop atmosphere the casting director knows you have only had about twenty minutes to make your acting choices.

• **I personally believe** you should feel pretty confident about your cold readings before being seen at a showcase. Learn about the acting of audition material from your acting teachers, have a few auditions, land a few roles and then show yourself to casting directors at showcase workshops. When you have acting experience, the casting director will have more to work with and will remember you as a good actor.

• **Sharon Lawrence of *NYPD Blue*** said when she first came to town she did casting director workshops. She chose the casting directors very carefully; picking shows she felt she would be right for. Sharon met casting director Junie Lowry Johnson's assistant, they called her and she booked a guest star spot on the series *Civil Wars*. When a part came up for a district attorney on *NYPD Blue*, Junie remembered her and brought her in for the interview. She was cast and then became a regular for several seasons.

• **Rebecca McFarland** was one of George's girlfriends on **Seinfeld**. It was her fourth Los Angeles job. She had moved here the year before with a college degree, many theater credits and SAG eligible. A friend asked Rebecca to audition with him for an agent he wanted—the agent took her and not him. She performs at a casting showcase each Tuesday night, sending a picture postcard in advance to the casting director she's meeting. Showcasing has helped her get to know casting directors and they know she will audition well.

• **Casting director's jobs depend on bringing in actors that read well.** I think you can also get a good return for your money by attending a casting director's own workshop for a month or six weeks. They will get to know you better because you worked with them over several weeks.

• **I know many experienced actors,** including myself, who have landed roles from both types of showcases. Again—go, watch and decide for yourself where your showcase dollars will be spent most wisely.

• **One of my students sends a picture, resume and short note** to the casting director before he does a showcase, typically saying, "I'm looking forward to meeting you at such and such showcase."

• **Actress Stacey Smithey, who is very ambitious** and active in promoting her career, sent me the following report about doing a three-night prepared scene showcase with the Actor's Showcase Company. (*Also see what Stacey has to say about producing your own projects*)

> • **It is a very pricey showcase,** $795 per person, but I think it's worth it. It is held at the Stella Adler Theatre at Hollywood and Highland. Each scene is five minutes long and introduced by the host. I liked that I knew who was there and exactly what they thought. They hold showcases every three months and you have to audition to get in. I know they turn away a lot of actors.
>
> • **To audition, you bring in a monologue** or they have you do a cold reading from their material. I did a cold reading and they called me the next day to let me know I was in. When you are chosen, the company pairs you up; I really loved my partner. You can, however, bring in your own partner as long as you both audition and are accepted. You choose the material—one pair even wrote original material.
>
> • **You really need to direct yourself** and be fully prepared. The coordinator of the event will also direct you and add input. There are two rehearsals before the event. One is acting oriented, you get one hour with the director. The director was great, but you don't have the luxury of time in this process. The second rehearsal is tech oriented. The whole show is run with scene changes, lighting, and

the host introducing the scenes. The tech rehearsal was the same day as the first performance. The acting rehearsal was the night before the first performance. So, as I said, you have to be on your toes and know your scene! The rest of the rehearsals with your acting partner are on your own. There were 13 scenes, a total of 26 actors.

- **The showcase went really well.** Every night was standing room only. There were 60+ industry guests: agents, managers, and casting directors. High caliber guests give written critiques of the scenes. They also indicate if they want you to follow up with them via phone, mail, or reel. I got called in after the first night by Rick Millikan to read for *Sabrina The Teenage Witch*. So, that was very rewarding.

- **Some of the guests were from:** GVA, NBC Casting, Jeff Greenberg Casting, Rick Millikan, Valorie Massalas Casting, The Blake Agency, The Chasin Agency, The Artists Group, Abrams, Paul Kohner Agency, TEG, Braverman Bloom, Levinson/Arvold Casting, Brillstein Grey, Zanuck Passon and Pace, Gersh, KSA, Commercials Unlimited, AKA, The Geddes Agency, GEM, Big Ticket TV, BBA, Valko Miller Casting, Identity, and some others.

- **A theatrical agent talks about the value of cold reading workshops with casting directors.**

  - **When your agent sends your picture and resume to a casting director,** that casting director may have received 700-2,000 submissions for the same role. First, they bring in who their bosses told them to. The second group of actors are friends who could do the job. The third group are professionals who work all the time who they know can do that job. And the last person is the unknown picture in the pile that they have no knowledge of. My feeling is, you can jump from kindergarten to first grade if you can do the cold reading workshops with the casting director. I think they're extremely valuable for the good actor. Out of 16-20 people they see in a workshop, they're looking for the gem. If you're very good, they're going to remember you. You've now put yourself past the picture and resume that's been put across their desk by an agent. You're now a human being and they know a little bit about you.

- **Beware of scams when looking into showcases.** There are some unethical people who call actors that have submitted their pictures to casting directors. The actors are told, "You need to showcase with me in order to work." Do not accept phone calls from people you have not submitted to, who say they don't know how they got your picture or who gave it to them. *Please see the Section on Scams.*

Resources

• PREPARED SCENE SHOWCASES

The Actors Showcase Company, 323/650-1294. 3940 Laurel Canyon Blvd., #675, Studio City, 91604. Email: actorshowcase@covad.net. They hold showcases presenting prepared scenes four times a year for an Industry audience. They bring in a minimum of 50 to 60 pre-announced A level Agents, Managers, Producers, Directors and Casting Directors to see and give written critique and feedback of the work. *See Stacey Smithey's comments above.*

The Showcase Company, Directed by Scott Sedita. Scott Sedita Acting Studios, 323/465-6152. www.scottseditaacting.com. 526 N. Larchmont Blvd., Los Angeles, 90004. $600 for a 12-week course for actors wanting theatrical representation. Direction by Scott to find and develop two scenes (Comedic/Dramatic) tailored to showcase the actor's unique talents. Rigorous rehearsal and input from guest teachers will culminate in a professional industry showcase which includes at least 15 top industry professionals. Limited to 14 and admittance is only through audition.

SAG & AFTRA members are eligible for the union showcases. Usually several casting directors attend these monthly showcases. You can perform once every six months. For AFTRA, request the casting showcase registration card from the membership counter (10-4:30) or call 323/634-8100. For information on the SAG showcases call 323/549-6540.

• COLD READING SHOWCASES

Following have good reputations. Please investigate carefully; reputations can change. Check out others in Back Stage West *and* The Working Actor's Guide.

Act Now!, office: 818/840-2795. www.actnownetwork.com. 1907 West Burbank Blvd, 91506. Their audition process consists of three cold readings by appointment only. $40 per session. Directors, agents and casting directors. Staff provides ongoing guidance and support to help each actor set and meet their professional goals. They are also in compliance with the LAAWC guidelines.

The Actor Site, JP Turnbolt 818/762-2800. www.actorsite.com. 5652 Cahuenga Blvd., North Hollywood, 91601 Seattle agent Carlyne Grager highly recommends this showcase for the actors she represents when they move to Los Angeles. You must audition for the showcase. Showcasing is just a small part of the services they offer for actors.

Casting Network, office: 818/980-6980. www.castingnetwork.net. Free orientations & cold reading auditions. 818/788-4792. Showcases are at La Bella Center, 12500 Riverside Dr., #202, Studio City, 91607. $30 per session, discount when you buy a series. Many sessions a week. Directors, agents and casting directors. Call for their brochure. Strong acting background and/or union affiliation required. They are affiliated with the LA Actors Coalition certified by the Labor Board of California.

Casting Break, 818/990-9994. www.thecastingbreak.com. 11965 Ventura Blvd., Studio City, 91604. Actors are given the choice of a cold reading, prepared monologue or scene. Casting directors, producers, directors and agents lead workshops. Individual workshops are $35 each; 6 workshops, $150; 10 workshops, $200; 20 workshops, $300; They only take trained actors; your first workshop is your audition. They are affiliated with the LA Actors Coalition certified by the Labor Board of California.

In the Act, 310 281-7772. www.itaproductions.com. 10015 Venice Blvd. LA, 90034. Audition required. There is a $45 processing new member fee for those accepted. This also gives you your own web page on www.casting911.com for one year. Regular priced workshops: $32. Series package available, six workshops for $162. They are affiliated with the LA Actors Coalition certified by the Labor Board of California

Now Casting / LA Actors Online, 818/841-7165. www.nowcasting.com. 60 E. Magnolia, Burbank, 91502. Auditing of one individual workshop available free of charge. (Observance only for audited workshop) Cold Reading audition required to participate. They occasionally offer free showcases. Average cost is $24. Now Casing/LAAO has a disclaimer form that every member is required to sign before taking a workshop there. This workshop is run by a good show business/networking organization. Members may receive a discount.

One On One, 818/789-3399. www.oneononeproductions.com . 13261 Moorpark St., Suite 202, Sherman Oaks. Office hours: M-F 11-5. Average $28, special for series. Audition required, they are held each Wednesday between 1-3:30, no appointment necessary. Guests include casting directors, agents, directors and producers. They are affiliated with the LA Actors Coalition certified by the Labor Board of California.

Reel Pros, 818/788-4133. www.reelpros.com. 13437 Ventura Blvd., Ste.220 Sherman Oaks. "The Workshop for Professional Talent." Run by actors, for actors. They are affiliated with the Coalition certified by the Labor Board of California. They take great pride in the showcase and have a very careful audition process. Workshop price varies, but starts at $29. They also offer series packages.

• *For Audition Material and Cold Reading Teachers, see Section One.*

NUDITY,
THE CASTING COUCH
AND SEXUAL ORIENTATION

NUDITY REQUIRED

• **Julia Roberts, John Travolta, Sandra Bullock, Cameron Diaz,** Freddie Prinze Jr., Sarah Jessica Parker, Sarah Michelle Gellar all put no-nudity clauses in their contracts. Many actresses use black electrician tape on their breasts so the camera operators won't shoot what they're not supposed to. Geena Davis advises, "If there are parts of you that you don't want the crew to see make sure the tape is very visible."

• **If you play a leading actress** you will most likely need to make the decision of whether or not you will do nudity in your career and under what circumstances. Diane Lane in *Unfaithful* and Kathy Bates in *About Schmidt* were nominated for 2002 Oscars. Christina Ricci in *Prozac Nation*, said it was "really difficult." Jenny McCarthy has built a career using her Playboy centerfold as a launching pad, although now she says she won't do nudity. Darryl Hannah and Jamie Lee Curtis both made the transition from nudity-required "B" movies to big budget mainstream films. In Debra Winger's first movie, she had her top off *(Slumber Party '57)*. Sylvester Stallone was nude in *The Italian Stallion*, a low-budget soft-porn movie. Many actors have appeared nude, yet they haven't hurt their careers—in fact they may have propelled them: Richard Gere in *American Gigolo,* Minnie Driver in *The Governess*, Camryn Manheim in *The Road To Wellsville,* Tim Curry in *The Rocky Horror Picture Show,* Isabella Rossellini in *Blue Velvet,* Natassia Kinski in *Cat People*, Glenn Close in *The Big Chill*, Kim Basinger in *9 1/2 Weeks*, Sharon Stone in

Basic Instinct, Emma Thompson in *The Tall Guy*, Heather Graham in *Boogie Nights* and others. Holly Hunter won the 1993 Oscar for *The Piano* where she had a beautiful nude love scene and Harvey Keitel exposed his penis. There are some roles where a body double was used. Jane Fonda in *Coming Home* and Julia Roberts in *Pretty Woman* used body doubles.

• **There are the low-budget**, teen-exploitation, horror or comedy movies. Often, an actress' career can get locked in this genre and—because they have done one or two—that's how they will be cast. The producer will say, "You did it for that movie, so you have to do it for mine." Elizabeth Berkley got typecast after she did *Showgirls* in 1995.

• **If you never want authentic nude pictures of your body on the internet**, then never allow yourself to be photographed nude. Alyssa Milano, Pamela Anderson and Dr. Laura Schlessinger went through law suits because old boyfriends had sold shots of them nude. Leonardo DiCaprio sued *Playgirl* because they used frames of his nude butt from his movie *Total Eclipse*. Charlize Theron's pictures ended up in *Playboy* because she had signed a release for pictures taken for her portfolio before she was famous.

• **Once you consent to work nude**, it is very difficult to take the decision back. Matthew McConaughey posed with his girlfriend in the nude in exchange for a few roles of headshots for acting pictures. When Matthew became a big hit, the photographer threatened to sell the photos. Beginning bids were half a million dollars. Remember the Vanessa Williams scandal—losing the Miss America crown because of the *Penthouse* magazine pictures? She survived and has gone on to become a major singer-actress. When Suzanne Somers was at the height of her sitcom success with *Three's Company*, *Playboy* ran pictures that she had modeled for when she needed money to raise her son. What is there to consider in making the decision? If it's a strong moral dilemma, don't compromise yourself. If it is not a moral issue, discuss it with your agent or manager in relation to your career. If you choose to do it, the things you have to consider are:

> • Are you able to be nude in front of the cast and crew of a movie set?
> • Will the scenes be shot in a tasteful way?
> • Is the nudity important to the story line or there just for the sake of nudity?
> • Videotapes and DVDs of your movies will live forever.
> • The time it will take to keep your body looking great.
> • Be honest with yourself; come to a decision you can live with.

• **I was director Joan Darling's assistant** when she directed William Katt and Susan Dey in their first nude love scenes in the feature film, *First Love.* Joan, a wonderfully sensitive director, discussed the design and choreography of each move. After the first day of shooting, the actors seemed to get used to it. They were both beautiful and in full body make up. After a week, cast and crew were all very bored and eager to get them out of bed and on to the rest of the shooting.

• **Olivia d'Abo** discussed her role with Armin Muller Stahl in *The Last Good Time.*

> • **After the film was edited,** the director asked me to reshoot the scene of me walking out of the bathroom and this time actually dropping the towel so the audience could see what Armin was reacting to. I decided that it was important to the film. When nudity is totally organic and motivated by the scene and the actor is comfortable within their own skin and vulnerable in that moment, it works.

• **I asked Olivia about having love scenes with such an older man.** She said, "He's got baby's eyes, it made me want to mother him, to take care of him." She also talked of her deep respect for him as an actor. These feelings also parallel the plot of the film.

• **Winona Ryder, Meg Ryan, Julia Roberts and Alicia Silverstone** have always refused to work nude.

• **Liv Tyler removed her top in** *Stealing Beauty,* but declined to do so in *Onegin.*

• **Leonardo DiCaprio;** *Total Eclipse* and *The Beach.* "Nudity is really tough but you have to do it if it's part of the film."

• **Mira Sorvino was nude in** *At First Sight.* When asked about it on Entertainment Tonight she said, "Have a sense of humor about it. Trust the people you are working with and have a generally good atmosphere on the set."

• **Daryl Hannah hid behind hair extensions in** *Splash.* She said, "If there was a role I really wanted to play and that was the only way I could get it, hell, I'd do it. Though I would really rather not."

• **Nicole Kidman and Iain Glen were both naked on stage** in New York doing the play *Blue Room.* Iain did nude cartwheels. *People* magazine asked Iain, "How did the decision to appear naked come about?"

• We shook hands and said, "I'll do it if you do it." And that's when we went for it, really. It's a very strange feeling being naked. It does make you feel vulnerable. But the thing that grounds us is trying to be inside the scene so that it's not about a thousand people watching you but one person—the character—watching you.

• **Bridget Fonda's first film was a** NYU **film,** *Aria.* There were 10 different directors directing 10 minute segments based on opera arias. There was no dialogue, just nudity and death. She "went for it all, first time out."

• **Gwyneth Paltrow says she used a body double** in a brief strip scene in *Great Expectations* because, "I would have had to not wear a bra, and I just didn't want to do that in front of the crew."

• **Angela Bassett says she was asked to undress** for *How Stella Got Her Groove Back.* She decided to keep her private parts private. That way, the audience "can put their own ideas of love and sensuality into it."

• **Halle Berry,** was lying facedown naked in *Introducing Dorothy Dandridge.* When asked if it was a body double or her body she said, "I'm not really comfortable with nudity in films. I doubt I'll do it again, but because that is how Dorothy was found dead, to stay true to history, I had to do it." She of course did do it again for *Swordfish* and her Oscar winning performance in *Monster's Ball.*

• **Sally Field** said in an Actors' Studio interview: "What is the big deal about taking your clothes off? It's about the acting work."

• **Holly Hunter** in an Actor's Studio interview, when asked what it was like to do the sex scenes in *The Piano.*

  • **Very easy. The sex scenes became integral to the story**. It was necessary to the movie to see the unveiling of those characters. No big deal— by then the crew were all family.

• **Julianne Moore was asked** in the *Los Angeles Times* how her family dealt with the many times she has done nudity, especially in *Boogie Nights.*

  • **My mother has always said, "I'd much rather see you naked than dead."** It's funny, but it's true. What's really disturbing, when you look at a movie, is seeing a dead body. But how scary is it to see your daughter walk across a room with no clothes on? Not very. But if you see her shot up a million times or have her head cut off, that's scary.

• **You just hope you're in a situation that's safe.** I did a nude scene in *Body of Evidence* that was just awful. I was too young to know better. It was the first time I'd been asked to get naked and it turned out to be completely extraneous and gratuitous. Ugh. It was a terrible film and a terrible performance by me. It was about nothing, and I didn't need to be doing it.

• **Ashley Judd** said that she won her applause prior to filming a lengthy nude scene. She arrived on the set in a robe and blithely announced, "Hi, I'm Ashley and I'm going to be nude for the next 12 hours. I'm not embarrassed and I hope you won't be either." The actress then dropped her robe and said, "This is my body." The ovation swelled.

• **Faye Dunaway,** in an Actors' Studio interview.

  • **What is really difficult is to reveal your soul,** your pain, your vulnerability. That's what has to happen, no matter whether you have clothes on or not. Nudity comes with the territory of movies. The actual clothes on or off is less important than the emotional nudity. In bed usually exposes moments of extreme vulnerability and openness— that's what is difficult.

• **Jennifer Jason Leigh says:**

  • **I don't have a problem with nudity** if I think it moves the story forward and says something about the character. But no matter how truthfully and honestly it's portrayed, it still seems to bother people.

• **Kate Winslet, when asked how comfortable she was** with her first nude scene in *Jude,* said:

  • **Not at all! No way! Oh, it was awful.** I was so nervous, I starved myself for a month beforehand. I went through all the paranoias: "My bum's massive. My breasts are saggy. I've got a spotty back. Chicken arms. I can't do it." I just had to keep remembering that the scene was a real turning point in the story and to get on with it. At the end of the day, you forget that you're completely naked.

• **Stephanie Stephenson,** after landing a choice role in the touring production of the Broadway musical *Les Miserables*, quit the next day when she learned she would also have to play a prostitute in an ensemble scene.

• **I have a friend who is very cute.** His first day on the set in his first starring role in a Showtime movie, he was required to be completely nude, making love with Laura Boyle. They didn't know each other and, right off the bat, they were both totally nude and in bed. He said it was uncomfortable but got on with the task and was proud of his work. Incidently, he is gay; but this was an acting job, not a date.

• **Nudity can be a perfectly wonderful part of artistic expression,** or it can be in poor taste and a career risk. It is such a personal decision—I suggest you search and follow your heart. Trust your educated instincts. *See manager Tami Lynn's remarks in the chapter on Personal Managers.*

CASTING COUCH

• **The so-called casting couch still exists.** There are people who will promise actors roles in film and television in exchange for their bodies and there are actors who will go for it. There are also actors who will make the offer first. Sometimes it works—the actor gets a job, but most often the actor gets no job, loss of self-respect and loss of reputation (a fragile commodity when you're trying to build a career.) I've seen actors waste enormous amounts of time trying to take this way to a career that resulted in one or two minor jobs and loads of broken promises.

• **Be honest with yourself**—have a fling if you choose because you think it might be fun and worth the risks, but don't fool yourself. With very few exceptions, the "casting couch" has not been a winning journey.

• **There are SAG regulations governing franchised agents** or sub-agents which make it a violation as a condition of representation "to request of an actor a nude or semi-nude interview, or to request that an actor engage in sexual activity." Any breach of this regulation should be reported immediately to SAG.

• **Three actors accused a writer** on the old *Arsenio Hall Show* of fondling their buttocks and genitals during an audition. These men had been called in for a skit spoofing Thighmasters. They claimed in a Superior Court lawsuit that the writer fondled their buttocks after each removed his pants and underwear during one-on-one auditions.

• **Agent Bonnie Howard of Howard Talent West** received a package addressed to "Mr. Howard." In it was a pair of sexy, new panties, a piece of candy, a condom and a letter requesting an interview.

• **Talent agent Wallace Kaye was tried**, found guilty and sentenced to five years and four months in jail for sexual attacks on eleven aspiring actresses and models ranging in age from 20 to 35. He would engage them in various improvisational scenes that were sexual in nature. The "auditions" were scheduled in the early morning or late evening behind locked doors. At a certain point in the scenes, he would force himself on them, putting his tongue in their mouths, fondle and kiss their breasts, grab their buttocks—all while they were physically restrained.

• **The law says that sexual harassment exists** when attention is unwanted or unwelcome. The moment your relationship with someone changes for you, and you say so, you are a victim of sexual harassment if that attention continues.

• **Sidney Poitier** advised Denzel Washington at the beginning of his career: "Be very careful of how you start in Hollywood. The first two, three or four movies will determine how the town looks at you. The choices you make then will affect the rest of your career."

• **Eve Brandstein**, producer, casting director and author of *The Actor: A Practical Guide To A Professional Career*, was a guest on my cable show. One of my students at the time, Cynthia Geary *(Northern Exposure)*, asked:

Q: Does the casting couch exist?

• **There is something like that going on all the time.** The casting couch exists in life, not just in a casting director or producer's office. This particular profession you're involved in is a very seductive profession. I believe what an actor brings to the audition or to the interview or movie is a certain amount of sexual energy, the creativity, charisma, beauty, the specialness of the person. You have to use that to make your work great, and that is sexy and at the same time you're trying not to be seductive. So you're doing two things—you're sending the message "Pay attention. Hey, how do I look? Do you notice me?" So there is something confusing; some people get mixed messages. Then there's the good old fashioned situation where you're attractive to somebody or you find them attractive. By the way, the casting couch goes both ways; it can be a two-way experience. Nobody is an unwilling victim.

• **Bottom line is it's a personal decision.** I recommend you walk out of the room if somebody's putting the make on you as an actor. I don't think it's worth the risk. A lot of times it turns out to be a very bad thing for the actor. The person in power is certainly less at risk. If you feel you're being harassed or asked to do something that is obviously inappropriate for that interview or that audition that deals with your sexuality, I say get out of the room as politely and nicely as you can. Do not be offensive; leave. You are dealing with someone who has problems you do not understand and it could possibly even turn against you. Leave but follow it up. Make sure your agent knows. Report it to someone.

• **A young actor I know arrived in town from Texas** with a list from his teacher of a few people to look up. I was one of them. We met and he enrolled in class. Three days later, I got a call from him. He was ready to leave town. He had met with a casting director who was on his list and the man was very nice and helpful. He asked the actor to pick him up at his home to go out to dinner to talk further about his career. The actor was very pleased to be having dinner with this well-respected person in the industry within his first week of hitting town.

• **During dinner, the casting director** spoke of specific actors he knew who were not gay but had sex with male casting directors in order to land their roles. My friend was shocked at the conversation and revelation and said he could never do anything like that. When they arrived back at the casting director's home, he invited the actor in to pick up some scenes to practice with. When they got inside, the actor stayed for a time talking, still reveling in being in this man's company. Eventually the man put on a porno tape and tried to seduce him. The actor fled, didn't sleep that night and called me early in the morning. I pointed out that perhaps he had been too nice during the dinner conversation when his instincts sensed it was going in a sexual direction. I also pointed out the casting director was wrong to take advantage of his profession in trying to seduce him. To give the casting director a break (a very big break), perhaps he felt the actor was hanging around waiting to be hit on.

• **It's been ten years since this incident** and the young actor has gone on to a very nice career in all areas of our business and may be on his way to stardom. I'm sure he smiles now at his naivete.

• **Make the decision as to how far you will go sexually** to land a part before you are in a situation where you must decide in the moment. Most actors have never faced a casting couch situation; I hope you never do. I hope it's always your talent, look and personality they want.

SEXUAL ORIENTATION

• **I believe in freedom of choice in matters of personal sexuality.** "To thine ownself be true." However, if an actor is perceived as gay due to certain types of mannerisms, this can be limiting to the actor's castability in certain types of roles.

• **On my cable show, an actor asked Eve Brandstein:**

Q: How do you advise actors who are gay in how honest they should be with their agents and casting directors?

> • It depends; I certainly don't think it's something you have to bring up since it's a personal issue in a very professional circumstance. If an actor has heard that they are perceived as gay, it may create a closing-in of how they'll be cast. If you don't want your casting possibilities perhaps narrowed, it's perfectly okay to make a decision and adjust to how you are perceived.

• **I would like to add to Eve's comments** that an actor must always be working on their image and must understand it is important to learn how you are being perceived. It's hard to look at ourselves honestly, but it's necessary.

• **An actor once came to me for private coaching** because he had accidently overheard the people in his theater group laughing and talking about him, saying he would be foolish to think he would be considered for a certain role because he was so obviously gay. The actor didn't understand what this meant. When he told me the story, he was choking back his tears. He had left the company and had been off sulking for a few weeks but then decided to face the truth of how he was being perceived.

• **When I met him, he did display mannerisms** that were probably inappropriate for the wide range of roles he was physically "right" for. The fact that he actually was not gay had nothing to do with his image problem. When we got on camera, he talked and walked and did some of his stand-up comedy act. Then I played back the tape so he could observe himself. He quickly developed an understanding of his own body language and appearance and was able to adjust his physical expression to create a more effective image. I saw him a few years later. He was fine and had gone on to a wonderful working career. While gay actors certainly play powerful, masculine roles, no actor can get such specific roles without the appropriate image.

• **Another actor was sent to me by a commercial casting director** who said "The actor is wonderful but with his mannerisms, he will never land a commercial." This actor happened to be gay, but the concern to me was not sexual orientation, but rather the actor's physical believability playing certain types of characters. After studying and analyzing the way he came across, he made some adjustments which improved his castability in a wider range of roles for his physical type. Within a year, he had landed eight commercials and continues to have a very lucrative commercial career.

• **What about playing a homosexual?** You and your agent must decide what's best for your career. You must decide if you can be comfortable showing affection in or out of bed with a person of the same sex if the script calls for it. Also, you must consider the idea of being typecast. Tom Hanks won the Oscar for *Philadelphia*, playing a gay man dying of aids. Hal Holbrook played a homosexual father in *That Certain Summer*; Matthew Broderick in *Torch Song Trilogy*, Aidan Quinn in the television movie, *An Early Frost*. William Hurt won the Academy Award for *Kiss Of The Spider Woman*. Will Smith *(Fresh Prince)* played a gay man in *Six Degrees of Separation*, but refused to do the sex kiss as it was written in the script, so they used a camera angle that looked like they kissed. These roles certainly didn't hurt the actors, but all of them had previously played roles as straight men.

• **More roles are opening up for men and women gay characters.** Ellen "came out" on her show. *Will and Grace* is a hit.

• **Agent Bonnie Howard went to a play,** *Bar Girls,* in which all the characters were lesbians—very sexually explicit. One of the women was seeking representation and asked to meet her. Bonnie assumed she was gay. She said, "No, I'm an actress." Bonnie signed her on the spot because she had been so convincing.

• **You do not have to divulge your sexual orientation;** it is nobody's business. You are an actor, and if you wish to play gay and straight characters, it is your choice.

WORKING ON THE SET

See On-The-Set Glossary of Terms on my website, www.JudyKerr.com.

• Katharine Graham said it best, "To love what you do and feel that it matters...how can anything be more fun."

• **First and most important, you have the job.** It is yours. You might as well act on that instead of thinking, "Oh no! Someone is going to take this away from me." Yes, it can happen sometimes actors are replaced because after casting, someone (producer, director, etc.) changes their concept of the character.

• **One day on *Seinfeld*,** all the actors and crew were on a New York Street rehearsing a scene. A guest actor was back on the stage complaining, wondering how long he was going to be there, generally pestering the 2nd AD. Jerry happened to hear over the walkie-talkies that there was a problem. He called the line producer, asked her to fire the actor and call casting to bring in someone else. The next season, this actor was the star of his own show and all the gossip was how horrible he was to work with. His show lasted just one season.

• **So yes, your worst fears are possible**—you can lose the job. But the odds are in your favor that you will do the job. Let go of the idea that somehow you won't live up to the role and that you can't deliver what is necessary. You can do it like no one else in the world can. So to say it again: The job is yours. Use your energy in *how* to do the job, not in fear of not being able to do it. Make that role come to life through you.

• **Fear starts with a "what if" thought.** You can stop making up the fear thoughts. Create thoughts of how wonderful you are going to be. "I'm going to be totally satisfied with my performance." Fear is a misuse of your imagination. Wait till the bad things happen, then worry.

• **Jerry Seinfeld told a good/bad story on the set one day.** The first sitcom he was hired on as a regular was *Benson*. When he came to the set for the table reading of the fourth show he would be shooting, the assistant director called him over and said they had forgotten to call him and tell him he was fired. He had to leave the stage. He said, "That is when I knew I had to have my own show, so that could never happen to me again."

• **When doing a situation comedy,** there will be a table reading. If you have a significant role, you will be at the reading. Prepare for it like you did for your audition. If you can't get the script the night before, see what time you can pick it up from the office. Go sit in your car or the commissary and mark your script and rehearse your role. The writers need to hear you deliver the lines so they can see what works. Dress close to what you wore for the audition and look like you looked when they gave you the job. You are the guest; you want everyone to see why you were cast.

• **In order to study the finest of sitcom acting,** tape *Seinfeld* reruns. Each of the characters have a different form of comedy. Study how they deliver the lines, notice how it is not about the line, but the delivery. Of course, *Seinfeld* also had brilliant writers.

• **Bobbie Eakes of *The Bold and the Beautiful* was a student of mine** when she first moved here. She had been Miss Georgia. Being cast on the daytime drama was one of her first acting jobs. She was on the show for 10 years, she talks about when she first started.

   • **The main thing for me when I was starting out and still very green,** was you fake it. You try to let them think you are completely confident even if you are nervous because they just want to know that you are going to be able to take the ball and run with it and do your job. Just try to be confident or exude confidence even if you are not.

• **For your first time working on a set,** here are a few hard and fast rules that cannot be broken:

• **If you accept a job, you must show up on time** and you must stay there until you are told you can leave or at wrap time. Always report to the Assistant Director when you arrive and when you leave the set for any reason. Sign out with the A.D. at the end of the day.

• **Being on time can be a chore.** Make a trial run before the first day if possible. Check out where the parking will be. If you are going on location there should be a map attached to the call sheet. If you are not on the set, have them fax it to you or your copy service where you receive faxes. You will probably have a ten or fifteen minute walk to the set from your car—wear comfortable shoes to get there. You may be delayed checking through security at the studio gate. Allow yourself the longest time it could take to get to the set, not the shortest.

• **Never look directly in the camera**; never talk or move when they have called "rolling" unless you are in the scene. Talk very quietly on the set, even when the camera is not rolling.

• **Never walk through a door** when a red light is on; it means the camera is rolling/shooting.

• **If you have an injury**, do not leave the set without reporting it to an assistant director. This happened to me. My finger was broken. I didn't realize it because I had been acting and the adrenaline was going. Luckily, the makeup person insisted I report it. Surgery was required to correct the break, which would have been very expensive if I hadn't reported it on the job.

• **When you are shooting you must focus** all your concentration on your acting work. You will be getting direction of where to hit your mark, you have to keep track of an activity you are doing to make sure you do the same thing on every take so the editor can cut in and out of takes. This may be your toughest assignment, there is usually so much activity going on around you.

• **Buy the book,** *The Camera Smart Actor* by Richard Brestoff. Read it the night before every new job. Take it with you, if you get scared and feel like you don't know what you are doing you can read it in your dressing room.

• **Michael Richards, Kramer on** *Seinfeld*, in an interview with the *Los Angeles Times* said,

> • **It is hard work. Deep down I always enjoy the process,** but I find you have to work very hard to get to the moments where you surprise yourself—spontaneous moments where something comes through that wasn't in the script, the table reading or any discussions. That's always exciting. It feels holy.

• **Mira Sorvino said in an interview,**

> • **I was absolutely neurotic doing** *Mighty Aphrodite.* Every night brought a new nervous breakdown. I'd cry and talk to God, I was so nervous. Then the next day, I'd show up and do my scenes.

• **In an interview in the** *Hollywood Reporter* the three following actors talked of what it takes to deliver on the set.

> • **Robbie Benson:** At a moment's notice, you can be transformed into another world. Ten seconds before the director says "Action!" you are yourself, yet with that one word, you put your entire soul into what you're playing. It becomes an obsession, especially when it works and you know that it's working. You realize that your performance contributed to the film in that one moment. Even if they cut it, you think about that one moment that works. That moment carries you through all the bad moments. It's like baseball and that one perfect crack of the bat. You're going to keep swinging to hear that crack once more.

> • **Rutger Hauer:** Actors make films for the same reason people go to see them—it's a chance to share the dream, the drama, the comedy, the horror, the fantasy of life. The audience wants to buy it and we want to give it. The key element is "Don't act." The moment the camera comes on, the moment it starts to roll, the actor's third eye goes into focus and he or she begins to live the part.

> • **Susan Blakely:** Besides knowing your craft, there should be the ability to be spontaneous, to be intuitive, to feel how much you are projecting in front of the camera compared to what you project in real life. The spontaneity is so important, especially in television because you don't do much rehearsing, if any. You need to be open and loose so you can change things and react at the right moment. The best actors are able to be creative on their feet.

• **When you are the star of a project you will set the tone** for the whole on-set family. I admire the actors who show up on time and ready to go; it is rude to be late, to keep sixty people waiting for you.

• **In television there will be times** when, as a guest, you won't be able to rehearse with the star because they don't want to work that hard any more. Give it your all, when rehearsing with the stand-ins. Don't let a situation like this hurt your shot on that show.

• **Gossip—the crew is full of it,** and when you are a guest you will be the target of some of it. There is so much empty time to pass and people who have been together for a long time have talked about everything there is to talk about so they are looking for anything new. Try to be a welcome addition to every set you go on.

• **Members of the crew often don't understand the way actors work.** They can't understand why you don't hit your mark and say your lines perfectly every time so they can go home. Don't look to them to judge how your acting truly is. The director and other actors can be trusted much more, although you may not get feedback.

• **Director Jim Burrows,** who's directed *Cheers, Frasier, Friends, Caroline in the City, 3rd Rock From the Sun, Will and Grace,* and many others, is said to hug everyone before the shooting of every show.

• **Director Robert Altman** was asked, how do actors act? He responded:

> • **They bring their personality to it.** Anybody can do this; it's just if they will. They can act if they get past that barrier of self-consciousness. All the experience you need is in your head. If they have the opportunity to do it and they have the confidence, they can break that shell and let the truth of themselves show. It's all in everybody's mind, it's in everybody's computer. We all sit there and say, "I'd do this or I'd do that"...that's all it is.

• **Steven Spielberg asked Dee Wallace Stone** why actors get so weird on the set. She gave him this explanation:

> • **Actors are like race horses**; they are trained to get in the starting gate and go. When in hair, makeup, and wardrobe, they are getting ready and when the gate doesn't open for five hours, they get worn out.

• **William H. Macy,** when asked if there was such a thing as overpreparing, told *Back Stage West*:

> • **Perhaps not over-preparing, but useless preparation.** I've been guilty of it, and I think many actors are. You're going to play the Pope, and so you start trying to figure out, What does it mean to be the Pope? What does the Pope read? What was the Pope's childhood like? What does the Pope do when he prays? And I think the mature actor ultimately realizes, There's no way I can know any of that, and even if I did know it, there's no way I can act on it. I *am* the Pope—end of story. So that ends my preparation. Sure, you've got to figure out how Catholics do the service and all of that stuff. But that ain't about acting; that's about physicalizations and anybody can do that. Who is the Pope? You are the Pope. Quit auditioning. You've got that role.

• **The set is the most grown-up place to be.** At first appearances it seems that there are a lot of people to take care of you. Wardrobe, Makeup, Hair, Script Supervisor, Dialogue Coach and the Director. Make friends with these people; they are your allies. But these people will not necessarily always know what you need. You must take care of yourself.

• **The costume designer and wardrobe assistants** can really help you. Your wardrobe is so much a part of your character, you have to be comfortable in your clothes. Do not settle for just anything; keep pushing nicely till your clothes are right for you. If the director is dead set on a certain outfit you can't stand, get the designer to help you become comfortable in it. Within limits, you can help design your makeup; it will depend on the look of the film, but you do have a say.

• **Costume designer Tom Baxter suggests:**

  • **If you are a visitor on the set,** guest starring or supporting, treat everybody the way you would like to be treated. If a wardrobe person asks you if you have clothes to bring in, tell them honestly what you have and if you think it will work or not. A lot of times they will think, "They said they had that so I don't have to cover that." Then you get there the next day and you find out they did have a white shirt but it was short sleeved and looked like a rag. It wasn't a white shirt you could use as a dress shirt. For the smaller parts you are always going to be asked to bring in your wardrobe, unless the show needs something specific or it's a period piece. When you get in and out of the clothes, hang them up. The wardrobe people aren't there to be maids; they are there to do a job. It's really quite a complicated one.

  • **Be someone everyone likes.** If you have an bad attitude, it doesn't work. The most successful people I've seen in television are the people who have that spark about their personality.

• **On one of the films I worked on,** I had to ask for a different makeup person. He was so negative; every morning I spent my energy warding off the negativity. One day, he got drunk in the afternoon and started making sexy remarks. I had a week's work left and knew I couldn't go through that turmoil anymore or my acting would suffer. I went to the head of the makeup department and he put me with someone else. The makeup person is the one you will spend your first hour with each morning—he or she is important. On a situation comedy, I like to be one of the first to be made-up.

• **Handle hair the same way.** You know what your hair will and will not do. My hair is curly so I know if they are straightening it out with hot rollers they can't keep them in too long or it will go even curlier. I have a friend who goes to the set in her own hot rollers because her hair is really straight and it takes longer to curl.

• **The script supervisor** has your lines and can help you match lines for other takes if you happened to change a word or two. Assume you are giving directors what they want unless they say otherwise. If it isn't *your* scene, you may not get much attention; learn to give it to yourself. Don't rely on the outside world to tell you that you're wonderful; assume you are. After you assume you are wonderful, then see what else you can find. It may be another acting choice or something special to do with one of the props. Make every tiny little thing count. Keep adding things you would do in your real life; some will work, some won't—take the chances. All kinds of surprises can happen in the editing room. Because of the master or a change in the concept of the scene, they may need to use your close-up because you were the most interesting and had the most life about you during the scene.

• **Your dressing room is your home** away from home. Bring with you things that make you feel comfortable. There is usually an abundance of time so you need things to fill the time. Depending on your type of dressing room, you can expand what you may need to feel safe and content. It's the place to prepare your acting work first and foremost. It is also the place to rest and conserve your energy, meet with other actors, work on your scenes, go over lines, have someone in to share lunch, make your phone calls and check your service. I try to keep most of my outside life away from me unless I'm having a real easy shooting day.

• **Jennifer Grey,** *Its like, you know...*, the first week we were back from summer break she went to Pier One and bought some great tables and a rug. She covered the ordinary couch with a lovely blanket and pillows. She brought in some pictures and favorite lamps. She made the rather drab place adorable and homey. She also snuck her little dog, Lu Lu, into her dressing room everyday for company.

• **I bring any little snacks** I need that I won't be able to get on location or at the studio. I bring incense because I like to make the room smell like me. I bring my own makeup (just in case) and, of course, a hairbrush. I always bring a book to read that I am loving at the moment—

something to look forward to get back to reading. I bring a good tablet to write on. Sometimes I use it as a kind of journal; other times to just simply write over and over "I can do this role," "Everything is working perfectly," or any other affirmation I may need at the time. Usually there is a bed or couch to lay down on; if not, bring an air mattress the next day so you can stretch out. I always bring an inspirational book or two. Sometimes, if I'm feeling insecure, just by opening a positive book a passage may catch my eye and make all the difference. Be careful of eating meat or sugar; it gives your body too much work to do and can take away from your acting energy.

• **When on location**, there is the additional burden of finding something to do because you don't go home at night. You go to a hotel room that you have had to make into a safe, homey place. A camera can really get you involved with everyone else. I like a Polaroid because you can give pictures to the people right away. If you do this, you must ask the still photographer and cameraman for permission to shoot. Also ask if there are any rules you should know about—when or where not to shoot.

• **Sally Field** said that the first time she worked with Burt Reynolds she filled books writing "I am worthy for Burt to like me" and other such affirmations. Obviously it worked; they had an affair that lasted several years and films.

• **You are the star in your own life** and you are the star in the role you are playing. When it comes right down to it, you are the one who the audience sees on the big screen, little screen, or stage. Your instincts are there to guide you. Keep your mind open, take in all the information anyone has to offer and then make your own decisions as to what is best for you.

• **No one can act your role for you**. Your job is to be prepared and to make yourself comfortable or uncomfortable, whichever appeals to you.

• **If you do get scared trying to figure out a script** or getting a handle on the character, pick up a phone—call your coach or another actor and talk about it. Joan Darling tells a wonderful story about a role she was in a panic over. She couldn't see what the part was about. She went to see her old friend and teacher, Walter Beakel and raved on for the whole evening about not knowing what to do. He finally said "It's easy— she is a Jewish mother." Joan saw immediately what he meant. She went out and bought a big mommy purse and filled it with things Jewish mommies have in their purses and she was home free.

• **I worked with Sharon Farrell** on a pilot where she was playing a ditsy social reporter who was very interested in how she looked. The part was flimsy, so the day before shooting she went out and spent $100 on makeup. When she came to the set, she had all these new things to play with that ended up making the part very funny.

• **So don't panic: there are solutions to every acting problem.** Just ask the universe for the answer and you *will* come up with the solution. And after all, this is the fun part of acting, solving the problems.

• **Now you have the job:** wardrobe, makeup, hair, director and best of all, the other actors. The best thing that can happen is you can play totally *in the moment*. This is where acting is at its easiest; it feels like flying. No matter how you may have prepared, leave yourself open for the wonderful surprises that happen when the camera starts to roll or the curtain goes up. Playing in the moment is what creates the real magical moments in any performance.

• **I talk so much about acting work** because when you are in trouble your work is your insurance. Just like life insurance, hopefully you won't need it. All your work is there if you need it, but it is okay to have everything going beautifully.

• **When I was coaching Dennis Erdman** (now a very accomplished director) in *Friendly Fire*, he called me from location. He said, "I don't know what happened; everything is gone. I was wonderful and then today I couldn't do anything." As we talked, it came out that he had been shooting for seven days and it was easy and fun. All the emotions were there, and he hadn't done anything but relax and hit his marks. Of course he wanted it to be that way, as we all do, but sometimes something happens for whatever reason (doesn't matter) and we *run dry*. All he needed was to start using the acting work. Well, he went back on the set the next day, used his work and came up with the same great acting he had been delivering. After that he had days when he would *fly* and days when he needed to call on his craft every moment he was shooting. Both ways work for the audience.

• **The more acting jobs you do,** the easier and simpler they get. If you are not feeling scared, that is okay. Yes, you may miss the feeling but you will get over it.

• **On every project** there are an abundance of ego trips, power plays, and politics. Ideally, the actors won't be involved in them. The director usually tries to keep these undercurrents away from the actors so you can do your job better. Of course, the gossip is always interesting and I am not saying not to listen to the stories going around. Sometimes they can be the most entertaining part of the job. But learn to not look at these trips personally. Don't get emotionally involved. If something is going on between some of the actors or even between you and another actor, it is most difficult to keep your personal emotions under control. But do it. Let's say, for example, you must insist on something you need to be able to perform and you can't get it—let it go. You will gain somewhere else. I'm not saying not to fight for what you want; but if you lose the fight, lose it and forget it. That way it can't really harm you. Feel good about the times you win and even let go of those too and move on to the next event.

• **Hopefully, your set will be a happy one** and a *family*. All sets end up being families but not necessarily the type of family we want. Whatever you can do to turn the people around you into the family you want, do it. Sometimes you may have to shield yourself from this family and other times you will die and cry when the project is over and you have to leave this family.

• **Relaxation. Keep relaxing and feeling all your feelings.** Don't cover up fear, anger, tears, frustration, joy, ecstasy. Relax and experience all of yourself. Then go out and use all of it. If you are feeling joy and the scene is about sadness, then let the joy be there over how sad you can be. If you are feeling angry and the scene is about ecstasy, be in ecstasy over being able to feel such anger. Most of the time after your relaxation and full experience of your feelings, you will come through to the perfect emotions for the scene. Do not censor or cover up your feelings from *yourself.* Sometimes it is very appropriate to not let others see your feelings. You can have all your defenses up off-camera but never on-camera.

• **One of the things I liked best about Jerry Seinfeld** was he was able to really feel and experience his feelings when they were happening. I saw him get angry a very few times and I saw him get his feelings hurt a couple of times. He dealt with it in the moment and didn't seem to carry any resentments. On the last day of shooting the show, I asked him how he felt. He said when he started driving to the studio that morning he had cried the whole way in. He then let it go and had a great day and evening.

• **We usually get what we intend to get.** Intend to have a good time doing your job.

• **When it's a wrap for the day,** find some way to entertain yourself and be good to yourself. We all have our own unique ways; use yours. Again, there are no rules to follow except your own.

• **Drugs and alcohol** will shortchange you and the people you're working with. *STAY IN REALITY.* Actor Kelsey Grammer, in the middle of the television season, went to the Betty Ford Center. While that is good for him, there are seventy or eighty crew members who are without jobs because all of the television jobs are filled for the season. There are probably an additional 20 employees the production will continue to pay until he can work again because they are too valuable to let go.

• **Safety, safety, safety.** Actor Kenneth Steadman was 27 years old; he had moved to Los Angeles to pursue acting five years before his death. His career seemed to have great promise, he had been on *NYPD Blue* and *Baywatch* and guest star on the premiere episode of *Maloney.* He died while guest starring on *Sliders* when a dune buggy he was riding in overturned. The dune buggy had seat belts, but he wasn't using his. Take care of yourself on the set, wear the seat belts, let the stuntmen do their jobs.

• **Firearms Safety:** After actor Brandon Lee's death, SAG put out some guidelines for using prop guns on the set.

> • **Use simulated or dummy weapons whenever possible.** Treat all guns as if they are loaded and deadly. Unless you are actually filming or rehearsing, all firearms must be secured by the prop master. Never engage in any horseplay with firearms or other weapons. Do not let others handle your gun for any reason. Never point a firearm at anyone, including yourself. Always cheat the shot by aiming to the right or left of the target character. If asked to point and shoot directly at a living target, consult with the property master or armorer for the prescribed safety procedures. If you are the intended target of a gunshot, make sure that the person firing at you has followed all these safety procedures. If you are required to wear exploding blood squibs, make sure there is a bulletproof vest or other solid protection between you and the blast packed. Check the firearm every time you take possession of it. Blanks are extremely dangerous. Even though they do not fire bullets out of the gun barrel, they still have a powerful

blast that can maim or kill. If you are on a set where shots are to be fired and there is no armorer or qualified prop master, go to the nearest phone and call the Guild. A union representative will make sure proper procedures are followed.

• **Whoopi Goldberg** comments on winning awards.

> • **It's never a slam if you don't win** because I always say to people the idea that you are one of five in any year makes you part of a very elite club. From now until the end of your life, you are an 'Academy Award nominee' or 'Academy Award winner.' Not everybody can have that. It's a title. So it's a no-lose situation. It's the greatest.

• **Reviews can be killers.** If you decide to read them, do you believe the goods ones and discount the bad ones? Glenn Close says she can't read them because even if they are good for her but mean to another cast member, it hurts her. I know many actors, myself included, that have gone to bed for days over bad reviews.

• **I want to encourage you to think of acting as a life-long career.** Brenda Blethyn did six films in the year following being nominated for an Oscar for *Secrets & Lies*. She did *Secrets & Lies* when she was 50 years old; it was the third movie of her career. Some actors do work in their older years; don't buy into "Your career is over at 40."

• **To read the TV ratings:** The first figure is the number the show comes in (currently, out of 131 shows); the next figure is percentage/share. For instance: *Seinfeld* one week was #2 with 22.0/34. *The Single Guy* was #7 with 16.3/26. A single ratings point equals 970,000 households, or 1% of the nations 97 million TV homes in the Nielsen Media Research universe. Share is the percentage of sets turned on at a given time that are tuned in to a particular show.

• **To obtain the overnight television ratings,** call Warner Brothers Television Hotline at 818/954-3482 or www.backstage-pass.com after 7AM. The nationals come in at 1PM. You can be the first on the set to know how your show did last night.

DIALOGUE AND ON-SET COACHES

• **Whenever someone asks me what I do** and I say I am a dialogue coach, they ask, "What does that mean?" Or they think it is a dialect coach, who corrects speech or teaches accents or dialects, which it is not.

• **Cherie Franklin, actress and acting coach,** is a well known dialogue and acting coach on feature films and television.

Q: What do you do as an acting/dialogue coach on a set?

> • **I try to isolate each actor's individual problem.** They might be frightened or lacking information or knowledge. I get to know the actor in order to find what might be stopping him from really nailing a script or understanding the emotion of a character and being able to use his own emotions to fuel that particular character's life. Our tools are our emotions and our facility to call those emotions up and down easily at 2:15 in front of 75 people and 50 crew members. It's my function to get the actor comfortable with being able to use his emotions. I build up a safe bed of trust where the actor can tell me his needs, can admit his flaws, can state his fears so that we can eliminate them. I am working with the director's vision, supporting the actor in his ability to take direction and to execute the director's request in performance efficiently.

• **Leigh Kilton-Smith, coach and director**, is a well respected on-set acting coach. She talks about coaching actors.

> • **On-set coaching is highly individualized.** The reason I am there is always very specific and my perspective is adjusted by those reasons. Somewhere along the way in the building of the hierarchy of the entertainment industry, actors became the only elements on sets expected to show up without a crew. Directors have assistant directors, key hair and makeup people have their assistants, even craft services has a crew. Well, I am the actor's crew.

- **It is my goal to have actors walk onto sets confident and prepared,** with a clear understanding that the 'preparation' not be confused for the 'actual work' which must always be free, spontaneous and inspired, in the moment, by the moment. I insist actors not get attached to the work we've done together, but instead have the courage to show up with a clean slate and allow the work to evolve. The actors I work with understand that the director will decide what is appropriate for their vision of the project.

- **In the end, my responsibility as an acting coach,** both on set and in private sessions, is to help the collaborative process run smoothly and efficiently.

• **Each dialogue coach** may give you a different job description. On some shows, I have been the acting coach where I prepare the actors for the director, rehearsing and helping them to make their acting choices.

• **On most shows,** I am there to run lines and rehearse with the actors, to help them memorize their lines and incorporate any line changes or new scenes that suddenly arise. Typically on sitcoms, there are changes each day and even while shooting, there may be changes between takes. Sometimes I just read the cue lines flat; other times I read the full lines of the other characters, close to the way the characters will be saying their lines so the actor I'm reading with can work out their moves, timing and reactions.

• **Sometimes we will have non-actors as guests on a show.** I usually work very intensely with them not only to help them to learn their lines but to help them sound real. When Los Angeles Mayor Richard Riordan appeared on *Its like, you know...*, he had all of his scenes with A.J. Langer who played Lauren. As I was running the lines with them, the Mayor said about himself, "Oh that didn't sound real." A.J. gave him such a great tip. She said, "Try and make each line just a little different, have a different attitude on each one." That was such an easy way to think about the lines. He understood what she meant and really gave a good performance and got laughs.

• **Each actor has their own personality** and their own way of working. The coach must try to be very sensitive to their needs because there is much more that goes into the acting process than the words. Some actors like me to be close by all the time (Jerry Seinfeld, Olivia d'Abo and Jennifer Grey); others prefer to work mostly on their own and ask me to run lines with them occasionally. Still others may like to just sit down and go over a difficult scene or some may just want to go over the line changes.

• **Jason Alexander, who played George on** *Seinfeld,* **has a photographic memory**; it seemed like he could look at the lines once and have them down. Before he shot a scene, I would hang around, available to run lines with him, although I knew it wasn't necessary. I'd run the lines with the guest actors as many times as they wanted, then I'd ask Jason to run them once with the guests. It would be tedious and unnecessary to run them more than once with him. I don't know how Jason made the despicable George likeable, but he did. Jason received a lot of fan mail from women because they thought he was adorable, which Jason is in real life.

• **Julia Louis-Dreyfus was a blast to work with.** Maybe because I have three daughters around her age; maybe its her curly hair (I also have curly hair). It certainly was her sense of humor and talent. I loved it best when we had a new script or were blocking and shooting and taking one scene at a time out of sequence. She would come into the makeup room and say, "I don't know the lines, I haven't looked at this." So for the next hour while she was getting her hair done, she would get the entire script down and have an idea of how she wanted to play each scene. She learns very fast and starts out running her lines flat and then, about the third time through, she follows her instincts and begins to flesh out her role. When she went on the set, she turned it up another 100 degrees and nailed it.

• **It seems to me Julia can make any line work.** I remember in one script Elaine had the line, "Tim Whatley." Jerry says he's talked to Tim Whatley and she responds, "Tim Whatley!" with so much emotion and body movement, the audience immediately got it that she is nuts about him, he is adorable and she would do anything to get him, loose woman that she is.

• **Michael Richards (Kramer) is so very talented and funny.** He was my first buddy when I started on the show—he had the flu that week and really needed my help. I think he may have worried more than anyone about his lines, but he always got them. He had so much to figure out besides the lines—the timing of his physical humor is so precise. It looked easy, natural and truthful, but he planed it meticulously. When he had a complicated scene to work out, we would go over it many times. Yes, there are surprises, like when he jumped out of a window while chasing Newman and just about ended his sex life. I think the most important thing for him is to be truthful; he was always working to achieve that.

• **In one scene, Kramer was supposed to be taking pictures** of George to impress the girl at the one-hour photo place. We were shooting the scene without an audience so Michael hadn't had any rehearsal. He had many props in the scene, supposedly lights to set, a fan to move and turn on, pictures to take from different angles and George to convince to relax and loosen up. Very precise movements, lines to be said and marks to be hit all at the same time, so the four cameramen shooting the show can each get their shots. Since there had not been a rehearsal, I had to run lines with Michael, anticipating the pace that Jason might use. It was so entertaining to watch Michael work out the crazy stuff he does and fun to be a part of his acting process.

• **Jerry Seinfeld was very particular** about getting each line exactly as it was written. Because he had the final decision of each word in each line, he liked to have the lines rewritten just the way they would be spoken. Each week I would pick out my favorite line in the show; most often it was one of his lines and wasn't really a joke line, it was a payoff or an attitude he had. Before each show, we would run through his scenes and then before each scene was shot, all the actors ran through as much of the scene as time allowed, as they were getting touched up with hair and makeup on the set. I tried to keep track of any problem lines and point them out to them before shooting.

• **Jerry is a "money player;"** he was great in rehearsal but when the cameras rolled, a whole new energy and dimension came out. When he was acting, he was also producing the show, deciding on how the scene was to be played. I don't know how he did i; he had control of it all, and yet he seemed to have a very good time working. One of my favorite things about Jerry is that he didn't mind looking like a fool. He could write the show so he always looked good but it was funnier when his character looked shallow. On show days, he liked to have a precise schedule which included light meals. His assistant, Carol Brown, made sure he had everything he needed to be comfortable. He meditated before each show. Jerry seems to have endless energy— I never saw him look tired on the set except the second to last show when he got sick and lost his voice. It was the first time in nine years we had to postpone the shooting for one day.

• **On *The Single Guy*, we had a good time**; the pace wasn't as fast and there weren't as many scenes as *Seinfeld*. Jonathan Silverman started working as a teenager and has never stopped. He is great on the set and is concerned about all of the cast and crew. When we did the pilot, he had *Single Guy* hats made for all of us, which is unusual for an actor to do on a pilot, but it made us all, cast and crew, a family.

• **Ernest Borgnine was so much fun**; he loves to laugh and has a thousand stories to tell. He used the script cover he's had since *Marty,* the movie for which he won his Academy Award. He brought in his Oscar to the set one day so we could see it. The set chair that he uses was made in Mexico for him when he was working on *The Wild Bunch.* At his age, he had plenty of energy, loved to work and was able to keep up with everyone on the set. He was always prepared with his script; we just ran lines a few times.

• **Shawn Michael Howard's first series regular role** was on the *The Single Guy.* He liked to run all of his lines in the script from the beginning to the end. He would get his lines down perfectly and then when we were shooting he would throw in some lines that he thought might work for his character. The producers encouraged him to do this because they were still developing the character.

• **Ming-Na just fascinated me.** *Joy Luck Club* was one of my favorite movies and the serenity and mystery of the character she played was so beautiful. But on *Single Guy,* she was snappy, hip and New York sarcastic. It is interesting to watch her listen. There is always so much going on in her mind; she listens actively.

• **Joey Slotnick (Sam on *Single Guy*) had a great amount of energy**, sort of an engine running inside. He always had some activity, something that was going on in the scene. He had a small role in the movie *Twister,* but every time he came on the screen, he was full of where he had been and where he was going. The same was true for *Blast From The Past*—he was so funny as that intense religious hippie, and that engine was running inside.

• **Olivia d'Abo (*Single Guy*) was great to work with**; she loved to rehearse so I got to spend a lot of time with her. She was always working out her activities and because she was new in the second season, she was trying to discover more things about who her character was. In one scene we were shooting late at night, she had to fly in the door, find out Jonny wasn't going to stop a friend's marriage, hit several marks as she was all over the room, tell a long story filled with emotion and then flop into the chair. The scene was playing too long so the producer decided to cut part of the dialogue. They cut a chunk out from the top and then a piece out of the middle of the monologue which changed the blocking. It is hard to remember cuts like that but Olivia tackled it like, "Oh, boy here we go; this is a challenge and fun." Each take was hilarious, it was always like it was the first time she was doing the scene; whether it was a different turn of her head or inflection in her voice, she kept discovering new things each take. Actors must develop discipline, concentration and focus.

• **I work with all of the guest stars on the shows**, which I hope all of you reading this book will be at sometime. Almost all the guest stars are good, have great respect for the shows and are happy to be there. It is important to remember that as a guest star, you are there just for that show, so always check out the set, the cast and crew, figure out where it is designed for you to fit in. There is always a chance that if they like working with you, you could be called back to do your character for another show.

• **If you get scared, just keep breathing** and there will probably be someone who senses it and will help you, though you don't want to seem needy. Occasionally actors have had panic attacks. They put so much pressure on themselves, they sort of short circuit. I don't think anyone else on the set has been aware of it and that is how I like to it to be. I will hang out with them, keep coming back to them, run their lines, laugh at their jokes, assure them that they can get through it. They always do.

• **It is important that you do your rehearsals at home** because you never know what your shooting day is going to be. On *Seinfeld,* an actor was doing one scene on a no-audience, block-and-shoot show. He was playing a repair guy making a telephone call to Kramer; working a half day, doing one scene and leaving. This was a show shooting on location all over the studio lot. I ran lines with the actor and we rehearsed where he would be shooting until he felt comfortable with the hard hat and the phone on the pole. He was a big fan of the show and was fighting his disappointment at not being able to work with the cast. The scene played great, just what the director wanted. There were two takes and then the crew moved on, so anti-climatic for the guest.

• **It helped this actor immensely that he came in prepared**, he had done his acting work, figured out who, what, when and where. If he had been planning on discovering his character during rehearsal, he would have been caught short.

• **The actor who played the cable guy** on that same show was wonderful. He had several long monologues outside Kramer's door, in the last one there was quite a dramatic emotional change; he convinced Kramer to open the door and they hugged. He almost cried, yet he was funny. The preparation, talent and guts to do that take after take was remarkable. I must have rehearsed those monologues fifty times with him so he could try a lot of different acting work he was thinking of. The crew applauded at the end of his last take—it is unusual to move the crew.

• **When you are a guest on a show, come in absolutely prepared**,. We had one actress who could hardly tear herself away from other stuff she was doing (reading a magazine, eating, talking) to rehearse. She would have a wad of gum in her mouth, casually go off her lines like they didn't matter, and just think she was so cute. Of course, this drove me nuts. I would try to work with her but she always wanted to get back to me later. Finally, right before the show she was ready to work with me. Well, my policy is to take care of the guests first so I can be fully available for the members of the cast who have so many scenes and a story line to think about. This girl had given a hard time to many of us on set who were trying to do our jobs. When you come to play on a team, jump in and be a team player.

• **One actor had fully prepared his work,** but in rehearsal he was completely flat. I knew he would be replaced if he didn't deliver the character. I took him aside to run lines and encouraged him to do all the stuff he had worked on. He said he was afraid of being too big. I said, "Go for it, they will tell you if you're too big." Well he did, and was so funny, they brought him back to do another show.

• **I love working as a dialogue coach,** I work closely with the script supervisor who, among other things, is in charge of making sure any missed or muffled lines are reshot so they don't lose a line or word the writer or producer wanted. Not everything can be fixed in the editing room. If a show doesn't have a dialogue coach, the script supervisor will run lines with the cast, in addition to their other work. I'm happy to say the script supervisors I've worked with are always glad I'm there to help the actors.

Commercial Print Modeling

By Cynthia Kerr

• **Print work is an additional source for actors to gain experience** and make extra money. Commercial print is a still picture of a commercial. It is the type of advertising you see in newspapers, magazines, on billboards and buses. Print models get paid by the hour. In the Los Angeles market models are paid between $150 to $200 an hour. There are no residuals, but depending on the format and product identification, it is not unusual to be paid a bonus on top of the hourly rate.

• **Aaron Marcus is an actor, commercial model and author** of *How to Become a Successful Commercial Model.* He says:

> • **A lot of very successful commercial models are actors.** Photographers love hiring actors because they can take direction, and provide a variety of believable emotions.

Q: What is the difference between commercial modeling and fashion modeling?

> • **Everyone knows about the fashion model**—tall, thin, very unusual and exotic looking. To even be considered as a fashion model, you must have very specific physical requirements. For commercial print work they hire everybody; there are no height, weight or age requirements. Fashion models normally promote high-end designer clothes; commercial models advertise everything else.

Q: **How can someone get started in the commercial print business?**

- **The most basic way would be with an 8x10 head shot.** Call the agents in your city and find out if they handle commercial print. Ask if they have open calls, or if you should submit by mail. Once you get an agent you will need to get a zed card. This is a collection of photographs that shows a variety of ways you can look and the different categories you can play. The agent can help you decide on the categories that would be marketable for you. The zed card is your calling card. It is what the agent submits to a photographer or an art director in order to get you work. It is not uncommon to get hired from your card, without having to audition.

Q: **How do you audition for print work?**

- **The audition for commercial print modeling is called a go-see,** because you go and you are seen. When your agent calls you with the audition information, make sure you find out what they are looking for, and dress the part. When you walk in the room you want them to say, "Yeah, that is the person for this job." Before signing in, look over the layout of the ad (copy of ad). It shows what the clients are looking for. Study it. What does this person look like? What are their facial and body expressions? Is there any copy, any words to the ad? Know the kind of expressions you want to show. When you feel prepared and ready, sign in. In most situations you will have a Polaroid shot taken and they will staple it to your composite sheet.

- **When you book the job, it is important that you understand the ad** and how it needs to be delivered. I view commercial print work as any other acting job. I say words or sounds that will allow me to feel the emotion that I need to present. It will make the shots look very powerful. When you are in touch with your expressions and emotions, there is believability in your eyes and your body will move naturally. Some photographers might say, "I really don't want to see any kind of talking," then you need to do an internal monologue. The key is to have some life going on in your brain.

Q: **When do you get paid?**

- **The client pays the advertising agency,** the advertising agency pays the photographer, the photographer pays the agent. Once the check clears, the agent takes out their 20% commission and then the model gets paid. In most cases it takes 90 days to get paid.

Real:

• **At the shoot there are two forms you need to fill out.** One is a voucher and the other is a model release form. The voucher is the contract that you sign at the end of every job. You get a copy, your agent gets a copy and the person paying you gets a copy. The other form is the model release form. Basically it says the photographer can use your image any way he wants to. You must get familiar with these forms, learn to fill them out correctly and make the necessary changes. If the changes are not made, you could lose a tremendous amount of money.

• **While researching the print modeling business,** I talked to several actors who supplement their acting income as "fit models." Fit modeling is basically a garment industry job. Every company that manufactures clothing uses fit models to make their patterns. The fit model goes to the factories and works with the designers. They drape their designs on them and decide what trim to use or what buttons would be best. Then the model goes to the fit room and tells the pattern maker what is uncomfortable, what is too tight or too loose.

• **The hours are flexible;** the manufacturers will work with your schedule if you are the size they need. The required size is "average" but one company's average might be a size eight for women, another's a size two. You do have to be well proportioned. The pay is $75 to $85 an hour minus the agency commission which is 15 to 20%. Models can work for several manufacturers; many fit models work non-stop.

• **Natasha at Peak Models, Inc., says her company handles many actors** that add to their acting income by fit modeling, print modeling or working conventions as hosts and hostesses. You can send a picture and resume along with snapshots, your measurements and the type of work you are interested in, to Peak Models, Inc., 25852 Mc Bean Parkway, PMB 190, Valencia, CA 91355.

Resources

How to Become a Successful Commercial Model, by Aaron Marcus www.howtomodel.com. 410/764-8270.
Ross Reports Television & Film: Commercial Casting Guide, by Back Stage West.
The Agencies: What the Actor Needs To Know by Acting World Books. Use this guide to look for an agent. Their listing will specify if they do print or not.
The Working Actor's Guide, L.A., Aaron Blake Publishing.

VOICEOVERS FOR COMMERCIALS AND ANIMATION ACTING

Voiceovers and animation acting take a special acting energy, coming from a different perspective. You should be a well-trained actor before studying voiceovers; it is a *very* lucrative field to get into. You must have an agent for this work; there are several of them in town. This is another very tough field to break into—you need a very special voice and talent. I would take classes with casting directors. Look in *Back Stage West* for ads. If you get in the circle of people who are doing voice-overs, you will learn a lot about it.

Go to www.voicebank.net and listen to the many demo voice tapes that are online and you will get a feel for the type of talent this work demands.

Voiceover Classes

Susan Blu, contact 818/783-9130. www.blupka.com. Great classes, she knows the business. Studio: 818/501-1BLU for voiceover demos. Susan is the author of *Word Of Mouth, A Guide To Commercial Voice-Overs.*

Terry Berland Casting and Voice Box Studios, 310/571-4141. "The place to go to move your voiceover career forward. The most progressive up-to-date creative workshops, seminars, marketing and networking strategies in the industry."

Dolores Diehl, The Voiceover Connection, Inc. 213/384-9251. www.voconnection.com. Teaches workshops in all phases of voiceovers, commercial, narration and animation, from basic to advanced levels. All basic classes taught by Dolores. Agents, casting directors and performers teach the intermediate to advanced to pro levels. Demo seminars, workouts and simulations.

Michael Bell's Voice Animation Workshop, 818/784-5107. "In my class, you will learn to paint the picture with your voice, test the limits of your pipes and your imagination and rediscover the fun of eating the scenery! Above all discover who's hidden inside, let them out and make them pay!" Teaches just a couple of workshops a year.

Joni Gerber, 323/654-1159. Private classes $65 per hour, all levels. One of the top working voiceover people.

Sandy Holt, 310/271-8217. Teaches voiceover/looping workshops and produces voiceover demos. Also teaches cold reading.

VOICE COACH

Robert Easton, "The Henry Higgins of Hollywood," 818/985-2222. He is also known as the dialect doctor. He has coached many, many famous actors over many years.

BOOKS

The Agencies: What the Actor Needs To Know by Acting World Books. This is the authentic, well-researched agent guide. There are other publications that look like this one—don't be fooled. You will find agents who specialize in voiceovers.

Word Of Mouth, A Guide To Commercial Voice-Overs by Susan Blu.

Voice and the Actor by Cicely Berry. This is not necessarily about voiceovers, but about using your correct voice.

Voice-Overs: Putting Your Mouth Where the Money Is, by Chris Douthitt.

WEBSITES

Voiceover demos plus much more, www.voicebank.net.

Voiceover resources, www.VoiceStarz.com. Classes on line, plus a lot of information.

LOOPING

• **Looping is another acting tool** to add to your tool box. Many actors have never heard about this lucrative work. Looping is done on a post-production sound stage; the actors replace or add voices to film and television productions after they have been edited. Loopers need strong improvisational skills because the main function is to supply the voices of the extras that are seen in the background. There are a few looping groups but they are very hard to break into. In general, TV shows may use just five actors and films may use six to 12 actors for all the voices.

• **There are several different modes** of looping such as "Wall to Wall," "Doughnut," "Pass By's" and others. You will be taught these in a work-shop or you may get the chance to observe a looping group in action.

• **The most important tool is your looping notebook.** This is where you write down sentences you might use in conversations at an airport, hospital, bowling alley, boxing match, nightclub, singles joint, computer lingo, dance studio, etc. You look for potential dialogue everywhere. Any lingo or jargon of different occupations is very valuable. Extensive research is usually required for each job you do, depending on the situation of the film. This all adds information to your notebook. Long time, experienced loopers arrive on the sound stage with several huge notebooks.

• **Toby Stone of *Sounds Great* looping group:** "When I worked on *Backdraft,* I needed to find out all about Chicago, including street maps. Then I called the burn unit ward at Sherman Oaks Burn Hospital to find out what the vitals are on a burn victim. What kind of drugs they would give, what kind of salve they would use." This information went into her looping notebook to be used for that job, and saved for any other project involving burn victims. This authentic type of conversation is what makes looping believable.

259

• **When you take a workshop,** the teacher will hand out sheets to begin your looping notebooks, including Police Codes and Traffic Violations, Police Dispatch, Police Precinct, Phones, General Conversation, Forensics/Crime Scene, Airport Pages and Airport Terminal Conversation.

• **In looping, the conversation can't be all that interesting** because the audience doesn't want to be aware of what the background voices are saying. There's a fine line between not being boring and having new things to say, something with a little spin to it. It's like walking and chewing gum at the same time. There are different kinds of restaurant conversations; it may be a Denny's kind of lunch place or it may be a very fancy upscale dinner kind of place. Depending on what you are seeing on the screen, you may change your voice or the type of attitude you have. If there are only six loopers on the sound stage, you have to be able to sound as if you are everyone in every situation.

• **Even if you are not planning** to seek actual looping work, I think all actors will find taking a workshop helpful because you could be called in to revoice or loop your own lines on film and television projects due to sound or other technical problems. With the experience you gain in a looping workshop, you can go on any sound stage knowing looping etiquette, what will be expected of you and what terms are used. Self-confidence is a real key to looping.

• **Sandy Holt** owns a looping group, *Loop Ease,* and runs looping workshops. "Sometimes we have to revoice a main character. We may do a teenage or baby's voice, also different dialects. All the actors in the company are incredible at improvisation. We're quick and creative on the spot; you have to be able to improvise while you're looking at the scene on the sound stage screen."

• **Loopers earn Screen Actors Guild minimum and residuals.**

Resources

LOOPING WORKSHOPS

Loop Ease, Sandy Holt at 310/271-8217 is a voice casting director. She holds weekend looping seminars on a professional sound stage.

Contact SAG for current list of Looping Groups.

STUNT AND ACTION ACTING

• **It is very hard to break into stunt work.** None of the stunt schools are recognized by any of the stunt coordinators who are the directors of the stunts on the set. Unless you have a real specialty—gymnastics, martial arts or your size is unusual—it's going to be very hard to break in. If you are an all around stunt person, usually the directors will not look at you as an actor for speaking roles. Stunt people are SAG and have all the benefits actors do. The stunt associations—Stuntmen's Association, Stunts Unlimited and International Stunt Association—are also tough to join.

• **There are groups of stunt people** who work out together. Try to meet them and be invited to work out. It's a real networking feat to get to know and hang out with these people.

• **Actor James Lew,** www.jameslew.com, is a member of the Stuntmen's Association. His martial arts training began at age 14, first in Korean style Karate. He studied a combat style developed by a member of the Green Beret, a Chinese style called "White Eyebrow" after the appearance of the original Grand Master and Kung Fu "Five Animals" style, the five animals being Tiger, Leopard, Snake, Dragon, and Crane. His favorite parts of the martial arts training were "the traditional weapons: spears, swords, many Chinese weapons; great for developing balance, speed, power, weapons are an extension of your body." James has successfully established credibility as an actor via the martial arts.

• **James is typically hired as a stunt coordinator** or martial art choreographer, which is somewhat like a dance choreographer, or as a second unit director.

Q: Tell me about your job.

• **I first read the script and break it down** in terms of the tone of the movie and the appropriate style of action to fit the telling of the story. My job is always to bring the vision of the director to life; he may want a certain feeling from the fight, a certain intensity, and a certain drama. You try to choreograph moves accordingly. If it's a real brutal, intense fight, you want to use more of a street feel to it. Or if there is a bit of comedy, then you want to lighten it up or find a situation to throw the old "banana peel on the ground." If things happen by chance, people fall or something breaks, you give it a different flavor. As a stunt coordinator my job is to bring the most exciting action for the best budget and all done with safety as the priority.

• **When I was working** on *Undercover Blues*, with Kathleen Turner and Dennis Quaid, we had approximately two weeks time in pre-production for them to train. We worked on the basics first, to provide a strong foundation, footwork. Rather than trying to give them a general training program, we gave a concept of what the fight scenes were actually going to be so they could work on specific moves. Kathleen had a personal trainer so she was in great shape. I came in also as a physical trainer for Dennis, using weights and stretching. Both actors were very athletic so they picked it up easily.

• **I am currently training Brad Pitt** for his upcoming movie, *The Trojan War*. He is playing Achilles, the greatest warrior in Greek history. The producers want to add a flavor of Kung Fu to his fighting style. We are working with the sword and the spear as his primary weapons. The challenge is to bring a different style to his fighting without making Mr. Pitt look like someone out of *Crouching Tiger*. My goal is to guide him to the level of proficiency that he does not have to think about his movements but rather just feel his natural reactions to how Achilles would fight.

Q: What training do you recommend for actors who want to do their own action work?

• **The most basic skills a stuntman** must train in are fighting skills. This also holds true for an actor wanting to perform his own action. Fight scenes are the foundation to build upon to becoming an action actor. A martial arts program would be a very wise investment because it teaches you how to throw your body, how to fall down without hurting yourself. The styles vary with different schools, different instructors. It's best to audit a class and get a feel for it. Ballet is great for general movement. For stunts, gymnastics is beneficial; you need to experience rolling and tumbling. On the original movie, *Buffy, The Vampire Slayer*, I trained Kristy Swanson in martial arts. She had dance training and enjoyed movement, so I had something to build on, a foundation. I would incorporate some dance principles to her training to make it her own fighting style.

Q: Is it hard to break into stunt work?

- **It's like getting a credit card without having credit.** People always want to know what you've done. If you haven't done anything, they don't want to hire you. Get some nonunion work; get some experience; get something on your resume. If you have a special ability, if you're a champion at something, it can open the door. Motorcycle riders, gymnasts, swimmers; doing something a little better than the normal person can do.

- **My first job** was on the original *Kung-Fu* series. They were looking for martial artists and I had that special ability. Then other projects came along, and I had a credit. Your last job is your audition for your next job. The stunt coordinator may have liked your work and will recommend you to someone else looking for someone with your abilities.

- **Make a demo tape of yourself in action.** With the economical costs today of digital video cameras and editing available you can put together an exciting reel of yourself performing action of your expertise. As in an acting reel, it should be under five minutes long. I feel the production value is not as important as the actual content. It is your talent that matters.

Q: What is the audition like?

- **The martial arts or stunt double audition** is the same as an acting audition. They're always looking for that spark, something special. So you want to come in with a lot of intense energy, to come across like you can really hurt the person that you're going to fight in the film. They'll ask you to do a demonstration. You need to get across in your body language and your eyes through sense memory or personalization that your opponent is someone that you really want to hurt, take care of, defend against. You've got to really sell it to the director. A routine is usually 30 seconds to a minute. If it is being taped, you play it directly towards the camera, as if that's the director or someone who would be watching it. If the director's in the room, you want to play it toward him and give him that impression personally. He can always watch it on the tape again.

Q: What advice do you have for martial artists or others wanting to break into action acting?

• A lot of people make the mistake of thinking that just because they are a martial artist or an athlete, they can be in movies. It's a totally different field; it's movie making, so I recommend acting classes. That teaches you to hold a feeling while doing a fight. Also to be able to handle dialogue; not just kicking and punching and screaming. You have to be able to open your mouth and talk.

• There's a bit of a difference between film martial arts and real martial arts. It can be difficult to grasp. In real fighting you don't want to telegraph to your opponent, "I'm going to kick or punch you." In film, you need to show the audience: "This is the kick that I'm going to use." Present it then go through with it. To make it a little more theatrical, you have to overemphasize certain moves.

• To be successful, the key word is always persistence; never give up. If you are a martial artist, you know what that means. If you want to do a certain kick, the only thing is to just do it over and over; be persistent about it. Finally, one day it comes. To be successful in the film business, it's the same thing; there's that big heavy door in front of you so you have to keep kicking, kicking, kicking until you kick it down. That's what I did for a long time.

Q. What about women in the stunt business?

• Never has there been a better opportunity for a female stunt person or a female action actress than today. The popularity of "chicks kicking butt" in the entertainment world is at an all time high and it is here to stay.

• My advice to any women interested in the action world would be exactly the same for the men. Total commitment to training to the level of a world class athlete is your best foundation. What distinguishes the successful stuntwomen is their ability to be just as good as a successful stuntman.

Q. What are your thoughts on achieving success in this business?

• The first and most important point to always remember in show business is that it is a "business." Part of any business plan should be short term and long term goals. Just like any business, the marketing approach can make or break your company. Survive with passion and persistence in your belief of yourself. But the one most vital thing you must do is. . . have fun!

• **Simon Rhee is a 7th Degree Black Belt** in Tae Kwon Do and a 4th Degree Black Belt in Hap Ki Do. www.simonrhee.net. He has been involved in the movie industry as a Martial Artist, Stunt Coordinator, Fight Choreographer, and Actor, as well as instructor to many celebrities. Master Rhee owns one of the top Tae Kwon Do centers and has trained thousands of men, women and children since 1980.

Q: Tell me about working with Madonna.

• **I was hired** by Mr. Eddie Braun to work on the *007 Die Another Day* Madonna music video. There were two of us and the script required that we push Madonna into the water and throw her against a wall. We had to manhandle her and he wanted someone who could act and look menacing without hurting Madonna. To look more menacing one of us had to get a military haircut, and I had to be bald. I was paid $1,250 extra for shaving my head.

Q: Was Madonna afraid at all?

• **I don't think she is afraid of anything.** We rehearsed for two days, and after she saw how we were handling her, she felt very comfortable that we weren't going to hurt her in any way. One time we tied her to an electric chair, and she was halfway tied down and the director told her to struggle more. While she was struggling, she kicked me in the head with her boot. We didn't rehearse that, but sometimes stuntmen have to take that.

Q: As a stuntman, do you ever get hurt?

• **Yes, I do.** A few years back, I was doing a TV series called *Dark Skies* and I had to ride this machine called an air ram—you step on it and it catapults you into the air and then an explosion follows you. One time I was about to step on it and the explosion went off a little early and the debris went into my eyes. Another time, on *Lethal Weapon 4*, I had to fall onto the freeway from a moving car and I banged my shoulder—but you survive and you move on.

• **It's better to be an action actor**, because the production will always provide you with a stunt double so you won't get hurt. When you do your own stunts there is definitely a chance of getting hurt.

Q: What is the best training for an action or stunt actor to have before they arrive in Los Angeles?

- **If you want to be an action actor**, you will have to know how to act. Make sure you have a good acting coach. It's very important to take acting classes. In a movie I did called *Best of the Best* there is a scene at the end where I am handing a medal to my brother and I'm crying. We had to shoot that ten times and every time we shot it I had to cry. That's not that easy.

- **Pick some kind of martial arts training.** You are selling your image in Hollywood so you've got to look that image. It will take a minimum of six months to get good at martial arts. You also need weight training for definition. It's like taking acting lessons; you don't learn everything in one day.

Q: What was the first movie that you were in?

- **I worked on *Octagon* with Chuck Norris.** I was a martial artist extra and I got to do some karate stuff. I saw myself up on the screen for maybe one second. *See the website for all of Simon Rhee's films.*

Q: How do stunt actors get work?

- **I have been doing this for more than ten years,** so a lot of stunt coordinators know me. They will call me directly and ask me for my availability.

- **The way to find jobs** once you are in Los Angeles is through EIDC, www.EIDC.com, which is a permit office. They post where productions are shooting. You can go to the office or to the website and download addresses. I go to the website, find out what films are shooting and who the stunt coordinator is and then give them my picture and resume.

- **To join EIDC, you write them a letter** requesting to join. They will ask why you want to know the addresses. You can tell them you are a stuntman, and normally they will give you a password.

- **You have to be a member of SAG to be hired as a stunt actor.**

- **Shoot a demo reel** that demonstrates your martial arts, fencing, highfalls to an airbag, mototcycle tricks, whatever are your stunt skills and submit the reel to stunt coordinators.

- ***The Hollywood Reporter* is a good source for films** that are in pre-production. You can get your resume to the stunt coordinator before the movie starts.

Resources

www.jameslew.com. James Lew has many links to other interesting websites for action actors.

www.simonrhee.net. Simon Rhee's official web site.

Karate, Simon Rhee, 818/224-3400. www.simonrhee.net. 22880 Ventura Blvd., Woodland Hills, 91364. Considered one of the best Karate studios, many celebrities have studied with Master Rhee. He is also a prominent action/stunt actor, *Best of the Best I & II,* and other films.

Action Actor's Academy, 310/558-1143. www.wgn.net/~actiona. They are a company of actors learning to tell stories through physical movement and acting techniques for projects such as *Zorro* and *Hercules.* Classes include martial arts, European, Asian and Filipino weapons.

Westside Fencing Center and Center for Stage Combat, 310/204-2688. 8737 Washington Blvd., Culver City, 90232. The largest fencing center in the country. Classes and private coaching. Call for their brochure; there is a coupon for a free fencing lesson. Some former students are: Geena Davis (*Cutthroat Island*), Teenage Mutant Ninja Turtles, Robin Williams, Shelly Long, Keanu Reeves and Eric Roberts.

Beverly Hills Karate Academy, 310/275-2661. 9085 Santa Monica Blvd., West Los Angeles 90069. Emil Farkas teaches motion picture stunt fighting and all forms of martial arts stunts. He is a stunt coordinator and frequently casts stunt people from his classes.

www.eidc.com. This is a website that delivers a show sheet that tells where productions are filming that day on location in Los Angeles. You have to register to receive the information.

EXTRA WORK

• **All actors should work** at least several days of extra work at the beginning of their careers. New actors have no idea what it is like to be on an actual film or television set. No person or book can explain what it is like to be working on location or on a sound stage. As an extra, you are part of the action and become familiar with studios and locations. If you are working part-time jobs to support your career, why not include extra jobs?

• **Keep a very low profile on the set** if you are already a trained actor; that way no one will really remember you as an extra. There is still a bit of a stigma attached to being an extra in Los Angeles; in New York it is not unusual to be an extra one day and a principle the next. If you are at the very beginning of your training, it is okay to be seen on camera and to be a stand-in.

• **There is a strict on-the-set protocol.** Never go on the set until you have read *Back To One: The Movie Extras' Guidebook* (see resources.) As an extra, you are the lowest in the pecking order so your needs will be barely considered. Bring water, snacks, sunscreen, chair and reading material with you. Have anything you might need packed in your car—clothes to layer, sun glasses, reading material, playing cards, loose change and small bills; anything you might need to be comfortable.

• **Your best friend on the set is the second assistant director (2nd AD).** Report in as soon as you arrive and always let the AD know when you are stepping away from the set. When you are called, answer immediately in a loud voice that you are on your way and start walking with haste to where you are needed. The AD will most likely tell you where to move and what to do during the filming. I have overheard a second assistant director tell the third AD that she never wanted to see a certain extra on the set again because he wasn't cooperative. Everywhere you work, you are building a reputation; make sure you can be proud of it.

• **There is a possibility of getting your SAG card**. When you get three SAG vouchers, you are eligible to join SAG. A voucher is your pay record and is a three-page multicolored form. Or, if they decide they need someone to say something like, "Hey, pull that truck over here," there is no time to go out and hire an actor, so they point to one of the extras. That means you get paid SAG minimum ($617) and are eligible to join SAG. Plus, you'll get residuals on that work for many years.

• **Samuel L. Jackson** was a stand-in for Bill Cosby for three years on the original *Bill Cosby Show*. He said he learned so much about the camera working on the show.

• **Rob Morrow** (*Northern Exposure)* had been on *Saturday Night Live* in 1980 as an extra, playing juror #11 in a skit with Jane Curtain, Bill Murray and Garrett Morris. 12 years later, he guest-hosted the show.

• **Judith Light** *(Who's The Boss)* began her career with a five-year role on *One Life To Live*. She landed that role after being an understudy on the soap. She took the understudy role—which is not even on-camera—because she was broke. Lucky for her.

• **Bruce Willis** in 1990 was on a TV show honoring Frank Sinatra's 75th birthday. He said in 1980, he was a photo-double and stand-in (extra) on Frank's movie, *First Deadly Sin*. Bruce said, "Frank had been such an inspiration on the set, talking to the actors and extras, telling stories of working on *From Here To Eternity."* Bruce went from a film extra to a multimillion dollar superstar in those 10 years.

• **Casting director Marvin Paige**, who cast *General Hospital* for years, said in an interview:

> • **I don't refer to our people in that category as "extras."** I refer to them as atmosphere people. The point is, I want every cast member to be an actor. I don't just want a body standing there because, among other things, if they aren't actors, there's always a chance they'll trip over the scenery. People who have the training and background respond much better to direction so I prefer to have people who really are pursuing acting careers even in small roles. For example, we have an actor who plays a bartender; sometimes he has dialogue and sometimes not. But he's been working with us three or four years and that's an actor's number one goal—getting work.

• **Other actors who worked as extras** at the beginning of their careers are Ben Affleck, Matt Damon, Sharon Stone (Woody Allen movie), Bruce Willis, *(The Verdict),* Brad Pitt *(Cutting Class),* Anjelica Huston, Dustin Hoffman, Kevin Costner, John Wayne, Bette Midler, Gary Cooper, Marlene Dietrich, Clark Gable, Robert Mitchum, Jean Harlow and Sophia Loren.

• **Cullen Chambers, actor, background artist, author,** has helped tens of thousands of people work as extras over the years. His best selling book, *Back To One: The Movie Extras' Guidebook,* is a manual with step by step instructions.

Q: Why would an actor want to work as an extra?

• **It's the first step toward an acting career.** It's like starting in the mail room and working your way up. You gain knowledge, experience and technical insight into the film making process. I've had to do more acting in the background on certain films than in principal roles; as a fireman, fighting fires, rescuing people in earthquakes, warping across the galaxy on the bridge of Starship Enterprise. You become aware of where the camera is and how to make a cross very precisely take after take so you won't block an actor who's delivering lines.

Q: How does a person get started?

• **By registering with one or more of the extra casting agencies.** I've listed over 100 agencies in my book and rated them. You'll also find agencies advertised in trade publications. Some agencies charge a fee. Scams abound in this business—don't register with any agency that charges more than $20 or insists on expensive photos. You can have your extra pictures taken for $25 by the best in the business.

Q: What tools does an extra need?

• **Here are a few: 3x5 color photos, telephone, an answering machine** or service and/or a pager, dependable transportation, Thomas Brothers Guide Mapbook, and wardrobe which can be picked up at yard sales or thrift shops. Put together a business and formal look and some period outfits from the '50s, '60s, '70s etc. It's all tax-deductible.

Q: What are some of the rules for an extra when on the set?

• **Number one rule is listen.** The director or assistant director's job is to tell you exactly what to do. Be on time. Bring three changes of wardrobe, pen and paper, book, small change, snack, and a folding chair. Sign in and out with the assistant directors or their assistants. Don't talk to or bother the principal actors—those with lines.

Q: How much does a nonunion extra make and how often can they work?

- **If they hustle, five to seven days a week.** The lowest pay is $6.75 an hour, $54 a day plus overtime and bumps which are for special bits. $101.24 for 12 hours. On many shoots you do work overtime.

Q: How can you work on your favorite TV show?

- **The end credits list the Unit Production Manager**, Stage Manager or Assistant Director, and where the show is taped or filmed. Call the studio. Ask for the show's production office and ask for the production manager or AD. Say you're interested in working as a background actor and ask what extra casting agency they use. Then contact that agency and follow up as instructed in my book. *Cullen also lists the casting companies of every show in his monthly magazine. See below.*

- **Wardrobe designer and costumer Tom Baxter gives a few hints to extras:**

  - **If you are working as an extra the best thing to do is to be polite** to the wardrobe person. A lot of times they can get you silent bits; sometimes they can even get you a line if you fit into a costume they have. I can't tell you how many times an extra who fit the mailman or cop uniform has gotten lines because I said that's who fits the costume. If you are wearing wardrobe from the studio's department, take care of it; watch where you put it down and never leave it lying around. We lost a jacket on a show that was loaned to an extra and he won't be back on the show again. The jacket cost more than he made. Make sure all of the clothes you bring to wear are clean and ironed perfectly.

- **I spoke with Judi Keppler of Judi's Casting.**

Q: What do you think it takes to be an extra?

- **People have no conception of the discipline and hard work it takes.** A lot of people aren't used to getting up early. When we were doing a two-day commercial shoot, our call time at the Johnny Rocket Cafe was 5:30 in the morning. It takes money. You need money to survive when you're not working. There's no guarantee you're going to work next week.

Q: Do you have any special advice for extras?

- **If an extra is really intent on getting ahead**, they should not only register with the different agencies, but they should learn how to network a little bit so they are not just a photo on a piece of paper.

They have to get an identity and a reputation with the agency and that takes time. And yet, it's a fine line because they can't be a pest. I've had actors who would call me up in the morning and say, "Do you need any cigarettes? Do you want a cappuccino?" They were very smart. You can't bring people flowers and booze, it's too tacky. But little things like, "I've got a half a day free. Can I come by and do some filing or something?" Those people you remember, obviously, and try to take care of them. It's a matter of perseverance, which means you don't give up.

• **Stand-in.** The stand-in takes the place of the principal actor. It frees the actor from tedious hours of lighting and camera blocking. They also are there to protect and take care of the actors they replace—by showing them any blocking changes. The stand-ins tend to get more respect on the sets they work on because they are there week in and week out. They are part of the crew.

• **Extra casting agencies** are listed in *Back Stage West*; I've listed a few here to get you started. All agencies require two forms of identification: social security card, driver's license, passport or birth certificate and either a 3x5 or 4x6 color picture of you against a white background.

• **Call-in Services.** Most of the people I know who are doing extra work say they have to use calling services to get their jobs. The service calls the agencies for you and books your work for the next day. They call your machine or beep you to tell you where to report. There is usually a fee for starting the service and then a monthly fee of around $60.

• **When I am working on a show, some of my best friends** on the set are the stand-ins. They are a great asset to the production and are hired year after year. Shows have several extras over and over again also, but there have been people who have come on a show and behaved in a manner as to never be asked back. The actors are pleasant but they are, in fact, working and can't be visiting with the extras. Never ask for an autograph or picture unless you are on the set as a guest.

• **At this writing,** SAG is investigating the call-in services and the easy accessibility of SAG vouchers. As in all areas of the business, changes can happen very fast. Investigate everything thoroughly. One of my students got her three SAG vouchers in a couple of weeks while she was interning at Bill Dance's Extra Casting Service. The interns in the office are first to hear about a film or television show that is giving out SAG vouchers. You have to work all the angles to get what you need.

Thanks to Cullen Chambers for the resources below.

Resources

Cullen Chambers, 323/969-4897. www.backtoone.net. *Back To One: Movie Extras' Guidebook, $24.95* or *Back To One: Movie Extra Work For Rocket Scientists*, a pocket-sized version of *Movie Extras' Guidebook*, $14.95. The books can be purchased at theatrical bookstores and many newsstands in Los Angeles, or you can call and mail order. Free trial subscription to the monthly *Hollywood Industry Insider Magazine* when you order a copy of either book. To receive a free Extra Pay Rate Schedule ($5 value) send a self-addressed, stamped envelope to Back To One, Attention: Pay Scale, P.O. Box 753, Hollywood, CA 90078. It fits in your wallet so at the end of day you can figure out how much you made. It also lists some extra casting agencies and other information.

Rich Hogan's Photos for Extras, 323/467-2628. At Hollywood and Vine. The best. Prices start at $25 for 3x5s. He registers extras for Sunset Casting and Idell James Commercial Extras. Also a great headshot photographer; see the photo sections.

www.eidc.com. This is a website that delivers a show sheet that tells where productions are filming that day on location in Los Angeles. You have to register to receive the information. This would be helpful if want to go to sets to see if they can use you as an extra that day.

Screen Actors Guild Extra scales: to 6/30/2003, $110; 2004, $115. Stand-ins make $115, by 2004 $130. Commercial extras and stand-ins make $275.

AFTRA Extra daily rates are: **General extra** network sitcom, $85; 30-minute serial, $99. 60-minute serial, $136.

AFTRA Extras Casting File. This is a file of pictures and resumes of paid-up members who are available to do extra and stand-in work on AFTRA programs. Producers and casting representatives call and request names and home telephone numbers from the file. To submit: send your picture and resume to Extra File, c/o AFTRA, or drop them off at the membership counter. Sometimes you may be hired without being in AFTRA. You can work 30 days without being a member and after that they will deduct the union payments from your paycheck. Two of my daughters worked on *Facts of Life* as extras, joining this way. Some situation comedies hire AFTRA members as extras or "under 5s" (under five lines). Pick up an AFTRA show sheet (printed monthly) then contact the production companies and find out who casts the extras. Call the person, ask if you can send a picture and/or come in for a meeting. Some Soap Opera Casting Directors attend cold reading showcases, so you can meet them that way. You can also send in a picture, etc. They will be listed on the show sheet.

EXTRA CASTING AGENTS

People registering for extra work must bring two original IDs: driver's license, passport, voter registration card, birth certificate or social security card. If in a union, bring union card. Also, bring exact cash or money order.

Central Casting, 818/562-2755. www.ep-services.com for information on how to register. 220 S. Flower St., Burbank, 91502. Fee: $25 union and nonunion. Cash only, exact change. For union members, bring your current union card. 818/562-2966 for address and directions only.

Kids! Background Casting, 818/239-1371. 207 S. Flower, 2nd Floor, Burbank, 91502. $25 registration and they take a 20% commission when the children work. Parents and children can get a good feel of what the business really is by working at least a few days as an extra. If you want your children to work extra jobs you will pay 15% to 20% as commission to the extra company. Adults wouldn't stand for this but I guess they figure the kids don't need to earn a living and they get the parent along to take care of the child for free.

Background Players/Axium Casting, 323/692-1783. 7201 Melrose Ave., #D, L.A. 90046. $15 for each agency.

Back to One Casting, 323/969-4897. Union and nonunion, commercials and print work. $25 photo imaging fee.

Christopher Gray Casting, 323/939-8502. 7204 1/2 Melrose Ave. Suite A, L.A., 90046. They try to help you get your union vouchers.

Bill Dance Casting, 818/754-6634. 4605 Lankershim Blvd. #401, North Hollywood, 91602. www.billdancecasting.com. Everyone says good things about this casting company. They also use interns if you want to learn all about extra work.

Idell James Casting, 310/230-9344. 15332 Antioch Street, PMB #117, Pacific Pallisades, 90272. Pictures: send 8x10 with resume. Union members for commercials. Likes beautiful young people. Very selective.

Producers Casting, 310/364-2300. Fee: $25. Casts for commercials. Very selective.

Jeff Olan Casting, 818/377-4475. 1059 Mc Cormick, #1, North Hollywood, 91601. Fee: $20 computer imaging. They will call you in; they prefer not to work with a call-in service. Jeff has been doing this for years and works hard for his people.

Sunset Casting Registration, 310/398-5904. Non-union commercials. EZM Studios, 1645 Vine St., #615, Hollywood. $25 Registration fee.

San Diego:

Background San Diego, 858/974-8970. There are several shows that shoot there. There is an information line giving full information and how to register. Free.

CALL IN SERVICES

Extra Management, 818/972-9474. Tell them Cullen Chambers from *Back To One* sent you for $75 off the startup fee.

Studio Phone, 310/202-9872. 10624 Regent St., Los Angeles, 90034. P.O.B. 34481, Los Angeles, 90034. The oldest calling service. Union only. Registration Tu, W, Th by appointment. They do take some non-union extras and will try to help you get your three vouchers.

FREE REGISTRATION EXTRA CASTING COMPANIES

To register at the following agencies, send a 3x5 color snapshot along with your general information.

Cast of Thousands, 818/325-2080. P.O. Box 1687, Burbank, 91507.

Creative Extras Casting, 310/203-7860. 2461 Santa Monica Blvd., #501, Santa Monica, 90404.

Extras Network Casting, 323/692-8289. P.O. Box 93549, Hollywood, 90092.

Xtraz Casting, 818/781-0066. P.O. Box 4145, Valley Village, 91617.

SHORT FILM PROJECTS
INCLUDING
STUDENT AND GRADUATE FILMS

• **Chris Cooper** is a character actor who works all the time. Some of his roles include his Oscar winning performance in *Adaptation*, the cruel father in *American Beauty* and the sheriff in *Lone Star*. He grew up in Kansas City and started working backstage in regional theatres there. He moved to New York, studied, worked on and Off-Broadway and eventually an NYU student film led to his big break. Director/writer John Sayles, cast him in his student film, then used him in other small roles and later wrote the lead in *Lone Star* for him.

• **Acting in student films** and projects can be your gateway to an acting career. It is not always easy to get the tape copy—you can probably expect a 50/50 chance of getting it and that is with a great deal of persistence on your part. Student films are not always shot under the best of circumstances; the directors are learning too. But if you are lucky and end up on a director's reel, you could be seen by every producer and agent in town, and possibly be seen at many film festivals. There is a possibility of being spotted and cast in a major production because of your acting work in a promising graduate director's reel.

• **If you are a beginner, you will gain valuable experience** in front of a camera—experience you cannot get in acting class or anywhere else. If you are a seasoned actor, you may get the chance to play a leading role, portraying the type of character that you may not be cast as in a commercial film. Circulating that tape or being seen at the screening may have casting people thinking of you for a wider variety of roles.

• **USC, UCLA, AFI** (American Film Institute), The Los Angeles Film School, Cal Arts and Loyola Marymount are the finest film schools in the world and their students need actors for their projects. They advertise in *Back Stage West* most heavily at the beginning of each semester or quarter. Crew work is also available. It is valuable to meet these future filmmakers when they are starting out. I wonder who acted in George Lucas' first films at USC.

• **When working on a student production** expect long delays, expect mistakes. You will learn how to size up a situation and to pick and choose the projects that you think will benefit you. Often student directors want actors to rehearse scenes from well known films to take into their directing classes. I feel it is of value to do this; their professors are working directors who may be in the process of casting a film you would be perfect for. You must open yourself to opportunities as often as possible.

• *Back Stage West* **writes an occasional column** about the hot talents in independent and student films. One of the things they reported on was the annual Student Academy Awards held by The Academy of Motion Picture Arts and Sciences. They honor student filmmakers from all across the country in four categories of filmmaking: alternative, animation, documentary and dramatic film. There were winners from Dartmouth, Rhode Island, NYU, Harvard, Stanford, Yale and Los Angeles. You can act in or produce student films anywhere you live.

• **Academy of Television Arts & Sciences Foundation** recently held their Annual College Television Awards with a screening for the industry held at the Directors Guild of America Theater. Winners were from AFI, Brigham Young, NYU, Missouri, Florida, Columbia and Northwestern.

• **Ang Lee, the director of Sense and Sensibility and The Ice Storm,** did his graduate film at NYU, winning the school's annual competition. The film caught the eye of a William Morris agent, who signed him.

• **Actor Al Sapienza was advised not to work** for first-time directors for no pay. He didn't listen and acted in director Danny Cannon's first film, *Strangers*. Four years later, Cannon gave Al a co-starring role in his film *Judge Dredd.*

• **Quentin Tarantino** optioned Reb Braddock's Florida State University thesis film, *Curdle,* and is planning to produce it.

• **USC student Laura Anne McCreary** turned in her senior thesis short film, "The Fourth John," to her professor, Carl Gottlieb, who wrote *Jaws.* He was so impressed he asked for a copy. When producer Ruben Hostka asked Gottlieb if he had any good scripts about young people, he gave him the tape. CAA is handling the script and Gottlieb and Hostka have become attached as producers.

• **Harvey Keitel** was studying at the Actor's Studio in New York in 1965. He answered an ad placed by film student Martin Scorsese, who was looking for actors to appear in *Who's That Knocking at My Door?,* a film he planned to make. Of course, they've gone on to make five feature films together. That student film was the turning point in Harvey's career.

• **At the 1991 Academy Awards**, Adam Davidson won an Oscar for his 1990 short film, *Lunch Date.* In his acceptance speech he said he was so surprised; he just did a 10-minute film for his film class and all "this" happened. He thanked the actors for contributing their talents.

• **Allen and Albert Hughes did a five-minute**, $250 short film that served as Albert's film school project at Los Angeles City College (LACC.) He used that as his demo reel. The 21-year-old twin brothers made their feature film debut co-writing and co-directing the $3 million New Line's *Menace II Society.* Suddenly every studio in town wanted to hire them as writers and directors.

• **Make it a priority** to gain experience by landing work in short films. Landing these roles is just as competitive as any other part of the business. This is where networking can come in handy. Get on some of the crews, come to know the filmmakers.

• **Anita Jesse's Studio**, www.anitajessestudio.com, produces two short film festivals a year. You do not have to be a member of the studio to participate in the productions. The acting in the films is very good.

Resources

www.filmfestivals.com. Gives schedules of all the film festivals.
www.48hourfilm.com. Make a film in two days of competition.

Back Stage West **and** www.backstage.com lists many student films that are currently casting; answer the ads. But also, you might submit your picture and resume to each school, each semester on the chance that you would be perfect for a project a student may be casting. On the web site you can get their Film Festival Guide.

Signatory Workshops, 323/549-6064. SAG, 5757 Wilshire Blvd., 8ᵗʰ Floor, Los Angeles. Held the second Wednesday of every month. They will walk you through the signatory process of SAG's Low Budget Agreements from start to finish.

Kevin Spacey has created a web site devoted to encouraging new filmmakers. www.TriggerStreet.com. Top industry people participating include Mike Myers, Sean Penn, Annette Bening and Bono. Elaborate online workshop and showcase for those who don't have a showbiz track record. View short films and scripts.

Annual Shorts Festival, www.actorsbone.com/shorts Event for filmmakers of shorts.

The Art Center, Film Office, 626/396-2274. Send photo and resume to be represented in the Film Department's files. Film Department Art Center College of Design, 1700 Lida Street, Pasadena, CA 91103.

California Institute of the Arts School of Film & Video, 661/253-7825. 24700 McBean Parkway, Valencia, 91355. www.calarts.com P&Rs are posted on the casting bulletin boards.

California State University Northridge (CSUN) Cinema and Televison Arts Dept., 818/677-3192. 18111 Nordoff St. Northridge CA 91330-8317. www.csun.edu Send P&R, the school maintains casting files.

Columbia College, 323/851-0550. 18618 Oxnard St., Tarzana 91356. Attn: Library. www.ColumbiaCollege.edu They maintain casting files. Actors receive a copy of their work.

Los Angeles City College (LACC) Radio/TV/Film Dept. Cinema Division, 323/953-4000. 855 N. Vermont Ave., Los Angeles, 90029. www.lacitycollege.edu They maintain casting files.

The Los Angeles Film School 323/860-0789. www.lafilm.com. 6363 Sunset Blvd., Hollywood, 90028. Attn: Headshot Files. This is the newest film school, opened in the fall of 1999.

University of California Los Angeles (UCLA) Film & TV Dept., 310/825-5761. 405 Hilgard Ave., Los Angeles, 90095. Attn: Gary Bailard www.tft.ucla.edu/tfthome.htm They maintain casting files.

University of Southern California (USC) Cinema School, Student Productions Office, 213/740-2235. www.usc.edu. University Park, Los Angeles, 90089. They maintain casting files.

DEMO REELS AND
AUDITION TAPES

DEMO REELS

• **Actors seeking agents, managers** and many film and television roles in Los Angeles need a demo reel. For actors with credits, this is not a problem—you simply get tape or DVD copies of films and television shows you have worked on and have a dynamite editor put together a three to four minute entertaining tape featuring your best acting work.

• **Planet Video's web site has useful information** about gathering tape and getting your raw footage ready to edit on your demo reel. www.planet-video.com. Go into their office and view hours of demo reels they have edited from actor's footage. *(Additional tips about gathering your tapes below.)*

• **Jan's Video tapes all night-time episodic television shows, and movies of the week.** They will probably have copies of shows you may have missed taping or need a higher quality copy. As I'm writing this, actor DJ Johnson had asked the production office at *General Hospital* to give him the exact dates his shows would be airing. They did and said, "Barring a nationwide emergency, those dates were solid." He arranged the airchecks. A few days later, sooner than he expected, he received a call from a friend saying he had seen him on the show that day. What a shock! But he was able to call Jan's Video and yes, they were able to retrieve a copy of the show from a company who tapes all the soaps. DJ picked up a copy of the episode that afternoon.

ACTORS WITHOUT FOOTAGE

• **For actors who have not worked in film and television** or if you can't get the tape from the projects you have worked on, you must get creative. Most agents, managers and casting directors say unless you have a network quality demo reel, don't bother. Yet, they still want to see your acting on camera. I believe laws can be broken.

• **Starmaker Jay Bernstein says**, "get an acting partner, shoot two minutes of a wonderfully acted original drama piece and two minutes of a good original comedy piece. Bottom line, fabulous acting with good material will showcase you well whatever the production values." Jay advises new actors to be well trained before letting anyone in the industry see you. He says, "They will remember you."

• **New actor Jordan Osher had an interview at a commercial agency.** They told him they were interested but would have to see something on tape. Jordan went to his commercial/acting class teacher, Stuart K. Robinson, who also happens to be a terrific writer/director/producer and asked for help. Stuart knew that one of Jordan's strong suits was comedy—a nerd or someone trying to be more important than he is. He suggested shooting a one page scene similar to *Swimming With The Sharks*. The tape is less than two minutes but it starts with Jordan in a suit and tie looking like a big shot with his feet on the desk, talking on the phone. All of a sudden the actual boss comes in and Jordan is scampering around trying to make nice and looking like the office flunky he really is and will be cast as. The scene is original, funny, directed and edited well and landed the agent. Jordan's cost was about $500. The important element, as always, was the acting. Jordan smartly gave this short film a name and it is on his resume.

• **Jordan wanted to have an additional character role** for his tape so Stuart K. wrote another minute and a half scene where Jordan is a low ranking hood, weaseling his way out of a sticky situation. It was shot outside featuring a great walk into and then away from the action that told a lot about the character. This took a little longer to shoot because of the outdoor location and cost around $600. This is also a short film and on Jordan's resume. Stuart K.'s philosophy is: If you need a piece of film for your reel, shoot an original very short film. Digital tape is used so much now it doesn't matter that a short film isn't shot on film. Jordan is looking for a theatrical agent and now has a dramatic piece on his demo reel.

• **Stuart charges according to the time he puts in.** He writes and rehearses the actors separately before the shooting day. He then edits and adds titles plus a score when it enhances the action.

• **PerfectReel Productions is a company that produces many demo reels** as well as larger projects. For actors, they specialize in shooting one to one and a half page short films. Michael Mc Clure is the owner and has two other filmmakers on staff. Michael believes that if an actor doesn't have anything on tape it would be best to shoot three shorts. For one short, shooting three and a half hours and editing for three hours, the cost would be about $300. The fee will rise if you want them to write a script, if you need coaching or another actor, or more people on the crew. He has computer programs to enhance your footage so it looks more like the piece was shot on film. If you have other footage he will edit in your new short for a dynamic reel. This is another location where you can view many of the reels they have done.

• **Michael is very helpful and suggests that two or even three actors** shoot together acting in each other's shorts and split the expenses. Each short is edited to feature the specific actor whose reel it is. At PerfectReel they also produce audition tapes; see below.

• **Richard and Miyumi Heeene of My You Me Productions** are a great team. They want all of their production work to look like quality films. Miyumi edits on the Avid using letter box and flicker effects when called for. I enjoyed the short films I viewed that had been shot to showcase actors. They will meet with you and design your shoot to fit in your budget. Shooting on location is a minimum of two hours for $180. Richard says for $600 and a 10-hour day including lights and sound, you can get a lot of coverage. It is, of course, more money for more crew. $800 to $1200 for a day will give you the top quality, including makeup. They will also shoot a twenty-minute short for $50. When you a have a three minute scene that you have rehearsed, perfected and that can be shot in their studio, you could get a master and two close-ups. This would be a good investment, as well as the experience of acting in front of a camera. They also will shoot an audition tape for the $50 rate. Again, the acting must be wonderful in order to actually use the tape as a demo reel.

• **Acting coach and director Joel Asher** is producing and directing three minute short films for actors' demo reels. He takes about a month to prepare to shoot with the actors. The cost is $1500 per actor. The original scenes are written to feature each actor as they may be cast. When the script is agreed upon, the actors are fully rehearsed and coached. The location is chosen and the "film" is shot with a professional crew and you are the star. The scene is then edited and packaged for each actor. Again, this is valuable experience—learning to work under pressure and another film credit for your resume.

• **Joel's students have had great results with these demo reels.** One actor was having a meeting with a prospective agent. She picked up the tape the moment the editing was finished, rushed to her meeting and as soon as the agent looked at the tape, they wanted to sign her.

• **Agent Bonnie Howard told me about an entertaining demo reel she viewed.** A new actor had captured famous actors in famous roles on the phone saying a line or two then the tape would cut to the new actor on the phone answering the famous actor in a character appropriate to the situation. The actor had written his own dialogue. Bonnie liked the concept but unfortunately the actor wasn't a good actor. She says, "On demo reels I want to see a name, headshot, no montage—just some really good acting of no more than three to four minutes long." Here is a case where the actor's ideas were good but he couldn't deliver.

• **Jill Jaress, acting coach, long time actress and career consultant,** teaches a three month intensive class which includes supplying the actors with five minutes of footage for their demo reels. They do two short scenes and one monologue. She is not aiming for network quality production values but she directs the actors to deliver good performances in roles that they can be cast in. She tells me several of her students in the last session got agents from their reels. In the demo reels I saw, all the actors were cast well and acted well. Poor production values don't bother me; poor acting does. This is not a demo reel that will look like a film you were in; it is an acting piece. I think Jill's class will work well for actors who are trained but haven't had camera experience. She helps actors create their business tools.

• **I've seen some terrific short clip location work** created by camera operators and editors for actors. Using a digital video camera, they shot the actor all over town, on Melrose, at the beach, on a hillside bluff, in the woods, on a motorcycle, whatever was appropriate for that actor. They included a short monologue; the tape was a personality piece. It is tough to get great sound but it is very important in this type of shoot. A microphone that attaches to the body is best when you are moving quite a bit, otherwise a handheld boom mike is good.

• **Photographer Mary Ann Halpin and her videographer husband Joe Croyle** are doing some great reels for beginners by shooting the actor looking like and talking like characters they can be cast as. They also shoot footage to be added to existing demo reels that show the actor doing characters they haven't been cast as yet.

• **I asked Mary Ann: When is it the right time for a novice actor to make a demo reel?**

> • **If you are a beginner, have taken some classes** and feel you are ready to put yourself in the market, you can create a personality tape with interviews and spontaneous monologues. This will capture the essence of who you are and the type of characters you might be cast as. This sort of demo reel should be no more than two minutes.

> • **Prepare by thinking about how you want to be cast** and about different sides of your personality that you want to bring forward. Then, find or write two monologues that show comedy or drama, or perhaps you could think of a clever through-line that will be the theme of your video. There is no excuse for not creating this important marketing tool.

• **Actress Mary Pinizzotto talked about shooting with Mary Ann and Joe.**

> • **At first it was a little intimidating** having to be characters without a script, but it really worked out well. There was one part where I was in my business suit trying to remember the motivational speech I used to do for a job—I got so frustrated with myself that I started to cry and we just taped it. I ended up going into some speech about how we are all supposed to have it all together and nobody does; we're all just dressed up to look good and faking it.

> • **I did some businesswoman stuff;** a cooking scene; a scene where I talked about the weird people in Nashville, using my Nashville accent; a ballroom Diva and me just talking about all those people. Should be good.

• **Mary Ann and Joe suggest having the footage they shoot** edited by Planet Video's David Conner or D.C. Douglas. They really do excellent work. You can make an appointment, go by their office, put on a pair of headphones and look at many, many of the demo reels they have edited. This is a great learning tool and will give you a good idea of how you will want your reel to look.

• **If you produce a project yourself** like those described above, you need talented, creative people with you. Research it carefully. You could get several actors and hire an excellent camera crew and split the expense. This is not cheap, but when a producer or director asks you for tape, you will have something of quality to show them. Of course, you have to look very good (lighting and makeup) and above all, the acting has to be of superior quality. See if you can get your acting coach involved in the project. Remember to keep this three to four minutes long—even two to three minutes, as long as it is 100% high quality.

• **Janice Allen, a long time student and now a director** in my class, was not able to use a piece of footage from a film she did. The production company lost their funds so they weren't able to complete their postproduction. The sound was awful, yet it was a good acting scene. Janice borrowed my Mini DVD camera, rented lights, a boom and mike. With a few friends, one a director/writer/editor, and three other actors they were able to shoot three short films in a day. Each actor got the footage they needed. The advantage was an editor able to edit on his work machines to come up with professional looking pieces. I saw a bit of Janice's close up; the acting was very good and it looked great. Remember—these demo reels aren't played in big screen theaters; they are played on TV screens and computer monitors.

• **Some of best acting** I saw in short films while researching demo reels was at a short film festival that the Anita Jesse Acting Studio puts on twice a year. Anita wants her actors to learn to network within the industry so she tells them to each star in their own three-minute maximum short film. She doesn't help them at all with scripts, rehearsal, contacts; they do it all on their own. They each had to learn where to get a camera, who they knew that could provide editing facilities, how to write a script, get a crew—all that goes into developing one's own project. Not all of the production values were great but in every single one, each actor delivered a wonderful performance. A short film like one of these could easily be used as a demo reel or part of a demo reel.

• **Look at demo reels** on many of the web sites below. All the businesses I talk about here have videos for you to view at their facilities. When you are putting out this amount of money you really want to get a lot of value. If you are not ready with your acting and the scenes aren't good, you will have purchased a lot of experience. I cannot emphasize enough that no matter how much money you invest, if the acting is not excellent you are wasting your time. This takes the same level of dedication and rehearsal you would do for a role in a multi-million dollar movie. You must always give 120 percent of yourself when you are acting.

• **Director Mike Nichols told Dustin Hoffman** on the set of *The Graduate*, his first major film role, "This is the only chance you have to do this scene today; we won't come back and do it again. Whether the picture is a flop or a hit nobody knows but it is going to be up there for the rest of your life. So how dare you not give it 120 percent." Dustin says he never forgets that.

HOW TO GET TAPE FOR WORK YOU HAVE DONE

• **When working on student or non-union productions** it is often a difficult task to get tape of your work, though the tape is usually the reason you are working for free. When you have been cast in this type of production, ask the director or producer what kind of tape or format you will receive your copy on. Also ask if it will be possible to get unedited takes of your closeups. Provide new high quality tapes, Beta-SP, 3/4", Mini DV and a high grade 1/2" VHS tape. Also have blank ready-to-record-on CD and DVD disks. Label these and give the producer or editor the type of format they request. Perhaps they will give you copies as you are shooting or while they are editing. For your demo reel purposes there is no need to wait until the filmmakers are finished editing and with post production.

• **All of the above may work to get copies of your acting.** If not, David Conner of Planet Video suggests, "Make friends with the editor and anyone who will be working on post-production; keep in touch and get a copy of your edited work."

• **You can buy tapes** at Good Guys, Best Buy and Edgewise Media; it is important that they are new. When you get a tape copy, take the best possible care of it. You will need to transfer the copy to a VHS tape on SP speed so you can watch it and decide what you want to use for your demo reel. Play this original master tape just once for the transfer because each time tape is run it loses quality. You will probably have to go to a tape editing facility to have it copied. It is worth the expense.

• **If you're in a film that is available on video or** DVD, rent it, cue it up and have an editing company copy your scenes, bypassing the anti-copy code. When you are copying shows from television to use for your reel, use a new high grade tape and record on SP, standard play, speed. This will give you the best quality from your home machine for editing. For the highest quality, pay to have a company record it on 3/4" or Beta tape for you; that is called an air check. Jan's Video is the best. *See Resources.*

• **Gather your pieces of tape**, interview editors, look at their demo reel demonstrations, choose one and have a smashing video tape designed. Four minutes maximum, with all the scenes featuring YOU. Don't worry about story points, only your acting moments. Your name should appear at the beginning and end of the tape.

• **Take your footage** to an editing company with a sharp editor and put your piece together using fades and all their goodies to enhance the production value. If you have some *extra* work where you are seen, you could mix that in too.

• **Packaging counts for a lot**; you want to look very professional.

• **Label your tape boxes** *and* your tapes in bold letters with your name and phone number. Use a white or black tape box that has a full plastic cover/sleeve over the whole box. Scan your picture on your computer. Create a good looking presentation for your box. Slip it inside the plastic cover and you are set. Imagestarter, as well as many other companies, creates wonderful video box graphics.

• **An editor can freeze a single frame** on your tape and download it for you, so you will have a production still to use for promoting your movie coming out or telling people when your television show is airing. This is especially valuable when you are in a scene with a star. These are also good photos to show in interviews, when you are talking about working with a well-known actor.

• **Bonnie Howard, Theatrical and Commercial Agent.**

  • **Demo tapes should be as short as possible**, and as high impact as
    possible. Just select the best work. Don't send out a tape unless it is
    requested, because you probably won't get it back unless you submit
    an envelope with postage.

  • **Until you have a tape of your work** that you are proud of, that can
    help you to get roles and shows a range of your talent, you are
    better off without one. Tapes are generally requested (a) if you are
    not available for a reading, (b) to see the range of your talent, (c) to
    show your work to a director who may be out of town, already
    shooting on location.

• **John Ingle**, Edward Quartermaine on *General Hospital*, tells how
he landed the role, replacing the actor who retired from the show. He
auditioned and was being considered. Eight weeks later, the casting
director, Mark Teschner, happened to turn on *The Young and the Restless*,
and there was John playing a judge. Mark called John's agent to see if it
had been taped. It hadn't been because it was a flashback on the show
and John wasn't aware it was going to be on. John called Jan's Video (they
tape everything) and asked them to find his scene, record it and messenger it to the casting director, who took it to the producer and said, "This
is our actor." They cast John right then, after a long search of auditions
here and in New York.

AUDITION TAPES

• **Brian Hibbert's manager wanted to interview agents** to find representation for him so he requested that Brian get an audition tape. The
manager wanted footage of him doing three short roles he could be cast
as. Brian plays in his teens to early twenties, is well trained, but new to
the business. He had a very tight budget, I gave him some appropriate
scripts and he hired Michael McClure of PerfectReel Productions to
produce an audition tape for him. Brian came in well rehearsed, bringing someone to read the other character's lines off camera. To change
the backgrounds they shot the scenes in different parts of the office;
the production value was wonderful. Brian's talent came through and
he landed an agent. Michael charged Brian $70 for the shooting and
editing; it is not a tape to be used as a demo reel but it did the job of
landing him an agent at a price he could afford.

• **Thomas Mills** wrote in one of his *Back Stage West Tombudsman* columns of overhearing a jubilant actor tell his friend how he just landed a role in a major film. It seems the actor had read the book, knew he was perfect for a certain role. His agent said he wasn't right but submitted him anyway. Word came back from the casting director that he wasn't right for the role. The actor got the sides, changed his appearance and shot an audition tape. He took it directly to the producer's office; the producer and director both looked at the tape. They brought him in and he landed the part.

Resources

Screen Actors Guild, 323/549-6064. If you are making a short film, attend a Signatory Workshop, held on the second Wednesday of every month from 6 to 8 PM at SAG, 5757 Wilshire Blvd., 8th Floor. Here you will learn how to produce your film under the SAG deferred payment plan. It's always best to use professional actors.

www.watchreels.com. This is a site with many types of demo reels; included are the directors, directors of photography and editors. Good research site.

Planet Video, 323/848-3662. www.planet-video.com. 8159 Santa Monica Blvd., #201, West Hollywood, 90046. Above Hoy's Wok on NW corner of Crescent Heights and Santa Monica. D. C. Douglas and David Conner are Avid editors extraordinaire, top in their field. $75 an hour for editing. $25 for your Beta Master. Archiving your demo is free. Go watch their demo reels after you have gotten all the wonderful, informative data off their website. The website takes you through the step by step process of how to get the best demo reel. When I interviewed David, he said he could deliver almost any actor's reel within a four hour session, $300. If you want to design your reel yourself, you know exactly what you want and are ready to go with your tapes cued to the best performance, you can get it done in two hours or less.

Jan's Video Editing, 323/462-5511. www.videodemo.com. 1800 N. Argyle #100, Hollywood, 90028. M-F 9-6. Make an appointment, Doreen will give her recommendations and assign you an editor. She believes actors need 1-1/2 to 2 hours for first time reels. You only pay for the actual editing time you use. All the editors are very well trained and have years of experience. Jan's Video will aircheck your shows for you from the air on 3/4" or Beta tape, $15 for an hour show, $10 for 1/2 hour. Best of all, they may have a copy of a show you did years ago, which would be impossible to obtain from any other source. Jan's has the most extensive library of tapes anywhere—most network series and all movies of the week taped from satellite. They can take stills from your videos. They can transfer formats from any country to our formats and they can put your reel on any format you may need. Jan's has been producing demo reels longer than any other editing house. *Entertainment Tonight, Inside Edition, Extra* and *Access Hollywood* are always calling to grab something from their archives.

Stuart K. Robinson of Robinson Creative, 310/558-4961. $80 an hour for ongoing students; $100 an hour for others. He meets with the actor or actors to see what the short film needs to say about the type of characters the actor can best market themselves as. He then writes a script and they meet to rehearse. Stuart believes that the preparation should not be mixed with the shooting. He shoots with his small crew, then edits and scores the short film when it enhances the scene. He teaches a motivating, positive acting philosophy and is very focused on actors landing the jobs.

PerfectReel Productions, Michael McClure, 818/752-6494. www.PerfectReel.com. 3749 Cahuenga Blvd. West, Studio City, 91604. Basics: Shooting, $49 per hour; Editing, $39 per hour. Options: Custom written scene, $45; Actor provided per scene, $55; Crew Provided per scene $50; Location, $95; Acting Coaching, $45. Their web site is full of information on shooting demo reels. In answer to, "Can I put this on my resume?" He says, "Of course, we are a legitimate production company known for our larger projects as well. Treat it like a short film. If we get any inquiry calls, we'll back you up."

Potty Mouth Productions, 818/846-1779. www.pottymouthproductions.com. 627 Cedar Ave., Burbank. Home of the $100 cash special for demo reels, including 10 VHS copies with box, face labels and DV master. Professional Digital Video Production. Shoot and edit your scene and 10 VHS copies for $200. David McClellan is an independent producer/director. "I shoot and edit projects for independent companies on a daily basis. I try to be fair in my prices and give repeat clients and referrals discounts." Good website, very informative.

My You Me Productions, 310/820-1772. www.myyoume.com. 2050 S. Bundy Drive, #104, West Los Angeles. They do air checks. They shoot demo reels on locations or at their studio; audition tapes; blue screen; demo reels to computer CD ROMS; check them out. $80 to edit a standard demo reel; $3 per copy for VHS tapes including laser labels. They create websites including pictures resumes and demo reels. Founded by actor Richard and Miyumi Heeene, this company is dedicated to helping actors achieve their marketing goals.

Joel Asher Studio & Michael Communications, 818/785-1551. www.Joel-Asher-Studio.com. Actors At Work Demo Reels. $1500 for writing, directing, producing, editing, graphics and titles, packgaging, duplication—the complete demo reel. His informative, instructive video tapes he has produced are: *Getting the Part, All About Cold Readings*; *Casting Directors "Tell It Like It Is"* and *Agents "Tell It Like It Is."* The newest is: *Directors on Acting!*

Halpin-Croyle Studios, 323/874-8500, www.maryannhalpin.com. By appointment. Mary Ann Halpin well-known for her very individualized head shots and her accomplished videographer husband, Joe Croyle have developed a technique of shooting footage to enhance the footage you have. If you don't have any footage they will create a reel that shows the types of roles you will be cast in. One of their demo reels shows an actor who only had a black and white IBM commercial. They used every angle of the commercial amidst the footage they shot. Top of the line professional digital camera, sound and lighting equipment and professional makeup delivers the makings for an exciting, entertaining reel. They give you the footage on digital tape and a 1/2" video work copy and then recommend you take it to Planet Video for editing. The "Creating Your Reel" package is $595 and the "Supplementing Your Reel" package is

$375. This is without the cost of editing which they estimate to be about $300. They give you a full explanation of how to work with the editor.

Allen Fawcett Productions, 818/763-7399. www.killerreel.com. View his sample demo reels on the website. $1500 to create a four minute demo reel from scratch. Also available to edit your own footage into marketable demo reels. Editing is $70 an hour. Gives an occasional free seminar on: *See reels that agents love; get your own reel—now!* They say, "We shoot and edit tasty demo reels that make agents drool." You can make an appointment and they will show you reels and all of the services they provide. They have packaging specials, they can also put your tapes on CDs. They offer readers of this book discounts on some of their services, be sure and ask about it. Also Hosts Actor's Websites: $60 set-up fee, $29.95 per month with a one-year commitment. Allen shoots audition tapes for $80.

Jill Jaress, coach and career consultant, 310/828-7814 or 888/576-4695. www.actorsconsultations.com. $240 a month for three months in a class called "Breaking In." This is a three-month intensive class which covers the information needed to break into the business and the acting skills needed to book the jobs. The class includes supplying the actors with five minutes of footage for their demo reels and giving them the opportunity to do a prepared scene for Casting Director, Penny Perry who has cast 65 major feature films, three of which have won Oscars for Best Picture. Jill is very supportive and interested in helping actors advance in their individual goals. She herself has had a long acting career that you can check out at www.imdb.com.

Firepit Productions, 818/558-6622, Richard Corbin produces professional digital video audition tapes, specializing in Demo Reels for actors seeking Hosting auditions. Shooting, $60 per hour, custom written scenes, editing services, and coaching available for an additional cost. For the actor without a demo reel who needs an audition tape to submit for representation, or auditions that require actors to be "put on tape". Mini DV Master and VHS copies available on the spot. Call for more information on the Host Demo Reels.

Dino Ladki, Casting Director, 323/654-8703. www.thecastlist.com. $90 an hour or $45 for half-hour, after the half-hour he bills in ten minute increments. Dino will rehearse and coach you on your audition and you leave with a VHS copy of your best take. He also shoots material to be used in your demo reel or to be posted on The Cast List site. Also, just a good place to go to see how your auditions are coming across in the actual audition room. It is one thing to do an audition in your acting class but going to Dino and putting audition material or even a monologue on tape will give you valuable feedback.

Imagestarter, Video Tape Packaging, 323/848-3663. www.imagestarter.com. 8159 Santa Monica Blvd., Suite. 201, West Hollywood 90046. (above Hoy's Wok) M-F 10-6. $45 includes 12 inserts and matching labels, including set-up, name, photo, spine, contact # and running time. Set up an appointment, bring in your photos, resume, reviews or any other information you think might be good on your tape box. They'll design a truly distinctive look with matching labels. Additional charges may apply for custom requests. They also do resumes, photoresumes, 8x10 quality lithos, business cards, postcards and other promotional items. Very classy and reasonably priced.

Dub-it, 323/993-9570 or 888/993-8248. www.dub-it.com. 1110 North Tamarind, Hollywood, 90038. Video and CD-ROM duplication and conversion. VHS custom packaging, only orders over 2500. Minimum of tape copies is 50. When you are doing large quantities, this is the place to go.

EZTV, 310/829-3389. www.eztvmedia.com. 1653 18th Street Santa Monica, 90404. M-SA 10AM to 7PM. Both studio and location production. They shoot demo reels at their facility. Prepare actor's reels and all dubbing, copying and editing in all formats. No air checks. I didn't actually go by this facility for this printing but they were the pioneers of this type of business. I worked with their editors years a go and they were very helpful, interested, caring and reasonable. Go in and look at the reels they have created.

Larry Eisenberg, 323/254-5312. www.larryeisenberg.com. See the site and view several demo reels. Editing $30 an hour. "Every reel is a unique and entertaining production." Larry graduated with a Masters in Film Directing from Cal Arts. He says he financed his education by cutting demo tapes for actors.

Post Wanted, 818/563-2230. www.uniquefilms.com. 1918 West Magnolia Blvd., Suite 102, Burbank, 91505. They produce actor demo reels. The price is comparable with the other listings. $1500 a day for two to three pages, plus editing. They use a 3 or 4 member crew, everything is professional. I have not seen their reels but I like the web site and their credits. If you had three short wonderful scenes you could possibly do this in a day and split the cost with one or two other actors.

Pro-Star Media, 818/509-9316. www.prostarmediagroup.com 11366 Ventura Blvd., Studio City, 91604. At the intersection of Ventura and Tujunga. M-F 10-6, Sa 12-5. Editing and copying. 10-minute tapes sell for $2; full sleeve tape boxes $1. Air checks $45 an hour for 3/4", $20 an hour for 1/2". Avid-computer digital editing system; Beta sp, $80 an hour.

Ross Hunt Productions, 818/763-6045 or 818/980-3812. www.rosshuntproductions.com. 12438 Moorpark, Studio City, 91604. Demo reels, inexpensive quantity duplication. Editing.

Speed Video Duplication SVD, 310/828-2239 2400 Wilshire Blvd, Santa Monica, 90403. Video copies from VHS, S-VHS, 3/4" Betacam SP, Betamax, 8mm. Hi-8 and VHS editing for demo tapes. Air checks.

Edgewise Media (formerly Studio Film and Tape), 323/466-8101. www.edgewisemedia.com. 1215 N. Highland Ave. Hollywood, 90038. Hours: 8am-Midnight, Sunday 9-4PM, 7 days a week. 3/4" Sony 30-minute tapes, in 10 tape bulk packs, BRS $11.21, XBR $13.43. 30-minute 1/2" VHS bulk tapes are $1.07 ea. for qty. 50, cardboard sleeve is $.25 extra. 30-minute tapes in 10-tape bulk packs. 60-minute bulk tapes. Black and white tape boxes with full plastic sleeves, $.85. Tapes for any use available. Call ahead and they will have your order ready.

The Tape Company, 323/993-3000 or 800/851-3113. www.thetapecompany.com. 1014 N. Highland Ave., between Melrose and Santa Monica Blvd. M-F 8-6, 9-5PM Sa. 3/4" Sony 30-minute tapes: BRS $12.21, XBR $12.57. 1/2" VHS Sony 30 minutes $2.82, includes sleeve and label. 50 Bulk tapes: Fuji 30-minutes $1.33 each. 40 bulk 10-minute tapes are $1.21 each. They have occasional blowout sales on bulk tapes. Bulk means 10 tapes in a package. VHS 1/2" 15-minute BASF tapes are $.84 each in bulk. Sony 3/4" 30-minute BRS $12.21; XBR is $14.09; BRS in bulk is $9.48. 1/2" plastic sleeve box $.74.

Point 360, 323/461-3726. www.point360.com. 1220 N. Highland Ave., Los Angeles, 90038. 24 hours a day, 7 days a week. Any copying from any type of format. These are the top of the line machines, including film to tape. The best quality. No editing or air checks.

Video Tech, 818/765-1778. 12120 Sherman Way, North Hollywood. 91605 M-F 9-5. Under 10-min. tapes, $2.00 (10-24); $1.19 (25-99); $1.15 (100-999).

World of Video, 310/659-5959, 866/900-DUBS. www.wova.com 8717 Wilshire Blvd., Beverly Hills, 90211. M-F 9-6, Sa 11AM-4PM. Demo reels. Editing and duplication for all formats, digital effects, film-to-tape and freeze frames. Avid editing, $129 per hour. Linear editing, $89 per hour. Air checks.

Digital Demo Reel at Breakdown Services, 310/276-9166. $120 for 10 CD copies includes two pictures, one resume, your reel up to four minutes converted to the digital format. These CDs can be played on a PC or MAC.

Producing Your
Own Projects

• **If you find it hard to break into the business,** or if it's been a while since you have acted, you have the power to generate projects for yourself. The people interviewed below are creating work in Los Angeles. If you are not in Los Angeles yet, start at home. If you are in Los Angeles, start now. If you aren't familiar with how stage or performance art is produced, apprentice yourself to directors and producers. They are always looking for unpaid hard workers in exchange for the education they will give you. *Back Stage West* lists ads for technical and back stage people all the time.

• **Once you have found material** that suits your own personal style, honed, rehearsed, and performed it, you may want to professionally tape or film parts of the production. A few minutes can be used for your audition tape, or perhaps you can find directors who need a 10, 15 or even 30-minute piece for their demo reels. Material is the hardest thing to develop. Once you have that, you may find all kinds of help from people who need to demonstrate their skills also.

• **Biff Yeager will make a movie starring you for $500,000.** Of course this is not for everyone but it's a very interesting idea. He produces the SAG project using industry writers, directors, a star name or two, dialogue directors and crew. He will make it any genre you want. www.ultimatewishgift.com.

• **Stacey Smithey, actress and producer,** has produced several plays. I asked her to write about what it takes to produce a play. She is always generating a place for herself to act.

- **I would strongly urge actors** to put up their own projects—plays, films, anything. One is able to control the quality and roles they will play and an actor then is responsible for generating their own work rather than waiting by the phone.

- **I learned how to produce theater by trial and error.** I found plays by going to Samuel French Bookstore and looking through their catalog of plays. The catalog breaks down plays by number of characters. It also lists the genre, a summary, past press quotes, any restrictions and royalty range (usually between $40 and $60 per performance and there is a security bond/deposit of $500 which you get back at the end). You can buy the catalog for $3. I then bought plays I thought were interesting and read them. I applied for the rights through Samuel French. You can send a letter to them stating the play, author, venue and number of seats, dates of performances, ticket price and type of performance (amateur, equity, etc.). It can take anywhere from one week to five months to get a response, so start early.

- **The most important choice is your material**, but the second most important choice is the theater. I called every theater in town and asked their prices, availability for performance and rehearsal. This is important because many theaters are not available at night for rehearsal as they are rented out for classes—and tech week starting at midnight every night makes it rough! It is better to pick a well-known theater, but they do tend to be much more expensive. You can also barter with the theater owner to bring down the price or throw in some extra re- hearsal time. I have always paid less than the price they have asked. You can also ask to pay for the first 2 weeks up front and then pay the rest after you have opened and made some money. Some theaters want all the rent up front, but some will work with you and your needs. You can also find better prices if you are willing to do weeknight productions as opposed to weekend productions. It is usually half price if not 75% less. As a producer, you will want to make sure you have insurance. Usually theaters require this. It is about $425 for 8 performances over a one month period.

- **You will need to cast and crew up your production.** A great way to raise funds is to split the cost between the actors. You need to agree upon this up front and you can't advertise this in *Back Stage West*. You can ask actors in your classes, friends, etc. You will need to find a director, lighting designer and operator, sound operator, set designer, graphic designer for postcards and flyers, press point person, box office/concessions attendant. Ask around—you will find these people. They will show up. It is wonderful when they do! Props and wardrobe are usually handled by the actors. You need a reservation phone number, reservation lists by date, cash box and cash change.

• **You will also need sound cues and music**, usually within your show. (Music within the play should be cleared through the music publisher. You can also ask unknown bands to use their music for free). It is also nice to have pre-show music, curtain call music, post-show music, and lobby music.

Other needs:

• **Rehearsal schedule**, usually four to eight weeks.

• **Other rehearsal venues** such as apartments, houses, etc..

• **Opening night reception** is nice.

• **Concession menu**, cookies, coffee, water, soda—you have to have a liquor license to "sell" alcohol, but many people serve it "for free" but accept donations.

• **Always bring extra toilet paper**, trash bags, paper towels—you never know!!!

• **Press Kit for reviewers and industry people**. This includes a press release, bios of cast and crew, actor's photos and press photos. They may want to feature your production and use still photos you provide.

• **Fax the press release** and invitations to press outlets for consideration for free listings and reviews at least one month in advance. Press outlets include *LA Times, LA Weekly, Back Stage West, Variety, Hollywood Reporter, New Times, Venice Magazine, Tolucan Times*—make follow up calls to make sure they received faxes and will be attending.

• **You may consider advertising**, but it is expensive. Only do this if you have a lot of money.

• **Lobby Board** with actor's headshots.

• **Awards**. Find out if you are eligible for the Ovation Awards, *LA Weekly* Awards, Drama Critic's Circle.

• **Program**. Include credits and bios of cast and crew.

• **Promotion**. Postcards, flyers, posters, map to venue and list of local restaurants you recommend. Opening night invites to casting directors and agents.

• **Web Tix offers your tickets at half-price** and On The House will give your tickets for free to their members and you get a free audience. This is good on press nights.

- **It is a joy to produce plays.** It is such a high when everything and everyone comes together. Live theater is like nothing else! And as Judy Kerr suggested, "You will look back on this time as sweet!" The first play I produced was with Judy as director. How lucky we were to have such a wonderful, generous woman to direct, guide and lead us. It was a cherished time in my life.

• **Pamela Munro, actress, producer,** studied, acted and produced theater in New York, London and Berkeley. Now in Los Angeles, she continues to act and produce.

- **I was a member of St. Ambrose** church and the church hall wasn't being used. Our first play was *George Washington Slept Here* by Kaufman & Hart. We produced it for $500, which was loaned to us by the Church. We made $500 and paid them back.

Q: How could you produce for so little money?

- **We basically had costumes and set pieces.** An artist friend did the art work for the program; we sold advertising in it and that paid for the printing. We did a lot of deficit financing where people would buy things, keep their bills and get paid back from the box office. The money we had up front was mostly for printing, postage and royalties. I picked a play that was the high end of summer stock; a comedy. It had to be new enough that we didn't have to hassle with the costumes too much. I had a large cast so I had more resources to draw on.

- **I produced classical plays.** At the Pasadena Library, I found an ancient translation of Chekov's *The Boar* which did not require payment of royalties. We did friends' plays who were willing to forego the royalties and Cabaret things in which everybody did their own thing.

- **All deals do not involve money.** There are a lot of swaps in the non-profit sector. They call it Non-Cash Donations. We call it sweat-equity. It requires a tremendous amount of work. It's also contacts, contacts, contacts. Someone I know spent $15,000 and lost $10,000 on a show. I spent $1,000, and didn't lose any money. The same reviewer saw both shows.

- **When you have an actor's co-op,** you can do all kinds of things together that you can't do singly. In financing, they call it a syndicate. It's more sensible to produce as a syndicate and share in the profits and the losses; everyone feels that they have a personal investment in what's going on.

- **I look for tech people** who are willing to be trained. For example, there was a film director who had just come into town and hadn't directed a play since college. He wanted his name all over the publicity and we said, "Sure." It gets the director's names out there. It's worth it to them.

- **I knew several women** who were doing one-woman shows, so I put together a compilation of excerpts from their shows for ANTA. I brought that in as a package. I've been piggy-backing other organizations, because the theater companies already have insurance and the spaces are sitting there.

- **The biggest expense is theater rental,** which really isn't necessary. You can produce little productions in a cabaret setting, a club. It's the high end of the poetry scene and you don't have to worry about the unions. They also do dramatic things and acoustic music. We did a show called *A Collage of Women's Moments* in the club and cabaret circuit. We worked at Highland Grounds, Natural Fudge, Pikmeup, the old Santa Monica Improvisation.

Q: How do you get people to see you?

- **There's the audience of the venue,** the audience of the friends and families of the actors, then there's the general public. If you're working for an existing venue, find out if they have a mailing list or a calendar and get yourself on it. Give all the people in the ensemble lots of flyers. If it's getting to the end of the week and the response is weak, get on the phone and paper the house saying, "This is the weekend that you can get all your friends in on two-fers."

- **To get industry people,** we put the flyers in the Breakdown Service. If you get seven people and it costs $70 to put the ads in Breakdowns, that's $10 a piece. It's more reasonable for actors to pay $10 each than pay for individual postage to the casting directors.

Q: What was the drive for you to produce?

- **My payment was that I had artistic control,** or artistic input. They were the kinds of things I wanted to do, the kinds of parts I wanted to work on. I didn't have the lead in every show, but there was always something there. Also, I kept myself working and learned a tremendous amount. Most of the things in L.A. are over-produced. I'm interested in getting results, not window dressing. You have a couple of well-placed chairs and some good actors; what else do you need?

- **Everybody should have an act.** I've developed a role for myself that's a combination of Renaissance and Celtic music, and I go to Renaissance Faires; there are a whole string of them. Sometimes I make money, sometimes I just pass the hat. My entourage and I get in for free; it's sort of like having a paid vacation. I work on my music and have a great time.

• **Anne Etue is an actor, director, producer and publicist** for several theaters and projects. Anne directs and helps produce performers Amy Hill's and Nobuko Miyanoto's one-woman shows.

Q: How did you get interested in one-person shows?

• **Amy had some material** that she thought would make a good one-person show, and asked me to direct it. Her first show, *Tokyo Bound,* had a theme of her at age 18 going to Japan to find her mother's roots. We put the ideas on 3x5 cards and she would go away and start writing. I was initially a sounding board for her on whether or not I thought the material worked and I did some editing for her. She also had a dramaturge involved in the process.

Q: What's a dramaturge?

• **A dramaturge is a person** who looks at the script and helps to shape it. It's common in most theater companies to help research the material or go through the material and give feedback on whether it should be produced. One mistake a lot of people make is not to have a director or someone outside the piece to formulate it. Amy was approached by the Japanese-American Cultural Center and that was the first booking.

Q: Was that for money?

• **It wasn't much, but we always had some kind of compensation.** We decided that we had a good half-hour of material. Then we workshopped it at West Coast Ensemble. We had maybe 10 people in to give us some feedback in preparation for a run at the East West Players. Amy applied for a $9,000 grant from the Cultural Affairs Department; that's how the first run was partially funded.

• **When you get a grant, they don't just hand you a check** but at least it validates the goal; it's the green light to keep on working on it. We had a run and it was a huge success. Sylvie Drake *(L.A. Times)* came and saw it, loved it and gave us the front page. All of the reviews were outstanding. At the 99-seat level, it probably was one of the most successful one-person shows. In the program I was listed as Hika Keltamaki, stage manager; Elizabeth Bennett, promotions; Anne Etue, director. It was basically me and Amy. We had a lighting designer, a set designer, a music designer. Amy felt very strongly about paying everybody involved.

• **Another fertile ground for these one-person shows is festivals** in Canada. We did the Montreal Fringe Festival. There is an entrance fee, maybe $200-$300, and you've got to get there. We had tons of frequent flyer miles to take care of that expense. They put you up at someone's house who's connected to the festival, then you keep all the box office receipts every night. We did extraordinarily. Tickets are $7, seating 100+ people and every single night for two weeks we sold out. Each night they gave us $700 in Canadian money. Amy and I split it right down the middle and had a great vacation.

- **We could've gone all summer.** There were people that went from Vancouver all the way across Canada. We have been to Vassar College, Boston College, Arizona State University, Michigan State University, and a whole slew of schools.

Q: How do these colleges know about you?

- **Every year, there's a Western Arts Administrators Conference** called WAA. At the conference there are people who book for public venues, but the biggest number are people who book for the art centers. For example, UCLA has Royce Hall and the Wadsworth Theater, so the guy that runs that would be at the WAA Conference. We showcase a bit of the show at the conference; you get 15 minutes.

- **The college circuit has been a big thing for us.** We were at the Public Theater in New York. George Wolfe came to see *Tokyo Bound* when we did it at East West Players, and liked it. A number of theaters have solo performers' festivals. Louisville has a *Solo Performers Festival*; San Francisco has *O Solo Mio*. You don't make enormous sums of money, but they do pay. They'll be willing to subsidize your airfare and find you a place to stay.

Resources

Biff Yeager, www.ultimatewishgift.com. Produces your starring movie for $500,000. I've known Biff for years. He is a great actor and can really put things together.

Anne Etue, 323/669-0553. She is available for directing, producing and publicity work.

The Larry Moss Studio, 310/399-3666. www.edgemar.com. 2437 Main Street, Santa Monica, 90405. All the teachers here encourage "story exercise"—creating a 15 minute monologue of a story based on your life that is difficult to tell, with you voicing each of the characters. Many one-person shows were developed out of this exercise.

Back Stage West www.backstage.com, produces an annual edition with theater and spaces suitable for rent. You can call them and get their most recent back edition with the theater listings.

Time Six Theatre League Alliance and Web TIX, 213/614-0556. www.theatrela.org. Most Los Angeles theaters belong to this group and they also take individual members. There is a monthly newsletter and you can keep up on everything that is going on in the theater in Los Angeles.

On The House, 310-399-3868. $195 a year for 2 tickets; many shows available every week.

PUBLIC ACCESS CABLE TELEVISION

• **Anyone living in Los Angeles County** can produce their own 1/2-hour public access television show. Some studios charge $35 plus the cost of a 3/4" video tape, while other studios are free. If you provide a 1/2" tape, they will record the show on both formats at the same time for no charge. The best bargain in town!

• **It is possible to serve as a non-paid intern.** Most of the technical people are interns, thus the programs are not network quality. They offer small workshops where you'll get actual hands-on experience with cameras, lighting, technical directing (TD) and even directing. You can apply by calling the cable company. I interned for about nine months when I first started producing my public access show so I would be familiar with all aspects of production. Many of the full-time employees at the cable companies started out as interns.

• **The cable companies offer classes for producers** in how to operate remote 3/4" camera equipment and how to use the editing bays. There is currently no charge for editing or using remote equipment. Cable company rules change frequently but any amount they may charge will be reasonable.

• I've been producing *Judy Kerr's Acting Workshop* for 18 years. My students do cold readings, scenes and monologues; it helps them gain three-camera experience and exposure to industry people who may be watching. The tape can also be shown to agents and casting people if the actor has no other footage.

• **I also do talk shows**, interviewing prominent people in the acting business who have information for the acting community at large. My students present questions to the guests. Sometimes we have guest teachers designing exercises for the actors.

• **You can produce any type of show you wish.** Why not give yourself, your friends and associates an opportunity to do some acting or talk show work? For very little money, you can learn about the television industry from the inside out. All of the studios have day, evening and Saturday hours available in which to tape your shows.

• **When you're ready to produce a show**, you can rehearse in front of your home camera. In fact you can tape your whole show at home and use the cable facilities to transfer from your 1/2" format to 3/4" tape and edit the pieces into a 28-minute show. After your tape airs with the cable company that recorded it, you can take the tape to each of the other studios and they will air the tape for no charge. You can even get a several-week regular time slot at many of the studios.

• **All possibilities are open to you and your imagination.** I've coached many public access producers, working with them on-camera, guiding them and offering tips so they can avoid mistakes in their first few shows.

• **Here are a few studios to get you started.** Call and they will mail the guidelines, the producer meetings schedule, and provide information on the classes and intern programs. See you on TV.

Resources

At this printing, none of these studios are charging for producing shows.

Adelphia Cable, 310/315-4444. 2939 Nebraska, Santa Monica, 90404.

Adelphia Cable, 323/255-9881. 3037 Roswell, Eagle Rock, 90065.

Adelphia Cable , 818/781-1900. 15055 Oxnard St., Van Nuys, 91411. Free; you furnish the tape.

ATT, 323/993-8000. www.ATTbroadband.com. 900 N. Cahuenga, Hollywood, 90038.

West Valley Cablevision, 818/998-2266. 9260 Topanga Canyon Blvd., Chatsworth, 91311.

Private Coaching: Judy Kerr, 818/505-9373. $100 per hour.

THEATER AND THEATER GROUPS

• **Working in the theater is a way to keep acting,** networking and giving yourself the opportunity to be seen by someone who has the ability to hire you for film and television work. *Back Stage West* lists auditions for plays. The directors often put the notices through the Breakdown Service, too. Sometimes, agents aren't very interested in Waiver stage work because there is no commission for them. Perhaps they will let you drop in once a week to look through the Breakdowns for stage work. Go to all the play auditions you can; it gives you a place to practice your auditioning skills.

• **After Robert Redford** had turned down the role of Benjamin in *The Graduate,* director Mike Nichols remembered seeing Dustin Hoffman in an off-Broadway play, playing a hunchbacked German transvestite, and flew him into Hollywood for a screen test. Dustin was cast to play his Oscar-nominated role. He was 30 and it was his first major movie role at a salary of $750 a week. He earned $20,000 in all and applied for unemployment benefits afterward.

• **Harry Belafonte told an understudy success story.** "In 1945, I worked as an assistant janitor; Sidney Poitier was a dishwasher. In our first play at the *American Negro Theater* in Harlem I had the lead and Sidney was my understudy. One day the young man covering my job called and said he couldn't work that night. I went off to haul garbage and Sidney went on to play my part. That performance turned out to be on the night a director from Broadway came to scout our company, saw Sidney in my part, and signed him on the spot for a role in *Lysistrata,* launching his brilliant career."

• **There are many theater groups.** Choose one where you feel comfortable; a good way to find friends who are working together towards common goals. You'll usually need a short scene or monologue to audition. Certain companies may want a classical and a contemporary monologue. Go to the theater you are considering joining and see a production to find out if you like the acting and the production values.

• **Kelsey Grammer** (*Frasier)* tells this story: He was doing an off-off-Broadway show of *Lonely Hearts*. Opening night was the first blizzard of the season, there were three people in the audience. One of those people was the casting director who cast him in *Cheers!*

• **Beverly Long, actress turned commercial casting director**, was in *Rebel Without a Cause*. "Every actor in the entire city went on the auditions for *Rebel*. I had done a few TV shows and Corey Allen (now a director) and I were doing a play. The director saw us and cast us both. This is why I tell actors to do plays—you never know who is in the audience."

• **Chazz Palminteri** is a real inspiration to me. *A Bronx Tale,* directed by Robert De Niro, written by and starring Chazz was released in 1993. Five years before that, Chazz was a nightclub bouncer, TV bit player, living in a crummy North Hollywood apartment. "I was angry, I wasn't going anywhere. I went to a drugstore, bought some pads of legal paper and started writing." He took his first five-minute bit and performed it at his theater company's workshop. Although it was well received, he kept writing and taking it back to class. Eventually he had a 90-minute one-man show he performed to critical raves at both the West Coast Ensemble Theater in L.A. and Playhouse 91 in N.Y. He was hot. Everyone wanted to buy his story. He held fast. He had $200 in the bank but he wouldn't sell unless he could write the screenplay and star in it. Robert De Niro had seen the play in L.A. and called him. They met and made the deal.

• **When you have landed a play for the first time**, throw yourself into rehearsals, learn your lines fast so you have more time to play with the words. Show up prepared to rehearse. Take care of yourself. Provide yourself with food and water and the comforts you need so it frees you for the fun that rehearsals can be. Your rehearsal time is often much more fun than the actual running of the play.

• **Stage managers are second-in-command** and often in charge after the opening night. Show them every respect you can. Always let them know when you arrive. If there is a sign up sheet, as there will be at all Equity productions, sign it. When the play begins its run, the stage manager will give you half-hour, 15-minute and 5-minute calls. Always acknowledge that you heard them with a thank you or some verbal word so they know that you heard it. This is proper etiquette. Stage managers can be your best friends if you get into trouble during the play. Be kind to them.

• **The last week before the play opens,** rehearsals are hard because you are into tech rehearsals with the lights, costumes, sound, curtains. The last dress rehearsal before opening will be awful. The second night is usually a let down from all the energy that went into opening night.

• **On your first dress rehearsal night, set up your makeup space.** You want to make it a safe place to return to between scenes. Take a box of tissues and a couple of lunch size paper sacks. You can tape one of the sacks to your dressing table in case there isn't a handy trash container. Take paper cups, straws and a bottle of water. Share your water and cups. Lay your makeup products out on a hand towel. I like to use a small glass for my makeup pencils, a regular pencil and a pen. Take a writing pad, post-it notes and scotch tape.

• **When you get your opening night notes,** tape them up on your mirror. Also tape something that is special to you, a picture of someone who loves you, or a saying that gives you inspiration. Get little opening night gifts for everyone. It might be a rose, candy bar, bag of jelly beans, T-shirt with the play's name on it, helium balloon, balloon on a stick with something printed on it, a little miniature prop (kids' toys) that pertains to the person's role. Write a little personal note to the actors, director and tech people. This will make your opening night even more special. If you've received flowers, when they're near death, pour the water out and let them dry. They will still look good and you can keep them for the entire run.

• **Your curtain call is the last time the audience sees you.** Go out with great joy, no matter how you think your performance went. Often, you won't get many rehearsals on the curtain call. If you have any influence, insist on a well thought out and rehearsed one. You owe it to the audience so they can honor you. Bask in the applause, let yourself hear it, stay in the moment. It is what we act for, to hear the approval. Do not judge yourself; do that in your car on the way home. You can always improve and you will the next night, next week or the next play.

• **When you have a small part**, there is bound to be a let down after you open. In rehearsals the play seemed all about you, now you see it's really the people in the leading roles who carry the play. Keep making sure you find something new you want in your scenes. Bask in the glory when you are on stage, and next time maybe your part will be bigger.

• **If you have a large role,** don't let up. Keep putting all the energy into your acting choices. If the reviews are good, yeah! If they aren't, console yourself and make the reviewers eat their words. Many actors choose not to read reviews till after the run of the play or never because they feel if you believe the good ones, then you have to believe the bad ones.

• **Each time you have a performance** the audience is different and it is such an adventure. What holds you up is your acting technique. No matter how you are feeling or how you think things are going, you will take the audience on a journey if you keep concentrated and focused on your work and your acting choices.

• **Never whistle in the theater.** Develop little good luck charms for every run.

Resources

On The House, 310/399-3868. $195 a year for 2 tickets; many shows available every week.

Time Six Theatre League Alliance, www.theatrela.org. 213/614-0556. This service provides up-to-the-minute information on what's playing where. You may also purchase half-price day-of-show tickets by phone. Tu-Sa 12-4. Mark Taper, Pantages, Kodak Theater, The Geffen, Pasadena Playhouse and other under-100-seat Equity houses.

Back Stage West prints an annual issue featuring all the theaters and theater companies in town. You can call them and get that back issue.

• **LOS ANGELES PROFESSIONAL THEATERS**

Geffen Playhouse, 310/208-6500. www.geffenplayhouse.com. 10886 Le Conte Ave, LA, CA 90024.

Mark Taper Forum, 213/972-7353. www.TaperAhmanson.org. 135 North Grand Ave, LA, CA 90012. Casting Director: Amy Lieberman.

Pasadena Playhouse, 626/792-8672. www.pasadenaplayhouse.org. 39 S. El Molino Ave., Pasadena, CA 91101

• THEATER COMPANIES

Actors Co-Op, 323/462-8460. 1760 N. Gower Street, Hollywood, 90028. www.actorsco-op.org. Send a picture and resume. They audition twice a year. Bring in a three-minute monologue for a three person committee. On the call back you can do the same monologue or a different one, a cold reading with one of their company members and an interview for a seven person committee. This is one of the top companies in town. No initiation fee, dues are $20 a month. Janet Raycraft is one of the administrators.

Actors' Gang, 323/465-0566. 6209 Santa Monica Blvd., Hollywood, 90038. www.theactorsgang.com. Artistic Director, Tim Robbins. Award winning theater. On the Board: Robert Altman, Annette Bening, Robin Williams, Susan Sarandon. Presents fine award-winning productions.

Actors' Forum Theatre, 818/506-0600, 10655 Magnolia Blvd., North Hollywood, 91601. Applicants can audition every last Saturday of the month from 12:30-1PM, or come to a workshop that meets on Tuesdays from 7:30-10PM. Dues $25 a month. No set season. Theatre looks for a variety of new plays. Workshop presentation on Thursday nights.

A Noise Within, 323/953-7787. 234 South Brand Blvd Glendale, 91204. This theater presents classic American plays as well as Shakespeare. They have a 26 member resident company. New members are accepted by invitation only and not until you have worked a year with the company. They will, however, audition for roles that cannot be filled within the company. They teach all levels of actors in their Shakespeare classes and have a summer program of the classics for teenagers.

Colony Theatre, 818/558-7000. 555 N. 3rd St., Burbank, 91502. www.colonytheatre.org. They audition two times a year. Send picture, resume and a self-addressed, stamped business envelope, c/o Denise. She will send you information on the company. If you are interested, call for an interview appointment. They hold a two-day marathon of interviews. Then they will notify you if they want you to audition for the company. Dues are $15 per month. Must work two mailings within four months of production, attend company clean-up weekend, usher six times and work a full running crew within first year of membership. Shows are selected with company members in mind. Industry comps are given to cast members. No workshops; they produce plays. Very prestigious company.

Company of Angels, 323/883-1717. 2106 Hyperion Ave., L.A. 90027. www.companyofangels-uk.org. Send in your picture and resume, c/o Janet Aspers. They have auditions at least once a year. If you are called in they like to see two scenes, not over five minutes each and they may ask for a monologue. Initiation fee is $35 and dues are $35 a month. This is one of the oldest companies in town. They have many productions going on for the members to appear in. They don't have workshops but do have play readings; always looking for material.

The Company Rep at the American Renegade Theater, 11136 Magnolia Blvd., North Hollywood, 91601. www.Thecompanyrep.org. Hope Alexander is the artistic director of this multicultural resident company creating both modern and classical works and developing new plays and playwrights. They hold auditions twice a year. Send photo and resume to The Company Rep, P.O. Box 807, North Hollywood, CA 91603. Audition consists of two monologues, one modern one classical. Membership dues: $40 a month (plus $25 initiation fee for new members, due upon acceptance into the company). Classes and workshops offered as announced. Requirements: Company meeting, held the first Saturday of every month. Eight hours work per month required in any area of expertise, plus one night of hosting or ushering during every production.

Open Fist Theatre/Los Angeles Playhouse, 323/882-6912. 1625 North La Brea, Hollywood, 90028. www.openfist.org. They hold auditions two or three times a year. Send photo and resume c/o Scott. They will call you with details for the auditions.

Theatre 40, 310/364-3606. 241 Moreno Drive, Beverly Hills, 90210. www.theatre40.org. Located on the campus of Beverly Hills High School. "For more than 26 years, Theatre 40 has been one of this town's most stable and consistent actor-run professional theater ensembles." *Daily Variety.* Mail picture and resume c/o Robert Cohen, P.O. Box 5401, Beverly Hills, CA 90210. They will contact you if looking for members. They have workshops and company dues.

Theatre East, 818/760-4160. 12655 Ventura Blvd., Studio City, 91604. www.angelfire.com/la/theatreeast. New members are by invitation only; interviews are held for 18-month apprentice program. Dues: initiation fee of $40, then $40 a month. Must have a union affiliation. Apprentices work crews and various other stage work instead of paying dues. Members, including apprentices, can participate in workshops, classes, seminars, industry showcases; productions cast exclusively from within the company.

Theatre West, 323/851-4839. 3333 Cahuenga Blvd. West, Los Angeles, 90068. www.theatrewest.org. You may submit your pictures and resumes to be considered for membership. A couple of months before the auditions, usually in the fall, the membership committee reviews the submissions received and on the basis of your experience you may be invited to audition for membership. Only the membership actors are in the productions. Initiation Fee is $60, dues are $40 a month. Free professional workshops are offered to their members: Monday night actor's workshop, Tuesday morning Shakespeare, Tuesday evening writer's workshop, Thursday evening musical comedy. The apprentice wing has their own acting workshop on Wednesday night for young directors.

West Coast Ensemble, 323/876-9337. Mailing Address: 3151 Cahuenga Blvd West. Ste.107, Los Angeles, CA 90068. www.wcensemble.org. Les Hanson is the artistic director. Auditions twice a year. Send a picture and resume, attention: New Members. They will notify you when the auditions will be held. You do a four minute scene for Les and then have an interview with the membership committee. Lots of workshops and productions to get involved in. Initiation fee is $100, monthly dues are $45. Plus you must donate five hours work time each month. You can reduce your dues to $35 by doing 10 hours a month. You must perform one production job a year. They offer a great intern program for beginners; if you are interested in that, mention it in your letter.

LIVING AN ACTOR'S

DREAM IN LOS ANGELES

• **For this edition I asked new actor Jordan Osher,** who plays in his teens to early twenties, to write his story of how he came to Los Angeles a year ago to seek his fame and fortune. I also asked him to keep a six-month diary recounting everything he did toward developing an acting career.

• **Following Jordan's diary is the story of Keith Johnson,** a man in his thirties. He tells of the events that led to changing his life completely in order to follow his dreams.

• **Since the eighth edition of this book,** I have included a diary of an actress, Jode Leigh Edwards, who was new to Los Angeles. In the ninth edition there was an epilogue and a two-week diary. Now in the tenth edition, Jode has been here five years still pursuing and living her dreams. She has written of some Los Angeles lessons and another two-week diary.

• **Just today, I received a printed postcard** with a great headshot of an actor named Simon Anderson. I had met with him a few months ago for a one-time career coaching session. He writes, "Thanks for the great advice and coaching! I now have headshots by Marina Rice Bader, am studying with Howard Fine and Michelle Danner. I've joined the Actors' Network, which is so informative, and Doug at GMA is submitting me for roles—all in two months! P.S. Just got an under-five on *Days of Our Lives*." I know from his card he is excited and working every day to live his life as an actor.

• **When Jordan Osher and I met at our initial career coaching session,** I immediately recognized his ambition and drive; he also had a great personality, sense of humor and style. He wanted advice on how to go about launching an acting career. The information and coaching I gave Jordan that day I have given to everyone who comes to me for career coaching. Bottom line it takes hard work, self-discipline, determination, perseverance and the ability to not get discouraged when faced with rejections. Jordan has a dream and he wants to fulfill it.

• **Many aspiring actors take my advice** but most don't, it isn't easy to work as hard as the people have in this section. Will they be stars? I don't know but it warms my heart to see that they are choosing to live the life of their dreams. If they don't become stars I trust they will find joy living their lives as artists.

• **Jordan has the backing and encouragement of his family.** To help get him started, his father agreed to pay for his acting classes and marketing expenses. Jordan landed a waiter job at a high-end restaurant in Malibu not too long after he arrived. He has two roommates and lives in Santa Monica.

• **He has a distant cousin with a high position** in the entertainment business and his father has some show biz connections. These friends of his father's may help in the future but at the beginning of his career they are at too high of a level to help directly. They will take meetings in order to encourage and give advice but will not be giving him entry level acting jobs. Like everyone, he will have to land those himself.

• **When Jordan does schedule an important meeting,** he is like an Olympic athlete training for the big competition; he prepares as though the meeting will be a turning point in his life. If it is an audition, he will train with me. If it is a general meeting, he may meet with Stuart K. Robinson to plan what stories he might tell, what questions he wants answered, how he can showcase his sense of humor.

• **All the while he is pursuing the business part of acting,** he is studying acting techniques privately as well as in several classes a week. He has a very high average of auditions, callbacks and bookings. At this writing, he is starring in a project geared for the Sundance Film Festival. His life is jam packed with acting and he seems to be loving it. It is exciting to watch his dreams unfold. *See Jordan's pictures on pages 112 and 113, commercial pictures on pages 170, 171 and his beginning resume, as well as his current one, as of this writing, on pages 154 and 155.*

• **Here Jordan tells his story** and following are the daily and weekly steps he took to develop as an actor.

> • **Three summers ago I went to Wilmington, North Carolina** in hopes of meeting some of the cast members of *Dawson's Creek*. Through a friend of my father's I was introduced to the casting director, she asked if I wanted to work as an extra. I was thrilled and began working the next day in a pep rally scene at a huge auditorium. There were probably 400 people there; over 300 extras, the football team, the cast, and the crew. I was chosen to play the school's mascot and had to wear a colonial style wig and uniform. I was on stage with a couple of the actors from the show as well as the football team.

> • **About 15 minutes into shooting**, the director shouted from the back of the room "This guy looks like Seinfeld!" I knew he was talking about me because I have been told that I look like a young Jerry Seinfeld. Everyone started laughing at the comparison. It was the best thing that could've happened because the cast and crew started talking to me and got to know my personality and humor.

> • **The director called me three days later** and asked if I would be interested in doing a featured role on the show. I was ecstatic. I came to North Carolina hoping to possibly catch a glimpse of the show being filmed, and now I was in the center of it. When I shot the scene the director kept saying what a great job I did and how I was a natural. It was so much fun.

> • **This experience of working on a television show** seemed like something I would love to do for a living. When I got back to Indiana University, I took acting classes for two years trying to "get good" before pursuing this new dream.

> • **I graduated in December 2001 and moved to Los Angeles** in January. The night before I left, my best friend gave me a going away present, the book *Acting Is Everything: An Actor's Guidebook for a Successful Career in Los Angeles*, by Judy Kerr. It was perfect because it answered every question I had. I arrived with my luggage, some money and my new book. My first day in Los Angeles, I went walking in Beverly Hills and got into a conversation with a guy outside a shoe store (Mike Johnson). I told him I just moved here and was pursuing acting. He said I should buy his teacher's book because it is so helpful. I asked who his teacher was and he said, "Judy Kerr." This was such of a coincidence, so I called Judy to arrange a career counseling appointment.

> • **What is ironic is that Judy was the dialogue coach on *Seinfeld*** but I didn't know that. I told her on the phone that I looked like a young Jerry Seinfeld; she thought that was why I was calling her. The real reason was because of her book and the recommendation from one of her students.

- **When we met, we outlined the goals I wanted to pursue.** We then started to strategize how to go about accomplishing these. She told me which classes that she thought I should take, who the best photographers were, the connections I needed to make, the networking that needed to be done, as well as answered the other 101 questions I had for her.

- **Over the course of the next six months** I took classes four days a week, went to any audition, booked some jobs, got call backs, didn't get call backs, met some important people, made some great connections. I wrote a short script, and whatever else I could possibly do day in and day out to better myself as an actor.

- **I met presidents of studios, producers, directors, agents**, managers, casting directors, and more. From each one of these meetings, I learned something different and made a connection. Along with this, I met with Judy for private coaching once a week and not only was she my teacher, but my mentor as well. If I had a problem, all I had to do was call Judy and she had the resolution. I landed a commercial agent (KSA) a few months after I moved here thanks to the help of Stuart K. Robinson. He too (like Judy) was a mentor to me and is known as one of the best commercial teachers in Los Angeles.

- **The first six months were a challenge,** as it is for anyone moving to Los Angeles. I like hearing how hard it is to make it in this business because that motivates me to work even harder. Joe Roth (head of Revolution Studios) told me, "You'll get rejected a lot of times in this industry and although it is personal, you cannot take it personally." This has been priceless advice because when I have been rejected, I take a step back and ask myself what could I have changed and what could I improve on. This has helped me more then I could possibly imagine.

JORDAN'S DIARY TAKEN FROM HIS PALM PILOT

Jan. 9   Moved to Los Angeles
Jan. 10   Movie. Saw Michael Jackson and Val Kilmer at the hotel.
Jan. 11   Setup a meeting with Judy Kerr. Worked out with Russell Crowe at the hotel.
Jan. 15   Career counseling appointment with Judy Kerr. Met with Joe Roth (head of Revolution Studios); he gave me great advice.
Jan. 16   Dinner w/ Bob Osher (co-president of Miramax); also my cousin. Met Dan Romanelli, president of Warner Brothers' licensing.
Jan. 17   Lunch with prod. Doug Drazen ("Fools Rush In")
Jan. 18   Private class with Judy. Dinner with family friend Judy Waxman (works for Stephen Bochco Prod.) Met with photographer Pam Springsteen.

Jan. 19	Met with Marina Rice and looked at her headshot books. Met with photographer Tom Lascher.
Jan. 21	Called Pamela Springsteen and booked her to shoot my headshots.
Jan. 22	Went to Hollywood and walked around; saw a movie.
Jan. 23	Private with Judy.
Jan. 25	Headshots with Pamela Springsteen.
Jan. 28	Nardulli's photo lab to look at my proof sheet.
Jan. 29	Private with Judy.
Jan. 30	Nardulli's photo lab to look at my 4x6's
Jan. 31	Showed my 4x6's to Judy to get her opinion.
Feb. 5	Started acting class with Sal Romeo.
Feb. 6	Private with Judy. Stuart K. Robinson's commercial class.
Feb. 7	Bought my first BackStage West. (BSW) Met with Stuart-see my 4x6s.
Feb. 8	Nardulli's and ordered 8x10's. Imagestarters to order my first resume.
Feb. 10	Went to Bob Osher's for dinner (Miramax)
Feb. 11	Private with Judy.
Feb. 12	Sal's class. Picked a scene to do with Andrea.
Feb. 13	Stuart's commercial class. Picked up headshots at Nardulli's and resumes from Imagestarters.
Feb. 14	BackStage West. Sent out first submissions.
Feb. 15	Ate lunch at Four Seasons. Rehearsed scene w/Andrea.
Feb. 19	Called Charles Newirth (head of casting, Revolution Studios) about dropping off my headshots. Performed my first scene in front of audience in Sal's class. Dropped off headshots to Charles Newirth.
Feb. 20	Stuart's commercial class. Went to Samuel French and bought Michael Caine's book on acting. Went to Universal Studio and walked around.
Feb. 21	Bought BSW and sent submissions.
Feb. 22	Class w/Judy. Called Charles Newirth to set up a 10 min. meeting.
Feb. 26	Acting class w/Sal. Private w/Judy/bring headshots.
Feb. 27	Call from Michelle Gertz-come in for a meeting (Casting director for Universal Studios; she cast: Legally Blonde, American Pie, and Big Fat Liar). Stuart's class. Started Hip-hop class w/Paul Douglas; another skill for the resume.
Feb. 28	Bought BSW, sent out submissions.
Mar. 4	Private w/Judy.
Mar. 5	Pick up business cards at Image Starter. Acting class with Sal.
Mar. 6	Commercial class with Stuart.
Mar. 7	BSW submissions.
Mar. 8	Called family friend Julie Waxman about going on set of NYPD Blue.
Mar. 12	Class with Sal. Met with Michelle Gertz at Universal Studios; my first meeting with a casting director; she gave me some good advice.
Mar. 13	Commercial class with Stuart. Met with my dad's friend Jimmy Gould at the Peninsula Hotel in Beverly Hills; he has ties with the managment company The Firm. Went to set of NYPD Blue.
Mar. 15	Jim Carrey came in restaurant. [Jordan's survival job] Call from Dave Baram (CFO of The Firm) asking me to meet with him; I'm excited!
Mar. 17	Waited on Ving Rhames and Dan Cortese today.
Mar. 18	Private w/Judy.
Mar. 19	Sal's class. Stuart's theatrical class.
Mar. 20	Private w/Judy. Met with Dave Baram-wants to set me up to meet with a manager. Met with Eric Klein about camera workshop class that meets on Tuesday nights.

Mar. 21   BSW submissions. Sent Dave Baram a Thank You card.

Mar. 22   Called friend, actress Kristin Herold; she said she will give my headshots to her casting director friend. Semi-private commercial class with Stuart Robinson.

Mar. 23   My mom and step-father came into town to visit; we went to the Getty Museum; loved it!

Mar. 24   Oscar party at family friends house; people from the biz there.

Mar. 25   Audition for student film; got it through BSW.

Mar. 26   Class with Sal. Got call; I got the lead in Loyola Marymount student film. Stuart's theatrical class.

Mar. 27   BSW submissions. Parents' friends for dinner; met agent for the late Milton Berle.

Mar. 28   Submissions BSW; Private w/Judy. Hip-hop class at "Swerve."

Mar. 29   Comm. w/Stuart. Private w/Stuart. Cover letters to casting directors and agents.

Mar. 30   Called Michelle Danner about taking classes with her at the Larry Moss Studio. Samuel French bookstore-got a book on developing a character. Open call for a Sigourney Weaver movie.

Apr.l 1   Picked up more headshots from Nardulli. Private w/Judy.

Apr. 2   Got call for extra on Sigourney Weaver movie; had to turn down - couldn't get out of work. Stuart's theatrical class.

Apr. 3   Stuart's class. Saw a play at the Tamarind Theatre.

Apr. 4   BSW Submissions. Met with Adam Asherton of The Firm; positive feedback.

Apr. 5   Called Michelle Gertz to say hello and update her on my progress. Met with Michelle Danner and signed up for her 2-day seminar; met Jasmine Guy (A Different World); she was so nice! Private w/Stuart.

Apr. 6   Saw my cousin Philip's play at the Tamarind Theatre that he co-wrote; it was so funny.

Apr. 8   Auditioned for independent film, "The Snitch" Worked on cover letter to commercial agents.

Apr. 9   I booked the lead role in "The Snitch." Went to Stuart's theatrical class.

Apr. 10   Stuart's semi private commercial class.

Apr. 11   BSW Submissions. Worked on script for audition. Private with Judy.

Apr. 12   Met with a writer about creating a short movie; I heard that was how Vin Diesel got his start. Sent P&R and cover letter to commercial agents. Private. Stuart worked on demo reel script.

Apr. 13   Call from a casting director to audition for independent film. Got the sides online; wow that helps!

Apr. 14   Joined BackStage West online; so much easier, and I get the audition notices earlier in the week.

Apr. 15   Got calls from two commercial agents wanting to meet me. Yeah!

Apr. 16   Two more calls from agents. Private w/Judy. Audition for USC grad film. Stuart's theatrical class. Also rehearsed scene for demo reel.

Apr. 17   Call from KSA about seeing some tape on me. Stuart's comm. class.

Apr. 18   Went to Planet Video about possibly using them to make my reel for potential agents. Got new headshots taken from Jillian; only $75 per role and she is great!

Apr. 19   Rehearsed for audition that I have on Saturday; more submissions to commercial agents. Shot the short scene for my reel with Stuart. It's funny, looks good.

Apr. 20	Audition independent film. Half-hour strategy session with Stuart on how to land a commercial agent. Went to LA Talent to meet with agent.
Apr. 21	Picked up proof sheet at Jillian's. Auditioned for spec Doritos commercial.
Apr. 22	Private w/Judy. Hollywood Sound to check out renting equipment if I decide to do a short film. Picked up edited scene from Stuart on DV and took to Lightning Dubs to make copies. Start shooting movie at Loyola Marymount University.
Apr. 23	Another day of shooting; Stuart's theatrical class.
Apr. 24	Met Michael Richards (Kramer) at Wild Oats Market; I told him I study with Judy and he told me to tell her hello. Stuart's Class. Final day of movie shoot.
Apr. 25	Took finished reel tape to KSA. Nardulli for 4x6's. Michelle Danner's Technique Breakdown Class at The Larry Moss Studio.
Apr. 26	Call from Josh Kaye of JGJ Mgmt bringing me in for their spec pilot.
Apr. 27	2nd half of Michelle Danner's Class.
Apr. 28	Prepared monologue for Michelle's class. BSW online for auditions. Private w/Judy.
Apr. 29	Pick up at Nardulli's. KSA called want to meet on Tuesday. Worked on audition for Needleworks Film.
Apr. 30	Stuart's class. Ask Stuart about writing and shooting another demo reel scene, also looked at 4x6's.
May 1	Nardulli's to get 8x10's. ImageStarters, re-did resume; Stuart's commercial class. Callback with Mathew Needleman.
May 2	BSW submissions. Performed first monologue in class at Larry Moss'. Lightning Dubbs to get more copies of reel tape for casting directors and potential agents.
May 3	Private w/Stuart.
May 4	Rented 4 classic movies to watch over the weekend
May 6	New resumes at Imagestarter. Found out Judy chose me to be featured in her book. Started to organize my Palm Pilot schedule. Met Stuart to work on new scene for demo reel.
May 7	KSA meeting went great. Stuart's class.
May 8	KSA called, wants to sign me. After narrowing it down to 2, I decided that KSA was perfect for me commercially. Stuart's comm. class. Also rehearsed the demo reel scene.
May 9	BSW Submissions. Went to KSA (Kazarian/Spencer & Associates) to sign paperwork. Class at Larry Moss Studio.
May 10	Nardulli's to proof the headshots. Shot action scene with Stuart outdoors. Met Larry David at my restaurant.
May 11	Take One Bookstore, bought "Audition" by Michael Shurtleff.
May 12	Spent the whole day reading "Audition;" It is amazing. Picked up DV edited copy from Stuart with added sound effects and music. Took to Lightning Dubs for copies.
May 13	Brought in headshots and resumes to KSA. Finished "Audition" Private w/Judy. Resumes from ImageStarter (took 2 weeks to be done). Picked up more head shots at Nardulli.
May 14	Found out about WMA Associates from Judy; they send out submissions for you. Worked on script for Judy's class. Went to Stuart's theatrical class.
May 15	Set up an appointment with WMA for next week. Stuart's commercial class

May 16   BSW submissions. Class Larry Moss's. Saw play at Tamarind Theatre.

May 17   Reproductions to get multiples - save so much money going there.

May 18   Started writing down an idea for a short film starring myself that will hopefully help launch my career. Went to Take One bookstore, got Uta Hagen's book "A Challenge for the Actor."

May 19   Saw a movie. Worked on a rough script for my short film.

May 20   Gave my friend Kristen Herold headshots for her casting director friend. Went to WMA Associates (talked to Doug). Private w/Judy.

May 21   Called Charles Newirth (at Revolution) and left a message. Private w/Stuart . Went to see Tina's play at the Tamarind Theater. Stuart's acting class.

May 22   Charles Newirth returned my call. Stuart's Comm. class.

May 23   Postcards to Charles Newirth, Joe Roth, Michelle Gertz, Adam Asherton and Dave Barum saying I just finished an independent film. BSW submissions. Class Larry Moss Studio.

May 24   Lightning Dubs to get more tapes; Picked up new postcards at ImageStarter.

May 27   Speech class to improve my New York dialect.

May 28   WMA, gave headshots to send out; what a time saver this is. Stuart's class.

May 29   Private w/Judy. Stuart's comm. class.

May 30   New York dialect speech class. Class Larry Moss Studio.

May 31   Postcards to Michelle Gertz, Adam Asherton, & Dave Barum saying I have new tape to show them.

June 4   Picked up headshots at Reproductions. Meeting with Adam Asherton at the Firm. Sprint commercial audition at Westside casting. Stuart's theatrical class.

June 5   Mail headshots to Dave Scotti who is writing a comedy in New Jersey; went to Stuart's comm. class.

June 6   Met with Charles Newirth; he is setting up a meeting for me with casting directors. Class Larry Moss Studio.

June 7   Went to Audition for Ex-Men (an independent film for film festivals).

June 10   Private w/Judy. Callback for Ex-Men. Audition for film called Lock Pick Kid.

June 11   Ex-Men called, I booked the part of a super-hero; shooting starts next week. Got a call from Jeanne McCarthy (a casting director). Stuart's theatrical class.

June 12   Call back for "Lock Pick Kid." Stuart's commercial class.

June 13   Booked "Lock Pick Kid"; I had to turn it down because it films the same dates as Ex-Men. Class at Larry Moss's. Met Michael Lynne, Chairman of New Line Cinema who told me to give him a call.

June 14   Private with Judy.

June 15   Audition for a play in Hollywood.

June 16   Call back for the play audition I had yesterday.

June 18   More headshots to WMA Associates. Worked on a scene with Zach Rowland (excellent actor) for one of my classes; he makes me a better actor when working with him. Stuart's theatrical class.

June 19   Andrew Duncan College Bound movie audition. Audition for McDonald's commercial. Stuart's comm. class.

June 20   Got a call to audition for the Maureen Mann Edith Piaf story. Class with John C. at Larry Moss's. Private w/Stuart.

June 22   Audition for "Ahead of the Game."

June 23   Michelle Mock called to audition Friday for the TNN pilot Giant.
June 24   Private w/Judy. Filmworks audition; Entertainment Industry Physicians: physical for the show Giants.
June 25   Audition for the Scarecrow at the Asylum 6671. Stuart's theatrical class.
June 26   Stuart's comm. class. Met with Jeanne McCarthy and Juel Bestrop (independent casting directors); had the best time.
June 27   Call from First Television ("Giant" pilot) saying I was picked to come back on Monday. Class/Larry Moss's. Meeting at the Firm with Adam Asherton.
June 28   Postcards to Jeanne, Juel, & Adam Asherton; work on script; Auditioned for Giant for TNN; there were 25 potential contestants.
June 30   First Television called. I am one of the three picked for "Giant."
July 1   Shot pilot "Giant" for TNN. Private with Judy.
July 2   Shot pilot "Giant" for TNN. Drop off tape to Jeanne and Juel. Stuarts theatrical class.
July 3   Shot "Giant." Stuart's commercial class.
July 5   Shot pilot "Giant." Class at Larry Moss Studio.
July 6   Shooting
July 8   Shooting
July 9   Final shooting day; now it goes to Network and hopefully they pick it up.
July 10   Stuart's theatrical class
July 11   New Line Cinema called to set up audition for "Girl Next Door." Went to Samuel French and bought the play "Trust" by Stephen Deitz for class. Shot Independent Film Ex-Men. Stuart's class.
July 12   Shooting Ex-Men. Class/Larry Moss's. Called Leanne at Mali Finn casting about "Girl Next Door." Call ImageStarter to add "Giant."
July 13   Sat in a meeting with a writer friend and a producer to work on a movie script.
July 16   Private w/Judy. Stuart's class. Rehearsed with Lara, "Trust."
July 17   Stuart's semi-private commercial class.
July 18   Picked up equipment at Hollywood Sounds to shoot a scene with some acting friends. Class at LMS.
July 19   Call from 3Arts Management company about meeting with a manager; Michelle Gertz set up the meeting; she is awesome.
July 20   Went to Take One bookstore and bought a couple plays to look for a monologue. More postcards to Charles Newirth; Jeanne McArthy, Juel Bestrop and Michelle Gertz the latest on my acting work.

This is an email I received from Jordan a few weeks before this edition went to print. He's been in Los Angeles one year and a couple of weeks.

- **I recently wrote a short film script** with two guys (a director and a producer). We got it financed and are shooting it mid-March. It is a SAG low-budget film and I will be eligible to join the union after shooting it. I am so excited and it could be a great opportunity.

• **Jordan continues living his life** as an actor in Los Angeles. Keep up with him on www.imdb.com.

KEITH'S STORY

*I met Keith Johnson (see his pictures on pages 120 and 121) and his fiance,
Bonnie Gillespie, the "Casting Qs" columnist at Back Stage West, for breakfast to talk to Bonnie about contributing casting director viewpoints for this
book. I was so intrigued with Keith's pursuit of his dream that I asked him
to write his story in hopes of inspiring others who think their lives have
fallen apart. You can pursue your dreams no matter your age or what
obstacles seem in your way. Keith is very much enjoying his adventure. He
wrote this mid October 2002. It covers one year and eight months.*

- **In February of 2001,** I was living in Grand Rapids, Michigan and
  my life was shattered. In late January, my wife informed me that our
  seven-year marriage was over. Two weeks later, the bank I was working for was bought out by another bank and I was going to be let go.

- **I went from knowing** what the next 20 years of my life was going to
  be, to sitting alone in an empty, 3 bedroom/2 bath house with no
  idea what the future held. I took stock of the things that I hadn't
  been doing for lack of time.

- **In March,** I signed up for an adult soccer league, started spending
  serious time writing "my great novel" again, and started looking to
  audition in local theatre. I had done one play in my life, five years
  earlier, "Dracula." I really liked acting, but it was not my dream,
  or so I thought.

- **In April,** I met a bunch of people on an Internet discussion group
  about an online, humor magazine. One of those people, a writer for
  the magazine, was Bonnie Gillespie. I became drawn to Bonnie's
  wit, charm, sass and intellect. I learned she worked in the Entertainment Industry, and she learned I thought acting was fun.

- **In May,** with Bonnie encouraging my pursuit of acting, I was
  suddenly open to the idea of dreaming differently. There was good
  chemistry between us, we had a lot in common and started talking
  on the phone. We decided to meet in person in the middle of July.
  My plan to take a year off to figure out who I was went out the
  window; I was in love. Fortunately for me, Bonnie was too.

- **She kept encouraging me** to explore the acting life and to come out
  to L.A. when my job in Michigan ended. She told me to come out
  to Hollywood, and she would make me famous. I fell for it. The
  thought was very appealing to me, and I was starting to dream about
  a career in show business. Bonnie helped me prepare to audition for
  the part of Teddy in "Arsenic And Old Lace" at my local community
  theatre, and I got it.

- **As summer went on with rehearsals**, it became clear that acting meant more to me than I thought it did. I made plans to move to L.A. when my job and my play were finished. As if it were a sign from heaven, my job ended on the Friday before the play was to close on Sunday.

- **I showed up closing night** in a fully packed Ryder moving van. We put on the show, struck the set; I said my good-byes, and drove forty-one hours to Hollywood. That was the end of October, ten months from the date that my life had flipped upside down.

- **I came to this town 35 years old with no training**, two non-professional plays under my belt and a dream. This is not the usual recipe for success when moving to Los Angeles.

- **In December**, Bonnie wrangled me a job as a production assistant (PA) on a SAG, Modified Low-Budget feature film. I had never been on a film set, seen professional actors or a film crew. Bonnie's advice was to stay quiet, listen to what everyone was saying, and do whatever I was asked. We felt confident that I'd make a good PA because I spent four years in the Marines; I could reasonably follow orders.

- **I was a great PA.** I learned what I needed to know to be comfortable behind and in front of the camera. I learned who's who and what's what. I learned about film crew etiquette and terminology. I got the chance to experience a lot of environmental setbacks, personnel setbacks, personality conflicts, and everything you might think of on a decently professional set.

- **Also in December, I took my first acting class.** I did four weeks with a coach who taught me the basics of scene study and character analysis. He made sure I understood what he meant and why it was important.

- **January of 2002** saw me working for the Sundance Film Festival in Park City Utah. Bonnie not only works as a newspaper journalist, but she also worked for the Sundance Institute as their Archive Director for the Sundance Collection, so she arranged for us to volunteer for the festival.

- **In February, I got my first headshots.** Again, Bonnie's experience in the industry meant that I had little research to do in order to find good value for my money. She had been shopping for photographers and lithographers for years, and she handed me to her best-value people.

- **In March and April,** money was running low, so I took a full time job doing computer consulting. One of the reasons that I have no stress involved with my acting career is that I came to the industry with a ton of marketable skills, so I will never have to worry about making a living. The way I look at it is this: unless stardom strikes I'll always make more money at my day job than I do acting. That's just a fact of my life.

- **In May,** Bonnie and I started heavily pushing my acting career. She submitted me on everything for which I might be right. We sent an honest cover letter with every submission. It said, I didn't have a lot on my resume, but I had already lived a life and brought that life to my acting. It also listed my training and I was pursuing more training.

- **The combination** of my headshot, resume, and skillful submissions by Bonnie led to getting lots of auditions, and it continues to this day. In the last five months I have been auditioning five to eight times a week, and have booked over twenty different projects. Over a dozen of those were paying gigs!

- **I view the audition as my job; I see booking as a bonus.**

- **When I am on a set** for a typical 14-hour shooting day, I may spend only 45 minutes on camera. For me, my on-camera stuff is small compared to the effort that everyone else is taking to make the picture happen. I want the people with whom I work to know that I understand that it's a team effort and I'm part of the team. I try to make everyone's job as easy as possible.

- *My latest email from Keith: www.imdb.com.*

- **January 10, 2003**, I had my TV debut, one of my non-union crime reenactment shows aired on The Learning Channel.

- **I sent 100 postcards** to casting directors and at least two tuned in. A casting director called the next day and wanted to know when I got my SAG card. I told her that I hadn't yet. She booked me for three days of voucher-earning extra work. While on the set, another casting director called and wanted to know if I was available to work on her Oxygen Network TV show for the following week. Yes!

- **Here I am**, nine months after getting my first headshots, with a SAG card and decent 2002 income from acting.

- **I am the luckiest man in the world.**

JODE LEIGH EDWARDS

• **This introduction and the three month diary appears as it did in the eighth edition** of this book. I believe Jode's activities are very typical of what a motivated person should be doing. Also see the following epilogues and subsequent two-week diaries.

• **Jode Leigh Edwards**, 20 years old, moved to Los Angeles from Dallas, Texas. My daughter, Cynthia Kerr, met Jode when they were both attending KD Studios' Conservatory program in Dallas. I saw Jode's work each semester when I taught a class for the Conservatory. Jode and Cynthia both worked hard and earned money acting while they were in school. Before graduation, Jode was signed by the Kim Dawson Agency, the top agency in Dallas. Although SAG eligible, she chose not to join until she landed her first SAG job here, so she could continue to work in nonunion independent films. She had the cash in reserve to join the union with a half-hour's notice.

• **Jode made an initial visit to Los Angeles** in January, with her parents and then in March with one of her agents to get a feel for Los Angeles. May 5th, she and her mother came to Los Angeles and rented an apartment in Studio City, furnishing it at Plummer Furniture. She was planning to move/drive out June 1st. But, she got a surprise audition and flew in on May 27th, while her dad drove her car to L.A.

• **When she finished my annual class**, which I teach during the television season hiatus, I suggested the Larry Moss Studio for Jode.

• **I asked her to keep a diary for me from the day she arrived.** She had a nest egg from her work in Dallas, some sponsorship from her family and a part time job that she does on her computer and fax machine. The only entries she included in her diary are the things she did for her acting career. She was well prepared for this move to Los Angeles.

May 27	Move to L.A. Private coaching with Judy to prep for Acapulco H.E.A.T. audition.
May 28	Acapulco H.E.A.T. audition - Sent thank you.
May 29	Met Tony at Judy's & picked up scene for Judy's cable show.
May 30	Dad drove into town with car and stuff. Rehearsed scene with Tony, Picked up Acapulco H.E.A.T. script for call back.
June 1	Appeared on Judy's cable show.

June 2   Sit in at Judy's workshop.

June 3   Phone gets hooked up. Call Michael at J. Michael Bloom (contact I
          made in Dallas).

June 4   Acapulco H.E.A.T. call back. Auditioned for casting director Beverly
          Long's commercial class.

June 5   Went to Samuel French, bought "The Agencies." Left another message
          for J. Michael Bloom. Had pictures reproduced-Quantity Photo-they're
          really quick. Started writing cover letter for agent submission. Signed
          up for Beverly Long's commercial class. Sent thank you for Acapulco
          H.E.A.T. callback.

June 6   Lunch with Darren Wadyko (new agent @Cosden, I worked with him and
          he cast me in a National commercial in Dallas, also a KD Studio
          Alumni). Picked up photos at Quantity. Finished agent cover letter and
          mailed. "Actor's Network" Orientation - I joined. Submitted P & R to
          Back Stage West notices.

June 7   Met with Doreen at Jan's Video for consultation. Picked up "Actor's
          Network" Notebook. J. Michael Bloom returned my message and set
          an appointment for me to meet with LeAnne Fader. Called Eddie
          Winkler (agent with CNA, he was my agent in Dallas at Kim Dawson).

June 9   Judy's workshop. Drove by J. Michael Bloom and CNA (scouting trip).

June 10   Met with Eddie, Lori, & Patrick at CNA (commercial dept.)

June 11   Met with LeAnne Fader at J. Michael Bloom. Worked scene with Phil
          for Judy's workshop. Looked for new monologue. Called Larry Moss
          Studio for more information.

June 12   Edited demo reel at Jan's Video. Sent agent thank you notes. LeAnne
          Fader at J. Michael Bloom set up an appointment for me to meet
          casting director Linda Francis. CNA wants to sign me commercially.

June 13   Worked scene for Judy's workshop. Drove by Linda Francis' for tomorrow's
          general. Bought video tapes and covers for demos (Studio Film &
          Tape). Submitted for Back Stage West casting notices.

June 14   Met casting director - Linda Francis (sent thank you). Sent thank you
          to LeAnne for setting up appointment.

June 16   Judy's workshop.

June 17   Met with CNA's theatrical department. "Actor's Network" session.

June 18   Worked scene for class.

June 19   Met with Michelle Danner (acting coach) at Larry Moss Studio.
          Dropped demo tape off at Tyler Kjar. Last touch to demo tape at
          Jan's Video.

June 20   Met with Producer Russell Gray to intern pre-production (tip from
          Actor's Network). 1st commercial class with Beverly Long.

June 23   Judy's workshop.

June 25   Russell Grey's office - intern.

June 26   Worked scene for Judy's workshop.

June 27   Russell Grey's office - intern. Worked scene for Judy's workshop.
          Beverly's commercial class.

June 28   Back Stage West submissions. Script coverage for a script for Russell
          Grey. Submitted to more agents.

June 29   Audition for student film (Back Stage West).
          Work scene with Terry for Judy's workshop.

June 30   Audition for independent film (BSW). Judy's workshop.

July 1	"Actor's Network" - met with acting teacher Kimberly Jentzen.
July 2	Interned for Russell Grey.
July 5	Saw play at Complex Theatre.
July 6	Saw "Moll Flanders" at DGA.
July 7	Audition for independent feature (Back Stage West).
July 9	Intern.
July 11	Intern. Rehearse scene with Tony for Judy's workshop. Beverly Long's commercial class.
July 12	Rehearse scene with Tony. Submit to Back Stage West.
July 13	Appeared on Judy's Cable Show.
July 14	Judy's workshop. Met agent Bonnie Howard in class - performed monologue.
July 15	Saw play reading at Canon Theatre.
July 16	Intern. Read screen plays. Booked commercial at Arts Center (Back Stage West).
July 17	Another actor approached me and asked me to join illegitimate managing group to get the breakdown service. I told him I wasn't interested.
July 18	Rehearse commercial. Met with Bonnie Howard again - she wanted to represent me. Beverly Long's Commercial Class. Submit Back Stage West casting notices.
July 19	Intern. Started taking technical acting classes with Michelle Danner at Larry Moss Studios.
July 20	Shot Arts Center Commercial.
July 21	Judy's last workshop.
July 22	Audition for independent film (Back Stage West).
July 23	Intern. Dropped tape off at Ann Waugh agency.
July 24	Saw a movie.
July 25	Met casting director Mark Tillman (Russell Gray set up). Class with Michelle Danner. Commercial class with Beverly Long.
July 26	I'm in San Francisco with parents and get a call from Schiowitz, Clay & Rose agency, they want to meet me next week (my own submission). Got a call - booked independent film.
July 29	Audition for independent feature (Back Stage West). "Actor's Network" meeting.
July 30	Intern.
July 31	Audition for independent feature (Back Stage West). Met student director to do scene for class at Arts Center.
Aug 1	Intern. Michelle Danner's class. Beverly Long's commercial class - met an agent.
Aug 2	Meeting with Schiowitz, Clay & Rose. Read thru for booked independent ("Roommates, Sex & Love").
Aug 3	Audition for independent feature - (Back Stage West). "Actor's Network" Summer Fling Party.
Aug 4	Rehearse scene at Arts Center for directors' class. Audition independent feature (Back Stage West) - "The Diary".
Aug 5	Audition/ independent film (Back Stage West) "Between Classes." Follow-up w/ Schiowitz, Clay & Rose - they like me, want to see a monologue. Michelle Danner's class.
Aug 6	Shooting "Roommates, Sex, & Love."
Aug 7	Reh. scene for director's class @ Arts Center.
Aug 8	Performed scene @ Arts Center - met a possible new cold-reading teacher. Back Stage West.

Aug 12   "Actor's Network" meeting.
Aug 13   Booked independent "Between Classes," met with director. Shot that
          evening "Roommates, Sex, & Love."
Aug 14   Michelle Danner's class.
Aug 15   Intern. CNA wants to meet with me theatrically again. Had 2nd
          meeting with Schiowitz, Clay, & Rose-they want to represent me.
          "Actor's Network" meeting. Back Stage West submissions to casting
          notices.
Aug 16   Rehearse "Roommates, Sex, & Love."
Aug 17   Call back for independent film "The Diary." Call back for independent
          film "What Do Women Want?"
Aug 18   "Actor's Network" meeting.
Aug 19   Filming "Between Classes."
Aug 20   Filming "Between Classes."
Aug 21   Started Kick Boxing classes. Called Eddie at CNA to set up
          appointment.
Aug 22   Intern (last day). Hooked up Voicemail/pager service.
Aug 23   Shooting "Roommates, Sex, & Love."
Aug 26   Filming "Between Classes."
Aug 27   Filming "Between Classes."
Aug 28   "Actor's Network" meeting.
Aug 29   Met Robert Costanzo at CNA - wanted to represent me.
          2nd call-back for indep. film "What do Women Want?" Booked it!
Aug 30   Audition for independent film - (Back Stage West) Church's Chicken
          wants to reinstate National Commercial - I'm in negotiations.
Aug 31   Start rehearsal for "What do Women Want?"
Sept 1   Filming "Between Classes."
Sept 2   Filming "Between Classes."
Sept 3   Filming "Between Classes."
Sept 4   Rehearsal "What do Women Want?" Started learning sign language
          for role.
Sept 6   Filming "Roommates, Sex, & Love." Prepped for theatre audition on
          Saturday.
Sept 7   Audition for play in Santa Monica "Picnic." (Back Stage West)
          Rehearsed "What do Women Want?"
Sept 8   Filming "Between Classes."
Sept 9   Filming "Between Classes."
Sept 10   Filming "Between Classes."
Sept 11   "Actor's Network" meeting.
Sept 12   Met with Robert at CNA second meeting. Called Schiowitz. Clay, &
          Rose -decided to go with them theatrically.
Sept 13   Audition independent film (Back Stage West) casting submissions.
          Filming "Roommates, Sex, & Love." Dropped pictures off at Schiowitz,
          Clay, & Rose.

• **Jode will be looking next for a commercial agent**; if she needs help or
referrals, Beverly Long will help her. Jode is a very commercial type and
has already done several commercials so she is a valuable client. It was
important for her to pursue the theatrical agent first. Jode is ambitious
and driven to be successful.

EPILOGUE

• **Jode wrote the diary above for the eighth edition** of *Acting Is Everything*. In June, two years later, I asked her to give me a copy of her next two week diary. As you will see she is busier than ever. She was writing this during the traditionally "slow time" in Los Angeles. Television shows are on hiatus, "grad films" are all finished, waiting for the schools to start up again and commercial interviews are slow. Jode creates places to act when many actors are just complaining about how slow things are. She has had career ups and downs but stays determined to live her dream fully in Los Angeles.

June 6	9-10	Kickbox
	12:15-12:45	Audition for a SAG independent short film.
	2-4	Industry party in Malibu.
	5-8	Rehearsed showcase scene w/director at the Actors Network.
June 7	10-11	Made calls, returned messages, found out I booked the film.
	12-1:30	Rehearsed showcase scene in Santa Monica.
	1:30-2:30	Private w/acting coach Michelle Danner for audition.
	3:15-3:45	Audition for a USA MOW in Burbank.
	4:30-5:30	Called casting directors, faxed flyers for the showcase.
	7:30-9:30	Filmmaker's Alliance in Hollywood - every other Monday they have a screenwriting workshop and they need/use actors to read their scripts.
June 8	8:30-1:30	Showcase tech rehearsal at The Coast Playhouse in West Hollywood.
	2:30-6	Called casting directors/faxed flyers for showcase.
	7:45-8:45	Therapy.
June 9	8:30-1:30	Showcase dress rehearsal.
	1:30-3	Getting last minute things together for show, stopped at laundry & picked up "good show" gifts.
	5:45	Call time for showcase.
	8:00	Showtime!! We had a packed house.
June 10		Spent most of day a vegetable after the show. The scene wasn't going as well as I'd hoped. I found myself pushing and not allowing moments to organically happen. I needed the day to regroup and figure out why.
	12:30-1:30	Kickbox.
	8-Midnight	Rehearsed the independent film.

June 11	12-5	Acting class, Larry Moss Studio, Santa Monica.
	8:00	Saw *Collected Stories* with Linda Lavin & Samantha Mathis at the Geffen, Westwood. Amazing show—I'm completely inspired by Linda Lavin's work. She is a lesson in specificity. I am so glad I didn't miss seeing it!
June 12		Day Off!!!
June 13	9am-Midnt	Filmed all day. I had a lot of fun. It always feels so good to get in front of the camera.
June 14	1:45-2:45	Pick-up rehearsal with showcase scene partner.
	6:00	Call time for showcase.
	8:00	Showtime!! Another packed house! All of my agents' assistants came tonight and loved the show. The scene felt better too.
June 15	10:30-11:30	Therapy.
	12:30-1:30	Kickbox.
	2-5	Final calls/faxes to casting directors for showcase.
	8-10	Saw a show at The Space Theatre, Hollywood. Written and directed by acquaintances of mine. A friend I saw there is producing *Miss Julie* and asked me to look at the character Christine.
June 16	9:45-1:30	Voice Class/Santa Monica.
	6:00	Call time for the showcase.
	8:00	Final Show! Another packed house! My agents, acting teacher, friends including Cynthia Kerr and, of course, Judy Kerr were there for support.
June 17	9:30-10:30	Jogged around Lake Hollywood. Spent the day regrouping from show. I analyzed the feedback I'd gotten from my teacher, agents and Judy. Called people to thank them for coming. I cried a lot! Some people loved the show and my scene. Some hated it. What's the lesson? I guess you can't please everybody. In my heart I know I did the best I could under my given circumstances, and that makes the whole process a success.
	2:00-3:30	Read *Miss Julie*, decided to pass.
	4-5	Prep tomorrow's audition. A lot of it is going to be improv, so I wrote up a couple of scenarios just to be prepared.
June 18	9-10	Prep audition.
	12-3	Acting class/Santa Monica.
	3:30-4	Audition/new show on the Internet that reviews movies.
June 19		Day Off!

• **JODE WRITES FOR THE TENTH EDITION:**

- **When Judy asked me to write** a little segment on my life in Los Angeles and what I've learned, my mind flooded with all the things I wanted to say. Instead, I'll keep it very meat and potatoes and pass on a few hints that have helped keep my head above water.

- **"This town is going to knock you on your ass, but you get right back up!"** Those were the first words out of my mother's mouth as we were flying into LAX and looking at the vastness of Los Angeles below us. Boy, was she right! This industry has knocked me on my ass, but I get back up, put myself together stronger than before, and give it another go. It will happen to you too! So don't be surprised when it does. That's the gift of living in Los Angeles and pursuing your dreams. You are constantly given the opportunity to expand yourself. Just say, "Ouch! That hurt," dust yourself off and give it another go.

- **Don't waste your time moving here** if you think you can get by without doing the work. My acting teacher Michelle Danner says, "Everybody eventually comes face to face with opportunity and there are only two reasons why people do not succeed. One they haven't worked hard enough on their craft; or two they haven't worked hard enough on themselves." I have seen many people with great business sense finally get an audition and then shoot themselves in the foot because they didn't have the chops to play the part. I've also seen talented actors lose an opportunity because their emotional garbage got in the way. I promise you there is somebody in the wings who has already done the work, and that person might just be me.

- **Create your own work!** This is something I have come to understand this year. When you create your own work, you are truly in control of your career. No matter what anyone else says, you can wake up every day, look at yourself in the mirror, and say, "I'm doing it! I'm really doing it!"

- **Remember, despite what** *Extra, Access Hollywood* and *Entertainment Tonight* might tell you, Rome wasn't built in a day!

- **Los Angeles is a magnificent place filled with angels and devils.** I've made amazing relationships with people in and out of the industry, but most importantly with myself. When you feel overwhelmed by the largeness of the city and our industry, just remind yourself that it's just a city. Your experience has everything to do with what you bring with it. Whether moving to Los Angeles or Idaho, you still carry the same bags.

- **What remains the same throughout these years** is my desire to act and create. I hope that is true for you, and if you can hang on to that then your path will be clear. Good luck, and I'll see you around town.

Mon. Oct.7,	5:30	Wake-up, meditate, and start the day
	7-8:05	Santa Monica College (I'm going to school to get my degree in writing/directing with hopes to transfer to USC).
	8:30-10	Rehearsal: "Fool For Love" (This is a play I'm working to produce and star in next March).
	12:30-1:30	Workout with my trainer, Joey.
	3-4:30	Private work on my character in "Fool For Love" and vocal warm-up.
	6:30-11	Acting Class with Michelle Danner @ Larry Moss Studio (Didn't get my scene up tonight. We did improvisations all night. Lots of fun.)
	12:30	Bed.
Tue. Oct 8,	5:30	Wake-up, meditate and start the day.
	7-9	Santa Monica College.
	9:30-10	Workout.
	10:15-11:15	Therapy.
	12-1:30	Catch up on e-mails from The Actor's Network, return calls, & misc. errands before I get ready for work.
	2:30-11:30	Work front desk at Mondrian Hotel (Survival Job).
	12:30	Bed.
Wed. Oct 9,	5:30	Wake-up, meditate and start the day.
	7-8:05	Santa Monica College.
	8:30-10	Rehearse "Fool For Love".
	11-12:30	I'm playing hookey from work and take a road trip to Santa Barbara with my girlfriends for some much needed wine tasting and spirit lifting!!
	1:30	Bed.
Thur. Oct 10,	5:30	Wake-up, meditate, and start the day.
	7-8:30	Santa Monica College.
	9-10:45	Rehearse "Fool For Love".
	11:30-12:30	Workout with my trainer, Joey.
	2:30-3:30	Back Stage West. [Sends out her submissions for castings]
Fri. Oct 11	8:00	Wake-up (Fridays are usually my OFF days).
	11:30-12:30	Workout.
	4:30:10:30	Tech Rehearsal for "Dancing Lady" (I'm running sound for a friend of mine who wrote a one-woman show called "Dancing Lady").
Sat. Oct 12,	6:00	Wake-up & meditate.
	7-3:30	Work front desk at Mondrian Hotel (Survival Job).
	4-4:45	Workout.
	7:30-12	Dinner and a movie. Saw Red Dragon. VERY SCARY!!!

Sun. Oct 13,	6:00	Wake-up & meditate.
	7-3:30	Work front desk at Mondrian Hotel (Survival Job).
	4-6:30	Work Study for Larry Moss Studio (I work to cover the price of the class. My duties are to organize a rehearsal schedule for the studio, call everyone with their times, and fax the schedule to the studio.)
	6:45-10	Work concession and ticket sales for "Danny and the Deep Blue Sea" (Some students I study with have produced this show on their own. We've made a deal to help each other with some of the crew work. You better believe I'll be calling in a few favors when I get my play produced.)
	10:30-12:30	Study for exam tomorrow.
Mon. Oct 14,	5:30	Wake-up, meditate, and start the day.
	7-8:05	Santa Monica College (Exam Day!)
	8:30-10	Rehearse "Fool For Love".
	12-1	Workout with my trainer, Joey.
	6:30-11	Acting class with Michelle Danner at The Larry Moss Studio (We did our scene tonight from "Fool For Love." I feel like we're making good progress.)
Tue. Oct 15,	5:30	Wake-Up, meditate, and start the day.
	7-9	Santa Monica College (I got a 100% on my exam!!)
	9:30-10	Workout.
	10:15-11:15	Therapy.
	2-11	Work front desk at Mondrian Hotel.
Wed. Oct 16,	5:30	Wake-up, meditate, and start the day.
	7-8:05	Santa Monica College.
	8:30-10	Rehearse "Fool For Love".
	12:15-11:30	Work at Mondrian Hotel.
	12:30	Bed.
Thur. Oct 17,	5:30	Wake-up, meditate, and start the day.
	7-8:30	Santa Monica College.
	9-10:30	Rehearse "Fool For Love".
	11:30-12:30	Workout with my trainer, Joey. Wrote a letter to a friend's agent.
	3-4:30	Back Stage West submissions.
Fri. Oct 18,	6:30-11pm	Run sound for "Dancing Lady".
Sat. Oct 19,	6:00	Wake-up and meditate.
	7-3:30	Work front desk at Mondrian Hotel.
	3:45-4:30	Workout.
	5:30-7:30	Work study for Larry Moss Studio. Saw "Runt of the Litter" an original one-man show at the Matrix
Sun. Oct 20,	6:00	Wake-up and meditate.
	7-3:30	Work front desk at Mondrian Hotel.
	6:45-10	Work tickets for "Danny and the Deep Blue Sea."

• **You must do something each day toward fulfilling your dreams—** there is plenty to do in this career you are creating for yourself.

Section Four
Professional Tools

Career Tips

• **This Professional Tools Section introduces you to the tools** you will need to create a business for your professional career. You are studying, you have your marketing tools (pictures and resumes), you've gained experience and you are now running your life as a professional actor.

• **Your career takes many roads.** No one road is the correct one; each actor's path is their own. I hope you are discovering many new paths in this book and, as you take a certain path, others will open up to you.

• **Following is information I find useful and that I pass on to people who come to me for career coaching.**

The Four Agreements, A Practical Guide To Personal Freedom by Don Miguel Ruiz. I believe the knowledge gained from this book enhances an actor's life and career. Buy the book or tapes. Here is an example.

1. **Be Impeccable with Your Word**

   Speak with integrity. Say only what you mean. Avoid using words to speak against yourself or to gossip about others. For example: When you say you are going to show up for a rehearsal, you are there; you don't cancel at the last moment. You will be careful and thoughtful about what you say you will do.

2. Don't Take Anything Personally

Nothing others do is because of you. What others say and do is a projection of their own reality, their own dream. When you are immune to the opinions and actions of others, you won't be the victim of needless suffering. For example: When you are told you are too old, young, short, tall, pretty, fat, thin, whatever, you will still feel good about yourself! That is their opinion, their world.

3. Don't Make Assumptions

Find the courage to ask questions and to express what you really want. Communicate with others as clearly as you can to avoid misunderstandings, sadness and drama. With just this one agreement, you can completely transform your life. For example: You will never end up with the wrong sides/script in the audition room; you will always ask, "Have there been any changes?"

4. Always Do Your Best

Your best is going to change from moment to moment; it will be different when you are healthy as opposed to sick. Under any circumstance, simply do your best, and you will avoid self-judgment, self-abuse and regret. For example: When you have prepared for your audition you will never have to leave the room feeling badly; you will have done your best.

• **The Internet Movie Database.** Look up every person you have met or who you are scheduled to meet on www.imdb.com. Never arrive at an audition without looking up the casting director, producer, writer, director, any actors that are involved. Do your research. IMDB also comes in very handy when that sleazy producer you've met at a party says what he can do for you. Look him up see if he is who he says he is.

• **Listening to tapes in the car** while driving is extremely valuable. Listening to good story telling helps to understand good stories. It is also helpful to have an entertaining time while in the traffic. I rent the tapes through the mail at the Los Angeles County Library, Books-On-Tape division. 800/253-0591. $10 per book includes postage both ways.

• **Know all you can about your profession.** I subscribe to all of the email newsletters below and find them very useful. Being a reader really helps in this business. Those of you outside of Los Angeles will find them valuable too.

• **Free Newsletters:**

Academy Of Motion Pictures, www.oscar.org, emails a monthly newsletter of Academy Events, film-related exhibitions, screenings, lectures and Student Academy Awards. To request, send an email: subscribe-calendar@lists.oscars.org.

Actorsite, www.actorsite.com. Great uplifting news about acting.

Now Casting, www.nowcasting.com. Acting, Casting, Marketing.

Razurdia Network, razurdianetwork@yahoogroups.com. Casting notices and industry info. Scott Taylor says many of his friends have booked.

Daily Candy, www.dailycandy.com. Great to keep up on cool things going on around you, places, clothing, play, movie or book.

Jeffrey R. Gund, jeffgmusic@mindspring.com. Request to be on email list; say I sent you. Networking, day job and acting opportunities. Savvy links at his web site, www.JeffreyRGund.com.

Hollywood Happy Hour. To subscribe: http://groups.yahoo.com/group/Hollywood-Happy-Hour, and sign up. Yahoo puts you through the paces. This site was founded by Bonnie Gillespie, Nelson Aspen and Kris Burtt. News, Schmooze, Reviews and Interviews, and networking opportunities.

Cynthia Turner's Cynposis, Cynopsis@optonline.net. The latest showbiz news everyday. Love getting this each day.

Planet Shark Productions, www.planetsharkproductions.com. They have over 200 show biz links. Free email newsletter.

Levine Breaking News E-lert, request at: Levinepr2@Earthlink.net. A little too political for me. Great website links, www.levinepr.com.

Show Biz Data, www.showbizdata.com.

• **Talk to any professional person** at the beginning of their career and you will hear of the many hours it took to establish themselves. As a competitive actor it will certainly take all the hours in the day to hone your craft, create your business and make a living. I am astounded at people's gall who think they can be lazy and have a career as an actor.

• **You have chosen the actor's way of life** over any other. Be the best that you can be.

MAKING A LIVING

• **An actor must have financial backing.** If you don't have a trust fund, supporting parents, spouse or angel, then you'll have to provide it yourself. Your "day job" will give you the cash flow to support you and your career. Like any other person in business, career expenses will always be a part of your life. You need enough to live on and to reinvest in your career.

• **Peter Elliott of Now Casting** (www.nowcasting.com) wrote an article I very much agree with titled "The Actor Cycle." Peter allowed me to extract some of it to emphasize how important it is to learn a skill or find a type of job that will pay for the kind of life style it takes for you to live in Los Angeles, pursuing your dream. You can read the full article on the website.

> • **In order to survive in Los Angeles**, you have to have money. And even if you work as an actor at SAG scale on 10 different projects in a year, with two days on each project (which is a pretty good year for most actors in LA in the first 3-5 years) you would only make a little over $11,000. That's just not a living.

> • **We all need to make a living.** There can be a balance between a full-time job and an acting career. *Every* actor needs to have another marketable skill. And there is *no* shame in working a full-time job. Success is not measured in the short term, but by the duration.

> • **If you are a planner,** you arrive in LA with no debt, $10,000 bucks in your savings account, a car, high hopes and plenty of dreams about your career. You pay the $300-800 to get your car registration transferred to California and find a place [most likely a single] to rent for $750 a month, paying a deposit and first and last month's rent. You feel on top of the world and you still have $6-7,000 in the bank.

• **You spend the first three months** trying to figure out what the heck is going on. You need headshots, classes, subscriptions and union dues ($1,300 if you become eligible to join SAG). You start using credit cards as your bank account dwindles. You get some nibbles and say "It's going to break any time now!" But it stays just a bit out of reach.

• **Your credit cards are getting higher**, but you know you can make it happen. You take a part time job so you can be available for acting jobs and auditions. It pays $7-12 an hour. On your ninth month, you find your bank account dry and the credit card debt piling up. So you keep the low paying job, increasing to 40 hours and only charge what you really need.

• **Soon you find yourself** $20,000 plus in debt with a job that pays you a few hundred dollars a week. You start doing the math and figure out that you can't pay this off unless you make a major change in your life. For many, this is the time they move back home, file bankruptcy and are beaten by the city. But it doesn't need to be this way.

• **Don't wait until it's too late and don't sugar coat it.** The next break may be around the corner, but that won't pay the big bucks. It takes time to be an overnight success and you have to be able to give it the time you need. Be realistic and stick to your dream. It can happen, if you can last long enough.

• **Most actors end up earning money** in many different aspects of show business, adding hyphens to their names: directors, producers, writers, teachers, dialogue and acting coaches.

• **Some jobs actors have had:** Jenna Elfman, clothing manufacturer. She put rhinestones on jeans and vests. Julianna Margulies: when people died, she would go in and pack up their belongings. Thomas Gibson worked in a bank vault, bagging coins. Tom Hanks, hotel bellboy (carried bags for Cher). Quentin Tarantino, video rental store. Ray Romano, washed trucks. Lucy Lawless, gold mining company, sawed rocks in half. Grace Jones, director's assistant. Ellen Barkin, waitress in Greenwich Village. Dom DeLuise, baby photographer. Elayne Boosler, waitress. Robert Duvall, post office. Meg Ryan, grocery checker. Harry Belafonte, assistant janitor. Sidney Poitier, dishwasher. Mary Steenburgen waitressed in New York for five years. Tuesday Knight, receptionist. Margaret Cho, Raggedy Ann Doll at F.A.O. Schwarz in S.F. Cameron Diaz, clerk at TCBY, the yogurt shop. Danny DeVito, hair dresser Mr. Dan. Michael Caine, donut maker. Bob Saget, deli clerk (he financed his student films in college from his earnings). Warren Beatty, brick layer's helper. Bill Cosby, shoe salesman. Sean Connery polished coffins.

• **Stella Adler,** one of the greatest acting teachers, said, "Waiting tables is excellent for the developing actor. To be a good waiter you need to communicate effectively with your customers, be responsive to their moods and needs and keep your memorization tools sharp." At the same time they are handling dishes, glasses and such. "A physical activity while responding to the others in your scene—exactly what the actor does."

• **Taye Diggs, Jennifer Esposity, Maxwell and Selma Blair,** Gillian Anderson, Sandra Bullock, Steve Buscemi, Jessica Lange, were waiters. Geena Davis and Julianna Margulies worked at the River Cafe; Geena says the owner used to say, "Relax! I can tell you're going to be a star."

• **Patricia Heaton, Amanda Peet, Ashley Judd and Gwyneth Paltrow** were hostesses. Bruce Willis and James Gandolfini were bartenders.

• **Brad Garrett** worked at T.G.I. Friday's restaurant in Woodland Hills for two years while working his way up with his standup act and acting.

• **Jeremy Gursey, at 19, when working at a coffeehouse** in Studio City, noticed the lines for ice-blended mochas. He decided to create his own version and take it to film and television sets. He saved $100 from three paychecks to buy a commercial blender and an ice chest. He said, "I figured if all else fails, at least I'll be able to whip up some damn good margaritas. At the time, I was charging $2 by the cup and I remember returning home with a fat stack of ones." One night, when watching *Seinfeld,* he scanned the credits for the line producer, called and worked his way in. He had somehow memorized all of our favorite blends. He would bring mine to the set because, most of the time, I couldn't get away. Everyone loved him. Last time I saw him, at age 24, he figured his company, Mocha Kiss, had prepared more than 75,000 coffee drinks on about 100 films and TV shows. His assets now include thousands of dollars worth of large-scale commercial cappuccino machines, a van and his own office. He and four employees shuttle between 12 and 20 productions a week. What would he really like to do? "Direct." He has several film ideas percolating.

• **Rachel Griffiths** says, "Oh, I was just a terrible waitress. So I became an artist's model instead because then all I had to do was take my clothes off, lie down on a nice rug and fall asleep. I was good at that."

• **While job researching**, a good exercise is to write down everything you love to do and see if you can possibly put them together in a job you would like. When you are on the job, you want to shine, to be the best at what you are doing. This will increase your chances to make more money, but most of all, you will be a champion at everything you do. This will raise your self-confidence and self-esteem; you will be contributing to a better work place. Striving to be the best that you can be is a valuable acting tool. You can train for it every day.

• **Keep your priorities straight.** If you are an actor, you need to be acting somewhere at all times. Pick a job that won't drain you physically or emotionally. It should give you some flexibility for auditions and the ability to take off for a few days if you land that one, two or three-day job. Generally, stage actors look for day jobs, and film and television actors look for night and weekend jobs.

• **It is in your best interest** to choose a job that is connected to show business or one that is in an area of town where people in the business will likely show up. There is the slim possibility that you will be discovered on your job—it does happen. At least you will make friends who are connected and interested in the biz.

• **Gretchen Mol**, in 1996, was working as a coat check girl at a restaurant named Michael's in New York—a lot of agents dine there. She says, "One day an agent asked for my picture and resume." She was cast in Woody Allen's comedy, *Celebrity*, and hasn't stopped working.

• **Ethan Erickson**, desk clerk at West Hollywood's Le Montrose. He was spotted by a casting director. He's is starring on daytime's *Guiding Light*.

• **Learn the skill of saving money** when you are working your "day job." An actor's paychecks can be few and far between. If you save your acting money and live fairly frugally, you can actually support yourself working relatively few days a year. *See Union websites for pay scales.* Inexperienced actors will make a major purchase when they receive their checks for six week's work on a film, then have to scrounge next month's rent. We never know when our next acting job will be. Knowing how to manage money is one of the keys to an actor's success.

• **Here are some ideas for jobs** that have worked very well for people I know. Some of these jobs take research to find out where to apply for them.

- **Starbucks**, all of their employees are hand picked for their personalities behind the counter. A manager told me last month he had 150 applications and only seven suited their criteria. All employees have benefits and profit sharing packages that become 100% funded after you work there five years. Flexible working hours and if you love coffee – why not?
- **Fit Model.** *See the Commercial Print section.*
- **Substitute teacher** can make a good living; the hours are great for our business.
- **The airlines** offer flexible hours, great benefits, trips to New York for auditions.
- **Work in restaurants or upscale grocery stores** (Whole Foods, Pavilions, Gelsons, Trader Joes, Ralphs) in Beverly Hills, Brentwood, Encino, Malibu, Santa Monica, Pacific Palisades, Studio City, West Hollywood or West Los Angeles.
- **An actress I know** works 20 hours a week, for 1-800-DENTIST, making $15 per hour. She can switch hours for her interviews.
- **Mystery Shopping.** One of my students does this earning about $200 a month.
- "**Acting as if you are a patient**" for doctor's tests.
- **A dog walking and grooming company** is a good way to be your own boss.
- **Traffic School teachers** work on weekends and make $100 a day, a good way to work on selling yourself to people, practice speaking and comedy.
- **Work as a messenger or delivering food** to offices and studios; landscaping or taking care of office plants; a mail clerk in a big theatrical agency; a secretary at a public relations firm; a limousine driver or a runner in an entertainment attorney's office.
- **Stage shows** at our local amusement parks, auditions are advertised in the trade papers.
- **Temporary agencies** furnish the studios with office workers.
- **People who know computers** can get jobs at night inputting information. The hourly rate is usually around $15 to $20.
- **Construction.**
- **A teller** at a Beverly Hills bank.
- **Extra work.** *(See Section Three)*

• **Dan Cortes** (*Suddenly Susan, Single Guy, Melrose Place*) began his show biz career as a production assistant at MTV. He was going to be let go in a month due to cutbacks. He wrote a treatment, mailed a copy of it to himself and left it sealed, for the postmark date. Then he pitched the concept for a sports show with him as the host. They said they weren't interested but in two weeks time they had developed the same show he pitched. The last day of his employment they were auditioning 15 guys for the host. One guy didn't show up on time, so they asked Dan to hop up on stage to hold the spot for the guy. Dan auditioned along with everyone else until the guy showed up. Two days later, the producer called and offered Dan the job. I asked him, why didn't you say I was the one who conceived it? He said, "I was grateful to get the job and knew they wouldn't give me a piece of it. If they had gone with another host and been a hit, eventually I could have gone to court with the treatment I had presented." Landing the job of the host was his opening into becoming known as a personality.

• **Andi Matheny**, one of the members of my theatre company, works in the Universal Studio Wild West Stunt Show. They have two casts of five, and five or six alternates for each role. They trained her and she rehearsed for a month. The auditions are advertised in the trade papers. As third and fourth alternate last year, she made $22,000. In a job like this you can always be available to take auditions because an alternate will fill in for you.

• **Steve Martin**, worked at Disneyland selling guides, then at Knotts Berry Farm at the Bird Cage Theater, learning balloon tricks and the banjo.

• **Mel Harris** made $85,000 in 1985 on the $100,000 Pyramid. She used the money to pay bills and finance her career. Five years later, in her third year on *thirtysomething*, she was on the $100,000 Pyramid as a guest celebrity. So if you like game shows, give it a try.

• **Craig Zisk,** a producer and director of *The Single Guy,* began his show business career as a production assistant (PA) on *Family Ties* during the summer of his junior year in college. After graduating, he held many different jobs. In 1995, he became the supervising producer on *The Single Guy.* After directing several shows in the first season, he became full-time director in the second season. He and Brad Hall, the creator of *The Single Guy* and *Watching Ellie* met working on *Family Ties.* This is how networking friendships are made in this business. Always do a good job, no matter what that job is; you will be remembered.

• **Catering, bartending, waiting, valet parking** and limousine driving jobs allow you the opportunity of seeing how successful people party. The hours are flexible and the pay is good. Like most jobs, you have to prove yourself in order to get the best parties and hours; a good place to work on your personality skills. Work for the companies that cater celebrity show biz parties. Read the gossip columns in the *Daily Variety* and *Hollywood Reporter* trade papers; they often mention who caters the parties and parks the cars.

• **Many actors do audience recruiting** for movie screenings and marketing research for studios. *(See Resources)*

• **Professional TV-studio audience member.** You get paid for sitting in sit-com audiences. *See Kidd's Temps on Time in Resources.*

• **Mystery shopper** can be a fun part-time job. You go undercover to stores you are assigned to and grade the employees and the condition of the store. Salary can be up to $100 a visit. You stay in the store 20 to 30 minutes and e-mail a two-page report within 24 hours.

• **Jill Hennessy** (*Crossing Jordan*) was a New York subway and street performer, playing the guitar and singing. She made a living and felt like she was performing and it kept her available for class, auditions and work when she could land a part. (*imdb.com*)

• **Bonnie Gillespie** is the casting columnist for Back Stage West and author of the book, *Casting Qs: A Collection of Casting Director Interviews*, www.castingqs.com. She is also a career consultant on the business of acting, and owner of Cricket Feet Management. Bonnie is a big fan of author Deborah Jacobson's book, *Survival Jobs*. Here are a couple of paragraphs from a letter she wrote to Deborah.

> • **The funniest realization**, upon reading your book, was that I had, at some point in my life, held no fewer than 30 of the odd jobs you detail. I never understood why people shook their heads at me in dismay, asking, "How can you do so many different things?" and, "When are you going to get a real job?" all while coveting the freedom and flexibility my job(s) of choice provided. Even though I'd already begun living a freelance lifestyle, while in my 20s, it wasn't until I read your book that I realized that there needn't be a stigma attached to that choice. What a wonderful discovery!
>
> • **Since clocking out on the last day** of my long-term temp assignment in 1999, [three years ago] I have held (usually six simultaneously) the following survival jobs: pet-sitter, interview transcriptionist, makeup artist, actress, singer, voiceover artist, hand model, hair model, Improv comedy traffic school instructor, Payroll/office manager, webpage designer, graphic designer, columnist, focus group participant, product tester, academic tutor, SAT course instructor, nanny, casting assistant, theatr0e director, film print archivist, restaurant reviewer, book reviewer, acting advice columnist, biz of the biz speaker.

• **Actress Stacey Smithey** says, "My advice to a new actor in town is to do extra work! It will allow them an opportunity to be on the set and make some money and contacts. And if they need more money, get a few temp jobs, catering, etc. but nothing that ties them down to a desk or responsibility. I wish I had done it that way, rather then the desk job way. I think I would be farther along by now."

Resources

CATERERS
Along Came Mary, 323/931-9082.
Scotty's Bartending & Waitress Service, 818/247-9968.

EDUCATIONAL THEATRE
Backstage West did a feature on this read the article online, www.backstagewest.com.
Kaiser Permanente's CareActors. Part time. Send P&R to Lisa Beezley-Lippman, Kaiser Permanente, Educational theatre program (CareActors), 393 E. Walnut St., Pasadena, 91188. Needs extensive theatre background. Training for physicians and health care professionals to improve communication skills and patient/physician skills.
Kaiser Permanente's Community Services. Touring Theatre Company with 25 full-time actors includes benefits. Tour schools, need young-looking actors. Send P&R to Edgar Garcia Educational Theatre, 825 W. Colorado Blvd., #222, L.A., 90041.
L.A. Troupe, Theatre-In-Education. Classical adaptations aimed at middle schools. P&R to L.A. Troupe, 9991 Maude Ave., Shadow Hills, 91040. 818/951-6882.
National Conference for Community and Justice. NCCJ Presents plays to high schools. P&R to Peter Howard, NCCJ, 1055 Wilshire Blvd., #1615, L.A., 90017. 213/250-8787, ext. 228. Equity contract. www.nccj.org.
Shakespeare and Friends. Small Equity company tours middle schools and high schools. P&R to Dee Mrie Nieto, 11824 Dorothy St., L.A., 9049. 323/820-2292.
Stop Gap, 17-19 actors play to youth, adult and senior groups. www.stopgap.org.
Storytellers and Troubadours, people with a ready-to-go finished project. P&R to Ken Frawley, President, P.O. Box 3831, Orange, 92865. 714/771-1981.

ENTERTAINMENT INDUSTRY JOBS
www.bu.edu/com-csc/html/Company_Links/company_film.html. Production companies and hundreds of job positions.
www.showbizdata.com.
Audience Recruiters, 1800-A-JOB-NOW, EXT. 1416, www.movieviewjobs.com. Also research assistants. You have to answer questions on an automated line, and if you pass they call you in for a physical interview, where you take a test and, if you pass, you are interviewed. I've known many people who work here, its tough but you can make a living with your own hours.
Robert A. Brilliant, Inc./CBS Screenings, 818/386-6605 Ext. 18, seasonal.

GENERAL

www.entertainmentcareers.net. All kinds of career advice.

Hiring On The Internet: JOBTRACK: www.jobtrak.com. Computer proficiency. **www.hotjobs.com.**

Hollywood Creative Directory: free job board: www.hcdonline.com.

Mystery Shopping. Feedback Plus, Inc., www.gofeedback.com. For other companies: www.mysteryshop.org, they have links to companies that use mystery shoppers.

Transcription Company, 818/848-0575. www.transcripts.net. They transcribe video footage into scripts, 24 hours a day. For those with good computer skills.

USC School Of Medicine, Dept. of Medical Education, 1975 Zonal Ave. KAM 200, Los Angeles, 90033. Actors portray actual patients to help train medical students. Strong improv skills a must. All ages, all types. Send picture and resume to Attn: Denise.

TEMP AGENCIES

Executive Temps, 818/563-2939. 2321 W. Olive Ave., Suite F, Burbank, 91506. "We Give Temps a Good Name."

Friedman Personnel Agency, 310/550-1002. 9000 Sunset Blvd., #1000, Los Angeles, 90069. Jobs in the industry, fees paid by employer.

Kidd's Temps On Time, 818/845-3030. 418 E. Olive, Burbank, 91501. Full range of employment needs. They also work with major studios supplying people for audiences. You get paid for seeing the show!

The Job Factory, 310/475-9521. www.thejobfactory.com. 1744 Westwood Blvd., Los Angeles, 90024. Unusual jobs and flexible hours. They've been helping actors for 25 years.

Our Gang Agency, 323/653-4381. 825 N. Fairfax Ave., Los Angeles, 90046.

PARKING SERVICES

Chuck's, 818/788-4300 (The best). **Valet Girls,** 310/457-6657.

THEME PARKS

Disneyland, Audition Hotline: 714/781-0111. www.disneyland.disneygo.com.

Knott's Berry Farm, 714/995-0088. www.knottsberryfarm.com.

Legoland California, Audition Hotline: 760/918-5454. www.legoland.com.

Sea World Of California, 619/226-3842. www.seaworldjobs.com.

Six Flags Magic Mountain, Audition Hotline: 661/255-4800. www.sixflags.com.

Universal Studios Hollywood, Audition Hotline: 818/866-4021. www.universalstudios.com.

Water Ski Shows, 818/622-8523. Contractor for Universal Studios.

BOOKS

Back Stage West, Hollywood Reporter and *Variety* and other trades have weekly listings.

The Working Actors Guide (**WAG**), www.workingactors.com, has many listings of where to find jobs for actors in Los Angeles. Order books through Take One Bookstore, 310/445-4050, www.take1filmbooks.com. or Samuel French Bookstore, 323/876-0570. www.samuelfrench.com.

Development Girl by Hadley Davis.

How to Be a Star at Work by Robert E. Kelley.

Survival Jobs by Deborah Jacobson.

CHANGING YOUR NAME

- **There are two reasons to change your name.** One, you don't like it and feel it doesn't suit you. Two, your name is already taken in SAG (Rule 15). I stayed with Kerr, one of my married names, because it fit, I liked it and my children are named Kerr. A numerologist once told me I would have more luck if I added an E as a middle initial or spelled my name Judie. I tried to do it, but couldn't; it didn't feel like me. I like my name so I will have to make more of my own luck. Listen to all opinions and then make your own decisions based on what feels right to you. Part of developing self-awareness is following your own instincts; they are there to guide you.

- **Jay Bernstein, personal manager, writer and producer:**

  - **A limousine driver/actor once asked me,** "Should I change my name, its Alexander Propapalis?" I told him to change his name, no one should have to get through your name to get to your talent. They're not going to say we have to get . . . They'll just cut you.

- **Salma Hayek says ten years ago Hollywood producers shunned her** because of her nationality. "When I first started, they said, 'Just don't say you're Mexican. With your name and your looks you can pass for Lebanese. Work on your accent so that it sounds more Middle Eastern.'" She refused. "I was born and raised in Mexico; I'm Mexican."

- **Michael Keaton's** real name is Michael Douglas.

- **Goldie Hawn'** was told, "You sound like a stripper." Goldie said so!

• **Actress Samantha Harper** had to change her name from Harriet Harper. Her fiancee, at the time, suggested Samantha. The minute she tried it she says, "My heart sang and I knew it was for me."

• **Bill Macy** (*Surviving Christmas; Analyze This; Maude)* had to change his name from William Garber. Later, William H. Macy had to add an initial in order to keep his name intact.

• **Meg Ryan** was Meg Hyra; Tori Amos was Myra Amos.

• **If you must change your name** because of the SAG rule, then choose a name that means something to you or your family. I would consult a numerologist with a list of possible names you could live with. Look for numerologists at psychic fairs and the Bodhi Tree Bookstore's bulletin board. (*See Bookstores.*) As with anything else, be cautious. Consultants will each have their own opinion based on their personal studies. When you are eligible to join SAG, call and ask about names before you join.

• **I asked actress Maddisen K. Krown**, who recently went through a name change, to tell of her experience.

> • **When I wanted to change my name**, I took the following steps. Purchased the book, *How to Change Your Name in California*, by Attorney Lisa Sedano. Visited my local Superior Court branch to pick up the Petition for Name Change forms. Contacted the Society of Kabalarians at www.kabalarians.com for assistance.

> • **California adults have the legal right** to change our names by "Usage," which is done without filing court papers. However, I decided to take the legal route because it can be difficult to get federal and state agencies to accept the new name without the official authorization.

> • **Once I had decided on my new name**, I filed the forms with the Superior Court; paid a Court Filing fee of $214.50, plus $95 for the Order to Show Cause for Name Change to be published in a local newspaper. On my court date I received my name change decree. I registered the new name with the actor's unions.

> • **The Society of Kabalarians** assisted me in choosing my new name. Their name change recommendations are based upon the principle that "through knowledge of the relationship of a name to a date of birth, one's inner potential and the mental characteristics, personality traits, and conditions in one's life can be determined. The right change of name can change your life."

• **Joel M. Barkow from** SAG wrote in the SAG newsletter about name changes on Social Security cards.

   • **Applicants who have legitimate business needs** for using assumed names (such as performers using stage names) are allowed to request additional cards. Apart from filling out an SS-5 form, available at all Social Security offices, you merely need to submit documents at the time of application that show use of the old name and current use of your stage name. A driver's license or similar ID would suffice for the former, while the latter can be evinced from a signed contract or pay stub using the assumed name.

   • **Since the employer submits only your Social Security number**— and not your name—you can wait to apply for the second card until you receive the initial pay check stub before filling out the necessary application. However, the transfer must be taken care of prior to tax time, when the IRS begins checking names against Social Security numbers. The second card is for ID purposes only—it is not a legal document and does not have the same effect as a legal name change.

• **In 1998,** SAG **approved changes** to its previously strictly-enforced Rule 15. They will continue to "urge membership applicants not to join SAG with a professional name that duplicates or can cause confusion with that of an existing member." I believe it is vastly better to use a name that doesn't closely resemble another actor's name.

• **Search for your name on www.imdb.com** before registering with SAG. you can also visit Academy Players and look in the books to see if your name is taken. You may use any name for performance purposes if you have the first claim on it. Vanessa L. Williams was forced to use her middle initial because Vanessa Williams (of Melrose Place) joined SAG first. However, Sean Hayes was able to drop his middle initial, although he is still listed as Sean P. Hayes in the SAG international database.

Resources

Legal Name Change, Los Angeles County, 213/974-5299. Call this line for recorded complete information of how to change your name legally. Currently the cost is $215, plus a publication fee of $95.
The Society of Kabalarians, (a registered non-profit society) www.kabalarians.com. Discover what's in your name.
www.imdb.com.
www.sag.org.
http://my.ca.gov to download name change forms.

HOME BUSINESS OFFICE

• **As a self-employed, self-motivated actor,** you are now in business and this requires an office, a private phone line (not to be shared with anyone), an answering machine, voice mail or message service and a cell phone with a message service. One lost message could mean the loss of a career break, as well as the loss of a day's income, which could pay for two years of phone service.

• **It's wonderful to have a separate room** for your office, but few of us have that luxury. So set aside an area devoted to taking care of business.

• **Your first order of business** is to get your pictures and resumes out to prospective buyers of your talent. Just as an employee shows up for work each day, you must make a commitment to look for acting work each day. It doesn't matter what that acting work is: big, small, paid, free; you are looking for experience in your new business. Free jobs are just as valuable as paying jobs in your career.

• **You need a desk or table, a computer** and file folder dividers, trays or file drawers. Designate a folder or tray for each different head shot, a place for letterhead stationary, business envelopes, 8x10 or 81/2x11 envelopes, postage scale, stamps, appointment book, acting notebook, networking card file, and bookshelf. You need a computer; until you can afford your own, some libraries and copy service stores have computers and printers available for your use.

• **Keeping track of incoming and outgoing phone messages** is an important part of every business. I find a valuable book for this is Avery's #50-111 In/Out Call Log, 100 pages. When I pick up my messages I write them in the book. My personal technique for checking calls off when I return them allows me to use both pages for incoming calls.

• **When my book is full**, (about two years) I file it away. There have been times I've had to refer to old books for the phone number of someone I needed to reconnect with. This is a small community and we do come in contact with the people we've worked with again.

• **Use a file box or file drawers to set up your files.** *Some suggestions for file folder titles are:*

- **Advertising/promotion.** Copies of any publicity about you.
- **Articles of interest.** Keep pieces on people you know, or would like to know; information on projects you'd like to work on; story ideas, etc.
- **Audition copy.** The sides and copy from your readings.
- **Bank statements.**
- **Cash receipts.** Keep for income taxes. Write any pertinent information on the back. Don't forget video rentals.
- **Commercial pictures.** Print work from magazines you could have done. Ideas of how to dress for commercials.
- **Correspondence.** Keep a copy of any letter you send out or receive.
- **Income statements of earnings.**
- **Manuals for equipment.**
- **Master head shots and negatives.** Labeled in a folder, you never have to worry about where to find your negatives or digital disks.
- **Phone lists.** Keep every phone list you're given from acting classes and productions you've worked on. Great for making a networking phone call.
- **Pictures.** I keep a few of each shot within reach.
- **Pictures of acting roles** I want to play or a characterization I think will help me. I take these along on my photo shoots to show the photographer.
- **Publicity, general.** I save copies of trade ads that I may want to emulate.
- **Receipts** from check and credit card purchases.
- **Resumes.**
- **Reviews.** Keep a copy of all reviews from every project you're in.

• **Organization** is one of the most important components of running a business. If you have no training for business, you can learn. Peter Elliott of Now Casting has written the book, *An Actor Organizes*, subtitled: *A Complete Organizer to Help You Create a Specific Plan and Track your Progress for an Entire Year.* It outlines goal setting, goal tracking and other important business tools for an actor to put a plan in place, keep track of it and to keep organized. Basil Hoffman, a mature character actor who has a very successful long-running career, says, "Every actor who expects to take charge of his own acting career needs to begin with *An Actor Organizes*. It offers a real plan for success and is the only workable step-by-step success program for actors that I've ever seen."

BOOKS

Working From Home, 5th Edition, by Paul & Sarah Edwards. www.workingfromhome.com. 664 pages and is part of the New York Review of Books Catalog of the best books in print. "On the subject of home-based business, this gets as close as possible to everything you need to know, from office layout to maintaining personal relationships. A must for anyone considering working out of the home."

An Actor Organizes, by Peter Elliott. www.nowcasting.com or Samuel French Books.

The #1 Home Business Book, by George & Sandra Delany.

Small-Time Operator, by Bernard Kamoroff, CPA.

AUDITION LOG BOOKS OR SYSTEMS
It is very important to keep track of all your auditions, who you met where you went. What you auditioned for. At the beginning of your career it is easy but as you get very busy it is hard to keep track with out a computer program or a log book.

Actors Callback, www.actorscallback.com. $50 looks very good but not available for the Mac yet. Put the information in once and the program organizes it in many ways.

Actor's Interview Log. A paper book to keep track of where you have been. $10

The Actor's Office, www.theactorsoffice.com. Mac and Windows $50. Track auditions and submissions, Print Postcards, cover letters, mailing lables, agent and casting director addresses

WEB SITES

Working From Home, www.workingfromhome.com. Paul & Sarah Edwards.

Work-at-Home Success, www.workathomesuccess.com. This site posts listings of companies that hire home-based workers, plus discussions of important issues, including effective ways to communicate with your boss on the telephone.

USED OFFICE FURNITURE

Steel Casey Traditional To Funk, 818/763-5667. 10624 Ventura Blvd., Studio City, 91604. M-F 9-5; Sat 11-5; Sun. 12-4.This is the absolute best place for used file cabinets with and without style. Desks, great desk and computer chairs. My husband and I have custom designed desks but everything else we have purchased at Steel Casey's. I especially love the used horizontal files. They take up less space, hold more and are easier for setting copy machines etc. on than the vertical file drawers. Stock changes all the time and Casey can get you just about anything you need.

Advanced Liquidators, 818/763-3470. 10631 Magnolia Blvd., North Hollywood. M-F 9-5; Sa, 10-4.

CAREER TOOLS

APPOINTMENT BOOK / PDA / TIME MANAGEMENT

• **Always have your "book" with you.** Write every appointment down: classes, rehearsals, interviews, workouts, meditation, dates for movies, plays, etc. All your phone numbers and addresses, and a place to jot down notes, career goals and future plans should be included. When you schedule your days be sure to allow for driving time. Sunday night is a good time to plan for the week. Purchase a system that has a full page for each day and lists the time of day down the left side of the page; a place for a To Do List and a place to write down directions to locations. I use the *Day Runner* in a 5x7 *Filofax* book. The daily log is valuable for verifying your tax deductions. You can file the year's log in the same file as the year's copy of your tax returns. I use a computer program for names, phone numbers and addresses. I update this every few months, print the pages and replace them in my book.

• **Personal Digital Assistant**—PDA—Electronic Palm Pilot Systems, also Handspring products. I use a Handspring Treo with the Palm Pilot System in it. I store all the phone numbers in my life and lists of anything I might need with me. I carry the PDA in my purse so I always have the information with me. I do not keep my calendar events and appointments on it. I find I need to look at them laid out on paper for the day, week and month.

• **I asked actress Tricia Gilfone to write about using the PDA.**

  • **A Personal Digital Assistant, or PDA,** is a good tool. The advantage is all the information on your PDA is stored and backed up on your computer. When you enter new information or make a change on your PC or Mac, it automatically appears on your handheld when

348

you synchronize, and vise versa. In the event of a computer crash or disappearance of your PDA, you always have your valuable networking information backed up. If you want to purchase a PDA but you're not sure if it's right for you, I recommend starting off with the Handspring Visor or the Palm Zire. Currently, these are the most basic and inexpensive on the market.

• **There are numerous companies** with a plethora of models to choose from, the most popular being The Palm Pilot; www.Palm.com, and Handspring; www.Handspring.com. Research at www.pdabuyersguide.com. Click on the links page for other related websites. You can download hundreds, of applications that allow you to view web pages, create detailed shopping lists, expense records, even de-stress with some cool games, www.Handango.com and www.tucows.com. Find everything from Dictionary/Thesauruses to Diet and Exercise assistants to GPS and Map software. Get the Rand McNally Streetfinder guide, www.Randmcnally.com, to find your way.

• **Another fabulous application** is www.Avangto.com. This software allows you to keep current with the latest industry buzz by downloading magazine subscriptions such as *Variety, Rollingstone, TVguide*, as well as the latest local and world news from CNN, USA today, and *The New York Times*. Keep up on Oscar picks with Yahoo or Hollywood.com to get your local movie theaters and show times.

• **Acting coach/actress Caryn West** keeps track of every casting director showcase she does. While there she puts in their name, address, where she met them, the scene she did and anything special she wants to remember. She can transfer to her computer and print out a complete list or just last month's list. When her agent or manager is submitting her for a role she will email them the history she has with the casting director. She finds the PDA very valuable in keeping organized.

• **The important thing about having a system to keep appointments** is the time management aspect. Time management can make the difference in having a successful career. You can educate yourself; there are time management courses. I have worked privately with expert Dr. Jo Christner and have taken a course from Dr. Jackie Jaye-Brandt. It is fun to manage your time and it can relieve that feeling of being overwhelmed. It will help every segment of your career and life.

Resources

Most stationery stores have inexpensive systems and books. The following systems are more expensive and prestigious.
Franklin System, at Franklin/Covey Store: 818/884-7791 or 800/996-1492. www.franklincovey.com. They hold time management seminars.
Filofax System: Fred Segal, 323/651-129. 8100 Melrose Ave., West Hollywood.
Time Design System, 800/637-9942. www.timedesign.com. 11835 W. Olympic #450, West Los Angeles.
Jo Christner, PsyD., 310/471-2773. Offices in Encino and West Los Angeles. Teaches you how to manage your time and to organize you and your environment. She is excellent for setting you up in your acting business. If you have a problem being late, get it straightened out with her. She is a Member of the National Association of Professional Organizers.
Jackie Jaye-Brandt, M.A., MFT, Corporate Communications and Psychotherapy, 818/ 505-1664. 3575 Cahuenga Blvd. West, #213, Los Angeles, 90068. Stress management, communications training, time management, group workshops, couples, groups and individual counseling.

TELEPHONE / VOICEMAIL / CELL PHONE / FAX MACHINE

• **You must have a private phone** with a 310, 323, 213 or 818 preface and message device, not to be shared with a roommate. If you share a phone number and message device, you will lose important messages. Don't do it.

• **Keep the outgoing message short and to the point.** People wanting to interview or hire you hate to wait through cute, long messages. It is important that your name or phone number, not both, be on your outgoing message so your callers know they have not dialed in error.

• **When you can't be reached on your cell phone,** check in for messages every 60 or 90 minutes during casting hours 10-6. You never know who may have a last-minute interview for you.

• **Show Biz is a phone business; when you call someone** and get their answering device, speak your name and phone number slowly and clearly first, as if someone is writing it down, then the rest of your message and then your phone number again. Voice mail systems often cut off but if you have given your name and number first, they know who has called. *Always leave your phone number,* even if you think they know it. Your calls will be returned faster! Why not make it the easiest thing in the world to return your call?

• **I believe you must have a cellular phone with voicemail** for emergencies, and it must also have a 310, 323, 213 or 818 preface. You never know when you will be stuck in traffic or in a deserted neighborhood in the middle of the night. The service companies usually have free phones if you sign up for two years; the least you can pay per month is $20. Have a car charger in case the battery runs down. At this writing Verizon is said to have the best reception. I have AT&T.

• **It is great to have your own plain paper fax machine.** If you don't, you must have a place where you can receive faxes 24 hours a day. You never know when you will need your sides faxed to you for tomorrow's audition. I prefer my fax machine on its own phone line. Some email addresses allow you to receive a fax like an email.

COMPUTER / E-MAIL / INTERNET / WORLD WIDE WEB

• **You must be computer savvy** if you want to be competitive in your marketing strategies. Before you have your own computer you can use one at a library. Get a free email address at yahoo.com, msn.com and many others. Don't make the address too difficult to tell people what it is. My Yahoo name is JudyKerrActing. Use your full name; if it is not accepted, add a word or number to the end. You will be including your email address on your business cards and resumes. When purchasing a computer I recommend Apple/MAC because of the ease of video editing and the great graphic applications. A PC will be cheaper and will do other functions just as well.

• **There is no charm in saying, "I'm not into computers."** You will miss out on casting, networking and friendship opportunities by not taking this educational step. You can do it. You learned to ride a bike and drive a car which opened up new worlds; so will a computer.

CABLE TV / TIVO / VCR-VIDEO TAPE RECORDER

• **All right, you are an actor,** you must know who is acting and where. You are a student of acting. You must have cable, you must have HBO, PBS, Showtime, Sundance and Bravo channels at the very least. Of course, you are not home to watch what you need to see, so you must have a TIVO and a VCR machine. This way you can view when it's convenient.

• **The TIVO is very easy.** You buy the machine and then you pay $300 for a life time subscription service for the machine. As long as you are using that machine the service will always set your channels for you to record. You can pay the manufacturer $100 to come out and set you up though that is also fairly easy. The truly easy part of TIVO is setting the programs you want to watch. One touch and you can set a whole season of *Friends*. Each week the show will be there ready for you to watch. Go to www.tivo.com to get all of the information.

• **You will use your VCR** when you want to keep a copy of a commercial or an actor's performance. That is also done with a click of a TIVO button, when the VCR is set up with the TIVO. You will need the VCR also to view tapes you rent or to watch your tape from acting class. These career tools make good gifts for loving families to give aspiring actors.

AUDIO TAPE RECORDER / VIDEO CAMERA

• **An audio tape recorder** can be used for learning lines, taping your teachers' feedback, or taping you and your acting partner rehearsing a scene. I like the kind that has a pause button on it, and that has a little speaker in it so I can choose to not wear headphones when listening to it. An Olympus Digital Voice Recorder W-10 is extremely tiny, and also takes digital pictures, very handy.

• **A digital MDV video camera would be a helpful tool.**

Tom Kelly, 818/730-1076 or 818/707-2424. Better prices than discount stores and he delivers, sets up and does repairs. He specializes in custom-designed systems. When he sells you equipment, he also trains you how to use it. Good bargains on computers, used equipment and trade-ins.

BUSINESS AND PROMOTIONAL PICTURE CARDS

• **Keep photo business cards** in your jacket pocket, purse, wallet, glove compartment. They are an important networking tool. Whenever you meet someone, hand them yours and ask for theirs. There is nothing more awkward than looking for a pen and scrap of paper when someone asks for your phone number.

• **File the business cards you receive.** Make a note of the meeting place, what the person looked like, your conversation. I keep mine in 8½ x11 clear-plastic sheets designed to hold business cards. The sheets are kept in a one-inch three-hole binder on my bookshelf, close to the phone and ready for instant reference. Your stationery store has different types of systems for filing business cards. *See Printing, and Picture Reproduction in Section Two.*

MAILING LIST / COMPUTER PROGRAM / CARD FILE

• **Start now and keep a 3x5 index card file of everyone** you come in contact with who is in the business. Include on the card where and how you met and something about them that will help you remember them 10 years from now. Also, if you read something about them or send them something about you, note it on the card with the date. Better yet is a computer address system that allows you to keep notes with the addresses. I have one on Filemaker Pro for my Mac. There is also a program for the Palm Pilot where you can make address labels and lists.

• **This is the beginning of your mailing list;** these are the people who will possibly help you get acting work. When you are doing showcases, you will get much more value from your money if you keep up with the casting directors you have acted for. When writing to them you can say: You saw me do a scene (give the name of it) at so and so showcase on (give the date).

• **I've heard it said:** it is best to mail your announcement, flyer, post-card, etc. on Tuesday or Wednesday because everyone else mails theirs on the weekend and the casting directors receive them on Monday or Tuesday. Yours will arrive on Thursday or Friday. Or better yet, mail them on your lucky day. I personally send a little spiritual wish with each one. Hey, we need all the edge we can get.

THOMAS GUIDE / LOCK BOX / EXTRA KEY / AUTO CLUB

• **The Thomas Guide is your absolute bible** for directions. This book is very clear and easy to use. If you don't know how to read a map, have someone teach you. Then buy the L.A./Orange County Edition of the Guide at Costco or any book store or newsstand. I cannot stress the importance of owning and knowing how to use this guide. You can't trust other people's directions and you *must* get to the job or interview on time. The Guide will help save your sanity. Most people who live and work in Los Angeles have a copy. Also, use www.mapquest.com.

• **You must have a lock box on your car** with a house and car key in it. Even though all of my students are given this book and hopefully read it, some will invariably lock themselves out of their house or car. Several times they have missed jobs, appointments and been late for auditions. Put this book down and take care of this now.

• **After you have the keys** made, test them. Do not trust that they will work. This is worth the extra effort to test the keys!

• **I keep a regular car key in my wallet behind my drivers license,** and a house key in the glove compartment, as well as a secretly hidden house key outside the house. If your car has one key for the door and another for the ignition, I would take it to a locksmith and have it rekeyed in order to use one key. But you can just keep an ignition key in the glove compartment. Take care of yourself.

• **The Auto Club Road Service Policy** is another protection you need for yourself. They will arrive to start your car anywhere, fix a flat tire, unlock your car, bring gas and, if necessary, tow your car. About $55 a year. Membership: 800/222-8794.

PASSPORT

• **You may land a job** because you are the only actor who can leave the country immediately. Have an updated passport and be ready to go. In December, 1995 the Passport Office closed for two weeks and no one could get a new or updated passport. Be prepared for all emergencies as well as all opportunities. New passports are generally $60, renewals $40. To expedite a passport request, the cost is an additional $35. The expedited passport will be mailed within three working days.

• You must provide two new 2-by-2 inch photos (with your head against a white or off-white background). To confirm identification, bring your drivers license. To demonstrate citizenship, they generally require a birth certificate, naturalization certificate or previous passport.

www.travel.state.gov. The Department of State's Internet site, includes state-by-state listings of all post office passport acceptance facilities. Also blank passport forms.
You can apply at some post offices or the L.A. Passport Agency at the federal courthouse. Ask at your local post office where the nearest location is.
Federal Courthouse, 11000 Wilshire Blvd., 13th floor, West Los Angeles, 90024. Office hours: M-F, 8-3.

PROFESSIONAL WORK HABITS

• **The chief cause of failure** is giving up what you really want for what you want at the moment.

PUNCTUALITY

• **Over and over in this book**, people being interviewed talk about the importance of being on time. This habit can make or break a career.

• **Garth Brooks** tells the story about when he had been in Nashville for a couple of years. He and his wife worked in a shoe store to make ends meet. He was scheduled to perform at 11:30PM at a songwriters' showcase. It was not a prime spot, as the record company reps usually left by 11PM. Suddenly at 9:30PM, the owner ran backstage and said, "You're up, Garth. Ralph Murphy, the second act, hasn't shown up yet." Garth jumped up on stage, sang his heart out, and Capitol Records signed him before the evening was over. Ralph is still looking for a deal.

• **Check in with someone** immediately when you show up for work or an audition to let them know you are there.

• **Practice being on time every day, for every event.**

ATTITUDE

• **In this business, if you get the job**, that means you are skilled and crafted in what you do. If you have to shoot a movie for the next 10 weeks, or do seven years on a television series, who do you want to work with? Most people will want to work with kind, helpful, considerate, gentle, warm, fair, fun, funny, professional actors.

• **There are all kinds of attitudes to adopt**. My grandsons, Austin and Jackson, are often told to change their attitudes when they are acting inappropriate. Their faces and tones of voice change. Very early in their lives, they knew all about attitude and how to fix theirs. So do you.

HARD WORK

• **Oprah's week-day schedule** was described by *People Magazine*. Her success is a result of hard work. How hard are you willing to work for your success?

• 5 AM:	Four-mile run.
• 7 AM:	Breakfast, makeup, hair and prep for shows.
• 9 - 2 PM:	Tape two shows.
• 2 PM:	Lunch.
• 3 PM:	Business and staff meetings. Phone calls.
• 5:30 PM:	Four-mile run, Stairmaster, sit-ups.
• 7-9 PM:	Tying up loose ends of future shows. Dinner.
• 10 PM:	Prep next day's show.
• 12 AM:	To bed

PREPARATION

• **Always have a pen or pencil** with you. Without a "note taking mechanism," you are minimizing your potential, rather than maximizing it. We think we'll remember a person's name or a phone call we need to make, but we won't. Keep notes throughout the day. Each night, process those notes: sort, file, transfer. Develop your own system of keeping track of valuable information.

• **Your success requires extraordinary, extreme actions**. The universe is giving us "whispers" all the time, many times a day. There are opportunities all around you; don't let them pass you by. Have your antenna up, your nose in the air, your ear to the ground, your sights on success.

• **Swoosie Kurtz**, film, television and Broadway veteran stage actress, in a *Women In Film* interview:

> • **In television and film there's no rehearsal.** In a one-hour television drama you do a different scene everyday and once you do the scene, you never do it again in your whole life. As far as preparation, if I have the time, I sort of do the same thing for film and TV as I do for the theatre, which is read the material over and over again, get as

familiar with it as I can. I don't mean in terms of learning lines but just the overall picture of the piece. What is the theme? What is this writer trying to say? And what is my part? What does my character do? And does she change? And, if so, what changes her?

- **Joan Darling, Emmy award-winning director,** talks about preparing for auditions.

  - **Have pride**—don't do anything less than the absolute best you can do. Work on the "given circumstances," pick two strong pieces of acting work, decide what function your character has in this painting. Am I the comic relief? Am I the villain? Do I drive the plot? If you know those very bold strokes and you know how to act, you can come in and give a pretty damn good performance very fast.

  - **I was in a television movie** with Dustin Hoffman called *Trap Of Solid Gold.* He had a tiny part as an accountant. There was so much texture to the portrayal; he so filled himself as an actor that when he first appeared, picked up his head and just looked at his fellow actor, you knew everything about his character. It was from the amount of work that he did. If you want to be doing leads, why not do all the work you do as if it were a lead?

CONCENTRATION

- **Being able to focus and concentrate** are two of your most important functions as an actor. Anita Jesse gives exercises to develop these tools in her book, *Let The Part Play You,* available at book stores.

- **Linda Buzzell, author** of *How to Make it in Hollywood; All the Right Moves,* gave some phone hints in the *Women In Film* newsletter.

  - **Lack of focus can create a reluctance** to get on the phone because you're not really sure what you're offering or what you're asking for, or whether you want it if you get it! It might help to put your Hollywood pitch (pitch for your talents, services, script, whatever) up over the phone where you can sneak a peek if you freeze up.

  - **Start out by calling a few friends** just to break the ice and get the day rolling. By the time you punch in the number of that studio executive or agent, you're nicely warmed up and ready to schmooze. Make your calls standing up and use your body to gesture as if the person were in the room with you. And smile! Research has shown that callers can actually hear the change in your tone of voice and will be more responsive. Making job search calls is a numbers game, not a reflection on your personal worth as a human being. It's important to remember that it may take 100 calls to land one serious job interview.

• **Phone etiquette is very important.** Return those calls promptly, before the end of the day. When you call and leave a message *always leave your number.* They will return your call quicker.

DISCIPLINE

• **When actors aren't acting,** they must be cleaning up their lives, their habits, their house, their bills, always preparing to go to work. Because when you are working as an actor, even in a class scene, you don't have time to do much of anything else. You can let everything else go and let your role consume you. All your discipline will go into your work. You will have trained yourself to have discipline by all the things that you intend to do each day and that you actually do each day. We ask 90% effort in acting—maybe it takes that much in life too—if you want to make a living as an actor. Effort has to do with commitment, intention and discipline.

• **Intention is keeping your agreements.** I intend to be curious, not judgmental; I intend to do my laundry; I intend to send out my pictures; I intend to change my life into positive stories; I intend to eat well; I intend to be on time, etc.

• **Not keeping your intentions** gives you anxiety which leads to guilt, which leads to failure. Don't waste energy on *trying* to keep intentions— just keep them. There is time for everything. Being in business for yourself, as actors are, takes a great deal of *self*-motivation; it won't be coming from anywhere else.

• **Discipline becomes easier** as certain sets of behavior become habits in your life. It has been proven: it takes about 21 days to unlearn a bad habit or to form a new positive habit. In those 21 days, it takes conscious effort and vigilance; but then the new habit is yours.

ACTORS' SECRETS

- **"Where there is mystery, there is power."** Charles De Gaulle.

- **"Talent is never using two words when one will do."** Thomas Jefferson.

- **"Whatever it is that makes a person charming**, it needs to remain a mystery." Rex Harrison.

- **"Mystery creates wonder** and wonder is the basis of man's desire to understand." Neil Armstrong.

- **Secrets are very valuable acting tools.** They give you energy, power and mystery; they draw dramatic, wonderful attention to you. I have heard it said: "Very good actors never talk about their art; very bad ones never stop."

- **Actors, as a rule, are great talkers**; they spend time and energy talking about what they are *going* to do, giving away all their secrets. In fact they talk so much to so many people, they don't do what they were talking about because they've expended the energy through the talking.

- **Learn to focus your conversation** on what you are actually doing, not on what you are going to do. If you decide you're going to send out 20 pictures and resumes to agents, don't tell a soul until they are in the mailbox. When you have an audition, don't tell anyone but your acting coach. If you're planning on getting a night job so you'll have your days free for auditions, get the job, then talk about it. So much energy will build up from your career plans that you'll be bursting to carry your plans out! When you take action, the payoff is that you can talk about what you are really doing. You become interesting to listen to, an inspiration.

• **Condense your stories**—get to the bottom line fast. You needn't go into boring details; assume the person you're talking with understands what you are saying. You can teach your mind to think in a concentrated form like a writer. The practice of conserving words can be developed without a loss of communication; in fact there should be an increase in communication. People (casting directors, agents, directors, loved ones) will want to hear more; they will ask you to explain if they don't understand. Don't give away more of yourself than is absolutely necessary. Mystery is an important asset.

• **When you have spoken a word, it reigns over you**. When it is unspoken, you reign over it. There's no point in speaking unless you can improve on silence.

• **In acting**, you may be thinking a paragraph or two in your mind but have only one line of dialogue to convey your thoughts. Dialogue is concentrated because a play, television show or film is limited in time. The writer knows the actor can portray much more than just the words and assumes that the audience will get the message.

• **By controlling the content of your conversation**, people will be more attracted to hiring and spending time with you. Be *responsible* for all of your words. Negativity is death to creativeness. Guard yourself! Talking about illness, everyone's flu, the car accident you just saw, the horrible interview, the awful casting person, smog, this town, lack of money—robs you of energy. When you hear this going on with yourself or the people around you, don't say anything about it or point it out; simply change the subject to something positive. It is difficult to drop old habits but change brings an *awareness* of self. Awareness is what actors are constantly searching for.

• **Finally, do not allow yourself** to make excuses or to blame someone or something else for your reality. Take responsibility for the words you speak and the deeds you do. If this is a new concept for you, there are many self-help books available at libraries and bookstores on creating your own reality.

• **Albert Einstein** said, "The most beautiful thing we can experience is the mysterious. It is the source of all true art and all science. He to whom this emotion is a stranger, who can no longer pause to wonder and stand rapt in awe, is as good as dead; his eyes are closed."

COVER LETTERS

• **Written communication is extremely important in this business.** When contacting people by letter or email you must sound professional, intelligent and personable. Have your personality show through, let them know you have a spark. Letter writing, when you are looking for representation or acting work, is not the type of letter you would write to a corporate executive when seeking a position.

• **Katharine Hepburn** said, "Show me an actor with no personality and I'll show you an actor who isn't a *star.*"

• **An audience judges your acting** by the way you bring a script alive. When your writing meanders, contains grammatical errors and fails to get to the point immediately, the reader (agent, manager, casting director, producer, director) will judge your other skills and aptitude by the way you write.

• **Technology has increased the volume** of communication, leaving little time for readers to do more than skim your writing. Getting to the point is essential.

• **Learn techniques to improve your writing.** Use short sentences. Lengthy sentences are ambiguous, tedious, aimless and needlessly time consuming. The first sentence should state what the paragraph is about. It is why I use this bullet and bold style in writing this book. I know people will scan to find the points they are interested in. I try to make the points easy to find.

• **Submissions to agents and managers** are almost useless without a cover letter unless your picture, or body of work is so outstanding it speaks for itself.

361

• **Stuart K. Robinson, commercial teacher**, says in his commercial class that your submission package is very important. Here he talks of the agent cover letter. *See the Commercial Section for more about the package.*

> • **A strong cover letter will tell me why I need to respond** to this right now. Cover three points in your letter.

> • **First, what is great about you?** Do not wait for them to discover it. If it is that you just finished two major motion pictures, your career is about to unfold and you are looking to get into commercials, tell them that. It could be that you have just finished the greatest commercial class and you feel like, "Ahhh, I know my calling now." Tell them that. It could be as simple as, "Everywhere I go, people ask me if I am an actor." Anything that will make them go, "oooh."

> • **Second, tell them why you do not have an agent.** Is it because you just moved here from another market? Or you have been in another business for a while and you are just getting started now as an actor. Or you have been with a smaller agency, or an agency that did not quite work for you and you want to move somewhere more proactive. Tell us why, if you are so great, no one has scooped you up before me.

> • **Third point, where you are going to make money.** Why are you going to book young mom spots or why you are going to book any spot that has soccer in it? Tell them the sure thing. Tell them why money is going to come in if they respond to this submission.

> • **Cover these three points in three very short paragraphs.** Add some personality, that is a big plus, and you will have a strong cover letter. Some cover letters are very colorful and some are right to the point. Either way, you want to catch their attention and give them the good news right away.

• **My daughter, Cynthia Kerr wrote the following cover letter:**

> I have just finished the greatest commercial class in the world with Stuart K. Robinson. I am continuing to work with him in his semiprivate classes. Having revived and sharpened my commercial acting tools, I am ready to go out and be competitive.

> I recently moved to Los Angeles after a successful commercial career in Dallas, Texas. I have booked many national commercials, including Mc Donald's, Chevrolet, Southwest Airlines and Applebee's Restaurants, to name a few.

> I book young mom spots, teacher, part of a couple, housewife, lady next door and business woman. I am also a champion black belt martial artist, so any spots in that category are mine.

> I am looking forward to meeting with you at your earliest convenience.

• **Jordan Osher wrote the following letter.** *See his pictures.*

> My name is Jordan Osher. On a trip to North Carolina, I booked a small part on *Dawson's Creek*. The episode's director proclaimed, "I love this guy! He looks just like Seinfeld!"
>
> My part was rewritten and expanded. I have recurred on several *Dawson's Creek* episodes, shot a motion picture in which I starred as a dorky, connoisseur of art and then made the decision to move to Los Angeles where I have been studying intensively in preparation for a career in film, TV and commercials. Both of my teachers, Stuart K. Robinson and Judy Kerr, admire and will vouch for my work.
>
> If you are looking for a character and leading actor who plays sidekicks (Anthony Michael Hall, Jason Biggs/*American Pie*), hip kids and various high school, college and beyond nebbishes, geniuses and heroes, I would like to schedule a meeting to continue my booking streak. Or at least call me in to see if you think I look like "little Jerry!"

• **Steven Nash, talent manager** and president of the Talent Manager's Association, gives some hints for writing a manager.

> • **A cover letter must be very short**, if you hope to have it read. Your objective usually is to get a meeting. Yes, do mention any important things about you that may attract interest. Your commitment to hard work and belief in yourself are not subjects to go into in this cover letter (as many do). These are things to talk about if and when you get a meeting.
>
> • **Be sure to give your phone number** and email address on your cover letter and on your resume. It can be effective to list two or three of your special points in your cover letter, so the reader can spot them easily. Do research on who you are writing to.

Dear Mr. Manager, [of course you would have the correct name here]

I am 17 years old and moving to Los Angeles in three months to pursue an acting career. I am looking for representation. A recent picture and resume is enclosed.

*Many roles in church, high school and community theater.

*Professional model in my local market.

*Speaker around my state for my Church teen program.

*Currently studying with: (Name well known Los Angeles teacher if you live here).

I heard of you in *Acting Is Everything*. (This lets me know you already have some understanding of how the business works.) Please let me know if you would be interested in taking a meeting.

Thank you

- **If you do not have important points**, then once again be brief and hope your age, look, or professional presentation will be meaningful to the person you are writing.

- **I personally do not like gimmicks** like attaching toys to the submission. Let yourself stand out by having a simple professional looking presentation. Actors should not call to see if we have received their package. If we are interested we will call you.

- **Letter writing is not a part of acting** but it is a part of the business of acting. Always know why you are writing and what you are asking for. Good writing is about editing. If you haven't edited your letter several times, it's not ready. There must be perfect punctuation and spelling. Always have someone else proof your writing.

- **When you are making online submissions** to castings or to agents or managers for representation consideration, label the downloadable file with your name. People who open attachments are taking a chance of downloading a virus. Many people have infected their whole system and are understandably wary. When the download file has your name on it the reader is more likely to download. Also, when it is downloaded onto their desktop your name will be visible and if they are considering you, the file will be easy to find again. Most such downloads are labeled a generic "Pic.doc" or "headshot.doc." Make sure yours will be welcome and identifiable.

ACTORS' WEB SITES

ACTOR'S WEBSITES

• **Many actors have purchased their own names** as their domain names: JudyKerr.com, for instance. My friend, who is now a series regular on American Dreams, has bought all combinations—WillEstes.com, .net, and .tv. As a new actor, people won't buy your name out from under you but profiteers will buy well known names. When the actual person goes to buy their name, they will have to pay hundreds or thousands of dollars to purchase their own name that could have been bought very reasonably before achieving a public persona. I urge you to buy your name; it is reasonable and you will want to have your own website— if not this moment, certainly sooner than you think. You can find out if your name (with the various extensions) is available at www.register.com.

• **Harry Governick, web master extraordinaire**, recommends, www.godaddy.com. $8.95 per year for new domains and $7.95 to transfer a domain from another registrar when it is time to renew. They are user friendly and inexpensive. Plus, someone answers the phone 24 hours a day. For a list of accredited registrars, go to: The Accredited Registrar Directory at: www.internic.net/regist.html. For complete information about domain names, see www.internic.net.

www.SitesForActors.com. has a whole site full of answers of how to launch a web site for yourself. Step by step instructions.

Resouces

www.zipp.net. Web Master Harry Governick says, "Here's what I do when I design for actors: $125 fee includes setup fee; home page with up to seven headshots (www.markcostello.com); resume page; contact sheet page if desired www.actingiseverything.com/photos, www.anitajessestudio.com/festivals/images; Bio page, Video page if needed and free domain registration for one year. The cost for hosting the site is then: $7 a month which includes10 E-mail Accounts, Unlimited Auto Responders, Unlimited E-mail forwarding, Domain Pointing, 5 Sub-Domains, FTP accounts, and much more." If you don't understand all this language beyond the E-mail accounts, Harry will explain all. Additional design: $50 an hour. Larger accounts available if needed.

www.actorsbone.com. Paul Molinaro runs this interesting site. $20 a year to post up to three pictures and resume, updated every month. Bonnie Gillespie recommended this site to me She finds it very valuable.

www.actorsite.com. L.A. Actor Site run by Jack Turnbolt. This is a great membership site. Free setup and website for members. Lots of free information and actor chat rooms. Great reputation, good investment. Free daily newsletter filled with uplifting information and encouragement.

www.backstage.com. *Back Stage West,* $9.95 a month. I believe you should be subscribing on line if you are actively seeking auditions because you will get advanced casting notices. One of the member features is your free page on their web site.

www.creativeactors.com. Creative Actors Alliance, 310/840-2240. Membership fee is $40 a year. Besides other benefits, they will post two pictures and a resume on their Affiliates Page.

www.killerreel.com. Allen Fawcett Productions, 818/763-7399. Hosts Actors' Websites: $95 set-up fee, $29.95 per month with a one-year commitment. Free email account; Domain name registration; Links to other sites. Three headshots and your demo reel digitized in 56k and DSL speeds.

www.jadetiger.com. Website designer Paul Giada is highly recommended by actress Tiana Hynes. "His work is excellent, quick and the prices are fair."

www.myyoume.com. My You Me Productions, 310/820-1772. 2050 S. Bundy Drive, #104, West Los Angeles. Richard and Mayumi Heene create websites including pictures resumes and demo reels. Dedicated to helping actors achieve their marketing goals. $80 to create a site and with a one-minute video reel $7.50 a month to host the site. You can you use your own site name or use their site with a slash and then your name. I always believe it best to have your own name established. For just straight web designing without using their hosting, they charge $80 an hour without watching the clock too closely.

www.nowcasting.com. Bob Stewart and all of the crew are actors. This is a membership organization that gives their members a free web site. It includes their pictures, resumes and demo reel. The actors can put the website on their cards, their resumes and whoever wants to check out their credits or view their reel just goes to the web site. The group offers so much; searchable, downloadable audition sides, labels for casting directors and agents, workshops and much more. Check the site for the price of the level of services you want to subscribe to. This is a wise investment.

www.nosotros.com. Nosotros is a non-profit organization formed to promote Latin actors. The membership is $50 a year. Members may post their headshots and resumes for $30 to $50 a year. You can have your posting connected to your own website and email for free if you wish. If you are Spanish-speaking I would think this is a must.

www.proactiveconcepts.com. Pro Active Concepts, 323/662-3337. Rick von Schnier owns this marketing company with an entire division dedicated to helping actors careers. Actress Kacie Taylor told me about Rick's innovative designs for a whole marketing concept for one's career.

www.SitesForActors.com. E-mail inquiries to sitesforactors@sitesforactors.com. $200 flat fee to design a 4 page website: welcome page, resume page, "clean printable" resume page, and a page featuring photos, reviews and anything you would like to highlight about your career. Demo reels and voiceover demos can be added to the site for an additional set-up fee. They understand performers' needs, and only design sites for actors. SitesForActors.com is also a resource center to help you through the confusing process of getting yourself onto the web. The website provides step-by-step guidance, as well as essential advice on how to protect yourself from being overcharged by web services. They are very kind people, experienced designers, and one of the best deals in town. E-mail to schedule a phone consultation.

www.websites4actors.com. Jonathan Levit has a special package. When you choose for him to host your site at $20 a month or $100 a year and sign up for the year, he will design the whole site for $20. That includes a home page with one photo; a headshot page with two more photos; a resume page and a contact page. Design for additional pages including video are $50 each or $75 for a larger video clip. For designing sites not hosted by their company he quotes a price according to the amount of work needed.

Free places to post your picture and resume:
www.zoetrope.com
www.actorplace.com
www.bigtalent.com
www.talentbank.com

THE
ACTORS' NETWORK

• **This is the organization for actors who are really serious** about getting work in this industry. I tell all of my students, as do many other acting coaches in town, to join. This is the best show biz bargain.

• **Actors Kevin E. West and Paulo Andres** have built a true acting community in our spread-out, industry-driven town. This is not an acting school, it is a group of information-sharing, working actors focused on the business side of their careers. The actors share trade publications, job leads, resources, tips, scams they've run across and general moral support and encouragement. They see special guest speakers, attend power groups and topical discussions all arranged and set-up by Kevin and Paulo.

• **The Resource Library is vast.** Most actors could not afford to own all the books and guides here, and they are certainly not available at the public libraries. They teach how to use these resources to make effective submissions for jobs. This is a place to go, an actual location. The Network will become your home away from home. You can receive faxes, use their mailing address and they have free computers too. They have also archived key stories and articles from *Back Stage West* since 1995.

• **I tell my actors who come to me for coaching**, this is a place to participate fully. If you aren't really ready to advance in your career, to jump in with both feet, then wait to join. If you are ready to take action, then hurry and join. Search their website for all the membership benefits.

• **The Network invites unpaid industry guests,** including casting directors, agents, talent managers, producers and acting coaches, to come in each month for question and answer sessions. They have no problem filling these spots with top people, proof of how respected and well thought of The Network is in the industry. They have activities such as improv workouts, cold reading workouts, demo reel review nights. The members sign up for these events. Talking to some of my students, they say the competition is tough to get in; you have to be there to sign up soon after events are announced. The monthly calendar can be seen on their website by anyone, but only members may attend.

• **The Actors' Network offers free orientation meetings** two times a month for actors to come in and listen to what they do. You most likely will be overwhelmed and empowered by what you hear. You will hear that you do not have to be a victim in this business. You are in charge of propelling your career.

• **Membership is $50 a month, with a four month commitment.**

• In *Backstage West's* column on The Actors' Network, Karen Kondazian quoted their philosophies. Paulo Andres: "Our philosophy is to help actors help themselves. Learning from each other can save them five years of struggling, of listening to the wrong people, and of going down the wrong roads." Kevin E. West: "One of our biggest mottos here is a quote of Margaret Mead's: 'Never doubt that a small group of thoughtful, committed citizens can change the world. Indeed, it is the only thing that ever has.' This is what I believe very strongly and why I started this place. It's how we feel."

• **Check out Jode Leigh Edwards diary** in *Section Three, Living Her Dream in Los Angeles,* to see all the things she did at The Actors' Network her first three months in town.

• **Online membership is available for $60 a year.** Many benefits, especially for those thinking of making the move to Los Angeles.

Resources

The Actors' Network, 818/509-1010. www.actors-network.com. "Where the Serious Actor Does Business." They are the only performer business information, education, consultation and networking organization of its kind. This is an organization I have a great deal of respect for. I believe dedicated actors can make a difference in their careers by working with this group.

ONLINE MEMBERSHIP GROUPS

• **There are many membership** online groups popping up. I've investigated these below and believe they will be great career helps. Many have informative actors forums. Always take with a grain of salt anything you read when you don't know who is doing the writing. On the other hand, you can meet industry people on line who will answer career questions. Remember we all have opinions; when you hear one that rings true with you, it probably is. If you hear something that you wish were true, it most likely isn't.

• **Now Casting**, 818/841-7165. www.nowcasting.com. 60 E. Magnolia Blvd., Burbank, 91502. The membership packages are $10, $15 and $20 monthly for their many services. As a member, you receive free unlimited sides; otherwise it's $25 a year. They post union actors pictures and resumes on the site for free. Non-union, unrepresented actors are charged $2.50 a month. Members receive casting notices almost on a daily basis and can submit to the projects and roles they are right for online. They also produce Casting Director Showcases for member and non-members.

• **L.A. Actor Site**, www.actorsite.com. Membership site. $10 a month or $89 a year. They post your pictures and resumes. Members can submit electronically. They post casting notices and have links to the Actor Access site. You can sign up to receive the free, very informative newsletter. They produce Casting Director Showcases, always focused on education.

• **Actors Bone**, www.actorsbone.com. You can post your headshot and resume for $20 a year, and there is an actor forum section. Paul Molinaro has been running the site since 1999 and has met many industry people. Many actors have been cast through the site. What I like best is the Shorts Festival—they accept shorts on video or film. This year's ten winners were both video and film.

• **Actors' Network**, www.actors-network.com. They also have an online membership is available for $60 a year. Many benefits for learning the business.

• **L.A. Casting Network**, www.lacasting.com. This is the newest online casting service. They plan to offer free services, such as sides and mailing labels. Check their website for current information. It may turn into a membership type group.

ACADEMY PLAYERS DIRECTORY
AND
ONLINE CASTING ORGANIZATIONS

• **As we go to press on the Tenth Edition,** there are great changes going on in this part of the industry. Online casting is gaining the momentum we have been predicting in the 8th and 9th editions but all the players and options are not fully in place. I am writing about all that I know at the moment in March of 2003. I believe in marketing, as in any business, it pays to advertise. Many of the organizations charge to post your pictures; some don't but you may pay for another service within the organization, such as receiving casting notices. When you do not have representation and are looking for acting roles on your own, it is important to have access to where the jobs are.

• **All of the organizations in this chapter** are reliable businesses. It would be helpful to be registered with all of them. If you must choose one or two, then select by doing your research and following your instincts.

ACADEMY PLAYERS—THE ONLY PRINTED CASTING BOOKS

• **The Academy Players Directory is a set of books** with actors' pictures and how to contact them. Casting directors, agents, producers and directors buy the set of four books. Until recently, they were used 100% of the time by 100% of the casting community. Their on-line, www.playersdirectory.com, service is included when you sign up.

• **To qualify for registration,** you must be a paid up member of a professional actors union. The Directory is printed twice a year in January and July. When you register and deliver your picture it can take up to six weeks before you appear in the Online Directory. You will appear in the next printing of the Directory and will remain for one year. $75 a year, for one picture, one category; two photos, $85; three photos, $95. If you are a character actor who also does leading roles, or a leading person who plays characters, you should appear in both categories if you can afford it. They will need a black and white 8x10 picture. I believe the Directory is a valuable marketing tool.

• **Actors do get called in to read for roles** because their pictures are in the directory or on line. A student of mine was called in to audition to play Tom Hanks' double from the Academy Player Directory. SAG scale plus 10% for four weeks, and an incredible experience. Another student was called in to audition and ultimately film *Space Camp* because the director spotted him while searching the directory for new faces. Many in the theatrical casting part of the business have not made the switch to online casting and prefer looking at the Directory and at actual photos and resumes. The commercial casting community seems to be making the switch to the online casting organizations.

ONLINE CASTING ORGANZATIONS

• **Computerized talent services** put actors' pictures, credits and sometimes short video or voiceover reels on their web sites. Some sites charge for posting pictures; others don't. Some are free when you are in the Union or if you have representation. Some are strictly for the casting and agent communities to use and others will accept email submissions from actors. Some have casting notices that you can submit yourself for. I think if you can afford it, they are all good investments. If you get one job, it will pay for five, six or more years of postings.

• **When making online submissions to castings** or to agents or managers for representation consideration, label the downloadable file with your name. People who open attachments are taking a chance of downloading a virus. When the download file has your name on it the reader is more likely to download. Also, when it is downloaded onto their desktop your name will be visible and when they are considering you, the file will be easy to find again. Most such downloads are labeled a generic "Pic.doc" or "headshot.doc." Make sure yours will be welcome and identifiable.

Resources

Academy Players Directory, 310/247-3058. www.playersdirectory.com. 1313 N. Vine Street, Los Angeles, 90038. M-F 9-5. Free parking behind the building; enter from Homewood Ave. They are non-profit and part of the Motion Picture Academy.

Breakdown Services, 310/276-9166. www.breakdownservices.com. Agents and casting directors use their online service for submissions. They have the Actor Access area where casing directors will post roles for unrepresented actors, as well as non union roles. I anticipate (but don't hold me to it) they will be adding the ability for unrepresented actors to be online at no charge and will be able to email submissions. The agents pay for their services so it will be free for actors to post pictures and resumes. Many changes are going on, keep checking all the websites.

L.A. Casting Network, www.lacasting.com. Beau Bonneau has developed this newest/ hottest online casting service. They started with actors who were represented commercially. Agents sign their actors up for free. If an actor wants to change or add a picture it is $25. Set up fee for unrepresented actors is $50, free hosting for six months, then a $10 monthly fee. They've branched into theatrical castings. The agents and casting directors I've talked with love their service. It will be interesting over the next few years to see all the changes in electronic casting. LACasting is planning on some free services for all actors, such as sides and mailing labels. Check their website for information.

Now Casting, 818/841-7165. www.nowcasting.com. 60 E. Magnolia Blvd., Burbank, 91502. They post Union actors pictures and resumes on the site for free. Non-union, unrepresented actors are charged $2.50 a month. Members receive casting notices almost on a daily basis and can submit to the projects and roles they are right for online. $10, $15, or $20 a month membership packages. They produce Casting Director Showcases. As a member you receive free unlimited sides otherwise they are $25 a year. They don't charge for casting directors to post their projects so many independent, non-union and student casting directors will favor this site for posting casting notices.

L.A. Actor Site, www.actorsite.com. Membership site. They post pictures and resumes and members can submit electronically. They post casting notices and have links to the Actor Access site. You can sign up to receive the free, very informative newsletter. They produce Casting Director Showcases always focused on education.

The Cast List, www.thecastlist.com. Membership site, they post pictures, have casting notices and other audition information.

Castnet.com, 888/590-9994, ext. 3603, 323/964-4900. www.castnet.com. Membership site, free for SAG members. Non union membership is around $500 with a monthly dues plan. Includes: free sides, talent search, agent submissions, resume updating, casting notices with email submissions. This is now an international site and there have been many changes. I still love the sides. **I do not recommend for LA nonunion actors.**

New York Players' Guide, 212/302-9474. www.playersguide.com. 123 West 44th, Suite 2J, New York, NY 10036. Players' Guide Book, Players' Guide Casting on the Web, Players' Guide CD-ROM.

TRADE PUBLICATIONS

BACK STAGE WEST

• *Back Stage West* **is a must-read.** You may reach a level in your career where you don't need to read it, but you may still enjoy the interviews and ads. Even when I am not actively seeking acting work, I still feel like it is part of my job to keep up with all of our trade papers. I sure want my doctors, dentists and plastic surgeons to keep up with their trades.

• **For your information:** you may hear the name *Drama-Logue* when actors refer to our Los Angeles trade paper. *Drama-Logue* was the only paper of its kind in Los Angeles for 20 years. *Back Stage* is *the* paper in New York. They moved a branch to Los Angeles thus *Back Stage West.* Five years later *Drama-Logue* and *Back Stage West* merged. The combined paper is published by the same company that publishes the *Hollywood Reporter* and the *Ross Reports.*

• **If you are seeking acting work**, I advise subscribing on-line, then you have a bit of a jump on the people who buy *Back Stage West* on the newsstand Wednesday afternoon and evening. You will definitely have a jump on the people who subscribe and don't get it till Thursday. Occasionally, it doesn't arrive in my mail until Friday. This is crucial when you are trying to be competitive and have your picture and resume opened first.

• **One of my acting students, Mark McKeel**, has an extensive theater background but needed film experience. In just a few months of class and following the directions in this book, his evenings and weekends were jam packed with auditions, rehearsals and work from USC, UCLA and independent films— all from ads in the trades. He is very serious about a career and is making it happen for himself. At first he landed smaller roles and then leading roles in several student and independent films, even earning some money.

• **When he had enough film experience** and had a short audition tape put together from his work, I advised him to do a few months of extra work to get his three SAG vouchers so he could look for an agent. He was an extra on *Apollo 13*, and Bill Paxton got to talking to him and said, "Hey, I'll help you." He called over the director, Ron Howard, and said, "I think Mark here should ask me for my gum before I put my helmet on." Ron said okay and Mark got his first speaking role and his eligibility for Screen Actors Guild.

• **There are listings for every type of acting work** in *Back Stage West*. Some jobs pay, some don't pay, but you earn audition experience, re-sume credits and sometimes a tape copy. As you send out each picture, keep of record of the role description and date, save up to three months. Don't call or deliver in person if the ad says not to.

• **Send out your pictures and resumes** as soon as you get *Back Stage West*. They post daily on their website. There are some newspaper stands that get the publication on Wednesday afternoon. There is a 24-hour stand in Hollywood on Cahuenga just south of Hollywood Blvd., and another one in Studio City on Laurel Canyon Blvd., at Moorpark. For every job, hundreds of actors submit their pictures; as always, it pays to be early.

• **Put the name of the role** you are submitting yourself for on the envelope and attached to your picture with a *post-it* note. No need to include a cover letter, unless you have some pertinent information— the part is for a golfer and you are a champion, or you've worked with the director and you want to remind them of that. Just writing a cover letter to say you want the job is unnecessary.

• **The free jobs that give you the most value** for your time and effort are usually, but not always, Equity-Waiver plays and graduate school sync-sound films. If you need experience in auditioning, then audi-tion for everything. One of my students, T. R. Richards, auditioned over 160 times in two years from ads in the *Back Stage West*. He's been in over thirty student films. Needless to say, with his studying and auditioning experience, he is moving his career right along. My career started from the first ad I answered (*Drama-Logue* cost 25¢ then), a USC student film, playing a waitress. The lead in that movie, Rick Davis, led me to my best friend, Samantha Harper, who led me to my mentor, Joan Darling.

• **Michael Lerner**, Oscar-nominated for best supporting actor for *Barton Fink,* said he owed his success to the *Drama-Logue.* He was living in a one-room Hollywood apartment with a pull-down bed. The phone was down by the gas station. He didn't have a car, lived on unemployment. He read about a play audition and got a part in *Little Murders.* Director Paul Mazursky came to see the show, put him in his movie, *Alice in Wonderland.* Director Michael Ritchie saw that and cast him in *The Candidate* and his career was launched.

• **New actor Robert Restraino** read an ad for a lead actor with intense eyes for a non union independent film, *Motor Psycho.* He ran a photocopy of his picture and erased the color of his eyes to lighten them. He landed the audition and the job.

• **Kevin Costner** credits his start from landing jobs he auditioned for out of the *Drama-Logue.*

HOLLYWOOD REPORTER AND *DAILY VARIETY*

• **When you have started a serious career**, it is a must to read one of these every day. You decide which is best for you and subscribe. I couldn't do without either one because in the social columns, my favorite, the same gossip isn't repeated. It's nice if you can share the expense and paper with another actor. You can also read them at the Beverly Hills or Hollywood libraries.

• **This information can be valuable** when meeting a producer or director; you will be able to discuss their projects because you are familiar with them. I keep files of articles that interest me or that may come in handy at a later time. I also have a file on types of publicity I like so I can refer back to it when I'm designing my own ads or mailings.

• **Jay Bernstein**, manager, writer, producer, publicist, taught a course called *Stardom, the Management of, the Public Relations for, and the Survival and Maintenance In.*

Q: Why should actors read the trade papers?

• **It's important to be educated** in anything you do. You're meeting people at parties. You may never know that you're meeting a director or a producer or who that person is unless you subscribe to the *Hollywood Reporter* or *Daily Variety*, read the *Los Angeles Times Calendar* section, and *People* magazine to get a feeling of who everybody is. You can spend a whole evening talking to someone and not connect their name or face to show business because a lot of people don't talk about it. You might have made a different impression if you had known. There are too many people, too many names. Also, learn the history of this business.

Resources

The Trade Papers can be purchased at almost any newsstand, 7-11 store or theatrical bookstore in the area.

Back Stage West, 310/474-6161, 800/458-7541. www.backstagewest.com. 5055 Wilshire Blvd., Los Angeles, CA 90036. Six months, $49; one year, $89; two years, $139. $1.85 per single copy at newsstands and 7-11's in the Los Angeles area. Some newsstands receive it on Wednesday afternoon around 2PM. It's owned by the *Hollywood Reporter*. *Back Stage* has been the bible in New York for many years.

Daily Variety, 323/857-6600 or 800/552-3632. www.variety.com. 5700 Wilshire Blvd., Suite 120, L.A., 90036. www.pubservice.com. $219 a year, three and six month prices available. Television productions listed every Thursday, film productions listed every Friday, cable listed every Monday.

Hollywood Reporter, 323/525-2000. www.hollywoodreporter.com. 5055 Wilshire Blvd., L.A., 90036. $219 a year for daily paper or $155 a year for Tuesday edition only. Film productions listed every Tuesday, television productions listed first and third Tuesday of every month. Their subscribers are affluent and trend setting: $180,000 average income; $659,000 average residence value; 26% are millionaires; 35% own real estate in addition to their primary residence. Sounds great doesn't it?

Los Angeles Times Newspaper, 800/LA TIMES. www.latimes.com. Every day, $15 a month; Sundays only, $8 a month. Another must. *Every morning*, read at least the Calendar Section. It will provide you with openings for conversation and again, more knowledge about the business and people in it. Much of film and television content, as well as style, relates to current events in the world. Your competition is reading the newspaper.

BOOKSTORES, LIBRARIES
AND
VIDEO RENTAL STORES

• **We are changing every second of our lives.** All knowledge gained is growth, even when some of the knowledge is rejected as not being valid. Just the act of making the choices of what is good for us is molding our unique selves.

• **Reading is an important tool for an acting career.** In *Dreams into Action,* Milton Katselas tells how reading can enhance your career. He gives exercises on how to improve your reading. I highly recommend this book from this respected director and teacher.

• **Sandra Bullock** loves, *"The Greatest Salesman in the World,* by Og Mandino. It was given to me by Matthew McConaughey on the set of *A Time To Kill.* It's really special."

• **John Singleton**, when living in South Central L.A., would catch the bus to Hollywood to go to the movies. "I'd hang out, spending hours in Larry Edmunds and Samuel French bookstores, read literature, wonder if I could ever be a part of the movie making environment."

• **Books on tape**: For Los Angeles travel time, audio tapes will save your sanity. If you live in L.A. County, the biggest bargain is through the Los Angeles County Library System, 800/253-0591. They will send you catalogues with hundreds of unabridged fiction and nonfiction titles. Each title is a flat $10, which covers the rental and mailing both ways. I always have three books going—one while exercising, one while I drive and another that my husband and I listen to on long drives. Books On Tape, 800/626-3333 also rents unabridged books, including the latest best seller at about $20 per title.

THEATRICAL BOOKSTORES

These stores are very important to your career. Besides all the plays, they have many reference books, including *Variety's Who's Who In Show Business*, seminar books such as *How To Get An Agent, How To Publicize Yourself* and videotapes on *How To Make It In Show Business*. Give yourself a treat and spend a few hours there getting acquainted with all the information that is available. Have fun, they don't mind. You can order online or by mail from any of the following stores.

Samuel French's Theatre & Film Bookshop, 323/876-0570. www.samuelfrench.com. 7623 Sunset Blvd., Hollywood, 90046. M-F 10-6, Sa 10-5. Valley location: 818/762-0535. 11963 Ventura Blvd., Studio City, 91604 (1 block east of Laurel Canyon.) M-F 10-9, Sa 10-6, Su 12-5. Closed some Sundays in the summer—call to verify hours.

Take One! Film & Theater Bookshop, 323/876-0570. www.take1filmbooks.com. 11516 Santa Monica Blvd., West Los Angeles, 90025, upstairs. At last, a great bookstore on the Westside. Five blocks west of the 405 freeway. Parking underneath and on the street. A very knowledgeable staff.

Larry Edmund's Theatrical Book Shop, 323/463-3273. 6644 Hollywood Blvd., Hollywood, 90028. M-Sa 10-6. This is a real Hollywood bookstore—lots of history here.

Performing Arts Books 818/703-7311. Outside Los Angeles County, 800/900-3949. 21530 Sherman Way, Canoga Park, 91303. M-F 11-7; Sa 11-5.

Elliot Katt's Theatrical Book Store, 310/652-5178. www.abebooks.com. 8568 Melrose, L. A., 90069. M-F 11-5:30, Sa 11-4. Some old and rare books.

BOOKSTORES

Book Soup (Bookstore and Newsstand), 310/659-3110. www.booksoup.com. 8818 Sunset Blvd., West Hollywood, 90069, across from Tower Records. Everyday 9AM-12 midnight.

Bookstar, 310/289-1734. 100 N. La Cienega Blvd., across from Beverly Center. 9-11 Su-Th, 9-12 F, Sa.

Bookstar, 818/505-9528. 12136 Ventura Blvd., Studio City.

Bodhi Tree, 310/659-1733. 8585 Melrose Ave., West Hollywood, 90069. A spiritual bookstore. New and used books. 10-7 (used books); 10-11 (new books) everyday.

Brentano's Book Store, 310/785-0204. www.borders.com. In the Century City Mall, next to the movie theaters. 10-10 Su-Th, 10-11 F, Sa.

Cosmopolitan Book Shop, 323/938-7119. 7017 Melrose Ave., Hollywood, 90038. M-Su 11-6. A wonderful used-book and magazine store. They will go to great lengths to find the publication you need.

Crown Books and **Super Crown Books**. Many locations. Most stores open M-Sa 10-9, Su 11-5. Discount prices on all books.

Heritage Books, 310/659-3674. www.heritagebookshop.com. 8540 Melrose Ave., West Hollywood. A special place.

Psychic Eye Book Store, 818/906-8263. www.pebooks.com. 13435 Ventura Blvd., Sherman Oaks. M-Sa 10-10, Su 11-8. Also Burbank, Woodland Hills, Torrance, Venice, LaJolla, Mountain View and S.F. stores. New Age, metaphysical, candles, incense and crystals.

VIDEO RENTAL STORES

These are stores that specialize in unusual videos, including classic movies and old television shows.

The Continental Shop, all things British, 310/453-8655. 1619 Wilshire Blvd., Santa Monica, M-Sa 9:30-6; Su 12-4.

Eddie Brandt's Saturday Matinee Video, 818/506-4242. 5006 Vineland Ave., North Hollywood, 91601. Tu-F 1-6, Sa 8:30-5, closed Su, M. Free catalogue, $2 by mail. 44,000 titles, from episodic TV *77 Sunset Strip* to Japanese sex epics *Notorious Concubine.*

Now Playing Video, 310/306-3336. 4718 Admiralty Way, Marina del Rey. Old classics, $2 for five days. New foreign or domestic releases, $3 for two weekdays, $3.50 for a weekend. The staff can help you choose a winning selection.

Odyssey Video, 818/769-2000. 4810 Vineland Ave., North Hollywood, 91606. M-Su 9AM-12 midnight. More than 25,000 movies to choose from. Tu & Th, 99 cents each. Hong Kong section which offers karate action flicks normally available only in Asia.

Rocket Video, 323/965-1100. 726 N. La Brea Ave., Los Angeles, 90038. 11-10 Su-Th, 11-11 F-Sa. Will find films by request. Huge foreign section.

Tower Video, 310/657-3344. 8844 W. Sunset Blvd., West Hollywood, 90069. Silents, B and C titles, cult, foreign and hard-to-find films.

Video Hut, 323/661-4680. 1864 N. Vermont Ave., Los Angeles, 90027. 10-11 Su-Th, 10-12 F-Sa. Also Asian films and special requests.

Video Journeys, 323/663-5857. 2730 Griffith Park Blvd., Los Angeles, 90027. 10-10 everyday. Library of 14,000 movies, 1,000 foreign films, and television series collections, documentaries.

Video West, 818/760-0096. 11376 Ventura Blvd., Studio City, 91604. Also 310/659-5762. 805 Larrabee Street, West Hollywood, 90069. 10-12 everyday. My favorite. These video stores are the best. Bargain days Tu, W, Th, $1.29 a tape. Have them give you a tour of the store—they've got classics, independents, foreign, comedies, stand-up comics. Just about anything you need to research. Fantastic!

Vidiots, 310/392-8508. 302 Pico Blvd., Santa Monica. Eclectic offerings at this alternative-video store. Large TV selection.

Web Sites and Order by Phone: B-Movie Theater, www.b-movie.com. Critics' Choice Video, 800/367-7765. www.vcatalogccvideo.com. Facets Video, 800/331-6197. Home Film Festival, 800/258-3456, www.homefilmfestival.com. Movies Unlimited, 800/466-8437, www.moviesunlimited.com.

LIBRARIES

Academy of Motion Picture Arts & Sciences, 310/247-3020. 333 S. La Cienega Blvd., Beverly Hills, 90211. Closed Wednesday, open other weekdays, 10-5:30. Scripts. You can also look up actor's agents.

Beverly Hills Library, 310/288-2220. 444 N. Rexford Drive, Beverly Hills, 90210. 10-9 M-Th, 10-6 F-Sa, 12-5 Su.

Brand Library, 818/548-2051. 1601 West Mountain, Glendale 91201-1209, located in Brand Park, at the top of Grandview Ave. Tu 1-9, W 1-6, Th 1-9, F-Sa 1-5. A very valuable source for music and art books, records, tapes, and over 4,000 CD's.

Burbank Central Library, 818/238-5600. 110 N. Glenoaks Blvd., Burbank, 91502. M-Th 9:30-9; F 9:30-6; Sa 10-6; Su 1-5. Scripts for use in the library.

Career Transition for Dancers, Career Resource Library, 323/549-6660. SAG Building, 5757 Wilshire Blvd., Los Angeles, on the 8th Floor. M-W 11-4; Th-F 10-6:30. Call for appointment to use the library or computer.

Glendale Public Library, 818/548-2040. 222 E. Harvard Street, Glendale, 91205. Information from Kelley Blue Book for prices on new and used cars.

Los Angeles Central Library, 213/228-7000. 630 W. 5th St., between Flower St. and Grand Ave., downtown L.A. Largest public library on the west coast. Open every day; call for hours.

Los Angeles City Library, Goldwyn Hollywood Branch, 323/467-1821. 1623 Ivar Street, Hollywood, 90028. M-Th 10-8, F-Sa 10-6, Su 1-5. All aspects of the industry including scripts and books on acting. *Free Money for People in the Arts* is one of their most popular books on grants, loans, money for film and video projects.

Los Angeles County Library, Culver City Branch, 310/559-1676. 4975 Overland Ave., Culver City, 90230. M-Th 10-8, F 10-6, Sa 10-5.

Los Angeles County Library System, Books on Tape Rental, 800-253-0591.

Los Angeles Public Library, Fairfax Branch, 323/936-6191. 161 S. Gardner St., Los Angeles, 90036. M-Tu 12:30-8, W-Th 12:30-5:30, F-Sa 10-5:30. Very limited selection.

North Hollywood Library, 818/766-7185. 5211 Tujunga Ave., North Hollywood, 91601. Large selection of plays; also books on acting.

Santa Monica Public Library, 310/458-8600. 1343 Sixth Street, Santa Monica, 90401.

Pasadena Public Library, 626/744-4052. 285 E. Walnut Ave., Pasadena, 91101.

UNIONS

• **Until you join a Union,** there are no restrictions. There are many opportunities for work that are non union. They may not be under the best conditions, and the pay will certainly be lower, but take a look at the ads for work in *Back Stage West* and other sources. Are you really ready to give up all these opportunities of gaining audition experience, the possibility of getting good film on yourself, building a reputation, and networking? Ask actors who have lived in a right to work state, their work almost dies if they join the Union.

• **Don't be persuaded by other actors'** impatience to join a union. You have your priorities; you are building a career. That means study, developing a demo reel and having a resume with legitimate credits and experience on it.

• **When you are starting out** and don't have an demo reel, in all likelihood you will not be able to land a theatrical agent even if you are in the Screen Actors Guild. It is easier to get a job on a non union project than on a SAG film. Do your non union work and your non signatory student films now. Those young film makers are trying to get into their respective guilds too. A few years down the line the producers and directors who hire you for student and non union productions will be hiring you for union productions.

• **Don't join the union until your second SAG job.** You can do all the SAG deferred roles you can land, you do not need to be a SAG member to be eligible to work on them. If you are in SAG, you cannot do any non union work of any kind without penalties.

• **When you are SAG eligible**, because you have three vouchers from your extra work, you can put SAG on your resume. You will be in the SAG computer as a "must join." When you land a SAG speaking role you will have to go in and pay your initiation fee and dues. Make sure you have that $1,300 available or you will lose the part.

• **I want to warn you** about some schemes actors have used to get into SAG using false credentials. These unlawful plans can get you barred from the union forever, besides costing you alot of money.

• **If you have decided** you must live your life as a professional actor, there are benefits for joining the American Federation of Television and Radio Artists, AFTRA, as soon as you can afford it.

• **If you plan to do game shows**, get your AFTRA card first so you will be paid for appearing. The shows don't seem to mind at all if you are union and you'll receive union scale payment for your appearance. The real bonus is: after belonging to AFTRA for one year, that work on the game show will make you eligible for SAG.

• **Most people reading this book** are not concerned with the SAG employment status known as "financial core," but I want to talk about it for a moment to dispel some rumors I've heard. Call the union if you have any questions. If you live in a right-to-work state and are not a member of the union, you may work both union and non union jobs. If you are a member of SAG you may not do non union work even in a right-to-work state. Taking a financial-core status means you pay 80% of your dues but you are not a member of the union and you can't put it on your resume. It is a very drastic step and the union makes it very difficult to rejoin if you change your mind. Investigate carefully what your advantages may be. I would strongly advise against it.

• **What does it meant to be Taft-Hartleyed into SAG?**

• **Taft-Hartley is a labor law** that basically says that you cannot force a person to join a union just because they did one job. If you go for a second union job, you are saying to everyone, "Hey, I'm interested in this as a profession." Now you have to join the union.

• **It is a catch-22**. You have to be in the union to get a job, and you have to have a job to join the union. SAG rules say that as long as they read 25 actors for a role, the production company will not be fined for giving a non union actor a job. If you are on a set and the director decides someone has to say a line and there is no time for casting, they can give you the line, a SAG contract and wages for the day. It is done through the Taft-Hartley Law. You can get your SAG card as soon as the paperwork is in the computer at the union; or you can wait years to get it. Always save your paperwork though.

• **The Guild has only 90 days from the day you perform the lines** to file a claim on your behalf. If you are told by anyone that you have to wait for the film to be released because upgrades apply only if the lines remain in the film, *do not believe that person*! An upgrade is warranted if you are directed to speak while the camera is rolling whether or not your lines are included in the final edit. If in question, call SAG Production Services at 323/549-6811. You should leave the set with a copy of the SAG contract.

• **The Union web sites** have all of the detailed up-to-date information available, so learn about the unions.

Screen Actors Guild

Screen Actors Guild, SAG, 323/954-1600. www.sag.org. 5757 Wilshire Blvd., Los Angeles, 90036. (between Fairfax and La Brea) M-F 9-5.

American Federation of Television and Radio Artists

American Federation of Television and Radio Artists, AFTRA, 323/634-8100. 5757 Wilshire Blvd., Suite #900, Los Angeles, 90036. M-F 9-5:30.

Actors Equity Association

Actors Equity Association, AEA, **also called Equity**, 323/634-1750. www.actorsequity.org. 5757 Wilshire Blvd., Los Angeles, 90036.

AFTRA/SAG Credit Union, 323/461-3041. 6922 Hollywood Blvd., Hollywood, 90028. M-F 9-4. Have your residuals automatically deposited in your savings account. It is a great way to save. If needed you can always take money out. There are many advantages as an actor being part of the Credit Union. They even make house equity loans.

INCOME TAXES
AND ACCOUNTANTS

Since *Acting Is Everything*, **many expenses you have are tax deductible.** You don't necessarily have to be earning money acting in order to deduct expenses. A tax specialist will determine exactly what is right for you.

• **When you start filing your income taxes** as a full or part time actor, seek an Entertainment Accountant. They will be aware of all the current deductions. Your part is to save receipts and to mark everything you do in your appointment book. Should you ever be audited, you will need to justify every expense.

• **An entertainment tax accountant**, financial consultant and finance manager, answers some income tax questions.

Q: Why should an actor hire an accountant to do income taxes?

• **The laws are very complicated** and change every day of the year. There are specific areas of deductibility for actors that are unique and an accountant has to be knowledgeable about them and must stay current on the changes in the law. In my experience, most actors are not knowledgeable about this and basically give the government excessive money in taxes every year.

• **In general, an actor can deduct anything** that has relevance to his career, the normal deductions relating to such things as union dues, use of their car for business purposes, subscriptions and books relative to their profession, going to theaters and movies where they can basically research current trends in acting, business travel, lessons as far as becoming an actor and numerous other specific items related to their unique career.

Q: Can you start deducting these expenses before you are earning money as an actor?

• **This is an area that is constantly changing** under the law. If the person is dedicated and exercising their efforts as an actor even though they are not earning money at this time, they can develop what is called business losses which they can utilize in one of the following ways: They can deduct those losses during the first two years of their profession and then accumulate any losses after that until they earn money. Generally this is not advisable because if they are not earning money the first two years the losses are not that beneficial.

• **I would recommend generally,** in the case of an actor whose career is accelerating, that they don't immediately utilize their beginning years' losses until they start to make better money because each deduction will create bigger tax savings. As they earn more money, they get into higher brackets. You list the losses on the year you spent the money but you put them into a reserve account that you can accumulate for future benefit. When you have future independent acting income, you can then extract those past losses and deduct them from your future income. It is necessary to list them in the year you spend the money, otherwise they are forever lost.

Q: How do you choose an accountant?

• **Usually clients pick an accountant on a friend's recommendation.** Then they decide to go with the accountant because they tell good jokes, have gone to the same college or for other wrong reasons. When actors are having a hard time deciding, I suggest they ask their potential accountant for three recommendations from current clients, three from former clients and the accountant's banker.

Q: How much does it cost to have your income tax done?

• **Accountants all have their own fees** based on the work involved. Minimum for a new client is $250. When actors start taking business deductions, their returns are no longer simple. Many new actors go to a general accounting firm like H&R Block and pay a smaller fee because generally their associates are not as qualified as an independent accountant.

• **It is a joyous day when your income tax return says occupation: actor.**
It is a time to take a moment and reflect on where you have come
from, to acknowledge that some of your dreams are coming true.
My return says occupation: actress/acting coach/producer/author;
it has expanded over the years.

• **Some tax filing categories:** Advertising and publicity, pictures,
resumes, audio/video tapes, Academy Players Guide, ShowFax; commissions paid; professional fees, tax preparation, attorney, bank charges;
office supplies, pens, pencils, paper, business cards, postage; dues and
initiation fees, unions, theatre groups; trade publications, including
Breakdown Services Casting Directors; supplies for research, plays, films,
scripts; career enrichment, workshops, classes, private coaching, video
rentals, movies; wardrobe and makeup; telephone, long distance calls,
fax, e-mail, website; equipment; auto, insurance, license, parking, gas,
repairs; business meals; business gifts, $25 and less.

• **At tax time, the trades run articles** about actors' taxes and ads for
accountants.

• *Working Actor's Guide* **has listings** for accountants, deductions
and business managers.

Resources

Feinstein & Berson: Scott Feinstein, 818/981-3115. 16133 Ventura Blvd., #800,
Encino, 91436. CPA and Business Manager, has a strong client list consisting almost
exclusively of SAG, AFTRA, IATSE and DGA members.
Pamela Price, 323/663-5727. 4527 Ambrose Ave., L.A. 90027. She used to be an
actress and specializes in people who are in the entertainment business.
Scott Rubenstein, E.A., 323/658-5271. 8350 Melrose Ave., Suite 204, L.A., 90069.
Tax consultant. Scott has given seminars for SAG. He has many clients in the biz
and photographer Alan Weissman recommends him.
SAG, Volunteer Income Tax Assistance Program. M-F 9:30 to 3:30. From February
through April 15. Union members help fellow union members with their taxes. They
hold classes in January for those who wish to be Tax Assistors. If you pass the test, you
are qualified to help other members prepare their own taxes. Every paid up SAG or
AFTRA member can get this free help.
California State Board of Accountancy, 916/263-3680. You can check to see if the
business manager or accountant you are considering is licensed and in good standing.
Working Actor's Guide (WAG), available at theatrical bookstores, lists many well
known accountants.

NETWORKING:

ORGANIZATIONS, CHURCHES AND CHARITIES

• **Increase your friendship circles** and social involvements. If you are not naturally a socially involved person, then this will be another task you will have to learn to do. Look for places within the show biz community where you can feel comfortable networking. Clubs or restaurants you frequent, tennis courts, such as Plummer Park, gyms, acting class, dance classes, charity volunteer, baseball or bowling teams, seminars, workshops, etc. Where do you have your morning coffee? Seattle agent Carlyne Grager told me of one of her actors being discovered by a Warner Bros. Producer because she had coffee at Priscilla's in Toluca Lake every morning.

• **The more people you know in the business**, the more likely you are to get a phone call from someone who wants you to work on a project. We all like to work with people we know and who are fun to be with. Also, by talking about the business, you pick up news and hints that will help you with your acting and career.

• **Publicist Joyce Schwarz** suggests attending or working at one charity event each month. Choose a charity that is close to your heart.

• **Camryn Manheim** says, "If you go to a play, don't go opening night; go during the preview week when everyone involved will be in the house." You may end up striking up a conversation with the producer, writer or director.

• **Jay Bernstein**, manager to the stars taught a course called *Stardom, the Management of, the Public Relations for, and the Survival and Maintenance In.* He advises actors to read *Emily Post's Etiquette* book. There is much to be said about knowing how to be polite and correct in social situations. He says, "If you are a woman join Women In Film, meet other women." In general he advises men and women to learn to play tennis and golf. "You can show up at a golf course and make up a foursome." And think of all the celebrity golf and tennis tournaments you can play in when you are a celebrity.

Resources

• ORGANIZATIONS

The Actors' Network, 818/509-1010. www.actors-network.com. They are a professional, unique, business networking, organization, created by actors. This is a membership organization I have a great deal of respect for. I believe dedicated actors can make a difference in their careers by working in this group. They have an office that you can drop by, check the bulletin board, look up something in the library full of all the current books and directories. Their members are pro-active and successful so you can create friendships with people who are on the same type of career path that you are on.

Take One Film & Theater Books, 310/445-4050. www.take1filmbooks.com. They hold free events most weeks on Wednesdays and Saturdays. A great way to meet people who are interested in the same topics as you. Casting directors, agents, writers, producers, and all aspects of show biz. Get on the mailing list.

The Creative Actors Alliance, www.creativeactors.com, holds a Monthly Showbiz Brunch. It is held at a restaurant. It's free; you pay for breakfast. On the website they tell you who the speakers will be at the next event. Actress Tiana Hynes tells me, "They are supportive, honest actors who realize the benefit of working together to uplift and challenge the entire group."

Film Industry Network, 818/985-5400. www.filmindustrynetwork.com. E-mail: FilmIndusNetwrk@aol.com. 12400 Ventura Blvd., #166, Studio City, 91604. Open to individuals from all facets of the entertainment industry. "We create the opportunity for industry professionals to: make key contact, develop solid industry relationships and exchange vital resources." Meets the second Sunday of every month from 3 to 6 pm. $60 for yearly dues. Monthly meetings are $6 for members and $12 for non-members. Topics have been: Show Runners; Packaging Yourself & Your Project; and Learn To Swim With The Sharks . . . But Not As Bait.

Nosotros, www.nosotros.org. They hold networking brunches every three months. "An event for the entertainment industry professional as well as the Hollywood hopeful. It is 'a place where we aspire to inspire' and honor special guest speakers from every aspect of the entertainment business." You do not have to be a member to attend. Membership is $50 a year and meetings are the first Wednesday of each month. If you are Spanish-speaking I would think you would want to be a part of this long established group.

Jeffrey R. Gund's Newsletter, email jeffgmusice@mindspring.com, to receive tell him Judy Kerr sent you and request to be put on the newsletter email list. Check out the links at his web site www.JeffreyRGund.com. Many networking opportunities.

IFP/West, Independent Feature Project West, 310/432-1200. www.ifpwest.org. 8750 Wilshire Blvd., 2nd Fl., Beverly Hills, 90211. Annual membership $85. "This non-profit membership organization is one of the largest and most dynamic groups supporting quality independent filmmaking today." They offer seminars, top level contacts, member gatherings, luncheons and the Breakfast Series.

Showbiz Softball League, 909/867-2327. Vic Puglisi. Play, but also go to games!

Entertainment Basketball Game: For men every Sunday at 5pm in Beverly Hills. For information, contact: Aurora411@earthlink.net.

Women In Film (for men too), 310/657-5144. www.wif.org. 8857 West Olympic Blvd., Ste. 201, Beverly Hills, 90211. Annual dues $125 a year plus initial fee of $75. You can volunteer to work in the office in order to meet people who later may sponsor you for membership. Great networking breakfasts and industry seminars and screenings.

Academy of Television Arts and Sciences, 818/754-2800. www.Emmys.Tv. 5220 Lankershim Blvd., North Hollywood, 91601. They will send you requirements to join; they are less stringent for non-voting members.

Audiences Unlimited Inc., www.tvtickets.com, 818-753-3470. Free tickets to live TV comedy and drama show taping sessions (no game shows). Hours and availability vary, mostly at Valley locations. Details also available online.

• CHURCHES
Agape Center of Truth, 310/348-1250. 5700 Buckingham Parkway, Culver City. www.Agapelive.com. Sunday at 8 and 10:30am. Wednesday 6:45pm. New age, large following, many celebrities.

Bel-Air Presbyterian Church, 818/788-4200. 16221 Mulholland Dr., L.A., 90049. www.Belairpres.org. Many programs for all ages of people, great singles groups, spectacular location and building.

Church On The Way, 818/779-8000. www.TCOTW.org. 14300 Sherman Way, and 14800 Sherman Way, Van Nuys. At Sherman Way and Van Nuys Blvd., Pentacostal Christian.

First African Methodist Episcopal Church, (F.A.M.E.) 323/735-1251. www.Famechurch.org. 2270 S. Harvard Blvd., Los Angeles.

First Baptist Church of Beverly Hills, 310/276-3978. www.firstbaptistbevhills.org. 9025 Cynthia St., Beverly Hills, 90210. Lots of actors and people in the business; very active membership.

First Presbyterian of Hollywood, 323/463-7161. 1760 N. Gower, Hollywood. 90028. www.fpch.org. Pastor Lloyd John Ogilvie is very well known. Great Choir. Lots of programs.

Grace Community, 818/782-5920. www.gracechurch.org. 13248 Roscoe Blvd., Sun Valley, 91352. Between Coldwater and Woodman. Fundamental Christian.

Hompa Hongwangji Buddist Temple, 213/680-9130. 815 E. First Street, Los Angeles.

Kabbalah, 310-657-5404. www.Kabbalah.com. 1062 South Robertson, Los Angeles, 90035. Tuesdays, 7PM, What is Kabbalah? This is where Madonna took lessons.

North Hollywood Church of Religious Science, 818/762-7566. www.nhcrs.org. 6161 Whitsett Ave., North Hollywood, 91606.

Performing Arts Synagogue, Wadsworth Hall, UCLA. First Friday of every month. Major industry attendance.

Self-Realization Fellowship, 323/661-8006. www.srf-yogananda.org. 4860 W. Sunset Blvd., Hollywood. 310/454-4114. 17190 Sunset Blvd., Pacific Palisades.

St. Ambrose Catholic Church, 323/656-4433. 1281 N. Fairfax Ave., Los Angeles, 90046.

• CHARITIES
www.networkforgood.org. Connects you to 33,000 volunteer activities. Thanks to www.dailycandy.com for this info.

Heal the Bay, 800/Heal-Bay. www.healthebay.org. Memberships start at $25. Fighting for a swimmable, fishable, surfable Santa Monica Bay.

Meals On Wheels, 310/208-3439. www.meals-on-wheels.net. Provides meals to the elderly.

PAWS (Pets Are Wonderful Support), 323/876-7297. www.pawsla.org. 7315 Santa Monica Blvd., West Hollywood, 90046. Provides pet care for ill people with pets.

Project Angel Food, 323/845-1800. www.angelfood.org. 7574 Sunset Blvd. Hollywood, 90046. Provides meal delivery to incapacitated people with terminal illnesses.

Union Rescue Mission, 213/628-6103. www.URM.com. 545 S. San Pedro St. LA, 90013. Provides food, shelter and clothing to the homeless. Need servers for Thanksgiving and Christmas.

SECTION FIVE
CAREER TEAM

AGENTS

• **Spike Lee said it best** on *Inside the Actor's Studio*, "Agents are not going to get you work if you are not established."

• **Your job is to establish yourself**, to make a mark, before you seek a theatrical agent. This book is written in sequence. First you study, you learn how to deliver a crafted, good performance, one you can deliver take after take. You have your pictures taken and develop a resume. You learn to audition by going to many auditions. You learn to work by working. You develop a demo reel, you prove that many directors have taken a chance on you, hired you and you have delivered. Maybe you've worked non union and made some money. Your next tool will be to become SAG eligible. Don't join SAG though until you book that second job, while you are SAG eligible you can work non union. You have developed your career tools; you are now ready to get your career team in place. An agent is usually your first team member.

• **There are the four distinctly different areas** of work requiring an agent. Theatrical, which includes work in films, TV and on stage; in commercials; in voiceovers and doing print work. A few agencies handle all types of acting work; some handle just one area of the market. Many individual agents specialize in one field; some may handle actors across the board. An agency may have one or several agents working in each department.

• **Agents are protected by California law;** only they can solicit employment and negotiate actor's fees. Some are franchised by the unions—SAG, AFTRA and AEA. At this time (March, 2003) SAG does not have a franchise agreement with the agents, though many agents continue to follow the guidelines of the franchise. Keep checking www.sag.org and www.agentsassociation.com for the most up-to-date information regarding signing agreements with agents. I must say I am an actor, I belong to all three unions and as misguided as I sometimes believe the union is, I still back them 100%. When SAG members voted down the Franchise Agreement, 62% of the vote were people without agents, 80% of the 25,600 votes were voters who earned less than $2,000 acting the year before. The franchise agreement was defeated by nonworking actors without agents. Talks are starting to form a new union including all actors and broadcasters to have a broader strength and representation within the business. AFTRA members did vote in the new union franchise and there are AFTRA franchised agents.

• **If you are a commercial type**, it may be easier to get a commercial agent first. They sign many more people than a theatrical agent; some agencies have several hundred actors on their rosters. A good theatrical agent would handle 30 to 50 actors alone; if there are three agents then perhaps 150 clients for one agency. These are very general figures just to give you an idea how it works. One of SAG's guidelines for agents is to accept only union actors—yet, if you have a great commercial look they will stretch the rules. If you are 22 or younger, it is easier for an agent to accept you as a non union actor.

• **My advice is to read one of the several books** on agents which you can buy at a theatrical book store. Then design a short, unique cover letter. *See Writing Cover Letters in Section Four.* Enclose your wonderful 8x10 photo that looks just like you, and your resume. Mail it to specific agents within the agencies that use the type of actor that you are.

• **When agents are interested,** they will call you to come in and meet them. Go in dressed looking like your picture. Something in that picture attracted them. What you have to offer the agent is your good training, background, and the experience you have been able to get for yourself. They want hard workers because when you are first starting out, they are not able to devote much time to you; they concentrate on the actors who are making money for them. Agents make 10% of what you earn. They do 10% of the work and you do 90% of the work of obtaining employment.

• *Back Stage West* has interviews on a monthly basis, talking to agents. Cut these out, save them, learn more about the way the business is run. Agent Billy Miller of Michael Slessinger & Associates told this story.

> • **When Jenna Elfman (*Dharma and Greg*) was looking for an agent,** her husband read an article in *Drama-Logue* about agent Michael Slessinger. He said, "Jenna, this sounds like the kind of agent you'd want to be with." She asked her commercial agent to set up a meeting. There wasn't a lot on her resume except a couple of student films and commercials. She had scenes from her student films on tape and they were great, so we decided to give it a try. And that's how we started representing her.

• **Anne Archer** *(Fatal Attraction, Patriot Games)* advises, when you have landed your agent:

> • **Learn how to keep friendly,** positive communication with your agent—always telling them the good news—something positive someone said, a great project you heard about, etc. Make them feel like you're a team. Be helpful; take responsibility for creating a warm relationship with your agent.

• **Tom Cruise's** producing partner, Paula Wagner, at an awards dinner, remembered her meeting with Tom during her agent days at Creative Artists Agency 15 years ago.

> • **Tom wore a great sports coat** (borrowed) that covered a ripped T-shirt. . . he was living in and out of his car, and I was impressed with his intelligence, presence, self-assurance, decency, capacity for good, and, as I came to know him, his curiosity, courage and conviction.

• **Theatrical agent Harry Gold,** of Gold/Liedtke Associates Agency told Karen Kondazian in *Back Stage West,* what he thought an actor should know about this business.

> • **There's so much more that you can do to get yourself work** besides waiting for your agent to call. The more you know about the business, the more empowered you are. The more you know your place within the structure, the better you can play the game. There's so much material to read to stay current with what is going on. Read the newspaper every day to keep up with current events, the trade papers to know who the principal players are that are making the decisions today. I find so many actors have no idea who, for example, is running ABC. You can be sure Al Pacino knows the head of every studio. He works the business as well as anybody. It's about understanding the business, about trying to look at the trends so you can follow them and be a part of them in some way.

- **The biggest stars in the world work the business.** It's a skill and it takes a certain kind of expertise. Seek to be in some kind of contact. You must be extremely resourceful in this business, even if you have an agent. The way you do it is by gaining a full understanding of the business and by networking well. If you can align yourself with good directors, good casting people that will help you get one extra little foot in the door, then you're playing the game a little bit.

- **Theatrical and commercial agent Bonnie Howard.**

Q: How can an actor get an appointment to meet with you?

- **A great 8x10 will attract attention.** By that I mean a 3/4 shot from the knees up in a natural setting, looking very relaxed, and not posing. I like to see more in a picture than *generic nice guy*. Something a little more specific, perhaps *grandfather,* or *driving instructor.* Something a casting director could look at and say, "Yeah, he would make a great IRS collector." A 3/4 shot has body language and tells you more about what the person is like. Leaning forward into the camera expresses more enthusiasm, more energy. If your picture is touched up, and you walk in with wrinkles that are not on the picture, it's disappointing and distracting. There's very little difference between commercial, theatrical and modeling pictures. I'm using them all for everything and getting good results. I look at every single picture that comes into my office because I'm interested in finding new talent.

- **A well put together resume helps.** Don't put any extra work information on your resume. Instead of listing the type or name of the character you played, I would rather see the billing. If you were featured, costarred, or even starred in something, brag about it and put that on there. Commercials should not be on a theatrical resume. The reason for that is you might sabotage yourself unknowingly. Someone might want to call you in for AT&T. If you have Pacific Bell on your resume, they may say, "That's a competitor company, let's not call him in." Only include modeling if you've modeled for a top designer, like Dior, in Paris or New York. I would leave broadcasting off, unless you're going for a voice-over agent. Student films are good. You should list the school that you did the film for. The resume should be the same size as the picture. I don't care whether the resume is stapled or glued to the picture; *I do care very much about grammatical and punctuation mistakes.* Have a professional proofreader read the resume before you mass produce it.

- **I attend the UCLA and the USC student film screenings** and I find talent there. Showcases are also good. I strongly suggest doing Equity-Waiver plays.

Q: On a day-to-day basis, what exactly does an agent do?

- **I subscribe to the Breakdown Service.** It's a breakdown of almost every project in production. There's a description of each character that they need to cast. I represent about 60 theatrical actors—from the age of five to the oldest actor, who is 85. I submit the appropriate pictures to the casting directors; then I try to get auditions for the actors. The actor goes on the audition and hopefully gets a call back. Once the actor goes to the audition, it's out of my hands.

- **I call casting directors to pitch my actors.** I receive calls requesting suggestions for roles not put out to all the agents. I meet with talent managers to discuss a client's career.

Q: What if the producer or director wants to hire the actor?

- **Usually the casting director or business affairs for a series calls me** to make the deal. The price of the job is determined by the prior history of the actor's work. It starts out union scale plus 10 percent for the agent. A good agent will always try to raise their actor's fee. Lately, the industry has been very tight-fisted. I like commercials a lot because I get to see my actors more frequently, and I get a great deal of pride from that. I also like it when the checks roll in. On national commercials, usually the actor works one day, and sometimes the checks come in for more than a year. Residuals are a big part of the business.

Q: If I have an agent, how can I help them to help me?

- **Don't bug them.** Don't call them frequently to say, "Why haven't I heard from you?" My pet peeve is, "I was just calling in to see what's new." If there is anything pertaining to that actor, the first thing we do is call them. Most agents represent a large number of clients, and it's very difficult if we get calls all the time. To help your agent, update your pictures; make sure your agent has a large supply of pictures and resumes at all times. I don't mind if my clients come in and check their supply themselves; it's a big help to me, but some agents may mind it. When you deliver your pictures and resumes, make sure your resume is attached to your picture.

Q: What about the actor's demo tape?

- **Demo tapes should be as short as possible,** and as high impact as possible. Just select the best work. Don't send it unless it is requested, because you probably won't get it back, unless you include an envelope with return postage.

• **Wondering who the top agencies are?** In 2002 the studios rated the leading agencies according to their dealmaking creativity and effectiveness. It was a tight race but CAA was slightly ahead, then Endeavor, UTA, William Morris and ICM. This lineup probably changes on a yearly basis. If you have one of these agencies representing you, you are at the top of your game.

• **I must caution you about certain scams.** *Never* sign with an agent who charges you any type of fee or insists you have pictures taken by a certain photographer or says you must study with certain teachers. Always call SAG to make sure the agency is franchised with the union. This must be strictly a business arrangement and it is your responsibility to get out of the office if things don't seem on the up and up. An agent's fee is 10% of what your gross salary and residuals are, period. They make their money when you work. When you terminate an agent, be sure to notify the unions. Some agents in this time of SAG uncertainty are having clients sign General Service Agreements, which are approved by the State Labor Commissioner. My understanding of that type of agreement is the agent can charge up to 20% as an agent fee.

Resources

BOOKS

Reference books date quickly; purchase only the latest editions. The following books may be purchased or ordered through Samuel French, 323/876-0570, and Take One Film Books, 310/445-4050. www.take1filmbooks.com.

Association of Talent Agents, www.agentsassociation.com.

The Agencies: What The Actor Needs To Know by Acting World Books. They list each agent within the agency. This is the best book when you are looking for a new agent.

An Actor's Workbook: Get The Agent You Need & The Career You Want by K. Callan. She is a working actress and has written several books for actors.

Screen Actors Guild, 323/954-1600. www.sag.org.

AFTRA, 212/532-0800. www.aftra.org. A national listing of AFTRA Franchised Talent Agents is available.

Personal Talent Managers

• **The professional talent manager is responsible** for all aspects of the client's career. This includes their client's artistic development, promotion of their career, working towards short and long term goals, maximizing their income, and protecting them along the way.

• **The Talent Manager's role is to advise**, consult and guide your career all along the way. A good manager understands your needs and goals, and they use their skill and concentration to help you move toward your objectives. They sift offers, deciding which to pursue and which to turn down. They usually have the final say on the agent's negotiation with the casting director or producer.

• **A manager takes a percentage of the money you earn**—usually 15%. Typically the Agent takes an additional 10% . Some actors fear these costs, particularly when the paydays get very big. Instead of looking at how much you must "give away," think about this: When the paydays are big, that is when you can most comfortably afford to compensate your team. And consider how little of your income that you must pay out to compensate your team. Plus they are working "on spec," meaning you only have to pay them when there is income. There are very few companies in America that get to pay their executives in such a manner!

• **Your manager works in every part of your life.** Managers have fewer clients than agents do and their clients sometimes speak with them daily.

• **A new actor would be very lucky** to get the services of an experienced manager. This is the era of the agent needing to focus primarily on the immediate audition. A good manager, by definition, looks at the longer term career development of the actor. An actor with opportunities needs as much expertise as they can get to make wise decisions and take advantage of opportunities. How many actors broke through with that one big job and then were never heard of again?

• **When you hire a manager,** hire one who you honestly believe can help you achieve your personal career goals. This means you must have goals and educate yourself on who the respected managers are and how you can appeal to them. Value yourself. Don't be lazy. If you are lazy there is not much hope for your having a career no matter how much money you have to promote yourself. You need to work every day on the business side of your career as well as your acting craft. To do any less will minimize your chances of reaching the big career.

• **Poppy Montgomery moved to Hollywood** from Sydney, Australia with no acting experience. She cold-called Julia Roberts' then-manager Bob McGowan to see if he'd help make her a star. She sent him pictures all the time. She says, "I think he thought I was kind of funny." Two months later he signed her. Two years later, by the time she was 23, she was working steadily on ABC's 1996 series *Relativity*, movies *The Other Sister, Life, This Space Between Us, Dead Man on Campus, Desert's Edge, Devil in a Blue Dress,* and her career continues to grow; she is now a series regular on *Without A Trace.*

• **Steven Nash, head of Arts and Letters Management,** came to management after years as an acting coach and as a prominent producer/ director in theatre and film. His clients have appeared in many films, commercials and television series. He is President of the Talent Managers Association and continues to produce feature films under the banner Arts and Letters Entertainment.

Q: Why does an actor need a manager?

> • As I said in *Acting World's Personal Manager Directory*, to break through to the big career in today's increasingly competitive market, an actor must have expert guidance at all steps of the journey. There are many people who call themselves managers, but I feel the professional Talent Manager is a breed apart. Managers who have true expertise and take a hands-on approach to developing and protecting careers is what to look for.

Q: Tell us about the Talent Managers Association.

- It was formed in 1954 as the Conference of Personal Managers. We changed the name in 2000 to the Talent Managers Association (TMA) to reflect the 21st century evolution of Talent Management. Members pledge to pursue the highest standards of professionalism and ethics in all we do. A member may not sell any goods or services to a client for profit. We are paid by commission only when our clients work. We also create networking and informational events for industry professionals, including actors.

Q: What sort of actors do you look for?

- Talented, of course, but I need to feel that I can help the actor to achieve an important career. I am attracted to well-trained actors who are marketable and appealing. I also consider an actor's ability to pursue a career aggressively in terms of time and resources. A really great look is always of interest.

Q: Would you consider taking on a client who is fairly new to the biz?

- While the last actor I signed had extensive film and television credits, if I see the potential of a "new" person, I could be interested. The time and effort that I put into each of my clients is quite substantial, so I have to be ready to commit.

Q: Where do you find clients?

- Referrals certainly. Our office receives many headshots sent by actors and will call those that we are interested in at that moment—please do not call us. I go to theatre and showcases and occasionally teach industry workshops as well as university seminars. Everywhere I go holds the possibility of meeting an actor with strong potential. One of my clients I met at a party, then spotted in an independent film. His screen presence grabbed me. This client is currently starring in a film that I have in production.

Q: Do you only manage actors?

- I sign people "across the board," meaning in all entertainment areas. Recently one of my actors booked a job directing a television pilot. Another actor wrote a screenplay which we sold.

Q: So you also manage writers?

- Most of my clients do work in related creative areas sooner or later. But please remind your readers that our office does not accept unsolicited scripts.

Q: How involved do you get in the actor's life?

• **I have been known to help find an apartment** and to help shop for a designer gown for an awards show. The actor and I are on a team together. I give support and guidance in almost any area, though I spend most of my time on their career and development. It takes all our best efforts to reach for the big career and then to hold onto it and grow it.

Q: Do you think your background as a director and acting coach helps your effectiveness as a manager?

• **Definitely. I think my understanding of the acting process** and the interpretation of material makes me more valuable to clients. I have been thanked by producers, directors and casting directors for appreciating their artistic needs or requirements.

Q: As a manager, what do you think it takes for an actor to get the job?

• **Getting the job in Hollywood** is initially about things other than acting.

• **There are so many trained actors today,** the competition is tougher than ever. Many good and deserving actors can rarely get an audition to "show their stuff." The challenge today is to be at your peak readiness on every level in case that key opportunity pops up.

• **I believe casting directors at an audition,** working efficiently in their high pressure jobs, have usually decided whether you are in the running before you even speak. This is particularly true in one of the many film and television auditions where your audition scene is three lines, and there is no event in the scene to sink your teeth into. In addition to having an appropriate look, I believe you need to have a carefully focused edge, an essence about you that is clear and instantly captures the casting director's attention. One can and should develop this edge intentionally. Figure out your unique traits, and choose the ones to put forward. I call this Image Definition.

Q: Any advice for the young actor?

• **The cold reading, camera technique** and result oriented classes are very important, but it is also significant to study basic acting. Learn how to interpret material. When you pick up a script, have a technique for making artistic choices into actable elements. On a business level, be organized and aggressive. Don't just wait for the phone to ring. There is always something you can do to progress. A good manager will certainly guide you and be a source of ideas and inspiration.

Q: Any final advice for my readers?

- **I love actors and I love the creative process** of developing careers. I sign clients with the expectation of success and long-term relationships. An actor who comes to me needs to be on the same page and understand our roles together.

- **If a quality manager** doesn't respond the first time you contact them, maybe keep them on your promotions list. There may come a moment when you are just what they are looking for.

- **The higher your career goes**, the more you will benefit from the expertise of a quality manager. Build your reputation with that manager.

- **Arthur Toretzky, a theatrical agent, talks about managers:**

  - **If an actor wants a manager,** he must remember that he's putting together a team. If you're with an agent, it's not a good idea to go out and sign with a manager and then come to the agent and announce, "Oh, by the way, I just signed with so-and-so." What if the agent doesn't like so-and-so? If the actor is with an agency and wants a manager, they should come to the agent and say, "Give me a list of managers you enjoy working with." At our agency the list is very large and we can set up the meetings. Similarly, if an actor doesn't have an agent but has a manager, the manager is going to take the actor to those agents he enjoys working with. It's just so important to make sure that the actor keeps everybody involved in the process.

- **Jay Bernstein, who has generated big careers** for such people as Farrah Fawcett, Suzanne Somers, Stacy Keach and Mary Hart, says:

  - **Look at the careers of actors you admire** and find out who their managers are, then try to attract them to you. You can find this out by reading the trades and making note of the managers who are mentioned in articles about their clients.

- **Tami Lynn**, Personal Manager/Producer, is past president of the Conference of Personal Managers (COPM) and became a lifetime honorary member in recognition of 30 years of personal management. She started the West Coast National Conference of Personal Managers.

Q: When is the right time to look for a personal manager?

- **When actors know that they need help,** they should seek representation whether they're just starting out or they are established.

- **A personal manager is one who guides** and gives direction to one's career.

Q: How does one look for a manager?

- **The best thing to do is to contact one of the organizations.** The TMA is based on the West Coast. Contact them and explain that you're looking for a manager. We usually have actors mail their pictures and resumes and I will present them to the organization. If there is some interest, then the manager will contact the client. If you want to investigate someone, ask the appropriate manager organization to have them checked out.

- **Every manager should, like an actor, have a biography.** You can see who their current clients are and other clients they have represented, how long they've been in management, what their record is. I give my clients my full biography.

Q: Could you name some of the people that you've managed?

- **Christina Applegate,** 11 seasons on *Married with Children, Jesse,* and many films. We've been together since she was seven years old. Valerie Bertinelli, Adam Rich, Mary Beth McDonough from *The Waltons,* and Katy Kurtzman.

Q: In Christina's career, before she got *Married with Children*, was she in that sexy mode?

- **Yes, she made many guest appearances on episodics.** She's a beautiful girl. At the age of 14 her career zoomed, which is usually a difficult age to hit. She had beautiful long hair which she cut all off like a punk hairdo. All the girls had long hair, and she would walk into interviews with this short, very unusual haircut. She got cast in *Heart of the City,* which really showed her acting ability. It was a wonderful hour-long series. She stood out. When the producers of *Married with Children* wanted to recast the role of Kelly Bundy, they came to us.

Q: Should an actor sign a management contract?

- **Once both people have done their homework** and the manager wants the actor and the actor wants the manager, most definitely there should be a three year contract. It takes a year just to put the whole thing together.

Q: What happens when a manager signs an actor?

- **The first thing is to evaluate their acting ability** and to make sure they are working with a good drama coach, that they have pictures that work. Most likely, they will need new pictures. Then get their resume together. A lot of times an actor doesn't realize that there are things that should be included. They think that school plays and things like that are not important. Anything they've done is important.

- **A manager will probably be in touch with a client daily** if they're working. If the actor isn't working, the two would be in touch to talk about something specific coming up or they would be sure the client is doing what is needed for themselves. If there is a problem on the set, the actor calls the manager, not the agent, because of the personal involvement that you have.

- **We can open up an interview for them.** Then the ball is totally in the actor's court.

Q: For a general interview, what kind of clothes are appropriate?

- **The simplest clothes are the best.** Casual clothes from jeans to simple skirts for girls, and for guys, just jeans and T-shirts. It should be a totally relaxed, simple situation unless there's a specific role that they're going for. Then they would most likely dress for that role. They shouldn't be investing in expensive clothing.

Q: What happens when the question of nudity comes up?

- **In advising the actor on what roles to take,** unless it's something like nudity, there's no role that should be turned down when you're starting out. Absolutely no role. I've heard actors say, "I'm looking for a particular role, or a particular path," or "I don't want to do this or that kind of role." That's insane. I think they should take the roles that are there whether it be feature films, television or cable, because you never know what you're going to get from that.

- **When you're talking about nudity, that's totally different.** There's nudity and then there's nudity. Pornography is an absolute no. It's the lowest type of work. All that does is to put you in the context of being a nude actor. It degrades you. I have actresses right now who will do nudity. That's fine as long as it's done in good taste and there's a reason for it. I will go in and say, for instance, both actresses are fine with their breasts but they do not want to show their butts. I will make sure in the contract, that whatever part of their body they do not want to show won't be shown. I'm there whenever they do a nude scene.

• **Al Onorato, personal manager** with Handprint Entertainment Inc., was a casting director for 15 years and one of the founding members of the Casting Society of America (CSA).

Q: When, in your opinion, is it time for an actor to get a personal manager?

- **There are a couple of schools of thought.** One is that you start right from the very beginning, to discover people who have x quality or x amount of talent and direct them toward the right productions, films, projects, teachers, etc. I've always thought in this business you have to trust some people. I have to put trust in the people that I want to handle, and they trust that with my guidance they will avoid some of the pitfalls. Everything costs money, and so when you're going to spend the money, you want to put it in the right area so you're not just spinning your wheels.

- **On the other hand,** someone may have a career that's already started but has gotten blocked or typecast into one area of television or stage, and they can't make the move into the next area they want to be in.

- **When I read actors,** sometimes they may not have had a lot of training but they have certain instincts that work for them, and they are able to transcend all the training that other people have had for years.

- **There is a great demand right now for young actors and actresses;** so if someone has the right look their chances are greater of getting a shot. More than ever, actors who have been on successful television series are making the leap into leads in movies.

Q: Where do you find clients?

- **Everywhere. I go to workshops, showcases, watch television,** and see both big budget and small independent films. I travel across the country doing workshops and looking for talent. Along the way you find some people you think have a certain amount of ability and desire; those are the ones you encourage to pursue a career.

Q: When should actors move to L. A.?

- **If someone really wants a career** they have to go where the market is. That is Los Angeles for film and New York for theater. That old adage about "I'm not going to go there unless I have a contract" or "I'm not going to go there unless I have a job," well, that's really pie-in-the-sky thinking. Before someone gets a job there are numerous steps one must go through first: tapes, auditions, callbacks, interviews.

Before I encourage anyone to relocate, I try working with them long distance by requesting that they put themselves on tape for projects.

• **At the International Model & Talent Association** we found a girl from Ohio who we felt had great potential. We started working with her this way, on tape. Eventually she and her mom spent some time in Los Angeles so she could be seen in person. She did land a role in an Ang Lee film.

• **I did a workshop in Phoenix** and there was a woman well into her 60s who said, "My family's grown up, my husband's passed away, this is something I always wanted to do. What do you think about my coming to Los Angeles?" I told her she was going to be battling folks who have had a lot more experience. But you know something, I'm one of those people who believes if you want to do it, do it. Don't be discouraged; if you've got the guts, the wherewithal and the desire, go for it. She did it, she came out here. And she's been working.

Q: What do you do on a daily basis? What is your job description?

• **We try to keep apprised of all the projects that are going on,** whether it be television or movies and the various roles in the particular projects.

• **Most all our work is on the phone.** It's checking and dealing with agents. You deal with the studios, casting people at the studios and casting directors on various projects. We try to get our clients to where they have projects working for them. We're aiming to get into production so that we can find projects that we think our clients are right for and put together the writer, actor and director. We also handle producers, directors and writers and a very successful music division.

Q: Do you have any advice for actors?

• **Acting in this business is very much like athletics.** You have to do it. You've got to study. The best athletes and Olympic stars are people who have been nurtured and have had coaches along the way to help guide them and keep them away from bad habits and the wrong training. The people we revere in our business, Meryl Streep, Al Pacino, Anthony Hopkins and that calibre of actor, have trained and continue to grow as artists.

• **Don't believe people who say, "I'll make you a star."** It's not an easy process and if you want to be a star, hopefully you want to be an artist as well, not just somebody whose name is on a billboard but somebody who can point proudly to the work that they do. I think it's important to uphold dignity and principles. There are no guarantees.

• **What is so often the hardest thing** for parents or loved ones of actors to understand is that it doesn't happen overnight. Every time they say, "What have you done?" or "What are we going to see you on?" though it's done with love, it also puts the actor in a precarious situation, because they feel like they've got to prove something. Loved ones don't understand how long it takes.

• **Terrance Hines, personal manager, Hines and Hunt Entertainment**, acting coach and author of the best selling book *An Actor Succeeds, Career Management for the Actor.*

Q: What do you look for in prospective clients?

• **I look for honesty, a sense of humor and a passion that fills the room.** I like the actor to have good reasons why they want management. They should do their homework by checking out my company. They should have a support system in place and enough money to invest in pictures that look like them and enroll in excellent acting classes.

• **They should be open and honest** about who they are, with an understanding of how others see them. They should have a grasp on the business aspect of the entertainment world. Are they prepared to trust and listen to those guiding their career and are they able and willing to block out the voices that do not have their best interest at heart? Are they prepared for rejection? Do they understand that there are valleys as well as mountains in long careers? Above all, do they have a sense of humor to get them through the worst of times?

Q: How do you work for your clients?

• **Our company interfaces with a network** of producers, directors, writers, casting directors and executives. When you have clients on a series or in films, the casting directors or producers call to have lunch and discuss the show. This gives the manager the opportunity to discuss their client list.

• **I find that going with clients to an interview**, especially a producer call back or the network, has proven very fruitful. Discussing the choices of material, adjustments in the direction of the career, changing physical appearance and working on the acting tools take up much of the management day.

• **Management offers a landscape** where the actor can have a sounding board at his beck and call. Every artist needs to be encouraged to beat their head against the wall one more time.

• **Casting director Joey Paul,** CSA.

Q: What is your feeling about working with personal manager?

  • **As a casting director,** I would love to spend more time finding new
    talent, but there are time constraints with the job that make that very
    difficult. Good talent that comes from the east coast or midwest re-
    gional theaters, who have their Equity and SAG cards but not a lot of
    TV credits, may have incredible difficulty just getting an agent. Smaller
    agents have difficulty getting their clients in to read for auditions. A
    personal manager who has both knowledge of the industry and certain
    relationships with agents, can get their clients representation. They can
    really make a difference in somebody's career when they're starting out.

  • **Actors can benefit** from the manager's experience and relationships
    and save themselves a lot of time. The manager might steer them to a
    good teacher, a good photographer and help them to redefine their
    look into something that's marketable. Many actors come here think-
    ing it's just about the acting or they hear it's all a look. They don't
    understand what a look is, what their look is. Many actors hear, "Well,
    you don't need a personal manager till you've got a career to manage."
    But there are personal managers who have developed careers right
    from the start. I think some of them are very worthwhile.

• **Anyone can be a personal manager,** as they are not governed by state
law. It may be wise to choose one who belongs to the personal manager
association (TMA). Before hiring a manager, check around to be sure
he or she has a good reputation. An inexperienced manager who has
not built any successful careers will be counting on you to put them on
the map. **Walk away from anyone who wants to charge you a fee
other than a percentage of what you earn.**

• **I want to alert you to some practices** that I believe are not helpful to
your career. Breakdown Services Ltd. over the years has sued and won
judgements against many pseudo/fake management companies who
go into business solely to charge actors $50 to $100 a month for access
to the casting breakdowns.

• **Actors defend paying these illegal fees** by saying it helps them to know
what roles are being cast. I believe there are legitimate ways to spend
money that will indeed really help your career. The Actor's Network costs
$40 a month and the return is of great value. Casting Showcases are a
valid way to open yourself to casting opportunities; they average $25 to

$30 a piece. Alicia Silverstone moved to Los Angeles when she was 14 to live with her acting coach Judi O'Neil. Soon afterward she was spotted at an actors' showcase by manager Carolyn Kessler. Within a year she was cast in *The Crush*. Her manager is shaping her successful career.

• **The best thing you can do for your career is to act** wherever you can make an opportunity for yourself. Submitting unsolicited pictures and resumes to casting directors is valid but one of the very least likely ways to be discovered. Doing showcases, short films, student productions and hosting or appearing on public access shows are legitimate ways of being seen.

Resources

Arts and Letters Management, Steven Nash, 7715 Sunset Blvd., #208, Los Angeles, 90046. They will consider mail submissions, from age 15 to 24 only. They will contact you if interested. No visits or phone calls, please.

Bonnie Gillespie, Cricketfeet Management, 323/871-1331. www.cricketfeet.com. $60 an hour. She works as a career consultant, see Keith Johnson's story in *Actors Living Their Dreams,* and gives career advice with pictures, resumes, marketing, career direction and how to approach a manager or agent for representation.

Tami Lynn Productions and Management, 818/888-8264. Fax: 818/888-8267.

Handprint Entertainment, Al Onorato, 310/481-4400

Hines & Hunt Entertainment, Terrance Hines and Justine Hunt, 818/557-7516.

Stein Entertainment Group, T.J. Stein, 818/766-6525. www.SteinEntertainment.com. 11271 Ventura Blvd., #477, Studio City, 91604. Children, teens and young adults.

Talent Managers Association, 310/275-2456. www.talentmanagers.org. Their purpose is to promote and encourage the highest standards of professionalism and ethics in the practice of Talent Management.

The West Coast Performer's Complete Personal Managers Directory of Managers for All Performing and Creative Talents, an Acting World Books Publication. At theatrical bookstores and www.actingworldbooks.org. This is much more than a directory; it has the information you need to shop for and land a personal manager.

Ross Reports, Working Actors Guide and *Hollywood Creative Directory* are other publications that list personal managers and are sold at theatrical bookstores.

Life Is A Contact Sport: Ten Great Career Strategies That Work, a book by personal manager Ken Kragen. Very inspirational, educating you on what a manager does for his clients. He talks about people and situations we all know of.

PUBLIC RELATIONS
AND PUBLICISTS

• **No one knows who you are or what you are doing** without publicity. All the networks and most of the production companies hire publicists, formerly known as press agents. These publicists get the press to write about the TV shows, movies and the actors in the projects. Even so, many individual stars hire their own representative to handle their publicity.

• **Alicia Silverstone, Jenny McCarthy and Matthew McConaughey** are actors who became household names even before we saw the projects they were promoting. This is because a publicity machine had put their faces and names in front of the public with such repetition that we wanted to know who they were. A while ago it was Sandra Bullock and Brad Pitt.

• **A publicist's basic responsibilities** include preparing written biographies of their clients to send to the press, keeping contacts in the media aware of any favorable newsworthy developments in their client's lives, taking the requests from newspapers, magazines and TV talk shows that want to interview their clients, and pitching story ideas about clients to these same requesters. The publicist can also decide how the public should see their client and proceed accordingly to create that image.

• **Rosie O'Donnell** mentioned in a live interview at the Oscar ceremonies that she was out of town and her publicist picked her gown and jewels. She flew in from location that morning and had the final fitting. Publicists can design the way their artists are presented to the public.

• **Marisa Tomei's** successful nomination for the Academy Award for *My Cousin Vinnie*, was directly due to her publicity team. They took out trade ads and got tapes to all of the Academy voters. When she was nominated they doubled their efforts and she won the *Best Supporting Actress*.

• **Many actors choose a publicist** for their capability of keeping them out of the news. Jason Alexander of *Seinfeld* told me when we were working on the show that he had been with his publicist for years because, "she doesn't like publicity." She didn't ask him to do openings and the type of things he didn't want to do.

• **When selecting a publicist,** as in other business choices, choose by reputation, personality and a mutual agreement on the way you want to be represented.

• **Liria Mersini is a public relations consultant and life coach currently working in Washington D.C.** When in Los Angeles, she coached individuals and led workshops on *Celebrity 101, The Power of Image and Creating Perfect Bios.*

Q: How do you help actors create PR?

   • **My goal is to de-mystify the PR process and help my clients** create powerful packages. I work with actors before they are ready for representation, as well as established actors who are ready to make a change in their image. In both cases, I help actors understand the PR process and package themselves so that they can gain more control of the image they and their team put forward.

   • **Understanding PR and the way it works can really help an actor** navigate the system and set reasonable expectations for their own PR campaign. Taking a workshop or interning at a PR firm is great exposure. It can take the mystery out of building celebrity and help a new actor think in terms of marketing.

Q: How does an actor start?

   • **An important first step is to create a bio that reflects their essence,** especially before they've done a great deal of work. This is one tool that can clarify their whole package and set the tone for meetings with agents, casting directors, managers as well as publicists. The point here is to have your package of materials (you, your pictures, bio, resume, and tape) deliver a strong, consistent message. It is never too early to begin this process.

- **I work with actors on becoming experts on marketing themselves.** In this business there is so much pressure on actors to conform to someone else's idea of who they are when it is really their uniqueness that generates interest and builds celebrity.

Q: Where do you see actors getting stuck?

- **The biggest mistake I see, both in new actors and in celebrities,** is that they tend to abdicate their power to experts. Remember, a good publicist is an expert at the process of building celebrity. They have training, experience and, most importantly, contacts. However, you are the world's foremost expert on you. When an actor knows who they are and what they want from the publicist, they radically increase their chances for success.

- **Often, an actor will hire a public relations firm** because of the "A list" artists that firm represents. Sometimes this strategy pays off, but there are no guarantees. It is also common for actors to present themselves as blank slates and ask for guidance on how to be marketed. Either way, the whole power structure is off. The actor is only one of many clients on a talent roster and that can be disempowering, especially when there are bigger names on that roster.

- **The bottom line is, if you are an expert on you,** then you can really benefit from a good publicist's ideas and contacts. It can be a very exciting process. At $2,000 to $5,000 per month, it is definitely a costly one. Doing your homework can prepare you to get the most from this important relationship.

- **Publicist Kelly Bush** of ID Public Relations works in entertainment publicity, representing actors, directors, composers and writers.

Q: Does an actor hire you on a regular monthly basis?

- **The publicist,** like the agent or manager, is part of the team. When an actor has a strong team supporting them, they are able to focus on doing great work while their team does its job. It is important the publicist, agent and manager are in constant communication.

- **I have an ongoing relationship** with my clients just like the agent or manager. People sometimes think a publicist can be hired only once in a while. When there is an opportunity to make something happen for someone, what happens if they are not "on" at the time? It is important to consider publicity for the entire career—not just for a particular project. For example, magazines work sometimes up to 4-6 months in advance.

Q: When you get a new client and you are the first publicist, what is the procedure?

- **If the client has worked** for 10 years and never had a publicist, they've probably done a mish-mosh of interviews based on what they were promoting at the time. I approach the entire career. I start with smaller things and work towards magazine covers. I look at all the photographs that have been taken and biographical information or feature stories that have been written. I write a new bio that is very straightforward. If necessary, I put together a photo shoot so we have something we're happy to send out.

- **It's about presentation** and packaging. If a client has never done any press, it's exciting because you can do it right from the beginning.

Q: Is there a great deal of expense for new clients?

- **The client doesn't pay** for the magazine or newspaper photo shoots; the publications do. If we're promoting a film or television show, usually the studio will pick up expenses associated with the publicity. The client only pays publicity fees and expenses.

Q: How are those fees determined?

- **It's a flat monthly fee.** Publicists charge anywhere from $2,000-5,000 a month. There are perfectly reputable publicists that charge less but in my opinion, you get what you pay for.

Q: How do actors shop for publicists?

- **Their agent or manager will know publicists** the client would get along well with and whose work they trust. I would take no more than three meetings, otherwise it gets very confusing. Ask the publicist about their approach to things, or what they feel are important types of publicity, and you will get a pretty good sense whether or not you agree with their ideas. If you trust your publicist, they can do their job and help take your career to a high level—which makes the agent's and manager's job easier. If a producer sees an actor in *Vanity Fair*, they may say, "If *Vanity Fair* thinks they're hot, then I want them in my next movie."

Q: When is it time to hire a publicist?

- **When the actor has something to promote.** A television show, a film, a theatrical production—with enough time in advance to do the proper job. Look at Rita Wilson from *Sleepless in Seattle*. She got a good amount of press with just a five-minute crying scene in the film. There have been a lot of small parts that stood out and received attention for the performer. A publicist can get your work in front of an editor, to convince them that your story is worth covering. The time to think about hiring a publicist is when you've done work you're really proud of.

- **My job is to educate** the magazine editors and television producers on who my clients are and why they should be on their shows or in their magazines.

Q: Does the publicist go to these interviews?

- **You accompany your client** on everything. For print interviews, I introduce the writer to my client and then I leave them. I'm there for every photo taken and every television appearance.

Q: Have you ever had a client who is really shy and publicity was difficult for them?

- **I don't put them in situations** where it's going to make them uncomfortable. I have clients that I would never put on *Letterman* or *The Tonight Show*. It's just not appropriate for them. There are a lot of other things you can do, though, that are more conducive for your client. If they're more comfortable with a one on one situation, everything they do is in print. They just don't do TV.

Q: How do you find clients?

- **The best way to get a client is to do a good job** for the ones you have and word gets out. Also, I go after clients. For example, at the film festivals you see movies before their theatrical releases. I hear about someone who is outstanding in a role, and I'll call their agent and say that I'm interested in meeting with this person.

Q: Do you have any advice for actors who don't have that movie or television project yet?

- **Do great work** and if you receive great reviews that gives you something to go on. I've met with people who wanted a publicist and once we had a meeting, I was able to tell them that it's not time for it yet. A person may have a supporting role in a successful television series and the media may have no interest in talking to them. The publicist really doesn't know what we can do for that person until we get out there and start working and see what kind of response we get.

Q: What advice can you give for actors who already have publicists? How can the actor help?

• **Doing press is almost like an audition.** You put on your acting hat and you're an actor. You put on your publicity hat and you're doing publicity. It's very different. You really have to know what you're doing. You really have to make an impression. The client can make a publicist's job easier by being good at it. It helps to see other people on TV shows like *Letterman*, read magazine and newspaper articles, see other actors doing press and the kind of impression you get after you read the article. You may say, "Do I like this person?" or, "This person sounded really arrogant" or, "This person I admire." You see someone doing a talk show and you say, "That was really boring."

• **You can learn from that.** You see a great actress like Geena Davis who brings on her inventions. That makes for good TV. These TV producers want to get great ratings. They want people to stay up late and watch.

Resources

Working Actor's Guide lists Public Relation Firms.

Guerrilla P.R. and *Guerrilla P.R. Wired* by Michael Levine are good books about doing your own publicity.

ID Public Relations: Kelly Bush, 310/204-6868. 3859 Cardiff Ave. Culver City, 90232.

Studio Fan Mail/Tamkin Color, 310/275-6122. 1122 S. Robertson Blvd., Los Angeles, 90035. When it is time in your career to have someone answer your fan mail, Jack Tamkin runs a wonderful business. They send out all color photos with authentic-looking autographs and personal messages. Their costs are lower than most black and white photos. When requested they will send a prospective client an interesting, thorough set of samples of their work.

ENTERTAINMENT ATTORNEYS

• **It is an exciting time** in an actor's career when the future holds so much promise that an attorney is needed. Be certain that the finances and terms of your deals are properly in place so that you can calmly enjoy your hard-earned successes.

• **As actors' careers grow**, they must seek the best support people for their team. It is important to understand what an entertainment attorney can do for you before you need one.

• **Your attorney can advise you** of your rights in a given situation and negotiate a contract—money, billing and terms are complicated areas but it's vital they are handled to your best advantage. The ins and outs of an entertainment contract are so complicated and abstract that you need a specialist. It can be dangerous to your best interests to rely on a family attorney—or even your agent—who is not an experienced specialist. Attorneys usually charge by the hour and a good one will estimate costs for you. When seeking an attorney, ask your friends in the entertainment industry for their recommendations. We all hear the attorney-bashing jokes, but your personal legal matters are no joke and you need a caring, honest, loyal attorney. Interview several and then go with your well-tuned instincts as to who will work the best for you.

• **Chandler Warren, entertainment attorney,** began his career in New York representing the producers of *As the World Turns* and *Another World,* also dozens of stage productions on and off Broadway and over 50 independent feature films. Today he represents writers, directors, actors, producers and designers in all phases of film, television, stage and recording. He works extensively in low budget features in New York and Los Angeles, including the complicated area of film distribution.

Q: Under what circumstances does an actor need an attorney?

- **For example**, when an actor is required to sign a test option for a television series, it may bind him for the next three to seven years of his/her professional life. The agent can negotiate the basic terms of the deal, but it is important to have the fine points of the contract negotiated by an entertainment attorney.

- **When an actor is engaged for a series of commercials**, the agent will handle the basic negotiation but an attorney should review and negotiate the fine points. Otherwise, the actor could find his/her picture on the product's labels, billboards and cardboard cutouts in super markets and wonder what happened. Every phase of the use of the actor's name, likeness, voice, etc. has to be carefully spelled out.

- **When the actor is cast in a good role** in a motion picture, the producer may want additional options, etc. This should be reviewed on the actor's behalf. There are any number of things in most "standard" actor contracts that need to be negotiated.

- **When the actor is cast in a legitimate stage production**, often the producer will want options to take the actor along with the play as it moves. And there are billing considerations, housing, per diems, etc. to be negotiated. Or the situation may be reversed, where the actor wants the option to continue and this has to be negotiated so the actor is protected.

- **When the actor is also a singer** there are other pitfalls, as the music business is complicated and dog-eat-dog. Those contracts can tie up an actor and/or the actor's writing talents for many years. This is an area that must never be entered without an entertainment attorney at the actor's side.

- **When an actor signs with a manager**, a lawyer is essential. A management contract can be in effect for a long period of time and usually encompasses money from all sources of the entertainment business. An actor has to be sure the contract allows him/her to leave if the manager is not fulfilling the job. Remember, an actor must never rely on an oral promise.

Q: How do you feel about agents?

- **I am a strong believer** in both agents and managers. Most attorneys are not acting agents; they don't get the Breakdown Service, they aren't in contact daily with casting directors, etc. But if an actor doesn't have an agent yet and has been cast in a series, a soap, a major part in a motion picture, or gets a recording contract, the actor only needs the services of an attorney. From that job, the actor may then secure a top agent or manager.

Q: In what other situations might an actor need an attorney?

• **No one should direct a play** without a written contract, especially if the play is a new one by a new playwright. What is the director's future option to direct? What is the director's billing? Should the director agree to a royalty pool? And so on.

• **An actor who writes a play**, or has a unique idea, will need a copyright. No one reading this book should ever lose sight of the fact that a copyright is probably the most valuable commodity a person can have; yes, even better than residuals because it lasts longer. Also, the writer needs to negotiate royalties, travel and per diems, billing, subsidiary rights, option terms, etc.

• **Actors often produce** their own 99-seat waiver shows in order to showcase their acting talents. All of the many legal headaches which every producer must face will have to be dealt with. No producer should remotely consider going into the producing business without an entertainment attorney who is familiar with legitimate stage contracts, SEC filing requirements, limited partnerships, etc.

Q: Can you give me a ball park figure of what it might cost for certain contracts?

• **It is hard to answer specifically** because every situation is different. Certainly if the negotiations get very complex or drawn out it will increase the hours that an attorney will need to spend in reviewing and negotiating. An average television series or day time soap contract could cost $1000 to $1500 to review and negotiate, a management contract, usually $250 to $500.

Resources

Chandler Warren, 323/876-6400. 7715 Sunset Blvd. #208, Los Angeles 90046. Extremely knowledgeable, fair, and easy to talk to. His walls are lined with pictures of famous actors and posters of shows he's worked on.

Los Angeles County Bar Association, 213/627-2727.

California State Bar Association, 213/765-1000. Ask for information on several attorneys who are listed as specialists in Entertainment Law.

BUSINESS MANAGERS

• **As actors develop in their earning capacity** and start saving money, the next person on their *career team* will be a business (financial) manager. Some actors or spouses of actors may have an educated background in business and time to research, but most of us need to seek a professional to manage our expenses and investments. Business affairs become very complicated when the actor is working on remote locations.

• **When you have landed that role on a series or a big movie** that is taking you on location for months, it might be time to look for a business manager. Gayle Futernick, in her *Drama-Logue* column, gave some great examples of when you would need some help.

   • **After 25 hours a day on a set spent learning your lines** and your marks, you aren't going to feel much like writing rent checks or doing budgets on Quicken. You need a new car, because you just can't drive to The Lot in your old, beat-up Chevy. Should you buy or lease a new car? Should you open a retirement fund? Maybe you should keep your bucks in a liquid, short-term investment just in case. Then again, the producer did smile and mention something about a starring role in the spin-off.

   • **Maybe it is time to buy a house.** Who is going to help you get a mortgage? Who is going to refer you to a reliable investment advisor? Who is going to reconcile your check book? Who is going to be on hold with the bank for 20 minutes while they figure out why your service charge quadrupled last month? Who is going to remember to deposit your residual checks in the investment fund and the weekly paychecks in the household account?

419

- **Who has time to keep up with your paperwork? Not you!** You're busy getting to sets on time and interviewing with the press. They need you in wardrobe at 7AM for a fitting and you're supposed to lunch with your agent at Le Dome. Life is a bit hectic and right now you're spending your time shmoozing with the right people at the right parties.

- **Tax planning is not exactly your strong point** and you're not really sure how to build a spreadsheet that will remind you when to pay your bills. And mom lives too far away to help . . .

• **I love Gayle's writing and I think she makes her point very well.** As actors, we all hope and yearn for the predicament she outlines. Here are a few more of her thoughts on using the right business manager.

- **There are no generic answers.** These decisions depend on you and your lifestyle. If you tend to lose control with money, think about your future. Remember how hard it was to get this gig. Remember how many people are trying to become working actors. Unless you are an established mega-celebrity, be conservative with your finances and use your business manager as your money conscience.

- **While you need to be able to depend on your business manager,** it is not advisable to totally turn over the reins and never check his work. It is your money and your financial health that are important. Request and review periodic (monthly or quarterly) reports. You are paying them to provide services for you and to educate you about your financial matters. Trust is a mutual understanding.

- **There are no licensing procedures for business managers.** You may want to find one who is a CPA (Certified Public Accountant). The advantage is tremendous: CPAs have passed the CPA Exam and have work experience in the accounting field. They are licensed and regulated by the state, and must abide by professional ethics and complete 80 hours of continuing education every two years.

- **Business managers can charge hourly, a fixed rate or a flat percentage** of your gross salary earned as their fee. Typically, business managers charge five percent of gross income that is earned from your professional services as their fee. Thus their fee would not be based on amounts earned on investments.

- **If your annual income exceeds $100,000,** it is probably time to consider using the services of a business manager.

• **At the beginning of Oprah's success**, she had Bill Cosby on her show. When discussing finances, Cosby said, "In order to know where your money is going, always sign every check and investigate and approve each investment yourself." Oprah credits his advice for much of her prosperity. I'm sure Oprah has a business manager to keep everything in order, but she runs the ship.

• **Shaquille O'Neal**: "When you're dealing with money, you have to take half of what you make and put it away. Then take half of what you have left and put that away. So you've put three quarters of it away and you play with the one quarter that is left. If you invest wisely, safely and don't take too many risks, you'll be all right."

• **Some actors are not interested in handling their money.** If you are this type, be selective in choosing your professional advisor. There are no regulations for financial managers so they have free rein. You sign your money over and trust they will do the right thing. Your hard-earned money could be gone—we have all heard the horror stories of business managers running off with all of their clients' money. On the other hand, most actors with money have been guided by financial consultants and managers.

Personal Manager T.J. Stein had an article in his newsletter by business manager, CPA Scott Feinstein about whether or not to incorporate. I am quoting some of the article to give you an overall view. Keep in mind this is general information and tax laws change every year.

> • **It comes down to one main issue, cost vs. benefit.** The costs of incorporation include initial one-time, out-of-pocket expenses plus on-going annual expenses such as legal and accounting fees and additional payroll and corporate taxes. On the other hand benefits of incorporation include the ability to establish a pension plan, the right to deduct medical expenses and the transfer of other expenses from your personal tax return to corporate tax return where there are no limitations and the financial advantages of fiscal year-end planning.

> • **The benefits fall into three basic categories:** pension plans, medical and business expense deductions, and fiscal year-end planning.

> • **As an employee of a production company/studio** and the recipient of W-2 income, the only retirement account you can voluntarily set up is an IRA. Unfortunately, if you are a member of a union, and although you have the right to contribute to an IRA, the contributions would <u>not</u> qualify as a tax deduction. With a loan-out corporation,

you can set up a corporate pension plan and take a deduction from your gross income of up to $30,000 per year. This would obviously save significant tax dollars.

• **Your employee business deductions are included on Schedule A** of your personal tax return and, as such, are subject to several limitations. In fact, if your deductions are large enough you could be subject to what is referred to as an "alternative minimum tax." In simple terms, you could lose a significant portion of the tax deduction. With a corporation, there are no such limitations. The IRS generally respects the deductions of a corporation. In other words, the standards for proof can be greater on a personal tax return than on a corporate tax return.

• **As for medical and other personal expenses,** a corporation can adopt a medical reimbursement plan which allows the corporation to pay directly and deduct all medical expenses (less amounts paid by insurance) including expenses for mental health, eye care, chiropractic, etc.

• **Finally, a corporation can establish a "fiscal" year-end** as opposed to the required December 31 calendar year-end for individuals. This enables you to manipulate income by pushing back or accelerating income between calendar years, depending on your particular financial status each year.

• **Since there are no regulatory bodies** or other ways to check on financial/business managers, you must do some extensive research before making any financial decisions. Ask your accountant, attorney, agent, manager, successful actor friend or any other trusted friends in the business for their recommendations.

Resources:

Feinstein & Berson: Scott Feinstein, 818/981-3115. 16133 Ventura Blvd., #800, Encino, 91436. CPA and Business Manager, has a strong client list consisting almost exclusively of SAG, AFTRA, IATSE and DGA members.

California State Board of Accountancy, 916/263-3680. You can check to see if the business manager or accountant you are considering is licensed and in good standing.

Working Actor's Guide (WAG), available at theatrical bookstores, lists many well known business managers.

CAREER AND LIFE
COACHES

• **Career and Life Coaches** have come to be a very important part of actors' teams. I wrote the first edition of this book in 1981 for my students because I felt they needed career coaching in order to compete at the highest levels. In the last several years many classes, seminars and workshops have been established solely to help people promote their careers. One of the largest areas of private coaching is now in building careers. Career building in no way replaces talent development, nor would any career coach of merit make that claim. I think career coaching is very valid and necessary in this competitive field. Each individual has to decide how much energy they want to put into art and how much into business. Sometimes we can do both at different stages of our lives. The truth of the matter is, it is always hard work. Perhaps the career coach can guide you in answering where best to focus your time.

• **Melissa McFarlane is a certified life coach.**

Q: How is having a life coach different from having a career coach?

>   • **A life coach helps your career within the context of your whole life.**
>   I help clients gain a clear sense of who they are, what they want, and
>   what ultimately matters to them in life. Then we work on a plan to
>   get there. With this foundation, actors are less likely to make choices
>   based on their fears, on what others say they must do, or what they
>   see another, more successful actor doing. Now the career is being
>   developed on a strong foundation. Career development is much more
>   successful and satisfying approached this way.

- **We all know that when one part of our life is out of balance**, the rest of our life is affected. Most people would agree that if they were offered both a wonderful life and a wonderful career they would take it. A life coach becomes your partner in making that happen.

Q: Why would an actor need a life coach?

- **Having a life coach is like having a personal trainer for your life.** This is a particularly important resource and relationship for actors. In an industry that requires you to take risks and face regular rejection, it is important to have ongoing support. A good deal of an actor's life is spent waiting between roles. It can be tough for even the most successful actors to stay focused. Part cheerleader, part taskmaster, part counselor and part mentor, your coach is there to support you in defining, refining and achieving your goals and dreams.

Q: What do you do as a life coach?

- **A coaching relationship is a business partnership** based on the client's desires and goals. I am committed to my clients and their own greatest vision of themselves. Coaching works whether someone wants to prepare for a move to Los Angeles, book a sitcom, break into film, or balance personal and career development. I know my clients are capable of having lives of deep personal fulfillment and brilliant career success—if they can keep their eye on the ball. That's where I come in. Our relationship begins with an extensive intake process; from there we establish goals and deadlines and work weekly to achieve them.

Q: How does the coaching process work?

- **Most of my clients choose to work privately**, in half-hour sessions by phone; others prefer to participate in a supportive weekly class. Some clients enjoy both. There are times when a person must focus so deeply that others are a distraction. Sometimes, however, the input and support of a group can carry us further than we could go alone.

Q: How can someone determine if coaching is for them?

- **Try it! Most coaches offer a half-hour coaching session without charge.** Others hold free introductory classes or seminars. Generally, people know right away whether they want to continue. My best advice would be: trust yourself; you know what is best for you. As with anything, if you feel pressured or uncomfortable, leave. If, on the other hand, you feel like a thirsty traveler who has just been given a huge glass of cool water, stay and enjoy the drink. Any coach worth their salt would say the same thing. Remember, coaches want you to win!

Q: You mentioned preparing for a move to Los Angeles. Could someone work with you over the phone while they are still living out of town?

- **One of the greatest uses of a coach would be preparing for the move.** Since this process is very effective by phone, an actor can have a strong support system in place before they arrive.

Q: Melissa, what is the process you use to help an actor get the most out of their career efforts?

- **I agree with former client/colleague, Liria Mersini, who describes the work as a seven-step process.**

1) **First, we look at how you see yourself and how others see you.** These things generally have a lot of power in a new client's belief system.

2) **Next, we look at who you are fundamentally.**

3) **Third, we examine the difference between the first two steps** and identify any gaps. These are gaps in identity and they are the root of a lot of suffering and angst.

4) **With all of that on the table, we begin to bridge the gaps** and gain the freedom to choose. Building a bridge and coming from choice is far more powerful than operating by default.

5) **Next is an opportunity to define your personal playing fields** and who you are on them. This is where you decide what you really want and how you're going to get there.

6) **Now begins the process of taking yourself public.** This includes new actions that are fueled by new perceptions, approaches, and attachments.

7) **The final step is all about consistency and building a discipline.** This is where ongoing support is critical because you are building muscles and learning to use them in new ways.

- **Taken together, these seven steps** are a prescription for a brilliant and rewarding career and life.

- **Having success as an actor** requires a particularly strong sense of self and persistence in putting that forward. The intuitive, consistent, empowering dialogue with a coach is a big help for any actor committed to staying on track mentally, emotionally and strategically, not only for the short term, but to develop a healthy long-term career.

• **Maddisen K. Krown, actress, student and contributor** to the tenth edition talks about working with Melissa McFarlane as her life coach.

> • **I have a good life**, and I'm fulfilled in most of the primary areas: personal growth, health, fun, recreation, friends, family, love, money, and physical surroundings. But there is one major area that has not kept up with the others, and that is career.

> • **Melissa is very good at sensing** what is really going on underneath the surface, and offering that up to me for examination in a way that is non-threatening and healing. And she most always follows up the discoveries with fun exercises and/or homework and with questions that spring forth empowering answers or at least options.

> • **Each session with Melissa** is a time of exploration and discovery, usually mixed with unexpected insights and emotions. I can clearly feel Melissa maintaining a structure that keeps us on track, but that also allows for natural zig-zagging. With her guidance, I have been able to access deeper levels of my psyche and spirit. As a result, I am now moving into wholeness and fulfillment with a successful acting career.

• **Carolyne Barry, commercial actress, teacher and casting director**, works with coaches Breck Costin, Barbara Deutsch and Laurie Johnson.

Q: Why do you like working with life coaches?

> • **I've done therapy where you are dealing with issues** that are far in the past. This work deals with the present—how you are hearing things, how you are seeing things, how your perception is. If you get in tune with all that, it really cleans up the past as well, but it doesn't stress the past. It is all about reality and perception. I use what I have learned from my coaches in my teaching all the time; the clearer my perception is, the better my teaching is. I know, on a personal basis, it has transformed me.

• **Laurie Johnson is a life coach, as well as a working actress.**

Q: How do you know if you need a life or career coach?

> • **There are two ways I approach it.** One is if you feel a block somewhere. If you feel like your shoe is nailed to the floor in a particular arena and there is some obstacle in the way. The second way is you are not feeling blocked but you don't know what the next step is. Everything is going great and I want to kick it to the next level. You can't quite see what that next level is or how to do that. One is handling an obstacle and one is a design conversation. The kind of obstacles I've dealt with are: trouble in auditions, fear, can't seem to move into action.

- For some people it can be, "**Am I in the right career?** Is this really my passion? Am I doing this because I told my high school friends and parents I am going to do this, so now I have to?"

Q: Would a coach help them find what they should be doing?

- **Yes, to discover what their passion is**, and also to relieve them in knowing that they don't have to do this. There is no contract that says they have to do this. This business is a choice, it is not an obligation. Many times I have to remind people I work with that they chose this. They are the ones who have the say, nobody is doing this to them. There is no "industry" per se; there are just a lot of people. There is not a big monolith somewhere.

- **The other thing I work with people on are conversations** that they buy into in the industry that are disempowering. Like, "If you are over 40, you are not going to work very much." I don't buy that, I am on the court with them because I walk my talk. I work and I'm almost 50. I just got into the business seven years ago, so if I can do it, anybody can do it. It is not a product of talent; turn on television and you can see it is not talent. Talent is a nice icing on the cake but it is not the requirement to work.

Q: What is the requirement to work?

- **You really have to take a very strong stand for working** and you have to have a very strong stand on yourself. You have to be unstoppable. If somebody says no—you don't go down the tubes. If one person out of 10 says, "I don't think you've got it," and nine people think you do and you go to the one person, then we've got to have a talk about that. That's not healthy.

- **Breck Costin, of BCC & Associates**, conducts many different types of seminars.

Q: What led you into seminar coaching?

- **I noticed actors acted as if they were uninvited guests** crashing a private party. Meaning they would get into situations or auditions, and find themselves not able to come up with the goods. I take them from uninvited guests to host of the party—it really all has to do with their ability to belong.

- **I work on the inner dialogue that prevents people** from fully expressing themselves, having full permission for their talents and having more freedom in their choices and expressions.

• **I'm looking to see when pressure is put on**, where they break down. They may not know how to do an effective cold call, how to generate auditions or how to manage their representation. I work on those tools.

Q: With 150 people in a class, how can an individual be helped?

• **I work with individuals, but it impacts the whole group.** Most of them have the same concerns.

• **They have a homework assignment each week.** It's very specific tools and language, whether it be marketing, management, closing deals, negotiating, or even how to move from guest starring to starring or how to move from recurring to regular roles on TV series.

Q: How would you expect a beginning actor to be affected by a three-month seminar?

• **I have a lot of beginners, people who have just gotten off the bus.** It probably saves them about a year and a half of time. Some of the people in the seminar are starring in features or have their own series, with strong agents or middle-of-the-road agents. The new actor immediately has the entire lay of the land. They are in a community of support where they can see the absolute possibility of beginning something, following through, and having something happen at the end. They have a much stronger sense of what it's going to take to produce in this town. They find out the inner workings so they don't have to go down blind alleys and spend a lot of money.

• **Laurie Sheppard is a master certified life coach** and career strategist. She is a pioneer coach, having started her business, Creating At Will® in 1994, when coaching was just coming out of the corporate environment and gathering more interest with the general public.

Q: How do you work with the clients you coach?

• **My work, individually and with groups,** is about assisting them to clarify their *Next Big Thing*—and develop a strategic action plan to get there.

Q: How do you describe the *Next Big Thing*?

• *The Next Big Thing* **is what's most important for you now**, a valued and worthy objective which challenges and rewards you.

Q: How do you start and what kinds of clients do you work with?

• **As a life coach I assist my clients** in looking at the whole pie rather than one slice of their life, to have their career and personal goals integrate smoothly. But all of my clients hire me initially for their career development or career transitions. Individuals meet with me by phone once weekly for a minimum of twelve sessions and we start by assessing their specific needs. Groups vary in length, depending on workshop, seminar, or training format, which often include individual coaching.

• **Clients are usually in four places:** 1) they are clear and ready to up-the-ante in their productivity or results; 2) they are feeling overwhelmed, confused or indecisive (though this is not a long-term pattern); 3) they have been working harder, not smarter and want to know how they can take a well-needed break, without losing ground; 4) they need to maximize their preparation time toward their objective(s), make clearer choices and prioritize their actions toward their goal.

• **I mainly work with entrepreneurs and professionals.** That is how I view the individual in the entertainment industry. They have a business. It is themselves they are selling, promoting, or perhaps repositioning in their industry. How to do it and not burn out the flame for their artistry in the process is the key.

Q: It sounds like you're talking a lot about balance with change?

• **Yes I am.** *Balance* is an overused term these days, which can dilute it's meaning, but I feel it is important. To me it means while achieving your next big thing you are able to maintain a connection to yourself, trust yourself, and have a certainty about your choices. We are bombarded with distractions as well as opportunities. We need a peaceful heart as well as a discerning eye and well-designed map to keep us on course. Understanding change, rather than being at the effect of it, gives us the necessary edge to expedite, as well as enjoy, the journey. My clients are more confidently accepting, more effortlessly maintaining their focus and direction, and able to repeat steps for the next challenge.

• **Sam Christensen's course is called Image Process.**

Q: Tell me about the unique course you teach.

- **The level-one class is an 18-hour course.** I have students that have just stepped off the bus two weeks ago, and I have people who have been at this for 30 years who are trying to focus. I begin with a basic introduction of how marketing works for any product and then adapt it to acting. I then work on an image system, which allows people to figure out how they are perceived by other people outside of themselves. For example, with Greta Garbo, there was always mystery in her photographs: the clothes she wore, the publicity the studio did for her. The studios used to develop themes with an actor.

- **Suppose an agent represented Goldie Hawn.** Goldie Hawn thought she was a serious actress and she wanted to play Juliet. The agent took her because she's kind of a giddy blonde. Meanwhile, the photographer is attracted to her and he's trying to catch all the sexiness. Instead, if Goldie, the agent, photographer, and haircutter are all in agreement around the theme that Goldie is wacky, upfront, bright, lively and a little suspicious, then everybody's talking the same language.

- **The actors come up with a set of words which are the primary themes** of what happens when they walk into a room—the stuff they bring to every part before they start making adjustments. It's the stuff that ought to be in a photograph of them.

- **For instance, from one of my classes,** there was an actress whose words are "urban, perplexed, genial, comic, direct, and impatient." Somebody else who is "tempered, amused, a tough-nut to crack, straight-shooting, embodied." Another person who is "hard-core, a mutt, motley, I land on my feet." Here's somebody who is "simmering, wild-eyed, mad-cap, conspiratorial, I know where the body's buried." These are not descriptions I give them. These are things that they choose through a rather involved process.

- **All of a sudden the actor has a language** and qualities to talk to the agent about so the agent can go out and use those same kinds of descriptions. When the actor comes in to meet the casting director, the actor is what the actor is comfortable in being, the actor is what the agent has introduced, he is what the pictures look like and everybody is in agreement. Improvements show up in all kinds of ways, not just in getting jobs.

• **In the ninth edition I asked actress Janice Allen** to talk about working with a life coach. I am keeping it for the tenth edition because Janice continues on a deliberate, motivated path. (*See Janice's pictures in Section Two.*)

Q: What are the biggest benefits in working with a coach?

• **I have been working with my coach for the past eight months** and my career and life are in better shape than ever before. I am hard-working, ambitious and motivated by nature. I used to push myself really hard, spending all my free time and energy pursuing my career. And then I would crash and need to take a month or two off to regenerate. Then I would have to gain my momentum back. It was a roller coaster and I was doing a lot of work without much reward.

• **My coach helped me find balance in all areas of my life**, and it's paying off! I gained the courage to quit my day job and now I am supporting myself as an actress and I am developing my career full-time. I haven't crashed in eight months (normally I would have crashed at least twice) and I am auditioning and working more than ever before. Professionally, the biggest difference is that now when I walk into an audition, I AM an actor and it isn't personal. That has given me a lot of freedom—and I'm booking the jobs!

• **We all hear people talk** about the reasons they are not making it. You know, the normal lines about not having the right agent, the right contacts and connections, even the right headshot. It's really easy to buy into that conversation. On the other hand, we all know some-body who believes in themselves no matter what. I used to look at people like that with a lot of skepticism. My coach has given me the tools to join that club... and now all the reasons and justifications don't stop me. I'm unstoppable.

Resources

Judy Kerr, 818/505-9373. www.judykerr.com. Private one-time class for $100 to $150. I critique pictures and resumes, help you choose clips for your demo reel, steer you toward teachers, photographers and services specifically suited for you, as well as guide you on long and short term goals. If you wish, I will also send you a script ahead of time so you can prepare it and test your audition skills. For people out-of-town, $50 half-hour phone consultation.

Artist's Way Workshop, 310/839-3424. www.creativelife.com. Remove seemingly insurmountable barriers to artistic confidence and productivity. Based on the book.

Linda Buzzell, MA, MFCC, 310/553-9660. Career counselor/therapist and author of *How to Make It In Hollywood*. Private consultations, call for brochure.

Sam Christensen, 818/506-0783. www.samchristensen.com 10440 Burbank Blvd., North Hollywood, 91601. Specializing in image definition and career marketing for actors and comics. "Today craft and talent are expected from the actor. Ultimately, it is their personal uniqueness that gets them hired and gains them an audience. An actor's ability to identify and market their unique qualities is 'make or break' in our business." Sam's studio offers the *Image Process* one-day marketing workshops, acting and audition classes and a gallery featuring 40 of Hollywood's best photographers.

Breck Costin, BCC & Associates, 323/848-9665. www.bccfreedom.com. 8033 Sunset Blvd., #8000, Los Angeles, 90046. Private, $250 an hour. Monthly *Conversation*, first of the month on Mondays, $30. Los Angeles Conversation, 8 session seminar, $400. "Come to be coached, get your questions answered and gain clarity about your life."

Barbara Deutsch, The Barbara Deutsch Approach, 818/508-9096. www.bdapproach.com. She works with actors, writers, directors and producers. Private sessions, $125 an hour. Actors' workshops, *Breaking The Rules, Your Own Way,* $225 a month. She moves your career to a higher level. *In The Biz,* interactions and role playing with powerful film and television professionals. Also in Vancouver, Toronto, N.Y.

Flash Forward Institute, 323/850-7392. www.flashforwardinstitute.com. Tools: How to get mentors, referrals, bookings and deals. Network with high-powered Flash Forward alumni from agencies, networks, studios, production and casting companies. They offer very inexpensive introductory courses: *One evening crash course!* $10. *The absolute scoop on how to get a great agent,* $10. The *Flash Forward intensive* is $425. SAG Conservatory had a two-hour session, which was informative and inspirational.

Bonnie Gillespie, Cricketfeet Management, 323/871-1331. www.cricketfeet.com. $60 an hour. She manages 10 actors (see Keith Johnson's story in *Actors Living Their Dreams)* and is available to help with pictures, resumes, marketing, career direction and the best way to market yourself to agents and managers.

Harriet Greenspan, 818/266-6698. A casting director for the past 20 years, she includes acting coaching, career issues, relationships, money and health matters. "Strives to help students create rewarding lives." Harriet has a great uplifting personality, is great to be with and knows all aspects of the business.

Jill Jaress, coach and career consultant, 310/828-7814 or 888/576-4695. www.actorsconsultations.com. Jill specializes in teaching new actors how to break into the business and working actors how to increase the number and quality of their bookings. Private consultations are one hour and can be conducted either on the phone or in person.

Laurie Johnson, 323/935-1528. Four sessions, $300. They are one-hour taped sessions. You walk away with a tape for life. "Once you finish the four sessions, that can be it or you can maybe come back for one. If there is a new issue we do another set of four."

Melissa McFarlane, 818/729-7858 or 323/697-0165. www.yourcoachandbiggestfan.com. An International Certified Co-Active Life Coach, and on a mission to bring extraordinary change to ordinary lives. She has over 15 years experience, as a coach, trainer and professional actress, working extensively in the area of professional development with a diverse spectrum of individuals including actors, producers, directors, writers, lawyers, salespersons, creative types and CEO's of small businesses. She holds workshops as well as private sessions in person and over the phone.

Kathleen Noone, 818/980-7234. knoone@webtv.net. Emotional coaching and entertainment business counseling. Over 40 years as an Emmy Award winning actress working as a primetime series regular, daytime series regular, episodic appearances, MOWs, films and theatre. "I have experienced the tremendous highs and lows and developed good techniques to help in relationships with agents, producers, writers and actors. We face the struggles of employment and unemployment as well as our own demons when dealing with a business that doesn't honor our talents."

Mary Pinizzotto, Life Purpose Coach, 760/809-6279. www.positivelyattractive.com. Her web site means: "Become positively attractive to what you really want." Mary coaches you to live the life of your dreams by helping you discover your true purpose. She lives in Encinitas. Most of the coaching is by phone and email. Call her for a complimentary session to experience her unique services. Mary has a great personality and lives her goals and dreams. I've watched her go for her goals, she's an inspiration.

Laurie Sheppard, 310/645-2874. www.creatingatwill.com. Certified life coach, $45 for one-hour coaching introduction. Twelve-session rate for start up. Call for private sessions, current workshop or adult school instruction class information and availability.

Cat Williford, Winning Ways, 818/562-6851. Personal best coach and self-professed joy junkie. Her clients are on a quest for a more successful, satisfying and balanced life.

IN BOSTON
Lori A. Frankian, Business Consultant for Actors, 617/437-0334. www.lorifrankian.com. In Boston, work one on one or via telephone. Lori says, "When actors work with me, they will: Gain the direction, respect, motivation they deserve as well as a solid understanding of how to pursue work/training with reputable professionals in Boston, New York and Los Angeles. Talent will develop and maintain their goals, receive personalized strategies and learn how to carry them out successfully. Learn the who's who, the how to's and what not to do's when it comes to networking, auditioning, marketing and training." She successfully prepares her clients for the move into the Los Angeles market.

SECTION SIX
CREATING YOUR STYLE AND IMAGE

STYLE, IMAGE AND WARDROBE
FOR ACTORS AND ACTRESSES

• **Much of who we are as actors** is how we look, what we wear, how we present ourselves. Some of us are born or raised with a sense of style and taste; others develop it. You must look successful. If you are not naturally talented in this area, you will have to learn how to dress yourself to present the image that you choose to project. You can cultivate taste and create your own *look*. Read books. Consult a friend whose taste you like. Try different styles; decide how you want to uniquely present yourself. Always practice looking your best, whether your style is beach dude or conservative homemaker.

• **When I've taken style classes**, I studied pictures of styles that were flattering to me and learned what types of clothing suited me best. I have hired stylists to go shopping with me to teach me the clothing style and color foundations I needed to build my wardrobe. It has been a great help to me professionally to be able to present the exact picture of myself that was right for the occasion.

• **If your funds are limited**, go to resale stores, discount designer stores, department store sales and factory outlets. I have listed a few. There are also countless books available with stores and their locations. When buying clothes, the fabric and fit are most important. A student of mine said she never shopped because she didn't have money to buy clothes. She had no idea what her size was, what current styles were up to date. You can educate yourself. Do lots of shopping and trying on, no buying. When you can afford to buy, you will know what and where to buy.

434

• **Consider the thought and money** that go into film wardrobes and you realize how important dressing is. Costume designers receive Academy Awards. When you are working on a production, see what tips you can pick up from the wardrobe design people. When I was doing my first film—*First Love,* directed by Joan Darling—on location in Oregon, Donfeld (nominated for an Academy Award for *Prizzi's Honor)* took me shopping to show me what styles would be good for me. I still use the information I learned that day; basic rules don't change.

• **Angela Lansbury**, film, stage and television star, said, "I made peace with myself early and decided I was going to be a rare bird." She understood her style and image and capitalized on it. She started acting at age 16 and made all the transitions, carrying her image with her.

• **Costume Designer Linda Serijan-Fasmer created the wardrobe designs for the first season of** *Felicity*.

  • **Felicity was a bit of a wallflower the first season.** She wasn't supposed to be too sexy or adorable looking. But Keri Russell looked gorgeous in almost everything we tried on her. Body-conscious clothes showed off her size 0 figure, so it became apparent that not only her legs, but also her waist would have to be off-limits. She's an extra small so we bought mediums. Everything was oversized. Flattering colors lit up her face, which meant that colors had to be restrained—navy, rust, olive, and burgundy. Felicity's closet revolved around pants (Levi's 501s were her favorite, followed by Army surplus or Abercrombie & Fitch khakis and other straight-legged pants), cotton shirts and dozens and dozens of sweaters—textured, nubby cardigans, turtlenecks and crew necks in patterns and earth-colored solids.

  • **We bought every DKNY turtleneck made.** Man-style shirts from stores such as the Gap, Banana Republic and Nordstrom were usually not tucked in. Every single one was recut to look somewhere between fitted and baggy, but never with darts. Darts are too sexy. Her shoes were strictly utilitarian, either Converse navy sneakers or Birkenstock boots or sandals.

  • **Keri was also a stickler for character consistency.** She didn't want to wear anything with stretch or sheen or big, groovy collars. She didn't wear anything in her hair or paint her nails. When I bought her a stainless steel Swiss Army watch, she didn't think it was right. "It's like, too much."

  • **Resident advisor Noel Crane** (Scott Foley) wore Big Star, Lucky and Diesel jeans because they are most flattering to the rear end.

• **See Photography Section,** for clothes to wear on your shoot.

• **Maddisen K. Krown** an actress in Los Angeles told me of her experience working with an Image Consultant.

> • **I was at a point last year** where I felt lost about my outer image. I was changing internally, but my wardrobe continued to reflect the old me. I heard about fashion designer and Wardrobe Therapist™ Kelima Fukumi and gave myself over to her and her amazing Wardrobe Therapy™ program. She listened and tuned into my inner changes, working closely with me to help create a new outer image.

> • **We emptied my closets** and put back only the items that met my new criteria: I must love the piece, it must be excellent quality and it must fit my inner image. I gave the rest away. Then I took the Image Book Kelima created for me and shopped for clothing using the same criteria. I transformed my outer image. The cool thing is, it continues to transform. Now, I have the knowledge and tools to match the outer with the inner changes as I evolve. I am more confident and am enjoying the edgier, more wildly feminine me. When I need it, I know I can contact Kelima for refresher consultations.

• **Maude Feil, costume designer, wardrobe specialist,** specializes in working with actors and actresses just starting to set their own style or in changing their style.

> • **I can put a man or woman together for about $1,000.** That includes my fee of $60 an hour. I know all the places downtown; I know where to get the look for less money. I work on commercials all the time and I'm used to staying within a budget. There are just certain wardrobe pieces you have to have. I work with all shapes, sizes and ages. If a client needs special hair and/or makeup styling, I bring in someone from one of the network shows I work on, to consult with them. That would be an extra cost of around $150.

> • **I don't work with color charts myself;** I find it too confining. But many times a client will give me their book of colors and I work within those colors for them.

> • **One of my clients called me recently because he wasn't happy** with the roles he had been auditioning for, strictly senators. He wanted a broader range. He has an abundance of white hair and a very tailored conservative East-coast look. I went through his closet, picked out some things he could use, got rid of some of the Brooks Bros. shirts. We added some soft t-shirts and softer clothes, and I advised a buzz cut for his hair. He is very pleased, has new pictures and now he is auditioning for and landing a wider variety of roles.

- **When I start working with someone, I get an idea of the look** they want to achieve, I pull magazine pictures, put them in a book. I'll look at their closet to see what they have. There are shopping, fittings, alterations, returns. I work with the client like I do when I am working for a director of a show.

• **Tom Baxter, Emmy-nominated wardrobe stylist, costume designer,** *Aldo Award* for "Most Influential Costumer in Fashion on Prime Time Television."

Q: What about audition clothes for the actor?

- **Let the dialogue in the script guide you.** For auditions, the actor should get the breakdown of the character from their agent and dress close to the person they are playing. For example:

- **Preppie, upwardly mobile, young male professional:** Go for the stereotype navy blue blazer, gray slacks, maybe a sweater vest with a tie and shirt, perhaps a crest on the blazer. A more casual look could be khaki pants, an oxford button-down shirt and a V-neck sweater. Visually, you need short to medium hair. If it says preppy and you have long hair, you might as well stay home, or wear a ponytail and tuck it in the back of your shirt.

- **A tough, over-the-hill broad:** if it's a comedy and the actress is busty, take advantage of that; a V-neck sweater and a pair of slacks with a big wide belt. She would be the girl sitting on a bar stool, 55 trying to look 35, with a cigarette hanging out of her mouth and a pink scarf tied around her neck. We did this exact look for an actress in *Pennies From Heaven.*

- **Upscale, trendy patron at an art museum:** For a woman 30-50, a suit would be nice; '40s gabardine styles obtained at resale or vintage stores. Guys in this setting can do it with a suit or khaki pants and a cotton blazer.

- **Men 21-50 with these few items can do anything.** A black blazer (sport coat), a navy blazer, one suit, a pair of khaki, grey, navy, black and white dress slacks. A business look with the suit, a nautical look with the blazer and white slacks (just stick a crest on the blazer on the pocket.) Put the black blazer with the black slacks and you have a black suit. The khakis with the black blazer and you have nice sporty look. Gray pants with the blue blazer you've got a nice business or preppy look.

- **Women's looks vary with their age**. 18-30 is one look, 30-50 is another look, and after 55 another look. Women need a rayon suit with a skirt. For the money, rayon looks and hangs the best and seems to be the easiest to alter. Make sure the skirt is a color that matches the jacket. Substitute a pair of slacks to make it more casual. A short or long black stretch evening dress for a young girl going up for sex-pot or modeling parts. Jeans, sweater or chambray shirt and sneakers. A sweatshirt for a housewife that lives next door. Secretary in a law firm, don't go in without a suit; you can always take the jacket off and put it on the back of the chair. It is a nice piece of business and something a secretary would do, unless you sit at the front desk—then it would stay on the whole time. Secretary in the car rental or super market manager's office: A skirt or a nice pair of slacks and blouse and cardigan or sweater vest. A tough secretary would wear jeans and sweater.

- **Gabrielle Zuccaro of Bleu Clothing** has advice for men's formal wear. My daughter Christina's husband Thomas Cobb is a graphic artist. Last year he was nominated for an Emmy and of course needed to wear a tuxedo to the ceremony. Gabrielle told Christina not to rent one because, "they are awful." She said, "Buy one at a department store have it altered to fit, then buy a beautiful black or dark gray shirt and a black tie. The black on black on black is a great look." It would serve an actor well to have good looking formal wear in his closet, you never know where you might be invited at a moment's notice and you can show up in "black tie" attire.

- **Illeana Douglas** (*Next Best Thing, Message in a Bottle, Grace of My Heart*) says she buys her t-shirts and sweaters in the children's department; "They fit much better."

- **The colors you wear** will determine how people perceive you: whether you look vibrant, washed out, cool or hot. This is valuable information when you are dressing to read for a specific role.

- **Have an expert or professional do your colors**. Your color consultant will hold different shades of all colors next to your face to see what looks best on you. Some color systems put people into four categories: fall, winter, spring or summer. Then there are variations within each season. (I'm a "gentle summer"; my husband is a "vibrant winter.") The expert will make an individualized color chart that you carry with you when shopping. If you stick to your color chart, you will be able to wear everything in your wardrobe mixed and matched; all your clothes will go together. This information will enable you to be a wise shopper and help minimize your expenses. Having your colors done is a one-time expense.

• **Know what your colors are** even when being photographed in B&W. You can help your professional makeup artist: When you sit in the makeup chair, describe what colors look best on you.

• **Jennifer Butler,** has a unique way of achieving color and style harmony for her clients. She has created a system of personalized design and color analysis that draws upon her 4,000 swatch color system. She gives a free seminar on colors and style once a month.

Q: Why are colors important?

- **How many times have you looked in your closet** and said, "I have nothing to wear!" even though you have a closet full of clothes. When you walk into a meeting, is your unspoken communication saying, "I'm approachable" or "Leave me alone!"? Do people think you are overpowering when your biggest challenge is overcoming shyness?

- **What may be a power color for one person** could signal romance in another. You can see what a dilemma this could cause. And if you send out the wrong messages, you may well be puzzled by other people's responses to you.

- **Have you ever noticed how one day** everyone you see tells you how great you look while on another day, you don't even get noticed? If you choose to wear clothes that are reflective of your personality and physical characteristics, you will experience more and more of those, "Gee, you look great" days. In fact, not only will those who see you notice how well you look but you, too, will see and feel the difference.

• **Color Consultant Jill Kirsh says:**

- **People think having their colors done can be very limiting,** that they can only wear a few colors, but what you see when you have your colors done is that everyone can wear every color. It is just finding the shade of the color that works best for you.

• **You can create different characters with the use of color.** When you have your colors done, you find out what colors make you look vibrant and alive, say for commercial auditions, but you also can create different effects for characters by using the wrong shade for you. What would you wear for a character that is out of step with the real world? For a trailer park resident? For a druggie? For a socialite? Homeless? Rich?

• **Tina Lynne, wardrobe stylist,** takes into account the color of your hair, eyes and skin though she doesn't adhere to a strict color palette. She believes everyone can wear certain shades of all colors.

Q: How do you dress a guy, 22-30, good looking, who has only worn jeans and t-shirts all of his life? What would it cost him to be "styled," including your fee and the clothes?

• **He will need a dressy look, a GQ look.** There is a great store called the Men's Warehouse. He can get a nice knock-off Italian suit that will make him look like a million bucks. Another basic sport coat, two pairs of pants, four shirts, four ties and one or two pairs of shoes, a nice belt, and he will look absolutely fabulous. The cost for the clothes might be $500. The cost for my services would be from $50 to $150 an hour, depending on where we have to go. For men, I also find the Beverly Center is a great place because they have hip looking, very Hollywood looking clothes. You don't have to get the name brands; you just have to know what looks good on you.

Q: How about an actress, thin, size 0-4, and 22 to 30, who doesn't know her image. How would you get her together for auditions?

• **When a woman walks into an audition,** she should be dressed for the part and comfortable with the type of person she's trying to portray. I coach them on how to wear the clothes and to project the image they want to sell. Depending on the build, the coloring and whether they have a hard or a soft look will determine whether we create a floral or a very simple kind of look.

• **Looking finished, put together, color coordinated** is probably one of the biggest keys in landing a role. Look at soap operas. When they decided to spend a great deal of money on the clothing, accessories, hair and sets, daytime TV changed forever and the ratings became huge.

• **If the client is on a budget,** I take them through Neiman Marcus and Saks Fifth Avenue so they can see what is available and what they like. That takes half an hour. Then I take them to a store that is reasonably priced and we match the look. You start with two skirts, two jackets, four tops, two pairs of shoes, one pants suit and two bags. You have one black dress. You can do this at a place like Ross or Loehmann's for $500, versus one Armani jacket for $1,000.

• **Loehmann's is a great place to start** because they have the more expensive clothing at a quarter of the price and you can get some fabulous basic clothes there. Jones of New York and Tahari (brands available at Macy's and Bloomingdale's) make some classy stuff that looks like Armani but is a quarter of the price. Marshall's and Ross are also good. You have to take the time to go through everything.

- **Dino Calabrese, clothing designer** and wardrobe, hair and makeup stylist, gives the following hints for actors with limited funds for clothes.

  - **Thrift store shopping is great.**

  - **Both men and women** should own: a pair of black slacks; a nice denim jacket, oversize so you can layer it; a pair of jeans; and a nice basic blazer, whether it's oversized or not, in rayon, not wool. Something in black is good and primary colors are good too. Combine colors, layer tank tops and t-shirts. Keep the same types of textures in your wardrobe; mix and match silks with lighter-weight rayons or cottons.

  - **A basic skirt** should be gabardine or a lightweight fabric to wear with silk. Wear a t-shirt with the skirt and thick obi belt and you have a nice casual look.

  - **Everyone should have a white shirt.** Plain form-fitting t-shirts can be worn under the shirt. Women need an A-line black dress. A pair of colored hose makes one outfit, belt it for another look, wear it as a tunic over a pair of bell-bottoms or pajama pants. A string of pearls works with a dress, sweater or t-shirt. Plain black boots with a medium heel to wear with skirts and pants are a necessity. Same with men— basic black boot; wear with tuxedo or jeans. Always keep shoes cleaned and shined and clothes pressed.

  - **Take t-shirts**, skirts and jackets all in the same fabrics but different colors to mix and match. Use blue, green and yellow and tie it together with a multicolored belt and you look great but if the texture's off, it doesn't work.

- **David R. Zyla was a fashion designer** and owned his own Seventh Avenue Fashion Company in New York. But what he loves best and has devoted his career to is helping people with their color palettes and planning wardrobes and home and business environments. He works with many, many celebrities. I asked him to talk about how he chooses the color palette.

  - **The first session is about two hours long.** I look at their skin, eye and hair colors. Everyone has a romantic, dramatic and tranquil color. There are about ten groups of color. I explain how to use each of these colors. At the end of the session, I tell them what type they are and the artist their palette is based on. I also go over a five-page checklist of the fabrics that will look best on them. We look at the types of patterns in fabrics that will work well. Some people will be able to wear sporadic confetti patterns, others look best in a tight geometric pattern. Some clients may not get many patterns in their palette; it depends on their type. I talk about the historical periods that relate to their type. That doesn't mean you run around in costume but if Grecian is one of your periods, the way to translate that would be in a crossover leotard top or a sandal evening shoe.

Q: Tell me a little about using the colors.

• The first basic color is your "black" and is a neutral. The second basic is your "brown," a little less formal and an everyday neutral. The third basic is your least formal neutral or your "khaki." The skin tone color is always flattering and is your version of "white." The eye color tone has a calming effect. The dramatic color is worn whenever a strong impression is desired. The tranquil color can be used whenever a subordinated effect is desired.

IMAGE MAKERS
Wardrobe consultants and Image Makers are listed in The Working Actor's Guide (WAG) and trade ads.

Kelima Fukumi, 323/363-1402. In New York, 212/207-6607. www.kelima.com. Image Make-overs, wardrobe design and personal shopping. Fashion designer and Wardrobe Therapist™ Kelima expertly walks you through the process of establishing a new self image, one that is aligned with your dreams and goals. She loves to help people who are looking for a dramatic change, or who have no idea what their image is. She helps you discover who you are and then guides you in selecting the correct clothing, accessories and attitude to project that image.

Bleu Clothing, owned by Gabrielle Zuccaro, 323/939-2228. 454 S. La Brea, Los Angeles. Bleu is one of the Editor's Picks in the book, *Where To Wear L.A. Shopping Guide.* My daughters are wild about her clothes and her eye for design. Cathy Kerr was at the Oscars last year, all over the red carpet and on all the preshows' cameras. Gabrielle had styled her, including what makeup to wear and what to do with her hair. She looked great, easily competing with the women who had spent many thousands of dollars. Gabrielle will help you find your own personal style. Twice a year she holds not-to-be-missed sales. Get on her mailing list.

Janice McCarty, 310/393-6858. www.janicemccartydesigns.com. 912 Montana Ave., Santa Monica, near 9th Street. Open M-Sa, 11-6. They are known for their classic and "modern retro" styles, sometimes using both vintage and unique buttons. They offer in-house production and personalized fitting. Styles that enhance a good figure and are forgiving to problem areas. Sizes 2-18+, ages 20 to 89. Large selection of fabrics. Rush 24-hour turnaround, if needed. They work with costumers, wardrobers, stylists and personal shoppers. Loves rayon. Call to get on her mailing list. Occasionally does free workshops with Jill Kirsh of The Color Company

Jennifer Butler, Color and Wardrobe Expert, 323/931-2626. 20 years experience in the art of color and design. She offers extensive services and is an expert on your whole image. She has introductory free seminars each month. She does wardrobe consultations, color palette design, shopping excursions and wardrobe classes. She can send you a brochure outlining her many excellent services. Very highly recommended. Why not check out her free seminar, you will gain new knowledge.

Deborah Gordon, Flying Colors, 818/784-2939. Wonderful color palettes. She creates quite a spectacular color notebook for your use. Call her studio for full information on her services.

Maude Feil, 310/545-0882 She will rearrange your closets and put together outfits so you won't have to wonder what goes with what; go shopping with you; in fact, she will shop and bring you the things to try on and return what doesn't fit or you don't like. It is more expensive that way, but working actors often don't have the time to shop.

Jill Kirsh's, The Color Company, 818/760-7798. www.jillkirshcolor.com. $150 for a color consultation. Featured in *L.A. Magazine, The Best of L.A. List*. Jill is known as the "guru of hue." She drapes you with all the colors and picks out the shades of each color that are best for you, making a swatch book for you to carry. For men, she uses suit fabrics to show what works best for them. She helps actors choose the right colors for audition clothes. She has developed her own makeup line and included in the fee, she does your makeup showing you the shades that are right for you.

Tina Lynne, Style Consultant, 323/939-9117. A specialist in the complete makeover, she can put you together from the inside out. She loves new actors and people new to town and is willing to work within a fairly small budget. Says she shops all the time and knows what is out there in the stores.

David R. Zyla, 310/769-7613 or 212/802-9237. Email: davidzyla@msn.com. Initial Color Palette and Style Session, $395. Palette Extension, $295. Personal Shopping/ Interior Design, $195 an hour. Package #1, Color Palette and three hours shopping, $800. Package #2, Color Palette Extension and two hours shopping, $500. I had my colors done years ago and had gotten out of the habit of using them. I had David do them and got excited again about wearing colors. My daughter, Catherine, was in a "what to wear, what to buy" slump, with a closet full of clothes, but she still felt she had nothing to wear. After he did her colors and closet, she said she could always find something to wear and knew what to buy to make all of her things work together.

WEB NEWSLETTER AND RADIO SHOW

Best Bargains by Geri Cook and Suzanne Conner, www.bargainsla.com. Their radio show is on Saturday mornings, KRLA, 870AM on the dial. They have only the highest quality of bargains. Subscribe to their free email bargain newsletter at the website.

SERVICES
• CLOTHING DESIGN

CoCo O'Connor of CoCo Jeans, 818/754-2558. She paints, beads and personalizes jeans, using your own or her vintage Levis. $45 to $90 a pair. "Wear Your Art."

Shawnelle Eveningwear, 310/230-2032. She specializes in costume design for feature films and evening gowns for award shows. Gowns average $800. She also does consultations for auditions and specializes in character development through wardrobe. By appointment only.

• ALTERATIONS AND CLEANERS

5 Star Cleaners & Laundry, 818/506-8960. 4356 Laurel Canyon Blvd., Studio City, 91604. M-F 6:30-8; Sa 6:30-6; Su 9-5. Great service and great prices! Alterations.

Suke at Beachwood Cleaners, 323/467-0021. 2699 N. Beachwood Dr., Hollywood Hills. Great cleaning, fast alterations and inexpensive.

International Custom Tailors, 818/509-9032. 12075 Ventura Place, Studio City. Good prices. He can alter just about anything beautifully. They are great people.

Golden Needle Tailoring, 323/666-3365. 2044 Hillhurst Ave., L.A. Expert tailor, can loosen trousers without making them baggy.

Studio Cleaners, 818/505-0828. 11302 Ventura Blvd. at Eureka, across from Bally's. $1.50 per item. Surprisingly good work. Very good alterations.

• EYEGLASSES

Oliver Peoples, 310/657-2553. www.oliverpeoples.com. The absolute best in eyeglasses. You really can tell the difference. They are very expensive but guaranteed and they will fix them up if they get twisted or broken. I love mine and will always have a pair. Their non-glare coating is really the best.

Westside Opticians, 323/653-0243. 817 N. Fairfax, Los Angeles, 90046. M,Tu,F 9-5; Th 10-7; Sa 9-1; closed W & Su. The best styles for good prices. Jeff can fix anything.

Happy Eyes,818/246-2202. www.happyeyesoptical.com. 114 E. Wilson, Glendale. Recommended in Geri Cook's Best Bargains, Tony the owner is very helpful. Great bargains and great styles.

• SHOE REPAIR

Sunset Shoe Repair, Manuel Keshishian, 323/654-7743. 8036 Santa Monica Blvd., L.A., 90046. (Crescent Heights & Santa Monica) "We rebuild your shoes like new." There has never been a shoe or purse problem this man couldn't fix for me.

Garbo Shoe Repair, 310/394-6306. 1450 4th St., at Broadway, Santa Monica, 90401. Very reasonably priced. "If your shoes are uncomfortable, he won't let you out of here until he's got the pad just right."

• LUGGAGE SALES AND REPAIRS

Beverly Hills Luggage and Gift Shop, 310/273-5885, www.beverlyhills.com. 404 N. Beverly Dr., Beverly Hills. Expensive but great.

H. Savinar, 323/938-2501. 4625 W. Washington Blvd., between Crenshaw and LaBrea, L.A. Valley store: 818/703-1313. 6931 Topanga Canyon Blvd., Canoga Park. 30%-50% off Tumi, Hartmann, Boyt, etc. Also replacement hardware.

Langers Luggage Shop & Handbag Hospital, 323/512-4710. 1512 Gardner St. Los Angeles, 90046. The best; they can fix anything. If you ever have luggage damage at the airport, report it, then take it straight to Langers; they take care of everything.

Luggage For Less, 818/760-1360. www.luggage4less.com. 5144 Lankershim, near Magnolia, North Hollywood. Do not buy luggage until you check this place out.

• WIGS

J & J Wigs of Hollywood, (men and women) 323/466-0617. 6324 Hollywood Blvd., 90028. Rent a wig for photo shoots for $25 or $29 and they will style it and put it on you. They have wigs to buy for as little as $35. You can get a good one for $60-$70. The real hair and hand-tied ones go for up to $250.

Naimie's Film & Television Beauty Supply. 818/655-9922. 12640 Riverside Dr. North Hollywood, 91607. Second location: 818/763-7073. 12801 Victory Blvd., North Hollywood, 91606. Discounts for actors.

Wilshire Wigs, 800/927-0874. www.wilshirewigs.com. 5241 Craner Avenue, North Hollywood. M-F9-5:30; Sa 9-4. One block east of Vineland, off Magnolia.

TRENDY/UPSCALE/RESALE/VINTAGE/THRIFT SHOPS

Geri Cook's Best Bargains, 310/203-9233. www.bargainsla.com. This is a must for truly good shopping! Bargains on everything.

The Ultimate Consignment & Thrift Store Guide, www.consignmentguide.com. Many links to other shopping information all over the country.

Aardvark's Odd Ark, (men & women) 323/655-6769. 7579 Melrose Ave., 90046. M-Th 12-8; F-Sa 11-9; Su 12-7. Other location: 310/392-2996. 85 Market St., Venice, 90291. Every day 11-7. Vintage and regular clothes.

Alice & Annie's, 818/761-6085. 11056 Magnolia Blvd., North Hollywood. Vintage, antique clothing. 1870's-1970's including couture hats, gloves, gowns. 12-6 Th-Sa, and sometimes open on Sundays. Love this place.

Armani Wells, (men) 818/985-5899. www.armaniwells.com. 12404 Ventura Blvd., Studio City, 91604. M-Sa 11-6.

American Rag, (men & women) 323/935-3154. 150 S. La Brea Ave., L.A., 90036. M-Sa 10-9; Su 12-7.

Baba's, (women) 310/360-9494. 517 N. La Cienega Blvd., West Hollywood. Custom couture, exquisite fabrics, and warm salon. Custom prices start at $350.

Becca's Chic Boutique, 818/703-0151. 19822 Ventura Blvd., Woodland Hills, 91364. T-Sa 10-6.

Cherie, (women) 818/508-1628. 12526 Ventura Blvd., Studio City, 91604. T-Sa 10-5. Very upscale designer clothes on consignment.

Cinema Glamour Shop (men & women) 323/933-5289. www.cinemaglamourshop.com. 343 N. La Brea Ave. (just north of Beverly), L.A. M-F, 10-4. Designer and vintage wear. Many stars donate their clothes; proceeds benefit the Motion Picture Home. They provide clothing to extras at affordable prices. They are having super sales on the last Saturdays of the month. Call first.

Claudia's Boutique,(men, women & children) 818/980-3473. 11930 Ventura Blvd., Studio City, 91604. M-Sa 10:30-7; Su 12-5. Really packed in tight, but she seems to know where everything is.

Collectible Glitz-Miss La De Das, 818/347-9343. 21435 Sherman Way, Canoga Park,Calif. 91303. One block west of Canoga Ave. M-Sa. 10-6; Su 11:30-5. The greatest and best priced vintage jewelry in LA, many believe. Huge selection available with jewelry arranged by color and type. Specializes in vintage jewelry, costume jewelry and sterling silver. A little new modern jewelry is also available.

Council Thrift Shops, (men and women) 310/477-9613, 11571 Santa Monica Blvd., 323/938-8122, 1049 S. Fairfax Ave., L.A., 90019. Also 818/997-8980, 14526 Victory, North Hollywood. Also 323/654-8516, 7818 Santa Monica Blvd., West Hollywood, 90046. This is one of my favorites, really good brands at low cost. Excellent men's sport coats and suits. They will pick up your donations. They provide clothes for homeless women and children.

Fashion Institute of Los Angeles Scholarship Store (FIDM), (men and women) 213/624-1201. www.fidm.com. 919 So. Grand, Los Angeles. M-T 9-5; F 9-4; only one Sat. per month—call for date. The institute operates a year-round fund-raiser to support their scholarship programs. Local manufacturers and retailers donate new merchandise, some quality, some irregulars and the public is invited for some excellent bargains.

Great Labels, 310/451-2277. 1126 Wilshire Blvd., Santa Monica. M-F 10-7; Sa 10-6; Su 12-5. 11th and 12th parking in rear of building.

Heaven 27, 323/871-9044. 6316 Yucca Street, Hollywood. Sofia Coppola, daughter of director Francis Ford Coppola owns this shop. She designs panty camisole sets, knit caps, logo tees, hooded sweatshirts and other things. Prices range from $20 for a t-shirt to $150 for a denim jacket. M-Sa 12-6.

Hubba Hubba, 818/845-0636. 3220 W. Magnolia Blvd., Burbank. Vintage 30's-60's clothing in good condition. Average selling price $50.

Iguana Vintage Clothing, (Men and women) 818/907-6716. www.iguanaclothing.com. 14422 Ventura Blvd., Sherman Oaks, 91403. Styles of the '40s, '50s and '60s. M-Th 11-7; F & Sa 11-8; Su 11-6. This is a huge store, very organized. Great shopping.

It's A Wrap! (men & women) 818/567-7366. www.itsawraphollywood.com. 3315 W. Magnolia Blvd. Burbank, 91505. M-Sa 11-6; Su 11-4. Large busy store; they have a lot of clothes from the film and television industry. Definitely a place to take people visiting from your hometown.

Jet Rag, 323/939-0528. 825 N. La Brea, Los Angeles. M-Sa. 11:30-8. They have everything from every era. For current and vintage styles. Winona Ryder, Juliette Lewis and Drew Barrymore have been known to stop in.

Junk for Joy, (men & women) 818/569-4903. 3314 W. Magnolia, Burbank, 91505. Tu-Sa 12-5. New and used vintage fashions, footwear & accessories. Kimonos, junk jewelry, gloves, bow ties, spats, hats and eyeglasses. Silly and ugly clothing of good and bad taste.

Lisa's N.Y. Style Resale, 818/788-2142. 13541 Ventura Blvd., Sherman Oaks. M-Sa 10-6. The clothing is top quality, and leans toward the exotic.

Nena's Fashions, (over 40 crowd) 562/697-7885. 581 W. La Habra Blvd., La Habra 90631. M,W,F,Sa 10-5; T-Th 11-5. The specialty at Nena's is the Levi bend-over pants, the pants that fit most women's bodies and which are hard to come by. They mail these pants all over the country, but at the store, you can try them on. They also come in every color. Sizes 4-24. 49 Years in business.

Out of the Closet thrift stores benefiting AIDS patients. 323/934-1956. 360 N. Fairfax Ave, West L.A. 323/466-7601. 1408 Vine. St., Hollywood. www.aidshealth.org. Many other locations.

P.J. London, (women) 310/826-4649. www.pjlondon.com. 11661 San Vicente Blvd., Los Angeles, 90049. M-Sa 10:30-6; Su 12-5. Highest fashion, lowest prices for clothes.

The Paper Bag Princess, 310/358-1985. www.thepaperbagprincess.com. 8700 Santa Monica Blvd., West Hollywood. Very upscale; shoppers are said to be: Elle MacPherson, Shalom Harlow, Demi Moore, Elisabeth Shue, Parker Posey, Courtney Love, Madonna, Sofia Coppola, Jennifer Nicholson. Puccis, Pradas, Guccis, prices range from $25 to $6,000.

Pasadena City College Flea Market, 626/585-7906. Pasadena City College, 1570 E. Colorado Blvd. at S. Hill Ave., Pasadena. 8-3 on first Sunday of the month. Like garage sales, it's free and showcases a somewhat haphazard mix of merchandise, offered by established circuit dealers and casual sellers who strew goods on the ground. The market is in four sections, three along the S. Hill Ave. side of the campus and the fourth off Bonnie Ave.

Playclothes, 818/755-9559. 11422 Moorpark, Studio City. Vintage fashions from the 30's to 60's. Some children's clothing. Good prices.

Polka Dots & Moonbeams, 323/651-1746. 8367 W. 3rd, Los Angeles, 90048 . Great vintage and funky new clothes for women. Great selection of vintage hats, bags, jewelry too.

Ragtime Cowboy, 818/769-6552. 5213 Lankershim Blvd., North Hollywood. Vintage clothing & costumes. This is one of the first vintage clothing stores in NoHo.

Ragtime on Green, 626/796-9924. 1136 E. Green St., Pasadena. Tu,Th F 10-5; W 10-6; Sa 10-3. Jammed with inventory with low prices. Brand names, also.

Reel Clothes, (men and women) 818/508-7762. www.rellclothes.com. 5525 Cahuenga Blvd. North Hollywood, 91601. M-Sa 10-6; Su 12-5. Clothes that are returned from film and television sets. I have good luck with men's clothes here.

Repeat Performance, (men & women) 323/938-0609. 318 N. La Brea, Los Angeles, 90038. By appt. only. Fine vintage clothing and accessories in perfect condition. Specializing in '40s & '50s attire. No Rentals.

Rose Bowl Flea Market, 323/560-7469. Rose Bowl Dr., Pasadena. More than 1,500 vendors. Second Sunday of every month.

Ross, 1-800-945-7677. www.rossstores.com. Men and women's new clothing, including women's plus sizes; home accessories.

Sacks SFO, (men and women) New clothing with extraordinary deals. SFO locations: 818/506-4787. 12021 Ventura Blvd., Studio City; 310/559-5448. 9608 Venice Blvd., Culver City; 323/939-3993.

Star Wares, 818/707-8500. Internet only. www.starwares.com. They only sell items that celebrities have worn or owned, movie wardrobe and props.

The Address (women), 310/394-1406. www.theaddressboutique.com. 1116 Wilshire Blvd., Santa Monica. M-Sa 10-6; Su 12-5. Clothes from very wealthy women who can't be seen in the same outfit twice, plus new clothes.

The Place and Company, (men and women) 310/645-1539. www.theplaceandco.com. 8820 S. Sepulveda Blvd., Los Angeles, 90045. (Half block south of La Tijera). M-Sa 10-6. 75% off the original price for suits worn by Jay Leno (44 long) and Pat Sajak. The best bargains.

DISCOUNT SHOPS

Citadel Factory Outlet Stores, 323/888-1220. www.citadeloutlets.com. Right off the I-5, Los Angeles. From I-5 southbound, exit at Washington Blvd. From I-5 northbound, exit at Atlantic Blvd. North. M-Sa 10-8; Su 10-6. 44 stores. Ann Taylor, Geoffrey Beene, Bass, Eddie Bauer, Gap, Harve Bernard, United Colors of Benetton and many others.

DNA, 310/399-0341. 411 Rose Ave., Venice. For jeans and t-shirts, everything from Calvin Klein to Point Zero, for less. Joseph jeans, normally $89, and Big Star jeans, $120, are only $14.99 and $39.99. Weaver's soft cotton loose-fitting t-shirts are three for $10.

Dressed Up!, 818/708-7238. www.dressed-up.com. 6000 Reseda Blvd., Tarzana. M-Sa. 10-5:30; Sun. 11:30-4:30. "L.A.'s only evening wear superstore." Designer dresses, cocktail suits, formal gowns and evening separates.

Foot Locker Outlet, 310/450-8178. www.footlocker.com. 115 Lincoln Blvd., Venice. 30%-50% off Nike, Reebok, Adidas, K-Swiss, LA Gear and others.

Loehmann's, 310/659 0674. www.loehmanns.com. 333 S. La Cienega, 90048. Just south of 3rd St. and across from the Beverly Center. M-Sa 10-9; Su 11-7. This is where Tina Lynne brings her image clients that are on a budget.

Marshall's, 800/627-7425. www.marshallsonline.com. Call for store locations and complete information.

Marrika Nakk, 323/882-8278. www.marrikanakk.com. Very romantic, beautiful clothes. Call and get on her phone list and they will call to tell you of their sometime sales at her house in West Hollywood. Fabulous bargains!

Nordstrom Rack, (men, women & children) 818/884-6771. www.nordstrom.com. 21490 Victory Blvd., Woodland Hills, 91367. M-F 10-9; Sa 10-8; Su 11-7. Plus other locations. You can find real treasures here.

Rick Pallack, (men only) 818/789-7000. 4554 Sherman Oaks Avenue, Sherman Oaks, 91403. They dress all the stars and design movie wardrobes. Twice a year they have a huge sale. Take advantage of looking like you are a successful actor. M,Tu,W,F 10-7; Th 10-7; Sa 10-6.

Sichel Promotional Sportswear, 818/255-0862. www.sichel.net. 10847 Sherman Way, Burbank, 91352. They make many of the T-shirts, caps and jackets for film and TV crews. About two weeks before Christmas they put a couple of racks on the sidewalk filled with the left overs. They are a steal, relatives back home love to get these treasures. M-F 9-5.

TJ Maxx Stores, for locations 800/285-6299. www.tjmaxx.com. In Culver City, 310/390-7944. Pavilion Shopping Center, 11020 W. Jefferson Blvd. & Sawtelle Blvd., north of Fox Hills Mall.

COSTUMES AND PERIOD CLOTHES
RENTAL AND SALES

CRC Costume Rentals Corporation. Rental only. 818/753-3700. www.costumerentalscorp.com. 11149 Vanowen Street., North Hollywood, 91605. Huge! Uniforms/research library, check them out.

Glendale Costumes, 818/244-1161. www.thecostumeshopp.com. 746 W. Doran, Glendale, 91203. Tu-F 12-7; Sa 12-6. Good prices.

Hollywood Toys & Costumes, 323/465-3119. www.hollywoodtoys.com. 6600 Hollywood Blvd., Hollywood, 90028. 4 blks. E. of Highland. 9:30-7 M-Sa; 10:30-7 Su. They have a huge selection.

Magic World Costuming, 818/700-8100. 10122 Topanga Canyon, Chatsworth. Rental: M-F 10-6; Sa 9-5:30. Retail: M-F 7:30-6:30; Sa 9-6.

Western Costume Co., Rental only 818/760-0902. www.westerncostume.com. 11041 Vanowen, North Hollywood, 91605. M-F 8-6. Probably the most famous and most expensive. They have everything you could possibly need.

HAIR STYLISTS,
MANICURISTS AND WAXING

For makeup stylists, eyebrows and makeup resources, see Section Two.

• **As an actor, how you look** has a great deal to do with getting your career moving. You need a hair stylist who can be trusted to deliver your hair the way you want it each and every time they work on you. Sometimes you are hired for a role two or three months ahead of time and the director expects you to show up looking the same as when they hired you. You want a hair stylist who will please you if you are maintaining a look, as well as contribute their own ideas on how to develop the unique "you" to the fullest. Cultivate your relationship with this most valuable person on your team of personal professionals.

• **Fernando Dejesus of the West End Salon** talks about hair:

  • **It is important to have the right look** when showing up for a casting call. Style, shape and color should be current with today's fashion world. The product you could sell or the series you could star in partly relies on your look. Updating your image can make the difference in a director casting you for the role that may have gone to someone else.

  • **A step beyond the new haircut is the color.** Not only can it highlight your features but it can actually change your image from comic, to that zany redhead! You can be as subtle as going from mousey brown to golden brunette. Take a good look at who is making it and ask yourself. "Does their look play a big part in their success?" "Yes!"

Stan Vogel (a/k/a Red), one of my favorite hair stylists, comments:

  • **If there's anything constant**, it's the change on a man's head of hair. Whether he likes it or not it thins out, he loses it, the hairline changes, grey starts coming in. Men aren't that knowledgeable about what hair

450

can do, so they need a lot more instruction. They might appear to be easier to deal with, but it's hard for them to accept change. Women are more adaptable. Culturally, it's cooler for women to color their hair, and we're getting there as far as men go; there is progress.

• **Attitude is everything. You can wear your hair the way you want,** as long as you have the right attitude about yourself. Barbra Streisand does all kinds of things with her hair and none of it is really right, but it's right because she's got the right attitude. If you're not satisfied within, it doesn't matter what you do on the exterior. All's fair in love and hair!

Resources

The following professional hair stylists work with men and women.

Stan Vogel (a/k/a Red) at Louis Michael Salon, 310/275-1322. 413 N. Canon Dr., Beverly Hills, 90210. A good guy, never runs late, never cuts too much, very talented in all areas of hair work, a color expert. I love the highlighting he does for me and when I was a redhead, he kept it the perfect red. He blows hair really straight. Because I have curly hair, this is important to me; not everyone can do it. He's fun and easy to be with. *See his comments above.*

Object Beauty Shop, 323/852-0978. 8237 W. Third St., L.A., 90048, at Sweetzer. Cuts start at $45. My daughters, long-haired Cathy Kerr and thin-haired Cynthia Kerr, love Hiroshi (his cuts are $50); he never cuts too short and you don't have to wait a long time for an appointment. Cynthia loves his special highlights. They rave about the massage shampoos. Hiroshi is a surfer so if you love the ocean you'll love this shop.

U Salon, 310/204-4995. 1772 S. Robertson Blvd., Los Angeles. Cut and blow dry is $26-$37 depending on hair length. $26 to blow long hair straight. Highlights only $54 to $64. This is a wonderful place to save money and get the latest fashion updates. Owned by Umberto's of Beverly Hills. I understand that the creme of the crop hair stylists work here developing their skills so they can move up to Umbertos. My friends Elizabeth Beim and Linda Small love it. Linda, especially, loves Daniel. "For short hair the price is $26, so after tips I walked out feeling fabulous for $33." I've heard nothing but raves about this place and they are open on Sundays and Mondays—seven days a week.

Borealis Holistic Artistry, Lisa Lowe, 310/260-2556. 1460 7th St., Santa Monica, 90401. For men and women. She is a very special stylist. Hair Balancing is the most sensitive and life-enhancing hair care system in the world. It is a holistic healing art that involves cutting the hair using the principles of Sacred Geometry, and is designed to achieve healthy, vibrant and beautiful hair. Each hair is balanced to every other hair on your head. The hair is cut vertically, horizontally and diagonally. With "hair balancing" you can expect these benefits: hair designs tailored to you, wash and wear hair, artful "grow-outs," reduces hair loss, hair grows thicker and faster, enhances curl and wave, maintains shape longer than other hair cuts. I love to have my hair balanced. Many people with thinning or unmanageable hair have benefited greatly. Also natural enzyme hair coloring.

Art Luna, 310/247-1383. 8930 Keith Ave., West Hollywood. Cuts $100-$200, color, $150 and up. Clientele includes Claire Dane, Kelly Lynch and Candice Bergen.

The Barber Shop Club, 323/939-4319. 6907 Melrose Ave., West Hollywood. Hot-towel shaves, shoe shines and games of chess. Listen to jazz while getting a haircut. Shaquille O'Neil, David Arquette and Vince Vaughn all are clients. *Featured on www.dailycandy.com.*

Brenda Ferreira at Studio B, owner/stylist, 310/395-8025. 1512 11th Street, Suite 206, Santa Monica, 90405. All services. She can be very trendy, if you want that. She will teach you how to style and manage the hairstyle she gives you. Her background is as an image consultant for men and women. She is good to talk to about how you look and how you would like to look. Great with men.

Byron Studio, 310/276-4470. 407 North Robertson Blvd., Beverly Hills. Small, three-chair, Zen-like studio offering haircuts, styling, color and makeup. Byron Williams has styled Rene Russo, Sharon Stone, Salma Hayek, Kirsten Dunst and Robin Wright Penn. *Featured on www.dailycandy.com.*

Colin Booker, 310/657-9172. Works privately through referrals. He works on many film and television productions including *Fraser*. Specializes in makeovers and rede-signing your whole "look." Very highly recommended by actress/coach, Caryn West. She recently did a redesign for her color photos taken by Klint Spillsbury, www.xlint.com, who works closely with Colin.

Julia Clay, 323/633-7328. Private and makes house calls. Highly recommended by stylist/facialist Tina Lynne. She is known for her transition free highlights and her unharsh custom coloring, she is an artist in all of her hair work and also has reason-able prices. Offers complimentary consultation.

Elements Spa and Salon, 323/933-0212, at Farmer's Market Place, Los Angeles. Richard Dalton was the official hairdresser to Diana, Princess of Wales for ten years. Providing glamour and the highest levels of service in a descreet, sleek environment. *Featured on dailycandy.com.*

Fernando Dejesus, The West End Salon, 310/855-0048. 520 N. La Cienega Blvd., West Hollywood, 90048 Fernando is from London; he specializes in corrective hair coloring. Beautiful custom stylized work. One of my students took in a magazine cover picture of Elizabeth Hurley to match the color and style; she got beautiful results.

Linda Kammins' Aromatherapy Salon, 310/659-6257. www.lindakammins.com. Th-Sa 11-6. 848 N. La Cienega Blvd., Suite 204, Los Angeles, 90069. Hair cut is $65, aromatherapy is $45. Services: Aromatherapy hair and scalp oil treatments; aromatherapy hair loss treatment, enzyme hair coloring and hair painting, herb coloring and texture developing, expert artistic hair cutting and styling, hair painting-botanical color, herbal facials, custom-blended aromatherapy beauty products. She brings thinning hair back!

Mauro, 310/273-0600. www.maurohair.com. 421 N. Rodeo Drive, Rodeo Collec-tion, Beverly Hills, 90210. Consultation on a new look, 30 minutes, $65. Restyling (first time clients) $80. Cut and blow-dry (existing clients) $75. Up-do from $75 -

$125. Full weave from $125-$225, partial weave, $125. Color correction (per hour) $80. My friend, Samantha Harper, has been loving his work for years. He does many celebrities as well as new actors just creating their individual "look." He has developed a great product line, as well. For information: 800/42-MAURO.

Pingatore Vern Salon, 323/932-8376. 7961 W. Third Street, Los Angeles. Enter from Edinburgh Ave. and go up the outdoor staircase. Gene Forget for men and women's great haircuts and expert color work in a low-key environment. Reasonable prices. Steven Nash says, "Gene is a skilled artist and cares a lot. He is especially sensitive to your special showbiz needs."

Quy Phu Nguyen of Empire Salon, 949-261-5856. 2967 Michelson, Suite K, Irvine, 92612. Monday thru Friday. Robin Gee says, "Quy gives great contemporary, fashionable haircuts that are easy to manage and to do yourself. He has a good sense of trends and being current. He listens to what you want, but always has great ideas of his own for you to consider." On Saturdays there is a special bargain at a salon that specializes in Asian women. $25 for haircut, shampoo and blow dry at Mossemo Hair Studio, 714-839-3738. 9433 Bolsa Ave. Suite #E, Westminster, 92683.

Rosiland Mitchell at Carlton's Hair Salon, 818/986-8750. www.carltonhair.com 14006 Riverside Dr., #249, Sherman Oaks, in Fashion Square Mall. She also has good products. Hair cuts start at $50. Highly recommended by makeup artist Rita Montanez.

Rudolfo David of Hair Design Studio, 818/754-4080. 12073 Ventura Place, Studio City 91607. Private salon by recommendation. Photographer, actor, Sean Kenney highly recommends his work.

Yuki's, 310/652-7474. 8640 Sunset Blvd., Sunset Plaza, L.A., 90069. Don Moran is very famous for color; he used to do Marilyn Monroe's hair. This is a very well known salon, lots of celebrities.

MANICURISTS AND WAXING

Chinoiseri, 818/752-4347. 12246 Ventura Blvd., Studio City. Sharon Stone says, "Tammie Ly will create any nail color polish you want.

Esfir Tselner of Esther's Place, 310/274-4552. 9399 Wilshire, #205, at Canon Drive. Hair removal. Legs and bikini lines, $40. "My customers tell me I don't hurt them as much as other people do."

Yolanda Frye Skin Care, 310/275-3981. 632 1/2 Doheny Dr, Los Angeles, 90069. She does manicures, pedicures and acrylics. Cathy and Chris Kerr love her weekly manicures. Cathy often has a manicure and pedicure when returning from a long, exhausting business trip; it perks her right up. Waxing, men and women.

WORKOUTS, EXERCISE AND DANCE

• **All actors need some type** of body movement class at least twice a week for body awareness, five times a week to change their bodies. The purpose of this is to become acquainted with every muscle and tendon. Acting is physical work, and if you don't know your body, you are denying a great many tools that could be available to you.

• **Working as an actor has a lot to do with how you look**, your weight, your health, discipline and stamina. There is no way to get around building your body and staying toned. If you don't have a steady, consistent work out program you will probably not be a working actor.

• **Glenn Close,** when talking about doing the stage play *Sunset Boulevard,* made these comments.

> • **It takes a great deal of stamina to do a play.** If I didn't do something physical every day, I wouldn't be able to make it through the show. You know those stairs you see me climbing? There are just as many stairs offstage that I climb to get to those stairs. I do a yoga class for forty-five minutes before each show. We do five shows each weekend. When working, I don't smoke or drink and eat very, very healthy. I have this policy that I can have two Oreos each performance. One of the things that gets me through the weekend is that I know I can have four Oreos on Saturday and four on Sunday.

• **Michael Richards,** who played Kramer on *Seinfeld,* introduced me to the practice of yoga. He is in such great shape, he can make his body do anything. In addition to his hour daily practice, he does a half hour of restorative yoga positions before each performance. Yoga enables him to do all of his physical comedy and not get hurt. He practices on his own, but when he takes a class it's at the B.K.S. Iyengar Yoga Institute.

• **Jerry Seinfeld** loves to exercise. Swimming, weights, treadmill, Nordic track and some yoga stretching before and after his workouts. During *Seinfeld,* he worked with a trainer at 6:30 AM. Jerry had a very tough schedule. Along with writing, casting, acting, editing, and promoting *Seinfeld* (of course with a talented, accomplished staff) he still got in his meditation and exercise.

• **Julia Louis-Dreyfus** of *Seinfeld* loves the treadmill and uses it most every day for an hour. She also has a trainer/physical therapist three times a week. She has a Pilates machine and a trainer to work out with her. She is tiny, yet very strong and looks great in whatever the wardrobe designers put her in. She always looks stunning in the spectacular dresses she wears to the award shows.

• **Jason Alexander** of *Seinfeld* trains in various ways. He does fight his weight so he always looks for an exercise he enjoys. He is proficient in Karate, he does the Stairmaster the Pilates machine. He is so tough and strong, yet when you see him dance he looks like he's floating on a cloud.

• **So dance, fence, run, lift weights, practice yoga**, anything that requires precision movements. Going to classes and the gym are good places to meet other actors and people in the biz who might have information about acting jobs. Your VCR can help too. There are a lot of good exercise tapes for sale or rent. You can also tape workout television shows.

• **Personal trainer Carla Jones talks about how to burn fat:**

  • **The only way to achieve long term weight loss, decreased body fat**, a firm and shapely physique and a higher level of overall fitness is to address both sides of the fitness equation. In order to maintain your current weight, your caloric intake must equal your caloric usage. If you eat more than you burn, you'll gain weight. If you burn more than you eat, you'll lose weight. Burning fat calories is crucial for any weight management plan. However to burn fat most efficiently, you must work within your fat burning heart rate zone. Many people don't realize that there are five heart rate training zones in all. Each training zone is at a different level of exercise intensity and is best suited for a particular purpose. Training in one or all of these zones can play a crucial part in your overall training program.

- **Moderate Activity Zone** (50-60% Max HR): the heart rate training level, if you are primarily interested in weight loss, beginning a program after being sedentary, are in extremely poor condition, or are rehabilitating from a medical difficulty. In this zone, the fuel used for energy is about 85% fat, 10% carbohydrates and 5% protein.

- **Weight Management Zone** (60-70% Max HR): starting at this intensity level and upward, your body begins to reap the positive effects of aerobic exercise. In this zone, your heart is working hard enough to become stronger and ready for a steady, pain-free, moderate pace. The fuel used for energy in this zone is also 85% fat, 10% carbohydrates and 5% protein.

- **Aerobic Zone** (70%-80% Max HR): training within the aerobic zone benefits your cardiovascular and respiratory systems (heart and lungs). If your goal is to become fitter, faster and stronger, this is the zone for most of your concentrated efforts. This zone has been known as the "target heart rate zone" for years. The fuel used for energy is about 50% fat and 50% carbohydrates.

- **Anaerobic Threshold Zone** (80-90% Max HR): this zone brings you near the point where aerobic training crosses over and becomes anaerobic training. Primary benefits of training in this range is to increase your body's ability to metabolize lactic acid allowing you to train harder before crossing over into the pain of lactate accumulation and oxygen debt. This training benefits athletes interested in high performance training. In this zone you will burn about 15% fat and 85% carbohydrates.

- **Red-Line Zone** (90-100% Max HR): train at this level only if you are extremely fit from extensive training and have a working knowledge of the principles of high performance training. While in the red-line, you will have crossed over the anaerobic threshold and will be operating in oxygen debt (your muscles will be using more oxygen than your body can provide).

- **Fat Burning:** you will need to exercise three to six days per week at a low intensity level, long duration (35 minutes or more) and moderate pace.

- **Weight Training:** In addition to your fat burning work, which will serve to reduce your percentage of body fat, you will need a comprehensive weight training program design. It would be prudent to seek the advice of a certified personal trainer to ensure that you are working at a safe, practical level of intensity and utilizing proper weight training techniques.

- **Proper Nutrition:** maintaining a healthy diet plan can be much simpler than most people realize. First, keep in mind that calories are provided by four nutritional categories: protein provides four calories per gram, carbohydrates provide four calories per gram, fat provides nine calories per gram and alcohol provides seven calories per gram. A healthy diet should include a wide variety of foods.

Resources

Shelly's Discount Aerobic & Dance Wear, 310/475-1400. 2089 Westwood Blvd., Westwood, 90025. (Between Santa Monica Blvd. & Olympic) M-Sa 10-6, Su 11-4.

• PROFESSIONAL DANCE STUDIOS

Dance Arts Academy, 323/932-6230. www.danceartsacademy.com. 731 South La Brea Ave., Los Angeles, 90036. They offer professional quality dance training and performing opportunities, in all dance disciplines, to students of all ages and levels of experience. Founder/Director, Carla Luna has created beautiful quarters with over 10,000 square feet of space, state-of-the art sprung floors and ample dressing rooms. My friend, Catherane Skillen, takes ballet here every day; she's very devoted and disciplined.

Ballet with Lisa Ebeyer at Dance Arts Academy, 731 S. La Brea, Los Angeles. Lisa's Direct Line: 818/892-0908. Lisa Ebeyer was a professional ballet dancer nationally and internationally before becoming a teacher. Teaching for more than ten years, her classes range from Intermediate to Professional level. The current schedule is Mondays and Wednesdays 11AM-12:30PM; Fridays and Sundays 10AM-11:30AM. Class rates are $15 for one class, $60 for five classes, $110 for 10 classes. Catherane Skillen says, "Lisa brings both humor and a sense of joy to her classes. Not only does she understand how the body can affect and help movement, she also has the actors' understanding of how to communicate this knowledge to her student

Edge Performing Arts Center, 323/962-7733. 1020 North Cole Ave., 4th Floor, Hollywood, 90038. All ages, beginning through professional; jazz, ballet hip-hop and tap. $11 a class; with SAG card, $10.

Debbie Reynolds Rehearsal Studios, 818/985-3193. 6514 Lankershim Blvd., North Hollywood, 91606. $10 a class, union $9. M-Sa 9-9. Adult and children. Jazz, ballet and tap, hip-hop, musical theatre, specialty classes in turning.

Jennifer Nairn-Smith, 323/938-6836. www.outbackstudios.com. Private and small classes specializing in changing your body. Jennifer is from the New York City Ballet and danced in the film *All That Jazz*. She teaches all types of dance and choreographs for films, music videos and commercials. Fosse style original jazz.

Moro Landis Millennium Dance Complex, 818/753-5081. 5113 Lankershim Blvd., NoHo, 91601. All ballet, jazz and hip-hop dance single classes are $11 and $10 for union. Dance coupons are 5 for $52 and 10 for $97.

Lauridsen Ballet Centre, 310/533-1247. www.southbayballet.org. 1261 Sartori Avenue, Torrance, 90501. This is a home for the serious student interested in celebrating the art of dance. The faculty is dedicated to nurturing, developing, and guiding dancers through the world of ballet in a professional, caring and healthy environment. Students are privileged to study in a traditional ballet atmosphere with live piano accompaniment. The school's teaching staff boasts professionals and guest artists from world-renowned ballet companies. Diane Lauridsen, Charles Maple, Colleen O'Callaghan and Alicia Head make up our senior teaching staff. Lauridsen Ballet Centre and its non-profit per-forming company, South Bay Ballet, are internationally recognized for integrity, strict guidelines and the highest quality training that provides pre-professional performances enjoyed by patrons throughout the Southland.

Pedro Montanez, 818/426-6895. Teaches privately ballroom, waltz, rumba, samba, salsa, fox-trot, hussle, hip hop, street dancing, ballet, jazz, and tap. He choreographs weddings and is hired to get people dancing at parties. He can be hired if you need to learn a dance step quickly for an audition. As an actor, you should know the usual dances for your resume.

• PERSONAL TRAINERS

Trisha Grant, 818/247-3911. For women only, $50 a session. She meets with you to discuss what you want to achieve. If she thinks you both can accomplish your goals she will take you on. She advises on what to eat and what to do on the days you are not with her. She requires two workouts a week in her great private outdoor gym. She takes before pictures and measurements and then pictures and measurements every twelve weeks. I've seen great results from her training.

Marcus Patric, 818/769-9635. www.getripped.tv. Marcus is ACE Certified. P.E. Diploma and holds a Second Degree Black Belt. On his web site he gives nutritional information for losing fat and exercises for burning fat. Also pictures of some beautiful bodies he trains. He comes to your home or you go to his gym. Marcus says, "I stress that health is the key to all success and happiness in life and in an exercise program."

David Brown, 323/957-9066. He is a great personal trainer, inexpensive, fun to be with and has a great looking body. He only trains at Gold's Gym, so you have to be a member there. He also teaches several spinning classes at Crunch!

Tony English Fitness Training Centers, 818/761-TONY. 11745 Ventura Blvd, #2, Studio City, 91604. Specializes is fat burning and toning. He has a small private gym or he will come to you.

Joey Kormier, 818/948-8108. www.kormierfitness.com. Jode Leigh Edwards says, "Joey uses a soulful approach to working out. By incorporating weight lifting, kickboxing, cardio, and stretching, Joey's helped motivate my physical fitness to new levels." He does in-home training or at his private gym. Joey gives a free consultation. Rates and packages available upon request.

Julie Fisher, Personal Fitness Trainer, 310/407-3537. $60 to $75 a session. She trains clients at home, at the gym or outdoors. Julie has been interviewed for both "Rosie" and "In Style" magazines for her expertise as a personal trainer. She came here from NYC, where she was a master trainer at Equinox and then started her own private training business. She is also a former ballet dancer—and she'll give you great exer-cises for toning your arms and adding definition. She now trains privately and has a number of celebrity clients. Actress Blythe Baten trains with her and says, "Julie is very energetic and supportive."

Javier at Hotte Bodies Technique, 818/508-4545. 11634 Ventura Blvd., Studio City, 91604. www.hottebodies.com. Training 3x a week is $50/session, 2x a week is $55/session, and once a week is $60/session. Body sculpting, weight reduction, strength training away from the crowds. Javier's specialized services: nutritional evaluation and guidance for weight loss and weight gain, cardiovascular conditioning, flexibility training, physical rehabilitation and stress reduction.

Carla Jones of Star Quality Fitness Training, 213/918-2906. Certified personal trainer. She distributes all natural supplements. My friend had great success working one on one with Carla. She is a tennis jock but says she has never been in better shape since weight training with Carla. One-on-one sessions; personalized program designs; fitness evaluations; nutritional evaluations. Single session in the gym, $45. In-home training, single session, $60. Body fat assessment, $15.

Tina Lynne, 323/939-9117. A specialist in the complete make-over. She does basic nutritional consulting. Instructs her clients in the proper exercises for posture lengthening and grace. Facial exercises for firming and toning. She teaches privately or in small classes. She also does facial and body work.

Pilates with Tawny Moyer, 323/650-0748. "With Pilates, we reshape the body for maximum strength and long, lean muscle." Specializing in women, focusing on muscle sculpting, strength training and flexibility. Recommended two to three times a week. Private sessions in her studio, $75.

Gyrotonic™ Instructor, Lisa Ebeyer, 818/892-0908. Lisa Ebeyer is a Level 1 Gyrotonic™ instructor working on the Gyrotonic Expansion System™ which stretches and strengthens the musculature while mobilizing and articulating the joints. Gyrotonic™ exercise is a non-impact workout done one-on-one so that the client has the instructor's undivided attention. Lisa also teaches Gyrokinesis Yoga as well as ballet. Call for more information, rates and Lisa's schedule.

LA Body Kinetics, 310/253-9500. www.labodyk.com. 3865 Cardiff Ave., Culver City, 90232. They offer an array of movement modalities but most popular are the Pilates and Gyrotonic Expansion System™. They have all of the equipment for both of the techniques; and offer Pilates group mat classes and Gyrokinesis™, which is a form of yoga that is the basis for Gyrotonic™. They are a certification studio as well. Lisa Marie Goodwin is considered a Master Trainer of Master Trainers in Gyrotonic™ and both of her partners are trainers in Pilates as well.

Winsor West Pilates Studio, 310/442-1030. www.winsorpilates.com. 12231 Wilshire Blvd., Santa Monica, 90025. Winsor Fitness Pilates Studio, 323/653-8767. 8204 Melrose Ave, West Hollywood, 90048. Both locations are fitted with shower and changing facilities. $70 an hour for a private class, utilizing the Cadillac and Reformer Pilates equipment. $15 for the group floor class with a trainer and maximum 10 people. Mats provided. Both types of classes can be bought in a series. Mari is well known for teaching the New York method of Pilates. She's written a book explaining the exercises and produced videos that can be used at home; sold on the website.

Rob Parr, 310/476-9172. Helped reshape Demi Moore, Maria Shriver and Tatum O'Neal after pregnancies. John McEnroe and Christy Turlington.

Michael Thurmond's Six-Week Body Make-over, 800/639-2639. www.bodymakeovers.com He advertises in L.A. Magazine. I met a mature actress on the set of *Thea* who had lost 40 pounds. She said she looked better than she had in years. She was working out with weights and said Michael's program really motivated her. Free initial consultation.

• WORKOUT PLACES

Angel City Yoga Center, 818/762-8291. 12408 Ventura Blvd., Studio City, 91604. www.angelcityyoga.com. Multi-method Hatha yoga, Sivananda Hatha; Iyengar; Astanga; Kundalini. $14 per individual class. 10 class card, $110. Unlimited: $135 per month, $325 for 3 months.

Aquatic Masters Program, Southern California, 310/390-5700. www.swim.net. Clay Evans has designed this program to aid injury recovery, as well as overall fitness and swimming ability. You are videotaped during stroke-technique exercises. Has trained many celebrities in swimming roles.

B.K.S. Iyengar Yoga Institute of Los Angeles, 323/653-0357. 8233 West Third Street, Los Angeles, 90048. Individual 1 1/2 hour class, $14; the noon one hour classes, $12; series of 10, $120; monthly unlimited, $140. First class is free. I love this place; the teachers are great. There are three levels so you don't have to worry if you are new. For your first class I would recommend Saturday morning 10:45 with Chris Stein or Tuesday morning 8:30 or noon or Tuesday night at 7:30 with Leslie. I love the 8:30 morning classes; they are small and Leslie and Sue really have the time and inclination to make sure you understand all the moves. All the teachers are very highly trained and are very aware of keeping you from injury. Marla, Karin, Larry, Sylvie, and Herb are great too. Alice teaches a special class Saturday morning at 9 for people with scoliosis.

Bikram Yoga, www.bikramyoga.com. Popular in Los Angeles for many years. Check the website for the style and locations.

Yoga Works - Montana, 310/393-5150. www.yogaworks.com. 1426 Montana Ave., 2nd floor, Santa Monica 90405.

Yoga Works - Main, 310/393-5150. www.yogaworks.com. 2215 Main St., Santa Monica, 90405.

Yoga Meditation & Insight (YMI), 323/964-5222. www.ymiyoga.com.

L.A. Yoga Center, 310/234-1200. www.ayogacenter.com. 1256 Westwood Blvd., 2nd floor, West Los Angeles.

Maha Yoga, 310/899-0047. 13050 San Vicente, #202. www.mahayoga.com. Corner of San Vicente and 26th, Brentwood. Meg Ryan, Goldie Hawn, Dennis Quaid, Elizabeth Berkley, Jim Belushi. High-energy power yoga classes as well as more meditative classes.

Body Sculpting, 310/657-4140. 624 N. La Cienega, West Hollywood. This is not a membership gym; the trainers pay to belong and then charge you for the workout. Many trainers. They generally charge between $50-$60/hr.

Bally's Total Fitness, 323/461-0227. 1628 N. El Centro, Hollywood, 90028. M-Th 5:30AM to Midnight, F 5AM –10PM, Sa-Su 8-8. www.ballyfitness.com. Swimming pool, running track, many treadmills and bikes, TVs to watch. 818/760-7800. 11315 Ventura Blvd., Studio City, 91604. Open 7 days a week, 24 hours. I love Bally's because I can always find a gym in another city when traveling. Not as fancy as others but the price is right.

Body and Soul, 310/659-2211. 8599 Santa Monica Blvd. Blythe loves this place. Her favorite class is Suzanne's Flow class. It is a beautiful studio, very zen inside: wall to wall bamboo and candle lit. Morning classes are usually small. They also have great spinning classes.

Bodies in Motion, 310/264-0777. 2730 Santa Monica Blvd., Santa Monica, 90404. www.bodiesinmotion.com. Also 310/836-8000. 1950 Century Park E., Century City. Kick boxing, boxing, yoga, aerobics, free weights, treadmills. Jode Edwards takes kick boxing and says this is a terrific workout. "When you finish hitting that bag it's like a release; you get all your anxieties out."

Critical Mass. 310/917-1199. $50-$100/session. www.criticalmassstudio.com 26th and San Vicente, Brentwood. Tori Spelling, Harry Hamlin, Anne Archer work out here. Private Training. Owner/trainer David Kelmenson.

Crunch, 323/654-4550. 8000 Sunset Blvd. at Crescent Heights in Virgin Megastores complex. www.crunch.com. Hours: 5AM–12AM daily. This corner is where the old Schwabs Drugstore used to be. Madonna's trainer and Lordes' father Carlos Leon works there. Afro-Brazilian aerobics. Marisa Tomei, Julianna Margulies, Laura Dern, Brad Pitt, Jeff Goldblum, Julie Delpy, Jon Favreau, Debi Mazar and Ben Stiller have all been spotted here.

Dolly Mama, Dawnn Alane. 310/230-0390. Pacific Palisades. Dawnn also teaches privates for $75-$125 hour.

L.A. Fitness at Warner Center Club, 818/884-1100. 6336 Canoga Ave., Woodland Hills. www.lafitness.com. M-Th 5AM–11PM, F 5AM–10PM, Sa-Su 7AM–8PM.

Gold's Gym, 310/392-6004. 360 Hampton Drive, Venice. Also 323/462-7012. 1016 N. Cole, Hollywood. www.goldsgym.com. M-F 4AM–12PM; Sa-Su 5AM–11PM. The Venice gym is filled with every big name from the world of bodybuilding plus the likes of Janet Jackson, Lisa Bonet and Jodie Foster.

Gymnastics Center, 310/838-4228. 8476 Warner Drive, Culver City, 90232. www.members.aol.com/smgcgym. Hours 9AM–10PM. Ask for adult gymnastic classes.

Carreiro's Gymnastics and Trapeze Arts, 310/652-3060. 722 N. La Cienega Blvd., L.A. 90069. 7:30-6:30PM. Package of 10 classes, $25/session. One class is $30, private is $80. Class size is 5 people or less. Bob Carreiro can turn even the most uptight body into one that is lithe, strong and obedient. The risk is higher; so are the rewards.

Easton Gym, 323/651-3636. 8053 Beverly Blvd. (near Crescent Heights.) 5AM to midnight. Cardio and strength training, personal training, complete locker facilities.

Karate, Simon Rhee, 818/224-3400. www.simonrhee.net. 22880 Ventura Blvd., Woodland Hills, 91364. Considered one of the best Karate studios, many celebrities have studied with Master Rhee. He is also a well-known action/stunt actor, *Best of the Best I & II,* and many others. Cathy Kerr is a Second Degree Black Belt—oh I hate to brag! Love my girls! *See Master Rhee's interview in the stunt-action actor section.*

Karate, Jun Chong, 323/658-7570. 6401 Wilshire Blvd. L.A. Also 818/769-9308. 5223 Lankershim Blvd., North Hollywood. www.karatejunchongtkd.com Danny Gibson is the manager here. Mr. Gibson is inspirational and keeps his students motivated. Cathy and Cynthia Kerr trained with him when they were teenagers. Masters Chong and Gibson are action actors. Third location: 310/449-1333. 11870 Santa Monica Blvd., Santa Monica, 90025 (two blocks east of Bundy).

Rock Climbing, Adventure 16, 310/473-4574. 1161 W. Pico, W.LA. M-F 10-9, Sa 10-6, Su 11-6. After training you go to Stoney Point in Chatsworth to climb boulders 30 to 60 feet high. Equipment is provided.

24 Hour Fitness, 310/652-7440. 8612 Santa Monica Blvd., West Hollywood, 90069. www.24hourfitness.com. Membership gym. Weight lifting; all types of exercise classes. M-Th 5:30AM-11PM, F 5:30-10, Sa&Su 7AM-8PM. Also 310/410-9909, Century City; 213/683-1400, downtown; 310/553-7600, West Los Angeles; 213/388-2700, Korea Town.

Sports Club L.A., 310/477-7799. 1835 Sepulveda Blvd., West Los Angeles. www.sportsclubla.com. Very expensive, but in! This is the gym to get a day job at!

Stair Climbing on the 4th Street Stairs, at 4th and Adelaide Streets in Santa Monica, 189 steps.

Stairs, in Santa Monica. They ascend from the 400 block of North Mesa Road to Amalfi Drive, 201 steps. Less crowded than the 4th Street stairs and redwoods, wisteria and live oaks.

Southern California Boat Club, 310/822-0073. 1355 Fiji Way, Marina del Rey. Wide array of classes and boats for rent.

Westside Fencing Center and Center for Stage Combat, 310/204-2688. 8737 Washington Blvd., Culver City, 90232. www.westsidefencing.com. M-F 3-10PM, Sa 7-3PM. The largest fencing center in the country. Classes and private coaching. Call for their brochure; there is a coupon for a free fencing lesson. Some former students are: Geena Davis (*Cutthroat Island*), Teenage Mutant Ninja Turtles, Robin Williams, Shelly Long, Keanu Reeves and Eric Roberts.

Workout Warehouse, 310/358-1838. 648 N. La Peer Drive, Los Angeles, 90069. Lots of celebrities. The gym's high tech resistance machines are known for flawless motion; Tectrix Bikemax stationary cycle gives a smooth ride. Great locker rooms, a staff massage therapist, rubdowns for a dollar a minute.

Working Actor's Guide lists many gyms and trainers.

AGE DEFYING AND
BEAUTY ENHANCING TECHNIQUES,
INCLUDING FACIALS AND MASSAGE

• **Your face is your billboard**; it's where the audience sees what you are feeling and thinking. The first time you see your face on a big screen·it is awe inspiring.

• **When you are wearing makeup** and working in it for hours, you need a thorough cleansing. A facial every month or so is a wonderful way to relax and treat yourself well. Aging can be slowed down; our profession is so youth oriented that it demands we look as young as we can for as long as we can. Surgery is a last resort because when they cut into the skin you never know how your body will heal.

• **Medical doctors used to say that nothing** rubbed on the skin can penetrate and help stop aging; it has to come from the inside. Then Retin A, glycolic acid, and chemical peels came along. Now the doctors are using these products and admit that they do retard the aging process.

• **Christie Brinkley** is known for her beautiful young looking skin; she has made a living with it. It is said that she never turns on her heat or air conditioner, as they dry out skin. I have an actress friend who has to be in her late forties, though she never tells her age, with the most flawless skin. She has never been in the sun and during the winter, layers her clothing so she doesn't use heat. She did this even while acting on soap operas in New York. It has paid off, she looks like she is in her thirties and is still being cast as that. Women have to stretch their young years as long as possible. Men need to stretch their mid years.

• **Kim Basinger,** in her forties, is still a great beauty. Her skin is luminous without a wrinkle. She says she has avoided the sun with a "fanatical determination."

• **Bernadette Peters** who is known for her flawless skin, is in her fifties but looks like she is in her thirties. "When I was thirteen and on a trip to Las Vegas, I got a slight tan—but no sun since. I use Coppertone WaterBabies Sunblock."

• **Rand Rusher,** R.N., C.N.O.R. www.randrusher.com. Botox, Collagen, Cymetra, Perlane and Restylane Injection Specialist of Solutions Skincare Medical Clinic in Beverly Hills, shares the following information about suntans.

  • **I'm afraid there is no such thing as a safe suntan,** no matter how carefully you want to "get some sun." Tanning is still a defense mechanism of the skin. With sun exposure, the skin produces more pigment to provide protection against the sun. The presence of a tan indicates there has been some degree of damage. This damage is responsible for 85% of aging.

  • **If this is not going to stop you from getting a tan,** here are some tips that will help reduce the damage. *Tan the hide, hide the face.* Use a heavy SPF on your face, lower number on your body. Good face products are available, low oil to oil free, paba free. The FDA is changing the rules on SPF's, with SPF 35 being the highest possible. Always make sure that you use *at least a* 30 SPF on your face, and at least a 15 SPF on your body. Some of the better sunscreens are Ti-silc, Leaf&Rusher, www.leafandrusher.com, or Environ products. *Avoid becoming sunburned at all costs.* The damage may not show up for years, but it will. *Always wear sunscreen even when it is cloudy,* even if you have very dark skin. *Lips need sunscreen too.* Neostrata makes an excellent product for this. *Fake tans are great; use self action tanners.* The trick is to find one that complements your natural skin tone. Chanel smells great but is a bit greasy, California Tan has no smell and not greasy but can streak. You really have to try the products out on your own skin.

• **Sylvie Archenault, owner of Sylvie's Advanced European Skin & Body Care System,** has been doing facials for thirty years. She works with three chemists and two laboratories developing her cutting edge Sonage skin products, importing the raw materials from Europe, Japan and Australia. Sylvie talks about the results people can expect from facials:

- **When you have a facial,** you should see a change right away; your skin will be glowing, energized, and cleansed. You are taking off all the makeup and grime, the skin is pure. If you have acne or a breakout, you should not be red when the treatment is over. A deep pore facial once a month is good for general cleaning and toning, but if there are skin difficulties or special occasions then you will need facials more often. The aesthetician can do things to make your skin beautiful for a photo shoot. Makeup responds beautifully when you have healthy skin underneath. The style now is very light makeup; you can't hide the imperfections so you must really clean your skin.

Q: How do you choose a skin care person?

- **Skin care is an art.** You will probably go to a facialist before the plastic surgeon and dermatologist. You want to choose a professional, first by their word of mouth reputation, then by the techniques they use and most importantly the results. Have a consultation or an over-the-phone interview. Finally, you must experience their facial. If it's too strong it can bruise the skin and leave you marked for a few days— that might interfere with your acting interviews. At Sylvie's we use the latest techniques and revolutionary ingredients; my goal is to fight aging.

Q: How can actors help their skin?

- **Drink a lot of water** because it provides energy, keeps the skin glowing and cleans up your system by drawing the toxins away from your body. Caffeine and smoking does a lot of damage. Exposure to the sun is damaging. It is easier to apply makeup on porcelain skin; you cannot take off the tan if you need a white skin.

- **Facialist and natural product developer Leah Ruiz** of The Vital Image gives some hints for skin care.

  - **Don't touch your face,** unless you are going to be gentle. Don't rub your eyes if they itch. Use your middle fingers and pat to keep from stretching your skin. Use short, firm strokes to apply products.

  - **In order to drink more water each day** make a pot of herb tea or add a splash of juice to your water and drink throughout the day.

  - **Increase oxygen intake to relieve stress.** Oxygen bath: add a full 16 ounce bottle of common 3% Hydrogen Peroxide to a warm bath. Soak for 20 minutes. Oxygen break: make a point of taking ten deep breaths, ten times a day.

  - **Acne skin is especially sugar intolerant.** Substitute a natural, sugar free sweetener such as stevia extract to sweeten drinks and food.

• **Be a fanatic** about your skin care routine at night before retiring. You will help your skin to rejuvenate itself by sticking to this good habit. Your skin is most actively regenerated between the hours of midnight and 4:00AM.

• **Don't sleep on your face.** Sleep on your back or side to avoid wrinkling and creasing your face while you sleep. It's easy for most people to train themselves into a favorable sleeping position. Satin pillow cases reduce friction that stretches and damages hair and skin. Look for pure silk rather than synthetic fabrics. To release tension around the eyes, put your head on the pillow, inhale deeply and with your thumbs, press upward toward the forehead on the eye socket—the sensitive area between the eyebrows. Exhale while applying pressure and relax the jaw, repeat three times. The results will amaze you.

• **Proper exfoliation can step up cell renewal.** You can use simple table sugar as an exceptional exfoliant. It has fine grains for gentle removal of dead surface cells, it is nondrying and rinses away completely. Wet your face and lather then add a half teaspoon or more of sugar to one lathered up hand. Dip the two middle fingers of your other hand into the sugar and gently wash your face using a circular motion. Rinse well and pat dry. Your face should look rosy but not irritated. After exfoliation, your skin will absorb more nutrients and moisture.

• **Perfume is okay but never directly on your skin.** It is best in your hair or on your clothes.

• **Tina Lynne, the creator of** *The Lynne Technique* answers the very important questions about how to look your best when you have overindulged.

  • **Our motto is: if you've had a "marguerita and salty chips" night,** don't wear it on your face the next day; do the *Lynne Technique*. When you do the technique it helps to clean out the lymph system, which is a filtering system that removes toxic bloat in your body. Open your mouth into the "long O" which is like the men's shaving position, put on your cleanser then blot the face with a hot compress, working down towards the heart hitting some of the pressure points, press down, with your knuckles on your chest, two, three, pump. Then pushing the knuckles into the armpits, one, two, three, pumping. Next take some deep breaths; the breathing is really important to oxygenate the body.

  • **You can continue to reduce swelling and puffiness** by pressing accupressure points while you're applying your undereye concealer and makeup, just by rolling your finger on the inside corner of the eye, out the side to the temple, walking your fingers out. This technique will help reduce dark circles and puffiness. Make sure you're never stretching the skin on your face.

Q: How does your technique done professionally help to defy aging and enhance beauty?

- **What I do is called the body clearing treatment.** It is the best part of a facial or traditional massage, which brings up circulation and carries away toxins. I clean out the lymph system. If your lymph system is clogged up it becomes inefficient. The analogy is: how poorly your dryer works when you don't clean the lint screen. You clean out the lymph system so your body is removing it's waste efficiently and quickly. A lot of massages swish around the toxins, but they don't end up leaving the body so people are still bloated afterwards. The treatment we do is to help dispose of the toxins though the kidneys, through both ends, so to speak. It's like a colonic without the machine.

- **Rand Rusher, R.N.,** describes products used for facial injections.

  - **Botox softens or actually can erase certain wrinkles.** As an actor you should be careful not to completely get rid of wrinkles; softening certain wrinkles can help if you have more than you want due to genetics, sundamage, etc. Botox works by blocking the nerve to the tiny facial muscles that relate to expression lines. Botox relaxes muscles so they do not contract. After the treatment, the overlying skin remains smooth. Botox has been used for over 10 years to treat many other disorders and has recently been approved for the treatment of wrinkles by the FDA, so not to worry.

  - **Collagen is a natural occurring protein** found in both humans and animals. It provides structural support for bones, skin, tendons, and is the most abundant protein in the body. Collagen is injected into the wrinkle to plump up the skin. Unlike Botox that stops the muscle from moving thereby softening the wrinkle, collagen fills out the wrinkle, while still allowing movement of the surrounding muscles. Since collagen is an animal product (bovine), it requires a skin test to ensure that you do not have an allergy. After the test implant is done (usually on the inner right forearm), you will need to wait at least 30 days to insure there is no allergic reaction.

  - **Cymetra works just like collagen** except that it is made of human tissue. Unlike collagen that is made up of beef collagen, Cymetra is based on human tissue and can be used for people who are allergic to collagen. Since Cymetra is made from human tissue, no skin test is required, so no wait is required.

  - **Hylauronic Acid**—also known as Restylane or Perlane, has not been approved for use in the United States at this time. It is a non-animal product that does not require an allergy test, and has been used widely in Europe with in the past seven years. Use of Hylauronic Acid requires advanced injection knowledge, so please research! Information on Restylane/Perlane can be found on their website, www.Restylane.com. FDA approval is likely to be in Spring 2003.

• **Facialist Margaret Tomaszewicz,** who works at the Burke Williams Day Spa and Massage Center, talks about men's facials.

> • **Men can shave in the morning,** if they're having a facial in the evening, but should not shave right before; it makes the skin too sensitive. Men tend to have good facial skin, but they break out on their backs due to sports and exercises. If there are just a few spots, an exfoliation treatment will be enough with an occasional maintenance. When there are a lot of problems, the client would have to come in every couple of weeks. I would also advise a topical medication for them to use. We do full-body facials for swimsuit and body photo shoots. It polishes the skin.

Q: Why is a massage valuable for actors?

> • **Doctors in Europe** prescribe massages for health reasons. A massage gives oxygen to the muscles and the tissue, even more than exercise can provide. It gives life, circulation, and relaxation as well. When directions on bottles of creams say to massage vigorously into the body, it's not the creams that are good, it's the actual massage that breaks up the toxins in your body. In short, it's great for relaxation and for long term effects; it's very good for your health.

• **My friend, actress Samantha Harper,** went through a complete body transformation in the last year. She worked with the technicians at Bella Vida, as well as with Connie of Allred Colonic Techniques for the detoxing. Samantha says, "I lost 24 lbs. by changing eating patterns and stress levels. The work with Julie and Connie helped my skin keep up with the weight loss and my tissues to release toxins/fat that were trapped in cellulite. I like my shape now, am loving how I wear clothes, and am having more fun when I take them off."

• **Julie Singer of Bella Vida Endermologie** talks about the work they do to help women reduce inches and cellulite through a detoxifying treatment.

> • **We all know how hard it is** for women to get rid of cellulite. In fact, even if you have a personal trainer and nutritionist, you can still have stubborn problem areas. At Bella Vida, we're dedicated to helping you feel more confident about your body whether you need to be in a bikini or just want to feel great in a pair of jeans.

- **Endermologie is unique** because it reduces cellulite and body circumference by working to release toxins in the fat cells of the hypo-dermis layer. This is the layer of skin that diet and exercise do not effectively reach. Endermologie is the first process cleared by the FDA for the reduction of cellulite and body circumference.

- **When you begin treatments at Bella Vida,** you'll notice your clothes feel looser, and your legs and hips feel lighter. Then you'll see smoother and more supple skin. Many clients tell us their significant others start to compliment them on the look and feel of their skin.

- **Our non-invasive, full body treatments** run 30 to 45 minutes in length. You will wear a body suit and relax on a massage table while a technician uses a gentle suction device with two rollers to create a symmetrical skin fold. You've never experienced anything quite like it; it's actually lifting and rolling the skin simultaneously. Clients tell us they love the way this feels and are thrilled with the health benefits.

- **Endermologie increases local blood circulation** which brings oxygen and nutrients to the tissues. After each treatment your circulation will increase up to 400 percent for the next six hours, energizing your entire body. The process also softens tightened connective tissue, which binds and traps fat, allowing fat and toxins to be eliminated more efficiently. Equally exciting is that Endermologie restores collagen and elastin to the surface layer of the skin, creating a more youthful appearance.

Resources

The Vital Image, 310/823-1996 or 800/414-4624. www.thevitalimage.com. Leah has a studio in Playa del Rey. $60 for an hour facial. Guaranteed quick results. She does minimal extractions so there is no marking at all. She believes the products will pull most of the toxins out. The facials, special Chinese lamp and all natural products heal skin damaged from age, sun and deep abrasion or laser work. I've had terrific healing with these facials. The three products, Face & Body Wash, Skin Renewal Complex and Phytohydrator (liquid moisturizer) are all you need to deliver fabulous skin. Among their many other products, they have a special under-eye bag cure, which removed my daughter Chris' inherited bags (from me, sorry Chris). Chris is thrilled with the results. I love their Shaving Miracle liquid; I've never gotten such a close shave. Men love it—no break outs. Newest is Lift & Firm, fights wrinkles and flaccid skin, eye lift, jaw-line and neck firming—it works! Sun Shield Moisturizer: amazing and 100% free of man-made chemicals, powerful nutrients. Call for their special product report.

Rand Rusher, R.N., C.N.O.R. Botox, Collagen, Cymetra, Perlane and Restylane Injection Specialist, 310/276-5558. www.randrusher.com Solutions Skincare Medical Clinic, 436 N. Bedford Dr., #104, Beverly Hills. "Los Angeles's most sought out Botox and Collagen Specialist." He is a master with the needle. I love Botox, Collagen and the latest: Cymetra, Restylane www.Restylane.com and Perlane; they do help defy the look of aging. A good technician will make all the difference; if they get too much botox in your forehead, your eyebrows can sag. Great for lines around the eyes and chin too, Rand leaves you with facial expression, which actors must have. The collagen fills in lines; especially chronic frown lines, and those pesky lines around the mouth. The Cymetra, Restylane and Perlane are for more extensive deep folds and fluffing up the lips. With Rand your lips look real not artificial and unattractive. Rand has a nursing and artistic background which is the best combination when working on the face. You want the artistic touch, he knows where and how much to inject for the best looking results. I've been going for years, always with great results, love my lips puffed a little! You need to make appointments in advance for Rand. He stays booked. He has been featured in many fashion magazines. Everyone in the office is very helpful. Appointments are mandatory.

August Denton, R.N. Botox, Collagen, Cymetra, Perlane and Restylane Injection Specialist, 310/276-5558. Solutions Skincare Medical Clinic, 436 N. Bedford Dr., #104, Beverly Hills. Three Baccalaureate's in Art, Physiology, and Nursing. August graduated with Honors from the top rated University Of Illinois at the Chicago College Of Nursing in 2000, and began his clinical work at the University of Chicago Hospital. His talents in sculpture and physiology have enhanced his skills giving his Botox and Collagen technique an artists touch.

Solutions Skincare Medical Clinic Inc. 310/276-5558. 436 N. Bedford Dr., Suite 104, Beverly Hills. www.leafskincare.com. They specialize in preventive maintenance, which can help reduce or forestall the need for restorative surgery. Lighter, non-invasive treatments can be adequate to bring back abused, over-stressed and over-exposed skin. Some of the treatments besides great facials are light peels, power peels, micro dermabrasion, laser hair removal and permanent make-up. Renowned plastic surgeon Dr. Norman Leaf, "surgeon to the stars" is known for his undetectable facelifts, has designed Solutions Skincare to be a bridge between commercial skincare, beauty salons and the plastic surgeon's or dermatologist's office. Ask them to send you their brochure with descriptions of their many services. My special Esthetician is Maya—amazing.

Dr. Jon Fong's Laser Facials, 818/766-0110 and 877-LFACIAL. www.LaserFacials.com. $375 for the first treatment and $250 for further treatments. Treating sun damaged skin is the goal. This is a laser process that treats the entire face, for men and women 20 to 60 including dark skin types. It treats fine lines, wrinkles, texture, tone, dark spots and sun damaged skin with no down or recovery time. I've had three over two years and will continue to do them. This is Dr. Fong's invention and is not like anything else others use. He is an emergency room doctor and is the on-set advisor for *E.R.* He also offers a lunch time Laser Facial that is cheaper and not as deep.

Sylvie's, 818/905-8815. 17071 Ventura Blvd., Encino, 91436. For men and women. Tu&F 9-5, W & TH 9-8, Sa 8-5. Deep pore cleansing facials start at $75. Micro-dermabrasion $125, vacupression body and face treatments $90, collagen treatment $130, seaweed facial $105, cell structure enhancement $85, enzyme $105. They do skin and body waxing, lash and brow tinting, permanent lip, brow and eyeliner makeup. One hour body massage $65. Varied prices for several types of massage including lymphatic drainage, reflexology, anti-stress detox, PMS treatment, exfoliation, cellulite, hair removal by electronic tweezers, electrolysis and European waxing. Aromatherapy. Manicures and pedicures. All of the aestheticians are trained by Sylvie using her techniques and methods. Her Sonage skin care products are healing, enhancing, concentrated, smell good; you see and feel a difference right away. Cathy Kerr's favorite. There is a discrete back entrance for clients who may not want to be seen.

Yolanda Frye Skin Care, 310/275-3981. 632 1/2 N. Doheny Dr, Los Angeles, 90069. Her special beauty treatment is Oxiana, a European skin therapy, she calls "a fountain of youth for men and women's skin!" With Oxiana it is possible to apply highly concentrated oxygen and skin-enhancing nutrients where needed. Especially recommended after all laser resurfacing as soon as bandages are removed; all skin peel recipients; acne conditions; following electrolysis, waxing and permanent makeup procedures; and in combination with deep cleansing facials. Her facials start at $60 to $150. Cathy Kerr especially loves her back facials, great for when you are wearing a low back dress; men love this too. Yolanda does lash and brow tinting, skin and body waxing, full nail service and makeup.

Bella Vida Endermologie, 310/804-9714. 1327 Ocean Ave., Suite M, Santa Monica, 90401. "We give personalized, reasonably priced sessions, and our clients enjoy a beautiful and soothing atmosphere with a great ocean view as they relax during their treatment." Endermologie reduces cellulite and body circumference by working to release toxins in the fat cells of the hypo-dermis layer. Make an appointment for a free consultation and demonstration.

The Lynne Technique **for Face and Body Care by Tina Lynne**, 323/939-9117. When actors overindulge, she can get them ready for their close-ups by taking the toxins and swelling out of their faces and body. Some of the symptoms her technique helps fight are puffiness, dark circles, facial lines, acne, headaches and jet lag. She combines a regimen of acupressure massage with a balance of minerals, herbs and emollients to firm muscles, clear sinuses and revitalize skin cells by inducing detoxification and faster metabolism of fats and other wastes and nutrients thus stimulating cell renewal and growth. She works pre/post-op plastic surgery treatment to maintain and enhance surgical results. She brought me through a major detoxification in a short amount of time. Incorporating her own designed products and exercises, you can carry on the work at home. Many celebrity clients including international and Hollywood royalty.

The Arcona Studio Holistic Beauty Therapy For Face and Body, 818/506-5192. 12030 Riverside Dr., Valley Village, 91607. Men and women. $75 for non-surgical facelift and facial contouring with essential oils. This treatment is what attracts many people to them; you can tell the difference. Many other treatments including natural fruit enzymes treatment and oxygen facials and European deep-suction cleansing. Arcona is booked six months ahead by many celebrity clients including Sharon Stone; Nicki and Meagan are her trained assistants – but you need to book them two weeks in advance. Samantha Harper loves this place.

Anna Marie Colavito, 310/577-8525. 520 Washington Blvd #218, Marina Del Rey 90292. She uses a new treatment called Lafleur reparer which is a controlled microcurrent system. Treatments rejuvinate from the inside out – Anna Marie says it's a very sophisticated—the only triple feedback loop computerized treatment available. A series of six treatments is recommended, complimentary consultation. Many models, actors and celebrities flock to her.

Beverly Hot Springs, 323/734-7000. 308 N. Oxford Ave., L. A., 90004. Everyday 9-9. This is not a fancy place but many celebrities go there. Built over a natural hot spring, they offer many services. Separate pools for men and women; everyone is naked. Admission M-Th. $40; F, Sa, Su $50 .

Burke Williams Day Spa & Massage Center, 310/587-3366. www.burkewilliamsspa.com. 1460 Fourth Street, Santa Monica, 90401 and 323/822-9007. 8000 W. Sunset Blvd., Hollywood, at Virgin Megastores complex at Crescent Heights. Have a facial with knowledgeable Margaret Tomaszewicz. Four-and-a-half-hour packages such as "Day of Beauty," and "Gentlemen's Choice" cost from $410-$420 or you can purchase services a la carte starting at $25. All sessions of $55 or more include free sauna and whirlpool.

Drew James, 310/395-1405. 733 10ᵗʰ St, Suite B, Santa Monica, 90402. Facials $100 and up. Glycolic and salicylic peels available. He's great at picking out your imperfections without marking you. Waxing and lash tinting. Large clientele of men and women.

Nina Bard, PME, 310/589-5385, on Pacific Coast Highway in Malibu. She does facials, waxing, corrective cosmetic tattooing including eyebrow enhancement and permanent eyeliner, plus her well researched products. Call for prices.

Spa Transcendental, Christina Marino 818/505-9511. www.christinamarino.com. 10645 Riverside Drive, Toluca Lake, 91602. At Christina Marino's spa, they have many specialized services and spa packages. Services include: acupuncture, herbs and nutrition and full service massage therapies; foot reflexology, 30 minutes, $40; deep tissue and sports massage, 60 minutes for $75. Body treatments and wraps. European Facial, 75 minutes for $65. Waxing, lash and brow tinting. Agent Bonnie Howard says, "You feel like you have been on vacation."

• MASSAGE & BODY WORK ONLY

Myrna Moss, M.T., 805/526-1636 or pager 818/372-9474. She is a massage therapist to the stars and regular folks too. 13 years of experience. For $75, she brings her table to you. Deep tissue work; she is a healer. Massage lowers your blood sugar and enhances creativity and productivity. Many production offices and shows hire her to come in and give neck and shoulder massages to cast and crew. What a great Christmas gift or end of season present for a cast or crew member to give to their fellow workers.

Joey Kormier, 818/948-8108. www.kormierfitness.com. 1 hour, $100. Joey uniquely combines Deep tissue Techniques, Swedish Massage, Trigger Point Therapy, Stretching, and Acupressure in a soulful blend of bodywork. Treat yourself to an in-home massage session that you truly deserve.

See above for *The Lynne Technique.*

HEALTH, DOCTORS, NUTRITION, THERAPY AND PLASTIC SURGERY

• **Choosing doctors, dentists, nutritionists, alternative treatments and therapists** are very personal decisions; what is perfect for one person may not work at all for someone else. I can only speak to you from my own and close friend's experiences.

• **I am inclined to investigate most everything.** I have received help and healings from many different types of traditional and nontraditional techniques.

• **As always, proceed with the utmost of caution.** By investigating and following your own instincts, I believe you will be led to the paths that are best for your life.

PHYSICAL HEALTH

• **It is imperative to have your body in excellent condition** in order to be the best actor you can be; your body is your instrument. The following practitioners are all specialists in their fields. I hope you are never sick and only need to consult doctors in order to improve your life's condition. In my experience, holistic doctors allow me to take an active part in my recovery so I seek them out.

• **Dr. Cynthia Watson, Medical Doctor and Naturopath.**

Q: What are your recommendations for staying healthy?

    • **Maybe the most important factor is life style.** Make sure that you try to eat a healthy and balanced diet, lots of fresh fruits and vegetables. Stay away from the junk foods and sugar. Smoking, drugs, coffee and alcohol really rob your body of nutrients. Important to take a good vitamin program on a regular basis. Many of the congestion problems in Los Angeles are related to the pollution. Take antioxidant vitamins, A, C, and E. These vitamins help your immune system and handle some of the heavy toxins we're dealing with. One of the first things that I do with patients who have postnasal drip problems is take them off dairy products. Enzymes are a very important part of what the body does to help break down toxins, chemicals and food. As we age, we make fewer enzymes. I've found that taking enzymes between meals can help with some of the congestion problems like allergies and some of the digestive problems that I see in my practice.

Q: How do you keep healthy and keep the energy up when you are working the long hours our industry demands?

• **Again, antioxidant vitamins** like vitamin A, C, E and Zinc are important. B vitamins are essential for the nervous system, the adrenal glands and the liver. There are also herbs that can help give you energy and keep your immune system strong. Siberian Ginseng is an herb that really helps; it can be taken over long periods of time and it helps to support those glandular functions. Echinacea is an herb that helps to support the immune system. It shouldn't be taken over long periods of time, but on a short term basis like those three or four weeks that you're on a shoot, is fine. There are products on the market that have Echinacea and Golden Seal root together that help fight infection. Start these herbs in the beginning, as a preventative, and you'll have a much better effect in keeping illness away. Eat well. You can substitute coffee with Siberian Ginseng or American Ginseng for women, the Chinese Ginseng for men. Bee pollen, royal jelly or B vitamins will give you a little extra energy.

Q: What about traveling on locations, especially to foreign countries?

• **One of the things that helps my patients** is to take a form of acidophilus. That is a product that you can buy in your regular drugstore. It's a culture that's in yogurt and various milk products, and is available in capsule form that doesn't need to be refrigerated. When you take these capsules while traveling, you're continuing to fill your intestines with the healthy bacteria that your body is used to. It helps to prevent traveler's diarrhea and stomach problems. You want to be really careful about your water supply. If you're on a long air flight, take a bottle of water with you on the plane; don't rely on the plane water—it's generally not very good. Flying is extremely dehydrating. A little atomizer bottle helps to spray your skin. For motion sickness there is a homeopathic remedy called Cocculus. There are other drugs, but they tend to make you sleepy and give you dry mouth; the homeopathic won't.

• **Dr. Theresa Gormly, Chiropractor and Founder of the Los Angeles Center for Healing, offers additional information on staying healthy.**

- **If people paid greater attention to their diet** they would not have as many physical complaints. I strongly recommend three meals a day consisting of 40% carbohydrates, 30% protein and 30% fat plus two small equally balanced snacks. The key is to eat high quality protein: lean red meat, turkey, chicken, fish and soy; low glycemic carbohydrates: vegetables, fruit, very little grain; and high quality fats such as raw nuts, cold pressed oils or avocado. For many people, it is also necessary to abstain from foods that they may be sensitive to, such as dairy and wheat.

- **Nutrition is one side of the triad of health** that I assess when it comes to staying healthy. It is highly beneficial to care for the physical structure of the body. The spine and extremities house our central nervous system, the brain and spinal cord. Chiropractic care and plenty of exercise are great ways to care for the physical structure.

- **Equally important is the emotional side of the triangle.** There are wonderful techniques that help clear the body of stored or toxic emotions such as Neuroemotional Technique (NET), Reiki and homeopathy. By paying attention to one's daily routine of nutrition, exercise, rest, work and play, it is easier to keep the triad of health in balance. EMOTION/CHEMISTRY/STRUCTURE.

Q: What do you recommend for delivering one's best performance when working long hours under a great deal of pressure?

- **It is important to center one's mind** through meditation or attunement at the beginning of the day. The tool for long term *sustained* energy is blood sugar stabilization. This is done with the right choice and amount of food and no longer than four to five hours of time between balanced meals. This routine takes the stress off the adrenal glands and sustained energy and a clear mind will follow. A second 20 minutes of meditation or rest in the later part of the day will give the body a second wind for the evening hours. By combining rest or meditation with the appropriate food plan, you can't miss.

Q: What about air travel? Is it a concern when traveling to locations?

- **Hobon Environs is a homeopathic remedy I recommend** for supporting the immune system during air travel and hotel lodging. This remedy helps prevent contracting airborne diseases that come through the ventilation systems. One capful per hour is recommended. It never fails. For jet lag, I recommend a Systemec Formula Gf to support the glandular system. It is to be taken at the beginning of the flight, mid-flight and every two hours on landing for about four to six hours. This helps the body handle the time zone changes.

Resources

Working Actor's Guide lists doctors, dentists, alternative type treatments, nutritionists, mental health services, as well as medical insurance information.

Free Clinics: Los Angeles Free Clinic, 323/653-1990. 8405 Beverly Blvd., Los Angeles, 90048. Valley Free Clinic, 818/763-8836. 5648 Vineland Avenue, North Hollywood. Hours: M-Sa, 10-5. Appointments are given out daily from 9 to 11am on a first call basis. They offer free pregnancy and HIV testing.

Low Cost Clinic: AIM Health Care Foundation, 818/981-5681. www.aim-med.org. 1421 Ventura Blvd., #105, Sherman Oaks, 91423. Tests for sexual transmitted diseases, no appointment needed. Exams and vaccines, by appointment only.

Cynthia Watson, M.D., Family Practice, 310/393-0937. 530 Wilshire Blvd., Suite 203, Santa Monica, 90401. Covered by SAG and AFTRA insurance; you file your own forms. A family practitioner treating men, women (obstetrics, gynecology included) and children, she combines conventional medical therapies with herbs, homeopathy, and nutrition. She is a nationally recognized authority in immune disorders and chemical toxicity. Her main interest is preventative medicine and longevity. Her book *Love Potions, A Guide To Aphrodisiacs and Sexual Pleasures* is a best-seller. She continues to write books on nutritional supplements that have healing capabilities.

Emily Bloom, M.D., 310/278-8811. 436 N. Bedford Dr., Suite 202, Beverly Hills, 90210. Dermatologist. Highly recommended by our wonderful healer, Dr. Theresa Gormly. My husband went to her for a skin growth and was very satisfied with the results. They give you a super bill and you file your own insurance forms.

Derek Jones, M.D., 310/246-0495. www.drdjones.com. 9201 W. Sunset Blvd., #602, Los Angeles, 90069. Board Certified Dermatologist also teaches at U.C.L.A. Besides skin problem expertise he's an expert in beauty treatments including the latest Vantage laser treatments. Good staff, many celebrities, special favorite of Steven Nash.

Harold Lancer, M.D., 310/278-8444. 9735 Wilshire Blvd., Penthouse, Beverly Hills. Dermatologist. Samantha Harper loves this office and says they are on the cutting edge and use all the newest techniques and discoveries.

Harvey Abrams, M.D., Wilshire Aesthetics, *A Dermatology and Plastic Surgery Group*, 323/936-1245. www.wilshireaesthetics.com. 5670 Wilshire Blvd., Suite 650, Los Angeles, 90036. Dr. Abrams and his associates are excellent. Laser dermabrasion, botox, collagen fill in lines, pump up lips and smooth out frowns. Nina Bard's facials (only there on Tuesdays) will not leave you marked but she gets everything out, $75 for cleansing and toning. They have vein and hair removal specialists and laser resurfacing. Dana has 23 years experience in hair removal.

Charles Schneider, M.D., **Eyes, Ear, Nose and Throat,** 310/201-0717. Century City. M-F 8–5 PM. Very highly recommended. He helped a singer friend of mine with chronic throat problems.

Uzzi Reiss, M.D., for women, 310/247-1300. 414 N. Camden Dr. #750, Beverly Hills, 90210. They will file SAG and AFTRA insurance forms for you. Obstetrics, gynecology, infertility. He's delivered many babies of famous people. Although an M.D., he will prescribe homeopathic remedies. Very thorough, explains in great detail. A wonderful man and Julia Louis-Dreyfus' personal favorite.

Vernon Erwin, D.D.S., **Dentist,** 818/246-1748. 620 E. Glenoaks, Glendale, 91207. Dr. Erwin uses all the latest technologies available. Ceramic fillings that last longer than metal ones; instant orthodontics, straightens teeth in weeks; implants replacing missing teeth; bleaching. He recently used a laser to correct my receding gums without surgery. They will file SAG and AFTRA forms for you. A homeopathic dentist, he will remove silver fillings and has all the equipment to test your body's reaction to what will be permanently put into your mouth. These types of dentists are hard to find. He does beautiful bleaching; repair and cosmetic work that looks like you have had nothing done, just beautiful teeth. He also treats TMJ. Theresa is the dental hygienist and she is excellent; very caring and gentle but thorough.

J. Alan Bloore, D.D.S., Orthodontist, 310/277-9700. 300 S. Beverly Drive, #101, Beverly Hills, 90212. M–Th 8:30–5:30, F 9–4. My daughter, Cathy Kerr, had her teeth straightened as an adult. She just had to wear a retainer for several months and now they are beautiful. She says, "He is the best."

Conrad Sack, D.D.S., Orthodontist, 310/273-5775. 9201 Sunset Blvd., Suite 200, Los Angeles, 90069. He specializes in Crozat, a removable appliance to take the place of braces. He treats many actors.

William Dorfman, D.D.S., 310/277-5678. 2080 Century Park East, Los Angeles. Cosmetic dentist. He is the inventor of Nite White, the country's most popular teeth whitener. He also does bleaching in the office. Used by the casts of *Friends, Melrose Place, Beverly Hills 90210, ER, Seinfeld.*

Dr. Huggins, D.D.S., Dentist, 888/843-5832. He is the author of the book *It's All In Your Head.* If you have some chronic medical problems that cannot be solved, you may be suffering from mercury poisoning which is caused from silver fillings in your mouth. This dentist is in Colorado. They will send you the book that lists all the symptoms.

• **The following two dentists are in Mexico.** Close friends of mine have used them to have their silver fillings removed and for some cosmetic work. Both dentists do beautiful work. Linda Small went to Dr. Morales. She took the train from Union Station to San Diego and then took a trolley, which is at the train station, to the border and the town of San Ysidro. You walk over the bridge and easily catch a taxi to take you to the dentist's office. A motel the dentists recommend is International Motor Inn, 190 E. Calle Primera, San Ysidro, CA 92173. Phone: 619/428-4486. Medical Clinic Discount rates, $50 per night. Free van service.

Roberto Villafana, D.D.S. Tijuana, Mexico, 619/428-1262. In Tijuana, 011/52-66-84-09-55. This Mexican dentist was trained at UCLA, one of the finest dental schools. He does holistic and cosmetic dentistry, removing silver fillings and uses the finest of materials. His office is very "high tech." His prices are about one third of L.A.s. My friends Leah and German Ruiz of The Vital Image have their work done there and rave about his wonderful techniques and great office. Leah is on the cutting edge of all that is healthy for the body.

Javier Morales, D.D.S., Calle 6Ta. 1217 Esq. Mutualismo Zona Centro, C.P. 22000 (01152664). From the U.S. tel. 688-32-48 or 688-32-42. Fax: 685-34-57. Tijuana, B.C. E-mail: drmorales_tj@yahoo.com. He has a wonderful booklet that talks about silver fillings, root canals, generating toxins, diseases arising from mouth infections and nickel. Also includes a vitamin supplementation program and information on their detox programs. They have a D.M.P.S. chelation therapy as well as a Vitamin C therapy. Both in the form of IV drips. They have a variety of treatments for detox, including a masseuse that comes in several days a week.

Warren Reingold, M.D., of The Reingold Eye Center, 818/763-3937. www.lasikvison.com. 12139 Riverside Dr., Suite 101, Valley Village, 91607. Optometry, contact lenses, fashion eyewear, diseases of the eye. He is a very caring person and I find the office very friendly and helpful. Covered by SAG and Motion Picture Industry Health Insurance, they take care of the insurance for you. He also does all of the laser vision correction eye surgeries.

Caster Eye Center, Andrew I. Caster, M.D., F.A.C.S., 310/274-1221. 9100 Wilshire Blvd., Beverly Hills. Laser vision correction. Frances Fisher says "I see the world through new eyes!" "Best laser Eye Surgeon in Los Angeles" *Los Angeles Magazine*.

Theresa Gormly, D.C., Los Angeles Center for Healing, 310/858-8886. www.center4healing.com. 1157 S. Robertson, Los Angeles, 90035. Covered by SAG and AFTRA insurance; you file your own forms. She is wonderful for relief of pain, stress, nutritional problems, candida, Epstein-Barr and general balancing. Networking and body integration. I cannot begin to explain the wonderful treatment I have received over the last fifteen years from Dr. Gormly. Upon hearing my age, people are always surprised at how well I've held up—I owe the insides to her. Many, many celebrities and models go to her. Just a small percentage is covered by insurance but you can deduct the rest from your income taxes. She has cured me of the flu, sore throats, and a few cases of the "blahs" in a few hours with her homeopathic or flower remedies. For those of you into alternative medicine, she and her associates are a gold mine!

Noel S. Aguilar, Ph.D., HMD, The DNA Health Institute, "The Power of Advanced Natural Medicine at Its Very Best." 310/858-8886. Los Angeles Center for Healing, 1157 S. Robertson Blvd., Los Angeles, 90035. Part of the Los Angeles Center for Healing. Dr. Aguilar uses many tests for diagnosis including electroacupunture to screen the body. Using pen-shaped metal rods (microcurrent probes) that are hooked up to a computer, he touches the probes to different acupuncture points, or meridians, on the hands and feet that correspond to specific organs or body parts. The machine measures the small flow of electricity through each meridian, the numbers show on the computer and he can tell where your weak areas are. Two of my friends have been going to him for years with remarkable results. I'm very happy with the work I've begun with him.

Health Within Holistic Center, 310/289-7872. 8601 Wilshire Blvd., Suite 700, Beverly Hills, 90211. "Health Within has established a reputation in the entertainment industry for offering the finest in holistic health care as well as a full service holistic facialist and massage therapist. We have an expert staff offering Accupuncture, Network Chiropractic, and Naturopathic care. By working with the body's energy, structure, matter and spirit, we create a level of health virtually unsurpassed in the healing arts." My friend Jonathan Levit loves this facility.

Dr. Murray Susser, a homeopathic doctor, 310/966-9194. 2211 Corinth Avenue, Suite 204, 5 blocks west of Sepulveda off Olympic in West Los Angeles. Also recommended by Sharon Stone, "He's created IV bags of vitamins and immune boosters, and when we were shooting *Casino* all night long, I was never tired. Also wonderful for jet lag; you take it the day before."

Eve Campanelli, Ph.D., 310/855-1111. www.evesherbs.cnoffice.com. 292 S. La Cienega, #301 Beverly Hills 90211. Remedies for healing, herbs, nutrition, minerals, acupressure. You can almost be healed from the website, you can certainly find out what's troubling you. Many celebrities including my friend Catherane Skillen.

Dr. Mallory Fromm and Therese Baxter of Sike Health Institute, 818/992-0713. www.sikehealth.com. Treatment facilities in the West Valley and West Hollywood. $110 for initial diagnostic consultation, $65 for subsequent treatments. Mallory and Therese spent over 20 years in Japan learning a modern revision of classical Chinese medicine based on Qi Energy. To this they added Western movement and alignment techniques to create the SIKE Technique. The treatment is non-invasive, non-manipulative, and extremely effective. My husband has scoliosis, and Mallory has done wonders by straightening his spine, realigning his entire body's musculature, and completely removing his pain. Therese keeps me in excellent posture and quickly heals me when my structure falls out of alignment. They have helped many of my friends and family members. Mallory is the author of "The Book of Ki: The Healing Principles of Life Energy," and "Qi Energy for Healing and Health." Therese is a graduate of England's Royal Academy of Dramatic Art (RADA), is a certified instructor of Physio-Synthesis, has 25 years experience of Alexander Technique, and is also experienced in Feldenkrais Technique.

Tawny Moyer–Reflexologist, 323/650-0748. $85, treatments are approximately an hour. Reflexology is an ancient healing technique used today which accelerates the body's own healing process by returning it to it's natural state of balance. It involves a steady, gentle pressure to specific reflex points on the feet that correspond to organs and glands throughout the body. Reflexology can provide relief for everything from minor aches and pains to chronic health conditions. It is also used for preventative health care and maintenance because it releases stress and tension through deep relaxation, as well as improving circulation, eliminating toxins, and revitalizing energy. It is a loving nurturing step toward better health and well-being. Tawny is a gifted reflexologist and very much in demand by actors and crew members when they have been working long hours on the set.

Duong Huy Ha, C.A., Acupuncture. 310/394-9747. 1326 A 5th St., Santa Monica, 90401. M-F 8-5:45PM, Sat 8-12:45PM. Partially covered by SAG and AFTRA insurance. He started practicing in China at age nine. His phone number is unlisted; people come to him only through personal recommendation. He helped me quit smoking. Yeah!

Wing Hsieh, Acupuncture, 310/859-7618. 9400 Brighton Way, Suite 208, Beverly Hills, 90210. I have never been his patient but Lily Tomlin spoke of having a bad fall while doing a stage play; he helped her recover quickly and get back to work again.

Christina Marino, L.Ac., at Spa Transcendental, 818/505-9511. 10645 Riverside Drive, Toluca Lake, 91602. They have many spa packages and acupuncture for facial beauty. "When mind and body are in complete harmony, creating a perfect balance between the physical and the spiritual, the result is a state of well-being which is the most natural condition of mankind."

John W. Davis, 310/398-9196. 12036 West Washington Blvd., Suite #1, Los Angeles, 90066. Healer, body work, Reichian emotional release work, based on the body armor theories of Wilhelm Reich. John's work helps actors find the true depth and range of their feelings; a center inside from which they can make the transformation into the character. Sees a lot of actors, directors, writers and producers. My husband Ron believes his monthly treatments have helped him to stay out of back pain.

Allred Colonic Technique, 310/390-5424. www.allredtec.com. $65-$70. 11739 Washington Blvd. West Los Angeles. Colonics. This is where you go when you are really getting ready to look great or you have over-indulged. Also anytime you need to get rid of toxins. All of the technicians have been trained by Connie Allred, the developer of the technique. This special place is recommended by many celebrities, doctors and healers.

• **Diana Lipson-Burge, R.D., nutritionist, has developed many new tools** to help with with weight management. She and co-author Jackie Jaye-Brandt, M.A., MFT, have written *Finally Free,* a book that teaches people how to release their diet mentality, which then releases their excess weight.

> • **I am struck by the enormous number of clients** who come to me for weight management tools and yet never apply the tools, or seem to be blocked when it comes to making a lifestyle change for results. I find it is important to learn, first, who they are and what they are doing daily to take care of their needs prior to addressing their weight issues. The weight issue is a direct reflection of individuals not focusing on themselves and their own inner needs.

> • **When working with clients, I find it impossible** to focus on the weight management tools (e.g. eating every three hours, listening to the hunger scale) when there may be so many other issues on the client's mind. By reminding them to daily observe their lives, it provides a tool to place the responsibility in the hands of the client to really address other areas that may be causing stress, like a feeling of being out of contol or feeling overwhelmed.

- **Clients come to notice the difference** between physiologically and psychologically fed hunger. They choose food types and amounts to meet their needs and health desires that they decide upon themselves, not those dictated by others. Above all, they learn the pleasure that can be obtained from food and eating.

Weight Watchers, 800/651-6000, www.weightwatchers.com. They offer a very sound nutritional way of eating and motivational speakers. They are now the "in" way of losing weight and keeping it off. Their program is all about health and eating education.

WEB SITES: FITNESS ONLINE

www.fitnessonline.com.
Rob Woods Home of Fitness Testing: www.worldguide.com/Fitness/hf.html.
In Fitness and In Health Site: www.phys.com/
Nutritiously Gourmet Web Site: www.nutritiouslygourmet.com.

Diana Lipson-Burge, R.D., Registered Dietitian and Director of The Energy Resource, 310/318-9767. E-mail: dianaburge@adelphia.net. Co-author of *Finally Free*. Owner and Director of the Energy Resource, and has been treating disordered eating for over 15 years. Eight-week workshop, "Optimal Life Through Nutrition."

Kristin Lundstrom, D.C., 310/858-8886. Los Angeles Center for Healing, 1157 S. Robertson, Los Angeles, 90035. Covered by SAG and AFTRA insurance; you file your own forms. She is wonderful for relief of pain, stress and nutritional problems. She taught my husband and me about eating in The Zone. She tests different foods on you to make sure your body can tolerate your prescribed nutritional plan. She uses Contact Reflex Analysis (CRA) and Network Spinal Analysis to accurately determine the body's structural, physical, and nutritional needs. The root of the health problem is uncovered or it is used as a preventative technique to stop a problem from becoming a health issue. "Find it early and correct it."

The Vital Image, 310/823-1996 or 800/414-4624, in Playa del Rey. www.thevitalimage.com. Call for their special product report. Power O2 Tonic+ is a charged organic nutritional powder that gives you enhanced focus, concentration and willpower while fueling your energy reserves and stamina. Great for those early morning set calls and the long extended working hours. *Also see their listing under Age Defying Techniques for all of their valuable treatments and products.*

HOMEOPATHIC MEDICINES

Santa Monica Drug, 310/395-1131. 629 Broadway, Santa Monica, 90401. M-Sa 9:30 to 5:15; parking south of building.
Capitol Drugs, 310/289-1125. 8578 Santa Monica Blvd., West Hollywood, 90069. Nice coffee and juice bar. M-F 9-9, Sa&Su 9-6.
Capitol Drugs, 818/905-8338. 4454 Van Nuys Blvd., Sherman Oaks, 91403. M-F 9-8, Sat 9-6, Sun 10-6.
Drug Stop, 323/655-9761. 8021 Melrose, Los Angeles. M-F 10-6; Sa. 10-5.

MENTAL HEALTH

• **Knowing yourself can help you know the characters** you portray better; finding your own essence will help you find the essence of the character. As you learn to deal with your own anger, fears and anxieties, you will probably become a better actor. Working with a therapist or a self-help program can bring you to a deeper self-awareness.

• **Dr. Sherie Zander** gives the following advice on shopping for a therapist:

  • **Choosing the best psychotherapist** for your particular needs is of utmost importance. You will not only be spending time and money, but you will be talking about some very personal issues. The person you work with must be someone you believe you can trust. Base your trust on gathered information and an inner reaction or gut-level feeling about that person. If a therapist is recommended by someone whom you respect, that is a good place to start.

Q: What questions should you ask when interviewing a therapist?

  • **Are you licensed** by the State? How long have you been practicing? What type of therapy do you practice? Do you have experience with my particular issues? Have you had positive results? Would you do in-depth work to get to the root causes or would you have a more immediate behavioral approach? What is your fee? How often would I need to come in?

  • **As you gather information**, you will begin to get a feeling about the therapist and to form an opinion. It is important to trust that inner response you are having. If possible, interview at least three psychotherapists and compare the information you get and the ways you respond to each one. Based upon all of this, make a choice.

  • **If, after several sessions**, you believe you have made the wrong choice, I would encourage you to tell your therapist that you are dissatisfied and then move on to someone else. It is far better to start over than to continue in a situation that is not working for you.

Q: What do you most enjoy about your work?

  • **It is a great source of encouragement** to me when I see someone move from a place of despair to a place of hope, when emotional pain is decreasing and wounds are healing, when someone begins to utilize new tools and techniques to handle old sets of problems, and when life is being viewed from a new perspective.

Resources

www.psychboard.ca.gov. The California Board of Psychology website has good consumer information as well as being able to verify whether a therapist is licensed by the state. www.apa.org. The American Psychological Association website has articles and can tell you if a therapist has been sued. They also have a referral system at 800/964-2000.

Sherie Zander, Ph.D., 310/472-9736. Very supportive. Private and group therapy; she also teaches a class in men/women relationships. She has been a guest on my cable show several times, discussing how she helps actors learn to deal with their anger, fears and anxieties. Call her to request a free guide she uses with clients to help them deal with anger. Dr. Zander also specializes in couple communications, family relationships, help with attracting a mate and addictive behaviors.

Jackie Jaye-Brandt, M.A., MFT, Corporate Communications and Psychotherapy, 818/505-1664. 3575 Cahuenga Blvd. West, #213, Los Angeles, 90068. Stress management, communications training, time management, group workshops, couples groups and individual counseling. Jackie has made a huge difference in my life. She works with people privately, usually for short periods of time; she wants you well in a timely manner. She is the co-author of *Finally Free,* a book that teaches people how to release their diet mentality, which then releases their excess weight.

Pat Allen, 310/553-8248, 800/303-1902. www.drpatallen.com. Specializes in finding and keeping a mate. She gives private or telephone consultations and her books and lecture tapes are available. Monday evening seminars from 7-8:30pm are $5 to $10. The location and price are subject to change; call for the latest information. A great place to meet singles. Author of the book *Getting To I Do!*

Stephen Felman, M.A., 310/535-0515. 1427 21st Street, Suite A, Santa Monica, 90403. Steven says he likes to "help people get in contact with the wisest part of themselves so they can start making the decisions they really need to make in their lives." He also works with dreams.

Jo Christner, Psy.D., 310/471-2773. Offices in Encino and West Los Angeles. She specializes in helping you feel your very best so that you can have peak performances and a better quality of life. She has appeared on my cable show and has assisted many from the acting industry, from the novice to the renowned. Mood disorders (depression, anxiety and panic attacks), eating disorders, stress management and geriatric services are among her specialities. Her services include confidential, individual and group psychotherapy, as well as educational seminars.

Clearmind Hypnotherapy, Alisha Tamburri, 818/775-1868 www.clearmindhypnotherapy.com. Certified clinical hypnotherapist and member of the American Counseling Association. Alisha has helped actors gain confidence, overcome their fear of auditions and achieve career success through hypnosis. She helps clients with performance anxiety, stress, panic disorder, weight control, smoking, poor memorization, fear of flying, and insomnia.

Hand Analysis with Terry-Linn Snider, 310/358-7695. E-mail: lifepurpose101@aol.com. Northern California 650/738-2363. $100 for a one hour private reading. $150 for a two hour couples reading. Terry says, "Hand Analysis reveals your purpose and lesson in life as well as your gifts, challenges, non-negotiable needs and much more. It is like discovering your own personal owner's manual."

The following clinics are available on an ability-to-pay basis.

Gay and Lesbian Center, Mental Health Services, 323/993-7640.
Maple Counseling Center, 310/271-9999. 9107 Wilshire Blvd., Lower Level, Beverly
Hills, 90210. Sliding payment scale for actors who live or work in Beverly Hills.
Open Paths, 310/398-7877. 12655 W. Washington Blvd. #101, Los Angeles, 90066.
Southern California Counseling Center, 323/937-1344. 5615 W. Pico Blvd., Los
Angeles, 90019. I've known people who have received good help here.
Thalians, 310/423-3504 at Cedars Sinai Hospital, 8730 Alden Dr., Los Angeles, 90048.
AIPADA-Alcohol & Drug Abuse Hot Line: 800/756-HOPE
Take 12 meets every Friday at 8:30 p.m. in the James Cagney Room at SAG. Closed
meeting for union members only. Marijuana Anonymous, 323/964-2370; Adult Chil-
dren of Alcoholics (ACOA); Overeaters Anonymous; HOW/Overeaters Anonymous; Nico-
tine Anonymous; Narcotics Anonymous; Anger Anonymous; Co-dependents Anonymous
(CODA); Debtors Anonymous; Gamblers Anonymous; Sex & Love Anonymous (SLA);
and for people who deal with alcoholics or addicts in their life or addictions not listed here:
ALANON 818/760-7122. Many meetings are held at the Crescent Heights Methodist Church,
1296 Fairfax Avenue, West Hollywood. Stop by and look at their posted schedules.
Alcoholics Anonymous (AA) Referral Service & Treatment: 800/711-6375
24 hour hotline; can help you locate meetings in your area.

PLASTIC SURGERY, LIPOSUCTION, VEIN AND HAIR REMOVAL, SKIN RESURFACING

• **The most important thing you can do as an actor** is to stay out of
the sun; it is what ages you. If you have already done the damage before
you knew you wanted a long career in front of the camera as a leading
actor. Unless you have fabulous genes you will need cosmetic correc-
tions done. Check the *Age-Defying Techniques Section* for things to be
done before the knife, including resurfacing, botox and collagen.

• **When considering breast implants,** understand that extremely large
breasts will limit your casting possibilities. Yes, it will open up some
roles but unless they call for nudity, you can do those parts with false
breasts; even the nude ones can be done with body doubles. There is no
way to make your breasts look smaller. Pamela Anderson removed her
very large implants for just large ones. She still can't play a small-breasted
woman. I think Demi Moore and Teri Hatcher have the best breasts
because sometimes they look small and other times big. The most
requested size for women getting implants is a full B or a C cup.

• **Liposuction, noses, eyes and breasts** seem to be the most popular procedures and I have found experts to discuss these and other procedures.
Be conservative in your surgery decisions. I know it's tempting to have it
all done at once because you save money, but it is wiser not to make
plastic surgery decisions because of cost. Not all doctors are the same;
they all have different views of the same surgeries. Choose carefully.

• **A new student of mine** came for a private class after having just been to a plastic surgeon. This girl is adorable, 22, looks 16, ample breasts and lips, fashionably thin, attractive face, nice nose, cheeks. She went to a very notable plastic surgeon (a family friend) because she had a couple of small growths under her skin that needed to be removed. She was correct in seeing a plastic surgeon. But he met with her for an hour and showed her all the possibilities of improving her face and body. When she arrived at my house, she was feeling ugly and asked me for advice of what to do first. I said 'leave yourself alone, you're unique and beautiful.' Earlier that day I had been talking with an agent on the phone about meeting one of my very talented students. He said, 'I hate her picture, looks like she's had her lips all pumped up.' What could I say? She had. I relayed this to my new young student and told her to please let her good acting talent beam through her natural good looks.

• **Plastic surgeons are salespeople,** as are most doctors. Our goal should be to have as few surgeries as possible. Follow your instincts.

• **Your surgeon of choice is "a human being" not "God."** Ask questions, get clear answers and make sure costs, procedures and recovery are understood. Bring along a friend for moral support. Pay attention to the surgeon's attitude, temperament and responsiveness to questions. Ask for recommendations, photos or videos of befores and afters. Check the American Medical Association for negative reports. Remember that when getting a facelift, incisions will be made into the hairline. The skin removed in this area contains hair follicles and could mean a possible decrease in hair. Discuss each procedure.

• **Dr. Harvey Abrams, the founder of Wilshire Aesthetics, A Dermatology and Plastic Surgery Group, talks about what liposuction can and cannot do.**

> • **Thanks to recent technological developments,** especially the development of smaller, more refined instruments, liposuction is much improved. It can be offered to many more patients for whom I am able to remove larger amounts of fat safely and with minimal risk. In addition, the recovery process is much shorter and more comfortable.

Q: Who performs liposuction, how do you choose a surgeon, and how much does it cost?

> • **Liposuction does not belong to any particular surgical specialty.** Board certified physicians, especially Dermatologists, Cosmetic and Plastic Surgeons who have performed many liposuctions and have an interest in liposuction, are the best choices.

- **Word of mouth is the best possible endorsement.** Get referrals from people who have had the procedure and are satisfied with the results and the care they received. It is important the physician is board certified in their area of specialization. It is best to find someone who has performed this type of surgery on a regular basis for many years.

- **Fees vary greatly** but generally range from about $3,000 to $7,000.

Q: Is this a good way to lose weight and does the fat come back?

- **Liposuction is not for weight loss.** It changes the shape of the body by removing unwanted fatty bulges. It is a very successful way of contouring for individuals who are within 10% of their ideal body weight.

- **Scientific evidence indicates** that removed fat cells do not grow back. If a person maintains a weight close to their normal body weight through proper diet and exercise, there is every reason to believe the body changes achieved will be permanent.

Q: Does laser hair removal work on everyone? Is it permanent?

- **The whole field of laser hair removal is very new.** It doesn't always work, that is why you have to go to someone who knows whether it will work for you or not. There are a lot of variables; it depends on the thickness and color of the hair and on the color of the skin. Not everybody is a good candidate. Go to a technician who has had a lot of experience and will level with you. In our office, Dana has had 23 years experience in hair removal. Hair can be removed from every part of the body and it can be expensive. There are many so-called bargains that turn out not to be bargains because the technicians can't deliver on their promises. New lasers are being developed all the time. It is an evolving field. You want to go to someone who keeps up with the latest research and owns the latest proven equipment.

Q: What can be accomplished with laser skin resurfacing?

- **Lasers are used to eradicate many different flaws on the skin,** including blood vessels, wrinkles, sun spots and other signs of aging. Wilshire Aesthetics has a full range of laser services including tattoo removal. The success rate depends on the tattoo. The ones that are a blue/black are very successful. The ones that have many intricate colors, such as blues, reds, yellows and greens, are much more difficult,and require many more treatments. It doesn't usually leave a scar, but sometimes you can't get out all the pigment, so don't start unless you are committed to finishing. It can take anywhere from eight to twenty treatments. A small tattoo could cost $1,000; a large one could be several thousand dollars.

- **Dr. Guy Massry, specializes in reconstructive and cosmetic surgery** of the eye, eyebrows, forehead, and mid-face lifting. I asked why some doctors choose to specialize.

  - **I think when a doctor specializes in a specific area** their experience will be greater, the surgical results superior and, most importantly, complications are minimized. For instance, in facial cosmetic surgery, a poorly done nose or eyes can cause significant disability to patients, as breathing and vision can be affected. It is vitally important that the surgeons performing these procedures are well versed and have vast experience in order to avoid post-operative problems.

  - **The way I developed my practice** is to combine the expertise of surgical subspecialists, thus creating a cosmetic team, in order to provide the best service and attain excellent results. A common example is the patient who desires a browlift, eyelid surgery and a rhinoplasty (nose job). I will evaluate the patient and perform the brow and lid surgery, while my associate who specializes in rhinoplasty will address that portion of the patients concerns. The patient gets the best of both worlds.

  - **A significant part of my practice is revision surgery.** This refers to patients who have had previous surgery who need further correction or are unhappy with the results. Typical problems are eyelids that won't completely close, lower lids that are pulled down or turned out, a "wide eyed" appearance, or residual puffiness of skin. These are complex problems that truly require the care of a specialist. For instance, when lower lids are pulled down, lifting the cheek to supply skin to the lower lids is often times necessary. Thus, to correct these problems, an understanding of mid-face surgery is essential.

Q: What about cheek implants?

  - **You can lift the cheek without an implant;** the implant just brings the cheek out. Lifting the cheek is a procedure which brings the thicker cheek tissue higher and makes the cheek more prominent. If I can avoid putting foreign material in someone's face for life, I will. I'm very cautious about a foreign substance. When necessary, we will put it in.

- **Dr. Garth Fisher is a board certified Plastic and Reconstructive surgeon.** He specializes in aesthetic/cosmetic plastic surgery of the face and breasts. His practice has predominately included entertainers, celebrities and executives from around the world.

Q: When doing breast implants, do you make the incisions around the nipple for actresses that do not want any noticeable scars?

• **A large majority of the Playmates are my patients.** They often work with their clothes off, so I am very careful with the scars. I close the incisions carefully so that the scars are difficult to find. That is taken into account on a daily basis here.

Q: Is silicone still available?

• **For first-time patients, we primarily use saline implants,** unless there are mitigating circumstances, then we can use silicone. For reconstructive patients, I often use silicone.

• **There is an inclusion criteria set up by the FDA** and implant manufacturers. If the client fulfills the guidelines, then I use silicone. There are advantages and disadvantages to silicone implants. They are especially helpful for patients that have very thin skin.

• **There are different types of implants.** Teardrop shaped implants are mainly used on top of the muscle. Round implants can be used on top or below the muscle. The implant that is used depends on the person's body.

• **The important thing is having the implants look natural.** Small or large, you want to make them look like natural breasts. I find that is what most patients want. They don't like the hard, round, beachball look.

Q: I understand that you often have to do reconstructive surgery when a patient has had bad surgery elsewhere.

• **They are challenging cases and I've had a lot of experience with them.** I've done over 4,000 breast implants and associated reconstructive procedures. We try to convert people to a more natural look, a softer look. It depends on the particular problem they have.

Q: Is there any advice you would give people when interviewing doctors for breast implants?

• **Bring in pictures, show the doctor exactly what you want.** Communication is very important. Let the doctor know exactly what you are trying to achieve. Hopefully, he'll be honest enough to tell you whether he can deliver it or not. In our office, a patient will bring in a Playboy magazine. We know most of those girls, so we know what they are trying to accomplish. Look at before and after pictures, review some of the results of the doctor's work. Does he get the results that the patients are after?

Q: How can you try out breasts before having surgery?

• **They can fill Ziploc bags with saline or rice** and put them in their bra if they want to approximate sizes. It is not very reproducible or exact, but it may help.

• Respected plastic surgeon Dr. Gregory Mueller talks about facial surgeries.

Q: What kind of corrective facial surgeries are popular?

  • **Eyelid lifts are the most common procedure** performed on patients in their thirties. Sometimes the upper lids will have excess skin; fat that can be easily removed under local anesthesia. The postoperative care consists of cool compresses to the eye area for 48 hours. The stitches are removed on the 6th day after surgery. Sometimes individuals also develop a creppiness under the lower eyelid—that too can be easily remedied with a mild chemical peel. For the individual with puffy bags under the eyes, lower lids can be improved by removing the bags under the eyes and any excess skin. Both procedures result in a rested, refreshed look.

  • **Another common surgery for younger patients** is called a platysmaplasty or neck muscle tightening and liposculpting of the neck. This procedure is done to improve and define the jaw line. Patents can usually return to work in just 4 to 5 days.

  • **Cymetra is an amazing material** that requires zero down time and has immediate result. Injections of this soft tissue replacement material correct many defects, including repairing depressed scars, decreasing the appearance of facial creases, adding fullness to the cheeks and minimizing the laugh lines. Enlargement of lips. Like collagen, this treatment is not permanent and requires touch-up injections every 3 to 6 months.

  • **Another procedure that is increasing in popularity** is male pectoral augmentation. The typical patient is physically fit, works out in the gym on a regular basis, but just cannot achieve the desired cuts and definition in the chest area. Other candidates include those born with a smaller muscle on one side, or someone who has injured the muscle. The surgery is performed on an out-patient basis, with the implants being inserted through a small incision in each armpit. The patient wears a compression vest for approximately 4 weeks. After this period, he may return to full physical activity.

Q: At what age should someone consider a face lift?

  • **It really depends on your genetics and how you age.** When people notice they are beginning to get jowls around the jaw border area, or if they notice that skin is sagging under their neck, they may want to consider a facelift. This procedure can dramatically improve a person's appearance making them appear younger.

Q: How do you hide the scars?

  • **The scars are very well concealed.** There is no way you can do surgery without scars, but putting them inside the ear can hide them. We actually pull the front part of the ear forward and we are able to make the incisions almost on the inside of the ear. And then we bring it right around the ear where the earlobe attaches to the head and then back behind the ear in the little crease where the ear meets the side of the head, and then along the hair line, or sometimes in women, we will go up in the hair. Done this way, it allows us to hide the scars within the natural contour of the ear. The scars are very hard to see after several months. It usually takes 6 months to a year for the scars to completely heal, but even after two weeks you can conceal the scars by putting on cover-up make-up.

Q: How do you keep from having a pulled artificial look?

• **When choosing a plastic surgeon**, ask to see photos of other patients. If you like the results, you will probably be satisfied with your result. If the look is "too pulled" or obviously surgical, I would choose another surgeon.

Q: What if you want to lift your forehead or raise your eyebrows?

• **There are a couple of different treatments for foreheads.** Probably the newest and the most popular is botox. Botox helps people who have wrinkles on the forehead. It is a medicine that you inject, in an office procedure that takes about ten minutes. It basically relaxes the muscles so that they are unable to lift the eyebrows. What happens over a few weeks is it will lessen the wrinkles that run horizontally along your forehead. It will also improve frown lines and the crows feet around your eyes.

• **Some patients have very low eyebrows**, so they aren't candidates for botox, which could actually cause them to have a further drop of the eyelids. They would be a better candidate for a brow lift.

• **There are two types of forehead lifts.** There is one where the incision is made across the head from ear to ear. You basically take out a strip of scalp and then just pull everything up backwards and sew it together. That is the traditional brow lift. The new one is more popular, especially with men, because of receding hairlines. It is called an endoscopic brow lift. A series of five small incisions are made in the front of the scalp. A scope and digital camera system is used to visualize the operation with the skin still remaining on the forehead. We are able to release the eyebrows from underneath and then by using little anchors or screws, we are able to suspend the forehead. Fibrin glue is then applied to hold the forehead and brow in position.

Q: How long after a face procedure does it take to look presentable?

• **I recommend that my patients** have two to three weeks of down time if they don't want people to know. With makeup, you can pretty much conceal most of the scarring. You're still going to have swelling, but the majority of the swelling is usually gone. Usually the majority of the bruising is lower on the neck, so a high collar will conceal alot. After five to seven days, you can return to work if the appearance doesn't concern you.

Resources

Cinema Secrets, 818/846-0579, www.cinemasecrets.com. 4400 Riverside Drive, Burbank. Face lifts without fear. Maurice Stein sells a nonsurgical face lift kit for $25 that purports to take 5 to 10 years off your face for four to six hours. Movie makeup experts have used these kits for years.

I give you the names of the following MD surgeons to start your research, Rely on your own medical advisors before taking drastic surgical steps.

LIPOSUCTION

Harvey Abrams, M.D. **of Wilshire Aesthetics,** a Dermatology and Plastic Surgery Group, 323/936-1245. www.wilshireaesthetics.com 5670 Wilshire Blvd., Suite 650, Los Angeles, 90036. Dr Abrams is the founder of the group and has been developing instruments and procedures for liposuction work for many years. He also teaches his procedures to other doctors. Dr. Abrams, in my mind, is "the artist of liposuction." The results depend on the artistry as well as the technique of the doctor.

AMERICAN SOCIETY OF PLASTIC AND RECONSTRUCTIVE

American Society of Plastic and Reconstructive Surgeons, 847/228-9900. When you call they will refer you to their web site for information, www.plasticsurgery.org. You can put in the name of the doctor and they will tell you whether or not they are certified. The web page also has other links. If you are not online, call 800/635-0635, give them the names of the doctors and they will mail a printout with the information.

American Board of Plastic Surgeons, 215/587-9322. They will look up three doctors per phone call.

PLASTIC AND RECONSTRUCTIVE SURGEONS

Norman Leaf, M.D., F.A.C.S., 310/274-8001. Plastic and Reconstructive Surgery, 436 N. Bedford Dr., Suite 103, Beverly Hills. www.leafskincare.com. Practicing over 25 years. Specializes and is known for his beautiful facelifts. He was recommended to me as "the doctor for facelifts," by Dr. Theresa Gormly. Many, many celebrity clients. "W" magazine named him as one of the "World's Best Plastic Surgeons." Dr. Leaf has created "Solutions Skincare Medical Clinic," a ground-breaking facility in the area of medical skin health and beauty. Recently teaming with Rand Rusher, R.N., to produce the new and very exciting Leaf&Rusher, www.leafandrusher.com, line of medical-grade skincare products.

Gregory Mueller, M.D. 310/273-9800. 436 N. Bedford Drive, Suite 103, Beverly Hills. www.drgregmueller.com. Dr. Mueller's practice involves all areas of plastic surgery, including plastic surgery for men. He is said to be "the brow lift king of Beverly Hills." Excellent bedside manner and aesthetic good sense. A famous retired plastic surgeon, when asked who would replace him, said, "Dr. Greg Mueller is the most talented up and coming surgeon in Los Angeles." Great, supportive staff. Dr. Mueller has pioneered several surgical techniques and has designed a pectoral implant for men. Dr. Mueller travels around the country teaching other surgeons his technique for pectoral augmentations, endoscopic brow lift technique and cymetra injection technique. He has been on several television shows including *Entertainment Tonight* demonstrating makeovers and surgical techniques.

Garth Fisher, M.D. 310/273-5995. www.garthfisher.com. 120 S. Spalding Drive, #222, Beverly Hills, 90212. Board certified. *Los Angeles Magazine* says "One of the best plastic surgeons in L.A." *Best Doctors in America Review* chose him as "One of the top facial cosmetic and breast surgeons." I am most personally impressed by his "tear drop" silicone breast implants. One of my students had implants that were too large, but Dr. Fisher replaced them. He went in through the nipple and performed a miracle, since this actress needed to have virtually invisible scars. I saw them after only three months —amazing results! International clientele. Very helpful staff. Laser skin resurfacing. Featured on television's *Extreme Makeovers*.

Guy G. Massry, M.D. 310/453-8474. www.ggmassrymd.com. 120 S. Spalding Drive, Suite 315, Beverly Hills, 90212. Dr. Massry specializes in reconstructive and cosmetic surgery of the eye, eyebrows, forehead, and mid-face lifting. He worked a miracle on my eyelids. They had already been through three surgeries; he cured my tearing problem, plus he brought back the natural shape that had been distorted. (yeah!) He also does laser skin resurfacing, treating skin that is sun damaged, wrinkled, pigmented and scarred. Dr. Massry performs a large amount of revisional work.

Dr. Harry Glassman, 310/550-0999. 120 S. Spalding, Suite 205, Beverly Hills, 90212. Very large celebrity clientele.

Dr. Glowacki, 310/540-0144. 4201 Torrance Boulevard, Suite 150, Torrance, 90504. Board certified. One of my students had implants that were too big for her body, saline double Ds. He replaced them with saline Ds and she was very happy with the outcome. Very reasonably priced at $2,000.

Dr. Steven Grifka, 310/204-4111. Board certified. I have received glowing reports on his work from readers of past editions.

Hair Transplants

Dr. Lee Bosley, Bosley Hair Instutite, locations all over the country.
Dr. Peter Goldman, 310/855-1160. 8631 W. 3rd St, #635. Los Angeles.
Dr. Toby Mayer, 310/278-8823. Specializes in hair transplants for complete baldness.
Dr. William Rassman, The New Hair Institute, 1-800-NEW-HAIR. 9911 W. Pico, Los Angeles. Considered the number one hair transplant surgeon in the United States.

Section Seven

Acting Is Everything

Love of Your Career and Show Biz

• **I decided I had to live my life as an actor**—that I could be nothing else—in January 1975, sitting in my car at the corner of Hollywood Blvd. and Vermont. That decision, ambition, drive, has guided my life every day since. If you can be anything else but an actor, be it. But if you can't, then forge ahead, and love your choice. It is great to learn to have fun in life.

• **Tom Hanks says,**

  • **Acting is one cool gig.**

• **Kate Winslet said,**

  • **Because of the person I am, I won't be knocked down—ever.** They can do what they like. They can say I'm fat, I'm thin, I'm whatever, and I'll never stop. I just won't. I've got too much to do. I've too much to be happy about.

• **Timothy Hutton said the most important lesson he learned about acting** was from his actor father, Jim Hutton. When Jim was working and things were going well, he was happy; when things weren't going well, he was still happy because he had such a great appreciation for just being in the business.

• **James Woods said,**

  • **Acting per se has never been a struggle for me** because I enjoy it so much. I enjoy the other actors, being on the set, the excitement and the tension of going for the gold.

- **Janine Turner** said, before she got *Northern Exposure,*

  - **I was very depressed.** I had been auditioning for something like 11 years. I was wiped out. I couldn't even get a job as a waitress. So I went down to the jewelry district with the ring. (At one time she was engaged to Alec Baldwin.) I didn't know who to trust and I ended up walking away—I just couldn't do it. I had $8 in my checking account and wasn't able to make the rent. With nowhere to go but up, I tried for the part of Maggie.

- **Life can turn around on that phone call for an audition.**

- **We plant many seeds. It is important not to dig the seed up** to see if it is growing. We trust and have faith that it is indeed growing and it will manifest itself at the perfect time.

- **Ed Marinaro says,**

  - **If you can understand the reality of the business** and find a logical way of approaching it, your chances of being successful are going to be a lot better. There's nothing fair about the business. It's all about luck. The only thing you can count on is being prepared. You have to know what you're doing, train and become as good an actor as you can. What you can't count on is getting a break. But if you do get a break, you better be prepared; and that's true for every actor that's ever been successful. They got lucky. If you're really emotionally down and feel like the world's dumping on you, the next day you might get a shot and you're not going to be prepared. You're gonna blow it.

- **When we use acting tools, we cannot go for results.** We have to *make the effort* and then be willing for nothing to happen. The results will take care of themselves. It is hard to trust this, but by filling our hearts with love it is easier to trust.

- **When we read 12 plays to find one scene** that we want to do in class, when we audition for 20 plays and finally get a walk-on role, when we send out 200 pictures and get one response, when we have 10 different odd jobs just to support our career, when we go on 20 interviews before getting one line on a television show, when we have 50 commercial interviews before landing one, we are *making the effort* and we will reap the benefits. All of these endeavors are our careers. "Happiness is found along the way, not at the end of the road."

• **Discouragement is a killer**—a heart killer—don't give it a chance to grab hold of you. Yes, there are the times of discouragement and depression, but we must emerge from those times with even more determination and faith that the efforts will bring forth the results.

• **William Hurt says,**

  • **There's nothing about being an actor that isn't silly.** That's one of the attractions. It is very important to focus on this side of the work or else life can become tedious. So much of the effort we put out does not seem to get immediate results. One of the important bonuses is that the work is fun.

• **Farrah Fawcett says,**

  • **No matter what the experience, good or bad,** I think in the long run it strengthens your character and furthers your career.

• **Be willing for the results to be different than you imagined.** Usually they will surpass your wildest dreams—that's why it is very important to dream big, bigger, biggest. Do not limit your dreams. Who do you know who is more worthy of their dreams coming true than you? I trust your answer is "no one." When your dreams come true, you can help others attain their dreams as others have helped you to attain yours.

• **Kevin Spacey said,**

  • **There is no prize out there.** The only prize is this one (pointing to himself), what you feel and what you want to accomplish. To want and to be ambitious is not enough. That is just desire. To know what you want, to understand why you are doing it, to dedicate every breath in your body to achieve it, if you feel you have something to give, if you feel that your particular talent is worth developing, is worth caring for. Then there is nothing that you can't achieve.

• **Matthew Broderick said,**

  • **Actors have this desperate need to get in front of people** and do something. I don't know where that comes from; I have it too. Sometimes I think about it and I find it totally embarrassing. It's some kind of exhibitionist quality that we all have.

• **Visualization is a valuable tool. See yourself driving to the studio,** saying hello to the guard and pulling into your parking place with your name on it. Hear those magic words on the phone, "You got the job."

Watch yourself driving in your new car to your dream house with all the worldly goods that would represent your monetary success as an actor.

• **Most of us are daydreamers living in fantasy worlds.** Put your dreams to work for you; instead of dreaming negatively—worrying about future problems—dream positively. Guard and treasure your fantasy world: it is the key to your future. If you can *picture* yourself doing something, you can attain it. Your dreams will show you how to fulfill your desires.

• **Mary Steenburgen,** at a tribute for Jack Nicholson, told of working as a waitress in New York for five years while dreaming of an acting career. She heard of a casting call for *Going South* which Jack was directing. When she went by the office, the casting director told her, "We're only seeing well-known actresses or very beautiful models." Mary says, "Shy as I was, I did insist on seeing the script. Suddenly I hear this unmistakable voice, which said, "Are you waiting for me?" And I answered, "No, I don't have a script." After he gave me a script, he promised he'd see me for 10 minutes the next day." Several days later, Mary got the call to go to Hollywood for the screen test, and we know of the great career that audition fostered.

• **Julian Myers,** a Hollywood publicist, wrote a column years ago that I keep as an inspiration. Here are some of the ways he suggests to keep happy working in Hollywood.

> • **Be individualistic. Be different. Have outside interests.** Entertain, even if necessarily modestly. Master the Internet, and use it. Attend many industry doings, including dinners and forums. Eat, drink and have your hair done where your colleagues do. Drive a more expensive car than you can afford, and keep it shiny. Keep in touch with prospective employers every few months, preferably by mail. Dress attractively. Work long hours if they are leading you upward. Set aside savings for when you are unemployed. You will be. Cheerfully fill special requests. Have time, interest and advice for those not yet up to your career level. Attend movies and observe what audiences react to. Try to see all important TV shows, and each series at least once. Average less than six hours sleep a night. You're in a tough race and you have to make each hour count. Read new books. Decide this is your industry and you'll always be a part of it, even when between jobs. Try to like almost everyone in the industry—and almost everyone will like you. Look for the good in Hollywood and defend it.

ACTORS WITH DISABILITIES

• **Otto Felix**, an able-bodied actor, is the founder of Handicapped Artists, Performers, Partners, Incorporated (HAPPI), the largest non-profit theatrical group for disabled performers in the country. Otto has done over 300 commercials, has been a regular on three TV series plus many guest-starring roles and worked in over 20 feature films.

Q: Tell me about HAPPI.

- • **I created HAPPI in 1986.** There are actors, musicians, comedians and athletes. HAPPI includes partners who are all able-bodied people that also have the same aspirations, and they work side by side. We have a 10 piece band made up of able-bodied and disabled people. We have workshops Tuesday and Wednesday nights, and it's been going strong.

- • **The honorary chairman is Fred Dryer** (*Hunter*). The students elect a president of HAPPI. Right now its Demott Davis. He's the fellow who broke his neck playing football at Harvard. The vice-president is Chris Warfield who wrote and produced his own movie, *Blind*. Pretty incredible, huh?

Q: How much does it cost to join the organization?

- • **Everybody pitches in and helps** pay for the space that I rent over in West L.A. which usually comes to $40 each a month. The space costs $400 a month. It's a voluntary thing. We have an agency that we started that's called the H.I.T. Agency, that's HAPPI International Talent. We help people get jobs. They give us 10% of what they do and the money goes back into HAPPI's account, which is a full non-profit association. I use it for buying stamps when I send their pictures out and make calls for them. It's not a big powerhouse agency by any sense of the imagination.

Q: How do you get work for your people?

- **I get calls from agents for work.** I got a call today for three blind guys that jog, and I've got three of them all lined up. The casting people know who HAPPI is. It's either Richard Wright, my partner, or myself. We have 180 or so people signed up.

- **Every other year, I do a showcase** at the Director's Guild. Last year the governor, the mayor, Keith Carradine, Carl Weathers, etc. were there. I had celebrities give out little Ottos. Jon Voight calls them little Oscars. We give them out to handicapped people who did outstanding work in the previous year. We're growing; it was a great show.

• **My thanks to Terry Correll**, an actor/producer in a wheelchair, who told me about Otto and HAPPI. Terry is a wonderful, sensitive actor. He did a showcase scene on my cable TV show and had a leading role in a play I directed. His chair never made a difference. We didn't have to make any adjustments. He took care of everything.

Resources

HAPPI, Handicapped Artists, Performers and Partners, Inc., 310/394-6625. P.O. Box 24225, Los Angeles, 90024. Workshops and classes to assist talented, disabled artists seeking careers in film, television, radio and other areas of show business. Interviews and auditions are held on a continuing basis by appointment.

Otto Felix Film Acting Workshop, 310/470-1939. Actor/writer/producer/coach. He teaches disabled actors in his regular cold reading classes and film scene work classes, as well as for HAPPI. He offers a special rate of $50 a month.

Deaf West Theatre, 818/762-2998. Reservations: 818/762-2773. Voice: 818/762-2782 (TDD) 5112 Lankershim Blvd., North Hollywood, CA 91601. Manager/artistic director is Ed Waterstreet. 99-Seat Equity Plan. Philosophy: to enrich the cultural lives of the two million deaf and hard-of-hearing Los Angeles residents, use of Sign Language Theatre (SLT), classics, contemporary and original works; other activities; professional summer school, children's workshops.

Media Access, Gail Williamson, 818/752-1196. Employment for actors with disabilities.

SAG Hollywood Affirmative Action/Diversity Department, 323/549-6645. Performers with disabilities.

Manager Terre Worhach, 323/850-8136. Terre represents actors with disabilities. She is very helpful and will answer any questions you have. She really knows what is available for the actors she represents.

WRITING AND DIRECTING
WORKSHOPS

WRITING

• **If you have a talent for writing,** it can indeed be one of your greatest career assets. You should certainly develop it. Final Draft is the industry standard scriptwriting software.

• **We have all heard of Sylvester Stallone's** *Rocky* script. He was living penniless in New York but refused to sell his script unless he could act in it. It could happen to you.

• **Actors Matt Damon and Ben Affleck** decided, "If you want a good role, write it yourself." They sold *Good Will Hunting* to Castle Rock for well over a half a million dollars and both starred in it.

• **Copyrighting and/or registering your script is a must.** There are two ways to do it; some writers do both. The federal copyright office costs $20 and they keep the script for 75 years. The Writers Guild of America West is $20. They keep the script for five years, which means you must re-register every five years. You do not have to be a member to register.

(Phone numbers, addresses and websites follow.)

Writing Resources

www.bender-spink.com. Chris Bender and J.C. Spink are producers and managers of writers. You can submit scripts to their website and if they are interested they will give feedback and try and sell your project. Well respected. Also intern programs.
www.storybay.com. This is a place to sell your script or to at least have it looked at.
www.scriptviking.com. 818/787-8202. John Winther is the founder of the script service, Script Viking. They have put together professionals with expertise to recognize script potential and financing. Visit the website for details and pricing.
www.inkspot.com, many tips for writers.
Truby's Writers Studio, 310/575-3050. Classes, videos and tapes. Very popular among studio people.
UCLA Extension courses, 310/825-1901.
The Writers Computer Store, 800/272-8927 or 310/441-5151. www.writerstores.com 2040 Westwood Blvd., Los Angeles, 90025. Final Draft is the industry standard software. M-F 10-6, Sa 10-5.
For Copyrighting: Register of Copyrights, Library of Congress, Washington, D.C. 20559. $20 fee. Forms and circulars hotline, 202/707-9100. The U.S. Copyright Office web site: www.lcweb.loc.gov/copyright Find answers to questions regarding copyright and download copyright forms.
For Copyrighting: The Writers Guild of America West, 323/951-4000. $20 fee. www.wga.com 7000 W. Third St., Los Angeles, CA, 90048.
Alliance of Los Angeles Playwrights, 323/957-4752. Email: alapnews@aol.com.
A.S.K. Theater Projects, 310/478-3200. www.askplay.org.
Beyond Baroque Literary/Arts Center, 310/822-3006. 681 Venice Blvd, Venice, 90291. Promotes reading, writing and publication of contemporary literature.
Broadway on Sunset, 818/508-9270. www.broadwayonsunset.org.
Dramatists Guild of America, Inc. 323/960-5115. www.dramaguild.com.
First Stage, 323/850-6271. www.firststagela.org.
Mark Taper Forum New Work Festival, www.taperahmanson.com.
South Coast Repertory, www.scr.org.
Writers at Work, 323/661-5954. www.writersatwork.com.
Writer's Guild of America, West, 323/951-4000. www.wga.org.

• BOOKS ON SCREENWRITING

Story: Story: Substance, Structure, Style, and the Principles of Screenwriting by Robert McKee. See him in Charlie Kaufman's movie, *Adaptation.*
Screenwriting, by Syd Fields, an industry legend.
The Writer's Journey, Mythic Structure for Writers by Christopher Vogel. Based on the work of Joseph Campbell. Recommended by Maadison Krown. Jeff Arch says, "This book should come with a warning: You're going to learn about more than just writing movies, you are going to learn about life."
Dramatists Sourcebook and Writers Market

Fade In: The Screenwriting Process, by Robert A. Berman.
From Script to Screen: The Collaborative Art of Filmmaking, by Linda Seger and Edward Jay Whetmore.
Making A Good Script Great and others by Linda Seger. She's a premier "script doctor."
Making a Good Writer Great: A Creativity Workbook for Screenwriters, by Linda Seger.
How To Write A Movie In 21 Days, by Viki King.
Plots and Characters: A Screenwriter on Screenwriting, by Millard Kaufman.
The Screenplay: A Blend of Film Form and Content, by Margaret Mehring.
The TV Scriptwriter's Handbook; Dramatic Writing for Television and Film, by Alfred Brenner.
The Script Is Finished, Now What Do I Do? The Scriptwriter's Resource Book and Agent Guide, by K Callan.
The Complete Guide to Standard Script Formats, Part 1: The Screenplay, by Hillis R. Cole, Jr., and Judith H. Haag. Also Part 2: **Taped Formats for Television**.

Directing Resources

Action/Cut Directed By: Industry Seminars, 800/815-5545. www.actioncut.com. In two days, gain first-hand career knowledge of the directing craft with a working director, Guy Magar, from page to film. The only film learning workshop that offers a professional study of actual script scenes from the shooting process to viewing the final film. Step-by-step and shot-by-shot.

The Los Angeles Film School, 877/9LAFILM or 323/860-0789. www.lafilm.com. 6363 Sunset Blvd., Hollywood, 90028. 6-Week Digital Filmmaking Program plus many other workshops seven days a week. Daily tours at 11:30am Monday through Friday.

New York Film Academy, 818/733-2600, www.nyfa.com. In Los Angeles the workshops are at Universal Studios. They hold classes internationally. Day and evening workshops start the first Monday of every month.

Sherwood Oaks Experimental College, 323/851-1769, www.sherwoodoakscollege.com. 7095 Hollywood Blvd., #876, Los Angeles, 90028. Many workshops for writers and directors.

Take the Director's Journey Workshop with Mark W. Travis, 818/508-4600.

Beyond Structure, 310/394-6556; (outside CA) 866/239-2600. www.beyondstructure.com. Workshop comes with a full money-back guarantee.

• BOOKS ON DIRECTING

Actors Turned Directors: On Eliciting the Best Performance from an Actor and Other Secrets of Successful Directing, by Jon Stevens.
Directing the Film: Film Directors on Their Art, by Eric Sherman.
The Director's Journey, by Mark W. Travis
The Film Director's Team, by Alain Silver and Elizabeth Ward.

SCAMS

• **In the years I have been writing this book** the number of scams has risen sharply. The first edition was published in 1985. I wrote it to help my students receive career services for good value.

• **If someone says they can make you a star or get you work** and you have no training and no experience, run! They want money or sex from you.

• **There is a scam going on where certain agents and casting directors** sell or make available to showcases or pseudo acting schools the pictures that are submitted to them for employment. You will get a phone call from a salesperson who will say that you have come highly recommended from a casting director or agent. They won't know how they got your number but they want you to come in and audition for possible work. An actress told me she did a charity showcase with 80 people there from the industry. Each of the 20 actors received a call with this scam. One of the industry persons had sold or given away their folders that contained the actors' pictures and resumes.

• **Keep track of who you submit your pictures and resumes to.** Many producers receive thousands of submissions—they might throw them in the trash or they might pass them on to someone who has a scam going on. Actors are vulnerable because they want to act and are eager for the opportunity to do so.

• **There is a non union casting director** who has a showcase company. When you submit to the casting director for casting you may get a call from the showcase company asking you to come in and audition for the showcase. They usually say they don't know how they got your number; you will know how they got your number. It is fine if you contact the showcase yourself. I object to their practice of soliciting students in this way. I am not mentioning the showcase because they seem to present good showcasing opportunities and they are **not** a scam operation.

• **If anyone calls you out of the blue**, do not talk to them. If you have an agent or manager tell the caller to speak to them and get off the phone. I know it is tempting but there are no short cuts; you are not the exception. Do not trust anybody who has not come to you through your own thorough research or a personal introduction. Even then you have to be cautious.

• **Reported in** *Back Stage West*, a 17 year old victim said he paid $25 to be given access to casting director Randy Callahan's casting "hotline" after being referred to him by photographer Bud Stansfield of Western Images Photography. When he called, the jobs were always for over 18. Nevertheless, Callahan did let the boy come in for a purported audition for a *Playgirl* video that would feature frontal nudity and simulated sex. The actor took a couple of friends to the casting director's house for the audition. Callahan told him he needed three nude pictures of him— one from the back and two from the front, with one depicting him in a state of arousal—to show the video's director. The friends waited outside near a window so they could hear everything.

• **The actor said the first two pictures** made him "very uncomfortable," but it was the third that made him most nervous. "Callahan took off his shorts and then he started playing with himself. He said, 'Look, you do it, too.'" The actor followed the casting director's instruction and let him take the third photo.

• **When the police came in to search,** they found the actor's pictures in a drawer along with a stack of similar pictures of other men. Callahan had never sent them to the so-called director. A spokesperson for *Playgirl* said that the magazine did not produce the videos that Callahan claimed to be casting for.

• **Video Scam, a pitch given to a** *Back Stage West* **reader** from a manager who somehow got her number to see if they could work together. The meeting took place in his apartment. He said he was putting 24 actors on video to be sent to selected agents and casting directors. Each actor got two minutes on the tape. The cost to each actor is $175 and $40 a month for the term of the contract. He talked for two and a half hours saying he needed a decision right away because he was shooting the next video in a few days. Look out for video scams!

• **Premier Casting, an extras' casting company** also known as Universal Casting, charges $89 for a registration fee. They say you will work within a few days. Thomas Mills, "Tombudsman," a weekly columnist for *Back Stage West,* asked in his column for information. He was overwhelmed with complaints. After paying Premier, the actors had obtained no work or received a few post-midnight phone calls offering work early the following morning in faraway areas. They were promised a shot at small speaking roles if they signed up for $280 classes at Hollywood Way Pictures. The Better Business Bureau has logged 1,136 inquiries and 36 complaints against this company. Other names for the same company are Matthews Casting, Charles Matthews Casting and Take Five Casting.

Durkin Artists Agency, Debbie Durkin and On-Camera L.A. have been luring actors from out of state as well as in Los Angeles. She was a state and SAG franchised agent. She insisted potential clients study at On-Camera, her company, and have pictures taken by a photographer she got kick-back from. It is illegal for an agent to charge anything or to insist you study at a particular place or have photographs from a certain photographer. She finally lost her SAG franchise when she negotiated a commercial reinstatement for a former client and failed to turn over his residuals earnings of $3,500 for more than a year. Debbie Durkin is now a personal manager and not under the watchdog of the state or SAG. You are holding a book in your hands that recommends plenty of legitimate photographers and teachers. Do not get ripped off by these type of promises. It takes a lot of violations and complaints for an agent to lose their SAG franchise. Don't even trust the list, investigate.

Kirk Owens was arrested for sexual battery of two actresses and probably more. He advertised for a 20-30 Caucasian, slender, blond, attractive actress for a one day nonunion shoot with pay. He used the name Tony Wilson, met one actress in a public place, then ask her to come to his apartment where the script was. He then ask her to take off her clothes down to her underwear because that would be how the scene would be shot. You are reading this and thinking, "Why would an actress do that?" but unfortunately they do. This is not the way to have a career—please hear me loud and clear.

• **Glamour Models** was reported to me by a reader of the 8th edition. She said they bragged of all the careers they had developed. They wanted to represent her, and there would be a fee of $500 for color pictures. Actress Tiana Hynes, a reader of the 9th edition, reported they wanted $750 for composite cards. She says, "Stay away from this company, it is a scam."

• **When auditioning for a "nudity required"** role you are never required to take your clothes off for the audition. You will have to do that after you have your contract which will spell out exactly what type of nudity will be expected.

• **West Coast Talent Ltd. Inc., Alexander Zafrin and David Leroy Harris** were convicted and sentenced to 30 days in jail for grand theft in connection with a scheme in which parents were enticed to pay thousands of dollars for promotional materials and acting classes for their children. These crooks are probably already operating again, look out!

• *Back Stage West* goes to extreme measures to make sure their notices are legitimate, but you still have to be extremely careful with independent, nonunion projects. There is no one to protect you. If you are the least bit suspicious, take someone with you to the audition location. If anything seems odd, leave. If you are asked for money for anything, even a $10 picture, leave. Report them immediately to *Back Stage West*.

• **Do not submit your picture and resume to any publications** other than the trades. The ads in other publications, such as free papers like *New Times* and *L.A. Weekly*, are paid ads and will come to no good.

• **Entertainment Studios** say they are a management company; they charge people $495 for a seminar.

• **John Robert Powers** advertises on Disney radio. One of my readers wrote and told me of what happened when she took her son in to the office. "They tried to entice me to sign my son up to the exclusive invitation only John Robert Powers Club for $5,000." Her son said, "No, Mom let's go." A bright boy. Subsequently they sent in a snap shot to Ford Models and they now represent him without putting any money out. You will always have to buy pictures, but you choose the photographer. I've actually had several complaints about John Robert Powers. Investigate carefully when investing your money.

• Stalkers and their Victims (published by Screen Actors Guild.)

The Stalkers:
47% Simple obsession: Stalker, usually male, knows target as an ex-spouse, ex-lover, or former boss, and begins a campaign of harassment.
43% Love obsession: Stalker is a stranger to the target but is obsessed and mounts a campaign of harassment to make the target aware of the stalker's existence.
9.5% Erotomania: Stalker falsely believes that the target, usually someone famous or rich, is in love with the stalker.

The Victims:
38% Ordinary citizens.
32% Lesser known entertainment figures.
17% Highly recognizable celebrities.
13% Former employee/employer; other professionals.

Resources

Gavin de Becker, 818/505-0177. A large staff of security people. Home-security systems, crowd, background checks. He is the author of *The Gift of Fear*, also an expert stalking consultant.

SAG, Affirmative Action, 323/549-6644 and **Legal Affairs**, 323/549-6627.

Bunko/Fraud Unit, LAPD, 213/485-3795 or 818/756-8323, if you are confronted by a dishonest operation.

Vice Squad, 213/485-2121. Deals with cases of immoral or lewd nature.

L.A. City Attorney's Office, 213/485-4515.

L.A. County Dept. of Consumer Affairs, 213/974-1452.

Actor Information Service @ Acting World Books, 818/905-1345.

Back Stage West **Casting Line**, 323/525-2356. If you have any suspicious occurrences during the auditioning process, call immediately.

SECTION EIGHT

BECOMING GEOGRAPHICALLY DESIRABLE

THE RIGHT TIME TO MOVE
TO LOS ANGELES
AND
THE SCOUTING TRIP

• **This section of the book was inspired** by an interview I had with Tony Shepherd. At the time he was Vice President of Talent for Aaron Spelling Productions, overseeing the casting of all of their television series such as *Beverly Hills 90210, Melrose Place, The Heights, The Love Boat, Colbys, Dynasty, Hotel, Family.*

Q: When do you think it's time for an actor to consider moving to Los Angeles?

• **If an actor** wants to earn a living in motion pictures or television other than doing commercials, they have to be in Los Angeles. It may be time to think of moving when you've outgrown the market you're in. That means if you're in Chicago and you're pulling 60-70% callbacks, booking 35-40% of the jobs, you're ready.

• **If you've never been** to Los Angeles, make a trial visit. It's a tough city to live in; it's expensive. When someone is moving to L.A., it's not the actor, it's the person. It's a question of whether you want to pick up stakes. To move to L.A., you need talent, marketability, desire, time, money and patience.

507

• **I agree with Tony. Make a trip to Los Angeles** and check out the town; see if you could live here before you move.

• **When you do move to Los Angeles** it is in your best interest to be debt free, computer/on-line savvy with your own up-to-date computer and a paid-for reliable car. You'll need money to set up a place to live, which is usually first and last month, a security deposit and for sanity, a two month cushion; this could total $5,000. Money for pictures and picture reproductions—figure $1,000 and it will take about a month to have them ready to go. It would be wonderful to know you have enough money to take two classes a week plus a networking group for at least six months. Conservatively, that would be $450 a month, so $2700. Keep in mind you are moving here to be an actor; it is most important to be acting. Next will be your spending money for three months. What is your life style? How much money do you need each week? This could be another $3,000. While you are preparing to move, keep track of your daily expenses. Most things in Los Angeles cost more than where you live, unless you're moving from Manhattan, and there are so many more things you will want to take advantage of here. Don't plan on being a different person when you move; it just doesn't happen.

• **When you arrive here with this kind of financial backing** it will still be a jolt—moving is one of the most stress-causing events a human can experience. With your above basic needs taken care of, you will be more likely to have a successful move. You will be more at ease while you are finding that survival job to eventually pay for these expenses after your hometown savings have been exhausted. You will be living your dream of being an actor in Los Angeles.

• **Do not count on a public transportation system** to get around; you will be sorry. In your home town, buy a Sunday *Los Angeles Times* newspaper or order it mailed to you, 800/966-2450, $4. You will find lots of information, possible survival jobs available and the costs of rents. When you get here, pick up the *L.A. Weekly* newspaper. It's free and can be found at most 7-11s, liquor stores, newsstands, theaters, restaurants and many other locations.

• **Carry this book with you** and purchase *The Working Actor's Guide* and *The Thomas Guide* (street map book). The *Los Angeles Times* newspaper puts out a book of places to see, *Curbside LA*. You can order on the phone, 800-246-4042. The *Working Actor's Guide's* Living Section is very good for the best housing areas, with maps and detailed information about the areas, referencing the zip codes and page numbers in *The Thomas Guide*. Many rentals will expect a six month or one year lease. There are bulletin boards and rental services where you can look for a roommate. Be careful, don't trust too easily.

• **When you are thinking of moving here**, choose an area close to town; do not live in Orange County, Riverside or Oxnard. These areas are all an hour away from Los Angeles early on a Sunday morning, but any other time, count on two hours. This is not close enough to be a part of the show biz community. If you are making the move, give yourself as many advantages as possible.

• **Jay Bernstein, manager, writer, producer, taught a course called** *Stardom, the Management of, the Public Relations for, and the Survival and Maintenance In.*

Q: What is your advice for actors who are moving here from out of town?

- **They should be studying the town**. It's very tricky with a lot of roads and some of them look like freeways. You have to be very careful where you're going. I tell people to spend a year like you were in college. If your parents paid for your college, they may pay for a year here. If you worked your way through college, then work a year here. Get a feeling of what's going on. Weigh every decision. There's plenty of time. Get that career team together.

• **If you are new, visit or call the local Police**, crime prevention section, and ask if where you are planning to stay is a safe area.

• **Always be on the lookout** for film and television personalities. You will see them.

www.Losangelesalmanac.com. All the L.A. neighborhoods.

• **HOTELS & MOTELS**

There are many hotels and motels here. You can probably pick up a guide book at your local bookstore or over the internet. The ones below are mentioned to give you an idea of some acceptable areas.

Grove Guesthouse, Bed and Breakfast, 888-LA-Grove or 323/876-7778. Located in a safe, celebrity filled West Hollywood neighborhood, it is central to everything you will want to see. This is a fabulous value and one of my special secrets. For under $200 a night you are the only guests in your own private one bedroom, three room, guest house with phone, cable, 2 TV/VCRs, CD player, beside a wonderful pool/spa and delightfully

landscaped yard. Parking and local phone calls are free and you'll save money preparing your own meals. Your hosts are very savvy entertainment industry folks. Major movie stars stay there because it is very special! Mention *Acting Is Everything* for a discount.
Extended Stay America, 818/567-0952. www.extendedstay.com. 2200 Empire Ave., Burbank 91504. A very good area. Walk to a big outdoor mall; many eating places. Stay a week or more for big savings. Two miles from Burbank airport. A good place to stay while looking for an apartment.
Banana Bungalow Hollywood at The Orbit Hotel and Hostel. 800/446-7835 www.bananabungalow.com. 7950 Melrose Ave., West Hollywood. Dorm rooms $17 to $20; private rooms are: one person $49, two people $59, three people $69, four people $79.
Best Western Farmer's Daughter Motor Hotel, 323/937-3930. www.farmersdaughterhotel.com. 115 S. Fairfax Ave., L.A. $78 single or double. Across the street from Farmer's Market and CBS Studio City, where shows are taped. Also the greatest little hip shopping center called The Grove.
Beverly Garland's Holiday Inn Hotel, 818/980-8000. www.beverlygarland.com. 4222 Vineland, North Hollywood. Right off the 101 Freeway. Moderately priced. $84-$164. Special rates for AAA, entertainment cards. Paradise Cafe is a favorite.
Beverly Laurel Motor Hotel, 323/651-2441. 8018 Beverly Blvd., Los Angeles. Near the Beverly Center Shopping Mall. $80 single, $84 double. Adjacent to Swinger's Coffee shop.
Beverly Terrace Hotel, 310/274-8141. www.beverlyterracehotel.com. 469 N. Doheny, Beverly Hills, 90210. Basic but in a safe, central spot across from a great little market. Single $90 a night or $550 weekly. Double $115 a night or $650 weekly.
El Patio Motel, 818/980-2176. 11466 Ventura Blvd., Studio City, 91604. Near Universal and CBS Studios. AAA recommended. $55 single, $59 double.
Holiday Lodge, 818/843-1121. 3901 Riverside Dr., Burbank, between Hollywood Way and Pass Ave. off the 134 Freeway. Very near Warner Bros., NBC, Disney and Universal Studios. $75 single, $85 double.
Holloway Motel, 213/654-2454. www.hollowaymotel.com. 8465 Santa Monica Blvd., West Hollywood. $85 to $95 a night. Weekly rates are less. Jim Morrison stayed here many times in the old days.
Hollywood Roosevelt Hotel, 323/466-7000. www.hollywoodroosevelt.com. 7000 Hollywood Blvd. Hollywood, 90028. Great old hotel in the heart of Hollywood. Not a great neighborhood but safe enough and very handy for getting anywhere. Rates are $199 to $399 in tower, $189 for cabana rooms overlooking pool.
Olive Manor Motel, 818/842-5215. 924 W. Olive, Burbank, at Victory and Olive. Close to Burbank; not too far from Hollywood and freeways. $66 single, $77 double.
Ramada West Hollywood, 800/845-8585. www.ramada.com. 8585 Santa Monica Blvd., West Hollywood. Great location. $90 a day includes breakfast. To get a corporate rate, sign up for their free RBC club when you arrive to check in.
The Graciela, 818/842-8887. www.thegraciela.com. 322 North Pass Ave., Burbank, 91505. The Graciela Burbank is a first-class hotel located two miles from Burbank/Glendale/Pasadena Airport. Rates are from $149 to $500.
Sportsman's Lodge, 818/769-4700. www.slhotel.com. Ventura Blvd. and Coldwater in Studio City. $120-$139 a day. Restaurants and shopping. Great place, great location.
The Standard Hotel, 323/650-9090. www.standardhotel.com. 8300 Sunset Blvd., West Hollywood. $135-$225. On the strip. Very much one of the "in" places to stay!

• CAR RENTALS

Very valuable web site: **www.lawa.org**. *LAX airport parking lots, rates and locations, car rental agencies, hotels, busses and shuttle vans, a map of the airport and nearby streets.*

All the national companies are here in Los Angeles. You generally get a better deal renting at either LAX airport (Century and Sepulveda) or at the Burbank airport (Hollywood Way, between Victory and San Fernando.)

Both of the companies below have many locations. They will pick you up if you are in the vicinity of their location. Good standby rates for the weekends.

Avon, 323/850-0826. www.avonrent.com. 7080 Santa Monica Blvd., Hollywood. Open every day. Rates are $29 to $50.
Enterprise, 323/654-4222. www.enterprise.com. 8367 Sunset Blvd., West Hollywood. Rates are $27.99 to $89.99.

• STREETS TO KNOW ABOUT

Beverly Blvd. and Beverly Drive. Beverly Blvd. runs east and west, the same as Melrose and Sunset. It starts in downtown L.A. and dead ends at Santa Monica Blvd. in Beverly Hills. Beverly Drive runs north and south in the middle of the Beverly Hills shopping district.

Cahuenga Blvd. and Cahuenga Blvd. East and West. *(cuh-wang-guh)* Cahuenga begins near Melrose and runs north through Hollywood and through the Cahuenga Pass (Hollywood freeway in the middle), it turns into Cahuenga Blvd. West and disappears for a little bit at Lankershim near Universal Studios, then picks up after Universal on your right. So if you are told Cahuenga, find out what part of town and a cross street.

Sepulveda Blvd. *(suh-pull-ve-duh)* is a great street. It runs from the San Fernando Valley alongside the 405 freeway over the hill past the LAX airport to Long Beach.

La Cienega Boulevard. If you arrive at LAX, rent your car and take Century Blvd. to LaCienega and turn left (north) and follow it all the way up to Sunset, where LaCienega ends. At Sunset Boulevard, turn right (east) to go to Hollywood or to the left (west) for the Sunset Strip scene. You can keep driving west on Sunset until it ends at the beach.

• THINGS TO SEE

Universal Studios, 818/508-9600. www.universalstudios.com. Go on a weekday. It is an actual studio lot with an amusement park-like tour for $45. Plan to stay all day so you can take the tram out to the back lot where you may see working productions. I've worked on many shows produced here and I still get excited driving on the lot. You enter from either Cahuenga Blvd. West or Lankershim Blvd. Take the 101 Freeway to Barham or Lankershim, then the signs will lead you. Don't miss City Walk; if you can't afford the tour, at least check out the movie theater and night life. You can park on Cahuenga Blvd. West and walk over the bridge and save the $6 parking fee. You can also take the Metro Line and get off at Universal. Take the tram up the hill.
Warner Bros. VIP Studio Tour, 818/954-1744. 9-3 weekdays, $32. Reservations and photo ID are required. Enter at gate #4 where Hollywood Way ends at Olive. One of the staff will lead you on a two-hour informal drive-and-walk jaunt around the studio. You will even get to go on some working sound stages and see the faux streets. You will most likely see famous faces.

NBC Television Studio Tour, 818/840-3537. www.nbc.com. 3000 West Alameda Ave., Burbank. A 70-minute walking tour of the TV production complex departs at regular intervals, weekdays from 9-3. $7.

NBC's Tonight Show with Jay Leno: Get in line before 8AM on the day of the show. Box office: Look for a small sign, "Guest Service, Audience and Gift Shop." Two tickets per person. Then line up around 3PM to get the best seats. Watch the show the night before to see who the guests will be.

Disneyland, 714/781-4565. www.disneyland.com. 1313 Harbor Blvd, Anaheim. From Los Angeles take the 5 Freeway South to either Harbor Blvd or Katela Ave. Turn right. Open M-F 10-6; Sa & Su 9AM-midnight.

See tapings of TV shows. It doesn't cost anything and you will see the actors working. For a half-hour sitcom, plan at least three hours. Eat first because you'll have a long evening of sitting.

Audiences Unlimited, 818/506-0067. www.tvtickets.com. The ticket office is located on the Van Ness Street side of the Fox Television Center Building, 5746 Sunset Blvd. between Gower and the 101 Freeway. M-F 8:30-6. There is recorded information for all the shows they have tickets for. Write for their monthly newsletter of current shows. Send a stamped, self-addressed envelope to Audiences Unlimited, 100 Universal City Plaza, Bldg. 153, Universal City, CA 91608. Tickets are available for more than 40 sitcoms, game and talk shows.

Fox Television Center, 310/584-2000. www.foxla.com. 5746 Sunset Blvd., Hollywood. M-F 8:30-6 and Sa Su 11-6. Tickets are offered on a first-come basis starting on Wednesdays for most shows scheduled for the following week. Tickets are sometimes available the day of the show, but early arrival is advised.

Paramount Visitors Center, 323/956-1777. 860 N. Gower St., Hollywood. Weekdays 8-4.

Beverly Center Shopping Mall, 310/854-0071. www.beverlycenter.com. 8500 Beverly Blvd., Los Angeles corner of La Cienega between Beverly Blvd. and Third St. This is really state-of-the-art cool. See-and-be-seen MTV generation.

Getty Museum, 310/440-7300. www.gett.edu. 12000 Getty Center Drive, Los Angeles. Closed Monday, $5 parking, museum is free. You have to call for parking reservation.

Griffith Park Observatory. 323/664-1191. www.griffithobservatory.org. Take Hollywood Blvd. east to Western Avenue then go north or toward the mountains. Just past the American Film Institute (on your left) will be a curve in the road where Western turns into Los Feliz Blvd. The next street is Ferndale; turn left and follow the signs. Great hiking and picnicking there too.

Hollywood Bowl, 323/850-2000. www.hollywoodbowl.com. 2301 N. Highland Ave., Hollywood, near the 101 freeway. Gift shop.

Hollywood Fantasy Tours, 310/326-8279. www.hollywoodfantasytours.com. 6231 Hollywood Blvd., Hollywood, 90028. Tour prices are $16 to $53 Tours are every day from 10:00 am to 4:00 pm every hour.

Hollywood Sign. From the 101 Freeway or Hollywood Blvd., go north on Gower, right on Franklin and left at the next street: Beachwood. As you drive up Beachwood, look up and there you are. There is no public access to the sign but this is one of the best views.

Beachwood Canyon is a lovely area. There is a small cafe where many locals eat. There's a great bulletin board outside for rentals, roommates and other stuff.

Lake Hollywood, where earthquakes and floods are filmed. From the 101 Freeway, take Barham Blvd. north. Turn right at Lake Hollywood Drive. Follow around until you see the lake. It's about 31/2 miles to walk around it. Drive past the lake, continue on

Canyon Lake and you will get a real close-up of the Hollywood sign. Continue down to the Beachwood area.

Los Angeles Sports Teams (star spotting at the Lakers Games).

Main Street, Santa Monica and Venice Beaches. Shopping and eating. Take the 10 West/Santa Monica Freeway, exit Fourth Street, turn left to Pico, then right to Main St., then left and that's it.

Montana Avenue in Santa Monica between 17th and 9th streets. Celebrities!

Third Street Promenade in Santa Monica, begins at the 4th Street Mall and runs north for several blocks of shopping, eating and people watching.

Grauman's Chinese Theater on Hollywood Blvd. between Highland and LaBrea. Go and put your feet in the foot prints of the stars!

Kodak Theater, Hollywood Blvd. and Highlind, opened in 2001, is the first permanent home of the Academy Awards show. The very first Oscar night was held across the street at the Roosevelt Hotel. Also at this location is a six-screen extension of Grauman's Chinese Theater, 70 shops and the Renaissance Hollywood Hotel.

Tackiest souvenirs are on Hollywood Blvd. around the Grauman's Chinese Theater.

FOR RESTAURANTS & HANGOUTS
See the L.A. Scene / Hangouts Section

• **Now we begin your scouting trip.** Refer to this section and the L.A. Scene section for locations. Plan to arrive in L.A. on a Thursday.

• **If I were planning your trip for you**, I would say bring your best friend, at least $2,000 plus money for car rental and accomodations. Drive in to your hotel or motel on Thursday afternoon. If you are flying, rent a car at the airport. Pick up a Thursday *L.A. Times* at the airport newsstand. The Thursday *Calendar Section* has everything that is happening on the weekend.

Day One - Friday

3 mile walk around Hollywood Lake. From Barham Blvd., find your way through the hills with the help of the Thomas guide. You will drive very close to the **Hollywood Sign**.

Breakfast at the Village Cafe in Beachwood Canyon below the Hollywood Sign, 323/467-5398. 2695 Beachwood, Hollywood. After breakfast, drive down Beachwood to Franklin, right to Gower then left to Santa Monica Blvd. Turn left then right into Hollywood Cemetery, drive slowly; lots of stars buried here. Come out, turn left and left again on Gower past Paramount Studios, right on Melrose, then an immediate left on Larchmont for two blocks, cross Beverly Blvd. and park.

Coffee at Starbucks and shopping in Larchmont Village. Back to Melrose, left for several blocks past La Brea; park and walk both sides of Melrose Ave.

Lunch. Plenty of places to eat here. Drive east on Melrose, turn left on Cahuenga, following it all the way over the hill to Barham, and turn right. Barham turns into Olive and the gate to Warner Bros. will be on your right.

3:30 Prearranged reservations for Warner Bros. Tour.

Hotel/motel/friend's or relative's. Rest and get ready for a movie or play in Westwood, Century City, Santa Monica or Burbank, depending on where you are staying.

Movie or a play.

Coffee or drinks at a local place.

Day Two - Saturday

Breakfast at Patrick's Roadhouse in Santa Monica, then walk the beach from there to the Santa Monica Pier, then past the pier south to Venice Beach. At the end of the merchants on the boardwalk, turn left and walk a few blocks inland to:
Main Street in Venice and walk back to Santa Monica along Main Street. When sights thin out, turn left to Ocean Blvd. Walk past the pier and turn right to the Third Street Promenade.
Lunch on the Third Street Promenade. Blocks of shopping and people watching.
See a play in a little theater. Pick up the early edition of Sunday's *L.A. Times* or the *LA Weekly* at any newsstand, 7/11 store or Starbucks. The *L.A. Times* Calendar section will have a complete listing of plays in little theaters. Choose a play that is recommended; see Pick of the Week. There are also plays listed in *Back Stage West*.

Day Three - Sunday

Disneyland all day and evening, till it closes. Get there early. When you have breakfast at the Disneyland hotel, you get into the park an hour earlier. If Disneyland isn't of interest then spend the day hanging out in Malibu at the beach.

Day Four - Monday

Breakfast at Good Neighbor Restaurant on Cahuenga Blvd West.
Universal Studios, till it closes. Go on a weekday when possibly you will see some shooting on the back lot.
Dinner at Universal's City Walk.

Day Five - Tuesday

Jerry's Deli on Beverly Blvd. for Breakfast.
Farmer's Market at Third Street and Fairfax, and The Grove for shopping.
See a television show taping or filming. Check with Audiences Unlimited for shows that are shooting. If you are going to a show at CBS at Radford, go to a late lunch/early dinner at Dupar's coffee shop. If you are seeing a show at Paramount, go for an early or late Mexican dinner at Lucy's El Adobe on Melrose.

Day Six - Wednesday

Breakfast at Duke's on Sunset Blvd.
Research (during breakfast) areas where you might want to live and map out a plan for looking at as many as you can tomorrow. Head east on Sunset to Stanley, turn left then turn right in the first driveway to park in the Samuel French Bookstore parking lot.
Samuel French's at 10AM. Plan two hours to hang out and look at all the information.
Coffee or lunch at Urth Cafe, 8565 Melrose, just west of LaCienega. Many young celebs.
Free afternoon.
Dinner at Yamishiro Restaurant, 323/466-5125. Overlooking the city, above the Magic Castle on Franklin Ave. between Highland and LaBrea Ave.

Day Seven - Thursday

Breakfast at Rose Cafe, 310/399-0711. 220 Rose Ave. in Venice.
Look all day at areas you think you may like to live; start on the Westside.
Grauman's Chinese theater on Hollywood Blvd. Hollywood Chamber of Commerce has a free book, "Walk the Walk" with the locations of all the stars on Hollywood Blvd.
Kodak Theater complex, in the same block.
Dinner at Hamburger Hamlet across the street. Shop for souvenirs.

Day Eight - Friday

Breakfast at Hugo's in West Hollywood, Santa Monica Blvd.

Griffith Park Observatory. Right on Los Felix to Hollywood Blvd. and lunch.

Lunch at Musso & Franks, 323/467-7788. 6667 Hollywood Blvd. Then take Cahuenga Blvd. over the hill, turn right on Barham, go past Warner Bros. Studio. When the street splits into Olive and Alameda, stay to the right for Alameda. 3000 W. Alameda Ave., Burbank. NBC is on your right.

NBC Television Studio Tour, a 70-minute walking tour of the TV production complex. Departures at regular intervals weekdays from 9-3. $7. 818/840-3537. www.nbc.com. 3000 West Alameda Ave., Burbank. When you leave, return on Olive to Hollywood Way, turn right to Magnolia, then right.

Visit "It's a Wrap." 3315 W. Magnolia. Used clothes from films and current TV shows.

Castaways Restaurant, 818/848-6691. 1250 Harvard, in Burbank, for cocktails. Continue east (toward mountains) on Magnolia until it ends. Turn left onto Sunset Canyon, right on Harvard all the way to the top of the hill. Free valet parking.

Night spots you think you'll enjoy.

Day Nine - Saturday

Walking tour of Beverly Hills. Park south of Wilshire around Bedford, Canon or Beverly.

Lunch at Barney's department store on Wilshire, then drive east on Wilshire to LaCienega, turn left to the Beverly Center.

Spend afternoon at the Beverly Center.

Play at a little theater, and nightclubbing

Late, late night. Canter's Deli on Fairfax after 2AM.

Day Ten - Sunday

Whatever you have been dying to do.

Day Eleven - Monday

Return home.

THINGS NICE TO FIT IN:

La Conversation, 310/858-0950. 638 N. Doheny Dr., West Hollywood, 90069, near Santa Monica Blvd. Lovely food, sit outside. Have a facial at Yolanda's next door. This is the way to live!

Beverly Hills Hotel's poolside Cabana Club Cafe, 800/283-8885. 9641 Sunset Blvd. Beverly Hills. Expensive—pay cash so you don't have to explain you aren't staying there.

360 Degrees, 323/871-2995. 6290 Sunset Blvd., Hollywood, the corner of Vine. At the top of a 19-story building; lovely view. Dinner or late drinks.

Book Soup and Tower Records on the Sunset Strip.

Starbucks and other coffee places like Priscillas in Toluca Lake, that are located close to studios. Hang out.

• **This is not a vacation for relaxing**; this is the type of pace it takes to work and live here. If you follow this plan, you will cover many of the areas that are part of a Los Angeles actor's life. When you arrive be prepared to go; you can relax when you get home. Meet people, talk to everyone you meet, ask them about living in Los Angeles. Your time is very precious here.

L.A. SCENE / LOCAL HANGOUTS

• **You have moved here to seek your fame and fortune.** Here are places you may wish to check out that will put you in the neighborhoods where some of the action is. I've picked places that are known to be hangouts for people in show-biz. Places of business have a way of disappearing, but find your own. Have fun finding your favorite hangouts. *L.A. Magazine* and the Sunday and Thursday editions of the *L.A. Times* Calendar Section will help you keep up on the latest happenings. A special thank you to actress Carol Hernandez for rechecking all the businesses that were in the ninth edition, getting their websites and adding the latest cool spots.

The L.A. Weekly is the free local newspaper and comes out on Thursdays. Pick it up at newsstands, 7-11s, liquor stores and businesses.

• **COFFEE HOUSES**

The Abbey, 310/289-8410. 692 N. Robertson Blvd., West Hollywood. Cappuccino and dreams of Tuscany midst all the fountains.

Coffee Bean & Tea Leaf, www.coffeebean.com. Ice-blended mocha drink, no fat, no calories, but fabulous.

Cyber Java, 323/466-5600. www.cyberjava.com. 7080 Hollywood Blvd. L.A.'s first online coffeehouse. Cruise the web for $9 an hour.

Lu Lu's Beehive, 818/986-CAFE. 13203 Ventura Blvd., Studio City, 91604. Wednesday open mike night. Los Angeles Magazine says "Best coffee scene in the Valley."

Highland Grounds, 323/466-1507. www.highlandgrounds.com. 742 N. Highland Ave., Hollywood. Live comedy, avant-garde music and readings every night.

King's Road, 323/655-9044. 8361 Beverly Blvd., West Hollywood. Always packed. I love to meet people here for lunch. Near the Beverly Center.

Library, A Coffee House, 562/433-2393. 3418 E. Broadway Blvd., Long Beach. Carries thousands of titles on metaphysics, psychology, etc. nothing over $5.95. More than cappuccino. Ted Danson and Mary Steenburgen stop in every week for the chili.

Lulu's Alibi, 310/479-6007. 1640 Sawtelle Blvd., West L.A. Open till 2AM.

Newsroom Cafe, 310/319-9100. 530 Wilshire Blvd., Santa Monica. Great coffee, sweets, sugar-free desserts. Many celebs.

Newsroom Cafe, 310/652-4444. 120 N. Robertson. Healthy menu selections. Spotted: Sharon Stone, Ellen DeGeneres, Chris Rock.

Urth Cafe, 310/659-0628. 8565 Melrose Ave., West Hollywood, just west of La Cienega. Indoors/outdoors. Many young celebs stop for coffee, snacks and lunch.

• RESTAURANTS—UPSCALE

360 Degrees, 323/871-2995. www.360hollywood.com. 6290 Sunset Blvd., Hollywood, at Vine St. At the top of a 19-story building; lovely view; dinner or late drinks.

Bistro Garden, 818/501-0202. www.bistrogarden.com. 12950 Ventura Blvd., Studio City.

Cabana Club Cafe, 800/283-8885. www.beverlyhillshotel.com. 9641 Sunset Blvd., Beverly Hills. Poolside dining at the Beverly Hills Hotel. Live large and pretend you are staying at a $700 per night bungalow.

Ca' Del Sol, 818/985-4669. www.cadelsole.com. 4100 Cahuenga, North Hollywood, near Universal.

Cafe de Paris, 310/358-0908. 650 North Robertson, West Hollywood. Another Sharon Stone favorite.

Cafe Med, 310/652-0445. 8615 Sunset Blvd., West Hollywood. Keanu Reeves favors the spaghetti Bolognese and James Woods enjoys the pasta with olive oil and garlic.

Dan Tana's, 310/275-9444. www.kerrymenu.com/Dan-Tana's. 9071 Santa Monica Blvd., West Hollywood. Northern Italian food in a busy restaurant. Celeb hangout. Great New York steak.

Divino, 310/472-0886. 11714 Barrington Court, Brentwood. Clientele ranging from Diana Ross to Billy Crystal.

Four Oaks, 310/470-3623. www.fouroaksrestaurant.com. 2181 N. Beverly Glen Blvd., Bel Air. Secluded garden; great.

Geoffrey's Malibu, 310/457-1519. www.gmalibu.com. 27400 Pacific Coast Highway, Malibu, 90265. Power place in Robert Altman's *The Player*.

The Spanish Kitchen, 310/659-4794. 826 North La Cienega Blvd., between Melrose Ave. and Santa Monica Blvd. All dishes are authentic and all ingredients are imported from Mexico.

The Ivy, 310/274-8303. 113 N. Robertson, L.A., south of Beverly. Minimum $25 for lunch. If you can afford it, eat here at least once.

Ivy at the Shore, 310/393-3113. 1541 Ocean Ave., Santa Monica.

La Loggia, 818/985-9222. 11814 Ventura Blvd., Studio City. Power dinners.

La Pergola, 818/905-8402. 15005 Ventura Blvd., Encino. Marlon Brando comes in often for the pastas and Italian cuisine.

Lavande, 310/576-3180. www.loewshotels.com. 1700 Ocean Avenue, Santa Monica. A favorite place of Goldie Hawn, Steven Bochco and Sharon Lawrence.

Le Dome, 310/659-6919. 8720 Sunset Blvd., Sunset Plaza, West Hollywood. Big music business hangout. They closed down for many months to do a fabulous remodeling.

Kate Mantilini, 310/278-3699. 9101 Wilshire Blvd. at Doheny Drive, Beverly Hills. Many celebrities. Great for power breakfast; also open late at night. Jerry Seinfeld sightings when he is in town.

Menemsha, 310/822-2550. 822 Washington Blvd., at Abbot Kinney Blvd. Candlelit tables on the outdoor patio.

Mr. Chow, 310/278-9911. 344 N. Camden Drive, Beverly Hills. Prices are high, cooking is good and celebs go there.

Ocean Front, 310/581-7714. 1910 Ocean Front Walk, Santa Monica.

Orso's, 310/274-7144. 8706 W. Third St., West Hollywood. Power patio dining, hidden from the street; used to be Joe Allen's.

Osteria Romana Orsini, 310/277-6050. 9575 West Pico Blvd. near Century City. Agents, producers, and studio executives from MGM and Fox hang out here. Spotted: Sean Connery, Michael Douglas and Cameron Diaz.

Pinot Bistro, 818/990-0500. 12969 Ventura Blvd., Studio City. Near CBS/Radford and Universal. Even Warner Bros. people go there for lunch and dinner. Decorated beautifully during the holidays.

Pinot Hollywood, 323/461-8800. 1448 N. Gower St., Hollywood. Close to Paramount lot; many celebs and executives at lunch and dinner.

Polo Lounge, Beverly Hills Hotel, 310/276-2251. www.beverlyhillshotel.com. 9641 Sunset Blvd., Beverly Hills. Have breakfast in the coffee shop and look around.

Reign, 310/273-4463. 180 N. Robertson Blvd., Beverly Hills. Owner is football star Keyshawn Johnson. Lots of celebrities from TV, film, music and sports.

Smoke House, 818/845-3731. 4420 Lakeside Drive, Burbank, very near Toluca Lake. The best garlic-cheese bread in the world.

Spago, 310/385-0880. www.wolfgangpuck.com. 176 N. Canon Drive, Beverly Hills.

Sushi Nozawa, 818/508-7017. 11288 Ventura Blvd., Studio City. When you sit at the counter, don't dare ask for what you want—you get what they are serving. People love it, including my daughters. Go figure.

Sushi Roku, 323/655-6767. www.splendora.com. 8445 W. 3rd Street, near LaCienega. Very popular, many celebrities. Calista Flockhart comes in once a week; has been spotted having a glass of water and half of a cucumber roll.

The Grill, 310/276-0615. www.thegrill.com. 9560 Dayton Way, Beverly Hills. Power lunch for agents.

The Palm, 310/550-8811. www.thepalm.com. 9001 Santa Monica Blvd., Los Angeles. Spotted: Courtney Cox Arquette, Adam Sandler, George Clooney, Leonardo DiCaprio, Denzel Washington, Madonna and Guy Ritchie. A favorite for years.

Trattoria Amici, 310/858-0271. www.tamici.com. 469 S. Doheny Dr., Beverly Hills. "Friends" buddies Jennifer Aniston, Courteney Cox and Lisa Kudrow are served delicious pastas.

Typhoon, 310/390-6565. www.typhoon.biz. 3221 Donald Douglas Loop South (off Centinela). View of the airfield at Santa Monica Airport. Lauren Bacall orders the salmon with ginger poached in banana leaves. Robert De Niro, Al Pacino and Harrison Ford dine here.

• RESTAURANTS—MEDIUM TO LOWER PRICES

The Apple Pan, 310/475-3585. 10801 W. Pico Blvd., West Los Angeles. Open Friday and Saturday until 1AM, other days except Monday until midnight. Great burgers and apple pie. All counters; people stand behind you and wait. Great after a late movie at Westside Pavilion. Love these hamburgers!

Amazon, 818/382-6080. 14649 Ventura Blvd., Sherman Oaks. The atmosphere is not to be missed.

Art's Delicatessen, 818/762-1221. 12224 Ventura Blvd., Studio City. Favorite of the Hollywood community that resides in the Valley, also the television stars working at the CBS lot. Best Black & White cookies!

Aunt Kizzy's Back Porch, 310/578-1005. 4325 Glencoe Ave., Marina Del Rey. Southern cooking. Actors and athletes love the fried chicken and baked ribs.

A Votre Sante, 310/451-1813. 13016 San Vicente Blvd., Brentwood. Gourmet Vegetarian.

Bungalow Club, 323/964-9494. 7174 Melrose Ave., Daily, it's almost like being poolside at a fancy hotel, dining in an outdoor cabana on a private patio with fluttering bamboo in the middle of Hollywood.

Barney Greengrass, 310/777-5877. 9570 Wilshire Blvd., Beverly Hills. Great fish straight from Barney's in New York.

Birds, 323/465-0175. 5925 Franklin Ave., Hollywood. Perched in the shadow of the Hollywood sign.

Broadway Deli, 310/451-0616. www.foodcowest.com 1457 Third Street Promenade, Santa Monica.

Bristol Cafe, 310/248-2804. www.bristolfarms.com. 9039 Beverly Blvd., West Hollywood. Located in the market. Home of the original Chasen's restaurant. Original Chasen's booth; order the famous Chasen's chili.

Cafe Brazil, 310/837-8957. 10831 Venice Blvd., Culver City. Excellent food, also vegetarian. Most dishes under $8.

Caffe Luna, 323/655-8647. 7463 Melrose Ave, Hollywood. 8AM-3AM. Outside seating (you can draw on the tablecloths.) Great for people watching. Mick Jagger and Christopher Lloyd like this place.

Caffe Capri, 323/644-7906. 2547 Hyperion Ave., L.A. Lunch and dinner, Wednesday through Monday. Italian food served in a cute, diminutive restaurant.

Canter's Fairfax Restaurant, 323/651-2030. 419 North Fairfax, L.A. Open 24 hours. Folksy by day; underground by night. In the old Jewish neighborhood. Great for the middle of night after play rehearsal. Bakery open all the time.

Carney's Restaurant, 323/654-8300. www.carneytrain.com. 8351 Sunset Blvd., West Hollywood, 90069. Restaurant is in an authentic railroad car. Also on Ventura Blvd. in Studio City.

Chez Nous, 818/760-0288. 10550 Riverside Dr., Toluca Lake. Breakfast meetings.

Chin Chin, 310/652-1818. 8618 Sunset Blvd., Hollywood. Indoor and outdoor seating; watch the crowd go by! Other locations. I love the light chicken salad.

Dimples, 818/842-2336. www.dimplesshowcase.com 3413 W. Olive Ave., Burbank. Lunch and dinner, continuous karaoke, 6PM-1:30AM. Cheap, fun.

Duke's, 310/652-9411. 8909 Sunset Blvd. Big breakfast place, served all day, parking in rear.

DuPar's, 818/766-4437. www.dupars.com 12036 Ventura Blvd. in Studio City; also 3rd & Fairfax at Farmers' Market, close to CBS lot. Great pancakes.

El Coyote, 323/939-7766. 7312 Beverly Blvd, Hollywood. Popular with the twenty-something crowd. Great margaritas.

Formosa Lounge, 323/850-9050. 7156 Santa Monica Blvd. Long time old movie star hangout.

Good Neighbor, 818/761-4627. 3701 Cahuenga Blvd. West, Studio City. Great place, near Universal. Look for my picture on the wall. Breakfast & lunch only; closes at 4.

Gladstone's 4 Fish, 310/454-3474. www.gladstones.com. 17300 PCH, where Sunset Blvd. ends at the beach. Fun place!

Greenblatt's, 323/656-0606. 8017 w. Sunset Blvd. Parking in rear. Next to the Laugh Factory. The best deli in town. Open till 2:00AM.

Home, 323/665-HOME. 1760 Hillhurst Ave. Breakfast, lunch and dinner daily. Homey dining room with a jukebox, romantic patio.

Hugo's, 323/654-3993. 8401 Santa Monica Blvd., just east of La Cienega, West Hollywood. Power breakfasts, many celebs.

Jerry's Deli, 818/980-4245. 12655 Ventura Blvd, Studio City, 91604; 24 hrs. Huge menu. A favorite of many celebs, including, when the show was shooting, the writers and cast of *Seinfeld*.

Jerry's Deli, 310/289-1811. 8701 Beverly Blvd., West Hollywood. Very "in," especially late at night. Celebs spotted: Billy Crystal, Garth Brooks, Jon Voight, and Paula Abdul.

Light House, 310/451-2076. 201 Arizona Ave. Santa Monica. All you can eat Sushi, under $10 at lunch time.

La Conversation, 310/858-0950. 638 N. Doheny Dr., West Hollywood. Adorable; open weekdays for late breakfast and lunch. My daughters love the soups and great pastries.

Lucy's El Adobe, 323/462-9421. 5536 Melrose Ave., Hollywood. Across from Paramount Studios. Lots of celebs. Very casual and old Hollywood!

Magnolia Grille, 818/766-8698. 10530 Magnolia Blvd. (at Cahuenga), North Hollywood, 91601. Great weeknight specials that include salad, drink and dessert for under $10. Very homey place, lots of regulars, including me and my husband.

Mel's Drive In, 310/854-7200. www.Melsdrive-in.com. 8585 Sunset Blvd., West Hollywood. 24 hours. Great outdoors and in, good people-watching. Second smaller location: 323/465-3111. 1650 N. Highland Ave., Hollywood. Close to the Kodak Theater at Hollywood and Highland.

Musso & Frank Grill, 323/467-7788. 6667 Hollywood Blvd., Hollywood. Old time hangout. You must check this place out!

Nate 'n Al's, 310/274-0101. www.natenal.com. 414 N. Beverly Dr., Beverly Hills, 90210. When you're in Beverly Hills, this is the deli! This is a power breakfast spot for the film industry. You must check this out!

Original Pantry, 213/972-9279. 877 S. Figueroa, Los Angeles. Figueroa & 9th Streets, downtown L.A. 24 hrs. Known for their breakfasts and long-time waiters.

Patrick's Roadhouse, 310/459-4544. www.patricksroadhouse.com 106 Entrada Dr., Santa Monica. Lots of celebrities for breakfast. Patrick was a legend; he is gone now but his son is carrying on the tradition.

Pig'n Whistle, 323/463-0000. www.pignwhistle.com. 6714 Hollywood Blvd., Hollywood, 90028. Old Hollywood eatery recently rebuilt.

Pink's Hot-Dog Stand, 323/931-4223. www.pinkshollywood.com 709 N. La Brea, just north of Melrose. Sean Penn proposed to Madonna there.

Roscoe's House of Chicken & Waffles, 323/466-7453. www.chicken&waffles.com. 1514 N. Gower, Hollywood. Also 323/934-4405, 5006 W. Pico, one block west of LaBrea. Best in the middle of the night; down home food. Another Sharon Stone favorite.

Russia, 323/464-2216. 1714 N. Ivar Avenue, Hollywood. A Hollywood version of a Russian style restaurant. Within walking distance of the Pantages and Doolittle theaters. Live music and dancing on the weekends.

Saddle Ranch Chop House, 323/656-2007. 8371 Sunset Blvd., West Hollywood. Rowdy steak-and-suds hangout. Gas "campfires" for self-serve s'mores and a mechanical bull for urban cowboys with something to prove.

Silver Spoons, 323/650-4890. 8171 W. Santa Monica Blvd., Hollywood. Usual crowd is breakfast and lunch. Big hangout. There's the swapping of Hollywood gossip, stories of pending deals, recent auditions and past glories.

Sittons Coffee Shop, 818/761-3341. 11329 Magnolia, N. Hollywood. 24-hour coffee shop. Good food and prices.

Swinger's, 323/653-5888. www.swingersrestaurant.com. 8020 Beverly Blvd. Very "in" hangout for actors and other entertainment people; good prices plus many healthy and vegetarian selections.

The Gutter, 323/256-4850. 5621 N. Figueroa St., Highland Park. The sort of roadhouse you might have found when Figueroa was still called Route 66.

The Rose Cafe, 310/399-0711. 220 Rose Ave., Venice. Simple cafe and patio where the locals do breakfast and lunch.

The Standard Diner, 323/822-3131 www.standardhotel.com 8300 Sunset Blvd. 24-hour, modern take on a coffee shop.

Toast Bakery Cafe, 323/655-5018. 8221 W. Third Street, between Crescent Heights and LaCienega. All breakfasts 'til 11am, $6. Great atmosphere. The best cupcakes!

Village Cafe in Beachwood Canyon, 323/467-5398. 2695 Beachwood, about one mile north of Franklin Avenue in Hollywood. Look up and see the Hollywood sign. Great hidden neighborhood and memo board outside.

Vitello's, 818/769-0905. www.vitellosrestaurant.com. 4349 Tujunga Ave., Studio City. This is where Robert Blake was eating and had to return to pick up the gun he left in the booth. His wife was killed on the adjacent street. Great food!

• HANGOUTS

Bar Marmont, 323/650-0575. www.committedinc.com. 8171 Sunset Blvd., Los Angeles. No cover. At this moment, it is the place to be.

Breakfast: Four Seasons Hotel, 310/273-2222. www.fourseasons.com. 300 S. Doheny Dr., Beverly Hills border. Self park under the hotel. Many celebrities stay here, especially at award times.

Breakfast: Belevedere at the Peninsula Hotel, 310/788-2306. www.peninsula.com. 9882 Santa Monica Blvd., Beverly Hills, near CAA.

Club A.D., 323/467-3000. 836 N. Highland Ave., Hollywood. Dancing ala Studio 54.

Daddy's, 323/463-7777. 1610 N. Vine Street, Hollywood.

Diane Bennett's Personal Introductions, Hotline: 310/859-6929. She plans parties at hotels for singles. Upscale, $12 fee.

Dome Billiards, 323/650-1886. 7901 Santa Monica Boulevard, West Hollywood.

Doug Weston's Troubadour, 310/276-1158. www.troubadour.com. 9081 Santa Monica Blvd., West Hollywood. Singer/songwriter-based shows. Cover.

The Downtown Standard, 213/892-8080. 550 S. Flower St., L.A. Space-age party center.

Dragonfly, 323/466-6111. www.dragonfly.com. 6510 Santa Monica Blvd. Hollywood club with a different type of music each night.

Drake's, 310/450-7055. 23 Windward Ave., Venice. Bohemian chici. Resturant and club.

Falcon, 323/850-5350. 7213 Sunset Blvd., Hollywood. Chic eatery. Star sightings.

Father's Office, 310/393-Beer. 1018 Montana Ave., Santa Monica. Excellent foreign draft beer.

Firefly, 818/762-1833. 11720 Ventura Blvd., Studio City. One of the valley's new, hot clubs.

Forty Deuce, 323/465-4242. www.fortydeuce.com. 5574 Melrose Ave., Hollywood. Live music comes from a bump-and-grind combo. Dancers who strip down to pasties and skivvies. Nicole Kidman, Sandra Bullock, Naomi Watts, George Clooney, Matthew Perry, Vince Vaughn have been spotted here.

4100, 323/666-4460. 4100 Sunset Blvd., Silverlake. Late-night entertainment.

The Garage, 323/662-6802. www.thegaragela.com. 4519 Santa Monica Blvd., Silver Lake. Devotees include celebs Jennifer Aniston, Brad Pitt and Jennifer Love Hewitt.

Harvelle's, 310/395-1676. www.harvelles.com. 1432 Fourth Street in Santa Monica. Smokey blues bar.

H.M.S. Bounty, 213/385-7275. 3357 Wilshire Blvd., Los Angeles. Across the street from the Ambassador Hotel. Free jukebox.

Hollywood Athletic Club, 323/462-6262. www.hollywoodathleticclub.com. 6525 Sunset Boulevard, Hollywood. Young industry types.

Hollywood Billiards, 323/465-0115. www.hollywoodbilliards.com. 5750 Hollywood Blvd., Hollywood. 35 tables, video games, snacks, open all night.

House of Blues, 323/848-5136. www.houseofblues.com. 8430 Sunset Blvd., West Hollywood.

Key Club, 310/274-5800. www.keyclub.com. 9039 Sunset Blvd., West Hollywood. This is the site of the old very famous Gazzarri's and Billboard Live. Cover varies. Call for bookings.

The Lounge, 310/888-8811. 9077 Santa Monica Blvd., West Hollywood. Deejays, occasional live bands.

Miceli's, 323-466-3438. www.micelisrestaurant.com. 1646 N. Las Palmas Ave, Hollywood. Singing waiters, fun.

Molly Malone's, 323/935-1577. www.mollymalonesla.com. 575 South Fairfax, Los Angeles. High spirited bar, band.

Maloney's Sports Bar, 310/208-1942. 1000 Gayley Ave., Westwood. 14 TVs and drink specials. Near UCLA but all ages go there.

Nacional, 323/962-7712. 1645 Wilcox Ave., Hollywood. Havana-style supper club.

Sunset Marquis Hotel Bar, 310/657-1333. www.sunsetmarquishotel.com. 1200 N. Alta Loma Rd., West Hollywood. Young, hip, celebs and music industry folk.

Standard Lounge, 323/822-3111. 8300 Sunset Blvd., Hollywood. This hip hotel bar has a retro feel thanks to Ultrasuede hammocks and go-go-booted waitresses. Spotted: Keanu Reeves, Tobey Maguire, Sofia Coppola.

The Parlour Club, 323/650-7968. 7702 Santa Monica Blvd., West Hollywood. Wild and eclectic.

The Roxy, 310/276-2222. www.theroxyonsunset.com. 9009 Sunset Blvd., West Hollywood. L.A.'s major showcase for rock, pop and jazz artists. Call for bookings.

The Scene, 818/241-7029. 806 Colorado Blvd., Glendale. Deejays, live rock, country, alternative, depending on the night of the week.

Viper Room, 310/358-1880 www.viperroom.com 8852 W. Sunset Blvd., West Hollywood. Johnny Depp's place; where River Phoenix died.

Whiskey a Go Go, 310/652-4205. www.whiskeygogo.com 8901 Sunset Blvd., West Hollywood. Loud; world famous in the '60s and '70s.

Whist at the Viceroy, 310/260-7500. 1819 Ocean Ave., Santa Monica. Elegant resturant and bar.

Yankee Doodle's, 310/394-4632. www.yankeedoodles.com. 1410 Third Street Promenade, Santa Monica. 29 table billiard parlor.

• JAZZ

Baked Potato, 818/980-1615. www.thebakedpotato.com. 3787 Cahuenga Blvd. West, Studio City. 7PM-2AM.

Catalina Bar & Grill, 323/466-2210. www.catalinajazzclub.com. 1640 Cahuenga Blvd., Hollywood.

Charlie O's Saloon, 818/994-3058. 13725 Victory Blvd., Van Nuys.

Jax Bar and Grill, 818/500-1604. 339 N. Brand Blvd., Glendale.

Jazz Bakery, 310/271-9039. 3233 Helms Ave., Los Angeles, off Venice Blvd. Tickets $10-$20; call for bookings. Concert style listening room.

LaVe Lee, 818/980-8158. 12514 Ventura Blvd., Studio City. Tu-Su 8PM-1AM. Specializes in Lebanese dishes. Latin jazz and R&B.

Lunaria, 310/282-8870. www.lunariajazzscene.com. 10351 Santa Monica Blvd., West L.A. Happening jazz scene in Westwood.

Spazio, 818/728-8400. 14755 Ventura Blvd., Sherman Oaks. Good food; good jazz.

• PLACES TO DANCE

Salsa dancing, www.salsaweb.com. Do a city search for clubs in Los Angeles.

Swing dancing, www.nocturne.com and www.theswingthing.com. This is for Los Angeles clubs.

Any type dancing, any where. There are many links: http://scarecrow.caps.ou.edu/~hneeman/dance_hotlist.html.

Cava, 323/658-8898. 8384 West Third Street, West Hollywood.

Cherry at the Love Lounge on Fridays, 213/896-9099. www.clubcherry.com. 854 N. Highland Ave., West Hollywood. Good music focusing on '80s new wave, glam and metal.

Coconut Club at the Beverly Hilton, 310/285-1358. 9876 Wilshire Blvd., Beverly Hills. Open Fridays and Saturdays. Full dinner menu. A supper club with dining, dancing and a cigar lounge. Visitors include Victoria Principal, Loni Anderson, Esther Williams and Mickey Rooney. Private booths, 900 square foot dance floor. A special place for a special occasion.

Conga Room, 323/938-1696. www.congaroom.com. 5370 Wilshire Blvd., Los Angeles. Co-owners are Jennifer Lopez and Jimmy Smits. Liva Salsa music and dancing.

Crush Bar Continental, 323/461-9017. 7230 Topanga Canyon Blvd., Canoga Park. Big dance floor.

The Derby, 323/663-8979. www.the-derby.com. 4500 Los Feliz Blvd., Los Angeles. Swing dancing , cool place. Featured in "Swingers" the movie.

Good Bar, 310/271-8355. 9229 Sunset Blvd., West Hollywood.

Harvelle's, 310/395-1676. www.harvelles.com. 1432 Fourth Street, Santa Monica. Oldest blues club.

The Hollywood Dance Center, 323/467-0825. www.hollywooddancecenter.com. 817 N. Highland Ave., Hollywood. Pedro Montanez tells me Pam is the owner, "a wonderful, sweet spirit!"

Sportsmen's Lodge, 818/755-5000. www.sportsmenslodge.com. 12825 Ventura Blvd., Studio City. Call for info. Disco, House Music, Jazz, Salsa, Swing.

Sugar, 310/899-1989. www.clubsugar.com. 814 Broadway, Santa Monica. Different DJs and themes five nights a week.

Swing Dancing, The Best place to find out what's happening now is to log on to www.nocturne.com, Southern California's most comprehensive swing site.

The Brig, 310/399-7537. 1515 Abbot Kinney Blvd. A casual Venice Beach vibe. Cast members from Ally Mcbeal have been spied strutting their stuff.

The Nacional, 323/962-7712. 1645 Wilcox Ave. Glamorous 30's Havana-style cocktail lounge in the former space of Fuel.

• GAY AND LESBIAN SCENE

Big scene in West Hollywood on Santa Monica Blvd. between Fairfax and Doheny Blvds. Many street festivals. Bars, clubs, restaurants, coffee houses and shops. Most welcome everyone, straight or gay. The dance clubs are also popular with straight young women, who want to dance and have fun without getting "hit on." Be sure to park legally; they tow-away fast.

Gay and Lesbian Community Services, 323/993-7400.

Celebration Theatre, 323/957-1884. 7051 Santa Monica Blvd., West Hollywood. Gay/lesbian theatre company; quality work in a beautiful small theatre.

• COMEDY CLUBS

Acme Comedy Theater, 323/525-0202. www.acmecomedy.com. 135 N. La Brea Ave., Hollywood. Call for times and reservation.

Laugh Factory, 323/656-1336. www.laughfactory.com. 8001 W. Sunset Blvd., Hollywood. Thanksgiving and Christmas dinner free to people in the biz.

The Improvisation, 323/651-2583. www.improvclubs.com. 8162 Melrose Ave., L.A. Top comedy acts. Talent nights and open mike nights.

The Original Comedy Store, 323/656-6225. www.thecomedystore.com. 8433 Sunset Blvd. Many actors have been discovered here. Open mike nights.

Groundling Theatre, 323/934-9700. www.groundlings.com. 7307 Melrose Ave., Hollywood. Improvisational group doing consistently good work.

• ACTIVITIES

Backbone Trail. Three-mile hike in Malibu Creek State Park, which takes you to the old *M*A*S*H* set.

Barbara Streisand's former Malibu estate, 310/589-2850. www.smmc.ca.gov. 5750 Ramirez Canyon Rd. Now part of the Santa Monica Mountains Conservancy, the two-hour tour offers a thorough look at the estate, including three of the five houses. $30.

Book Soup, 310/659-3110. 8818 Sunset Blvd., You may never go back to a chain book store. Especially strong film section.

All Star Lanes, 323/254-2579. www.highoctane1.com. 4459 Eagle Rock Blvd., Eagle Rock. Home of Bowl-A-Rama on alternate Saturdays. A blend of rockabilly, punk fashion and bowling.

Canoga Park Bowling, 818/340-5190. 20122 Vanowen Street, Winnetka. Open 24 hours. 32 lanes, billiards and video arcade.

Casablanca Tours, 323/461-0156 or 1-800/498-6871. www.casablancatours.com. A four-hour van tour includes stops at the Hollywood bowl, Mann's Chinese Theatre, Sunset Strip, Rodeo Drive and a look at 25 to 30 celebrities homes.

Coldwater Canyon Park. Just east of the intersection of Coldwater Canyon and Mulholland Drive. Five miles of marked trails.

Culver City Western Hemisphere Marathon, 310/253-6650. www.culvercity.org. Early registration, $25; race day, $35. Expansive views of the Pacific Ocean above Dockweiler Beach.

Dodgers Adult Baseball Camp, 800/334-7529. www.dennismc.com/baseball/lad/dtnhmpg1.htm. Fantasy Camp. $4,000

Equestrian Center, 818/840-9063. www.la-Equestriancenter.com. On Riverside Drive in Burbank. This is our horse country. Many stables, restaurants, ice skating rink.

Gaona's Trapeze School, 818/710-8191. 5702 Lubao Ave., Woodland Hills. Students at Richie Gaona's Trapeze School must check any fears at the door. Within 30 minutes they're strapped into the safety harnesses, ready to ascend the 24-foot ladder and reach out to clutch a trapeze bar.

Glendale Batting Cages, 818/243-2363. 620 East Colorado Blvd., Glendale. Softball or hardball batting cages.

Hiking: Mount Hollywood Trail, Griffith Park. Enter Griffith Park from Los Feliz Blvd. and turn onto Griffith Park Drive. Parking lot next to the carousel. 800-foot uphill trek from the carousel to the planetarium. There are also easier trails.

Hollywood Bowl Rehearsals, 323/850-2000. www.hollywoodbowl.com. 2301 N. Highland Ave., Hollywood. During the Hollywood Bowl season from June to September, mostly Tuesdays, Thursdays and Fridays, you can see the program scheduled for that evening for free.

Hollywood Boxing Gym, 323/845-1420. www.hollywoodgym.com. 1551 La Brea Ave., Hollywood.

Hollywood Fantasy Tours, 800/782-7287. 1710 McCadden Place, Hollywood.

Los Angeles County Museum of Art, 323/857-6110. www.lacma.org. 5905 Wilshire Blvd., Los Angeles.

Los Angeles Downtown Walking Tour, 213/623-2489. www.laconservancy.org. All downtown walking tours begin at 10 a.m. and last approximately 2-1/2 hours (except the Biltmore Hotel tour which begins at 11 a.m. and is 1-1/2 hours long and the City Hall tour which begins at both 10 a.m and 11 a.m and is 1-1/2 hours long). Tours are free to Los Angeles Conservancy members and $8 for the general public (Angelino Heights is $5 for members and $10 for the general public). No strollers or young children. Advance Reservations required.

Indoor Climbing at Rockreation, 714/556-ROCK. www.rockreation.com. 1300 Logan Ave., Costa Mesa. 10,000 sq. ft. of sculpted artificial rock.

J. Paul Getty Museum, 310/440-7300. www.getty.edu. 1200 Getty Center Drive. Reservation for parking a must. They are completely redoing the museum in Malibu, 17985 Pacific Coast Hwy. Spectacular! Both museums are a "must see."

Laser Storm, 310/373-8470. www.gablehousebowl.com. 22535 Hawthorne Blvd., Torrance or 818/999-3150. 20929 Ventura Blvd., Woodland Hills. Laser tag venue lets you shoot at one another or at electronic objects in an arena filled with black and neon lights. Everything glows in the dark.

Mar Vista Bowl, 310/391-5288. 12125 Venice Blvd., Mar Vista. Call for open bowling times. Also has a great coffee shop for an inexpensive breakfast.

Melrose News, 323/655-2866. 647 N. Martel Ave., L.A. Celeb newsstand. Eddie Murphy allegedly stopped by the night of his infamous adventure with a transvestite.

Merchant of Tennis, 310/855-1946. 1118 S. La Cienega Blvd., Beverly Hills. 9-6. $15 per hour, per group. Lessons 6:30AM-1PM, $45 an hour.

Moore-N-Moore Sporting Clays, 818/890-4788. www.moorenmoore.com. 12651 N. Little Tujunga Canyon Road, San Fernando. Practice your marksmanship skills with clay pigeons. Celebs John Milius and Charlton Heston have been spotted here.

NBC Television Studio Tour, a 70-minute walking tour of the TV production complex. Departures at regular intervals, weekdays from 9-3. $7. 818/840-3537. www.nbc.com.

Poetry Readings, Beyond Baroque, 310/822-3006. 681 Venice Blvd., West Los Angeles.

Natural History Museum, 213/763-3466. www.nhm.org. 900 Exposition Blvd., Exposition Park, Los Angeles, near USC.

Paramount Ranch, 805/370-2301. http://www.nps.gov/samo/. Hit "In Depth" button. 401 W. Hillcrest Drive., Thousand Oaks. Free, this location has played the role of colonial Massachusetts, ancient China and countless Wild West towns. Take 101 Frwy. west to Kanan Road, south on Kanan half a mile to Cornell Way. Follow Cornell three miles to Paramount Ranch Road and turn right into parking lot.

Power Pools. Swim in the pools if you buy lunch at The Mondrian, Chateau Marmont, Regent Beverly Wilshire, Hollywood Roosevelt, or Sunset Marquis hotels. Takes a great body and nerve.

Romantic Rides/Hermosa Cyclery, 310/374-7816. 20 13th St., Hermosa Beach, Calif.

Runyon Canyon Park. Franklin Ave., 1 blk. east of La Brea, on Fuller. Past old Errol Flynn estate; foundations, old swimming pool still visible. At top, a bench and a view.

Santa Monica Pier, at the end of Colorado Blvd., in Santa Monica. Historical carousel and a whole amusement park, rides open on weekends, but plenty to do during the week. Bands play on the pier early evenings during the summer.

Shatto 39 Bowling Lanes, 213/385-9475. 3255 W. 4th Street, L.A. 19 pool tables, bar and coffee shop.

Sports Center Bowl, 818/769-7600. 12655 Ventura Blvd., Studio City. 32 lanes. Lots of industry clientele.

Stair Climbing, 4th Street Stairs, 4th and Adelaide streets in Santa Monica (189 steps).

Stairs in Santa Monica. They ascend from the 400 block of North Mesa Road to Amalfi Drive (201 steps). Less crowded than the 4th street stairs. Redwoods, wisteria and live oaks.

Sunset Beach, one of the best surfing spots. Take Sunset Blvd. west and park on Pacific Coast Highway, just south of Gladstone's 4 Fish.

Sunset Ranch Hollywood Stables, 323/464-9612. www.sunsetranchhollywood.com. 3400 N. Beachwood Dr., Hollywood. Friday night rides on horseback in the Griffith Park Hills.

Train Ride, Fillmore & Western Railway, 800/773-8724 or www.fwry.com. Two-and-a-half-hour excursion between Fillmore and Santa Paula. Barbecue dinner and dancing.

• AREAS

Beverly Hills, between Santa Monica and Wilshire Blvd., Canon on the east and where Santa Monica and Wilshire cross on the west.

Farmers Market, 323/933-9211. www.farmersmarketla.com. On Third and Fairfax, Los Angeles. M-S 9-7. Su 10-6. Great shopping and eating. The Grove, L.A.'s new and beautiful outdoor mall.

Hollywood Farmers Market, Ivar Avenue between Sunset and Hollywood Boulevards, 8:30AM to 1PM. Attracts a lot of Hollywood types.

China Town, in downtown Los Angeles, Hill and Broadway. Experience a dim sum tea breakfast for an unusual treat.

Fairfax Avenue, from Melrose to Sixth Street. The heart of the old Jewish district.

Koreatown, Olympic Blvd. from Vermont to Western. The Korea Plaza mall on Western features designer clothing, housewares, a bakery and large Korean grocery store.

Larchmont Blvd., between Melrose and Beverly Blvd. and Rossmore (Vine) and Gower. Old world village shopping and dining district.

Little Tokyo, 1st and 2nd streets between Los Angeles Street and Alameda in downtown L.A. Check out the new National Japanese American Museum. The Japanese Village features shops and restaurants. Also visit Yaohan Plaza at 4th and Alameda to see an incredible Japanese super grocery store, restaurants and an extensive Japanese bookstore. There's also a karaoke lounge where you can book private karaoke rooms by the hour.

Melrose Avenue, between La Brea and Fairfax. Underground chic shopping, eating and looking.

Montana Avenue, at 16th St. in Santa Monica. Great place for shopping and eating. A small town environment; lots of celebs live close.

Mulholland Drive. Enter from Cahuenga Blvd West (off Barham and the 101 Freeway.) On a clear day you can see the ocean, downtown L.A., and Century City Towers. 20-minute drive to the 405 freeway. Take in the Valley and the City. If it is not a clear day, you'll be above the smog.

Old Olvera Street, by Union Train Station in downtown L.A., off the 101 Freeway at Alameda. Permanent Mexican street festival.

Old Pasadena, 134 Freeway east, exit at Colorado. Check out Green Street and Fair Oaks. Antiques, dining, hot night scene, very in!

Third Street Promenade, 3rd Street between Colorado and Wilshire Blvd. in Santa Monica. Pedestrian mall with restaurants, movie theater and live street performers. A fun evening of strolling and browsing.

Santa Monica, Malibu, Zuma, Laguna, Newport Beaches!

Venice Beach Boardwalk, great shopping, walking, looking. Take Venice Blvd. west. Funky and crowded.

Walk By Moonlight, 626/398-5420. www.ecnca.org. On Friday nights closest to the full moon, walkers gather at 190-acre Eaton Canyon Natural Area in northeast Pasadena, at the base of the San Gabriel Mountains, for docent-led moonlight hikes.

World Book & News, 323/465-4352 1652 N. Cahuenga Blvd., Hollywood.

• BOOKS

The Ultimate Hollywood Tour Book, by William A. Gordon. Fantastic!
The Underground Guide to Los Angeles, by Pleasant Gehman, Editor.
Curbside L.A.: From the Pages of the Los Angeles Times, by Cecilia Rasmussen.

• NOVELS ABOUT L.A.

The Big Sleep by Raymond Chandler.
What Makes Sammy Run by Budd Schulberg.
Ask the Dust by John Fante.
The Day of the Locust by Nathanial West.
City of Quartz by Mike Davis.
A Red Death by Walter Mosley.
Maps to Anywhere by Bernard Cooper.
Golden Days by Carolyn See.
I Should Have Stayed Home by Horace McCoy.
Sad Movies by Mark Lindquist.
Armed Response by Ann Rower
Los Angeles Without a Map by Richard Rayner.
L.A. Is the Capital of Kansas by Richard Meltzer.

• MOVIES ABOUT L.A.

Adaptation	The Bad And The Beautiful
Barton Fink	Beyond The Valley Of The Dolls
The Big Sleep	Blade Runner
Boogie Nights	Bowfinger
Boyz N The Hood	Chinatown
Detour	Devil In A Blue Dress
Dogtown And Z-Boys	The Doors
Double Indemnity	Echo Park
Get Shorty	Heat
In A Lonely Place	Jackie Brown
Killing Of A Chinese Bookie	Kiss Me Deadly
L.A. Confidential	Laurel Canyon
The Long Goodbye	Lost Highway
Mulholland Dr.	The Party
The Player	Pulp Fiction
Short Cuts	Singin' In The Rain
Sunset Boulevard	Swimming With The Sharks

SECTION NINE

CHILD ACTORS

• **If your child really wants to act—really wants to work**—it can happen with your help. This is the consensus of all the experts I have interviewed. Children, as well as adults, need dedication, talent and luck to make it.

• **In the writing of this Tenth Edition, Austin Tovar** my 14-year-old grandson is in the 8th grade and has retired from acting for the time being. He worked on several long running Jack-In-The-Box commercials playing Jack Jr.—yes, he is wearing the big head. He loved working and being on the set but got to where he didn't like being pulled away from his activities to drive an hour to audition. His parents opened a bank account for him as well as the mandatory trust fund. He pays for special things he wants to participate in from his own earnings. He gets to spend $5 to $20 from each paycheck he receives, depending on the amount of the check. He is still receiving residual checks and holding fees. (*See his pictures at the end of this section.*)

• **Last year my seven year old grandson, Jackson Tovar,** called to tell me he wanted to be an actor and asked, "Could you help me?" I said, "Yes, of course." Jackson had been watching his brother go in for auditions and thought, "That looks fun." My daughter, Cynthia, had just returned to work in the hot real estate market and her husband, Hank, had left the turbulent record business. He runs a marketing business from home, as well as the care of the house and children. I asked Hank if he was willing to take on the rigors of an auditioning child. He said, "Yes" and took some great headshots of Jackson. (*See Hank's instructions on how talented amateur photographers can shoot their child's pictures, page 559.*)

• **I then made an appointment for Jackson to have a private lesson** with kids' coach Tracy Martin. I wanted her to evaluate his talent and readiness to meet agents. She said he was ready, so I arranged a meeting with agent Judy Savage. Jackson did another private with Tracy to prepare him to talk to the agent on his own; the parents wait in the outer office. He met with Judy, she liked him and thought he would do well on auditions.

• **At the end of this section Hank** gives a parent's eye view of the process he goes through. There is also a log that Hank kept of all Jackson's auditions for the first several months.

• **Scams abound in the children's field.** We all think our children are fabulous. We can get swept away by the praise for our children and the promise of stardom. I have heard horror stories of families losing thousands of dollars after paying money up-front to illegitimate talent companies or acting schools for services that were promised but never provided. Throughout this section, I have quoted respected professionals in the business. Please read it carefully. Do not get ripped off.

• **There are expenses involved in getting any business started.** Your child will need classes, pictures and a working wardrobe, but you only pay for these at the time of service, not before. Agents and managers get paid commissions only after the child gets paid for working. At the end of this section I list teachers, photographers, agents and managers that I know personally or who were recommended by friends. Check these resources out, do your own research, find out what you are paying for and follow your own intuition.

• **Carlyne Grager of Dramatic Artists Agency, Inc.** in Seattle is a mother of child actors and for the past 15 years has been an agent and co-owner of an agency that represents many children in the Northwest. I asked for her views of child actors as a parent and agent.

> • **I think every parent's level of investment** grows beyond what they originally intended and they all get caught up in the industry more than expected, but some parents nearly imprison their children within the Hollywood cycle of networking, classes, showcases, auditions etc.

> • **It is far better for a parent** to think that a career should be developed in much the same manner that they would develop their child athletically or scholastically. In those areas they start small and

invest as their child's interest grows, skills develop and passion increases. Sports and academics can affect children's lives in many of the same ways that acting for film and television can. Good or bad, it all depends on the attitudes and character of parents, coaches and professional guides such as agents/managers. How will the child's self-esteem and cultural enrichment be developed?

• **In my opinion, acting has been a saving grace** with my children when school wasn't going well or athletics were too political and competitive. It gave them another "arena" in which to shine or excel. Their acting friends always remained a separate entity outside of the social politics at school and in sports, giving them a "port" in the storm.

• **Acting can enhance the natural skills** and alter the course of a child's life in a very positive manner. I've had actors with "issues" that were overcome with the artistic expression found in acting. My own son overcame a high functioning form of autism because of acting for the camera. I've had several A.D.D. and Dyslexic children excel at acting when they were struggling in school. I've had a few kids who were dealing with substance abuse issues that found acting to be their survival and reason to stay recovered. It's my personal belief that acting has prevented many of its disciples from ever straying in the first place towards drugs, alcohol or delinquency. Mainly, because it provides calculated risk and the type of "highs" or peer support that can never be maintained through drugs or alcohol.

• **The enrichment and exposure** that a child receives in acting teaches tolerance, acceptance, discipline and camaraderie. It gives the child a venue to explore and dream that it is seldom found elsewhere. Where can a child live the moments of being crowned homecoming queen or being an international spy or even becoming a cartoon character when clearly "real life" doesn't always allow that? When do they get to be Peter Pan or Harry Potter other than in their imagination? The answer is that they get to be those types of characters and live different life scenarios every time they step into a casting office, or acting class. My oldest son, a sports enthusiast, got to spend a day talking to Olympic Medal Athletes on the set of *Prefontaine*. My daughter, got to bowl for free all day while doing a photo shoot at a bowling alley. Some experiences are great, some are simple, but often the experiences are unique.

• **The very behaviors** that young actors are trained to develop and display. . . social manners, memorization skills, character insight, action and reaction (scientifically referred to as "cause and effects") are all the behaviors that contribute to academic or athletic success.

• **T.J. Stein of Stein Entertainment Group was a child actor** himself and then evolved into management representation.

Q: What is the first step to get your child into the business?

> • **I think the first step would be enrolling your child in an acting class.** Basically to get in front of the camera, get an idea of where the camera is and what to do, following directions and to see themselves on TV. They will learn about being creative and using their imagination.

> • **Most children really have no idea what to do** when they first walk into a room to interview with an agent or to audition. In class they get the experience of what is going to be asked of them. Class for kids is really a training and a practice ground for them to go into the audition.

• **When the child gets to know how to work with the camera,** feels comfortable and wants to pursue acting professionally, it would be time to look for an agent. A SAG franchised agent makes 10% of any fee your child is paid for work. There are never any up-front charges for you to pay to the agent.

• **Manager Diane Hardin of Hardin/Eckstein Management,** along with her partner, Nora Eckstein, manages careers of some of the top working young actors in town. Some of their kids are: Aaron Lohr currently in a play at the Public Theatre in New York, Ryan Malgarini *(Freaky Friday)* and Lyndsy Fonseca is Colleen on *The Young and Restless*. Diane owns and teaches at the Young Actor's Space in Van Nuys, California. She also teaches three times a year in New York.

Q: What is the best way to find an agent for your child?

> • **If the parent doesn't know any agents** they can go to the Screen Actor's Guild and get a copy of the SAG franchised agents. It will say which agents handle children. Take some good color snapshots of the child, close-ups and full body shots. The children should look like real kids wearing play clothes, like they've just come from school or the playground. Get 3x5 or 4x6 copies made and send them with a cover letter listing their birthday, interests, skills to all the franchised agents.

> • **Have a meeting with the agents** who call you. Look at their track record, at the other clients they represent. What sort of reputation does the agent have? You should sign with the agent who shows the most enthusiasm for your child.

• **Hettie Lynne Hurtes, actress, newscaster and manager** of her children's careers responds to the question: "On the child's interview with the agent, what will they talk about?"

> • **It is important to know the child will be going into the agent's office alone.** The parents will be waiting in the front office. The agents want to find out if the child is open to talking to strangers, to people they are not familiar with. This can be a difficult situation for young actors because they are used to their parents telling them not to talk to strangers. The parents will have to tell the child, "This is an atmosphere where your mom is right outside the door and you can feel safe talking to these business people."

> • **The best thing a child can do is to be themself** and talk about anything they want to. Sometimes they will have specific questions like, "How old are you? What school do you go to? What grade you are in? What is your favorite subject?"—things that they know you know. The way they find out about your personality is to ask questions about your everyday life. They want to see if you are an out-going kid. That is very important in a child actor. The kids who are gregarious and precocious are the ones who usually work. If you are shy and quiet you will not be interesting to the agent.

• **Tracy Martin, acting coach for kids and teens** has coached many actors for their auditions and their roles. Her actors are currently working on series, in films and commercials.

Q: How would you advise a parent to help their child on an audition?

> • **It is the "trend" now in Hollywood** for young actors to be real and natural. Gone are the days of overacting and super cute smiles. Casting directors want to hire kids that look like "kids" and act like "kids." For that reason, some agents are discouraging their clients from being coached. I had a young girl come to me from a very reputable Hollywood agency. Her mom told me that the agent told her not to get coaching because they wanted the girl to remain "natural". The young girl arrived and actually read the stage directions out loud! She also "yelled" all of her lines as she did in her last "school play." Again, be a smart shopper. My students train hard with me and remain real and natural because that is how I train them. Find the coach or teacher that will help your child to book the job.

> • **If you must coach your child yourself,** here is what to look for. No acting. Have them read the lines to you as though they were really the character, having a real conversation. Encourage them to be themselves!

- **Understand the material.** You cannot play something you do not understand.

- **In comedy, it's about beats and timing.** If you do not have a good comedy coach at your disposable, watch classic sitcoms like *I Love Lucy* and *All In The Family*. You can actually count out the beats in a joke and between the jokes.

• **Agent Judy Savage of the well-respected Judy Savage Agency, represents children and very young adults.** She started with her own three children, then opened the agency when her youngest son was 14. The children she represents work in commercials, movies, television and stage.

Q: When you get a picture in the mail and you are interested in that child, will you call?

- **I look at all the pictures that come in.** One Saturday a month, we set up a time where the children come in and do a monologue for me if they're old enough, or I have them read something. I spend about 15 or 20 minutes with them and also with the parents. Usually out of a Saturday where I'll see 15 or 20 kids, I'll find maybe three or four new ones. You always have to build from the bottom up in an agency. You've got to get new little ones.

Q: At what age do you start them?

- **In California, the legal age to work is six.** I do start interviewing at three years old, but I prefer not taking them until they're old enough. When producers hire children under six, they usually want twins or they want a six year old to play four so they can work them more. It's a business. If they can save money, then that's what they're going to do.

Q: How would you advise parents?

- **Make sure that they're with an agent who cares about children.** There are some agents and acting classes that make the kids cry. Protect them. Make sure the team around them supports, loves and nurtures them. When they go on an interview, it's a really special time for a mother and a child. They should play games in the car or whatever they can think of to make it fun. If you make it fun, they're going to do better. When my children were little, I used to take all kinds of toys. When you get to the interview, take them aside, teach them the dialogue, make sure that they know it, and then relax and have a good time. Don't hound them to death by combing their hair, etc. When they come out of the interview, don't insist on knowing everything that goes on. The kids hate that.

Q: How do you get children and parents started?

- **We talk to them about the business,** the good and bad points. This business is very good for children, especially those who are extremely intelligent or have a lot of energy, even children who have a bad time in school. Some wanted to be in this business so badly they have gone from F's to straight A's, because in order to get and keep a work permit, you have to maintain a C average. The parents are astounded.

• **When you have interviewed and signed with an agent,** you will need your career tools. T. J. Stein talks about pictures, resumes and work permits.

- **The picture is the calling card for the child.** It is important to research the photographers you are thinking of using. Agents and managers have photographers that they will recommend. The Screen Actors Guild requires that an agency recommend at least three different photographers. The parents can base their choice on which photographer's work they like and how the photographer works with the child. Pictures cost $100-$250, depending on the photographer and how many rolls you will get. I would not pay anything over $250 for a child getting a head shot. The pictures should be taken after you have signed with an agent so that the agent and/or manager can help you choose which picture to blow up into an 8x10. The commercial shot will tend to be a smiling shot because commercials are always happy. The theatrical shot shows a more serious side of the actor.

- **Resumes are attached to the back of the 8x10.** On the resume you have the child's name, birthdate, unions, a list of the projects the child has worked on, name of the show, the part played. List the child's special skills and the acting classes they have taken.

- **It is necessary to have a work permit for the child.** It allows them to work in the entertainment industry. Go to the Department of Labor Standards—there is one in Van Nuys at 6150 Van Nuys Blvd. Fill out the application; if the child is of school age there is a section for the child's teacher to complete. During the summer, a current report card will take the place of the teacher's signature. The parent can do all of this without the child being present. Each time you work, the permit will be stamped. The child must maintain a C average in order to be eligible and the permit must be renewed every six months. It can be renewed through the mail and must be kept current or the child can lose a job.

- **When your child is on an audition** they are not covered by the state's strict laws because they apply only when your child is actually employed. So you must be on guard that there is never a situation where your child is in danger. If you have any misgivings, remove your child immediately.

• **Doreen Stone, known for her photography of children**, recommends when having your children's pictures taken to keep it simple. Bring simple Gap looking clothes, no logos. What they wear everyday is perfect for the pictures. When she shoots she actually plays with them, gets down on the floor, makes it fun.

• **More from Diane Hardin:**

Q: What is required of the parent?

> • **Constant vigilance.** The parent has to be ready at a moment's notice to run on interviews and to sit on a set. A parent, grandparent or somebody who is really connected to that child should be with them. Children have to attend three hours of school every day and maintain a high grade average in order to keep their work permit. There are a lot of wonderful experiences and nice people involved, but it's also a lot of pressure.

Q: How old do you think a child should be before they start?

> • **I wouldn't do it before six.** Children may be asked to be in uncomfortable situations and they don't understand the difference between an angry scene on the set and an angry scene in real life.

Q: When is it time to put your child in the business?

> • **Only when your child is constantly begging you** to be in the business. It should come from the child's saying, "Oh, I can do that. I want to do that." And if the child wants to try out for all the school plays and really seems to have a need to do it, then I think that they should have every encouragement in the world, just like you would encourage someone who wanted to play Little League or the violin.

Q: How do the young actors take rejection?

> • **My main suggestion is to make it about the work**, about doing the best acting job every time they go out and not about getting the job. When they land the job it's a nice surprise.

Q: How should a parent interview acting schools?

> • **There's only one reason for a child to take acting classes**, and that's because it's fun. I don't think it should be too psychological or too critical. I am very strongly based on positive reinforcement, rather than the negative. I will be quick to tell them what I believed in their work, rather than what I didn't believe. You can't build your confidence if you're constantly being torn down. If it's a chore and it makes them feel bad about themselves because somebody is tearing them down, then that's not the right place to study acting.

- **You can't really teach someone to act.** You can just give them a way to discover how to be real in the moment—how to listen and react. They have to learn to make very quick decisions and strong choices.

- **At the Young Actor's Space** we help these young people discover what it feels like after they've made strong choices about who they are, where they are, and what they want in the scene. They read it, make those choices, relax, listen and react within the given situation.

- **Every class at the Young Actor's Space** is based on improvisation. The first hour is improv warm-ups, improv scenes of different kinds. They have scenes to do every week. I tell them the scenes have to look like an improvisation, like this is happening for the first time, every time they do it.

• **Kids and teens coach Tracy Martin's students** are now appearing on television in series regular, recurring and guest-starring roles. In films, they appear in lead and supporting roles. Numerous students are working consistently in the commercial world.

Q: What does it take for a child to land jobs, luck?

- **Luck? No one will deny the magic of luck and timing.** But, to really make it these days as a child actor in Hollywood it takes more. It demands more. They will need passion, a good attitude and the ability to work hard. They will also need self-discipline, intelligence, talent, energy and a loving and supportive family.

- **Why passion? A working child actor** may miss sporting events, class trips, birthday parties and family vacations. They may have their heart broken when the part they "really wanted" goes to a "name actor" at the last minute. They may have the sniffles and want to stay in bed, but they have a callback they need to be at in one hour. They may be tired after a long day at school and have to learn seven pages of dialogue for a TV audition that very afternoon. The family may miss presenting a united front at one siblings school play because "Johnny" has to be on the set late one night.

- **My working students all have one thing in common.** They love to act. They love to act more then they love anything else and they are fortunate that their families support them. A family life may be turned inside out and upside down to support such a "passion."

- **Q: What kind of training does a child need?**

  - **There are many different classes** depending on the direction you are taking with your child's career. As a general rule, I discourage school plays for the simple reason that most of this kind of acting is over the top. Most film and TV acting is more understated and real.

  - **A good improv class is invaluable.** It will help build confidence in the child, help them to think on their feet and will help them greatly if they get into commercials.

  - **Scene study is very helpful when first starting out.** Make sure the class provides feedback. Just reading lines with a scene partner will not provide the skills that are necessary for successful auditions.

  - **There are some good on-camera commercial classes** out there. Try to get referrals.

  - **Audition technique.** Depending on where you live, you may not be able to find this kind of class. I teach the students how to break down the scenes, (make notes) and then they read against me as though I were the casting director. I try to duplicate the audition process for them so that they feel prepared and empowered when they walk into the casting directors office. I also hold "mock" producers' call-backs so they can get a sense of that as well.

- **Tracy Martin advises parents:**

Student Rights

  - It is your right as a student paying for a class (and parents paying for classes) to expect the following from your coach.

  - That your coach is clued in to the current trends in casting. This means that they are in communication with top kids agents and casting directors.

  - A supportive and nurturing environment. You will not grow as an actor if you do not feel safe.

  - That your coach will push you to your limit and help you to be the best actor that you can be. Many teachers will "praise" you, but that does not necessarily mean that this kind of feedback will help you to book jobs.

- That your coach will give you the tools necessary to book a job on your own. A good teacher is all about you, the student!

- That you pay a reasonable amount of money for the class you are taking. Call around and compare prices. Be a smart shopper.

• Agent Judy Savage:

Q: How do the kids turn out as adults?

- **I think I've known every child actor since Jodie Foster and Ron Howard** when my kids were working. It is absolutely, positively the family structure that makes the difference. If they have a good family, ethics, morals, some sort of spiritual background and the work is treated like a hobby they get paid for, they turn out just great.

Q: What about scripts with violence or sexual abuse? How do you deal with that?

- **We are alerted by the casting directors.** They'll call us, or they'll have on the breakdowns, "This is really sensitive material; make sure you alert the parents." We get the material ahead of time. We let the parents look at it and decide if they think their child is able to handle it. Some do and some don't. I've had people turn down major work. I believe these children have to have a life first because show business can come and go but they have to have a life afterwards.

Q: Anything you think parents should know?

- **It is very, very competitive in this business,** and there are many, many, many rejections. You may go on a hundred interviews before you get something. People are almost never discovered overnight. Some people think that they can come to Hollywood and get work in three months. My experience in working with really talented kids who are in training every week has been it takes about three years to get some-body started. There are twice as many parts for boys than there are for girls, yet there are probably 10 times as many girls in the business. If you're a 6-year-old, there are maybe 10 other kids, and by the time you are 14, there are 400, and by the time you are 18, there are 2,000.

- **It's a myth that child actors make all this money** that their parents spend. When a child works, 25% of their money goes into a trust fund, 10% goes to the agent, 15% goes to the manager, if they have one. Because they are making a high amount of money each week, they are in a 40% tax bracket. When a child actor works, their check is about 10% of their salary but they do have a nice trust fund when they turn 18. Usually their mother has to give up a job and work full-time as a driver. By the time you're on a series for eight years, you may be making $30,000 an episode, so even if you take home 10%, that's $3,000 an episode. Actors making their first movie usually earn scale plus 10% for the agent, even for adults. By the second movie, they make $40-$50,000; by the fourth movie, $100-$125,000. They may make $200,000 if it's a lead part, unless they luck out and it's a hit movie, like Macaulay Culkin did. Macaulay is the only child since Shirley Temple that's received a million dollars a film. Everybody thinks, "I want to do movies so I can make money like Macaulay." *Home Alone* was Macaulay's third or fourth movie. He made $100,000.

• **Agent Arletta Proch:**

Q: Have you ever had a child or parent who was distraught over losing a role?

• **Yes. I have suggested that they take a break from show business** or just get out of it entirely. The parents have a harder time than the child; if they can't deal with it, I have suggested that they get a manager for the child who can handle the career on a management level. The parent can then be a parent. It's worked for some problems we've had.

• **Manager Diane Hardin:**

Q: What are the manager's duties?

• **My partner and I are, perhaps, a little different than some managers;** we meet our clients on every single audition and give them hands-on coaching. We also coach them when they get the job. If they get a series, we coach them on their weekly scripts. Nora and I feel our main job as managers is to nurture their talent through coaching, exposing them to theater, recommending books for them to read, such as Uta Hagen's *Respect for Acting,* insisting that they take acting classes and that they stay in class. We do offer our clients as many acting classes as they care to take at the Young Actor's Space. It's all part of the management fee.

Q: What is the manager's fee?

• **We take 15% of their salary.** We take 5% of commercials, because we don't go with them on commercial auditions. But we do know that the good training does affect their commercial potential.

• **Manager T.J. Stein:**

Q: When do you think is the right time to look for management?

> • **I think that you really need the guidance and support right away.**
> Some people say, "Well, what do you have to manage if you are
> brand new?" You have a lot to manage. You need to get to the
> right people, you need to make sure that I, in my position, open
> the right doors. A child is a child for a very short period of time.
> There is a lot of competition.

• **Diane Hardin:**

Q: Can you talk about Kellie Martin's career?

> • **Kellie came to study at the Young Actor's Space** when she was eight
> years old. We knew right away she was a special little talent. Her
> mother asked, "Would you manage her?" We took Kellie on, and she
> started hitting everything she went on. She did some movies of the
> week and a recurring role on *Hogan's Family.*
>
> • **She was offered two pilots at once,** *Life Goes On,* an hour drama
> and *Mars Base One,* directed by Dan Ackroyd. We had to choose
> between the two.
>
> • **Kellie's mother, the agent, my partner and I were a team.** I like to
> think of it like a circle. Kellie's in the center, and we're all working for
> her, to keep her safe. The highs are so high and the lows are so low.
>
> • **She was on *Life Goes On* for four years.** When it was over, she did a
> movie, *Matinee,* and the series *Christy.* She went to Yale, and was cast
> on *ER* when she graduated.

• **Debbie Martin, Kellie Martin's mom.**

**Q: Did your younger daughter feel slighted because Kellie had so
much notoriety?**

> • **When Kellie was at home,** she was not treated any differently than
> anybody else. Heather I'm sure was jealous at times, but it was always
> exciting to go to shows and meet celebrities. The drawbacks would
> be that I wouldn't be home quite as often as I'd like to be.

Q: Kellie's working was really a full-time job for you, wasn't it?

> • **Yes. Kellie started working when she was seven,** and I taught school

until she was 11. The first time she got something that lasted for a month, I quit working and never went back.

Q: Why did you put her in the business?

- **She was an outgoing child.** She did a play at school where she had to memorize tons and tons of pages. Her teachers thought that she was wonderful, and I thought why not give it a shot.

- **She played with Michael Landon's children.** My sister was their nanny. Kellie would tell Shawna, his daughter, that she wanted to be on her dad's show. Shawna called her dad and said, "My friend wants to be on your show," and he said, "Okay, have her come in and talk with me." She went in and two days later he called Shawna and said, "Tell your little friend I found her a part."

- **She got an agent** and we said we'd give it a shot for a year. At the end of the year she had done six or eight commercials. One of the product companies was having a convention and they took us all to Hawaii for her to be introduced before they showed the commercial. It was really exciting and fun.

Q: What are the drawbacks?

- **For us, there were no drawbacks.** We always took it one year at a time. Up until Kellie was a freshman in high school, she went to a regular school and our life was regular. She just happened to go on interviews, or she just happened to work once in a while. It was not disruptive; it was just something she did. She got the series and we were very excited. For Kellie, there was never a drawback.

Q: Any advice for parents?

- **My advice would be to only do it for as long as it makes your child happy.**

- **Brigitte Burdine is a working actress**, casting director and commercial and theatrical teacher for children and teens. Brigitte started working as a teenager when she was living in Maryland. As an actress some recent commercial credits include: several Honda spots, Acura, Sizzler, Palm Pilot, Denny's, Prudential Real Estate, numerous regional spots, plus many animation voices. She cast, produced and directed the voice talent for Spider-Man I and II video games. The commercials she teaches in her classes are those she has followed from the beginning of casting through the production. She knows who the advertising clients wanted to see and why the children were picked for the spots.

Q: How should young actors get experience before they move to Los Angeles?

- I started acting and modeling when I was 14 years old in the Washington D.C. area. I think it is a good idea to get as much experience as you can in a small market. There aren't as many opportunities, but there isn't as much competition either. Expect that there will be some traveling involved. I had to commute to NY from time to time.

- If you are outside the LA or NY area, the best place to start is by checking with your local SAG office for reputable representation (www.sag.org). The same rules apply in a small market that apply here. Never pay for representation. Agents get 10% of your earnings when you work.

Q: When does a parent know it is time for their child to study? Should they try to get an agent first?

- Generally speaking, a child is ready to start training at 5. It is fine to seek representation by an agent before you begin to study. Usually the agent will want you to take a class before they send the child out on auditions. Children are able to be themselves easier if they are in a comfortable situation. A class will help with that. Think of it this way: we tell our children not to talk to strangers. Then we proceed to send them into a room on an audition with a bunch of people they aren't familiar with and expect them to feel safe and be their wonderful, uninhibited selves. From casting for more than 14 years, I can tell right away when a child enters the casting room whether or not they have had a class. They will have a confidence about them that other children don't have.

Q: How can the parents help their children at the auditions?

- The best way is to explain to them what they are going to do and make sure they understand what it means. Do not try and give them line readings. (Don't tell the child, "Say it like this.") Once you have directed them into a line reading, it is very hard for the director to change what you have told them to do. The more prepared and relaxed you are, the more prepared and relaxed your child will be. Have you ever noticed how your mood and state of mind directly affects your child's? Treat auditioning like a fun after school activity like baseball or dancing. It is important to take it seriously, but it isn't the cure for cancer.

Q: When Jackson was in your class, he enjoyed the voiceover class. Do they hire children?

- **It is true that they will usually hire an adult** to do the child's voice (I play a 14 year-old Chinese princess and a 15-year-old boy in a cartoon called *The Flute Master*). However, over the last few years, the voiceover field has opened up more to children. That is why I decided to include voiceover as part of my on-camera class. A lot of the commercial agents have voiceover divisions now. Just last week, I hired five children to loop a music video.

- **Al Burton, executive producer for Al Burton Productions:**

Q: What are some of the shows you've done?

- **My list of shows that children worked on would include** *One Day at a Time,* which introduced McKenzie Phillips and Valerie Bertinelli, *Diff'rent Strokes* with Gary Coleman, Todd Bridges and Dana Plato, *Silver Spoons* with Ricky Schroeder. In that show, we introduced Jason Bateman when he was 12. I worked with Michael J. Fox in *Palmerstown, U.S.A.*, a Norman Lear show that predated anything Michael had done in the U.S. The cast of *Square Pegs* was Sarah Jessica Parker, Jamie Gertz, Tracy Nelson, all teenagers, varying in ages from 15-19. Molly Ringwald started at age 12 in *Facts of Life*. She was a regular in the first year, then she got *The Tempest* with Mazursky, which shot her into a movie career.

- **Then** *Charles in Charge* **and** *The New Lassie*. In *Charles in Charge* we had Josie Davis, Nicole Eggert, Alexander Polinsky and Christina Applegate, very early in her career; Erika Eleniak who went on to become Ellie May in *Beverly Hillbillies* and starred in *Baywatch,* and Pamela Anderson who played the girlfriend of Charles for several weeks. I recommended both Nicole and Pamela to the *Baywatch* people and they became *Baywatch* stars. *The New Lassie* starred Will Estes, who is now starring on *American Dreams*.

Q: When you were casting *Facts of Life* and *Diff'rent Strokes,* you saw a lot of kids, didn't you?

- Yes. I was not satisfied until I felt I had cast the very best actors in the United States. We sent casting people to New York, Atlanta, Dallas, Denver and Boston to look for kids.

Q: How would they find kids in other states?

- **They start with little theater people.** If they had cast six kids in the previous year, we would see every one of them. We would put many on tape. I remember a casting director who went to Chicago, was told by somebody he ought to see a little kid in Zion, Illinois. He went up to Zion and found Gary Coleman. I got the tape when it came back and I looked at this little pair of eyes and this little nose peering over the desk. I ran and showed the tape to Norman Lear, he agreed and we brought Gary out and signed him to a contract from just the first meeting. He was perfect. His delivery was fabulous from day one.

Q: You seem to understand working children.

• **I feel very protective about children.** I have conversations with my directors and writers where my argument is, "Protect the kid." Don't ever say, "the kid can't act" or "the kid is bad." Your material needs to be fixed or your directing needs to be fixed. I often show a documentary on Steven Spielberg directing a 13-year-old boy in *Empire of the Sun* to directors. Spielberg gives direction that shows he unconsciously cares for, works with and has respect for the kid. I admire him a lot.

Q: If a child has that desire, what should they do to be discovered?

• **There are ways to get exposure** in Sheboygan, Dallas, Atlanta, etc. Acting is acting, whether it's in school, community theater or church, and I think experience in acting gives you the where-with-all to begin having a career. I began my career in Columbus, Ohio. By the time I was 15, I had engineered every opportunity I could find, which included producing shows for the Boy Scouts and local radio shows, just to give myself a part. It turned out that I liked the producing better than the acting, but it didn't start out that way. I created my own opportunities every step of the way.

• **In my heart of hearts**, I always want to say that if you're a parent and you see your child wants to be in the entertainment world, encourage it, and then get them close to a production center.

Q: How did you cast Will Estes on *The New Lassie* series?

• **Will was just a terrific 10-year-old.** We made him come back, I think, seven or eight times to audition because we weren't quite sure. He was littler and younger than we wanted in that part and, other than Lassie, it was the starring role. He kept having something that we didn't want to let go of. He never lost his cool or got disgusted. He just came and was the same sunny Will he always was. I've known him for 12 years now and we remain friends.

Q: What is it that makes you pick the kids that you pick?

• **I'll use Will Estes, as an example.** His engine in the office worked very well. He's a dynamo, and yet he's not hyper. He had something in him that was very, very good, and it looked to me very promising. When it was Jami Gertz or Sarah Jessica Parker or Tracy Nelson, they had a package that was great. It wasn't just a voice or just acting or timing. It was everything: great eyes, great presence. They were interesting and had a totality. Norman Lear used to say, "They have to have television eyes." I think everybody I have liked did have eyes that could give a great close-up.

Mary Lu Chasteen is the mother and manager of her son, Will Estes.

Q: How old was Will when he got into the business?

- **He started when he was nine.** Friends of ours referred us to the Kelman/ Arletta Agency who had been in the business for years representing all but one of the kids on *The Brady Bunch.*

- **Arletta said, "Yeah, we'd like to sign him."** He has an All-American look they liked. Within the first month he booked a print ad for Lee jeans. Then he got his first commercial, Fruit of the Loom. It was real exciting for us. From that point on it just kind of snowballed.

Q: How did you know what to do?

- **Well, the agent tells you but it's learn as you go.** The agent would call and give us the interview, the time, what he should wear, what he should take with him like a skateboard, skates or anything, and then we'd go on the audition. In a few days if they were interested they'd call him back. Then sometimes he'd book the commercial.

- **Within the first year** Arletta started sending him out for theatrical auditions. He tried out for a part on *The New Lassie.* There were eight call backs over a few month's period.

Q: How long did he work on that series?

- **It turned out to be one of the greatest experiences we've had.** We did 48 shows. He was there nine-and-a-half hours a day, five days a week. To this day he still keeps in touch with some of the friends he made on the set, people he worked with and the owners of *Lassie;* it was really like a family situation for him. I think that's hard for kids as they get older; when the show stops, the family stops. Will did tell me, not too long ago, that he was glad he was old enough to have his own self-identity before he started this business.

Q: What about his schooling, grades and outside activities?

- **Some of the money Will made went for his private schooling.** It was a half day, straight academic school. When he worked, they prepared his lessons for the set. If he missed, they would tutor him to catch him up. Because of the concentrated studies he skipped a grade and graduated one year early with honors.

- **All the things he's interested in** seem to stem from things he did on jobs. He's really into gymnastics, and that came from a job he did on a commercial where he had to use a trampoline. They had a coach from UCLA work with them. He got the bug for gymnastics and is still taking classes. When he worked on *Lassie,* the guys on their lunch hour would ride bikes; they took him and now he's into mountain biking. Karate is something he initiated on his own. But the agent said parts come up that call for karate. So he has enhanced his ability to get jobs.

- **I made sure the teachers on the set** were accredited and able to teach him what he needed. The thing I was always most concerned with was that his educational needs were met. I don't want to jeopardize his education with the business. I don't want to compromise anything for him. That's why parents really have to watch out for the kids.

Q: How did you pass the time on the set?

- **When you are on the set there is observing to do.** For instance, one time when Will was younger, he was inside an airplane prop where I couldn't hear him so I was listening to him on the headset. I heard him say to the guest actress that she had a mustache. I knew I had to tell him that you aren't supposed to say that to women.

Q: How are the finances and show-biz life style for you?

- **You put a percentage of the child's earnings away.** When he works we usually let him buy something like a skateboard, video game or something to reward him but not all the time. The busier he got, the less I could work. My job is pretty much taking care of Will, of what he needs as far as getting to auditions, taking care of his finances, going with him when he works on the set. We've had to travel to different areas. So we have to be ready at a moment's notice to go wherever.

- **I loved spending time with my kid**, being with him, going places; we did a lot together. It's been exciting, to say the least. I'm really proud of him. It's changed my life because it enables us to do things we would probably never do. When we went to Miami, we saw the Everglades. We've been to Hawaii twice, Vancouver, New York, Texas, Chicago, Italy.

- **If children want to work**, I think it's important that the parents are supportive and helpful. Having the support of their families helps them get through the tough times.

• **Will Estes** (www.willestes.com) **has appeared in 40+ commercials** and as a regular on four series, *The New Lassie*, *It Had To Be You*, *Kirk* and *Kelly Kelly,* plus guest starring television and supporting film roles. Now as a young adult he already had four starring roles in the films, *Terror Tract*, *U571*, *Blue Ridge Fall* and *The Road Home* and now is starring on the NBC series *American Dreams*. (*See his resume in Section Two*)

Q: What about rejection?

• **I've never really had a problem with rejection**, it never bothers me. There are other things I have a lot of fun doing. I go to an audition and then head on down to gym class. I'll get in the car and it'll just leave my mind; I don't even think about it.

Q: What is it that your mother does that helps you in your career?

• **Well, before I could drive, she took me to all my auditions.** She would sit in the waiting room and I would go into the actual audition by myself. She would read the other characters lines in the script to help me memorize my lines. Sometimes she gives me suggestions; that's cool. I like having her opinion.

Q: What do you do on auditions?

• **If there are lines, I'll look over those.** If I have my lines down or there are no lines, as the case with some commercials, sometimes there will be people there I know, I can talk to them and hang out.

Q: What about young actors getting on drugs?

• **I don't see that acting relates to drugs.** I've never even come across it.

Q: Do you have any advice for kids?

• **If you really want to do it, then give it a try.** Don't take it too seriously, when it comes to an audition. What's the big deal if you don't get the job? It's not worth being stressed over.

• **Acting coach Tracy Martin says:**

• **Young actors today work just as hard as adult actors.** It is an honor and privilege for me to work with all of my students. They remind me on a daily basis that acting is fun. I hope that you enjoy your child's path of discovery into the acting field. Whether they show up on the "big" screen or they simply use their acting skills to present a book report in school, I hope they have fun. Break-a-leg!

• **Following is Hank Tovar's account of a child actor's parent:** The title refers to the 101 Freeway. The Tovars live in Ventura, which is an hour away in decent traffic from all of the audition offices.

ACTING on the 101. . . A Parent's Tale
By Hank Tovar

THE AUDITION CALL
When your agent calls and tells you your actor has an audition, try and make sure the following things are known –

- TIME
- STUDIO or LOCATION
- CASTING DIRECTOR
- WHO THE CLIENT IS
- NATIONAL / REGIONAL / INDUSTRIAL
- WHAT TO WEAR
- WHAT AGE IS THE CHARACTER?
- DOES THE CHARACTER HAVE A NAME?
- ARE THERE SIDES?

TIME is important especially if you have another audition or callback the same day, or if there is a long drive time or long down time between auditions. If you have an audition at 2:05PM and another one at 6:10PM, see if your agent can get you into the 6:10 audition earlier. The casting director may have a particular reason for the 6:10 call, such as all the 6-8 year old boys are coming in at that time, or they have paired your actor up with a similar looking adult actor. If they can move the time, great; if not, live with it.

STUDIOS vary in size, from closets to massive rooms. After a while you will learn them all, and be able to figure out how much change to bring for the parking meters.

CASTING DIRECTORS all have different ways for handling auditions. Some are incredibly organized and run on time, and some. . . well, you'll see.

CLIENT and the type of commercial—NATIONAL / REGIONAL / INDUSTRIAL is important to know when your child books the spot. Will it be seen on your TV, or just shown in Milwaukee, or only for stockholders at a corporate meeting?

WHAT TO WEAR and AGE go hand in hand. My son is 7, but plays kids 5 to 9. If the part is for a 5 year old wearing "kid casual" clothes, I will bring clothes that have a "younger look" than if he was playing a 7 or 8 year old. There are so many kinds of "casual". We have been to auditions that have been "Kid Casual", "Fun Casual", "School Casual", "Athletic Casual", and "Real Casual". Remember if this is a regional spot, Southern California casual can look very different from Boston casual. Plan your wardrobe carefully. No shirts with huge logos, and nothing too busy. Tip of the day — Blue looks great on camera!

The NAME OF THE CHARACTER is incredibly important at some auditions, especially if they are shooting multiple scenes with lots of children. If I know up front that he is auditioning for the "swimmer" or for the "Flashlight kid" it will save me time when I go to sign him in. There might be an entire roomful of boys all his age, and 5 or more sign in sheets, and if I sign in on the wrong one, I just blew through 6 more quarters in the parking meter.

SIDES should be faxed over to you right after you get off the call from your agent. If not, there usually will be copies of the dialog at the sign in table. Remember, those actors who were faxed the sides ahead of time, have already been rehearsing their lines. Always ask if there are sides.

THE "STATS SHEET" There are many ways to keep track of all the information for each audition, from a yellow note pad to Palm Pilot. I have found that the little "STATS" Excel spreadsheet works best for me. It logs all the information mentioned above, plus a VERY crucial detail — what Jackson wore. We had 2 auditions on Monday, one on Wednesday, and a callback on Friday for the Monday audition, and the agent tells me the client wants Jackson to wear exactly what he wore to the audition. NO PROBLEM! I pull out my "STATS SHEET" sheet for Monday, and there it is. Of course the clothes are dirty, but that's another story. That's why I always buy multiples on most of Jackson's basic "kid casual" clothes. I learned that the hard way.

GETTING THERE The majority of the casting studios are either in the Hollywood area or on the west side of LA. Getting to them after school, in the middle of the afternoon can be tricky. Always be prepared for traffic. The last thing you want to be is late, hurried and hysterical. Your little actor riding with you will copy the way you are acting, and could blow that audition. You've got to keep them occupied with homework, books, Legos or Game Boy. Bring some crossword puzzles or his favorite CD. Bring plenty of snacks (sticky, gooey and chocolate don't work that well, I've found out), and juice or water. Don't sugar them up quite yet. DON'T HAVE THEM WEAR THEIR AUDITION CLOTHES in the car. One glob of Reese's Peanut Butter Cup down the front and there goes the cool calm drive. My son also misses soccer and baseball practice, play dates, pool parties and beach trips. That's hard on him, and hard on all kids, so constant reinforcement is very valuable. Make it fun! Let him know that all the time and energy he is putting into acting is making him so much better, and he is doing a wonderful job.

WARDROBE So the audition calls for "casual" but the client wants to know if your actor plays ice hockey, and if so, could he wear a jersey. Yikes. Ice Hockey! So, it's off to one of the greatest wardrobe stores on the planet — the thrift stores. Sure I could buy a new Mighty Ducks jersey at Sports R Us for $47, or drop by the Goodwill and get one for $1.50. Soccer team shirt, football jersey, Hawaiian shirt, cowboy hat—it's all there.

THE SIGN IN You have a call time and you hit no traffic and now you are 30 minutes early. What should you do? I say, "Sign in". Always remember your call time (there's a spot for call time on the sign in sheet), even if your agent gave you a new one due to a conflict. The reason is that the casting director may have matched up your actor's headshot with several other adult actors and scheduled you all at the same time. If that was not the case, you are already signed in, and you might get to go in early, and beat the traffic going home. Of course you can watch and examine the constant flow of fresh faces filling the audition room.

Remember while signing in —
- Check the callback dates and shoot dates
- Fill out the size sheet
- Get a copy of the sides (they may have changed since yours were faxed over)
- Look at the storyboard
And most important —
- **READ THE HANDWRITTEN SIGN ABOVE THE SIGN IN SHEET.**
It's the one on the dry erase board, or in big bold letters. It tells you exactly what they want. It might say DO NOT STAPLE, or fill out a nametag, or do not read lines 4 and 5.

THE AUDITION More than likely your actor's part will include "parents", either a "Mom" or a "Dad" or perhaps an entire "family". They might have lines, or they will just appear in the back of the car, or around the dinner table. The storyboard will give you a good understanding of the scenes to be shot. One important lesson I learned was if they cast a "Mom" with jet-black hair, chances are that they are not going to cast my redhead, even if he is perfect. So explain that little fact to your actor. Also, the client knows what the "family" should look like, so if your actor doesn't have the "look" the client has in mind, you're done. It's not about the actor; it's about the client's vision. Explain that too. Some auditions take 30 seconds, some take 10 minutes, but most, I've found, take about 3 minutes. So you got there early and you have signed in. They have had their snack, they went to the bathroom, they are in outfit, and their hair is perfect. Now, they are in a room full of kids their own age, and they want to play! KEEP THEM BUSY. Bring in that Game Boy, those Legos, and playing cards, whatever. Try to keep them from running around and playing tag with the other bored kids. The casting folks are trying to work and tape their fellow actors, so remember to be courteous. It is a place of business, after all.

THE CALLBACK They whittled down the number of actors seeking the job to a handful or two, and that's what the callback is. Many times the client wants the actor to wear the exact same outfit, so that is why the logging of the outfit on the "STATS SHEET" is so important. I have been to auditions where there have been 88 boys trying out for the role, and at the callback, there were 20. Your child made the cut! That is incredible. Congratulate your actor. He or she did a tremendous job to be noticed in such a large pack of acting children. I have started packing a little surprise (like a Matchbox car) in with the water, juice and cheese and crackers. It's a small way of letting my little actor know that he has done something special, and that I am proud of him.

ACTING CLASSES

Just like piano practice and soccer practice, acting practice is essential. There are many teachers and coaches for your young actor to work on their craft and improve their chances for callbacks and bookings. Some are actors themselves who can teach their students the ins and outs of life in front of the camera. Some are casting directors who can give your actor an insider's look at what the casting professionals and the clients are looking for. Research them all and enroll in as many as you can. All of them offer important lessons, instruction and guidance for the young star-to-be.

COUPLE MORE THINGS

SECURITY Very, very important thing to remember. NEVER PUT YOUR CHILD'S SOCIAL SECURITY NUMBER ON THE SIGN IN SHEET! Just write "on file" under that section. Also, when you are filling out the size card for your actor, DO NOT GIVE YOUR HOME ADDRESS, HOME PHONE OR SS# ON THIS FORM. Leave them blank! They know how to reach you. Once the callbacks are completed, all those size cards, with all that PERSONAL INFORMATION of yours is tossed into a trash can. Not shredded, just tossed out. BE CAREFUL!

PASSPORT Get your actor (and you, too) a passport and keep it current, and then let your agent know that you both have one, just in case the shoot is out of the country.

WORK PERMIT Keep track of your child's work permit and know when it expires (most casting sign in sheets ask for the expiration date) and keep it current as well.

RÉSUME Constantly update your actor's resume. Every acting class should be added. Any performance, from school talent show to church play, should be listed and updated. Don't list your actor's commercial (if they have booked some), just say, "Conflicts are available upon request". Your actor grows taller all the time. Make sure that their resume reflects that fact in the height and weight portion.

HEAD SHOT You might have to update this shot more often as your actor grows, and loses teeth. Take a good look at the shot you are submitting to your agent, and make sure that it REALLY does resemble what your child looks like these days. If the shot was taken when they were 6, big smile with baby teeth, and now they are almost 8, and huge front teeth, its time! (See the section on photographers and photography.)

SIZES Clothing sizes from shoes to shirt are listed on all the sign in sheets, so make sure you know their current sizes, top to bottom.

WATCH COMMERCIALS ON TV All those commercials on Saturday morning TV are exactly what your actor is trying out for. Try and make sure that your actor is aware of the product. If you don't know either, go to the Internet and look it up. Commercials will also show your actor what the client is looking for in an actor. The kids in the Chuck E Cheese commercials do basically the same thing in all their commercials. Watch and learn.

JACKSON'S JOURNAL: "ACTING ON THE 101"

Week 1 - Jackson had an interview with agent Judy Savage, head of the Savage Agency. He sat in her office for 40 minutes while they talked one on one. Then, I heard her laughing out loud. He must have told her his Indiana Jones joke. She invited us in to her office and signed him as one of their clients. Proud day!

Week 2 - Jackson has his first audition - *L'Oreal Kids Shampoo*. It was on a Saturday afternoon in Santa Monica. The room was packed with all kinds of kids. Jackson was excited.

Week 3 - Jackson has his first theatrical audition at Sony Pictures for a character on "Family Law". It was inside the studio in the Jimmy Stewart Building. Very cool! Sides to read and learn. Had a *Carl's Jr* commercial audition that was packed with redheads. Signed up for commercial acting classes w/ Pamela Campus.

Week 4 - 2 auditions this week, *Charmin'* and *Arco AM/PM*. One commercial is to be shot in Spain. His agent checked to see if we had valid passports. First acting class.

Week 5 - No auditions. **Jackson was asked to be in a new film "Manhood"** that was being filmed at a school in West LA. His Aunt Chris was working on the film with our friend Pamela Springsteen and her husband, director Bobby Roth. Jackson went to the set, and was in 3 scenes. Great fun! Acting class #2.

Week 6 - Had 2 auditions in one day - *Circuit City* and *Jiffy Lube*. Acting class #3.

Week 7 - Jackson has his second theatrical audition. The part was Jody for the "Family Affair" pilot. Had several pages of lines to read. We hired Tracy Martin, a private acting coach, to help him run the lines. Had a commercial audition for *Ballpark Franks*. Busy week. Acting class #4.

Week 8 - Kind of quiet this week due to Passover and Easter holidays. One audition for *HGTV*, and it was a zoo. No Acting class.

Week 9 - Jackson's had his first print audition. It was for *Kodak*. This was a very different experience. Long sign-in sheet, lots of kids, a 45-minute wait and a then, we both were invited into the studio and they just took a Polaroid, that's it. Had a *McDonald's* audition. Acting class #5.

Week 10 - 2 auditions in one day – *Cellular One* and *Zeller's Dept. Store*.

Week 11 - Nothing this week.

Week 12 / 13 - Booked out—Spring Break.

Week 14 - Nothing this week. Started a new acting class with Brigitte Burdine.

Week 15 - One audition this week for *Noah's Bagels*. Acting class #2 with Bridget.

Week 16 - One audition this week. It was for *Kellogg's Crispix Cereal*. Acting class #3

Week 17 - Jackson's first callback for Kellogg's Crispix. Jackson was grouped with an all redhead family for the callback – Mom, Dad, sister, brother and Grandma. Looks like a real TV family. 3 auditions for the week (*Red Lobster, J C Penney,* and *Home Depot*) and 2 of those were on Friday. Busy week. Acting class #4.

Week 18 - First time Jackson was placed on "avail" for Kellogg's. Cool! Looks like the redheads are in for the commercial. Another busy week with 3 auditions (*Freddie Mac, National Children's Week,* and a *Scooby Doo* toy) The Scooby Doo was non-union. Got the word from the agent that one of the redheads in the "family" could not get cleared and they opted for another family. So close!

Week 19 - *Scooby Doo* callback. Jackson read for a different part than the first time. Acting Class #5.

Week 20 - Nothing this week.

Week 21 - 2 auditions this week (*Direct TV* and *Nintendo*).

Week 22 - 3 auditions this week.(*State Farm, Flintstone Vitamins, and Betty Crocker Au Gratin Potatoes*). Acting class #6. Very busy for a short week due to July 4ᵗʰ.

Week 23 - *State Farm* and *Betty Crocker* callbacks!! We were told that the actors would have to eat the potatoes during the commercial, so we headed to Vons and bought a box to try out. 2 auditions—*Target* and *Walt Disney World*.

Week 24 - 3 auditions this week for Jackson. A non-union *Disney Channel*, a *Honda* and a *Nike* spot.

Week 25 - **Callbacks for *Disney Channel* and *Honda***. Auditions for *General Motors* and *Tyson Chicken*.

Week 26 - *Hyundai, Brinks Security* and *Old El Paso* auditions and then a callback for *Old El Paso* all in one week. Half a year since we signed and we are busy. Jackson loves it.

Week 27 - *JC Penney, Fuji Film, Mc Donald's* and *Applebees* all this week. Keeping us running. **Jackson was filmed in several scenes for an opening montage for a new NBC TV weekly sitcom.** The Thomas Cobb Group shot the scenes for the show "Hidden Hills." Hopefully, the scenes will make the final edit and be on every week.

Week 28 - *Medicine Shoppe* and *Petsmart* auditions this week. Started Acting classes again with Bridget Burdeen.

Week 29 - Callback for *Medicine Shoppe*. Strange thing happened at the callback. I had to sign a consent form that included things like my child agrees to: "Kissing between boy and girl, could be open mouth", and " eating food that has been dropped on the floor". The second one didn't bother him, but the kiss, Omigod! Auditions for *V-8 Splash* and *United States Postal Service*. Acting class #2

Week 30 - Audition for *Homestyle Bakers*. Acting class #3 – voiceovers.

Week 31 - Nothing this week. Acting class #4.

Week 32 - Auditions for *Chevrolet, Infinity,* and *Ace Hardware*. Callback for *Ace Hardware*. Acting class #5. **Final edit from the Thomas Cobb Group was approved by the network and the producers, and Jackson made the cut. He is in the opening montage!**

Week 33 - Callback for *Infinity* on Sunday afternoon. Audition for *Medicare* on Monday, *McDonalds* on Tuesday. Callback for *Medicare* and audition for *GPS* on Wednesday. Callback for *GPS* on Friday. Last acting class. What a week. Jackson is starting to feel like an actor.

January 10, 2003. Jackson started studying at The Young Actors Space with Nora Eckstein.

TAKING BLACK & WHITE HEADSHOTS AT HOME
by Hank Tovar

• **Be prepared to shoot through a few rolls of film** until you find a shot that works. There is black and white film that you can develop at your local one-hour photo store. Several manufactures make the film—Kodak Black and White + Select, Ilford XP2 or Ilford XP2 Super. All are 400-speed film. 400 speed film is very forgiving, versatile and can be used in a variety of different settings, lighting, and has good overall contrast. If the box says C-41 processing, then you can only develop it at the one-hour photo lab, not at a black and white custom lab. If the C-41 film has been developed at a one-hour store, you can take the negative to a black and white lab to have the master made.

• **Choose an outdoor area with indirect light,** but bright. Choose a non-busy background, one that has contrast or texture like a wood fence, stone wall, barn door, etc. Make certain your camera is focused squarely on their face and head and their eyes are looking directly into the lens at all times. The head can be turned, but those eyes must be focused directly on the lens. The more open the eyes, the better. Talk to them, ask for something so they can react to it. Give me a funny look; show me excitement; react like they were on a rollercoaster; jumping off the high dive. Have their eyes speak to the camera lens.

• **Once you're done,** bring the rolls to a one-hour lab. If they print the shots on color paper, you will get a tinted, cibachrome look. If they print on black and white paper, you should get the right results. When you find a shot you like, take the negative to a custom black and white photo lab to have them make your master 8x10 print that will be used to make the reproductions. The masters cost $5 to $10 and should be printed on fiber, not rc or glossy paper; it does make a big difference. If you don't have a lab near you, mail the negatives to Isgos or one of the photo labs listed in Section Two. Have fun and save your receipts. *See Hank's photos of Austin, Jackson and Rebecca Trosky.*

Actor: **Jackson Tovar**

Photographer: **Hank Tovar**

Photographer: **Hank Tovar**

Photographer: **Rich Hogan**

Photographer: **Kevin McIntyre**

Actor: **Cami Raich**

Photographer: **Marina Rice Bader**

Actor: **Skyler Cavalier**

Photographer: **Carrie Cavalier**

Actor: unknown

Photographer: **Doreen Stone**

Actor: **Rebecca Trosky**

Photographer: **Hank Tovar**

Actor: **Austin Tovar**

Photographer: **Kevin McIntyre**   Photographer: **Rich Hogan**

Photographer: **Hank Tovar**   Photographer: **Hank Tovar**

Actor: **Chance Onody**

Photographer: **Doreen Stone**

Photographer: **Doreen Stone**

Photographer: **Diana Lannes**

Photographer: **Diana Lannes**

Actor: **Carrara Onody**

Photographer: **Diana Lannes**

Photographer: **Diana Lannes**

Photographer: **Doreen Stone**

Photographer: **Doreen Stone**

Resources

• PHOTOGRAPHERS

Marina Rice Bader, 310/859-4687. www.marinarice.com. Packages range from $175 to $250. Her comfortable studio is located in Burbank. She is the mother of three young ones herself and truly understands the dynamics of children. *See picture of Cami Raich on page 561, theatrical picture of me on page 111 and commercial shot on page 172.*

Carrie Cavalier of Cavalier Photography, 818/840-9148 and 818/566-8291. www.cavalierphotography.com. Children's headshots are $150 which includes the negatives and one 8x10. Studio and outdoor available, although most of my work reflects creative locations using natural light. Make-up and hair $50. 8x10's are $16 each. *See Skylar Cavalier on page 561; and Keith Johnson's theatrical shot on page 121, and commercial shot on page 171.*

Gayle Garnett, 310-712-3911 www.photographybygayle.com. 155 W. Washington Blvd. # 944 L.A. 90015. Ages 4-12 years are $165 for one roll and $195 for two rolls. Includes proof sheets and negatives. 4x6 proof prints are also available for a nominal fee. Keep clothing simple. The key is focusing on your child's energy and personality! Babies and children under 4 years are also very welcome; the fee may be slightly higher depending on what is needed. *See Gayle's picture of Carly Althoff theatrical on page 114 and commercial on page 173.*

Rod Goodman, 818/760-0733. For children over five. $50 per 36 exposure roll of B&W; 4x6 preview prints $3 each; 8x10s $17 each. Proofs available the next business day. $70 per 36 exposure roll of color; 8x10s $22 each. All prints take 3-5 days. Two looks allowed per roll. Both studio and natural light are available. His studio is set in a stress-free homey environment. Hours: Tue-Fri 9-5, Sat 9-1. He is usually booked two to four weeks ahead. *See Keith Johnson's theatrical shots on page 120 and commercial shot on page 171.*

Rich Hogan, 323/467-2628. One roll, one 8x10, $125 shot in the studio. No children under three years old. He's fun and the kids love working with him. He took Austin's very first picture when he was seven and got great results. *See Austin Tovar's shot on page 562 and Jackson Tovar's on page 560, theatrical shot of Keith Johnson on page 121 and Keith's commercial shot on page 171.*

Sean Kenney, 800/505-7698. One roll with two 8x10s, $175. Two rolls, two changes with four 8x10s, $250. Many top children's agents in town recommend Sean. He also travels all over the country taking children's pictures.

Diana Lannes Photography, Voice Mail: 213/427-8096, Studio: 323/465-3232. $175-$250 depending on the package. Diana has been shooting the little ones for seven years and recently started shooting for children's fashion catalogues as well. She really enjoys the kids. *See Carrara Onody's picture on page 564 and Chance Onody's picture on page 563. Also see Janice Allen's theatrical shot on page 118 and commercial shot on page 169 and the retouching example on page 140.*

Kevin Mc Intyre Photography, 818-761-6081. www.kevinmcphotograph.com. Specializing in beautiful natural light photos of children and adults. 1 roll $145 and 2 rolls for $250. Mention Judy's book and receive 3 rolls for the price of 2. Negatives are always included. Kevin believes that by putting a child into the natural light, it encourages openness and confidence. Kevin is comfortable photographing kids of all ages. Work is guaranteed. He is recommended by many top agents and managers and has been shooting in Los Angeles for 6 years. *See pictures of Austin and Jackson Tovar on page 560 and Carly Althoff's theatrical shot on page 114 and commercial shot on page 173.*

Doreen Stone, 323/876-2636. Ages 3 to 21, $160, one roll. 8x10s are $15. Highly recommended by agents, managers and coaches; many say, "She is 'the' photographer for children." T.J. Stein of Stein Entertainment Group says, "She catches the child's personality and energy in the way that really sells the child; triple A rating!" Doreen tells parents, "Keep it simple; simple clothes. And don't worry, a child can't do it wrong." *See the pictures of Carrara Onody on page 564, Chance Onody on page 563 and the little girl on page 561.*

Hank Tovar, 805/650-6611. www.feetfirstmarketing.com. For children in Ventura. $125 a roll for the proofsheet, negatives and one 8x10. He is an award-winning photographer and his pictures are very expressive. *See Jackson Tovar's picture on page 560, Austin Tovar's on page 562 and Rebecca Trosky on page 561.*

• CHILDREN'S ACTING CLASSES

Young Actor's Space, 818/785-7979. www.young-actors-space.com. 5918 Van Nuys Blvd., Van Nuys, 91401. $440 for an 11 week session. Several types of classes are offered. You can audit a class for free but they encourage people to take one class for $40 to see how they like it. Diane Hill Hardin developed these supportive classes. She was a student of Joan Darling and her husband and daughter are actors. She and her partner Nora Eckstein also manage a few lucky young actors. At the end of each session they have a demonstration class where agents, managers, friends and parents are invited to watch the actors perform. I have attended several of their demonstrations and was very impressed with the talent I see in their classes.

New York/Young Actor's Space, www.young-actors-space.com. Check the website for dates and information.

Brigitte Burdine's Kids and Teens On-Camera Commercial and Theatrical Workshops, 818-377-9538. Robinson Creative, 8950B Ellis Avenue, Los Angeles, 90034. $275 for six-weeks. For commercials: learn how to audition, improv, short and long dialogue, voiceovers and great advice to the parents who watch the playback at the end of class. Plus she brings in an agent for the last session so the kids and teens get a real audition. In the theatrical class: $275 for eight-week on camera workshop. Kids and teens learn how to audition for TV and film. She emphasizes the child actor getting out there working while having fun.

Tracy Martin is Koaching Kids & Teens, 818/752-8487, email: mstracyco@aol.com. $325 for 8-week Audition Technique Class. Breaking down sides, listening, reacting, call backs and booking the job are part of what the classes contain. Tracy earned a BFA from NYU's Tisch School of the Arts. Highly recommended by agents and parents. She works with each child individually at whatever level they are at and helps them to be confident when they walk into the audition room. "We have fun every week in class and the students show great growth in their work." Classes held in Toluca Lake. "My students work and are real and natural." Audition coaching $60 an hour. Private lessons; rates depend on how many lessons booked. Free career coaching for parents who have children in her classes. Many working students.

TotaLook Young Actor Classes, 818/763-8063. Email: TotaLookCares@aol.com. $25 a class or $100 a month for ages five thru teens plus a one-time $25 family registration fee which includes the required workbook and the optional weekly parent workshop/discussion group. Maximum six students per class, grouped by age and experience. Extensive on-camera work with commercials, scenes and monologues. Weekend classes are taught by three professional teachers who each have over 20 years of active experience in the Industry. Parents select the dates they can attend and receive evaluations weekly. Discounts for siblings. The workbook: *How to Get In & Stay In Show Biz,* plus *101 Ways to Avoid Being a Stage Parent* is filled with "tricks of the trade." Private pre-audition coaching, $35 an hour. "There's only one chance to make a good *first* impression! Classes give the child the necessary skills and tools."

Dee Wallace Stone's Acting Studio, 818/876-0386, Ext. 3. www.dwsactingstudio.com. 4-7 year olds, $100/mo. 8-11 year olds, $140/mo. 12-17, $140/mo. This highly respected actress, acting coach and mother of a pre-teen daughter is now offering children's and teen classes. Place your child with a working professional who nurtures self-esteem. She creates a truly supportive, encouraging environment.

Class Act: The Young Actor's Studio, 310/281-7545 www.youngactorsstudio.com Noho Actors Studio. Full conservatory based on the work of Stanislavski. Jeff Alan-Lee heads the very experienced staff. Call for prices. Kids and teens 7-17. They also produce new original plays for the kids. Their brochure lists all their classes.

Academy Training Center, 818/771-8687. 4942 Vineland Ave., North Hollywood, 91601. $235 for new students and $185 for ongoing students, starting at age six. "Our workshops encourage the young actor to develop the skills and confidence needed to perform in film and television. New students may try the first class for free. Our Saturday sessions are six weeks long and on the last week we have TJ Stein, President, Stein Entertainment Group and other industry guests." Academy Training's director is Helen Anzalone, a New York trained professional actress who has coached many young performers and has successfully helped them land series regular roles for such shows as *Go Fish, Gideon's Crossing* and *The Agency.*

Laura Lasky of Quit Acting! 818/623-8830. 5044 1/4 Colfax Ave., Valley Village, 91602. Ages 4-17, $175 for four weeks of group class. The Quit Acting! Acting Workshop is on-camera for children pursuing a professional career in TV, film and theater. Skills necessary for the pre-read to the screen-test; geared to the individual needs of each student; a safe self-esteem building environment. Laura says, "An actor's ability comes from a strong foundation and trust of him/herself. Find out what's holding you back—and quit it! You are never acting a role; you are the role. Understand the difference between acting and pretending. The audition is the job." Private coaching available, $45 an hour.

Pamela Campus, casting director, 310/398-2715 or 818/897-1588. Has cast over 3,000 commercials and taught over 10,000 adults and children. Children starting at age three. Jackson Tovar began his first classes here and learned so much. They are always taught personally by the casting directors. Very highly recommended by agents.

Kevin McDermott's Center Stage L.A., 310/837-4536. www.centerstagela.com. He is also an on-set children's coach. "Acting classes provide the young actor with an opportunity to practice their craft in a safe and creative environment." They offer theatrical workshops for ages five to 20, scene study, cold reading, improv, character development and interview techniques. Private coaching with Kevin is $45 per half-hour. A friend of mine, Lee Alexander's son Tyler, was very happy with the approach.

Hines & Hunt Entertainment, 818/557-7516. $235 for six classes. A children's and teen class is taught by staff teachers. Besides acting and improvisation, they cover the pilot season, the audition, the interview and dealing with rejection. Terrance is a very highly respected personal manager along with his partner, Justine Hunt. Terrance is also the author of *An Actor Succeeds.*

Improv Class and Performing Group, 818/784-1868. www.laconnectioncomedy.com. 13442 Ventura Blvd. Sherman Oaks. Class meets every Sunday. Performances every Sunday. $300 for 10 sessions.

Paul Ryan Comedy Studio, 323/936-9524. www.PaulRyanProductions.com. CBS Studio Center, 4024 Radford Avenue, Studio City, 91604. Classes for teens: Saturdays, $195 a month.

Kids! Background Casting, 818/239-1371. 207 S. Flower, 2nd Floor, Burbank, 91502. $25 registration and they take a 20% commission when the children work. Parents and children can get a good feel of what the business really is by working at least a few days as an extra. If you want your children to work extra jobs, you will pay15% to 20% commission to the extra company on the $40 a day pay scale. Adults wouldn't stand for this but I guess they figure the kids don't need to earn a living and they get the parent along to take care of the child for free.

A very good training ground is right on-the-set. If you have the time and your child really wants to see what it is like to be on a set. Why not get their work permit and do some extra work? Your child will not make much money but they will gain the experience of being on-the-set and they will get to watch professional actors acting! Maybe they can earn enough to pay for acting classes.

• VOICE AND DANCE TEACHERS

Rosemary Butler, 310/572-6338. www.rosemarybutler.com. Works with teen singers.

Claire Corff, 323/969-0565. $35-$45. www.corffvoice.com. She is an associate of the very famous Bob Corff, specializing in children and young adults, beginners through advanced. Singing, speaking and accent reduction. My grandson Austin Tovar loved working with her; he learned how to slow down and to be easily understood. He loves the exercises she gave him.

Godeane Eagle, 310/450-5735. She has an M.A. combination in music, theatre and clinical speech. $50 to $75 an hour. Specializing in speech defect correction, projection and accent reduction, she has worked with many children over her long career.

Dance Arts Academy, 323/932-6230. www.danceartsacademy.com. 731 South La Brea Ave., Los Angeles, 90036. Carla Luna, director. They have classes for children from age six and up in ballet, tap, jazz, funk jazz, flamenco and hip-hop. See their website for the extensive schedule or call for brochure.

Dance at the Outback Studio with Jennifer Nairn-Smith, 323/938-6836. www.outbackstudios.com. $15 for a single class, $135 for 10 classes.

Lauridsen Ballet Centre, 310/533-1247 or 323-933-0117. www.southbayballet.org. 1261 Sartori Avenue, Torrance, 90501. Starting at age three. The faculty is dedicated to nurturing, developing, and guiding dancers through the world of ballet in a professional, caring and healthy environment. The students are privileged to study in a traditional ballet atmosphere with live piano accompaniment.

Musical Theatre Summer Training For Teenagers at: Idyllwild Arts Song and Dance Workshop in the San Bernardino Mountains, 909-659-2171. Two-week session in July, price $1650. In this musical theatre workshop, designed for high school and junior college students with background in either musical theatre (or vocal music) and/or dance, all students will receive intensive training in voice and dance, with a final performance which will include individual solo work and full company production numbers from recent and classic Broadway shows. The experienced staff has been lauded year after year for their ability to bring out the best in each student.

• MANAGERS

Hines & Hunt Entertainment, 818/557-7516. Terrance Hines and his partner, Justine Hunt are highly regarded. Terrance is also the author of *An Actor Succeeds*.

Stein Entertainment Group, T.J. Stein personal manager. 818/766-6525. www.SteinEntertainment.com. 11271 Ventura Blvd., #477, Studio City, 91604. Children and young adults.

The West Coast Performer's Complete Personal Managers Directory of Managers for All Performing and Creative Talents, an Acting World Books Publication. At theatrical bookstores and www.actingworldbooks.org. This is much more than a directory— it has the information you need to shop for and land a personal manager.

• AGENTS

• *A few children's agents out of the many listed by SAG.*

Screen Actors Guild—SAG Young Performers Committee, 323/549-6420 or 323/549-6419. www.sag.org. 5757 Wilshire Blvd., Los Angeles, 90036 M-F 9-5.
SAG Child Actor Hotline, 323/549-6420
SAG Franchised Agents List, 323/549-6733.
The **AFTRA-SAG Young Performers Handbook** is downloadable on the website.

The Savage Agency, 323/461-8316. 6212 Banner Ave., L.A., 90038. Ages 3 to mid-20s. Contact: Judy Savage.

Buchwald/Talent Group Inc., (TGI), Youth Division, 323/852-9555. 6500 Wilshire Blvd., 22nd Floor, Los Angeles, 90048. Ages 3 to early 20s. Contact: Debbie Palmer and Eddie Windler, commercial; Philip Leader and Emma Stashin, theatrical.

Acme Talent & Literary, 323/954-2263. 4727 Wilshire Blvd., Ste. 333, L.A., 90010. Ages 4-25. Contact: Kendall Park.

Alvarado Rey Agency, 323/655-7978. 8455 Beverly Blvd., Ste. 410, L.A. 90048. Ages 5 and older. Especially Latinos and diverse ethnicities. Contact: Jaime Ferrar.

Brand Talent & Model Agency, Kids Dept., 714/850-1158. 1520 Brookhollow Dr., Ste. 39, Santa Ana, 92705. Ages 3 and older. Contact: Melanie Rolson.

Howard Talent West Agency, 818/766-5300. 10657 Riverside Dr., Toluca Lake, 91602. Ages 5 and older. Contact: Bonnie Howard.

Innovative Artists, 310/656-0400. 1505 10th Street, Santa Monica, 90401. Ages 8 and older. Contact: Amy Abell, Abby Bluestone, Jeff Respress.

• *Consult your State Film Advisory Board for agents in your area.*

www.actorsite.com. Membership site but a lot of free information. Great support group.

www.startips.com. Richard Jay Ward, a personal manager, regularly posts updated material about children actors.

www.showbizkid.com. Casting director Judy Belshe runs this website for young performers.

www.moviesbykids.com. Summer in Cinema: Acting, Art, Film Making, Theatre and Animation Camps. For kids 7 to 16. A creative program taught by industry professionals.

• BOOKS AND TAPES

• *How to Get In & Stay In Show Biz, plus 101 Ways to Avoid Being a Stage Parent*, by Coral Leigh. Cost is $25 sent to 10543 Valley Spring Lane, North Hollywood, CA 91602. Email: TotalLookCares@aol.com. Coral Leigh has been an agent, personal manager, casting associate and a stage mom. This Guidebook is filled with "tricks of the trade" to help the child actor as well as showing parents what to do to help and how to understand how the Industry works. I highly recommend it for all parents who want to help make their children's dreams of being an actor come true. This workbook has exercises for the actors and instructions, everything you need to know for the babies up through the teens. *See above for information about the classes with the TotalLook group.*

• *By Kids for Kids*, by Catherine Gaffigan. Monologues for children 6-18 years old.

• *It's a Freeway Out There*, $30 by Judy Belshe. Agent Bonnie Howard insists all of the parents with new kids in the business read this book. It is easy and fast to read.

• *Launching Your Child in Show Business*, by Dick Van Patten. He should know how, having started on Broadway at age seven, as did his sister Joyce. "My mother was a real stage mother. On the other hand, it's terrible if a stage mother pushes a child into the business. People berate stage mothers—but how about mothers who push their kids to become doctors or lawyers?"

• *The Parents' Guide To L.A.*, $19.95, in bookstores. "Over 650 pages of detailed information that puts everything you need right at your fingertips."

• *Your Kid Ought To Be In Pictures: A How-To Guide For Would-Be Child Actors and Their Parents*, by Kelly Ford Kidwell and Ruth Devorin.

• *Fresh Faces by Arggie Gold*, one of the top managers of child actors in New York. No-nonsense, easy-to-read, what to do, what not to do.

• The trade papers put out annual special issues for Show Business Kids with many agencies, managers, photographers and teachers listed.

Mail Order Tape: *Lights, Camera, Kids! How to Get Your Child in TV Commercials*, by Carolyne Barry, 323/654-2212. Actress/commercial coach Barry produced this very informative tape and booklet.

Mail Order Tape: *Show Biz Kids: The ABCs of Getting Your Child in the Biz*, 310/275-5755. Special price for mentioning this book, $19.95. This award-winning video will help you avoid getting ripped off.

SCAMS

West Coast Talent Ltd., Inc., WCT, Screen Artist Talent, Alexander Zafrin and David Leroy Harris illegally operate an employment counseling service enticing parents to pay thousands of dollars for promotional materials and acting classes for children. They've been charged with many crimes, including making false and misleading statements and making false and deceptive representations. By the time you read this, these two men have probably changed the name of their business and continue to steal from parents. Be your child's watchdog!

A Photographer tells me of a current scam. A person approaches you in a public place, like a shopping mall and tells you your child is great looking. They say they are a casting director, gives you a business card and asks you to make an appointment. That person gets $100 for everyone who makes an appointment. If you do meet with the promoters, they give many promises, and if yu believe them and enroll in their "program," you pay alot for nothing.

GOOD ADVICE
Tracy Martin, Acting Coach, warns: Stay away from studios that offer pictures and lifetime classes and more for an outrageous amount of money. Call around. Compare class fees and photographer fees. Again, see if these people are "in the know" with current agents and casting directors. Ask questions. Find out if they have students who are working. Often a snapshot and good cover letter is enough to submit to an agent. If the agent is interested, they will recommend several photographers.

SECTION TEN

CITIES OUTSIDE OF LOS ANGELES

• **Many of you reading this book** are outside of Los Angeles and wondering how you will make the leap into the Industry. Here are some ideas to speed you on your way.

• **Al Burton gives an excellent interview** in The *Child Actor* section about the work you can do in your hometown. Throughout the book the information can be used to gain your training and experience to help you achieve a satisfactory artistic life where you live. If you can become a big fish in a little pond, you can gain a great sense of accomplishment.

• **My daughter, Cynthia Kerr's,** husband was transferred to Dallas, Texas. She had been an accomplished actress as a teenager; and after marriage, motherhood and a successful real estate career, she wanted to return to her first love, acting. This move was her opportunity.

• **The first week,** I visited and we checked out the town. I had asked actors from Dallas who studied with me, where to look. KD Studio was mentioned by several. We met with the director and knew we had found a home.

• **Cynthia enrolled in KD Studio Actors Conservatory of the Southwest.** She thrived on going to class every day, the voice and body work, the rehersals, the camera, acting classes and the friendships. She had her pictures taken and interviewed with four agents; one offered to take her on the spot. Because of the excellent schooling and networking at KD Studio she was in two plays, three industrials and a McDonalds' national commercial during her first year. At the time of her graduation, she had paid for her education and expenses from her acting work, plus the residual payments continued. She had another baby and then, at last, they have been transferred home, to Los Angeles.

• **Janine Turner** of *Northern Exposure*, originally from Dallas, was brought into the acting world in 1980 by a producer who met her in a hotel gift shop. She landed three episodes in a bikini on *Dallas*.

• **Photographer Sean Kenney** works in Phoenix several times a year.

• *Back Stage West* lists casting notices and local resources monthly in Northern California, San Diego, Las Vegas, and occasionally other states. Call for a back issue. 323/525-2356. www.backstage.com.

• **Judy Carter, the author of** *Stand-up Comedy: the Book*, published by Dell Books. "We have a complete listing of clubs, agents, and managers in the appendix. No matter where the readers live, there is a comedy club or a comedy venue near them. If they call us at 1-800-4COMICS, www.judycarter.com, they'll have a free subscription to our newsletter, which is published quarterly and is full of inspiring talks and tips and everything that goes on across the country."

• **Mid-America Performing Arts Conference or MAPAC** in the Branson, Missouri, area has opportunities for developing and expanding your talents for acting and modeling. Beyond special classes and career counseling, top agents, managers, and casting directors attend to scout for talent. MAPAC is being produced by Steven Nash, President of the Talent Managers Association in Los Angeles (*see his interview in the Personal Managers Section*) and Scott-Arthur Allen, a very well-respected Hollywood acting teacher (*Heather Locklear, Sela Ward, Tea Leoni*) who is now living and teaching in Missouri. Perhaps I will see you there. The web address is www.MapacOnline.com.

• *The Actor's City Sourcebook* by Andrea Wolper. She gives a complete rundown on: Boston, Chicago, Dallas, Los Angeles, Miami, Minneapolis/St.Paul, New York, Philadelphia, San Francisco, Seattle and Washington, D.C.

• *How to Start Acting In Film And Television Wherever You Are In America* by Lawrence Parke. Order at www.actingworldbooks.com.

• **Order books** through Take One Bookstore, www.take1filmbooks.com or Samuel French Bookstore, www.samuelfrench.com.

• **Contact your state's Film Advisory Board** for agents, films and extra casting agencies that will be casting in your area.

• **See Internet and World Wide Web listings,** *Section Ten*.

• **In the following are some recommendations** from readers of previous editions of the book you are holding. Let me know yours.

WEBSITES:
For Casting Directors see the CSA website: www.castingsociety.com.
For SAG Franchised agencies located all over the country go to: www.sag.org/agents.
www.RedbirdStudio.com/AWOL/acting. Many acting links. They do a great job!
www.ShowBiz.com. Casting and an Industry Online Directory, $10 a year fee.
www.wildogre.com. A general actor's chat room.
www.actorslife.com. Actor chat rooms.
www.nowcasting.com and www.actorsite.com - great free email newsletters.
www.actors-network.com. Great way to get familar with this organization before moving to LA. $60 a year. Go to website and click on Online Members.
www.actorsbone.com. Actor forum plus the Shorts Festival open to all.

• **ATLANTA, GEORGIA**
• **Contributed by Bonnie Gillespie**, the casting columnist for *Back Stage West*, author of *Casting Qs: A Collection of Casting Director Interviews*, consultant on the business of acting, and owner of Cricket Feet Management. Bonnie lived and worked as an actress in Atlanta before moving to Los Angles. Georgia is a right-to-work state. The work will be industrial, commercial and film. I had agents in NC, TN, KY, and FL, as well as GA.

CLASSES
YourACT 404/417-9898. http://www.youract.tv/classes.html. Great for classes.
Image Film & Video, 404/352-4225. This studio rocks. Good for on-camera technique.
Atlanta Workshop Players, 404/998-8111. Classes in everything.
Alliance Theatre School 404/898-1131. Biggest and best acting school.

PHOTOGRAPHERS & SERVICES
Best Photographers: Brian Doughtery, 404/294-4739.
Ned Burris, 404/339-4343.
Photo Retouching: Mack Leslie, 404/758-7551.
Photo Reproduction: 417/869-9433. ABC Pictures, 1867 E. Florida Street, Springfield, MO 65803. Call for free catalog.

NEWSLETTER/HOTLINE:
Georgia Film Office 404/656-6497 and 404/656-3591. Monthly newsletter on what's being shot where and by whom. Hotline—what's shooting. when, who's casting.
SAG & AFTRA, 404/239-0131. www.sag.org.

AGENCIES
These agents work hard for their talent. No exclusive agreements, work with agents.
Houghton Agency, 404/850-0888. They take beginners.
John F. Templeton Talent, 404/688-4101.
Linda Lange, 404/261-2278.
Stay away from: William Reynolds Agency; LanMar/L&M/Chadz' Agencies; Alpha Talent Management; Serendipity.

BOOKS AND NEWSPAPERS
Acting in Atlanta by 2 Working Actors.
Creative Loafing on Wednesdays at any newsstand.
Weekend Leisure Guide in Saturday's *Atlanta Journal* & *Constitution*.

• BOSTON, MASSACHUSETTS AREA

• **Contributed by Lori A. Frankian.** www.lorifrankian.com. Lori has been working in the entertainment industry for over seventeen years as an Actor, Business Consultant for Actors, Independent Casting Director, Arts Administrator, Public speaker and Model. Our 245 theatres (professional, small professional and community) produce dramatic, classical, experimental, comedic and musical productions. As for on camera work, Clint Eastwood filmed "Mystic River" in Boston cast 30 local actors in principal roles. In 2001, we had 35 feature films and TV projects produced, in 2000 it was 45 projects. You can land work in features, independent and student film projects, commercials, industrials, trade shows, and voice overs. We have 175 signatory producers within the greater Boston area and many non-signatory producers that hire non-union talent on a daily basis.

PROFESSIONAL SUPPORT FOR ACTORS

Lori A. Frankian / New England's only business consultant for actors, 617-437-0334. www.lorifrankian.com. *See the Life Coach section.*

CASTING DIRECTORS

Boston Casting, 617/254-1001. www.bostoncasting.com. 129 Braintree Street, #107, Boston, MA 02134. Angela Peri.
CP Casting, Inc., 617/451-0996. www.cpcasting.com.
Kevin Fennessy Casting, Inc., 617/547-1447. www.kfcasting.com. 25 Mount Auburn St, Cambridge, MA 02138. Kevin Fennessy.
Lori A. Frankian Casting, 617/437-0334. www.lorifrankian.com. Astor Station, P.O. Box 475, Boston, MA 02123. Lori A. Frankian.
LDI Casting, 401/364-9701. www.ldicasting.com. P.O. Box 7105, Warwick, RI 02886. Ann Mulhall.
Tighe & Doyle Casting, 617/424-6805. www.tigheanddoyle.com. 142 Berkeley Street, Boston, MA 02116. Maura Tighe.
Susan Willett Casting, 781/581-8846. 65 King Street, Swampscott, MA 01907. Susan Willet.

HEADSHOT PHOTOGRAPHERS

Lynn McCann, 617/451-0299.
Charles Matter, 617/541-4060. www.matterlight.com.
Lynn Wayne, 617/451-1223. www.lynewayne.com.

HEADSHOT REPRODUCTION

Pro Black & White, 800/932-9354. www.probw.com.

MODELING AGENCIES

Candy Ford Group, 617/266-6939. www.candyford.com. 277 Newbury Street, Boston, MA 02115. Candy Ford.
Click Models, 617/266-1100. 125 Newbury Street, Suite 5A Boston. Amy Garbo.
Image Makers, 617/482-3622. www.imagemakersmodels.com. 77 Franklin Street, 3rd Floor, Boston, MA 02110. Suzanne Crosby.
Maggie Inc., 617/536-2639. 35 Newbury Street, Boston, MA 02116. Maggie Trichon.
Model Club, Inc., 617/247-9020. www.modelclubinc.com. 329 Columbus Avenue, Boston, MA 02116. Ed Slyney.
Models Group, 617/426-4711. 374 Congress Street, Boston, MA 02110. Kathy Baxter.

STUDIO / INDIVIDUAL TRAINING

Classes@kfcasting.com, 617/547-1447. www.kfcasting.com.
The Studio at CP Casting, 617/423-2221. www.cpcasting.com.
Improv Asylum, 617/263-1221. www.improvasylum.com.
The Lyric Stage, 617/437-7172. www.Lyricstage.com.

New Repertory Theatre, 617/332-7058. www.newrep.org.
New Voices - New Visions, 978/232-9901. www.newvoices-newvisions.org.
Shakespeare & Company, 413/637-1199, x1149. wwwshakespeare.org.
Southwick Studio, 978/266-1165. www.southwickstudio.com.
John O'Neil (vocal coaching), 617/247-6787. www.cabaretfest.com.
Jeannie Deva Voice Studios (vocal coaching), 617/536-4553. www.thevoicestudio.com.
Jordan Rich/Chart Productions, 617/542-8251. www.chartproductions.com.
Wren Ross (v/o training), 617/924-7464. www.wrenross.com.
Dossy Peabody (private), 617/547-6977. www.dossypeabody.com/actors.
Derek Stearns (private / class), 617/388-6947. www.derekstearns.com.
Fran Weinberg (private), 781/453-0927.
Williamstown Theatre Festival (summer training), 413/597-3388. www.wtfestival.org.
Jeannie Lindheim's Hospital Clown Troupe, 617/558-2834. www.hospital-clowns.org.

TRAINING - COLLEGE / UNIVERSITIES

ART/Institute for Advanced Theatre Training, 617/496-2000. www.amrep.org.
Boston College (Undergrad/Graduate), 617/552-0823. www.bc.edu.
The Boston Conservatory (BFA), 617/912-9153. www.bostonconservatory.edu.
Boston University (BFA/MFA), 617/266-7900, x1657. www.bu.edu/cfa/theatre.
Brandeis University (BFA/MFA), 781/736-3340. www.brandeis/edu/theatre.
Brown University / Trinity Repertory Theatre, 401/863-3283. www.brown.edu.
Emerson College (BFA/MFA), 617/824-8780. www.emerson.edu.
Northeastern University (BFA/MFA), 617/373-2244. www.dac.neu.edu.
Suffolk University / C. Walsh Theatre (BA), 617/573-8282. www.cartah.cas.suffolk.edu.
Tufts University (BA/MFA/PhD), 617/627-3524. www.tufts.edu/as/drama.
Wellesley College (Course Offerings), 781/283-2029. www.wellesley.edu/Theatre/thst.html.
TRADE RESOURCES (On-line / Print)
VSA Arts Massachusetts, 617/350-7713. www.vsamass.org.
Adweek, 617/482-0876. www.adweek.com. On-line and print subscriptions.
Boston Pheonix, 617/536-5390. www.bostonpheonix.com. Auditions of all kinds. Some auditions call for, lets say, an open mind, be careful and use your gut. 90% on-line.
Imagine News Magazine, 617/576-0773. www.imaginenews.com.
New England Entertainment Digest, 781-272-2066. www.jacneed.com. A trade newspaper that lists auditions, covers the New England and New York markets.
NewEnglandFilm.com. Endless information. Get on their mailing list!
New England Theatre 411. www.netheater411.com. Production opportunities.
The Source / The Greater Boston Theatre Resource Guide. www.stagesource.org. A thorough directory that lists hundreds of contacts. A must!
Theater Mirror. www.theatermirror.com. An on-line resource and chat rooms.

ARTS SERVICE ORGANIZATIONS

Each organization and their web site is more than worthy of your time!
AFTRA, 617/742-2688. www.AFTRA.org.
Arts and Business Council, 617/570-8346. www.artsandbusinesscouncil.org.
Arts/Boston, 617/262-8632. www.artsboston.org.
Boston Association of Cabaret Artists, 866/639-9410. www.BostonCabaret.org.
Boston Dance Alliance, 617/482-4588. www.bostondancealliance.org.
Boston Film/Video Foundation, 617/536-1540. www.bfvf.org.
Cultural Access Consortium, 617/357-1864. www.culturalaccess.org.
Filmmakers Collaborative, 781/647-1102. www.filmmakerscollab.org.

New England Foundation for the Arts, 617/951-0010. www.nefa.org.
New England Theatre Conference, 617/424-9275. www.netconline.org.
StageSource/The Alliance of Theatre, 617/720-6066. www.stagesource.org.
Women in Film and Video / New England, 617/924-2766. www.wifvne.org.
UNIONS
AFTRA / SAG, 617/742-2688. www.aftra.com / www.sag.com.
BOOKS / SCRIPTS
Bakers Plays, 617/745-9891. www.bakersplays.com.
SelectPlays.com, 401/946-3537. www.selectplays.com.
THEATRE DIRECTORIES, 802/867-2223. www.theatredirectories.com.

• CHARLOTTE, NORTH CAROLINA
See below for more information about acting in the Southeast furnished by Agent, Beverly Brock.

• CHICAGO, ILLINOIS
Ed Hooks, www.edhooks.com. Well-known teacher and writer of several books
• Lexi Livengood, a reader of the Ninth Edition, recommends:
PHOTOGRAPHERS:
Brain McConkey, www.gratefulheads.com. Most popular, very distinctive shots.
Suzanne Plunkett, 773/477-3775.
Rick Mitchell, 312/829-1700.
Michael Brosilow, headshots@brosilow.com.
Pete Stenberg, www.petestenberg.qpg.com.
Larry Lapidus, 773/235-3333.
ACTING SCHOOLS
Steppenwolf Theatre Company, www.steppenwolf.org.
Piven Theatre Workshop, 847/866-6597.
The Second City Training Center, www.secondcity.com.
Actors' Center, 773/549-3303. www.actorscenter.com.
The Audition Studio, 312/527-4566.
Victory Gardens Theatre, www.victorygardens.org.
BOOKS AND NEWSPAPERS
PerformInk Newspaper is where most all auditions are posted. www.performink.com.
The Book, *An Actor's Guide to Chicago.* Everything you need, including all agents.

• CLEVELAND, OHIO
Actor, Michael Brown's contribution - ActorMKB@aol.com.
Docherty Talent Agency, 216/522-1300. Cleveland, Ohio. Gretchen, Julie or Deb.
North Coast Stunts and Movie Extras, Ray Szuch 216/651-5441. www.worldEonline.com.
Acting classes.

• DENVER, COLORADO
THEATRES
Denver Center Theatre Company, 303/893-4000. www.dcpa.org. 1050 13th Street,
Denver, CO. Casting: holds open calls.

• FLORIDA
Acting Studio in South Florida, 954/929-4553, www.actingstudio.org . 2450 Hollywood Blvd., #308, Hollywood, FL 33020. Full conservatory program plus classes for adults, children and summer programs. I taught a weekend seminar here and was impressed with the high level of actors. Robert Alpert is the Executive Director, they produce plays and showcases. The web site Links open a huge world. Wonderful job for Florida actors, bravo!
Photographer: Bob Lasky, 305/891-0550. www.boblasky.com. North Miami. You can use pictures taken by him in Los Angeles. Another great web site for South Florida.
Red Barn Theatre. 305/293-3035. Box 707, Key West, FL 33401. Casting: Open call for AEA actors in October. managing director, Mimi McDonald. Opportunities for interns.
Riverside Theatre, Inc. 772/231-5860. 3250 Riverside Park Drive, Vero Beach, FL 32963. Casting: auditions through Florida Professional Theatre Assoc..
Florida Stage, 561/585-3404. 262 South Ocean Blvd, Manalapan, FL 33462. Casting: open calls during the summer months, send pix to Nancy Barnett, managing director.
Marc Durso, www.acttrue.com. Teaches, among other places, in Ft. Lauderdale and Miami. This is a wonderful site for all actors, lots of information and insights.

• KNOXVILLE, TENNESSEE
Clarence Brown Theatre at the University of Tennessee. 865/974-6011. 206 McClung Tower, Knoxville, TN 37996. Casting: locally on a show to show basis. Pictures and resumes to Betty Tipton, company manager. MFA program in Acting.

• LAS VEGAS, NEVADA
Casting director, Marilee Lear, CSA. 41 N. Mojave Road, Las Vegas, NV 89101.
Nevada Talent Guide, www.nevadatalentguide.com. Great site for actors in Nevada and for Los Angeles based actors who want to go to Vegas to work. You'll be considered a "local hire." Must be on site in order to be considered. Chat rooms and information.
Back Stage West, www.backstage.com, or email: las.vegas@backstage.com.

• MASSACHUSETTS
North Shore Music Theatre. 978/232-7203. 62 Dubham Rd., Beverly, MA 01915 Local auditions for each production. Submit headshots. Internships available.

• MEMPHIS, TENNESSEE
Playhouse on the Square, 901/725-0776. 51 South Cooper, Memphis, TN 38104. Most outside roles cast from intern company. Whitney Jo, managing director.

• MILWAUKEE, WISCONSIN
www.redbirdstudio.com. Writer's group plus much more.

• NEW JERSEY
Two River Theatre Company. 732/345-1400. P.O Box 8035, Red Bank, NJ 07701. Casting: Cindi Rush Casting, 36 W. 25th Street, 2nd Floor, NY, NY 10010. Internships.
Paper Mill: The State Theatre Of New Jersey. 973/379-3636. Brookside Drive, Milburn, NY 07041. Casting Info: contact Alison Frank, Casting Director x 2366.

• NEW YORK
Making It in New York City: An Actor's Guide, by Glenn Alterman. www.glennalterman.com. This is a great book for you lucky New Yorkers.
Caryn West, bicoastal actress and acting coach gave me the following information.

Michael Howard Studios 212/645-1525, 152 W. 25th St, NY, NY 10001.
www.michaelhowardstudios.com. Beginners and the very advanced actors study here.
Caryn West teaches Audition Intensives there in December and June/July each year.
The School for Film and Television, 212/645-0030. 39 West 19th St, 12th Floor New
York, NY 10011. www.filmandtelevision.com. Caryn used to teach Commercial
audition technique there, has great admiration for owner Joan See. Camera based school.
The New Actors Workshop. 212/947-1310. 259 W. 30th Street, NYC.
www.newactorsworkshop.com Two year conservatory program, created and designed by
founders Mike Nichols, George Morrison and Paul Sills. Great for beginning actors, teaches
a hybrid of methods from Stanislavski to Viola Spolin. Blythe Baten is a graduate of
NAW; and wouldn't trade the experience for anything. Website has overview of program.
PICTURE DUPLICATION:
Reproductions: 800/647-3776. www.reproductions.com. Simply the best!

• NORTHWEST
• Wonderful Seattle agent, Carlyne Grager of Dramatic Artists Agency, Inc., gave me
an interview and provided all of the following information on the Northwest market.
• Breaking in to the Northwest Film and Television Industry is far easier than in LA or
New York. However, the work is much less bountiful and hundreds of actors are com-
peting for a relatively small slice of pie. Many projects have migrated to Vancouver.
• It's a bitter pill for Seattle, Portland and Spokane/Boise actors to swallow.
• The "Indy" market is starting to flourish and that means more opportunities for actors
wishing to participate in film. Even if the pay isn't high, the experience is very rewarding.
• The Northwest is primarily a commercial market and well over 50% of the projects are
non-union. Unlike LA, joining SAG or AFTRA will knock actor out of contention for a
many film and video projects.
• There are approximately 30-40 talent and modeling agencies of varying sizes. Eleven
are franchised by at least one of the unions. Consequently, finding a legitimate, qualified representative for your talent can be dicey.
• The "Big 4" Northwest talent agencies are Actors Group, Dramatic Artists Agency
and Topo Swope, in the Seattle market and Ryan Artists in Portland. They are the
oldest and most well established agencies, franchised by both SAG and AFTRA. The top
three modeling and print agencies are Seattle Models Guild, Heffner Management of
Seattle, and Cusicks in Portland.
• Contact the SAG or AFTRA office or website and get thelist of franchised agents. They
may also venture an opinion on a non-union agency that operates in an ethical fashion.
• Many Northwest agencies do not wish to adhere to the rules of the actor unions.
Commissions or fees for processing modeling and headshots packages, fees for acting
classes and industry seminars are often a significant source of income to these agencies.
They stock their files full of hopeful talents willing to spend several hundred or even
thousands of dollars to get their chance at auditions and bookings. Children's agencies
have been particularly notorious for preying on parents wishing to help their children.
If ever an agent says that it is customary to charge fees or commissions other than for
securing employment, move on. If a union agent pressures you to pay for picture packages or in-house seminars or classes, report them to the local union office.
• I always recommend that they take an on-camera class with one of the local casting
offices that offer beginning workshops. The classes are usually under $100 for the day
and will put the student through the paces of the "on-camera" fundamentals. The casting director will quickly see how advanced the student's skills are and make adjustments
in their curriculum to accommodate them. The casting directors also know who the
local agents are and can give a reference on behalf of their student if they deem them

ready for representation. In addition, casting directors are usually very well versed on who the best acting coaches are and can refer a student in that direction as well.

• **If you have an extensive theater background it's likely you will have** skills for a successful career in film and television. However, casting directors will be cautious about calling in an actor who doesn't list some type of camera training on their resume.

• **Before seeking agency representation, get a professional headshot taken,** but choose a high quality photographer. Print about 50 headshots. Once you secure an agent they will likely choose a different headshot proof for marketing purposes. Don't print a modeling zed card until you have agency representation. Fashion and commercial print agents can determine their level of interest based on the talent's physical statistics and a few snapshots or Polaroid's. Once a talent is offered representation the print agent will make a recommendation of a photographer that will best capture a particular "look."

• **If you are interested in voiceover work, start with training.** Even if you are a master of voices or people say you sound as smooth as butter, get training. Voiceover is very technical and without proper instruction you will not present your voice in a competitive manner. Also, the good trainers are often producers and can help you prepare a demo CD or MP3 file (tapes are rarely used anymore.) You have to have a voiceover demo in order to be professionally marketed by an agent. Every thing is produced onto computer and auditions are submitted in the same fashion. You will need an understanding of the market you're entering and classes are the best way of getting that information.

• **Is it necessary for Northwest actors** to have the level of professional training, headshots and other marketing tools that the LA actors have. The local casting directors and producers have to market you to industry professionals from other markets such as LA or New York. Though remember, no marketing tool will override lack of ability or novice skills. You are presenting yourself as a total package of talent.

SEATTLE CASTING DIRECTOR OFFICES:

Big Pants Casting, 503/274-8555. 1600 Dexter Avenue N. Ste. A Seattle, WA 98109. Jodi Rothfield and Heidi Walker.

Stephen Salamunovich, 206/903-6500. 219 1st Avenue S. #315 Seattle, WA 98104.

Kalles/Levine Casting, 206/522-2660. 8116 Greenlake Dr. N. Seattle, WA 98103. Patti Kalles and Laurie Levine.

Spokane Casting & Production North By Northwest, 509/324-2949. 903 W. Broadway Avenue Spokane, WA., 99201. Boise: 208/345-7870.

PORTLAND CASTING OFFICES

Lana Veenker Casting, 503/233-4017. 755 SW Viewmont Dr.Portland, OR. 97225.

Megann Ratzow Casting, 503/251-9050. P.O. Box 56343 Portland, OR. 97238. In addition to her regular casting Megann has added a new "Extras" Casting Division.

The Cast Group, 503/692-8926. 20645 SW 90th Avenue Tualatin, OR 97062. Suzi Smith and Kaylin Chaves.

Emily Dunlap Casting, 503/244-3014. 6200 SW Virginia St. Suite 200 Portland, Oregon 97201. Emily also features an "Extras" Casting Division.

NORTHWEST TALENT AGENCIES

Actors Group – Adult Talent. Tish and Jamie Lopez, 603 Stewart St. Suite #214 Seattle, WA 98121. Full Service Agency

Dramatic Artists Agency, Inc. – Adult and Youth Division, 206/624-9465. www.dramaticartists.com. 50 16th Avenue Kirkland, WA 98033 Full Service Agency, Carlyne Grager and Nancy Fox.

Topo Swope Talent – Adult Talent. 1932 First Avenue Suite 700 Seattle, WA 98101. Full Service Agency, Topo Swope.

Ryan Artists, 239 NW 13th Avenue Suite #215 Portland, OR 97209. Adult and Youth Division TV/Film/Commercial: Jeffery Hasseler; Fashion & Print Kit JustSports and Youth Division: Faye Lewis. Full Service Agency.
Mashia Talent Management,503/331-9293. 2808 NE MLK JR Blvd. Suite L, Portland, OR 97212. Full Service Agency, Adult and Youth.
Erhart Talent, Inc. 503/243-6362. eti@ipns.com. 037 SW Hamilton St., Portland, OR, 97201. Full Service Agency. Lo Erhart.

NORTHWEST FASHION AGENCIES
Heffner Model Management, 206/622-2211. 1601 Fifth Avenue Suite #500Seattle, WA 98101
Seattle Models Guild, 206/622-1406. 1809 Seventh Avenue Suite #608 Seattle, WA 98101.
Cusick's Talent Management, 503/274-8555. 1009 NW Hoyt Street Suite 100 Portland, OR 97201.

SEATTLE UNION OFFICES:
SAG, 206/270-0493. Joan Kalhorn, Executive Director. www.sag.org.
AFTRA, 206/282-2506. John Sandifer Executive Director. www.aftra.org. 4000 Aurora Avenue N. Ste. #102 Seattle, WA 98103.

PORTLAND UNION OFFICE:
SAG/AFTRA, 503/279-9600. Wendi Weiss, Executive Director. 3030 SW Moody Ste. #104,Portland, OR 97201.

LA ACTING CLASSES AND COACHES IN THE PACIFIC NORTHWEST
The Northwest Connection, 206/686-2206. Email: roycben@msn.com The Northwest Connection regularly features drama coaches, casting directors and other industry professionals from LA, New York and Chicago. The partners in the Northwest Connection do not collect commissions or salaries for themselves and they operate with a very small overhead budget, marketing mostly by word of mouth and student referrals from the Northwest Talent Agencies and Casting Offices. Because they operate more like a non-profit than a commercial business, they provide outstanding instruction at a very low cost to actors. Their list of industry guests is prestigious and highly regarded by the Film and Television Industry
Gary Austin, LA 206/781-4279 – Kay Byrd coordinates his classes. Gary Austin, creator of LA's Groundlings Theater and acting coach to Helen Hunt, Jennifer Grey, Lindsay Crouse, the late Phil Hartman and many other celebrity talents, makes his way to Seattle approximately every 4-6 weeks. Gary's classes are hard to top at the low cost of only $55.00 for a 4-hour workshop. Northwest actors who work with Gary swear he is the reason for their remarkable acting success in such a lean market.
Steven Anderson, 310/284-8282. www.s.anderson@actorswork.com. Steven travels from LA to the Seattle market a few times each year to conduct an excellent intensive weekend workshop. Through the weekend's teaching he will get his actors to trust that they are "always ready" to perform and how to keep their power in the room. He demonstrates how to integrate nervous energy and how to prepare audition material to get the job!
The Voice Project, Mary Beth Felker, 503/284-9488. Mary Beth is the Northwest associate to Seth Riggs, LA voice/singing coach. Her prices are reasonable relative to the Northwest market (much less than her mentor Seth Riggs, whose clients include many Grammy award winners.)

OTHER TOP ACTING COACHES IN THE NORTHWEST MARKET:
Richard Liedle, 206/367-2313. Drama Coach (Richard teaches in both LA & Seattle).
Terry Edward Moore, 206/729-7985. Drama Coach.
John Jacobsen, 206/325-4915. Drama coach – Seattle.
Sandra Peabody, 503/245-8525. Children's Acting coach – Portland.

Valerie Mamches, 206/524-9231. Theatrical and Voice-over coach – Seattle.
Patti Kalles, CSA and Laurie Levine, 206/522-2660. On-Camera Audition - Seattle.
Jodi Rothfield, CSA 206/448-0927. On-Camera Audition Technique – Seattle.
The Cast Group, 503/692-8926. Audition fundamentals, actor development – Portland.
Kathryn Luster, 425/378-0223. Voice-over coach– Seattle.
Jessica Stuart, CSA, 503/246-4111. Drama coach with excellent credentials– Portland.
Veronica Wiekle & Steven Mitchell – Voice-over Classes & Demos 206/ -Seattle.
Gloria Manon, 503/972-8117. Voice-over coach – Portland.

ACTING STUDIOS:
SAG, AFTRA & Equity Conservatory – 206/ 270-0493.
Freehold – 206/323-7499 - Seattle (Richard Brestoff in particular on staff) Drama.
Northwest Actors Studio – 206/ 324-6328 – Seattle.
Taproot Theater, 206/781-9705. Adult & Children.
Actor's Avenue, 503/234-2399. www.theactorsavenue.com. Portland Owner/Laurel
Smith. Private coaching, scene study, Meisner and audition technique.
Professional Actors Studio, Valerie Raymer, 425/829-5908. Seattle
Seattle Children's Theater (Children) – 206/443-0807.
Village Theater (Children) – 206/392-1942.
Youth Theater Northwest (Children) – 206/ 232-4145.

THEATER AND FILM BOOKSHOPS:
Cinema Books, 206/547-7667. 4753 Roosevelt Way NE Seattle, WA 98105.
Samuel French Book, 818/762-0535. 11963 Ventura Blvd. Studio City, CA 91604.
Mail orders and make it easy for Northwest actors to get the literature they need.
Drama Book Shop – New York 212/944-0595 or 212/730-8739.
www.dramabookshop.com. Huge inventory, nearly 4 floors of plays, books etc.

WASHINGTON THEATRES
A Contemporary Theatre (ACT), 206/292-7660. www.acttheatre.org. 700 Union,
Seattle, WA 98101-2330. Casting director: Margaret Layne
Intiman Theatre, 206/269-1901. www.intiman.org. P.O. Box 19760, Seattle, WA
98109. Casting director: Kate Godman.
Seattle Repertory Theatre, 206/443-2210. www.seattlerep.org 155 Mercer Street,
Seattle, WA 98109. Casting director: Jerry Manning.

OREGON THEATRES
Oregon Shakespeare Festival, 541/482-2111. www.ossashland.org. Box 158, Ashland, OR
97520. Casting directors: Libby Appel, David Dreyfoos, Penny Metropulos, Timothy Bond.
Portland Center Stage, 503/248-6309. www.pcs.org. 1111 SW Broadway, Portland,
OR 97205. Casting Director: Rose Riordan

TIPS FOR HEADSHOT PHOTO SESSION:
Bring several different types of tops (sweaters, dress shirts, t-shirts, turtlenecks) and
slacks (Twill, jeans) in a variety of solid colors. Stay away from prints, loud plaids and
geometric patterns. Business suits for both men and women. Women should bring a
dress or two. Don't forget matching shoes and stockings! Arrive with clean hair styled
in a traditional fashion (unless you don't mind having your headshots updated yearly or
you're a character actor and don't mind being stereotyped.) For men, faces should be
cleanly shaven with beards and mustaches neatly trimmed. For women, arrive with a
clean face and bring your make-up favorites along with you. Children should get plenty
of rest the night before a shoot (adults, too!) and a good meal before arriving. Bring
bottled water and no-mess snacks. Also, with children the same rules apply as above for
appearance. In addition to the clothing items mentioned, if your children are shooting
a color session, you may wish to bring sports uniforms and equipment, pajamas, slippers, dance costumes and favorite toys. Check with your photographer regarding their
preferences on the latter items.

Parents should stay out of the way. "Well meaning" parents often distract their children and make it difficult for the photographer to do their best work. Friends and spouses often do the same, leave them home.

Make sure you have made payment arrangements prior to the shoot and are clear about their prices. Don't ask the photographer to do extra rolls of film or special shots and settings that weren't mentioned in the price quote—unless you're willing to pay extra. Request that the photographer take a few 3/4 body and full body shots as well as headshots. Be cooperative when the photographer suggests a different look or mood for a photo because you will want a range of looks to select from. Be on time!

BLACK & WHITE HEADSHOT PHOTOGRAPHERS:
Wayne Rutledge 206/ 729-6014 – Seattle
David Hiller (800) 466-1918 – davidhiller.com – Seattle
Anita Russell (425) 746-6506 - Seattle
Susan Rothschild (425) 335-3277 - Seattle
Dave Ross 503/ 329-4178 – Portland
Bruce Gillette 503/ 331-6992 – Portland
Kevin Clark (604) 669-7577 – Vancouver, BC

COMMERCIAL/FASHION PRINT PHOTOGRAPHERS
Aaron Rakoz 206/ 718-3152 – Seattle – Editorial Fashion
Wayne Rutledge 206/ 729-6014 – Seattle – Commercial
Dave Ross 503/ 329-4178 – Portland – Commercial/Fashion
Bruce Gillette 503/ 331-6992 – Portland – Commercial/Fashion

HEADSHOT PRINTING SERVICES
Most of the printers offer lithographs only and they are generally more expensive than the LA market by 50-100%. I tend to refer business to Hollywood or Burbank services. The exception is Rocket Repros in Vancouver BC, their prices are competitive with LA and they produce a fine quality headshot.

The services I most often refer to are:

Rocket Repros, 604/682-6000 – Vancouver, BC.
ISGO, 818/848-9001 – Burbank, CA.
Reproductions 323/845-9595. 3499 Cahuenga Blvd. West. Los Angeles (close to Lankershim and Universal Studios) and Isgos have the highest quality lithos, they look fantastic.

MODEL ZED CARDS/LITHOGRAPHIC HEADSHOTS
Media Prints, 206/363-5473 or 800/825-0748. 20024 Ballinger Way NE Seattle, WA 98155. This is only business in the Western Washington market that produces a professional quality model zed card and they have all the top Seattle agencies as their clients.

HAIR AND MAKEUP STYLISTS
Mr. Thom, 541-779-8406. 59S. Stage Road, Medford, Oregon 97501. This is a full service day spa and hair salon. They perform all services including hair extensions. Many high-end clients including the current Miss America. Mr. Thom also travels to Portland and Seattle; call for his travel times.

Bocz Salon, Karen Bocz owner, 206-624-9134. 1523 6th Ave. Seattle, Washington. Masters with color and styling, will do consulting . All of the agencies send their models here.

Hair Lounge, Mike Hall, 253/941-3680. 1626 S. 310th Street, Suite A, Federal Way, WA 98003. Mike is a master. He does all the high end jobs at Fashion Shows (Halston, Hilfiger, Versace etc) Film Set Styling and fundraisers. Respected throughout the Northwest.

• ORANGE COUNTY/COSTA MESA/LAGUNA BEACH, CA

South Coast Rep, 714/708-5500. www.scr.org. Box 2197, Costa Mesa, CA 92628-2197. Casting director: Joanne DeNaut.

Laguna Playhouse, 858/550-1070. www.lagunaplayhouse.com. P.O Box 1747, Laguna Beach, CA 92652. Casting director: Wally Ziegler.

• PHOENIX, ARIZONA

WEBSITES:

Auditionnotice@durantcom.com An e-mail based audition service, it's fantastic. Free.
www.azproduction.com This is a web site for auditions. Hit the "Valley Auditions" www.geocities.com/sceneheard then go to box-office and there is a current listing of professional and community theatre in AZ.
www.durantcom.com. This site is great to submit your email to for a listing of auditions both professional and non-professional. When you get to her site you give her your email and she emails you with any listing for auditions.

COACHES:

Elayne Stein, 602-266-3498, for commercials, on-camera work.
D & D Company, 602/956-8604, for beginners to advanced.
Faith Hibbs-Clark 602/385-9228 faithhibbsclark@earthlink.net.
Commercial acting, film acting, and audition skills, adult classes and private coaching; Private lessons are $60 per hour and classes are $99 to $280 depending on the class.
Ramona Richards, 602/274-2881
Marla Finn, 480/922-9267, for voiceover.

PHOTOGRAPHERS:

Still n' Motion, 602-253-1035
Richard Petrillo, 480/921-8366.
Scottsdale Community College has a film making dept.
There are many theaters in Phoenix and they have their auditions on the www.Durantcom.com service. There are four SAG sanctioned agencies in town; see the SAG web site. www.sag.org.
John Janezic writes:

AGENCIES:

Dani's Agency (My agent) 602-263-1918. www.danisagency.com. One E. Camelback Rd #550, Phoenix, AZ 85012. Recorded information line for submissions: 480-929-1382.
Ford/Robert Black Agency Phone: 480/966-2537 Info: 480/966-2537 x150. www.fordmodels.com. 4300 N. Miller Rd. Ste 202, Scottsdale, AZ 85251.
Leighton Agency Inc. Phone: 602/224-9255 Info: 602/468-6880. www.leightonagency.com. 2231 E. Camelback Rd Suite 319, Phoenix, AZ 85016.
Signature Models & Talent Phone: 480/966-1102 Info: 480/902-0186. www.signaturemodelsandtalent.com. 2600 N. 44 St. #209 Phoenix, AZ 85008.
These listings are the big 4. When I first relocated here and went searching for an agent, I found these four. The other ones in town were the typical "Give us $500 for classes and pictures" and some even wanted a monthly fee for representation. Those are the one's that really made me mad. I think of the young people who may get suckered into that because they put on a lot of *razzle dazzle* with the beautiful office and all the many movie posters hanging up!

• PITTSBURG, PENNSYLVANIA

Docherty Talent Agency, 412/765-1400.
Bristol Riverside Theatre. 215/785-6664.

• SACRAMENTO, CALIFORNIA

My student Taylor McCluskey credits The Burton Group for helping him realize his dreams of living the life of an actor in Los Angeles. Taylor was discovered by his current manager at the showcase produced by the group.

The Burton Group 916/558-1555, 2110 K Street Suite # 22, Sacramento. Theburtongrp@aol.com "Where we find stars and make stars. We, at the Burton Group establish this by: *Strategically developing talent through Training and Academics Resulting in Success.* "STARS!" We are dedicated to the aspiration and dreams of each individual talent by training, encouraging, supporting, and personal grooming each star individually. You must have self growth as an actor. You cannot have the method and theory without the creative artistry. The Burton Group specializes in showcasing the person's talent and making their dreams in show business an obtainable reality. We help stars use their talent with strength and confidence."

Sacramento Theatre Company, 916/446-7501. www.sactheatre.org. 1419 H St., Sacramento, CA 95814.

• SAN DIEGO, CALIFORNIA

San Diego Actor's Resource, www.sdresource.com. This is a very valuable guide written by Alicia Cole. When you purchase a copy of the book from the website, you will be added to° the email newsletter list. She sends out notices for castings and anything of interest going on in San Diego!

Carolyn Bishop, an actress in San Diego, provided these resources. She also says, "Acting coaches/classes are listed on some of the websites below, but I'm not familiar enough with them to give any recommendations."

SAN DIEGO CASTING DIRECTORS:

Barbara Balsz Casting, 858/455-6225. She also teaches acting classes.
Samuel Warren & Assoc. Int'l Casting Service, CSA, 619/264-4135. Tricia and I are in his acting workshop.
Tina Real Casting, 619/298-0544. Specializes in extras casting.
Background San Diego, 858/974-8970. The exclusive extras casting agency for Stu Segall Productions. www.stusegall.com for more information.

SAG/AFTRA AGENTS:

Agency 2 Model & Talent Agency, 619/645-7744. 2425 San Diego, CA 92110.
Artist Management Agency, 619/233-6655. 835 Fifth Ave., #411 San Diego, CA 92101.
Elegance Talent Agency, 760/434-3397. www.eletalent.com. 2763 State St., Carlsbad, CA 92008.
Nouveau Model & Talent Agency, 858/456-1400. 909 Prospect Pl. #230, La Jolla, CA 92037.
San Diego Model Mgmt. Talent Agency, 619/296-1018. www.electriciti.com/sdmm. 438 Camino Del Rio South, San Diego, CA 9210
Shamon Freitas Talent Agency, 858/549-3955. www.shamonfreitas.com. 9606 Tierra Grande St., #204 San Diego, CA 92126.

PRODUCTION COMPANIES:

Stu Segall Productions, www.stusegall.com (where I worked as an art department co-ordinator on the episodic series "The Chronicle," and MOW called "Play'd," which is currently airing on VH1.)

From Stu's website: Stu Segall Productions is the only Motion Picture and Television Studio located in San Diego County. The studio was created in 1991 when San Diego was chosen as the location for the hit television series "Silk Stalkings". Since that time the studio has grown to encompass over 11 acres. Over 500 hours of prime time, network quality television series, 6 feature films and 30 two hour telefilms have been produced at the studio.

Four Square Productions, www.foursq.com. Commercials and industrials.
The Dakota Group, www.dakotagroup.com. Commercials and industrials.

THEATRES

The Globe Theatres, 619/231-1941. www.theglobetheatres.org. Box 122171, San Diego, CA 92112.
San Diego Repertory Theatre, 619/231-3586. www.sandiegorep.com. 79 Horton Plaza, San Diego, CA 92101. Casting director: Delicia Turner.
La Jolla Playhouse, 858/550-1070. www.lajollaplayhouse.com. P.O Box 12039, La Jolla, CA 92039.

OTHER RESOURCES:

San Diego Film Commission – See www.sdfilm.com.
Actors Alliance of San Diego – See www.actorsalliance.com.
www.sandiegoforum.com. Chat board for San Diego actors, models, and production crew.
www.sandiegoplaybill.com. What's playing, auditions, classes/workshops.
www.sdtheaterscene.com. Similar format to San Diego Playbill.

• SAN FRANCISCO, CALIFORNIA / BAY AREA:
COACHES

Richard Seyd, 323/665-9782.
Robert Weinapple, 510/559-1029.
Thanks to Joie Seldon, a well-known acting coach in San Francisco, for introducing me to Full Circle Productions.
John Howard Swain of Full Circle Productions tells me: "The one thing we are doing, which I think is very unique, is that we are also a production company. To date we have produced four films. The current one is being prepped to enter into the Sundance Film Festival. All the actors in our productions come from our school. Our goal is not only to train actors but to be able to employ them as well. I don't know if anyone else in the country is doing this, at least not on the scale we are doing it."
Full Circle Productions, 415/982-2024. www.fullcircleproductions.com. Email: fullcirclepro@aol.com. 1725 Clay Street, Suite 100 (Van Ness and Polk) San Francisco, 94109. Founded by John Howard Swain, it has become the Bay Area's premier school for actors interested in film and television. All of the teachers and facilitators have extensive acting and/or directing credits and use no-nonsense, cut-to-the-chase techniques to ensure you'll get the best training possible. FCP's students enjoy an unparalleled booking ratio in the Bay Area. In 2001 FCP began the production phase of their company. They have produced four films. All the actors in their films come from the Acting Wing of the company. Teaching staff: John Howard Swain, Marsha Mercant, Joie Seldon, Celia Shuman, Billie Sheppard, Mary Mackey, Barbara Scott, Elizabeth Ross. Check the web site for much more information. They are said to be, "the best on-camera acting school in town."
Joie Seldon of Full Circle Productions teaches a very unique class called, *Accessing Your Emotions*. $425 for eight weeks. "Can you cry on cue? Express fear or anger without being cliched? And after you've done it once, can you do it again? One of the most challenging aspects of an actor's job is to be able to access a wide range of genuine emotions on demand, whether shooting a scene over and over, or performing night after night on stage. This class will help you develop the emotional 'muscles' you need for even the most difficult roles." *This is the beginning class, the advanced gets even better. This explanation makes me want to fly up to S.F. and take it.*
The following websites provide information and many links for more actor related news.
Reel Directory, www.reeldirectory.com.

Beau Bonneau Casting, www.sfcasting.com
Nancy Hays Casting Director Site, www.hayescasting.com.
Bay Area Casting News, www.bayareacasting.com.
Casting Connection, www.castingconnection.com.
Thanks to actress Susan Yost for the following contributions for the San Francisco area.

ACTING SCHOOLS

Jean Shelton Actors Lab 415/433-1226. Union Square in the theater district. The studio teaches Method acting. Susan Yost says that Jean has extensive experience, is very intense and is wonderful to work with. Must study first with other instructors at the studio for Technique 1, 2 and 3 to get to her Scene Study and Script Analysis classes. If you have good credentials, you can bypass the Techniques classes and audition to get into the advanced classes. "I was green when I went there and learned so much." High Marks.

Rob Reese. He claims to be Method but his classes seem to be more into psychoanalyzing students. If you're interested in therapy, this class might be for you. I didn't get much acting training from the class. I notice that he is advertising in Backstage West with an LA number too.

Marin Theater Company, Artistic Director, Lee Sankowich, 415/388-5208. Lee is great. He also has other instructors come in to teach classes. The Theater Company is excellent; high caliber performances.

Ross Valley Players, 415/456-9555. Marin County. Community theater that is highly professional. They have a great following, usually sold out and well respected. They are located in The President. Ken Rowland, played the father role in *Heiress* (I played the aunt.) Fabulous actor and mentor.

THEATRES

American Conservatory Theatre (ACT). 415/834-3200. www.act-sfbay.org. 30 Grant Avenue, San Francisco, CA 94108. Casting: annual general auditions for AEA actors. Internships in theatre production and administration. MFA program in acting. Contact Heather Kitchen, managing director.

Berkeley Rep (Berkeley - East Bay), 510/204-8901. www.berkeleyrep.org. 2025 Addison Street, Berkeley, CA 94704. Casting director: Amy Potozkin. Berkeley Rep is top notch. I didn't take classes there but talked with others who did and they gave it rave reviews. The theater company is excellent. Went to many of their productions.

California Shakespeare Festival, (510) 548-3422. www.calshakes.org. 2531 Ninth Street, Berkeley, CA 94710. Casting director: Shana Cooper.

Foothill Theatre Company, 530/265-9320. www.foothilltheatre.org P.O Box 1812 Nevada City, CA 95959. Casting director: Carolyn Howart.

• SAN JOSE, CALIFORNIA

American Musical Theatre of San Jose. www.amtsj.org. 1717 Technology Drive, San Jose, CA 95110. Casting: auditions held in San Jose, NY and LA, both AEA and non-union. Limited internships available.

San Jose Rep, 408/291-2266. www.sjrep.com. 101 Paseo de San Antonio, San Jose, CA 95113. Casting director: Bruce Elsperger

• ST. LOUIS, MISSOURI

www.TheatrGroup.com., hosted by Harry Governick, Artistic Director. 314/832-1199. 5039 Gravois, St Louis, Mo, 63116. This is a great site with oodles of information for actors everywhere. Harry has worked in New York and Los Angeles and brings his great training and gifts to the Mid-West; you lucky people!

• SPRINGFIELD, MISSOURI

Scott-Arthur Allen 417/725-8267. www.creativeactorsworkshop.com. A well-respected Hollywood acting teacher who has returned home to Springfield and is teaching classes and privately. His many students over the years include Heather Locklear, Tea Leoni, and Sela Ward. Classes for all levels are $100 a month.

The Mid-America Performing Arts Conference or MAPAC www.MapacOnline.com

• SOUTHEAST MARKET – NORTH CAROLINA

• **Joan Darling**, 919/960-8233. Acting coach, teaching classes and privately.

• **You most fortunate actors**; if you've read the acting section of the book it is filled with "Joan Darling Techniques." For a limited time, she is now teaching at the University of North Carolina, Chapel Hill. You can not get any finer training anywhere and you have this treasure sitting in your backyard. If you've ever thought of studying acting, call her.

• **Kevin E. West of The Actors' Network**, www.actors-network.com, introduced me to Beverly Brock. Thank you Kevin!

• **Beverly J Brock of The Brock Agency, Inc.** an agent in North Carolina for the last 12 years has contributed the following information for studying and pursuing an acting career in the Southeast market. She tells me, "These are only partial listings and more can be accessed through the avenues given."

• **Living in North Carolina can really be delightful**, however we don't have as much work as the bigger markets. When things are slow here they are almost non-existent.

• **North Carolina as most of the Southern States** is a "right to work state." Meaning you can work here if you are SAG, AFTRA, or Non-Union. Both Non-Union and Union work comes to NC. Many non-union actors get their SAG cards by doing a SAG project here and becoming SAG eligible. When they move to New York or Los Angeles they will be required to join the union in order to do more union roles.

• **You can become SAG eligible** by being a Principle character in a commercial with or without speaking lines, or by having a speaking role in a SAG film or television production. Being in a SAG project entitles you to residual pay. It is important for our actors to learn all the SAG rules. Ask questions of the right people. Beware of those who think they know it all!

• **If you do not have an agent**, first contact The Screen Actors Guild (SAG) Office in Atlanta, GA, 800/724-0767 or 404/812-5342. The President is Brad Karl and he knows all the answers, if he doesn't he will find out for you. Always trust the people in charge for they won't guide you wrong.

• **For information on Talent Agents and Casting Agents** in NC go to www.telefilm-south.com then click on Film and Video Production Guides; then on the state you want to learn more about. Be careful, if someone wants you to pay money, always check the company with the Better Business Bureau in their city and check to see how long they have been in business. Longevity in any business is the key, but especially in this business.

• **Acting coaches are not as easily found here** as in New York or Los Angeles. Once or twice a year I bring a coach in to give a good, solid acting seminar. Some Talent Agents and Casting Agents teach their own classes here in NC.

TALENT AGENCIES – PARTIAL LIST

The Brock Agency, Inc., Beverly Brock, 828/322-8553. www.thebrockagency.com. Email: beverly@thebrockagency.com. 329 13th Ave NW Hickory, NC 28601.

Beverly's website www.thebrockagency.com has information on how to purchase the very important Southeast Actor's Guide. Actors living in this area are lucky to have this most valuable guide! There is also other interesting information and links on the site.

Actors and Entertainers, Phil Newsome and Nancy Krull, 336/993-1611. P.O. Box 486 Kernersville, NC 27285.

JTA Talent, Inc., Linda Newcomb and Kecia Michelle, 704/377-5987. Email: janoneill@jta-talent.com. 820 East Blvd., Charlotte, NC 28203

Capital Artists of NC, 919/467-8682. Email: caiofnc@aol.com. 1405 Bloomingdale Drive, Cary, NC 27511.

Marilyn's, Inc., Kathy Moore, Agent, 336/292-5950. Email: models@marilyn-s.com. 601 Norwalk St., Greensboro, NC 27407.

Talent One, Anne Greene, 919/872-4828. Email: tlntone@aol.com. 7125 Capital Boulevard, Raleigh, NC 27616.

William Pettit Agency, Bill Pettit, 704/643-8880. Email: billpettit@aol.com. P.O. Box 11798, Charlotte, NC 28220.

Talent Link, Inc., Vince Paul and Rosa Paul, 704/333-5304. Email: director@talent-link.com. P.O. Box 560337, Charlotte, NC 28256.

Carolina Winds, Donna Ehrlich, Agent, 803/581-2278. 141 Gadsden Street, Chester, South Carolina 29706.

CASTING DIRECTORS

Corrigan & Johnston Casting, Mitzi Corrigan, Paige Johnston and Gigi Wasiak, 704/374-9400. www.cjcasting.com. 3006 North Davidson Street, Charlotte, NC 28205. See their site on how to submit to them.

Marty Cherrix, 828/648-2843. P.O. Box 216, Canton, NC 28716.

Taylormacy Casting, Inc., Kristin Vining, 704/449-0572. www.taylormacy.com. 7701 Sharon Lakes Rd., Suite T, Charlotte, NC 28210. See this site for castings.

M&M Casting, Marti Siu, 704/770-0228. Email: MMCastingCompany@cs.com. Charlotte, NC.

• **Tons of student films are done in North Carolina**. NC School of the Arts in Winston-Salem is big for that and many are done in the Raleigh/Durham area too. On the web, go to NC Universities under any search engine; click on the listing that says "list all." You'll be able to find all of the schools.

The Film School at North Carolina School of the Arts in Winston-Salem holds semi-annual open casting calls. Directors will be casting for their film projects. For further information call Janice Wellerstein in the Production Office, 336/770-1322. This is an extremely impressive school and student filmmakers have won the top prize at the prestigious 2000 Angelus Award. One of their senior thesis films won Showtime's Black Filmmaker Showcase.

Piedmont Community College, 336/694-5707. www.piedmont.cc.nc.us. 331 Piedmont Drive, Box 1150, Yanceyville, NC 27379. Sarah Costello, Co-coordinator, Michael Corbett, Director.

Lees-McRae College is known for it's great stage company and musicals. Auditions are held, usually in February, for students who are interested in being a part of Lees-McRae Summer Theatre. Professional auditions in order to hire the best possible performers for the company.

East Carolina University in Greenville, NC is also a great theatre school and a great beginning for new actors. Diversity in the theatre offerings as well as apprenticeships.

The state listings below will assist actors in finding information about upcoming film projects.

North Carolina Film Commissions, 828/687-7234. www.awnc.org. Email: 121webb@bellsouth.net.

Western North Carolina Regional Film Commission, Mary Nell Webb, Director, P.O. Box 1258, Arden, NC 28704.
The Charlotte Regional Film Office, Marcie Kelso, Director, 800/554-4373 or 704/347-3942. www.charlotteregion.com. 112 S. Tryon St., Suite 900, Charlotte, NC 28284.
Winston Salem Piedmont Triad Film Commission, Jodie Klumpenhower, Director, 336/393-0001. 7614 Business Park Drive, Greensboro, NC 27409.
Research Triangle Partnership, Charles Hayes, Executive Director, 919/840-7372. www.researchtriangle.org. P.O. Box 80756, RDU Airport NC 27623.
Durham Film Office, Amy Higgins, 919/687-0288. Fax: 919/683-9555. 101 E. Morgan St., Durham, NC 27701.
Wilmington Regional Film Commission, Johnny Griffin, Director, 910/343-3456. www.wilmington-film.com. 1223 N. 23rd St., Wilmington, NC 28405.
Global Transpark Commission, Tom Greenwood, Ex. Dir., 252/522-2400. www.gtp.net. 2340 John Mewborne Road, Kinston, NC 28504.
Northeast Regional Film Commission, Chris Holland, Director, 888/872-8562 or 252/482-4333. www.ncnortheast.com. Email: nceast@ix.netcom.com. P.O. Box 29, Edenton, NC 27932.
Child Labor Requirements are best answered by the NC Department of Labor at 800/LABOR NC for copies of the Youth Employment Certificates. Request can be made by mail at NC Dept. of Labor, Labor Building, 4 West Edenton St., Raleigh, NC 27611.

• TEXAS
Alley Theatre, 713/228-9341. www.alleytheatre.org. 651 Texas Ave, Houston, TX 77002.
Dallas Theater Center, 214/526 8210. www.dallastheatercenter.org. 3636 Turtle Creek Blvd, Dallas, TX 75219-5598.
Theatre Three, 214/871-2933. www.theatre3dallas.com. 2800 Routh Street, Dallas, TX 75201.
KD Studio Actors Conservatory of the Southwest, 214/638-0484. www.kdstudio.com. Dallas, Texas. They have a four-semester program where you can earn an AA degree. Includes every phase of actors' development including opportunities for gaining actual working experience. Evening and weekend classes for actors not involved in the Conservatory program. The website provides actors a great deal of information.

• TUCSON, ARIZONA
Arizona Theatre Company, 520/884-8210. www.arizonatheatre.org. P.O Box 1631, Tucson, AZ 85702. Accepts head shots and resumes.

• SALT LAKE CITY, UTAH
www.actionacting.com. They list acting classes and casting information. This looks like a good place to get started in Salt Lake.
Pioneer Theatre Company, 801/581-6356. www.ptc.utah.edu. University of Utah, 300 S. 1400 E., Salt Lake City, UT 84112.

• VIRGINIA
Mill Mountain Theatre, 540/342-5730. www.millmountain.org. One Market Square, SE Roanoke, VA 24011. Casting: Auditions held locally Fall and Spring. Contact Doug Patterson, production manager. Opportunities for interns.

REFERENCE SECTION

SHOW BIZ WEBSITE ADDRESSES

• **There are many websites to search involving show business** and acting and there are new ones coming on line every day. You can find actors, casting directors, directors and producers in Los Angeles or in your area. The computer and internet will open your world to many possibilities.

• **Following are many websites**, where you'll find links to related websites. This is a fast moving world and some addresses may have fallen by the wayside, but there will be many to explore. You can find scripts of your favorite films and television shows too. Another book that lists valuable websites, including many casting director sites, is *Casting Qs: A Collection of Casting Director Interviews* by industry insider Bonnie Gillespie. www.bonniegillespie.com.

• *Variety* **reported the following account of an actor being discovered:** Producer Gene Corman was surfing the Internet one day when he decided to enter Actors World, where he was met with scads of actors' photos and resumes. One picture intrigued him: Donald Hoffman, an unknown living in Bismark, ND, who was a dead ringer for the elderly Orson Welles. He was flown to L.A. to read and subsequently cast in the role for a four-hour miniseries project "Orson Welles: The Later Years." Corman marveled, "It's amazing what you can do on this internet."

• **If you are interested in having your own website,** look in this section and also go to *Section Four: Actors' Websites*. Harry Governick, www.zipp.net, designed mine and my husband's, www.rongorow.com, I love this guy! Check out his site at www.theatrgroup.com/showbiz.

You will find a lot of useful information and the voice of experience for actors. He is currently located in the Midwest but will soon be back in Los Angeles.

• **Judy Kerr,** author of *Acting Is Everything: An Actor's Guidebook for a Successful Career In Los Angeles:* www.actingiseverything.com or www.judykerr.com. My husband and I bought .com domain names of both our names and the names of our books. Both domain names go to our respective websites.

• **Actress Tricia Gilfone** researched all of the following websites.

Internet Addresses

Academy of Motion Pictures Arts and Sciences: www.oscars.org Also the official site of the Academy Awards.
Academy of Television Arts and Sciences: www.emmys.org.
Academy Players Directory: www.acadpd.org.
Acting Classes: www.candacesilvers.com for Candace Silvers Studios.
Acting Coach Howard Fine: www.howardfine.com.
Actorsite, Resource site for actors: www.actorsite.com; www.vl-theatre.com; www.geocities.com/broadway/Mezzanine/4089; www.BroadwayArchive.com. The Broadway Theater Archive is the world's largest collection of Broadway plays adapted for television. www.wirebreak.com. Original live action shows.
Actors Access - Breakdowns for Actors: www.breakdownservices.com.
Actors Studio, The New School University www.newschool.edu.
Actors Equity Association, AEA, also called Equity, www.actorsequity.org.
Actor's Worldlink: members.aol.com/aworldlink.
Airport Information/Car Rentals/Hotels - great web site: www.lawa.org.
Aisle Say: www.escape.com/~theanet/AisleSay.
Alexander Technique: www.alexandertech.com.
American Federation of Television and Radio Artists: www.aftra.com.
American Film Institute: www.afionline.org.
American Women in Radio and Television: www.awrt.org.
Aquatic Masters Program, Southern California: www.swim.net.
Artist Rights Foundation: www.artistsrights.org www.film-foundation.org.
Artist's Way Workshop: www.creativelife.com.
Ask Theater: www.askplay.org.
Auditions Online: www.auditions.com.
Backstage West: www.backstagewest.com. Includes casting notices, articles, reviews, performing arts directory and more.
Best Bargains in Los Angeles: www.bargainsla.com.
Best Books Online: www.speaking.com.
Biff Yeager: Making a Movie: www.ultimatewishgift.com.
Body Make-over, Michael Thurmond's Six-Week: www.bodymakeovers.com.
Book Wire for Book Lovers: www.bookwire.com.
Breck Costin, BCC & Associates: www.bccfreedom.com.

Business and Communication Resources:
www.callwave.com; www.ureach.com; www.thefetcher.com; www.homefair.com;
www.dealmac.com; www.techtracker.com.
Casting: www.castingnet.com; www.castingnotices.com; www.castweb.com/casting;
www.lathespian.com/casting.html. Lists projects currently casting.
Casting director Stuart Stone: www.stuartstonecasting.com/actors.
Casting Workbook: www.castingworkbook.com.
Celebritiy Information: www.mrshowbiz.go.com or www.seeing-stars.com.
Cinewomen: www.cinewomen.com. Dedicated to promoting women in the film industry.
Comedy: Steve Kaplan's Comedy Intensive: www.comedyintensive.com.
Comedy with Judy Carter: www.judycarter.com.
Commercial Casting Director, Lien/Cowan: www.liencowancasting.com.
Consumer Information Center: www.pueblo.gsa.gov.
Cosmetics:www.gloss.com,www.shiseido.com; www.brownsbeauty.com;
www.spacadet.com; www.target.com. **Natural skincare and cosmetics:**
www.Eccobella.com; www.Burtsbees.com.
Bob Corff and Clair Corff: voice teachers. www.corffvoice.com.
Coupons: www.valpak.com. Thousands of on-line coupons are available that you just
print and use. Other sites include: www.coolsavings.com; www.valuepage.com;
www.hotcoupons.com; www.directcoupons.com; www.ralphs.com.
Create Your Own Website: www.crewdynamics.com; www.netcom.com;
www.earthlink.net.
Daytimer: www.daytimer.com. Free stuff.
Dialects Sources online: International Dialects of English Archive. www.ukans.edu/
~idea/ or www.rinkworks.com/dialect. This site'll learn ya'll howda talk jes like a hick.
Dining: www.zagat.com; www.epinions.com/res. Restaurants: www.dinesite.com.
Directing Workshop: Action/Cut Directed By: www.actioncut.com.
Directors Guild of America: www.dga.org.
Discounts: www.umdn.com. Union Members Discount Network. Discounts at over
200 businesses in the L.A. area for members of the entertainment industry.
Domain Names/Registrars: www.godaddy.com, at $8.95 per year for new domains,
and $7.95 to transfer a domain from another registrar when it is time to renew.
Episodic guide: http://epguides.com/grid/index.html. Guide to episodic TV.
Extra Work on Hollywood Sets: www.actingdepot.com/extrawork.html. Experiences
of a Hollywood Extra. home.earthlink.net/~ryalh/contents.html.
Film Festival on the Web: www.reeltimefilm.com. An online festival of indie shorts
available in the RealVideo format. www.filmfestivals.com; www.withoutabox.com.
Filmmaking for Kids Workshops: www.youngfilmmakers.org.
Film, TV & Commercial Employment Network: www.employnow.com.
Film School: The Los Angeles Film School: www.lafilm.com.
Fitness Online: www.fitnessonline.com. **Rob Woods Home of Fitness Testing:**
topendsports.com/testing/main.htm. **In Fitness and In Health Site:** www.phys.com;
www.caloriescount.com; www.prevention.com/weight/wlwb. **Nutritiously Gourmet:**
www.nutritiouslygourmet.com.
Geri Cook's Best Bargains Newsletter: www.bargainsla.com.
Getty Museum: www.getty.edu.
Getting The Job, An Audio Tape: www.carolynebarry.com.
Greeting Cards, Free: www.thebigday.com; www.birthdayexpress.com.
Health: www.healthyideas.com; www.onhealth.com.
Hollywood Actor's Network: www.hollywoodnetwork.com/hn/acting/index.html.

Hollywood Creative Directory: www.hollyvision.com.
Hollywood Film Institute: www.hollywoodu.com.
Hollywood Mall: www.hollywoodmall.com.
Hollywood Network: www.HollywoodNetwork.com.
Hollywood Radio & Television Society: www.hrts-iba.org.
Hollywood Reporter: www.hollywoodreporter.com. Has a Hollywood Hyperlink
area where you will find hundreds of addresses revolving around show business,
including all of the film commissions, unions, casting tools & actor resources, scripts
& screenwriting, production & equipment rentals.
HollywoodWeb: www.hollywoodweb.com.
Independent Feature Project: www.ifp.org.
Internet Movie Data Base: www.imdb.com. Look up your favorite actors.
Internet Resources: www.brandonu.ca/~ennsnr/Resources/Welcome;
www.everyrule.com. Gives you the rules for games and sports. www.refdesk.com;
www.freetranslation.com; www.britannica.com; www.onlineconversion.com;
www.skymaps.com; www.xe.net/ucc. Universal currency converter. www.kbb.com. Car
retail value. www.rentals.com. Housing. www.rxlist.com. Database of medications.
www.10minuteresume.com.
Site will generate a resume for you. www.webtender.com. Cocktail recipes.
Jobs: www.jobtrak.com; www.hotjobs.com; www.superjobsearch.com.
LA.temp.agencies.html; www.internweb.com; www.freeskills.com. Free online
training courses on the internet.
Jobs, Entertainment related: www.Getgigs.com; www.Mandy.com;
www.showbizjobs.com.
Judy Belshe Casting: www.askjudy.biz.
Learning Annex: Inexpensive classes. www.learningannex.com.
Life/Career Coaches: Breck Casting: bbc & Associates: www.bccfreedom.com.
Los Angeles Film School: www.lafilm.com.
Los Angeles Almanac: www.Losangelesalmanac.com. All the L.A. neighborhoods.
Makeup: www.naimies.com; www.cinemasecrets.com; www.makeupmania.com;
www.drbukk.com for character teeth.
Maps and driving directions: www.mapquest.com.
MGM's Video Savant: www.mgm.com/savant/index.html.
Modeling: www.howtomodel.com.
Models-Net: www.models-net.com; www.millionairesclub123.com.
Monologues:www.whysanity.net; www.themonologueshop.com.
Movies: www.atomfilms.com; www.apple.com/imovie/gallery; www.bmwfilms.com;
www.cinemanow.com; www.icebox.com; www.ifilm.com; www.movieweb.com.
Music: www.Hollywoodsheetmusic.com; www.wholenote.com. The place to go for
interactive guitar lessons.
New World Order Theater: www.yurope.com.
News Sites: www.cnn.com; www.msnbc.com; www.latimes.com.
New York Wooster Group: www.escape.com/~philbus/wooster.
NowCasting: www.Nowcasting.com. Great site; very useful.
Nutrition: www.zoneperfect.com/Site/Content/index.asp.
Office Depot: www.officedepot.com.
Office Max: www.officemax.com.
Onstage:geocities.yahoo.com/search?p=broadway.
Overnight television ratings: www.backstage-pass.com.
Paragon Photo & Digital Imaging: www.paragonphoto.com.

PDA: www.pdabuyersguide.com.

Personal Managers, Conference of: www.talentmanagers.org.

Photographers: David Laporte: www.Davidlaporte.com; **Raffi Alexander,** Spiderbox Photography: www.spiderbox.com; **Carrie Cavalier** of Cavalier Photography Studio: www.cavalierphotography.com; **Alan Weissman:** www.alanweissman.com; **Mary†Ann Halpin:** www.goddesshood.com. *See photo section.*

Plastic Surgery: www.garthfisher.com.

Plastic and Reconstructing Surgeons, American Society: www.plasticsurgery.org.

Playbill: www.playbill.com. World-wide theatre information.

Productions & locations going on in L.A.: www.eidc.com.

Publications: www.backstage.com; www.hollyvision.com; www.showbizdata.com; www.showbizltd.com; www.hollywoodreporter.com; www.reelwest.com; www.variety.com; www.latimes.com.

Resource Center for Actors: www.caryn.com.

Resumes: www.Imagestarter.com.

Reviews of movies, including film festivals: www.filmscouts.com.

Samuel French Book Store, to purchase theatrical books & plays: www.samuelfrench.com; www.dramabookshop.com.

Second City Improv Group and Training Center: www.secondcity.com.

Screen Actors Guild: www.sag.org.

Screen Actors' Guild Health Directory: www.sagph.org.

Scripts: www.script-o-rama.com; www.screentalk.org; www.moviepage.com; www.screenwriting.about.com.

Scripts: www.geocities.com, then Hollywood, then scripts.

Search engines: www.about.com; www.altavista.com; www.anywho.com; www.beaucoup.com; www.bigfoot.com; www.directhit.com; www.dogpile.com; www.excite.com; www.google.com; www.hotbot.com; www.infoseek.com; www.infospace.com; www.lycos.com; www.magportal.com; www.northernlight.com; www.overture.com; www.savvysearch.com; www.Teoma.com; www.whitepages.com; www.worldpages.com. For retail sites and web auctions: www.scour.com. For movies, music and cartoons: www.webcrawler.com; www.yahoo.com.

Shopping, Thrift Stores: www.consignmentguide.com; www.bibisworld.com; www.chelsea-girl.com; www.designerexposure.com; www.diamond.com; www.incagirl.com; www.leftgear.com; www.windowshoppinginparis.com. **Buy from chains supporting social causes:** www.shopforchange.com. **QVC Shopping Network:** www.qvc.com. **Clothing and accessories:** www.bluefly.com.

Sides Faxed: Showfax: www.showfax.com; www.nowcasting.com.

Software and Screensavers: www.screensavershot.com; www.galttech.com; www.tucows.com; www.Avantgo.com.

Stage Presence: www.sikehealth.com; www.alexandertech.com.

Stars' Driveways: www.driveways.com.

Starring Role In A Movie: www.ultimatewishgift.com.

Take One! Theatrical Bookstore: www.take1filmbooks.com

Talent Agencies: www.bossmodels.com, www.omnipop.com.

TalentBank International: www.talentbank.com.

TalentWorks: The Online Casting Source: www.talentworks.com.

Theater: www.playbill.com; www.theatre.com; www.theatermania.com.

Time Management Systems: Franklin System: www.franklincovey.com.

Train Ride, Filmore & Western Railway: www.fwry.com.

Transportation: www.subwaynavigator.com; www.trafficlinq.com.

Transportation Related: www.gaspricewatch.com. A timely site that allows you to check the lowest gas and oil prices in your neighborhood.

Traffic school, online: www.onlinetraffic.com.

Travel: www.travel.state.gov/passport_services.html. Passport Information. www.travelocity.com; www.expedia.com; www.cheaptickets.com; www.lowestfare.com; www.hotwire.com; www.lastminutetravel.com; www.11thhourvacations.com; www.site59.com; www.webflyer.com. Airline Tickets: www.travelweb.com; www.placestostay.com. For Hotels, Resorts, B&Bs and Inns: www.towd.com. Tourism Offices Worldwide Directory: www.topozone.com; www.gorp.com; www.flightarrivals.com; www.weather.com.

Travel Related: www.royal.gov.uk; www.abcparislive.com; www.musee-orsay.fr; www.theaustralian.news.com.au.

UCLA Extension: www.ucla.edu.

UCLA School of Theater, Film and Television: www.tft.ucla.edu.

Union Member Discount Network: www.umdn.com.

Unions: www.actra.org; www.aftra.org; www.dga.org; www.actorsequity.org; www.sag.org; www.wga.org.

Video Sellers: www.reel.com.

Virtual Headwork: www.xmission.com.

Voice: www.mnusa.com/corff.

Voice Overs: National Voice Database: www.voicedatabase.com.

Wake Up Call: www.mrwakeup.com. This is a free way to get wakeup calls. You have to register and listen to some advertising during the call, but I think it's worth it for that double way to wake up: alarm and phone call.

Weight Watchers: www.weightwatchers.com.

Web Site Design: www.zipp.net (designed my website); www.actorsite.com; www.Nowcasting.com; www.websites4actors.com. Offering free actor websites.

Wilshire Aesthetics, Dermatology & Plastic Surgery Group: www.wilshireaesthetics.com.

Women In Film: www.wif.org.

Woody Harrelson's O2 bar and restaurant: www.o2bar.com.

World Wide Stars: www.worldstars.com.

Generally interesting sites:

www.aedes.com.	www.beertravelers.com/roadtrips.html.
www.curiousgeorge.com.	www.Dailycandy.com.
www.designeroutlet.com.	www.drugstore.com.
www.inshop.com.	www.money.net.
www.shelleyabraham.com.	www.threedog.com. Gourmet treats for dogs.
www.women.com.	www.ams.usda.gov. Farmers Markets Nationwide.

www.ilrg.com. Access and download a variety of legal forms from basic buy and sell agreements, leases, loans,etc.

www.swell.com. The latest surf reports, forecasts and travel tips from Hawaii to California to Florida.

AN ACTORS' PRAYER

Oh Lord, Give me successes that are not just successes, but contain just enough quality to let me feel I haven't wasted my life. Give me long enough runs to pay my bills, and then when I am rich, get me into Repertory. Let me make wise decisions with regard to my career but when I cannot be wise, let me be undeservedly lucky. Let me be praised, let me be paid, let me be proud. Give me the strength never to announce my plans beforehand, give me the grace to get through interviews safely, give me the fortitude to survive my collaborators. Humbly, I ask all this...and Sardi's (NY) Spago's (LA), too. Amen.

Please wave "hello" to me as we
pass through the studio gates.

INDEX